D1272977

❧ Chaucer's General Prologue to the *Canterbury Tales*

An Annotated Bibliography 1900 – 1982

The General Prologue to Chaucer's *Canterbury Tales* is one of the most enduring works of English literature. Beloved by scholars, teachers, students, and general readers, it has been given a great many different interpretations. This annotated, international bibliography of twentieth–century criticism on the Prologue is an essential reference guide. It includes books, journal articles, and dissertations, and a descriptive list of twentieth–century editions; it is the most complete inventory of modern criticism on the Prologue. The extensive annotations provide uniquely convenient access to many publications that are otherwise difficult to obtain.

In her introduction, Caroline Eckhardt provides a careful and comprehensive overview of modern trends in criticism, trends which can be traced through the bibliography. At the beginning of the century, for example, Chaucer's Prologue was often described as a 'portrait gallery' and praised for its realism — social, psychological, and dramatic. Later in the century came emphases on irony, rhetoric, Freudian interpretations, elaborate allegories, and stylistic complexities. At present, the Prologue is often interpreted as a system of signs and symbols in which realism, if it exists at all, serves purposes beyond itself. The smiling and serene poet of the earlier period has been replaced by a self–conscious ironist, sometimes with a split personality. The portrait gallery of the beginning of the century is still there, though the spectator who walks along it tends to see something less fixed textually (the Prologue is now commonly discussed as work–in–progress) and more complicated structurally, generically, and thematically. It is the spectator, of course, who has changed.

CAROLINE D. ECKHARDT is a professor of English and Comparative Literature at Pennsylvania State University.

The Chaucer Bibliographies

Chaucer's General Prologue to the *Canterbury Tales*

AN ANNOTATED BIBLIOGRAPHY

1900 to 1982

Caroline D. Eckhardt

Published in association with the University of Rochester by

UNIVERSITY OF TORONTO PRESS

Toronto Buffalo London

©University of Toronto Press 1990
Toronto Buffalo London
Printed in Canada
ISBN 0–8020–2592–7

Printed on acid–free paper

Canadian Cataloguing in Publication Data

Eckhardt, Caroline D., 1942–
Chaucer's General prologue to the Canterbury tales

(The Chaucer bibliographies; 3)
ISBN 0–8020–2592–7
Includes index.

1. Chaucer, Geoffrey, d. 1400. Canterbury tales.
Prologue—Bibliography. I. Title. II. Series.

Z8164.E34 1990   016.821'1   C89–090531–2

For R.B.E.

Contents

❧ General Editor's Preface

The Chaucer Bibliographies will encompass, in a series of sixteen volumes, a complete listing and assessment of scholarship and criticism on the writings of Geoffrey Chaucer, and on his life, times, and historical context. Two volumes — on Chaucer's lyrics and *Anelida and Arcite*, and on the translations, scientific works, and apocrypha — have already appeared. The present volume, on the General Prologue, initiates work on the *Canterbury Tales*. It will be followed by the volume on the *Knight's Tale*, and by other volumes on the *Tales*, though publication of volumes on Chaucer's other poetry will appear in the next years as well. Each volume will center on a particular work, or a connected group of works; most contain material on backgrounds or related writings, and several will be topical in their coverage (music, visual arts, rhetoric, the life of Chaucer, and so on). Like all bibliographical projects, the series places unswerving emphasis on accuracy and comprehensiveness; yet the distinctive feature of the Chaucer Bibliographies, as this and the earlier volumes make clear, is the fullness and particularity of the annotations provided for each entry.

The individual volumes in the Chaucer Bibliographies series do not therefore constitute a reference work in the ordinary sense of that term. While they will enumerate virtually every publication on Chaucer worthy of notice, and give complete coverage to materials from the twentieth century, they go far beyond the usual compilation, bibliographic manual, or guide to research. The bibliographies are not mechanical or machine-produced lists. Each volume makes use of the intellectual engagement, learning, and discretion of a scholar actively at work on Chaucer. The series therefore serves not simply as the collection of all relevant titles on a subject, but as a companion and reliable guide to the reading and study of Chaucer's poetry. In this, the Chaucer Bibliographies represent an innovative and penetrating access to what Chaucer means, and has meant, to his readers. The project offers the full richness and detail of Chaucer's thought and world to a much wider audience than these have, even after one hundred years of energetic scholarship, ever before reached.

Before all else, then, the series provides a means of making practical headway in the study of earlier literature in English and its cultural context. These volumes will make the writing of Chaucer—the earliest figure in the canon of great writers in the English language—more immediate and more directly accessible to all readers. Although readers for six centuries have often praised Chaucer as a moving, superb, complex writer, even teachers of his writing sometimes feel less than fully informed. Moreover, despite his canonical stature, Chaucer has often remained unread or not fully appreciated because of the obstacles of language and historical distance. The goal of this project, at its first level, is to increase the numbers of those who read with understanding and pleasure by increasing the kinds of things that can be readily known about Chaucer. The Bibliographies will effect a major change in how Chaucer gets read, at what levels, and by whom.

The Chaucer Bibliographies seek to intensify the comprehension and enjoyment of beginning readers in university, college, and high school classrooms, presenting themselves as tools to both students and teachers. The series will move undergraduates more quickly from the generalizations and observations of textbooks and instructors to a direct access to the richness and variety of Chaucer's writing, and to its connections with medieval realities and modern understandings. For graduate students, the books will constitute a crucial resource for course work, exam preparation, and research. For non-specialist teachers of Chaucer in survey, masterpiece, and special topic courses, the series offers the means to a broader base of knowledge and to a more intense and shapely preparation than instructors, given the constraints of their work time, were previously able to manage. By clarifying and connecting both recent and long-available materials, and by making them readily accessible, the Chaucer Bibliographies can renew the teaching and reading of Chaucer, and enable the development of alternative approaches to understanding his writing.

The series promises still more for specialist readers. The fullness and detail of the annotations in each volume serves, in the first instance, as a check against duplication and redundancy; scholars and editors will be able to chart the place of new or proposed work quickly. Likewise, Chaucerians engaged with a topic or set of issues will be able to advance or situate their work more quickly by reference to the materials in the appropriate volumes in the series. In consolidating the massive work that has been done in the last century or so in medieval studies, and particularly on Chaucer, the Bibliographies provide the ground on which new work in Chaucer can build. Their presence will encourage more efficient research on minute as well as expansive topics, and will likewise facilitate work on the larger patterns and themes of Chaucer criticism, and on the ways in which institutions have fostered and used the reading and study of his writing.

In addition to Chaucerians, the Bibliographies benefit other specialists in medieval literature in offering ready access to publications on Chaucer that take up a variety of materials relevant to other fields. Whatever use the materials gathered in these volumes have for particular queries or problems, they will also address the interests of a range of scholars whose expertise extends to Chaucer, but whose contributions to Chaucer studies have been inhibited by the daunting mass of Chaucer scholarship. The Bibliographies place interdisciplinary research by Chaucerians at the disposal of scholars in history, art history, and other related areas, and so make multidisciplinary, collaborative work more possible and even more likely. In short, this massive effort to bring knowledge about Chaucer together strives to open up, rather than to close off, further innovative work on pre-modern culture.

The first three volumes in the series have analyzed, on average, more than six hundred items each. These include editions of Chaucer's writing, studies of language, manuscripts, and audiences, his sources and their contexts and intellectual connections, directly relevant background materials (eg, estates satire, medieval science, the tradition of Boethius), and all publications (in whatever language) bearing directly on Chaucers's poetry. The first volumes in print have thoroughly fulfilled the promise of the series to sort out and make accessible materials that are confused or obscure, including early philological publications in German and Scandinavian languages, privately printed or scarce volumes, and recent work in Australia and Japan. But even more strikingly, in bringing together all the materials on specific poems and subjects, these volumes have given new definition to the boundaries of Chaucer studies. Rather than working as a mopping-up operation, telling readers what they already knew, these volumes have taken their place in the new flourishing of Chaucer research and criticism, enabling and even inspiring fresh and solidly grounded interrogations of the poetry. They stand not simply as the summation of a great tradition, but as an impetus for more intense and expansive understandings of Chaucer. The sweeping vision of late medieval writing offered in each volume represents a reconfiguration of knowledge that justifies and encourages work by an expanded community of scholars, of whom Chaucerians form merely the core.

In producing volumes that record all relevant titles and that specify — and, in effect, assess — the content and interconnections of Chaucerian criticism, the Chaucer Bibliographies define a new space for themselves in their own field, and perhaps more widely among other reference tools as well. The volumes, published and projected, differ markedly in purpose and use from other introductory bibliographies and cumulative listings. Those unmarked, or minimally annotated listings are in essence on-going reviews of research, and as such they offer limited help to the specialist, and still less orientation or access to the uninitiated. Volumes in the Chaucer Bibliographies project take these publications as a base of information (and make reference to them), but the aim of each volume is to offer in-depth coverage of the work(s) at hand. Contributors initially review annual and collected listings, but acquired learning, developed instincts, and the extensive reading demanded for the preparation of each volume together provide titles and leads that complete the search. The series as a whole seeks to stand as a definitive companion to the study of Chaucer, a starting point from which future work on the poet will proceed. It addresses itself to an audience beyond the community of professional Chaucerians, inviting non-Chaucerian scholars and non-specialist teachers and students to take part in the continuous process of understanding Chaucer.

The series achieves this inclusiveness through exhaustive itemization, full and strategic commentary, attention to backgrounds and corollary issues, demonstration of interrelationships and connected themes through annotation, cross-referencing, and indices, and the report of significant reviews. Its design entails an examination of every relevant published item, in all foreign languages, though contributors will trust their own expertise and discretion in determining the choice and extent of annotations. Information on a 'ghost' or an inaccessible but useless item may prove as valuable to users of these volumes as careful assessments of central books in the field ; contributors have consequently taken special pains not to pass over inadvertently or to deliberately omit any 'trivial' writings. The specification of items in these volumes should obviate the need for many pointless struggles with the trammels of scholarship as readers of Chaucer pursue their special interests.

The Chaucer Bibliographies have been produced through the work of a diverse and distinguished array of experts. Such a format — where the individual efforts of autonomous scholars take their place within the well articulated, coherent framework of a single project — represents in a peculiarly appropriate way a project like this, with its broad base and wide appeal. The authors of individual volumes include both quite distinguished and younger Chaucerians, all of whom have demonstrated their learning and their engagement with the project. The expansive work for each volume has been carried out over a period of years by an individual scholar or a team in close collaboration, conceiving each volume as a single, coherent intellectual project giving access to Chaucer's poetry. Having a collective of two dozen Chaucerians actively engaged in the same project has already led to a more thorough cross-checking, a richer array of suggestions and shared information, and a larger number of surprising finds—some obscure, some obvious—than any individual or more limited collaborative effort could produce.

Since materials for the entire series will be on magnetic tape, floppy disks, or hard disks, it will be possible for the University of Toronto Press to issue revised editions of volumes, or to provide updated versions of the Bibliographies. It will also be possible to issue a general index to all sixteen books, though at present no decision has been made on this. The comprehensive and accessible character of the materials gathered for this entire project makes them the possible substance of a Chaucer data base. Although the production of an on-line data base is not a feature of the Chaucer Bibliographies project, several scholars have expressed interest in this further use for the work of the series. Inquiries and suggestions on this possibility will be welcomed by the General Editor and the University of Toronto Press.

The Chaucer Bibliographies as a project, and its individual volumes, have demanded extraordinary commitments of time and of intellectual and financial support. J. Paul Hunter, Dean of the College of Arts and Science, University of Rochester, and Brian J. Thompson, Provost of the University of Rochester, both provided initial assistance towards realizing the project's goals. At the University of Toronto Press, Harald Bohne, the Director, offered special support and encouragement at a crucial time; Prudence Tracy, the series' Editor at the Press, has carefully seen the volumes through production. Individual authors and the Editorial Board have made this a genuinely collaborative project; among the latter, John Leyerle has been especially active and effective in forwarding the work of the Bibliographies. At Rochester, Robert Lee Taylor and his associates at Taylor Hall have been patient and acute in offering help with the preparation of volumes for the Press. Mary Heinmiller did initial work on the present volume. Susan Sandell Draper, the Editorial Assistant to the Project, worked with intelligence, resourcefulness, and persistence in producing several volumes, and Nandini Bhattacharya has shown patience and resilience in attending to the interminable number of 'final' details for several volumes.

Thomas Hahn
Rochester, NY
9 March 1989

Preface

The aim of this bibliography is to record and annotate all books, articles, and dissertations published between 1900 and 1982 that are directly pertinent to the *General Prologue* of the *Canterbury Tales* — but within certain limitations. First, the *General Prologue* must be dealt with as a written text in Middle English: I have excluded modernizations, translations into foreign languages, imitations and parodies, adaptations for the stage, films, recordings, and videotapes. Second, with few exceptions I have scanned only publications dealing primarily with Chaucer. I have not attempted to seek out all the traces of the *General Prologue* in histories of literature, encyclopedias, surveys of medieval culture, anthologies, or other general works, though I am sure that this widely read poem is often mentioned in such contexts. Nor have I included studies of later writers' indebtedness to Chaucer. Third, I have omitted such relatively inaccessible items as master's theses and unpublished conference papers. Fourth, I have not recorded reprints of books first published before 1900. Finally, book reviews have been included only occasionally, as an indication of the reception of a book or as a supplement to a point being made about the *General Prologue*; comprehensive lists of reviews are available in *Book Review Index* and other sources. Aside from these intentional limitations, my coverage is probably quite incomplete for items published in the Far East and certain other parts of the world. I would welcome notification of material that I have missed.

Because the *General Prologue* is not only a section of the *Canterbury Tales*, but is in fact the opening section and the one that establishes the storytelling framework, it is not always easy to differentiate between topics that should be assigned to the present bibliographical volume and topics that might belong, instead, to volumes dealing with other parts of the *Canterbury Tales*. Questions of the order of the tales are not dealt with here, since there has been no doubt (at least so far) about the position of the *General Prologue* at the beginning of the collection. Discussions of the pilgrims' activities in the links between the tales are also omitted, unless there is a direct applicability to the *General Prologue*, since commentary on the links will be included in other volumes planned for this series. Debates about the suitability of tales to tellers are similarly excluded, except for those which analyze the *General Prologue* portraits, since later volumes will deal with each of the tales. However, general discussions of the state of the text at Chaucer's death, manuscript relations, etc, have been included insofar as they relate to the *General Prologue*.

The cultural, literary, and historical background has been represented only selectively. For example, items investigating whether the *General Prologue* is indebted to the framework of Boccaccio's *Decameron* are included, but nothing on the *Decameron* (or any other proposed literary source) as a work in its own right. Of the many studies of Thomas Becket have included only a handful. Similarly, I have cited a few standard studies of the English guild system (in the section on the Guildsmen), but have not attempted to supply a general bibliography on such broad subjects as armor (with reference to the Knight), or *amour courtois* (with reference to the Squire and perhaps the Prioress), or agriculture (with reference to the Plowman and the Reeve). The footnotes within the items listed here will usually provide sufficient guidance to such topics, as will Louis J. Paetow's *Guide to the Study of Medieval History*, Gray Cowan Boyce's *Literature of Medieval History, 1930–1975* (a supplement to Paetow's work), and the semi-annual *International Medieval Bibliography*.

One other matter may need clarification. I have endeavored to collect twentieth-century scholarship on the *General Prologue* without separating the wheat from the chaff. Much that is included here will surely seem trivial or redundant in the eyes of some users of this book, and I say that their opinion is good. In searching through more Chaucer material than any reasonable person should read in short compass, I have been many times impressed by the cogency of insights, but also repeatedly disappointed by unsubstantiated arguments, amused by announcements of discoveries that are far from new, enraged by arrogant and self-indulgent manipulations of the text, disturbed by scholars' misrepresentations or ignorance of each other's work, and bored by tediousness and baffled by jargon. In annotating the entries included here I have nevertheless tried to suppress these judgments, since what to my taste is chaff may be to someone else's taste the finest wheat, suitable for making the Prioress's dainty *wastel breed*. Furthermore, to understand the history of Chaucer criticism, and to assess the influence of major studies, it is necessary to read derivative pieces as well as highly original work. And it may save time for other researchers if they know that a book or article only makes a point that previous work had already established, or does not discuss their topic at all.

A note about the organization of this bibliography: the Editions section is arranged chronologically, all other sections alphabetically (with multiple items by the same author sequenced by date). The initial sections on (I) Editions, (II) Bibliographies, Indexes, and Other Research Tools, (III) General Criticism and Cultural Background, and (IV) Language, Metrics, and Studies of the Manuscripts and Early Editions are followed by twenty-five sections on the sequential parts of the *General Prologue*, from the opening description of the springtime setting and the gathering of the company at the Tabard Inn, through the series of portraits and the establishment of the storytelling plan at the end. Discussions of basic form and structure, literary affiliations, and unifying principles, as well as discussions of more than one individual pilgrim, are usually categorized as General Criticism. Since the narrator is first introduced at lines 20–21, most treatments of his persona and function are included in section V, which spans lines 1–42. Many items, though devoted primarily to one pilgrim or topic and categorized accordingly, also make reference to other pilgrims or topics, so the index should be consulted regularly.

Each publication has been annotated in terms of its pertinence to the *General Prologue*, which means that the overall argument or range of a work may not necessarily be evident here. Furthermore, though it is relatively easy, in annotating, to state the main point of short notes, it is difficult to briefly do justice to the complex arguments that appear in some of the longer articles, and probably impossible to adequately represent books. I fear that many readers who are also authors will find their entries here perfunctory or not entirely to their taste: nobody likes to be reduced to an abstract. Certainly I have not intended to offend and, like the Parson, *I wol stonde to correccioun.*

Quotations from Chaucer's works are given according to Robinson's second edition (see item **42**), except when they occur within passages being cited from a critic who has chosen another version of the text. (The third edition of Robinson's text, under the general editorship of Larry Benson, appeared too late to be used here.) Line numbers, unless otherwise indicated, refer to the *General Prologue*. Boldface numbers refer to the item numbers in this book. In supplying page numbers, since many items have been reprinted and the pagination frequently changes in reprints, in the first quotation from such items I have given both the year and the page in order to identify the edition from which I am quoting (eg, '1957, p 33'). Although I have included reprint information when it was readily available, I have made no attempt to record the complete publication history of each book. Skeat's critical edition (**3**), for example, has been many times reprinted, with different dates for different volumes, and it would probably occupy half a page, without adding materially to our knowledge of Chaucer criticism, to supply all those publication details here.

The indebtedness of Chaucer's Merchant remains mysterious (see line 280); mine too is difficult to express. I initially located many items through the cumulative bibliographies of Hammond (120), Griffith (119), Crawford (114), and Baird (100), and the annual bibliographies published by the Modern Language Association (129), the *Chaucer Review* (110), and *Studies in the Age of Chaucer* (98). Members of the library staffs at the Bodleian Library, the British Library, and the Pennsylvania State University were generous in providing access to their materials. I am particularly grateful to the Interlibrary Loan Department of the Pattee Library at Penn State, which ordered perhaps 500 items for me to scan. The Associate Dean for Research and the Department of English at Penn State provided funds for travel, manuscript preparation, and other necessities. Tony Colaianne, general editor of this bibliographic series when I began this volume, gave sound and courteous advice. Tom Hahn and Russell Peck, both of the University of Rochester, provided warm hospitality and splendid administrative and editorial guidance, as well as supplying large doses of both patience and encouragement and obtaining funds for computer processing. David Mycoff read the entire volume as it was prepared for the printer, caught many errors, and made many stylistic suggestions. Bob Yeager helped to solve a number of practical problems. Monica McAlpine called my attention to several important items on the Knight, read two long sections of my draft, caught errors, and suggested improvements. I am grateful to Larry Benson for sharing with me the notes to the *General Prologue* section of the *Riverside Chaucer*, prior to the publication of that work. For help with unfamiliar languages I turned to several colleagues and friends. Professor Toshiyuki Takamiya of Keio University sent me the *Bibliography of Publications on Medieval English Literature and Literature in Japan* published by Tokyo University in 1983; Yuko Ezaki translated all the Japanese bibliographical data on Chaucer included there and read selected items to me. My sequential research assistants at Penn State — Joseph Hynes, Shu-hua Wang, Sherilee Carpenter, and Alexander Jacob — made photocopies, kept files, typed index cards, and remembered when the library books were due. Kathy Leitzell, Kathy Itinger, Shelie Waite, and others typed; Jennifer Eckhardt, Amy Eckhardt, Jonathan Eckhardt, and Kathryn Cahir proofread and alphabetized. Sherilee Carpenter read two sets of proofs and prepared index entries. Mary Heinmiller entered the text into the computer, with Susan Draper's help on revisions. My best associate in this endeavor, as in others, has been my husband.

C.D.E.
The Pennsylvania State University

Abbreviations and Master List of Periodicals

CHAUCER'S WORKS CITED

ABC	*An ABC*
Anel	*Anelida and Arcite*
BD	*The Book of the Duchess*
ClT	*The Clerk's Tale*
CT	*The Canterbury Tales*
CYT	*The Canon's Yeoman's Tale*
FranT	*The Franklin's Tale*
FrT	*The Friar's Tale*
GP	*The General Prologue*
HF	*The House of Fame*
KnT	*The Knight's Tale*
LGW	*The Legend of Good Women*
ManT	*The Manciple's Tale*
Mel	*The Tale of Melibee*
MerT	*The Merchant's Tale*
MilT	*The Miller's Tale*
MkT	*The Monk's Tale*
MLT	*The Man of Law's Tale*
NPT	*The Nun's Priest's Tale*
PardT	*The Pardoner's Tale*
ParsT	*The Parson's Tale*
PF	*The Parliament of Fowls*
PhyT	*The Physician's Tale*
PrT	*The Prioress's Tale*
Rom	*The Romaunt of the Rose*
RvT	*The Reeve's Tale*

ShT	The Shipman's Tale
SNT	The Second Nun's Tale
SqT	The Squire's Tale
SumT	The Summoner's Tale
TC	Troilus and Criseyde
Th	The Tale of Sir Thopas
Truth	Truth
WBT	The Wife of Bath's Tale

JOURNALS AND OTHER PERIODICALS CITED

ABR	American Benedictine Review
Acta	Acta (Binghampton, New York)
AI	American Imago
ALLCJ	Association for Literary and Linguistic Computing Journal
AN&Q	American Notes and Queries
Anglia	Anglia: Zeitschrift für Englische Philologie
AngliaB	Anglia Beiblatt
AnM	Annuale Mediaevale
Archaeologia	Archaeologia
Archiv	Archiv für das Studium der neueren Sprachen und Literaturen
Archives	Archives of Dermatology
AS	American Speech
Athenaeum	The Athenaeum (London)
Balcony	Balcony
BBSIA	Bulletin bibliographique de la Société internationale arthurienne
BenedictineR	Benedictine Review
BJRL	Bulletin of the John Rylands Library
BlakeS	Blake Studies
Bridge	The Bridge: A Yearbook of Judaeo-Christian Studies
C&L	Christianity and Literature
CDBK	Chukyo Daigaku Bungakubu Kiyo (Chukyo University, Japan)
CE	College English
CER	Catholic Education Review
CF	Classical Folia
ChauN	Chaucer Newsletter

ChauR	*Chaucer Review*
CHJ	*Cambridge Historical Journal*
CL	*Comparative Literature*
CLAJ	*College Language Association Journal*
Comitatus	*Comitatus: A Journal of Medieval and Renaissance Studies*
CR	*The Critical Review* (Melbourne; also *Melbourne Critical Review*)
Crit	*Criticism*
CritQ	*Critical Quarterly*
CSSH	*Comparative Studies in Society and History*
CW	*Catholic World*
DA	*Dissertation Abstracts* (continued by *DAI*)
DAI	*Dissertation Abstracts International*
DR	*Dalhousie Review*
E&S	*Essays and Studies* (English Association)
EA	*Etudes anglaises*
EEK	*Eigo Eibungaku Kenkyu, Hiroshima Daigaku Eibun Gakkai (Hiroshima Studies in English Language and Literature)*
EHR	*English Historical Review*
EIC	*Essays in Criticism*
EJ	*English Journal*
ELH	*Journal of English Literary History*
ELN	*English Language Notes*
EM	*English Miscellany*
EngR	*English Record*
EngRev	*English Review* (London)
ER	*Erasmus Review*
ERon	*Eibungaku Ronshu, Kansai Daigaku Eibun Gakkai* (Kansai University, Japan)
ES	*English Studies*
ESt	*Englische Studien*
Expl	*The Explicator*
FForum	*Folklore Forum*
Florilegium	*Florilegium: Carleton University Annual Papers on Classical Antiquity and the Middle Ages*
FSUS	*Florida State University Studies*
Gaulois	*Le Gaulois*
Genre	*Genre*
GR	*Germanic Review*
Greyfriar	*Greyfriar: Siena Studies in Literature*
GRM	*Germanisch-Romanische Monatsschrift*

GSLI	*Giornale storico della letterature italiana*
HLQ	*Huntingdon Library Quarterly*
Horizon	*Horizon*
HSCP	*Harvard Studies in Classical Philology*
HT	*History Today*
Inozemna	*Inozemna filolohiia* (L'vov, USSR)
Italica	*Italica*
JAF	*Journal of American Folklore*
JAMA	*Journal of the American Medical Association*
JE	*Journal of Education*
JEGP	*Journal of English and Germanic Philology*
Katahira	*Katahira* (Chubu Katahirakai Academy, Japan)
KN	*Kwartalnik Neofilologiczny* (Warsaw)
KJDD	*Kiyo Jinbunkagaku, Daitobunka Daigaku* (Daitobunka University, Japan)
KJDR	*Kobe Jogakuin Daigaku Ronshu* (Kobe Women's College, Japan)
L&P	*Literature and Psychology*
LangQ	*Language Quarterly*
LAT	*Los Angeles Tidings*
LeedsSE	*Leeds Studies in English*
LHY	*Literary Half-Yearly*
LQR	*London Quarterly Review*
M&H	*Medievalia et Humanistica*
MÆ	*Medium Ævum*
Manuscripta	*Manuscripta*
McNR	*McNeese Review*
Mediaevalia	*Mediaevalia: A Journal of Mediaeval Studies*
Memoirs	*Memoirs* (Yamanashi University, Japan)
MH	*Medical History*
MHLS	*Mid-Hudson Language Studies*
MichA	*Micigan Academician: Papers of the Michigan Academy of Science, Arts, and Letters*
MLN	*Modern Language Notes*
MLQ	*Modern Language Quarterly*
MLR	*Modern Language Review*
Month	*The Month* (London)
Moznayim	*Moznayim* (Tel Aviv, Israel)
MP	*Modern Philology*
MQ	*Midwest Quarterly*
MS	*Mediaeval Studies*
MSCS	*Mankato State College Studies*

MusQ	*The Musical Quarterly*
N&Q	*Notes and Queries*
Names	*Names: Journal of the American Name Society*
Nation	*The Nation*
NCent	*The Nineteenth Century*
ND	*Nihon Daigaku Rikogakubu Ippankyoiku Kyoshitsu* *Iho* (Nihon University, Japan) .
NDKK	*Nagasaki Daigaku Kyoyobu Kiyo* (University of Nagasaki)
Nebulae	*Nebulae, Meiji Gakuin Daigaku, Daigakuin* *Eibungaku Senko* (Meiji Gakuin University, Japan)
NEJM	*New England Journal of Medicine*
Neophil	*Neophilologus*
NM	*Neuphilologische Mitteilungen*
NNPL	*Nachrichten aus der Neueren Philologie und* *Literaturgeschichte* (Göttingen)
NS	*Die Neueren Sprachen*
NYSJM	*New York State Journal of Medicine*
NYTM	*New York Times Magazine*
OGD	*Osaka Gakuin Daigaku Gaikokugo Ronshu* (Osaka University, Japan)
OL	*Orbis Litterarum*
OSDR	*Osaka Shogyo Daigaku Ronshu* (Osaka University of Commerce, Japan)
PAPS	*Proceedings of the American Philosophical Society*
Parergon	*Parergon: Bulletin of the Australian and New Zealand* *Association for Medieval and Renaissance Studies*
PBA	*Proceedings of the British Academy*
Phoenix	*Phoenix* (Hiroshima University)
PLL	*Papers on Language and Literature*
PLPLS-LHS	*Proceedings of the Leeds Philosophical and* *Literary Society, Literary and Historical Section*
PMLA	*Publications of the Modern Language Association*
PP	*Past and Present*
PQ	*Philological Quarterly*
PsychQ	*Psychoanalytic Quarterly*
RBPH	*Revue Belge de Philologie et d'Histoire*
REL	*Review of English Literature*
RES	*Review of English Studies*
RevG	*Revue germanique*
RLC	*Revue de littérature comparée*
Romania	*Romania: Revue consacrée à l'étude des* *langues et des littératures modernes*

RomR	Romanic Review
RP	Romance Philology
RSH	Revue des sciences humaines
RUO	Revue de l'Université d'Ottawa (University of Ottawa Quarterly)
SAB	South Atlantic Bulletin (now South Atlantic Review)
SAC	Studies in the Age of Chaucer
SAQ	South Atlantic Quarterly
SatR	Saturday Review of Literature
SDB	Saga Daigaku Bunrigakubu Eigo Eibunka Kiyo (Saga University, Japan)
SB	Studies in Bibliography
Scrutiny	Scrutiny
SE	Studies in English (University of Texas, continued by TSLL)
Seminar	Seminar: A Journal of Germanic Studies
SFQ	Southern Folklore Quarterly
SM	The Scientific Monthly
SMC	Studies in Medieval Culture
SN	Studia Neophilologica
Soundings	Soundings (Academy for English Language and Literature, Japan)
SP	Studies in Philology
Spec	Speculum
SR	Sewanee Review
SRAZ	Studia Romanica et Anglica Zagrabiensia
SRL	Studies in Romance Languages
SSF	Studies in Short Fiction
Standpunte	Standpunte (South Africa)
StHum	Studies in the Humanities
Style	Style
TCA	Transactions of the Connecticut Academy of Arts and Sciences
TGD	Tokyo Gakugei Daigaku, Kenkyo Hokoku (Tokyo University of Arts and Sciences, Japan)
Thoth	Thoth
Thought	Thought
TLS	Times Literary Supplement (London)
Topic	Topic: A Journal of the Liberal Arts
Traditio	Traditio: Studies in Ancient and Medieval History, Thought, and Religion
TSE	Tulane Studies in English

TSLL	*Texas Studies in Literature and Language*
TWA	*Transactions of the Wisconsin Academy of Sciences, Arts, and Letters*
UTQ	*University of Toronto Quarterly*
VLR	*Virginia Law Review*
Volcano	*Volcano, Kagoshima Daigaku Eibun Gakkai* (Kagoshima University, Japan)
WHR	*Western Humanities Review*
WVUPP	*West Virginia University Bulletin: Philological Papers*
YES	*Yearbook of English Studies*

❧ Introduction

More than sixty years ago, when the twentieth century was young, a major writer who was reading Chaucer complained that 'year by year the sediment of muddy comment and criticism thickens round the great man's bones' (item 300, p 194). The sediment — if that is what it is — is far thicker now, but not all of it is muddy or serves primarily to bury the poet from view. There has been praise too, and much clarification, and revision of the assumptions that guide the way in which readers interpret the famous *General Prologue to the Canterbury Tales* (*GP*), not to mention Chaucer's other works. I will begin with a brief description of the modern editions, since one of the most important achievements of recent scholarship has been to make the text available in more accurate and more detailed versions than ever before.

Editions

The editions listed here begin slightly before the year 1900 in order to include the contributions of two very important modern editors, Walter W. Skeat and Alfred W. Pollard. In 1891 Skeat published a school text of *GP* (1) and in 1894–1897 a multi-volume *Complete Works* (the 'Oxford Chaucer,' 3), an immensely influential critical edition that dominated Chaucer scholarship for forty years. It was rivaled only by the collaborative 1898 *Works* edited by Pollard along with H. Frank Heath, Mark H. Liddell, and W.S. McCormick (the 'Globe Chaucer,' 4, with the section on *GP* prepared by Pollard). Both Skeat and Pollard chose the Ellesmere manuscript as the basis of their texts, though they consulted other early copies, and thus as the new century opened the authority of the Ellesmere version was doubly endorsed. Ellesmere was to hold sway, in fact, until 1958, when E.T. Donaldson challenged its status, basing his text (63) instead on the Hengwrt manuscript — about which more later.

After the Skeat and Pollard editions, the next major edition including *GP* was the 1933 *Poetical Works* of F.N. Robinson (42). Especially in its revision, which appeared in 1957, Robinson's edition became the text most commonly cited by scholars. At the present time it still functions as the standard, despite being outdated; another revison under the general editorship of Larry Benson appeared early in 1987 (when this bibliography was in press) and, if well received, may replace Robinson 1957 as the text typically cited.

Between Robinson's first and second versions, and affecting the text of *GP* in the second, there was published in 1940 *The Text of the Canterbury Tales* by John M. Manly and Edith Rickert (49), an edition important not so much for its text as for its listing of the variant readings from all the manuscripts. The ready availability of the variants in Manly-Rickert aroused interest in the question of whether the Ellesmere manuscript really provides the best copy after all. Recently the general weight of opinion has shifted somewhat towards the Hengwrt manuscript, which has been chosen as the basis of the Variorum Chaucer project now underway (93). But the final verdict about these manuscripts, if there is ever to be one, is not yet in: the 1977 collected edition by John H. Fisher, *Complete Poetry and Prose* (91), took the Ellesmere manuscript as its base, while the 1980 *Canterbury Tales* edited by N.F. Blake (95) used Hengwrt.

Though the Chaucer tradition in the twentieth century has been established by Skeat, Pollard, Robinson, and a few other giants of the editorial realm, one of the most remarkable aspects of modern scholarship is simply the sheer number of editions. This bibliography lists 96 Middle English editions of *GP*, either alone or with other parts of the *CT* (and I am certain that I have missed many others, particularly some published outside England and America). In compiling this inventory I have not listed either English modernizations or translations into foreign languages. Nor have I attempted to record the great number of instances in which *GP* is anthologized in surveys of English literature, collections of world masterpieces, or other general sources. Only editions devoted mostly or wholly to Chaucer, with the text given in something resembling the original language, have been included. Many of these editions are school texts, yet this does not mean that they can be wholly ignored by the scholar. Others yet are facsimiles of important older versions — the major fifteenth-century manuscripts and the early printed editions, or, in the case of the Kelmscott facsimiles (64, 87 and 90), a splendid nineteenth-century book.

On the average, more than one edition of *GP* has been published for each year of the twentieth century. That is surely strong testimony to the vitality of those nine-and-twenty pilgrims, more or less, who set out on an April journey six hundred years ago.

Criticism

As the century opened, many of the major concerns of modern criticism were already in view. The essential work of annotation and elucidation — which will probably never be completed — was being actively pursued. There were discussions of single terms and phrases, such as the meaning of *purchas* and *rente* in the Friar's portrait, and of larger topics, such as the guilds of fourteenth-century London or the practices of medieval physicians. Questions were raised about manuscript relations and literary sources or analogues; the still unresolved issue of whether *GP* is indebted to the framework of the *Decameron* was being debated. Historical models were suggested for the Host, the Physician, the Knight, and the Prioress. It was a commonplace to describe *GP* as a portrait gallery in which Chaucer had depicted, simultaneously, types and individuals. The basic groupings of pilgrims within the series were noted, as was the dramatic and realistic quality of the portraits. Jenks commented that 'the pilgrims are more real than the personages in their stories' (**307**). Legouis (**334**) and others anticipated the later viewpoint of Kittredge (**317**, p 155) that the tales were intended, like the speeches in a play, to express or illustrate their speakers' personalities. Legouis, in pointing out that the narrator assumes the guise of a simple reporter (**334**), foreshadowed many later analyses of the narrator's personality. The sophisticated use of conventional diction was examined by Lowes (**345**), who demonstrated that the terms *simple* and *coy* in the Prioress's portrait echo the stock phrases of the courtly romances. Chaucer's own attitude in *GP* was thought to be cheerful, comic, tolerant, or lightly ironic. All of these topics appear in the criticism published between 1900 and 1910 — and many of them were already venerable at that time. Salter and Pearsall have argued, for instance (**567**), that a recognition of the pilgrims' dramatic qualities is evident in the layout of the Ellesmere manuscript itself.

Until somewhat after mid-century the course of criticism, while hardly smooth, ran mostly in those familiar channels. Issues of Chaucer's relationship to his contemporary world continued to be raised: Tatlock considered whether the Parson's portrait shows Wycliffite sympathies (**472**) and Kuhl proposed that the Guildsmen were chosen with an eye towards London's political controversies (**1076**). Manly, suggesting historical models for several of the pilgrims (**362**), gave new strength to the interpretation of Chaucer as a realist who accurately depicted his contemporary world. The drama-thesis too picked up energy, with Kittredge describing *GP* as the first act of a social comedy (**317**). Probing into the minds of the *dramatis personae*, Maynard pictured the Monk as a young novice (**896**), Sister Madeleva defended the Prioress's motivations (**821**), and Pratt speculated about the

Miller's lost youth (1220). The narrator became more and more recognized as a character in his own right — Chaucer the pilgrim as distinct from Chaucer the author (Donaldson, 596, and others). In another development of earlier ideas, the realization that the pilgrims represent not only individuals, but also abstractions or types, became linked with the estates-satire tradition (Jones, 309); or, alternatively, with the Seven Deadly Sins (Tupper, 482–485); or, alternatively yet, with the conventions of medieval physiognomy (Curry, 1208). Thus the abstract or symbolic value of ostensibly realistic details in the portraits was being recognized. In this spirit, for instance, Barnouw commented upon the sexual significance of the Wife's being gap-toothed (1132).

Though Coghill in 1949 (198), Ruggiers in 1956 (440), and others were still describing GP as a portrait gallery, its relationship to earlier traditions of verse portraiture was being reassessed. Cunningham, for example, associated GP with the dream-vision prologues that described a series of people or images (207). There was greater interest in the internal structure of GP, in its manipulation of point of view, and in the way in which its twin secular and sacred perspectives are established. One could subsume several of these subjects under the rubric of an increased emphasis on style and a concomitant positive regard for Chaucer's use of literary conventions. His debt to formal rhetoric was considered — but minimized — by Manly (361), while others set about collecting examples of rhetorical figures. Language, versification, and manuscript relations continued to be studied. An awareness of oral performance and its influence on the text occasionally appeared, with Bronson writing about Chaucer's responsiveness to a listening audience (176) and Everett writing about his 'good ear' (237). Textual studies noted the possibility that revisions were made to GP. But despite genuine advances upon the earlier topoi of criticism, much of the work of this period still reflects the assumptions of the nineteenth- and early twentieth-century commentators.

Yet if the subjects and themes are mostly a further development of earlier concerns, sometime between 1900 and about 1950 a more subtle shift occurred. Criticism became far more formal, technical, and academic in its manner, and thereby made itself less accessible to readers outside the universities. Some of the most memorable of the older criticism was almost conversational in tone and relatively innocent of footnotes, as if the critic were spending a friendly evening with a group of acquaintances. In 1915 Kittredge could make a broad claim — such as 'the Pilgrims do not exist for the sake of the stories, but vice versa' (317, p 155) — without feeling the need to bolster the assertion with references; his own authority sufficed in print, as it would have sufficed in his parlor. But by 1950 almost nobody in the main currents of Chaucer criticism was writing that way, and one might argue that the older style was already mostly gone by the 1930s. The reasons behind the shift are social and demographic as well as intellectual: the small community of scholars was expanding into a vast network of strangers, the generalist was giving way to the specialist, and Chaucer was becoming an academic industry. There will always be fine attempts to recapture a wider public with books written in a nontechnical style, but these works now tend to exist at the margin of a scholar's main endeavors, rather than constituting the center or the norm.

And in the 1960s occurred the burst of Robertsonian interpretation that sent Chaucer scholars delving into footnotes all the more thoroughly, learning new arcana, and disputing about the technicalities of medieval theology as never before. The Robertsonian thesis — that medieval characterization was intended not as realism, but as Christian allegory (427) — can itself be traced to earlier insights, since the symbolic implications of many details of the GP portraits had been examined before. As has been mentioned, Tupper had associated certain pilgrims with the Sins, Curry had correlated physical traits with diseases or other conditions carrying moral implications, and that lecherous gap in the Wife's teeth had been explicated more than once. However, Robertson and his followers now brought an immense weight of theological and art-historical reference to bear upon the question of Chaucer's allegorical intentions, so that to be either a Robertsonian or an anti-Robertsonian required expertise in aspects of medieval culture that were not in themselves literary. The Robertsonian 'historical criticism' movement has not focused on GP, but GP has certainly felt its effect. Nevertheless the drama-thesis has also remained productive: in 1962, the year of Robertson's Preface, Neuse (390) and Cohen (766) were discussing the pilgrims as dramatic characters whose personalities could be analyzed as such; Crane in 1966 (963), Beidler in 1968 (665), and others have continued to do the same.

In the 1970s two earlier concerns came to the fore: one was related to Chaucer's treatment of social and economic issues, the other to his irony and satire. Mann's book on GP as estates-satire (363) and other studies associated the pilgrims with fourteenth-century class systems, occupational labels, kinds of work, sources of income, or attitudes toward bourgeois values. (The similarity of this approach to Marxist critical assumptions is clear, and it had appeared earlier in the century, as one would expect.) The socio-economic school, seeing in GP not simply realism but a critique of a reality that was undergoing change, resembles the second tendency mentioned just above, that of emphasizing Chaucer's irony and satire. This was an anti-heroic period in Chaucer criticism, as in many other aspects of Western thought, and it is perhaps not surprising to find my lady Prioresse interpreted as a country bumpkin (768) or the Knight as a merciless mercenary (**689**). Nevertheless, studies of other kinds, such as rhetorical analyses, were also continuing, along with new ways of setting *GP* within the literary context. Howard, for example, described *GP* in terms of medieval works on artificial memory (**287**) and in terms of travel narratives (**289**).

This survey has so far ignored the steady twentieth-century production of research aids. In 1908 Hammond published the first systematic, comprehensive Chaucer bibliography (**120**), to be followed by the bibliographies of Griffith, Crawford, and Baird (**119, 114, 100**) and by indexes, glossaries of special terms, concordances, etc. Researchers have been provided with summaries of criticism, collections of contemporary documents, reports on work published and work in progress, and several dictionaries of proper names. Most of these sources cover more than *GP*, though occasional separate research tools for *GP* do exist (**104, 136**).

Looking over this century's work on *GP*, from 1900 to 1982, one might note that a great many publications, perhaps the majority, reflect no special school or theory but concentrate on the work of textual elucidation. However, insofar as an overall theoretical change is visible, at the beginning of the century *GP* was more commonly regarded as a work of realism (social, dramatic, or psychological), while in the 1980s *GP* is more commonly interpreted as a system of signs and symbols in which realism, whether of types or of individuals, serves purposes beyond itself. The smilingly serene poet of the earlier period has been replaced by a self-conscious ironist, sometimes with a split personality. The portrait-gallery of 1900 is there still, though the spectator who walks along it now tends to see something less fixed textually (*GP* now tends to be discussed in terms of revisions, work in progress, or incompleteness) and more complicated structurally, generically, and thematically. It is the spectator, of course, who has changed.

Brief comments on the main critical preoccupations of each section of *GP* follow.

The springtime setting, the narrator, and the gathering at the Tabard (lines 1–42). Many literary sources have been proposed for the remarkable *Natureingang* with which *GP* begins, and many commentaries have been written on such topics as the syntactical structure of the first verse-paragraph, the sexual metaphors of impregnation, the drought that is either literal or conventional or symbolic, the astronomical references and the implied dating, the intertwined secular and sacred imagery, the Biblical evocations, the rhetorical and rhythmical complexity of the verse, and the appropriateness of Becket's shrine as the goal. Lines 1–18, sometimes said to be the best known passage in English poetry, are often quoted, though it is acknowledged that their style is not typical of *GP* as a whole.

At line 20 the narrator is introduced ('In Southwerk at the Tabard as I lay ...'). Modern critics have attempted to compose the portrait of this pilgrim whom Chaucer himself did not explicitly describe. Donaldson (596) and others have presented the narrator as a persona who is not to be confused with the poet himself: the persona is naive, credulous, and impressionable, while the poet is none of these things. The double or ironic presence of Chaucer in his poem has become a new commonplace, though a few voices have been raised in protest. At line 24 a well-known crux appears: *Wel nyne and twenty* pilgrims are said to arrive in a *compaignye*, but the number identified in the portrait series does not total twenty-nine. Several of the proposed solutions to this discrepancy involve a revision or special reading of either line 24 or line 164 (see below).

The Knight (lines 43-78). Many details of the Knight's career have been annotated — the locations of his battles, the exact meaning of beginning the board in Prussia, the possibility that historical individuals such as the Earl of Derby served as models, etc. Two textual cruces concern whether *hors* (line 74) is singular or plural, and whether the Knight has participated in many a noble *armee* or many a noble *arivee* (line 60). The ethical terminology of the portrait — honor, truth, courtesy, worthiness, freedom — has been examined, with the Knight usually perceived as an idealized figure of the warrior class, perhaps matched by the idealized figures of the Parson and Plowman in an echo of the traditional three estates concept, which defined the fundamental social functions as fighting, praying, and laboring. As long ago as 1920, however, Jack argued that none of the pilgrims is wholly ideal (305), and touches of humor, or of imperfections such as egotism, have repeatedly been seen in the Knight's portrait. The negative view culminated in 1980 with Jones's claim that the Knight is a 'shabby mercenary' without redeeming moral qualities (689). This revisionist interpretation has been sharply disputed, as one might expect, and recently the Knight's defenders have at least partly restored him to favor.

The Squire (lines 79-100). The resemblance of the Squire to literary figures representing youth and love, and to visual images representing springtime, has been pointed out, as have the contrasts between his behavior and that of his father the Knight. His military activity is usually identified with the so-called crusade of 1383. Most critics have seen the portrait as favorable, perhaps even partly autobiographical, though the Squire's showiness of dress, devotion to secular loving, and participation in an inglorious continental campaign have been interpreted as negative traits.

The Yeoman (lines 101-17). The modest amount of commentary on the Yeoman has concentrated on the question of whether he accompanies the Knight or the Squire, on the green and brown coloration of his portrait, and on his rather elaborate accoutrements, especially his peacock-arrows.

The Prioress and her companions (lines 118-64). The Prioress has attracted more attention than any other pilgrim. Much of it concerns specific details in the portrait: which saint her *St Loy* represents (line 120) and why she swears by him, the implications of her affiliation with the nunnery of St Leonard's, her manner of speaking French, her smiling, her attitude toward animals, her brooch and beads, her forehead, her fastidious table manners, her name *Eglantyne* (line 121), and the color of her eyes. The literary sources and analogues of some of these traits have been identified and her resemblance to Chaucer's Criseyde has been pointed out. A few critics have seen her as an older woman, perhaps even fat, though the predominant viewpoint is that she is ladylike and dainty. On a larger level, the problem has been (and remains) one of overall evaluation. Is the Prioress depicted as an admirable, though perhaps slightly worldly, example of her kind; or as a misfit in her calling? In general, Catholic critics have defended her behavior, certain others have seen sharp satire in it, and many, like Lowes (814), have contented themselves with establishing its complex ambiguity.

The Second Nun, the *chapeleyne* of line 164, has received very little comment — understandably so, since the *GP* portrait states virtually nothing about her beyond her existence. As for the *preestes thre* who complete line 164, it is precisely their existence that is at question. Many Chaucerians have wished to reduce them to one priest, the Nun's Priest who later tells the tale of Chanticler, while others have defended their triple presence on the pilgrimage. On this matter, perhaps more than on any other single line of *GP*, elaborate theories have been constructed. *Diverse folk they seyden diversely* (Fragment I, line 3857). The problem not only touches the Prioress, who is characterized partly by the size of her entourage, but also raises questions about the overall number of pilgrims, possible revisions to the text of *GP*, and purportedly complex ironies on the narrator's, or on Chaucer's, part.

The Monk (lines 165–207). Commentators on the Monk's description have focused upon his hunting, his physical appearance (particularly his head and eyes), the word *recchelees* (or perhaps the correct reading is *cloisterlees*, line 179), the possibility that William de Cloune served as the model, and the meaning of *outridere* (line 166). Whether his hunting is sexual has been debated, as has the degree of negative judgment that should be attached to the portrait. His fundamental sin may be *acedia*, sloth (Berndt, 867); the worldliness he shows in *GP* has been correlated to qualities in his tale.

The Friar (lines 208–69). The implications of *purchas* and *rente* (line 256), *lovedayes* (line 258), *in principio* (line 254), and the Friar's name *Huberd* (line 269) have occasioned commentary, as have the Friar's curious lisping and his practice of arranging the marriages of young women. Tatlock (951) and others have speculated about which order of friars he represents. His corruption is generally recognized, though he has also had partial defenders (eg, Bloomfield, **916**). A gradation towards increasing evil and increasingly explicit sexuality in the Prioress — Monk — Friar series has been pointed out.

The Merchant (lines 270–84). The Merchant's mysterious indebtedness and his anonymity have evoked contrasting interpretations, with some critics thinking that he is not in debt (or that he owes money only in the way that any successful businessman might) and that he engages in normal, legal financial transactions; and others thinking that his indebtedness is damaging or deceitful and that his activities are thoroughly illegal indeed. The London merchant Gilbert Maghfeld has been proposed as a model.

The Clerk (lines 285–308). Though the Clerk is most often perceived as an idealized young student, Severs and Ussery have interpreted him as an older or more eminent person (**997, 1002**). Several historical models have been suggested; the cost of the books that he would like to have by his bedside has been estimated. From time to time comic or ironic intentions have been seen in the portrait. Axelrod went so far as to propose that the Clerk is sexually interested in the Wife of Bath (**976**), Crane that he steals the money he needs to buy books (**963**).

The Serjeant of the Law (lines 309–30). The phrase *In termes* (line 324) has been several times explicated, as has the relationship between the Serjeant's legal training and the legalities described in the tale of Constance, which he later tells. The Serjeant's very high social status is usually taken to be a central fact in his characterization, though Eliason suggested that he is of humble origin (**1015**), and tensions or ironies have been pointed out in the portrait.

The Franklin (lines 331–60). The main controversies over the Franklin's portrait have concerned his social status — whether he is to be regarded as a comfortable member of the gentry, or as an insecure parvenu; and his Epicureanism — whether he exemplifies a charitable superabundance, or a misguided and self-indulgent materialism. Historical and literary models have been proposed, and the details of his cuisine have been correlated to medieval concepts of diet and health.

The Guildsmen (lines 361–78). The tradesmen have been studied primarily in terms of contemporary guild politics and economics. The fraternity to which they belong has been thought to be a guild-merchant, a local parish guild, or a craft guild; specific London guilds have been proposed. Chaucer's choice of the five trades he names (lines 361-62) has been associated with the London political dispute between the victualling and the non-victualling guilds in the 1380s. The satiric qualities in the group portrait have also been examined, particularly by Goodall (**1072**) and Lisca (**1077**).

The Cook (*lines 379-87*). The most popular trait of this pilgrim, as far as criticism is concerned, has been the *mormal* on his leg (line 386). He has been identified with the historical Roger of Ware, a man of dubious reputation.

The Shipman (*lines 388-410*). Several attempts have been made to identify the Shipman with the historical owner or captain of a ship named, like his, the *Maudeleyne* (see line 410). The Shipman's responsibility for the wine he transports — and apparently steals — has been explained in terms of the Laws of Oleron, a code of behavior for seagoers. There is general agreement that he cheats and commits murder; Lumiansky found his presence on the pilgrimage puzzling (**1098**).

The Physician (*lines 411-44*). Most commentators have pointed out the presence of both positive and negative traits in the Physician's portrait: his competence and learning as a medical practitioner have been seen as positive, his materialism as sharply negative. The balance between good and bad has been differently assessed, however, with Nicholls finding the Physician to be an image of the better medical men of the time despite his faults (**1125**), while Brown and Curry have questioned not only his character but also his professional abilities, doubting that he understands medical causation or has really read the treatises of the experts he talks about (**1115, 1118**).

The Wife of Bath (*lines 445-76*). Like the Prioress, the only other woman given a detailed portrait, the Wife is often discussed. Throughout the century she has been interpreted as both symbolic and realistic — which may, of course, be how Chaucer intended her. The symbolic implications of details such as her hat, her teeth, her redness, and her deafness have been examined according to medieval concepts of astrology, physiognomy, or Biblical allegory. The portrait has also been analyzed in terms of fourteenth-century social realities, with suggestions that a specific historical woman served as the model, discussions of the weaving industry in Chaucer's time, and comments on the contemporary plausibility of her multiple pilgrimages. She has been regarded as a dramatic, realistic personality, so that we can speculate about her sexual proclivities and her reasons for joining the pilgrimage; or, less individualistically, as a folktale archetype, a representative of the new bourgeois economy, or a stock figure in the antifeminist tradition. The possibility of revisions in the portrait has been suggested.

The Parson (*lines 477-528*). The main textual crux in the Parson's portrait has been the exact meaning of *spiced conscience* (line 526), a phrase that also occurs in the Wife of Bath's Prologue (Fragment III, line 435). Otherwise, there has been general agreement that he represents the ideal priest, though the relationship between the ideal depicted here and fourteenth-century realities has been debated. Some interpreters have thought that the Parson's portrait constitutes approval of the Lollard (Wycliffite) movement, while others have found the portrait orthodox, though critical of contemporary abuses.

The Plowman (lines 529–41). Commentary on the Plowman has not been extensive, perhaps because he tells no story. The small amount of work on his portrait has focused on its satirical or political implications: in depicting a contented, idealized peasant, was Chaucer expressing his disapproval of the Peasants' Revolt or criticizing other ways in which real peasants were behaving?

The Transition (lines 542–44) and the Miller (lines 545–66). The listing of the remaining pilgrims at lines 542–44 has been recognized as a pause useful to the audience, or interpreted as evidence of revision. The Miller's stout head, which he uses to break doors down, has received several comments, as have his bagpipe, his hair, the animal comparisons in his portrait, and other traits. His similarity to the Miller within the Reeve's tale has been noted. He has been thought to resemble an ape, to be a caricature of a knight, and to evoke Pilate and the medieval tradition of the devil-as-hammerer.

The Manciple (lines 567–86). Aside from the general recognition that the Manciple is a shrewd trickster, and that his tale is appropriate to his GP portrait, there has been little commentary on this pilgrim.

The Reeve (lines 587–622). The Reeve's age in GP has been debated: is he middle-aged or elderly? His close-shaven beard, his horse, his garments, and his position at the end of the pilgrimage group have received attention, as has the way in which GP seems to foreshadow his later quarrel with the Miller. The portrait specifies that he lives near Baldeswelle in Norfolk (lines 619–20) and historical models have been proposed.

The Summoner (lines 623–68 and line 673). The Summoner's skin disease has provoked a variety of medical diagnoses, some with symbolic implications. The sexual suggestions in such traits as his singing burdoun with the Pardoner (line 673), his pulling of finches, and his interest in the young girls of the diocese have been explored, with some debate as to whether homosexuality might be intended. His liking for garlic, onions, and leeks has been correlated to the Biblical mention of these foods (Numbers 11:5), which are thought to represent depravity and other spiritual faults. Most critics have found the Summoner to be an unpleasant character, though clinically interesting.

The Pardoner (lines 669–714). As one of the strangest literary figures of all time, the Pardoner has elicited quite diverse responses among his commentators, some of whom see him as an utterly lost soul, others as living proof that God loves all creatures, even such as he. Everyone agrees that he has a sexual problem, though not everyone agrees on exactly what it is, or what it implies in spiritual terms. His hair, cap, purse, relics, pardons, and other accoutrements have been studied for their allegorical as well as literal significance; his companionship with the Summoner is seen as reinforcing his corruption. His motives for going on pilgrimage have been debated, with certain commentators finding him wholly hypocritical, while more sympathetic interpreters suggest that he seeks Becket's shrine at least partly in hopes of redemption. The contemporary scandals at the hospital of St Mary's of Rouncival, to which the Pardoner is apparently attached (line 670), the liturgical references in the portrait, and other details have been explained.

The narrator's comment on his descriptions and his apology for his style (lines 715-46). It has been pointed out that the reputation of the house called the *Belle* (line 719) was none too good. The narrator's claim that words must be cousin to the deed has been traced to Boethius, the *Roman de la Rose*, Plato, the *Decameron*, and other sources; Huppé argues that the narrator misinterprets both Plato and Christ (1345).

The Host and the establishment of the storytelling contest (lines 747-858). The Host has been compared to the chorus in a Greek drama, to a tour guide, to a secular ruler establishing a government, to Christ as Servant-and-Master, to the devil, to the Eagle in Chaucer's *House of Fame*, and to a surrogate for the author. His resemblance to the historical Harry Bailly, innkeeper, has also been noted, and its significance debated. Commentary on the storytelling contest that he devises has drawn upon political theory, modern games-theory, religious contexts such as the Last Judgment, and principles of medieval literary criticism, with some debate over whether the plan for each pilgrim to tell four tales is Chaucer's idea or the Host's, an early estimate or a late revision. The Host is usually regarded as a comic figure, though with serious overtones. The appropriateness of having the cut fall to the Knight, whether that happened *by aventure, or sort, or cas* (lines 844-5), has been acknowledged.

What amounteth al this wit?

In moments of irreverence towards scholarship one might be tempted to ask the Host's impatient question (Fragment I, line 3901)—and even to answer it with the Pardoner's phrase, *superfluytee abhomynable* (VI. 471). It is easy enough to identify articles that should never have been published, faddish interpretations that do not bear the test of time, and other manifestations of Queen Mab's cobwebs in the brain, children of an idle fantasy.

The present compilation may make it even easier to play that game. And yet I would suggest that the typical quality of the work published on *GP* is quite high and that in fact we need more of such work, not less. Despite the productivity of the past few generations, certain aspects of *GP* have not been much explored. At the risk of setting further projects into motion, I might venture to mention a few topics that, in my view, deserve our attention.

We are accustomed to reading, and some of us to teaching, *GP* as a separate literary work. It is often anthologized in textbooks intended for survey courses in English or in Western literature. Among well-educated people who are not Chaucerians, *GP* is the single part of Chaucer's oeuvre that is likely to be recognized, even if not read in the original language or studied in detail. However, did Chaucer's own audience perceive *GP* as a separate poem? Aside from one excerpt, it does not occur as a text by itself, without other parts of the *Canterbury Tales*, in any known manuscript. How did *GP* originally exist, and how was it received? We might imagine that Chaucer read it aloud at one sitting, which would have taken an hour or somewhat more, but *GP* is clearly a cliff-hanger at the end, so that the evening's session, if that is what it was, may not have come to a very definitive close. Or we might imagine that Chaucer never read it aloud, but that he worked on it from time to time, planning to make it known to his public when the whole collection would be finished, which never occurred. Perhaps the mise-en-page of *GP* in different manuscripts has something to tell us, at least about how the fifteenth-century scribes interpreted it. (I am convinced that we need more manuscript studies.) At any rate, despite the many investigations that are broadly historical, placing the work in its early context, I do not recall any great number that deal with the issue of the mode of existence of *GP* in Chaucer's time and immediately afterwards.

Still within historical approaches, one might also pursue the effects of the allusiveness of *GP*, an allusiveness that embraces not only literary sources and conventions, or religious and allegorical concepts, but also contemporary realities. The allusions themselves are often identified, but we need to know more about why they are there and what response they would have provoked. The Reeve lives near Baldeswell in Norfolk, for example, and Chaucer's possible connections with that district have been traced, but what difference does it make? That kind of question is not often enough asked, or adequately answered.

Aside from historical approaches, users of this book will notice that other forms of criticism have been unevenly applied. The Wife of Bath is no stranger to the Robertsonians, but there may be more to say from their perspective about some of the less-studied pilgrims, such as the Manciple. If the fundamental Robertsonian thesis about characterization is valid, perhaps it can yield somewhat more complete results. Similarly, modern assumptions about intertextuality — the realization that one literary text implies or recalls another — have been applied to *GP* only sporadically, or in the form of the older source-studies. Existing analyses of the Prioress's resemblance to Criseyde and the narrator's kinship with earlier Chaucerian narrators might serve as starting-points for further investigations of the ways in which *GP* embodies other literary works, particularly Chaucer's own. (The Pardoner has always reminded me of Pandarus, though I am not wholly sure why.) Furthermore, what might be called, in current usage, the interior intertextuality or the self-referentiality of *GP* — its tendency to repeat certain of its own words or phrases or rhymes and so to establish self-echoes — has been analyzed primarily for the rhetorical signal *Ther was* that introduces many of the portraits, for central ethical terms such as *worthy*, and for a few other repetitions; here too there may be more to discover.

Finally, to suggest only one further realm of exploration, the ground-work has been laid for a new generation of structural studies (not the same as 'structuralist' studies) that would advance our understanding of the sequence of the portraits within *GP* and also the relationship, if any, between that sequence and the probable sequence of the tales that follow. To my knowledge all of the manuscripts agree upon the order of the portraits; Chaucer's intentions on that matter were presumably consistent and clear. The major groupings or sections of *GP* were pointed out long ago, and recent work (such as that of Howard, **287**) has refined those groupings, but puzzles remain. Why exactly do the Guildsmen follow the Franklin? Why are certain adjoining portraits linked by sharing a couplet-rhyme, others not? The Knight, who is given the first portrait in *GP*, tells the first tale, as the close of *GP* itself specifies, but after that point there is no obvious correlation between the sequence of the portraits in *GP* and either of the two sequences of tales that most modern editors accept. It might be worth wondering whether the Clerk–Merchant sequence in Fragment IV has anything to do with the Merchant–Clerk sequence in *GP*; or whether the Monk–Nun's Priest sequence in Fragment VII has anything to do with the *preestes thre*–Monk sequence (again the pair is reversed) in *GP*.

I may have merely sketched out a few of my own immediate *desiderata*, rather than identifying topics that will seem pressing to anybody else. My point is only that there is certainly work left to do. It may not always be true that *glosynge is a glorious thyng* (Fragment III, line 1793), and one must admit that critical schools and arguments often revolve in the same patterns, *now up, now down, as boket in a welle* (I.1533), rather than running straight and true. Nevertheless, surely we will benefit from at least the best of our interpretive endeavors. And, just as surely, Chaucer can withstand even the worst of our mistakes. As the six hundredth anniversary of the General Prologue passes into history, the firm durability of the work is beyond question.

Chaucer's General Prologue to the *Canterbury Tales*

Part 1: Editions

The editions prepared at the end of the nineteenth century by Skeat and Pollard, and the twentieth-century editions through 1984, are listed chronologically. If more than one was published in a given year, within that year they are listed alphabetically by editor (editions that have no named editor are given at the end of the year's group). For an overview, see the Introduction, pp xxi–xxii above.

The earlier editions, beginning with that of Caxton (ca 1478), are conveniently described by Hammond (**120**, pp 114–49 and 202–19). The first editor who, in Hammond's words (p 205), 'attempted to construct and to annotate the text' was Thomas Morell in 1737; the other important eighteenth-century edition was that of Thomas Tyrwhitt in 1775–78. Between 1868 and 1877 the Chaucer Society issued the eight parts of F.J. Furnivall's 'Six-Text' edition of the *Canterbury Tales*, so called because it presented parallel texts from six manuscripts: Ellesmere, Hengwrt, Cambridge Gg.iv.27, Corpus Christi College (Oxford), Petworth, and Lansdowne 851. The fascicle containing the General Prologue was the first one (1868). The publication of the 'Six-Text' and other Chaucer Society editions of manuscripts reflected the desire to establish an authentic Chaucer text. This approach also characterized the critical edition of Skeat (**3**), who relied heavily upon the 'Six-Text'. Since Skeat's work in turn influenced the major twentieth-century editors, considerable continuity in editorial traditions can be seen from Furnivall's time onwards. An argument could even be made that the main editorial tradition, at least for the *General Prologue*, goes back to Tyrwhitt (see **540**).

Among the twentieth-century editions listed below, particularly important for scholarly purposes have been those of Robinson in 1933, revised in 1957 (**42**), Manly and Rickert in 1940 (**49**), Donaldson in 1958 (**63**), Baugh in 1963 (**69**), Pratt in 1974 (**88**), Fisher in 1977 (**91**), Ruggiers et al in 1979 (**93**), and Blake in 1980 (**95**).

1 *Chaucer: The Prologue to the Canterbury Tales, School Edition.* Ed. Walter W. Skeat. Oxford: Clarendon Press, 1891; London: Henry Frowde,
1891; New York: Macmillan, 1891. Rpt 1897, 1899. Rev (3rd ed.) 1906;
rpt 1940, 1949, 1980. Clarendon Press Series.
A school edition: the text of *GP* (based on the Ellesmere ms, with inconsistencies remedied and emendations from six other mss) is preceded by a
brief introduction and followed by substantial notes and an index of words
explained. For Skeat's critical edition, see **3**.

2 *The Student's Chaucer, Being an Edition of His Works Edited from Numerous Manuscripts.* Ed. Walter W. Skeat. New York and London: Macmillan,
1895. Rpt 23 times by 1976. Also published with imprint of Henry Frowde
and of Oxford University Press.
A school edition: this is a one-volume text based on Skeat's critical edition (**3**). A short general introduction, notes on textual variations and
emendations, and a glossary are included.

3 *The Complete Works of Geoffrey Chaucer, Edited from Numerous Manuscripts.* 6 vols with a supplement, *Chaucerian and Other Pieces* (vol 7).
Ed. Walter W. Skeat. Oxford: Clarendon Press, 1894–1897. 2nd ed. 1900.
Often rpt (different volumes at different dates). 'The Oxford Chaucer.'
This major edition, which has formed the basis of many other twentieth-
century editions, provides (in vol 4, pp 1–25 in the 1st edition) a *GP* text
that is based on the Ellesmere ms collated with ms Harley 7334 and the five
mss that had been published by the Chaucer Society, along with Ellesmere,
as the 'Six-Text' print [see introductory note on p 1 above.] The text thus
produced is extensively annotated (in vol 5, pp 1–59). For comments on
specific passages, from the first edition, see **652, 708, 751, 851, 906, 1032,
1257, 1350**. The general treatment of *CT* sources (in vol 3, pp 371–504)
examines the frame-tale tradition, the date and plan of the pilgrimage, the
question of the number of pilgrims in the group, and the 'dramatic and
masterly' quality of the sketches, which are 'doubtless original, with the
remarkable exception of certain lines in the descriptions of the Prioresse
and the Wyf of Bathe, which are transcribed or imitated from *Le Roman
de la Rose*' (3:389). Vol 6 includes general discussions of language and
metrics, an extensive glossary, and an index of proper names.

4 *The Works of Geoffrey Chaucer.* Ed. Alfred W. Pollard, H. Frank Heath,
Mark H. Liddell, and W.S. McCormick. London and New York: Macmil-
lan, 1898. 'The Globe Chaucer.' Many reprints, including Freeport, NY:
Books for Libraries Press, 1972.

Reprinted 14 times by 1928, this edition was widely used. The *CT* section, general introduction, and general glossary were prepared by Pollard. (For his separate editions see **9**, **12**, and **18** below.) The introduction to the *CT* briefly discusses the dating of *GP*, the pilgrimage setting, the mss, and sources. The text is based on the Ellesmere ms with conservative modifications from the other five mss of the 'Six-Text' edition [see introductory note on p 1 above], along with Harley 7334. *GP* appears on pp 1–13 in the 1898 edition, with brief glosses on the page; for specific comments see **641**, **837**, **900**, **942**, **1018**.

5 *The Complete Works of Geoffrey Chaucer.* With an Introduction by Thomas R. Lounsbury. New York: Crowell, 1900.
A school edition: after a short general introduction, the text is presented (its basis in the mss or earlier editions is not stated) and followed by a glossary. Crowell apparently published this edition in two volumes also — not seen. Cf Lounsbury, **11**.

6 *Chaucer: The Prologues to the Canterbury Tales, the Knightes Tale, The Nonnes Prestes Tale.* Ed. Mark H. Liddell. New York and London: Macmillan, 1901. Rpt 1922.
A school edition: an extensive discussion of the Middle English language is followed by briefer considerations of Chaucer's life and the *CT* mss, by the text (based on the Ellesmere ms, collated with others), by explanatory notes, and by a glossary.

7 *The Cambridge MS. Dd.4.24 of Chaucer's Canterbury Tales, Completed by the Egerton MS. 2726 (the Haistwell MS.), Parts I and II.* 2 vols. Ed. Frederick J. Furnivall. London: Kegan Paul, Trench, Trübner & Co., 1901 and 1902. Publications of the Chaucer Society, First Series, 95 and 96.
GP appears on pp 7–25 of vol 1. Lines 1–252 and 505–758, missing from the Cambridge ms, are supplied from the Egerton. Woodcuts of the Ellesmere and Cambridge illustrations are included in vol 2.

8 *Geoffrey Chaucer's The Prologue to the Book of the Tales of Canterbury, The Knight's Tale, The Nun's Priest's Tale.* Ed. Andrew Ingraham. New York and London: Macmillan, 1902. Rpt 1903, 1904, 1905, 1938, 1939.
A school edition: the text is followed by discussions of Chaucer's life, works, and language, and by notes and a glossary. The ms basis of the text is not stated, but it appears to be that of Skeat (**3**), with some regularization of spelling. Six ms versions of lines 1–11 are provided, along with scansion for 49 (non-consecutive) lines from *GP*. 'The Prologue, though it has been shown that Chaucer might have caught some of the traits from literature, appears to be the result of personal observation of English folk' (p 230).

9 *Chaucer's Canterbury Tales. Reprinted from the Globe Edition.* Ed. A.W. Pollard. London: Macmillan, 1902.
A school edition: apparently a re-issue of the *CT* part of the 1898 collected works (4); not seen.

10 *The Select Chaucer.* Ed. J. Logie Robertson. Edinburgh and London: Blackwood, 1902.
A school edition: after an introduction on Chaucer's life, times, and language, and a brief introduction to the *CT*, the text (based on the Ellesmere and Harleian mss) is presented, followed by notes and a glossary. *GP* is segmented: the beginning and ending are presented together as if continuous; the portraits then follow separately.

11 *The Canterbury Tales by Geoffrey Chaucer.* With an Introduction by Thomas R. Lounsbury. New York: Crowell, 1903.
A school edition: after an introduction on Chaucer's life, times, works, and language, the text is presented (its ms basis is not stated) and followed by a glossary. Cf. Lounsbury, 5; the present volume is based upon that one.

12 *Chaucer's Canterbury Tales: The Prologue.* Ed. Alfred W. Pollard. London and New York: Macmillan, 1903/rev 1932. Rpt London: Macmillan, 1967, and New York: St. Martin's Press, 1967.
Reprinted nine times before the 1932 revision and at least sixteen times since, this school edition has been widely used. The general introduction discusses Chaucer's life, poetry, place in English literature, use of the framework principle, language, versification, and astrology — as well as the text of this edition, which is based on the Ellesmere ms with corrections from a few others. *GP* is followed by extensive notes and a short glossary. In the revised edition Pollard accepts the general plausibility of Manly's suggestions (see 35) that several of the pilgrims may be drawn from life.

13 *Chaucer: Canterbury Tales, The Prologue & Nun's Priest Tale.* Ed. A.J. Wyatt. London: Clive, 1903/rev 1929. University Tutorial Series. General Editor, William Briggs.
A school edition: after an introduction on Chaucer's life, language, and meter, the *CT*, and *GP*, the text is presented with notes and a glossary. The basis of the text in mss or previous editions is not stated. An appendix groups the information provided in the portraits into categories: mounts, weapons, clothing, beards, facts not depending on observation alone, and similes and striking metaphors. The flyleaf indicates that *GP* is also available, in this series, with *KnT* or *MLT* (these editions not seen). See also **14, 17, 36**.

14 *Chaucer: The Prologue to the Canterbury Tales.* Ed. A.J. Wyatt. London: Clive, 1903 [perhaps 1900?]. 2nd ed. 1927. University Tutorial Series. General Editor, William Briggs.
A school edition: first edition not seen; in the second edition the treatment of *GP* is the same as in Wyatt, **13**.

15 *The Poetical Works of Geoffrey Chaucer From the Text of Professor Skeat.* 3 vols. London: Grant Richards [1903–1906]: imprints vary; imprint of vol 3 (1906) is London: Oxford Univerisity Press. Vol 3 rpt 1910, 1921, 1925, 1930. World's Classics Series vols. 42, 56, 76. Vol 3 of this set contains *CT*.
The text is followed by a short note on language and meter, and a glossary. (For Skeat's edition, on which this is based, see **3**.)

16 *Chaucer: The Prologue to the Canterbury Tales.* Ed. C.T. Onions. London: Horace Marshall, 1904. The Carmelite Classics.
A school edition: after a brief preface, the text (based on the Ellesmere ms) is presented, followed by a brief note on meter, a set of study questions, and a short glossary.

17 *Chaucer: The Canterbury Tales, The Prologue and the Squire's Tale.* Ed. A.J. Wyatt. London: Clive, 1904. University Tutorial Series.
A school edition: the treatment of *GP* is the same as that in Wyatt, **13**.

18 *Chaucer's Canterbury Tales [Vol 1]: The Prologue, the Knightes Tale, The Man of Lawes Tale, The Prioresses Tale and the Clerkes Tale.* Ed. Alfred W. Pollard. London: Kegan Paul, Trench & Co., 1905. The Dryden Series.
A school edition: after a short introduction, the selections are presented and are followed by a brief glossary. The texts are based upon 'the Harleian manuscript and those of the Six Text edition' [see introductory note on p 1 above], using the principle of 'taking the easiest reading' in 'a large concession' to 'modern laziness' (p xxv).

19 *The Works of Geoffrey Chaucer and Others, Being a Reproduction in Facsimile of the First Collected Edition 1532 from the Copy in the British Museum.* Intro. Walter W. Skeat. London: Alexander Moring for the De La More Press and Henry Frowde for the Oxford University Press, 1905.
In 1532 Thynne printed the first collected edition of Chaucer's works (along with some non-Chaucerian pieces). This edition provided the standard Chaucer text for more than two hundred years — until that of Tyrwhitt (1775–1778), which returned to the mss. In the present facsimile the text of *GP*, which is called 'The prologues,' appears on pp 11–20. Fifteen woodcuts of pilgrims are included, most of them taken by Thynne from Caxton's second edition of *CT*; the illustrations are placed at the tales, not in *GP*.

20 *Selections from Chaucer.* Ed. Edwin A. Greenlaw. Chicago: Scott, Foresman and Co., 1907.
An introduction, notes, and a glossary are included; the text is based on Ellesmere.

21 *The Prologue to the Canterbury Tales of Geoffrey Chaucer.* Ed. E.F. Willoughby. London and Glasgow: Blackie, 1907. Blackie's Standard English Classics.
A school edition: after a general introduction emphasizing Chaucer's language, the text (said to be based upon Wright's revision of the Harleian ms and Morris's text) is presented, along with notes and a glossary. (For the later edition in Blackie's series, see **50**.)

22 *The Prologue to the Canterbury Tales of Geoffrey Chaucer.* Designs by Ambrose Dudley. London: Arnold Fairbairne, 1907. Rpt London: Chatto & Windus, 1909.
In this artistic edition the text is said to be based on that of Skeat (**3**?); there is no critical apparatus.

23 *Chaucer's Canterbury Tales for the Modern Reader.* Ed. Arthur Burrell. London and Toronto: Dent, 1908; New York: Dutton, 1908. Rpt 1909, 1910, 1913, 1915, 1926, 1930, 1936, 1948. Everyman's Library. Series Editor, Ernest Rhys.
A school/popular edition: after a general introduction, the text, somewhat modernized, is presented. The basis of the text is not stated; there are no notes or glossary. (For the later Everyman's Library edition, see **62**). Cf. Burrell, **27**.

24 *Chaucer: The Prologue and the Knight's Tale.* Ed. M. Bentinck-Smith. Cambridge, England: Cambridge University Press, 1908; New York: Putnam, 1908. Rpt 1909, 1915, 1923, 1929. Also *GP* issued separately as *Chaucer: The Prologue*, 1929 [not seen]. Pitt Press Series.
A school edition: the text (based on the Ellesmere ms) is preceded by a substantial general introduction on Chaucer's position in English literature, his life and works, his language, the *CT* as a whole, and (briefly) *GP*. Notes, bibliography, and vocabulary are included.

25 *The Ellesmere Chaucer Reproduced in Facsimile*, vol 1. Preface by Alix Egerton. Manchester: Manchester University Press, 1911.
The Ellesmere ms, owned by the Huntington Library in San Marino, California, has been used as the basis of many editions (see other items in this section) and is the most lavishly decorated of the extant *CT* manuscripts. In this facsimile edition the text of *GP* appears on folios 5r–13v (not numbered in the reproduction). For reproductions of the Ellesmere illustrations of the pilgrims, see **562, 572, 575, 580**.

26 *Poems of Chaucer: Selections from his Earlier and Later Works.* Ed. Oliver Farrar Emerson. New York: Macmillan, 1911.
A school edition: after an introduction on Chaucer's life, times, chronology, language, and versification, the text is presented 'on the basis of the reprints of manuscripts by the Chaucer Society, these being independently examined for this edition' (pp v-vi). Notes and a glossary follow.

27 *The Canterbury Tales by Geoffrey Chaucer: Part I, Prologue, The Knightes Tale, The Clerkes Tale.* Ed. Arthur Burrell. London: Dent, 1913. English Literature for Schools.
A school edition: after a brief introduction, the texts (based on those in Burrell's larger edition, **23**) are presented.

28 *The College Chaucer.* Ed. Henry Noble MacCracken. New Haven: Yale University Press, 1913; London: Humphrey Milford, 1913; Oxford: Oxford University Press, 1913. Rpt seven times through 1929.
A school edition: a brief preface is followed by the *CT* (from the Ellesmere ms), other Chaucer selections, an appendix on Chaucer's language, life, writings, dates, and sources, a discussion of the *CT* as a human comedy, and an extensive glossary.

29 *Selections from Chaucer.* Ed. S.E. Winbolt. London: G. Bell, 1913. Bell's English Texts.
A school edition: a brief introduction is followed by *GP, KnT,* and the Prol to *LGW.* The basis of the texts in mss or previous editions is not identified.

30 *The Canterbury Tales of Geoffrey Chaucer Illustrated after Drawings by W. Russell Flint.* London: Philip Warner for the Medici Society, 1913. Riccardi Press Books.
The text of this artistic edition is based on that of Skeat (**3**). There is also apparently a three-volume version, of the same date (not seen).

31 *Geoffrey Chaucer's Canterbury Tales nach dem Ellesmere Manuscript mit Lesarten, Anmerkungen und einem Glossar.* Ed. John Koch. Heidelberg: Winter, 1915. Englische Textbibliothek 16. Series Editor, Johannes Hoops.
A school edition: after a general introduction — emphasizing the mss, the development of the *CT*, their sources, and previous editions — the text is edited from the Ellesmere ms. Notes on the variants, the Latin marginal glosses in several mss, and an extensive glossary are included.

32 *Chaucer-Handbuch für Studierende: ausgewählte Texte mit Einleitungen, einem Abriss von Chaucers Versbau und Sprache und einem Wörterverzeichnis.* Ed. Max Kaluza. Leipzig: Bernhard Tauchnitz, 1919.
A school edition: after an introduction on Chaucer's life, works, reading,

and the mss and editions, Kaluza presents selections (with headnotes) from most of Chaucer's works. The text of *GP* is taken from the Ellesmere ms. A discussion of Chaucer's verse and language and a glossary follow.

33 *Selections from Chaucer.* Ed. William Allen Neilson and Howard Rollin Patch. New York: Harcourt, Brace & Co., 1921.
A school edition: after an introduction on Chaucer's life, times, literary art, and language, the text (based on that of Skeat, **3**, with some normalization of spelling) is presented, with a list of variants and glossary.

34 *Chaucer and Spenser, Contrasted as Narrative Poets.* Ed. Guy Boas. London: Nelson, 1926. The 'Teaching of English' Series. General Editor, Sir Henry Newbolt.
In these selections from the works of the two poets, chosen to facilitate comparisons, *GP*, in the version of 'The Oxford Poets' (**3**), is preceded by an introduction and accompanied by glosses.

35 *Canterbury Tales by Geoffrey Chaucer.* Ed. John Matthews Manly. New York: Holt, 1928; London: Harrap, 1928.
A school edition: after an extensive introduction, which includes a brief bibliography, a section on 'The Pilgrims — Types or Individuals' (pp 70–4), and much other material pertinent to *GP*, the text is presented. Detailed notes and a glossary follow. This version 'is in no sense an attempt at a critical text' (p vi); for Manly's critical text see the Manly-Rickert edition (**49**). The basis here is the Ellesmere ms only, with minimal corrections. Many of Manly's characteristic viewpoints about *GP* appear here in the introduction or notes — for example, the possibility that Chaucer expanded, rather than reduced, his overall plan, since 'the Prologue contained some of Chaucer's latest work' (p 68); the absurdity of three priests accompanying the Prioress; and the likelihood that there were historical models for at least some of the pilgrims. Cf. **881**, **1017**. This edition, which does not include the complete *CT*, may be the same as *Canterbury Tales, Selected Tales*, ed. John M. Manly, 1928, listed in the British Library and National Union Catalogs — not located.

36 *Chaucer: The Prologue to the Canterbury Tales and The Nun's Priest's Tale.* Ed. A.J. Wyatt. London: Sidgwick and Jackson, 1928. Rpt 1929 [1930? — rpt not seen].
A school edition: after a general introduction, the text (based primarily on the Ellesmere, Hengwrt, and Harley mss) is presented, with glosses. Appendices on the zodiac and the humors are included.

37 *The Works of Geoffrey Chaucer.* 8 vols. Oxford: Blackwell (printed at the Shakespeare Head Press, Stratford), 1928 (vol 1) and 1929 (vols 2–8).

In this artistic edition, illustrated with miniatures modelled upon the Ellesmere illustrations, the text (*GP* is in vol 1) is based upon that of Pollard (4).

38 *Geoffrey Chaucer: The Canterbury Tales.* Ed. Walter W. Skeat. Intro. Louis Untermeyer. New York: Modern Library, 1929. Rpt 1957.
A school/popular edition: after a brief introduction on Chaucer's life and times, the text (based on Skeat's edition, 3) is presented, followed by a short statement on language and meter and a glossary.

39 *The Canterbury Tales by Geoffrey Chaucer.* Vol 1. With Wood Engravings by Eric Gill. Waltham Saint Lawrence, Berkshire, England: Golden Cockerel Press, 1929.
The text of this artistic edition is based on that of Skeat (3).

40 *The Canterbury Tales of Geoffrey Chaucer, Together with a Version in Modern English Verse by William Van Wyck.* 2 vols. Illustrated by Rockwell Kent. New York: Covici, Friede, 1930.
This artistic edition is limited to 931 copies. Not seen: according to the review by Robert K. Root, *SRL*, 7 (January 24, 1931), 545–6, the text is based upon that of Skeat (3). Van Wyck provides a parallel-column modernization, and Kent contributes full-page illustrations of the pilgrims.

41 *Complete Works, in Poetry and Prose; with Introduction, Aids to Chaucer's Grammar, Versification, and Pronunciation.* Boston: Cornhill, 1930.
Listed in Willard E. Martin, Jr., *A Chaucer Bibliography 1925–1933* (Durham, NC: Duke University Press, 1935), p 15; but not located—a ghost?

42 *The Poetical Works of Chaucer.* Ed. F.N. Robinson. London: Oxford University Press, 1933; Cambridge, MA: Houghton Mifflin, 1933. Also published as *The Complete Works of Geoffrey Chaucer*, Student's Cambridge Edition. Boston: Houghton Mifflin, 1933. 2nd ed., with title *The Works of Geoffrey Chaucer.* Boston: Houghton Mifflin, 1957. Rpt (paperback) London: Oxford University Press, 1974. 'The New Cambridge Chaucer.'
A general introduction on Chaucer's life, works, language, and meter, and on editorial principles, is followed by an introduction to the *CT*. The text is based on the Ellesmere ms with modifications from other mss. A glossary, bibliography, and extensive notes are included. Many bibliographical references are provided in the notes. Robinson's second edition has been the one most cited by scholars in recent years, having superseded Skeat (3) as the standard. The second edition's expanded notes are supplemented by a list of changes in the text (1957, p 883): the Manly-Rickert edition (49), with its inventory of textual variants, had appeared in the meantime. (Eg, the *Aprille* of line 1 in Robinson's first edition has become *Aprill* in his

second.) In the second edition the text of *GP* is on pp 17–25, with notes on pp 649–69 and 889–90. For a few of the more important notes on individual lines of *GP*, from the second edition, see **646, 704, 843, 1063, 1104, 1191, 1289.** A third collaborative edition, under the general editorship of Larry Benson and entitled *The Riverside Chaucer*, appeared in 1987 as the present book was in press.

- Review [of 1st ed.] by Albert C. Baugh, 'Fifty Years of Chaucer Scholarship,' *Spec*, 26 (1951), 661: 'It is hard to overpraise this monumental edition. Not only has it given us the best text of Chaucer that we have, but the careful digest of Chaucer scholarship in the notes and commentary, and the very full record of the scholarly literature ... make it the indispensable tool of every student of Chaucer.'

- Review [of 2nd ed.] by Richard L. Hoffman, 'The Canterbury Tales,' in *Critical Approaches to Six Major English Works*, ed. Robert M. Lumiansky and Herschel Baker (Philadelphia: University of Pennsylvania Press, 1968; London: Oxford University Press, 1968), pp 41–80: the second edition is 'the most valuable single volume which any student of Chaucer can own' since its text 'is the most accurate complete version available, superseding even the very estimable editions of Skeat and Pollard' (p 42).

43 *Chaucer's Canterbury Tales: The Prologue.* Ed. Sanki Ichikawa. Tokyo: Kenyusha [1933? 1934?].
A school/popular edition: after a brief introduction, *GP* is presented, with a facing-page phonetic transcription and an English modernization at the foot of the page. Notes and glossary follow. The basis of the text, in mss or earlier editions, is not stated.

44 *Chaucer: The Prologue & Three Tales: The Prologue to the Canterbury Tales, the Prioress's Tale, The Nun's Priest's Tale, the Pardoner's Tale.* Ed. George H. Cowling. London: Ginn and Company [1934]. Selected English Classics. General Editor, A.H.R. Ball.
A school edition: an introduction on Chaucer's England, language, and the *CT* is followed by the texts indicated in the title, with explanatory notes and a glossary. The Ellesmere ms, with its spelling normalized, forms the basis of the edition.

45 *The Prologue and Four Canterbury Tales [by] Geoffrey Chaucer.* Ed. Gordon Hall Gerould. New York: Nelson, 1935.
A school edition: after a brief introduction on Chaucer's life and works, the text is presented, with glosses at the foot of the page, notes, and a glossary

at the end. The basis of the text is not stated, though the editions of Skeat (**3**) and Robinson (**42**) are mentioned.

46 *The Prologue, the Knight's Tale, and the Nun's Priest Tale from the Text of Chaucer's Canterbury Tales by F.N. Robinson.* Ed. Max J. Herzberg. Boston: Houghton Mifflin, 1936.
A school edition: after an introduction on Chaucer's life, times, works, and language, along with excerpts of statements in his praise and a brief discussion of *GP* and its pilgrims, the text (see **42**) is presented. Annotations on the page and a brief glossary at the end are provided.

47 *The Canterbury Tales of Chaucer.* Ed. Edwin Johnston Howard and Gordon Donley Wilson. Ann Arbor, MI: Edwards Brothers [reproduced from typescript], 1937. Revised as *The Canterbury Tales by Geoffrey Chaucer.* Selected and Ed. Edwin Johnston Howard and Gordon Donley Wilson. Oxford, OH: Anchor Press, 1942. Rpt New York: Prentice-Hall, 1947.
A school edition: after a general introduction on Chaucer's life, times, works, and language, the text is presented, followed by notes and glossary. In the 1937 and 1942 editions the basis of the text, in mss or previous editions, is not stated (1947 reprint not seen).

48 *Canterbury Tales: Prologue, Nun's Priest's Tale, Squire's Tale.* [Ed. G. S. Dickson? — name given on half-title page only.] London: Thomas Nelson, 1938. Masterpieces of English Series.
A school edition: a brief introduction is followed by the texts indicated in the title, along with explanatory notes. The basis of the text is not specified.

49 *The Text of the Canterbury Tales Studied on the Basis of All Known Manuscripts.* Ed. John M. Manly and Edith Rickert. 8 vols. Chicago: University of Chicago Press, 1940.
This edition makes available the text of *GP* as represented in every known ms. (For this project photostats of the mss were made; copies of the photostats are available in the British Library, the University of Chicago Library, the Pennsylvania State University Library, and perhaps also elsewhere.) Pertinent to *GP* are vol 1, *passim*, descriptions of the mss; vol 2, pp 78–96, classification of the mss; vol 3, pp 1–37, the text, with textual notes and the glosses and rubrics found in the mss; and vol 5, pp 1–79, the variant readings from all mss. The main text as printed was derived by traditional processes of recension, ie, analyses of textual variants in order to establish the probable readings of the 'archetypal ms' — the author's or scribe's copy from which the existing mss presumably derive. (This archetype may itself

have included errors and did not necessarily represent Chaucer's final intentions.) On the mss containing *GP*, see **552** below; for a few of the more important notes to individual lines, see **634, 697, 825, 894, 936.**

50 *The Prologue to the Canterbury Tales by Geoffrey Chaucer.* Ed. R.F. Patterson. London and Glasgow: Blackie, 1940. Blackie's Standard English Classics.
A school edition: after a general introduction, the text (based on Skeat, **3**) is presented, along with notes and a glossary. (For the earlier edition in Blackie's series, see **21.**)

51 *Geoffrey Chaucer, Contes de Cantorbéry: Contes Choisis.* Ed. Joseph Delacourt. Paris: Aubier, 1946. Bibliothèque de Philologie Germanique, 10. General Editors, A. Jolivet and F. Mossé.
A school edition: after an introduction on Chaucer's life and works, a short bibliography, and a substantial treatment of Chaucer's language, the text (based on the Ellesmere ms, with modifications from others) is presented. Notes and glossary are provided.

52 *Canterbury Tales: Chaucer for Present-Day Readers.* Ed. H.L. Hitchins. London: Murray, 1946. Rpt 1946, 1948. Enlarged 1949. New ed. with preface by John Betjeman, 1956.
A school edition: the text, based on Pollard's Globe edition (**4**), is somewhat modernized. See **55.**

53 *Canterbury Tales by Geoffrey Chaucer.* Ed. Robert D. French. New York: Appleton-Century-Crofts, 1948. Rpt 1964. Crofts Classics Series.
A school edition: after a brief general introduction, the text (based on the Ellesmere mss) is presented and followed by a glossary.

54 *Chaucer's Canterbury Tales (Selected): An Interlinear Translation.* Ed. Vincent F. Hopper. Great Neck, NY: Barron's Educational Series, 1948. Rpt 18 times by 1962.
A school edition: after a short general introduction, the text — along with an interlinear translation — is presented. A few notes follow. The basis of the text, in mss or earlier editions, is not stated.

55 *Canterbury Tales: Chaucer for Present-Day Readers ... Adapted for Schools.* Ed. H.L. Hitchins. Adapted by Frank Mosby. London: Murray, 1949.
A school edition: the selections, including *GP*, are based on Hitchins' somewhat modernized edition (**52**).

56 *A First Chaucer.* Ed. W.E.W. Carpenter-Jacobs. Exeter, England: Wheaton, 1952. English Inheritance Series.

A school edition: after a general introduction, the text (based on Skeat, **3**), is presented, with notes and glossary. *GP* is somewhat abbreviated.

57 *A Chaucer Reader: Selections from the Canterbury Tales.* Ed. Charles W. Dunn. New York: Harcourt Brace Jovanovich, 1952.
A school edition: the text is based on that of Manly-Rickert (**49**). The general introduction on Chaucer's life, works, language, and versification uses passages from *GP* as illustrations; a short separate introduction to *GP*, notes, glosses, and brief bibliography are provided. *GP* presents a 'survey of medieval society, embracing the three large categories — feudal, ecclesiastical, and urban' (p 5). See also **774**.

58 *The Canterbury Tales, Selections, Together with Selections from the Shorter Poems, by Geoffrey Chaucer.* Ed. Robert Archibald Jelliffe. New York: Scribner's, 1952. The Modern Student's Library.
A school edition: after a short introduction on Chaucer's life, times, and language, the text (based on the Ellesmere ms) is presented, followed by a glossary.

59 *A Chaucer Selection.* Ed. L.J. Lloyd. London: Harrap, 1952. Life, Literature, and Thought Library.
A school edition: after an introduction on Chaucer's life and works, the text, based on Skeat (**3**), is presented, followed by brief discussions of Chaucer's verse, vocabulary, and grammar, and by notes, a short bibliography, and a glossary.

60 *Chaucer: The Prologue to the Canterbury Tales.* Ed. R.T. Davies. London: George G. Harrap, 1953.
A school edition: after an introduction on Chaucer's life and work, rhetoric, the *CT*, *GP*, and pilgrimages, the text (based on the Ellesmere ms) is presented, followed by notes and appendices on Chaucer's English, meter, astrology, and astronomy, a brief bibliography, and a glossary.

61 *Canterbury Colloquies: A New Arrangement of the 'Prologue' and 'End-Links' of 'The Canterbury Tales' to Show Their Dramatic Significance.* Ed. N. Hardy Wallis. London: James Brodie, 1957.
The text of *GP* (according to Skeat's 'World's Classics Edition,' **38**?) is re-arranged to coincide with the order in which the pilgrims later tell their tales. The portraits of the pilgrims who do not tell a tale are grouped at the end, followed by 'Colloquies' consisting of the speeches of the pilgrims in the links.

62 *Geoffrey Chaucer: Canterbury Tales.* Ed. A.C. Cawley. London: Dent, 1958; New York: Dutton, 1958/rev 1975. Everyman's Library.

A school/popular edition: after a short introduction, the text (based on Robinson, **42**) is presented, along with annotations and glossing. It is followed by notes on grammar and versification and — in the revised edition only — a note on pronunciation that uses *GP* for its examples. (For the earlier Everyman's Library edition, see **23**.) See also **88** (review by Brewer).

63 *Chaucer's Poetry: An Anthology for the Modern Reader.* Ed. E.T. Donaldson. New York: Ronald Press, 1958. 2nd ed. 1975.
The text of *CT* is based on the Hengwrt ms but with standardized spelling. *GP* appears on pp 5–34 (1975 ed.), with glosses on the page. The text is followed by substantial commentaries on Chaucer's language, life, and individual works (on *GP*, see pp 1034–61). In *GP* 'the pictures are profoundly vital, though they have no chance to come down off the wall and participate in the dramatic action implicit in them' (p 1034). To counteract a static effect Chaucer provides suggestive juxtapositions, 'the comedy that arises from the simplicity of the narrator' (p 1034), and diversity in length and technique. Chaucer's realism does not lie in simple naturalistic accuracy, or in his meticulous detail, but in his ability to combine different kinds of ingredients and so produce characters who 'are at once perfect types and perfect individuals' (p 1036). For specific comments, see **597, 676, 739, 964, 1141, 1246.**

- Review by J.B. Bessinger, 'Chaucer: A Parliament of Critics,' *UTQ*, 29 (1959-1960), 91–6: Bessinger notes Donaldson's 'spirited commentary treating Chaucer as a highly sophisticated poet' and finds that the book conveys 'an engaging critical attitude' (p 91). Donaldson's division between poet and pilgrim means that 'the reader joins the pilgrimage as an exercise in double audition, during which he must constantly twiddle the dials of his dramatic-ironic-paradoxical preamplifier'; this 'subtle reading' is seen as 'valuable corrective' to older views (p 92).

- Review by Richard L. Hoffman, 'The Canterbury Tales,' in *Critical Approaches to Six Major English Works*, ed. Robert M. Lumiansky and Herschel Baker (Philadelphia: University of Pennsylvania Press, 1968; London: Oxford University Press, 1968), pp 41–80: Hoffman objects to Donaldson's modification of spelling, given 'the several dangers of acquainting students with a standardized brand of Middle English' which neither Chaucer nor any scribe actually wrote (p 43). Nevertheless, Donaldson's commentary provides 'thoughtful and lucid criticism' (p 43).

64 *The Works of Geoffrey Chaucer: A Facsimile of the William Morris Kelmscott Chaucer with the Original 87 Illustrations by Edward Burne-Jones.*

Intro. John T. Winterich. Cleveland and New York: World, 1958.
In this facsimile of the 1896 Kelmscott version, whose text was edited by
F.S. Ellis on the basis of Skeat's edition (3), the size of the original volume is slightly reduced for the convenience of readers. Winterich supplies
a short introduction on Chaucer and Morris; a selective glossary is based
on Skeat's annotations. See also **87** and **90**.

65 *Selections from Chaucer: The Prologue, The Nun's Priest's Tale, The Pardoner's Tale, The Squire's Tale.* Ed. Marjorie M. Barber. London: Macmillan, 1961; New York: St. Martin's Press, 1962. The Scholar's Library.
General Editor, Guy Boas.
A school edition: after a general introduction, the text (based on Pollard's
Globe Chaucer, 4) is presented, with glossary, notes, and brief discussions
of Chaucer's astronomy and language.

66 *The Canterbury Tales of Geoffrey Chaucer: A Selection.* Ed. Daniel Cook.
Garden City, NY: Anchor (Doubleday), 1961.
A school edition: after an introduction on Chaucer's life, language, and
CT, the text (based on the Ellesmere and Hengwrt mss) is presented, with
glosses on facing pages.

67 *Geoffrey Chaucer: The Canterbury Tales.* Ed. Mario Praz. 2nd ed. Bari:
Adriatica, 1961. Biblioteca italiana di testi inglesi, 1. General Editors,
Gabriele Baldini, Agostino Lombardo, and Giorgio Melchiori. [First ed.
not located; perhaps = *Geoffrey Chaucer e i Racconti di Canterbury*, ed.
Mario Praz, 1947 — not seen.]
A school edition: the extensive introduction includes discussions of Chaucer's
life, learning, indebtedness to French and Italian influences, the *CT* in gen-
eral, and Chaucer's language. The text, followed by notes, is based on
Robinson's first edition (**42**).

68 *Geoffrey Chaucer. Ausgewählte Canterbury Erzählungen Englisch und
Deutsch.* Ed. Martin Lehnert. Halle: VEB Verlag Sprache und Literatur,
1962.
According to the review by Siegfried Wenzel, *JEGP*, 62 (1963), 680–83,
this edition includes the portraits of the Miller, Reeve, Cook, Wife, Friar,
Summoner, Pardoner, and Shipman, based on Robinson's text (**42**), with
annotations [ed. not seen].

69 *Chaucer's Major Poetry.* Ed. Albert C. Baugh. New York: Appleton-
Century-Crofts, 1963; London: Routledge & Kegan Paul, 1963.
After a general introduction to Chaucer's life, language, and versification,
a short bibliography, and an introduction on the *CT* specifically, the text
(based apparently on the Ellesmere ms) is presented. *GP* appears on pp
237–56, with notes and glosses on the page. A general glossary is also

provided at the end. Chaucer was able to 'endow most of his pilgrims with vivid personalities, besides making them representative of a class' (p 229). In addition, 'some of the portraits may have been drawn from life' (p 229). When Chaucer noticed that the number of pilgrims (see line 24) was not accurate, rather than revise *GP* 'he achieved the desired number' by adding the Canon's Yeoman's episode (p 233). See also **88** (review by Brewer).

- Review by John Burrow, *EIC*, 14 (1964), 307–10: Baugh's glossary is better than Robinson's, but 'the commentary proper is often disappointingly slight' (p 309). Baugh's introductory material is 'generally sound, conservative stuff' (p 309), but sometimes 'inert and questionable' (p 309), or 'more or less indifferent to much recent criticism' (p 310).

- Review by D. Fox, *MLR*, 59 (1964), 624–5: The 'historical and factual bias of the edition' leads to 'irrelevant or misleading' notes, from the viewpoint of beginning students (p 625). The annotations on lines 9–10 and on the Prioress's portrait are cited as examples. Nevertheless, the glossary, sections on language, and 'thorough, accurate, and lucid summary of modern scholarship' make the book useful (p 625).

70 *The Prologue to the Canterbury Tales (Chaucer)*. Ed. A.B. Chatterjee. Calcutta: Susmit Chatterjee (New Mahamaya Press), 1963.
A school edition: the extensive introduction discusses Chaucer's life and works, the content of the portraits, realism and the depiction of Chaucer's contemporary world, and the knowledge of Chaucer the man that can be inferred from *GP*. The text (based on that of Skeat, **3**) is provided with glosses and notes. In the portraits Chaucer follows a method of determining one central trait or 'fixing the ego of a person and then working out details of dress, habits, profession etc. from this ... The Prioress, for example, is an innocent exhibitionist' and all the details attributed to her are manifestations of this 'one motive force' (p xxviii). *GP* provides 'not only a wonderful picture-gallery but also a very faithful image' of Chaucer's times (p xxxiii), though Manly's attempt to seek historical models for the pilgrims (**362**) was inappropriate. For comments on the Clerk and Shipman, see **981, 1094**.

71 *Chaucer*. Ed. Louis O. Coxe. New York: Dell, 1963. Laurel Poetry Series. General Editor, Richard Wilbur.
A school edition: after a short general introduction, the text ('based on those of Skeat and Robinson,' p 25) is presented and followed by a brief glossary.

72 *Chaucer: Canterbury Tales/Tales of Canterbury.* Ed. A. Kent Hieatt and Constance Hieatt. New York: Bantam Books, 1964. Bantam Dual-Language Series.
A school edition: after an introduction on Chaucer's life, works, and language, the text (based on that of Skeat, **3**) is presented, along with a facing-page modernization. A brief glossary of names, Latin phrases, etc, is included.

73 *The General Prologue to the Canterbury Tales by Geoffrey Chaucer.* Ed. James Winny. Cambridge: Cambridge University Press, 1965. Rpt 1966, 1969.
A school edition: the text (based upon Robinson's revised edition, **42**, with modified punctuation and spelling) is preceded by a substantial general introduction and followed by extensive notes and a glossary. The techniques of portraiture depict 'personal character as an immediately tangible presence,' so that although the 'pilgrims can be fitted into various contemporary categories' none of those classifications 'is ample enough to account for all the varieties of human personality which the portraits describe' (1965, p 16). The approach is that of a psychologist, not a moralist, and the pilgrims' faults 'interest Chaucer not as evidence of a breakdown of moral values but for what they reveal of individual character' (p 18). The object of Chaucer's satire, instead of being contemporary morals, is 'the comic self-ignorance which gives man two identities — the creature he is, and the more distinguished and inscrutable person he imagines himself to be' (p 18). Stylistically, in *GP* Chaucer writes with a 'vernacular plainness' (p 28). The opening sentence is offered as 'a sample of the poetic tradition which Chaucer had abandoned' (p 29). *GP* shows the enthusiasm and vitality of life as being threatened by 'negative forces, whose purpose is to bring to a standstill the system which nourishes and renews natural life' (p 41); the Pardoner, Reeve, and Summoner are negative figures. For specific comments, see **1005, 1172, 1386.**

74 *Geoffrey Chaucer: A Selection of His Works.* Ed. Kenneth Kee. Toronto and London: Macmillan, 1966; New York: St. Martin's Press, 1966. College Classics in English. General Editor, Northrop Frye.
A school edition: after a general introduction and one on *GP* specifically, the text (based on the Hengwrt and Ellesmere mss) is presented, along with glossing and notes.

75 *Geoffrey Chaucer: Selections from the Tales of Canterbury and Short Poems.* Ed. Robert A. Pratt. Boston: Houghton Mifflin, 1966. Riverside Editions. General Editor, Gordon N. Ray.
A school edition: after a general introduction and a note on the problem

of the order of the tales, the text (based on that of Robinson, **42**, but 'less conservative' and intended to 'recreate the text as Chaucer wrote it,' p xxxviii) is presented. Both glosses and notes are provided on the page. Cf Pratt's complete edition, **88**. Here, as there, line 164 is left unfinished after *chapeleyne*, reflecting Pratt's viewpoint that 'Chaucer must have left the line unfinished' (p 7).

76 *Geoffrey Chaucer: The Prologue to the Canterbury Tales.* Screen Prints by Ronald King. London: Editions Alecto, 1966. Rpt Guildford, Surrey, England: Circle Press, 1978; London: Eaton House Publishers, [1978].
This artistic edition, with its text based upon the Ellesmere ms, includes original prints or lithographs with each copy.

77 *Introducing Chaucer.* Ed. Raymond O'Malley. London: Heinemann, 1967. A school edition: after a general introduction, the text (based on Robinson, **42**, with simplified spelling) is presented, with notes and glossing. From *GP*, this edition includes the opening 42 lines; the portraits of the Squire, Prioress, Monk, Franklin, Shipman, Wife, Parson, and Miller; and the closing section, slightly abbreviated.

78 *Chaucer: The Prologue to the Canterbury Tales.* Ed. Frederic W. Robinson. Bath, England: James Brodie, [1967?].
A school edition: after a general introduction that includes a brief summary of each portrait, the text is presented and followed by notes and a glossary. The basis of the text is not stated, though editions by Skeat (**3**?) and Manly (**35**? **49**?) are mentioned.

79 *Geoffrey Chaucer: The Works, 1532, With Supplementary Material from the Editions of 1542, 1561, 1598, and 1602.* Ed. D.S. Brewer. Menston, Yorkshire: Scolar Press, 1969. Rpt (with slight editorial changes) Ilkley, Yorkshire, and London: Scolar Press, 1974, 1976.
This facsimile edition makes several early printed versions of *GP* available. Its purpose is to indicate how Chaucer 'appeared to readers in the sixteenth and seventeenth centuries' (intro, not paginated). Brewer gives bibliographical details of each edition identified in the title, along with brief comments on other early editions not reproduced here. The edition of 1561 includes woodcuts of the pilgrims in its printing of *GP*.

80 *Chaucer: General Prologue [to] The Canterbury Tales.* Ed. Phyllis Hodgson. London: Athlone Press, 1969; New York: Oxford University Press, 1969. Athlone Press Texts for Schools and Colleges.
A school edition: the text of *GP* (based on the Ellesmere ms) is accompanied by about a hundred and fifty pages of explanatory notes and discussions of Chaucer's life, times, language, and art, with detailed attention to

such contemporary preoccupations as astronomy and astrology. A book-list, glossary, and list of proper names are included. Hodgson comments that some of the pilgrims are stock figures: the Monk, Friar, Pardoner, and Parson all have well-established literary analogues. Chaucer's audience would also have recognized moral personifications, with the Monk and Friar suggesting Pride, several others Avarice, etc. There are 'two kinds of apprehension': that of 'the reporter, adjusting himself to this nonesuch fellowship with wide-eyed wonder' (p 26), and that of the omniscient poet. Lines 542–44 divide the whole of *GP* into two parts, as well as establishing the fifth and final group of pilgrims, the rogues. The other four groups are formed by (1) the Knight, Squire, and Yeoman; (2) the Prioress, Monk, and Friar; (3) a middle-class group 'bound by their attitude to material possession' (p 32); and (4) the Parson and Plowman. See also **616**.

81 *Geoffrey Chaucer: The Canterbury Tales; A Selection.* Ed. Donald R. Howard with the assistance of James Dean. New York: New American Library (Signet Classics), 1969; London: New English Library Limited, 1969. Signet Classic Poetry Series. General Editor, John Hollander.
A school edition: after a general introduction on Chaucer's life, times, and works, the text (based on that of Manly-Rickert, **49**, but 'eclectic,' p xxxix, and with normalized spelling) is presented, along with glossing. In the opening lines the voice we hear is that of the poet, which conveys '*authority*; the poet's voice is steeped in tradition, learning, science'; however, when the pilgrims are described 'we get (so he says) *experience*, for the pilgrim-observer claims to be telling us what he saw and heard. Authority plus experience — that is really the "method" of the General Prologue' (pp xi–xii). The three ideal portraits (the Knight's, the Parson's, and the Plowman's) represent the structured conception of the three estates. Against this conception Chaucer sets 'harsh reality' (p xiv) and 'an intentional quality of haphazardness and randomness' (p xv). *GP* presents 'a world of game, of carefree assent, a topsy-turvy world where social rank is set aside, where drawn straws turn out miraculously right "by aventure, or sort, or cas" [line 844] — a holiday atmosphere surging with discord and tension, its goal the Martyr's shrine' (p xviii). In *GP*, which 'encapsulates and sets the nature and governing principles' of the entire *CT*, 'a structure of memories and received ideas takes shape and, like consciousness itself, renders up the design of the whole in vivid associations of feeling and perception' (p xx). On the narrator, see **619**.

82 *Selections from Geoffrey Chaucer's The Canterbury Tales.* Ed. Francis King and Bruce Steele. Melbourne, Australia: F.W. Cheshire, 1969.
The text of *GP* (pp 1–58) uses Hengwrt spelling, with reference also to

Ellesmere and other mss as presented in Manly-Rickert (49), and modifications of punctuation. Notes and text are presented on facing pages. The commentary on *GP* (pp 338–61) includes a short analysis of each pilgrim. The discussions of related topics such as Chaucer's versification, the terms *curteisye, gentil,* and *sentence,* and medieval astrology, medicine, and courtly love (pp 312–403) are also pertinent. For comments on specific passages, see 692, 988, 1052, 1368. See also 84.

83 *Geoffrey Chaucer: The Canterbury Tales.* Ed. John Halverson. Indianapolis and New York: Bobbs-Merrill, 1971. The Library of Literature. General Editors, John Henry Raleigh and Ian Watt.
A school edition: after a general introduction on Chaucer's life, works, and language, the text (based on Robinson, 42, but 'a trifle closer to Ellesmere,' p xxi) is presented. Annotations at the foot of the page and a glossary are provided.

84 *Chaucer: The Prologue and Three Tales.* Ed. Francis King and Bruce Steele. London: Murray, 1971.
A school edition: the texts of *GP, PardT, PrT,* and *NPT* (based on the Hengwrt and Ellesmere mss) are accompanied by glosses and followed by explanatory notes, substantial commentaries, and short appendices on medieval topics such as courtly love. This edition is a shorter version of 82.

85 *A Choice of Chaucer's Verse.* Ed. Nevill Coghill. London: Faber and Faber, 1972. Faber Paper Covered Editions.
Lines 1–18 of *GP* and the portraits of the Prioress, Wife, Pardoner, Parson (shortened somewhat), and Squire are included, with some modernization. The basis of the text is Skeat (3).

86 *Geoffrey Chaucer: The Canterbury Tales.* [No editor specified. Introductory note by J.A.W. Bennett.] London: Cornmarket Reprints in association with Magdalene College, 1972.
This facsimile edition reproduces Pepys's copy of Caxton's second (1484) edition of the *CT* — the Caxton edition that adds the woodcuts of the pilgrims in *GP*. Also apparently published London: Paradine, 1973 — not seen.

87 *Ornamentation and Illustrations from the Kelmscott Chaucer* [Printed by William Morris]. Intro. Fridolf Johnson. New York: Dover, 1973; Toronto: General Publishing Company, 1973; London: Constable, 1973.
The illustrated opening to *GP* is included among these reproductions from the Kelmscott Chaucer (see 64 and 90). The introduction concentrates on Morris' artistic contributions.

88 *The Tales of Canterbury, Complete [by] Geoffrey Chaucer.* Ed. Robert A. Pratt. Boston: Houghton Mifflin, 1974. Rpt NY: Holmes & Meier, 1976.
After a general introduction on Chaucer's life and works, with emphasis on the *CT*, the text is presented, in a version based on Robinson (**42**) but modified in an attempt 'to recreate the text as Chaucer wrote it' (1974; p 561). *GP* appears on pp 1–26, with notes and glosses on the page. The 20 readings in *GP* which differ from those in Robinson's version are listed (p 562). For example, in line 11 *Nature* is capitalized; line 164 is left blank after *chapeleyne*. A general discussion of Chaucer's language, a short bibliography, and a basic glossary are included. Fictionally the pilgrims seem to have gathered by chance, but artistically they 'are most carefully selected' for diversity and for potential interplay (p xx). The descriptions often 'reflect self-revelatory monologues which the poet has elicited from his subjects; and which he passes along to us with sufficient comment to show that he is not taken in' (p xxii). See also **1380**.

This edition includes, in revised form, much of the material from Pratt 75.

- Review by Derek Brewer, *YES*, 7 (1977), 205–8: Using lines 152–93 of *GP* as a sample to evaluate the edition's annotation, Brewer concludes that 'Pratt aims at a less intelligent audience ... than do Baugh [**69**] and Cawley [**62**], but Baugh gives more information than either' (p 207). The edition's virtues 'do not seem to give it preference over works already in the field' (p 208).

- Review by R.T. Davies, *N&Q*, New Series 24 (1977), 170–1: The revision of Robinson's text is thorough, but Davies would 'have liked to see a still fuller attempt to increase our understanding of what Chaucer is doing in the various character descriptions of the General Prologue' (p 170).

89 *Geoffrey Chaucer: The General Prologue to the Canterbury Tales and the Canon's Yeoman's Prologue and Tale.* Ed. A.V.C. Schmidt. London: University of London Press, 1974.
A school edition: after an introduction emphasizing Chaucerian realism and satire, the text of *GP* (based on the Ellesmere ms and glossed) is presented. A detailed commentary on individual pilgrims and specific lines follows, along with appendices on Chaucer's verse, textual notes, and suggested readings. The 'length and elaboration' of *GP* indicate that Chaucer 'regarded it as rather more than a mere introduction'; it can be read as 'a self-contained poem' (p 5). Chaucer's aim was 'to register *his impression* of reality' (see line 39, *as it semed me*), not necessarily to provide a complete

transcription of reality (p 9). For comments on specific passages see **651, 750, 1256.**

90 *The Works of Geoffrey Chaucer Now Newly Imprinted.* [Facsimile of the Kelmscott Chaucer.] London: Basilisk Press, 1975 (1974?).
This facsimile of the 1896 edition that was printed by William Morris, with the text edited by F.S. Ellis and the illustrations designed by Edward Burne-Jones, makes available at full size one of the most famous artistic productions of *CT*. The text is based upon Skeat (**3**). The edition's artistic aspects are examined by Duncan Robinson, *A Companion Volume to the Kelmscott Chaucer* (London: Basilisk Press, 1975). See also **64** (a reduced-size facsimile) and **87.**

91 *The Complete Poetry and Prose of Geoffrey Chaucer.* Ed. John H. Fisher. New York: Holt, Rinehart and Winston, 1977. Rpt 7 times by 1982. Glossary added in 3rd printing (1979); bibliography revised in 7th printing (1982); however, the reprints carry the unchanged copyright date of 1977. A brief introduction precedes *GP* (pp 9–24). The text is based on the Ellesmere ms with variants from Hengwrt and other mss. Despite recent interest in Hengwrt, Ellesmere has been chosen as the copy-text because it is 'more regular in dialect and spelling ... and more complete, with the tales in the order which many scholars today regard nearest to Chaucer's intention' (p 967). Glosses on the page and (from the 3rd printing onwards) a short glossary at the end are included, as are discussions of Chaucer's literary place, time, and language and versification. The extensive bibliography (pp 975–1032) records 'all books and articles from 1964 through 1974' (p 975) and selected items before and after; from the 7th printing onwards the bibliography includes items through 1979. *GP*, a 'self-contained commentary on what William Blake called "the lineaments of universal human life"' (p 7), introduces two unifying motifs for the *CT* as a whole. One is the 'literary persona of the poet, who provides here, as elsewhere, Chaucer's individual voice and who enables him to punctuate his poetry with ironic comments that warn us not to take any character or statement at face value.' The other unifying motif is 'the personage of the Host and the game he proposes' (p 7). On the springtime opening, see **609.**

- Review by Roy Vance Ramsey, *SAC*, 1 (1979), 163–70: Ramsey praises the bibliography, the introductions ('pointed and at times provocative in a useful way,' p 170), and the usefulness of the notes. However, he finds that the explanatory notes should have been fuller and that the choice of the Ellesmere manuscript for the whole of *CT* was inappropriate, though 'there might have been warrant for Fisher to use Ellesmere for *The General Prologue* and *The Franklin's Tale*' (p 168).

92 *Wynkyn de Worde and Chaucer's Canterbury Tales: A Transcription and Collation of the 1498 Edition with Caxton² from the General Prologue through the Knight's Tale.* Ed. William F. Hutmacher. Amsterdam: Rodopi, 1978. Costerus: Essays in English and American Language and Literature, New Series 10.

Hutmacher's introduction discusses Wynkyn de Worde's career and the importance of his 1498 edition of the *CT*, here reproduced in part. A bibliography emphasizing the fifteenth-century book trade and its effect on the circulation of the Chaucer text is included. This book is a version of Hutmacher's dissertation, *A Transcription and Collation of Wynkyn de Worde's 1498 Edition of the Canterbury Tales with CX², The General Prologue through the Franklin's Tale*, Texas Tech University, 1976, Dir. Joseph J. Morgan; abstract in *DAI*, 38 (1977), 779–A.

93 *The Canterbury Tales, Geoffrey Chaucer: A Facsimile and Transcription of the Hengwrt Manuscript, with Variants from the Ellesmere Manuscript.* Ed. Paul G. Ruggiers. Intro. Donald C. Baker, A.I. Doyle, and M.B. Parkes. Norman, OK: University of Oklahoma Press, 1979; Folkestone, England: Dawson, 1979. A Variorum Edition of the Works of Geoffrey Chaucer, 1. General Editors, Paul G. Ruggiers and Donald C. Baker.

The Hengwrt ms, presented here with a primarily palaeographical introduction, will serve as the base-text for the Chaucer Variorum Edition of the *CT* (in progress). *GP* appears on pp 2–45, with facing-page plates and transcription.

- Review by George Kane, *Mediaevalia*, 5 (1979), 283–8: The volume is 'very well produced' (p 284) and the palaeographical introduction is 'a model' (p 285), but Kane raises doubts about the choice of Hengwrt as the base-text for the Chaucer Variorum project. 'As a physically damaged, imperfect, disarranged and sophisticated copy it is a strange choice for any kind of basic text' (p 286).

- Review by William C. McAvoy, *Manuscripta*, 25 (1981), 183–5: 'Questions remain. What specifically is the provenience of Hengwrt? What evidence, if any, is there to justify the implication that the Hengwrt scribe may have had access to Chaucer's papers?' (p 185). However, the typography and 'the very careful transcription' are praised (p 185).

94 *Poetical Works, Geoffrey Chaucer: A Facsimile of Cambridge University Library MS GG.4.27.* Intro. M.B. Parkes and Richard Beadle. 3 vols. Cambridge, England: D.S. Brewer, 1979 (vol 1), 1980 (vols 2–3).

The text of *GP* as preserved in this ms is incomplete because leaves are missing: *GP* begins at line 37 and ends at line 756 (vol 1, fols. 132–41 in the facsimile). Color plates of the remaining illustrations of the pilgrims — some of those too are missing from the manuscript — are also reproduced (in vol 2, see the unpaginated section of plates prior to p 1 and the brief discussion of the illustrations on pp 58–9). The illustrations included are those of the Reeve, Cook, Wife, Pardoner, Monk, and Manciple.

95 *The Canterbury Tales by Geoffrey Chaucer. Edited from the Hengwrt Manuscript.* Ed. N.F. Blake. London: Arnold, 1980. York Medieval Texts, Second Series. General Editors, Elizabeth Salter and Derek Pearsall.
Blake bases his edition on the Hengwrt manuscript, which may be the oldest one extant and whose scribe may have 'had access to Chaucer's own copy' (p 11). The introduction concentrates on the mss. A brief discussion of language, a bibliography, and appendices that provide Ellesmere ms material not found in Hengwrt are included. *GP* appears on pp 29–65, with notes and glosses on the page. The *GP* portraits are 'more abstract' for those pilgrims who were already 'well-known types in medieval literature'; while for others (eg the Miller), who had previously 'appeared infrequently, if at all,' Chaucer was 'forced to rely on his own ingenuity' and therefore concentrated 'more on physical appearance' (p 29). The groupings of pilgrims represent 'social or professional links or simply similarity of outlook' (p 29). Aside from, perhaps, Harry Bailly, 'it is unlikely that Chaucer expected his audience to recognize any personal allusions' (p 29) among the pilgrims. (For comments on specific passages, see 586 and 1242.)

96 *The Canterbury Tales, Die Canterbury Erzählungen: Mittelenglisch/ Deutsch.* Trans. and annotated by Heinz Bergner, Waltraud Böttcher, Günter Hagel, and Hilmar Sperber. Ed. Heinz Bergner. Stuttgart: Reclam, 1982.
A school edition: after a general introduction, the text (based on Robinson's second edition, 42) is presented, along with a German prose translation. It is followed by a brief commentary and annotation on *GP* (by Heinz Bergner), mentioning such topics as sources and analogues, descriptive techniques, and attitudes of the narrator.

Part 2: Bibliographies, Indexes, and Other Research Tools

Except for items focusing on Chaucer, the coverage is selective only. For example, the bibliographies devoted wholly to Chaucer are listed, but among general bibliographies for the study of literature or the study of the Middle Ages, only those likely to be of major and frequent importance for research on *GP* have been included. At the present time, the most comprehensive lists of annual publications on *GP* are those provided by *ChauR* (**110**), the *MLA Bibliography* (**129**), and *SAC* (**98**).

97 Alderson, William L. 'A Check-list of Supplements to Spurgeon's Chaucer Allusions.' *PQ*, 32 (1953), 418–27.
Alderson offers corrections to Spurgeon (**134**) and provides a bibliography of further collections of Chaucer commentary and allusion. The additional items reported range from ca 1400 to the early twentieth century.

98 'An Annotated Chaucer Bibliography, 1975—.' *SAC*, 1 (1979), —.
The series of cumulative Chaucer bibliographies to 1973 consists of Hammond (**120**), Griffith (**119**), Crawford (**114**), and Baird (**100**), with Baird's coverage, 1964–1973, being nearly paralleled by that of Fisher (**91**), who in the first six printings of his edition included an extensive bibliography for 1964–1974. The *SAC* bibliographies are planned as a continuation of Hammond, Griffith, Crawford, Baird, and Fisher (*SAC*, 1 [1979], 201), but with some revisions of the categories and with short annotations. *SAC*, 1 (1979), 201–55, lists items for 1975–1976; *SAC*, 2 (1980), 221–79, items for 1977–1978; *SAC*, 3 (1981), 189–259, items for 1979; *SAC*, 4 (1982), 193–246, items for 1980; all compiled by John H. Fisher. After *SAC* 4, the listings continue to be annual and are compiled by Lorrayne Y. Baird. Cf the annual bibliography in *ChauR* (**110**): the *SAC* bibliography provides

annotations for published work, while the *ChauR* bibliography lists not only publications but also work in progress, etc, though ordinarily without annotations.

99 *Approaches to Teaching Chaucer's Canterbury Tales.* Ed. Joseph Gibaldi. Consultant Editor, Florence H. Ridley. New York: Modern Language Association of America, 1980. Approaches to Teaching Masterpieces of World Literature. Series Editor, Joseph Gibaldi.
In the section on 'Materials' (pp 3–32), resources such as editions, recordings, and films are described.

100 Baird, Lorrayne Y. *A Bibliography of Chaucer, 1964–1973.* Boston: G.K. Hall, 1977. Reference Guides in Literature. General Editor, Everett Emerson.
Planned as a continuation to Crawford (114), this listing makes a few organizational changes, such as the assignment of item numbers to each entry and the addition of new or expanded categories (eg, recordings and films appear here in a separate section, as do Festschriften and collections of articles). On *GP*, see primarily pp 78–9, though several other sections are also useful. For Baird's compilations in *SAC*, see 98.

101 Baugh, Albert C. 'Fifty Years of Chaucer Scholarship.' *Spec*, 26, (1951), 659–72.
Baugh provides an overview of major scholarly concerns between 1900 and 1950, mentioning editions, reference sources, and secondary works. The treatment is selective, not comprehensive. For comments on the Prioress, see 753.

102 ——. *Chaucer.* New York: Appleton-Century-Crofts, 1968. 2nd ed. Arlington Heights, IL: HHM Publishing Corp., 1977. Goldentree Bibliographies in Language and Literature. General Editor, O.B. Hardison, Jr.
In this selective bibliography for student use, some 270 items on *GP* in general and on the individual pilgrims are listed (1977, pp 79–91).

103 Benson, L.D. 'A Reader's Guide to Writings on Chaucer' and 'Chaucer: A Select Bibliography.' In *Writers and Their Background: Geoffrey Chaucer.* Ed. Derek Brewer. London: Bell, 1974. Pp 321–51, 352–72.
Benson provides a general overview of Chaucer publications (mostly twentieth-century items) and a corresponding bibliographic listing.

104 Bowden, Muriel. *A Commentary on the General Prologue to the Canterbury Tales.* New York: Macmillan, 1948. Several times rpt (4th printing, 1954). 2nd ed. New York: Macmillan, 1967; London: Souvenir Press, 1973,

rpt 1981. Portions rpt in *Critics on Chaucer*, ed. Sheila Sullivan (London: Allen and Unwin, 1970; Coral Gables, FL: University of Miami Press, 1970), pp 97–104.

This detailed study provides a summary of scholarship. The second edition includes additional pages to supplement the text and bibliography: pages 1–316 remain the same in both editions; pages 317–28 appear in the revision only. Bowden also presents background material on fourteenth-century life to enable us 'to hear what the poet's own contemporaries had to say about the social types the company represent and the social scene to which they belong' (p 1). After introductory chapters on the years 1380–1387 and on medieval pilgrimage, separate chapters are provided on the individual pilgrims or groups of pilgrims (though not on the narrator). The general influence of Manly's historical approach (see **362**) is apparent throughout. An extensive bibliography follows. For a representative selection of comments, see **666, 714, 754, 917, 960, 1009, 1113, 1354**. See also **167**.

- Review by George Kane, *MLR*, 45 (1950), 363–68: Although the book is 'a diligent and careful compilation' (p 363) and will be widely used, it is flawed by faulty logic and misconceptions about 'the relation of art to actuality' (p 364). Kane does not accept the likelihood of historical models for the pilgrims: 'It seems inconceivable then that anyone with a high opinion of Chaucer's creative powers should think of his pilgrims as actual, historical persons' (p 367).

- Review by Morton Bloomfield, *MLQ*, 11 (1950), 105–6: Bloomfield criticizes the book for an excessively historical orientation, for assuming that real people underlie the portraits, for accepting 'basic aesthetic and philosophical assumptions which are at least questionable,' and for 'logical solecisms and other examples of the uncritical acceptance of hallowed beliefs' (p 106).

105 Braddy, Haldeen. 'The French Influence on Chaucer.' In *Companion to Chaucer Studies*. Ed. Beryl Rowland. Toronto, New York, and London: Oxford University Press, 1968. Pp 123–38. Rpt 1971. 2nd ed. 1979. Pp 143–59.

In this bibliographic essay, Braddy summarizes work on the French sources and antecedents of *GP* and the pilgrimage framework; see especially pp 131–2 (1968), pp 151–2 (1979).

106 *Chaucer: The Critical Heritage*. Ed. Derek Brewer. Vol 1, 1385–1837; Vol 2, 1837–1933. London: Routledge and Kegan Paul, 1978.

Selections from earlier criticism, including many items pertinent to *GP*, are collected.

107 *A Chaucer Glossary*. Compiled by Norman Davis, Douglas Gray, Patricia Ingham, and Anne Wallace-Hadrill. Oxford: Clarendon Press, 1979.
The edition of Skeat (3) and the Tatlock-Kennedy *Concordance* (135) are used as the basis of the glossary; a selected list of proper names is also included.

108 *Chaucer Life-Records*. Ed. Martin M. Crow and Clair Olson. Oxford: Clarendon Press, 1966.
Documents pertaining to Chaucer's activities during the time he wrote *GP* and to biographical interpretations of *GP* are included in this collection. For example, there are several records of Gilbert Magfield, who has been associated with the Merchant's portrait.

109 'Chaucer Research in Progress.' *NM*, 70 (1969)—.
Edited by Thomas A. Kirby, this compilation of research projects underway (ie, work not yet published) appears annually.

110 'Chaucer Research, Report No.—.' MLA Committee on Chaucer Research and Bibliography. 1937—.
This periodic report has emphasized the Chaucer research of North American scholars. Initially the listings circulated in mimeographed form [not seen]. Since the compilation for 1966 ('Report No. 27'), the bibliography has been edited by Thomas A. Kirby and has been published annually in *ChauR*, vols 1—, except that volumes 5 and 13 of that journal include no annual report from the Committee, while volumes 9 and 15 include two annual reports each. Listings of current research, completed research, published books and articles, and other notices are provided.

111 *Chaucer: Sources and Backgrounds*. Ed. Robert P. Miller. New York: Oxford University Press, 1977.
Translated excerpts from many medieval works pertinent to *GP* are included. A few examples: there are selections from medieval rhetorics, from statements about the three estates, from complaints against the clergy, and from the *Roman de la Rose*.

112 Corson, Hiram. *Index of Proper Names and Subjects to Chaucer's Canterbury Tales together with Comparisons and Similes, Metaphors and Proverbs, Maxims, etc, in the Same*. Intro. W.W. Skeat. London: Kegan Paul, Trench, Trübner, & Co., and Henry Frowde, 1911. Chaucer Society Publications, First Series, 72. Rpt New York: Johnson Reprint [1967].
The index of names and subjects (including Biblical allusions) is followed by separate listings of comparisons and similes (29 in *GP*); metaphors (only 1 in *GP*–line 823); proverbs, maxims, and sententious expressions (7 in *GP*); and prayers, entreaties, and imprecations (none in *GP*).

113 Courtney, Eleanor Lewer. *Geoffrey Chaucer's Canterbury Tales: An Anno-*
    tated International Bibliography, 1964–1971. University of Arizona Disser-
    tation. 1975. Dir. Christopher F. Carroll. See also *DAI*, 37 (1976), 327-A.
    After a survey of trends in *CT* criticism in the years indicated, Courtney
    presents an annotated bibliography of books, editions, articles, disserta-
    tions, reprints, and reviews.

114 Crawford, William R. *Bibliography of Chaucer 1954–63.* Seattle: University
    of Washington Press, 1967.
    Planned as a supplement to Griffith (**119**), this listing includes reprints of
    items first published prior to 1954 and an introduction on 'New Directions
    in Chaucer Criticism' (pp xiii–xl). Items on *GP*, some with annotations,
    appear on pp 55–63, but other sections are also pertinent. See also **100**.

115 De Weever, Jacqueline Elinor. *A Dictionary of Classical, Mythological and*
    Sideral Names in the Works of Geoffrey Chaucer. University of Pennsyl-
    vania Dissertation. 1971. Dir. Robert A. Pratt. See also *DAI*, 32 (1972),
    4559-A.
    Names are listed and explained in both their traditional and their Chauce-
    rian contexts [description from *DAI*; diss not seen].

116 Dillon, Bert. *A Chaucer Dictionary: Proper Names and Allusions, Exclud-*
    ing Place Names. Boston: Hall, 1974; London: George Prior, 1974.
    Brief entries on the names in *GP* (except for place-names, on which see
    Heidrich, **121**; Huff, **123**; and Magoun, **127**) are included. A sample: 'HU-
    BERD, the name of the Friar' (p 146). Biblical allusions are noted. The
    compilation is based on Dillon's dissertation, *A Dictionary of Personal,*
    Mythological, Allegorical, and Astrological Proper Names and Allusions in
    the Works of Geoffrey Chaucer. Duke University. 1972. Dir. Holger O.V.
    Nygard. Abstract in *DAI*, 33 (1973), 5118–5119-A.

117 French, Robert Dudley. *A Chaucer Handbook.* New York: Crofts, 1927.
    Rpt 1929, 1932, 1935, 1936, 1939, 1941/rev ed 1947.
    In a section on 'The Prologue,' pp 202–9 in both editions, French reviews
    opinion on the use of the framework, the date of *GP*, its sources (*GP* is
    seen as a primarily original work, so that it is not profitable to search
    for complete literary sources or real-life models, though some details of
    the portraits are indebted to sources such as the *Roman de la Rose*), the
    scientific concepts behind the portraits, and the illuminations in the mss.

118 *Geoffrey Chaucer: A Critical Anthology.* Ed. J.A. Burrow. Harmondsworth,
    England, and Baltimore, MD: Penguin, 1969. Penguin Critical Anthologies
    General Editor, Christopher Ricks.

Excerpts from criticism pertinent to *GP* are reprinted here; brief comments on *GP* are also included in the introduction.

119 Griffith, Dudley David. *Bibliography of Chaucer 1908–1953*. Seattle: University of Washington Press, 1955.

Planned as a supplement to Hammond (**120**), but with separate sections for general treatments of *GP* and for each of the portraits (pp 163–84), this listing includes master's theses and reviews and provides some annotations. Several sections of the book are pertinent. For example, the general section on *CT* (pp 151–63) includes items on frame-tales and lists phonograph recordings; the section on modernizations and translations (pp 49–57) includes illustrated versions and children's adaptations. The book incorporates Griffith's earlier work, *A Bibliography of Chaucer, 1908–1924*, University of Washington Publications in Language and Literature, 4, 1 (1926). See also **114**.

120 Hammond, Eleanor Prescott. *Chaucer: A Bibliographical Manual*. Boston: Macmillan, 1908. Rpt New York: Peter Smith, 1933.

This first comprehensive and systematic collection of bibliographical materials for modern Chaucer-study includes sections on his life, canon and early editions, manuscripts, sources, *CT*, other works, linguistics and versification, etc. On *GP* Hammond summarizes previous work on the date, the sources, the number of pilgrims, and the Canterbury pilgrimage and shrine (pp 265–70). A few individual lines of *GP* are also treated in her sections on individual tales: the annotation for line 60 comments on whether the reading should be *ariue* or *armee* (p 273); for line 120, on the Prioress's oath; for line 125, on her French; and for line 164, on her chaplain and three priests (pp 286–7). Many references to earlier criticism are supplied throughout. The final group of pilgrims may have been an addition (p 254; cf Huppé, **295**). Successors to Hammond's *Manual* are Griffith, **119**; Crawford, **114**; and Baird, **100**.

- Review by John Koch, 'Die Chaucerforschung seit 1900,' *GRM*, 1 (1909), 490–507: the *Manual* is an essential resource, diligently prepared. However, some individual statements require correction and too much personal judgment intervenes (see pp 492–3).

- Review by John L. Lowes, *JEGP*, 8 (1909), 619–27: 'It would be hard to speak too highly of the wealth of material which Miss Hammond's *Manual* offers' (p 620). Lowes suggests that some of the book's valuable 'fresh and independent contributions' (p 620), which go beyond bibliography per se, might have received more notice if published separately.

121 Heidrich, Käte. *Das geographische Weltbild des späteren englischen Mittelalters mit besonderer Berücksichtigung der Vorstellungen Chaucer's und seiner Zeitgenossen.* Albert-Ludwigs-Universität Dissertation (Freiburg). 1915. Dir. Prof. Brie. Published Freiburg: Hammerschlag and Kahle, 1915.
The place-names in *GP*, beginning with *Southwerk* (line 20) and ending with the *Watering of Seint Thomas* (line 826), are each briefly discussed. Cf 123, 127.

122 Hoffman, Richard L. 'The Canterbury Tales.' In *Critical Approaches to Six Major English Works.* Ed. Robert M. Lumiansky and Herschel Baker. Philadelphia: University of Pennsylvania Press, 1968; London: Oxford University Press, 1968. Pp 41–80.
The first part of this chapter (pp 41–52) is a bibliographic essay concentrating on works other than those dealt with in Crawford's introductory essay to 114. See also reviews at 42 and 63. (The rest of the chapter recapitulates parts of Hoffman's book on Ovid and the *CT*, 285.)

123 Huff, Lloyd Dickason. *Place-Names in Chaucer.* Indiana University Dissertation. 1949. Dir. Henry Holland Carter.
The annotated list of place-names that comprises most of this study is preceded by discussions of their implications. In the chapter 'The Relation Between the Place-Names and the Tellers of the Tales in the Canterbury Tales' (pp 53–60), Huff divides the pilgrims into three groups: 1) the locals, who probably did not travel outside England; 2) the continentals, who probably crossed the Channel to visit nearby European locations; and 3) the cosmopolitans, who journeyed to more remote locations (p 53). Huff suggests that 'the Friar is not a native Englishman' (p 56). The Knight, Squire, Wife, and Shipman have traveled the farthest. In most cases the place-names of *GP* correlate with the pilgrims' later use of place in their tales, though the Shipman is an exception — the place-names in his tale do not fulfill 'the fair promise' of the names in his portrait (p 60). Cf 121, 127.

124 Kirby, Thomas A. 'The General Prologue.' In *Companion to Chaucer Studies.* Ed. Beryl Rowland. Toronto, New York, and London: Oxford University Press, 1968. Pp 208–28. Rpt 1971. 2nd ed. 1979. Pp 243–70.
In this bibliographic essay, Kirby reviews work on many of the preoccupations of twentieth-century criticism of *GP:* the art of the springtime opening (lines 1–18); the use of the narrator as a persona; the rhetoricians' precepts underlying the plan (lines 35–42); the organizing principles in the portrait series; the descriptive devices evident in the portraits; the possibility of historical models for some of the characters; the narrator's apology (lines

725-46); the personality of the Host; and the proposal for the storytelling contest. The second edition reprints the essay, adds a section, and brings the bibliography up to date.

125 Koch, John. 'Die Chaucerforschung seit 1900.' *GRM*, 1 (1909), 490-507.
Koch's survey of early twentieth-century Chaucer publications is particularly useful for European materials. See also his further bibliographic essays: 'Neuere Chaucer-Literatur,' *AngliaB*, 22 (1911), 265-82; articles of the same title in *ESt*, 46 (1912-1913), 98-114, and *ESt*, 48 (1914), 251-81; 'Neuere Beiträge zur Chaucer-Literatur aus Amerika,' *AngliaB*, 25 (1914), 327-42; 'Neuere amerikanische Chaucerschriften,' *AngliaB*, 28 (1917), 152-60; and 'Der gegenwartige Stand der Chaucerforschung,' *Anglia*, 49 (1926), 193-243.

126 Leyerle, John, and Anne Quick. *Chaucer: A Selected Bibliography*. Toronto: University of Toronto Press, 1981.
This item is included here in order to lay a ghost to rest. Although listed in *SAC*, 5 (1983), 218 and 223, and again (with a 1984 publication date) in *SAC*, 8 (1986), 289, this useful bibliography was evidently not published until 1986, when it appeared under the title *Chaucer: A Bibliographical Introduction*.

127 Magoun, Francis P., Jr. *A Chaucer Gazetteer*. Stockholm: Almqvist and Wiksell, 1961; Chicago: University of Chicago Press, 1961.
Explanations are provided for the place-names mentioned in *GP*, including (for example) the locations of the Knight's battles. The book is a conflation (by Ojars Kartins) of three articles by Magoun: 'Chaucer's Ancient and Biblical World,' *MS*, 15 (1953), 107-36; 'Chaucer's Great Britain,' *MS*, 16 (1954), 131-56; and 'Chaucer's Mediaeval World Outside of Great Britain,' *MS*, 17 (1955), 117-42. Cf 121, 123.

128 Martin, Willard E., Jr. *A Chaucer Bibliography 1925-1933*. Durham, NC: Duke University Press, 1935.
Reviews, translations into foreign languages, imitations, and children's versions, etc, are listed here, as well as scholarly books and articles.

129 *MLA Bibliography* 1922—.
Beginning as 'American Bibliography for 1921,' which was published in *PMLA*, 37 (1922), 1-29, this annual bibliography, international since 1956, has grown into a multi-volume separate publication with a comprehensive section on Chaucer studies. (Book reviews and unrevised reprints are not included. For reviews see the publication *Book Review Index*.)

130 Ross, Thomas W. *Chaucer's Bawdy.* New York: Dutton, 1972; Toronto: Clarke, Irwin & Co, 1972.
The bawdy implications of many words from *GP* are explained: *amor* (line 162), *grace* (line 88), *juste* (line 96), *hoote* (line 97), *priken* (line 11), etc — see Ross's index. Cf **647**.

131 Scott, A.F. *Who's Who in Chaucer.* London: Elm Tree Books (Hamilton), 1974.
The names of the people (and of the one animal, the Reeve's horse *Scot*) that are identified in *GP* are briefly glossed, along with other Chaucer names. A separate (unglossed) list of the names in *GP* alone is also included.

132 Shackford, Martha Hale. *English Literature, Chaucer: Selected References.* Wellesley, MA: Wellesley College Department of English Literature, 1918.
Based on *Chaucer: Outlines and References* by Sophie Jewett (1896), this selective bibliography concentrates on cultural and historical contexts. Editions and annotations of *GP*, works on the Canterbury pilgrimage, a few items on the pilgrims individually, and reproductions of the Ellesmere miniatures and other pictures are listed.

133 Spurgeon, Caroline F.E. *Chaucer devant la critique en Angleterre et en France depuis son temps jusqu'à nos jours.* Paris: Hachette, 1911.
Editions of *GP*, translations, and critical responses in England and France are recorded. The compilation is a published version of Spurgeon's dissertation of the same title, Université de Paris, 1911 (not seen).

134 ——. *Five Hundred Years of Chaucer Criticism and Allusion, 1387–1900 A.D.* 7 parts. London: Kegan Paul, Trench, Trübner & Co and Oxford University Press, 1914–1924. Chaucer Society, Second Series 48 (1914), 49–50 (1918), 52 (1921), 53 (1922), 54 (1922), 55 (1924), and 56 (1924). Rpt Cambridge: Cambridge University Press, 1925 (as 3 vols).
The index provides ready access to the many *GP* references included in this collection. See also Spurgeon's *Supplement Containing Additional Entries, 1868–1900* (London: privately printed, 1920), and Alderson, **97**.

135 Tatlock, John S.P., and Arthur G. Kennedy. *A Concordance to the Complete Works of Geoffrey Chaucer and to the Romaunt of the Rose.* Washington, DC: Carnegie Institution, 1927. Rpt Gloucester, MA; Peter Smith, 1963.
Pollard's text (4) is the basis for this concordance. Many entries are pertinent to *GP*. For example, among other words whose significance in *GP* has been debated, *vavasour* (line 360) is shown to occur only in *GP*, while

bourdon (line 673) occurs in four other Chaucer locations and *chevyssaunce* (line 282) in five.

136 Tsuchiya, Tadayuki. *A Concordance and Glossary to the General Prologue of the Canterbury Tales.* [Tokyo?]: privately published, 1975.
Not seen. According to *SAC*, 3 (1981), p 197, this is a 'complete concordance to *GP* based on Robinson's second edition [42]. All the words in *GP* are glossed on the basis of *OED* and [*MED*.]' Also cited (as published by the Shoei Publishing Company) in *A Bibliography of the Publications on Medieval English Language and Literature in Japan* (Tokyo: Center for Medieval Studies, Tokyo University, 1983), p 153, #8.

137 Wells, John Edwin. *A Manual of the Writings in Middle English, 1050–1400.* New Haven, CN: Connecticut Academy of Arts and Sciences, 1916. Rpt 1917, 1923, 1926.
In the chapter 'Chaucer' (1916, pp 599–747, bibliographical notes on pp 866–81), Wells provides a bibliographic essay; on *GP* see especially pp 671–92. 'Chaucer was enabled to present in the Prologue figures that are not only individual and as well typical for his own day, but also representative of human nature and conduct in all time' (p 690). Nine supplements were issued, 1919–1952. The complete revision of Wells' *Manual*, however (under the general editorship of J. Burke Severs and Albert E. Hartung), which has reached seven volumes to date, does not include a Chaucer section because of the availability of other bibliographic sources.

138 *The Year's Work in English Studies.* London: Oxford University Press and Humphrey Milford. 1921—.
In this annual collection of bibliographic essays, the section on Chaucer discusses selected publications. From vol 1 (1921) to vol 15 (1934), the Chaucer items are included in the general 'Middle English' chapter; beginning with vol 16 (1935), there is a separate chapter on Chaucer (though the first such chapter includes work on Gower and Lydgate as well).

Part 3: General Criticism and Cultural Background

Several kinds of items are presented in this section, including studies of (1) the structure, style, composition, rhetorical devices, organizing principles, etc, of *GP*; (2) groupings of pilgrims within the portrait series; (3) recurrent themes or images; (4) the date of *GP*; (5) the poem's sources, analogues, and generic affiliations; (6) *GP* as realism, humor, irony, paradox, social criticism, etc; (7) Chaucer's audience; and (8) the general literary and cultural background of *GP*. This last category is represented only very selectively. There are hundreds of books (and thousands of articles) on medieval pilgrimage, horsemanship, battle tactics, cooking, disease, monasticism, economics, religious controversies, art and music, marriage patterns, and many other topics whose investigation can enrich our reading of *GP*. It has been possible to include only a few such items here.

139 Adams, George Roy. *Chaucer's General Prologue: A Study in Tradition and the Individual Talent.* University of Oklahoma Dissertation. 1961 (degree 1962). Dir. Paul G. Ruggiers. See also *DA*, 22 (1962), 2382.
Adams examines the narrator, the opening eighteen lines, the rhetorical structure of *GP*, the traditions behind the portrait series, and the style of the descriptions. *GP* includes an ironic vision, with the narrator functioning sometimes from a limited point of view, sometimes from an omniscient point of view. The springtime opening 'has a climactic and multilayered structure' (p 27) involving multiple elements: a rhetorical *Whan ... Whan ... Than* pattern; a progression from the vegetable to the animal to the human world; a progression from the natural to the classical to the Christian world; and a linear concept of pilgrimage and a cyclical concept of rebirth. Chaucer's use of standard rhetorical devices is extensive. As for levels

of style, *GP* combines the high and the conversational tones as another aspect of its dualism. Analogues to the portrait series, beginning with the *Characters* of Theophrastus, are discussed, with emphasis on Benôit's *Roman de Troie*, the *Roman de la Rose*, and medieval estates satire as practiced by Gower and other writers. The medieval rhetorical precepts and practices (*descriptio*, etc) that underlie Chaucer's individual portraits are examined, as are his applications of rhetoric to individual portraits and his repeated use of the motifs of pilgrimage, love, rebirth, cupidity, the chain of being, etc. The repetitions of techniques and motifs help to establish links among the pilgrims. *GP* 'embodies Chaucer's own artistic vision, but is also the product of traditional themes and rhetorical principles' (p 142).

140 ——. 'Sex and Clergy in Chaucer's "General Prologue."' *L&P* (1968), 215–22.

The portraits of the clerics in *GP* identify their sexual propensities and constitute a series on this subject. The sequence of Prioress, Monk, Friar, Clerk, Parson, Summoner, and Pardoner is intended to place at the center the Clerk and Parson, the two clerics whose love is *caritas*. Thus 'they show that *caritas* is at the heart of any definition or manifestation of human love' (p 216). Before and after this center, Chaucer becomes progresssively more overt in his information about the clerics' sexuality. The portrait of the Prioress is ambiguous, but to the extent that sexuality is present, it is clearly heterosexual; that of the Monk is also ambiguous, but with even stronger hints of heterosexual activity. The Friar may be bisexual, while the Summoner 'unquestionably is condemned as an exemplar of unhealthy, perverted bisexual propensities' (p 218), perhaps including child molestation. The Summoner, an active homosexual, is followed by the Pardoner, a passive homosexual. The two idealized representatives of *caritas* at the center 'separate the three clerics who might yet be saved, the Prioress, Monk, and Friar, from those two who seem clearly damned, the perverted Summoner and Pardoner' (p 218). The theme is reinforced by permutations on the words for 'love' and by recurrent imagery — pointed objects, eyes, animals, etc. The seven clerics represent icons of *Luxuria* as a whole. Individually, the Prioress represents *Ira*, the Monk *Accidia*, the Friar *Luxuria*, the Summoner *Gula*, the Pardoner *Avaricia*, and the Clerk and Parson remedies for *Invidia* and *Superbia*. It was perhaps Chaucer's wish to have only seven clerics in this series of portraits that led him to omit a description for the Nun's Priest.

141 Alexander, Michael. *Geoffrey Chaucer: Prologue to the Canterbury Tales.* London: Longman, 1980; Beirut: York Press, 1980. York Notes Series. General Editors, A.N. Jeffares and Suheil Bushrui.

Summaries, commentaries, and suggestions for student responses to study assignments are provided.

142 Allen, Judson Boyce, and Theresa Anne Moritz. *A Distinction of Stories: The Medieval Unity of Chaucer's Fair Chain of Narratives for Canterbury.* Columbus, OH: Ohio State University Press, 1981.
GP is considered in the chapters 'Axioms of Unity and their Consequences' (pp 3–43) and 'Medieval Notions of Structure' (pp 85–116). Allen and Moritz emphasize the importance of Ovid's *Metamorphoses,* 'a morally normative array of tales,' as a precedent for the *CT* plan (p 15). They also propose a new order for the tales, based on Natural, Magical, Moral, and Spiritual groups. In accordance with this concept, *GP* is interpreted as a *distinctio,* a 'classification of kinds considered as a meaningful and normative array' (p 90). 'It is by analogy with the *distinctio* that the list of pilgrims in Chaucer's Canterbury prologue can be understood most profitably. These people are a normative array, sufficient for the definition of the category "man" ' (p 90). Howard's symmetrical division of the portraits into three groups of seven (**287**) is taken as the basis for analysis of *GP* as a *distinctio.* Howard's first group, for example, represents people distinguished for what they are; his second group, people distinguished for what they know; his third group, people distinguished for what they do. The first group presents seven types of men; the second, seven types of learning; the third, a 'normative array' of types of work done in stewardship for others (p 91). Although the pilgrims thus form a normative array, they are also particulars. *GP* begins with Chaucer's variation on the proverb that in springtime men think of love, and 'proverb plus pilgrims gives us a world very much in medias res, and determined to stay that way,' since these pilgrims 'are not penitential, not serious, not even very religious — pilgrimaging, more than Canterbury, is their goal' (p 91).

143 Ames, Percy W. 'The Life and Characteristics of Chaucer.' In *Chaucer Memorial Lectures, 1900, Read before the Royal Society of Literature.* Ed. Percy W. Ames. London: Asher, 1900. Pp 143–71. ·
'The highest and at the same time the most essential and characteristic quality of Chaucer's genius is his dramatic power,' a power that 'is most strikingly exhibited in the "Canterbury Pilgrims." These are not only realistic and vivid, but each is a type of class, as definite as the characters in Shakespeare' (pp 164–5). The pilgrims 'are described with extraordinary vigour and animation in the general "Prologue" ' (p 165). In addition to these descriptions, some of the pilgrims describe themselves in their own prologues and illustrate 'the leading feature of their character' in their tales (p 165). The Wife is briefly discussed as an example; other pilgrims are mentioned as being both realistic and representative of a class. Chaucer's

basic plan is superior to Boccaccio's since it allowed 'of a great variety of typical characters being brought together. And the journey was an admirable device for bringing out the peculiarities of the travellers' (p 167). *GP*, a 'rich piece of descriptive writing,' is also 'of the highest value historically, as furnishing the fullest, most accurate and vivid pictures of the various special and particular types of human society in the later Middle Ages' (p 169).

144 Andersen, Jens Kr. 'An Analysis of the Framework Structure of Chaucer's "Canterbury Tales."' *OL*, 27 (1972), 179–201.

The pilgrimage framework established by *GP* is connected to the individual narratives in several ways. Harry Bailly's injunction that the tales should report adventures that have befallen (line 795) creates a demand for 'authenticity' (p 180), to which the pilgrims respond in varying degrees. There is an 'interdependence of the storytellers' ranks and their literary tastes' (p 193), so that the tales can be classified as intended primarily for amusement, or for edification. Within these two categories, further groups can be discerned — eg, 'Fairy tales are told by members of the middle classes' (p 184). Andersen disagrees with Baldwin's description of the dualism between Chaucer the Pilgrim and Chaucer the Poet (see 148), postulating instead that there are 'two planes of time immanent in the work, the period of perception and the period of committing to paper' (p 189). The narrator of *GP* is conscious of 'telling something belonging to the past' (p 189). Chaucer's own persona is divisible into three components: the writer before writing this text, the character acting within this text, and the author of this text. Chaucer's overall management of the framework, thus examined, suggests that he did not use Boccaccio's *Decameron* as a model.

145 Andersen, Wallis May. *Rhetoric and Poetics in the Canterbury Tales: the Knight, the Squire, and the Franklin.* University of Detroit Dissertation. 1979. Dir. Edward J. Wolff. See also *DAI*, 41 (1980), 239-A.

Concentrating on the tales of the three pilgrims named in the title, and on the rhetorical techniques of *occupatio*, *brevitas*-formulae, *digressio*, and *descriptio*, Andersen suggests that *CT* involves a debate on poetics and that the 'story-telling "game" seems to be at least as important to the structure of the entire work as the spiritual pilgrimage' (p 204). After a two-line recognition of the pilgrims' spiritual purpose (lines 769–70), Harry Bailly spends much longer on their secular plan for the journey. Lines 1–18 and 769–70 'are the only parts of the *General Prologue* that treat the pilgrimage as a pilgrimage. In contrast, the last eighty-odd lines of the *General Prologue* are given to Harry Bailly's speeches about his ideas for having fun along the way and to the pilgrims' assent to his proposals' (p 205). On the Knight, see 663.

146 Azuma, Yoshio. 'The Canterbury Tales, the Prologue Ni Tsuite.' [About the Prologue to the Canterbury Tales.] *Katahira*, 11 (1975), 15-25.
Not seen; listed in *A Bibliography of Publications on Medieval English Language and Literature in Japan* (Toyko: Center for Medieval Studies, Tokyo University, 1983), p 141, #4.

147 Badendyck, J. Lawrence. 'Chaucer's Portrait Technique and the Dream Vision Tradition.' *EngR*, 21 (1970), 113-25.
Developing Cunningham's thesis that Chaucer's portraiture is indebted to that of the dream-vision tradition (207), Badendyck argues that Chaucer's modification of this tradition consists in the way he has linked his characters to reality. Chaucer did not rely simply on extensive visual detail, for he 'realized that visualization alone was insufficient to guarantee a sense of the presence of a person and that this effect could be achieved without such detailed picture painting' (p 124). Instead he has included information about the characters' activities and occupations — eg, the Knight's battles, the Squire's carving before his father, the Merchant's beard having been shaken in storm — so that with 'one line he forces us to envision the figure' (p 121).

148 Baldwin, Ralph. *The Unity of the Canterbury Tales.* Copenhagen: Rosenkilde and Bagger, 1955. Anglistica, 5. General Editors, Torsten Dahl, Kemp Malone, and Geoffrey Tillotson. Portions rpt in *Chaucer Criticism*, 1, ed. Richard J. Schoeck and Jerome Taylor (Notre Dame and London: University of Notre Dame Press, 1960; 10th printing 1978), pp 15-51; and in *Discussions of the Canterbury Tales*, ed. Charles A. Owen, Jr. (Boston: Heath, 1961), pp 25-27.
Baldwin offers a detailed stylistic analysis of *GP*, emphasizing the rhetoric of lines 1-42, the techniques of characterization and the management of time and verb tenses in the portrait series, and the voice of the narrator. Despite 'what appears to be a tendency to disregard the conventions of his era,' Chaucer was quite aware of them, as his handling of different levels of style in *GP* shows. His techniques for describing the pilgrims (*descriptio*) correspond to the expected rhetorical *notatio* (moral description) and *effictio* (physical description), though by modern standards there is little physical detail — some pilgrims, in fact, have none. Baldwin provides a tabular list of kinds of traits. 'Chaucer's innovation in the *descriptio* was the inorganic, disordered, and inconsequent piling-up of details' (1955, p 48). He uses hyperbole so that 'every pilgrim is the best of his kind' (p 49), assigns each pilgrim a *radix trait* or 'single dominating characteristic' (p 49), offers a 'quick glimpse of the interior man' (p 50), and, especially, chooses disparate detail: 'discontinuity and incongruity of detail are Chaucer's stock in trade' (p 51). The 'deliberate artistic dualism

of Chaucer the Pilgrim and Chaucer the Poet' (p 67), as well as the complex 'voice structure' (p 71) of the poem in view of this dualism, are discussed. (In reply see **144**, on the dualism.) Baldwin's dissertation, *The Unity of the Canterbury Tales*, Johns Hopkins University, 1953, is the basis of this study. On the springtime opening, see **584**. Cf **723**.

- Review by Ursula Brown, *RES*, New Series 8 (1957), 281–82: Brown finds that Baldwin's 'arguments are congested and his style is a nightmare' (p 281). 'Nevertheless, though much in Mr. Baldwin's book may not seem new, and much may seem nonsense, he has suggestions to make which are fresh and illuminating' (p 282).

- Review by Marguerite-Marie Dubois, *EA*, 10 (1957), 147–48: Baldwin is praised for his reasoning, his argumentation, and, for the most part, his convincing deductions ('Son raisonnement est précis, ses arguments valables, ses déductions pour la plupart convaincantes,' p 148). He is also praised for his historical approach, which places Chaucer into his own period ('les écrits du moyen âge doivent être considérés à la lumière de leur époque,' p 148).

149 Barney, Stephen A. 'Chaucer's Lists.' In *The Wisdom of Poetry: Essays in Early English Literature in Honor of Morton W. Bloomfield*. Ed. Siegfried Wenzel and Larry D. Benson. Kalamazoo, MI: Medieval Institute Publications (Western Michigan University), 1982. Pp 189–223.
The French literary form of the *voie*, or 'way,' 'presents a seer or dreamer guided through an otherworldly or allegorized landscape by an authoritative figure' (p 205). *GP*, as 'an important variation on the *voie*, lists in series the pilgrims themselves ... The usual phrase introducing each pilgrim is *was ther* or *ther was*, and something about the intimacy and vividness of the portraits almost makes those *thers* epideictic rather than merely expletive. The narrator tells us about them "so as it semed me" [line 39], and we have the sense that we walk along with him through a portrait gallery brought strangely to life' (p 206). On the Reeve, see **1239**.

150 Barnouw, A.J. 'Painting and Poetry.' *GR*, 8 (1933), 1–9.
'If Lessing had known the Canterbury Tales, he might have quoted the General Prologue as a telling illustration of his thesis in Laokoön, that time is the poet's sphere and space the painter's. Chaucer, exceptionally gifted with a retentive optic memory, saw the group of banqueting pilgrims before his mind's eye when he sat down to compose his Prologue. But since he used the poet's medium, he was forced to describe in succession what he remembered having taken in at a glance, and thus the guests at the banquet, portrayed one after the other, assumed the garb and equipment

that went with this single-file arrangement' (p 2). *GP* depicts not primarily the banquet at the Tabard, but 'the line of pilgrims on the road' (p 2) — or both images, like a double-exposure in photography.

151 Baum, Paull F. *Chaucer: A Critical Appreciation.* Durham, NC: Duke University Press, 1958; Cambridge: Cambridge University Press, 1958.
GP is examined within the chapter 'The Canterbury Tales' (pp 60–142). Baum points out a mixture of formal and casual styles, so 'interwoven that one is often at a loss to distinguish between the artless and the well concealed artistry' (p 60). There are some 'bothersome details' in the springtime opening; for example, in lines 17–18, are we to understand that the pilgrims are visiting Becket's shrine because they are 'gratefully convalescent' (p 61)? Later, the meaning of the narrative *I* is ambiguous. The three categories of description mentioned in lines 37–41 — general character, rank, appearance — are present in some portraits, but abandoned in favor of 'a most effective disorder' (p 63) in others. 'Variety is the guiding principle. The formula was introduced only to be neglected' (p 65). Having 'a quick eye for faults,' Chaucer includes in the portraits 'some carefully noted blemish' (p 178): the Knight's *bismotered* tunic (line 76), the Squire's lavishness of dress, etc. The Miller, Reeve, and Summoner may have been added to *GP* in a revision. 'Each figure is in its own way a type and also an individual,' so that Chaucer is able to 'rely on the attractive possibilities of identification to stimulate interest while honestly denying any intentional portraiture' (p 67). The length of the portraits varies independently of such qualities as vividness: 'the Cook with his nine lines is as memorable as the Parson with his fifty-two' (p 69). When Langland's prologue to *Piers Plowman* is compared to *GP*, we notice 'the earnestness of the one and the detachment of the other,' although both of them are vivid, 'equally clear about the folly and wickedness of mankind' (p 70), and alive to humor. *GP* is Chaucer's 'one finest achievement because along with composition, as structure and as expression, it called for the best qualities of his genius and did not require of him qualities which he possessed in limited measure' (p 111).

- Review by Martin M. Crow, *MP*, 58 (1960-1961), 53–55: Crow finds the book 'a stimulating, provocative, and at the same time irritating appraisal' by someone who 'frequently delights the reader by his penetrating and aptly worded observations, but who, the reader cannot help feeling, has an ax to grind' (p 55).

- Review by Howard R. Patch, *MLN*, 75 (1960), 50–53: 'This is a book written with malice toward all and with charity for almost none' (p 50). It produces a 'meager Chaucer' who is suited to 'the confusion

and meaningless disorder of the modern world' (p 53), but who is not
the same as Chaucer himself.

152 [Beeching, Henry Charles.] 'The Poetry of Chaucer.' In *Conferences on
Books and Men*. London: Smith, Elder & Co. 1900. Pp 269–99. Rpt in
Rare Early Essays on Geoffrey Chaucer, ed. Carmen Joseph Dello Buono
(Darby, PA: Norwood Editions, 1981), pp 155–85.
Beeching agrees with the poet Dryden's comment that he (Dryden) can see
the pilgrims as distinctly as if he had supped with them at the Tabard.
Beeching then adds: 'And not only can we see them, we can see through
them. Chaucer has given us more than dress, features, and humours;
with these he has given us their characters, and almost always sympathetically. His method is, from the circumstances, entirely different from
Shakespeare's, whom in his benignity and in his humour he not a little
resembles; he cannot to any great extent put his pilgrims before us and let
them speak; he has to describe them; and therefore there cannot fail to be
about the portraits a slight touch of caricature. But it is of the slightest.
The portrait is clearly recognisable as the portrait of a type, but it is none
the less individual' (1981 rpt, pp 174–5). Beeching notes that 'some of the
best portraits are those of country folk' (p 177), that Chaucer reserves his
'sarcasm' chiefly for the clerical pilgrims (pp 178–9), and that he 'shows
himself a sympathiser with Wyclif' in attacking friars and pardoners (p
178).

153 Bekus, Albert J. *Tradition and Innovation in the Prologues of Chaucer*.
Auburn University Dissertation. 1973. Dir. Thomas L. Wright. See also
DAI, 34 (1973), 1232-A.
Background principles from the rhetoricians, as well as earlier medieval
prologues, are considered. The traditions of 'dream-vision beginning, descriptions in medieval romance, and descriptions of vices and virtues, do
not account for the complex art of the *General Prologue*' (p 212). 'The
various aspects of the *General Prologue* may have their origins in the traditions and conventions that Chaucer inherited, but it defies placement in
a literary tradition' (p 222). Dante is not proposed as a specific source, but
'one cannot ignore the series of characters and the realistic descriptions' (p
212) in the *Divine Comedy*; that work also shares with *GP* the quality of
being structured as a remembered experience.

154 Bennett, H.S. *Life on the English Manor: A Study of Peasant Conditions
1150–1400*. Cambridge: Cambridge University Press, 1937. Rpt 1938,
1948.
This book on rural life in medieval England provides background information on topics such as agricultural practices, village customs, occupations,

the cycle of the year's labor, rents and services owed to various lords, manorial administrative structures, the situation of widows, the advantages of life in the towns, and the role of the Church in daily life. On the Parson, see **1174**.

155 ——. 'Medieval Literature and the Modern Reader.' *E&S*, 31 (1945), 7–18. Bennett argues that without adequate historical research 'we shall get only the barest surface meaning' (p 18) when we read medieval authors; in particular, we will miss their subtleties and ironies. Thus 'a considerable knowledge of medieval life and literature is required if we are to get the full flavor from Chaucer's great series of portraits in the *Prologue*' (p 9). The Prioress's and Monk's portraits are examined. The passage on the Prioress's manners is compared to the very similar description of how a fashionable woman should eat, if she wishes to attract masculine attention, in the *Roman de la Rose*; many of the details are identical. The passage on the Monk's hunting is read in light of the visitation of the Bishop of Winchester to Selborne Priory in 1387; the tendency of some of the monks to ride out from the cloister, or to hunt, is there deplored. Similarly, in 1337 Benedict XII had forbidden monks to use *grys*, the expensive fur of gray squirrels — which the Monk nevertheless wears at his wrists. Only a knowledge of medieval sources enables us to interpret such passages as the Prioress's or the Monk's portrait properly.

156 ——. *Chaucer and the Fifteenth Century*. Oxford: Clarendon Press, 1947. Brief comments on *GP* are included in this general treatment of Chaucer's life and works. On the framework device, Bennett remarks that 'the idea of a pilgrimage was masterly .... Chaucer was able to assemble the greatest possible variety of people, all linked by a common purpose, and to allow them to jog forward with a certain loosening of the stricter rules of etiquette and precedence which divided them in everyday life .... We are privileged, in short, to see this group of fourteenth century men and women, not as in a picture, or in the stiff attitudes of a tapestry, but as they laughed and talked, unconscious that the sharp highly trained eye of Geoffrey Chaucer was upon them. The result is not the story, but the *drama* of the *Canterbury Tales*' (p 68).

157 Benson, Robert G. *Medieval Body Language: A Study of the Use of Gesture in Chaucer's Poetry*. Copenhagen: Rosenkilde and Bagger, 1980. Anglistica, 21. General Editors, Norman E. Eliason, Knud Sorensen, and T.J.B. Spencer. In *GP* the pilgrims' gestures are presented as static rather than as active — ie, as 'potential or habitual actions' (p 67) rather than as actions taking place specifically at the moment. Gestures serve 'to individualize

the pilgrims whose physiognomies emphasize their more typical traits' (p 67), so that we can see them both as individuals and as representatives of types. Gestures also serve 'to identify Chaucer's portraits as delineations of character' (p 67). The *GP* lines referring to gesture are collected in an Appendix. Nearly all are classified as demonstrative gestures; the lines noted are 69, 133–5, 138–41, 148, 201–2, 264–5, 267–8, and 857. Cf Benson's dissertation, *Gesture in Chaucer's Poetry*, University of North Carolina, 1974; abstract in *DAI*, 35 (1974), 3670-A.

158 Bhattacherje, M.M. *Pictorial Poetry*. Folcroft, PA: Folcroft Press, 1969. [Originally published as *Research Bulletin (Arts) of the University of the Panjab*, 14 (1954) — not seen.]
Much indebted to Legouis (**334**), Bhattacherje briefly discusses the pictorial quality of the portraits, noting the presence of strong colors associated with the Prioress, Franklin, Wife, Summoner, and Miller. 'Gaudy and strong colours fatigue the eye,' but relief is provided by the 'duller tints' of pilgrims such as the Clerk, Serjeant of Law, Reeve, and Parson (pp 23–4).

159 Bickford, Charles Gray. *The Influence of Rhetoric on Chaucer's Portraiture*. University of Pennsylvania Dissertation. 1973. See also *DAI*, 34 (1974), 5091-A.
The rhetorical traditions pertaining to feminine portraiture, and then to masculine portraiture, are surveyed. Both Matthew of Vendôme and Geoffrey of Vinsauf imply that for male characters one should use *effictio* (physical description) sparingly, and 'Chaucer gives far fewer physical descriptions of males than he does females' (p 55). Nevertheless, 'two main streams of masculine portraiture, the realistic and the ugly' (p 56), existed in the rhetorical tradition. Chaucer draws upon the realistic tradition for the Squire, the ugly tradition for the Summoner, and a blending of both masculine traditions for the Miller, who is 'a modified Wild Man' (p 107). The Squire's portrait, associated with bird imagery in *GP* (lines 97-8), shows similarities to that of Chanticler in *NPT*. Chaucer frequently provides physical traits for 'men of amorous inclinations' (p 115). Handsome portraits are used 'only when there is need to describe an egoistic and self-important male' (p 116).

160 Biggar, Raymond George. *Langland's and Chaucer's Treatment of Monks, Friars and Priests*. University of Wisconsin Dissertation. 1961. Dir. Helen C. White. See also *DA*, 22 (1962), 1992.
Both Langland and Chaucer are concerned with the lower ranks of the clergy: monks, friars, and parish priests. Chaucer's treatment of the Monk is purposely ambiguous. Lines 184–9 are 'the key to Chaucer's somewhat ambiguous attitudes towards the monks of his day. The questions may be

questions which the Monk directed at the Narrator ... But this passage can also be understood as the Narrator's own buttressing of line 184, where he tells us that he has agreed, verbally at least, with the Monk's discarding the old texts against hunting and riding out' (pp 193–4). Parallels between the Monk's and the Friar's portraits are pointed out; for example, as the Monk 'was nat pale as a forpyned goost' (line 205), so the Friar 'was nat lyk a cloysterer' (line 259). Although the idealized Parson reflects views shared by Wycliffe, this is because 'Wycliffe often gets his ideas on priests from orthodox sources' (p 312), not because Chaucer or the Parson is Wycliffite. Chaucer may have read *Piers Plowman.* 'Both poets contrast the monks' unspiritual behavior and prosperity and neglect of their role to an ideal of their founders from the past. Both poets present their friars dramatically ... letting the rascals reveal what they really are by their own words and actions .... Both poets show their parish priests quietly performing their duties in the background' (p 323). Where Langland depends upon allegory, Chaucer's 'more tolerant, balanced, and moderate attitude' depends upon the 'more indirect methods' of 'irony, satire, suggestion, implication, and contrast' (p 325).

161 Blake, N.F. 'Chaucer in his Time.' In *New Views on Chaucer: Essays in Generative Criticism.* Ed. William C. Johnson and Loren C. Gruber. Denver, CO: Society for New Language Study, 1973. Pp 1–7.
Blake argues that the tone of a Chaucerian poem 'is more likely to be revealed in its larger linguistic patterns than in its choice of individual words' (p 3). 'Thus in the General Prologue Chaucer has presented a gallery of individuals. But he has not sought to encapsulate their characters in one or two pithy expressions; rather he has presented each pilgrim in the space of about a dozen lines. The vocabulary is not usually specific or exceptional, and it is doubtful whether we should think of the people as particularised individuals. ... Even if in any one description several of the words were changed or some of the lines rearranged the difference would be small, for our view of the knight or the monk depends on the overall effect of the paragraph rather than upon certain key words' (pp 3–4). Units such as paragraphs are related to each other by parallelism and contrast. 'The General Prologue is a collection of portraits which stand in relation to one another' (p 4). We need not assume that the narrator provides a tone of smirking or supercilious irony. 'There is no need to assume this tone since the interrelationship of the characters provides all the comment and tone that is necessary' (p 5).

162 —. 'Critics, Criticism, and the Order of "The Canterbury Tales."' *Archiv,* 218 (1981), 47–58.
Blake argues that the 'tales cannot have been written or developed in a

particular way to illuminate the character and prejudices of their tellers. The favourite critical assumption that the tale reveals the teller will have to be handled more discriminatingly,' since Chaucer seems to have composed the tales first, allocated them later, and not been 'much concerned with the relationship between a tale and its teller' (p 57).

163 Bloomfield, Morton. 'Authenticating Realism and the Realism of Chaucer.' *Thought*, 39 (1964), 335–58.
Bloomfield discusses various concepts of realism and the devices through which writers authenticate their fictions. 'Chaucer's realism of detail in the authenticating frame seems to be largely original with him' (p 353). In the initial title or announcement *Here bygynneth the Book* ..., Chaucer functions as 'the author speaking directly to the audience,' and at that point he is 'not the pilgrim who is reporting the Canterbury pilgrimage, although he is related to him very closely' (pp 355–6). As an authenticating device, *GP* exists not for itself 'but for what is to come' (p 358).

164 Bookis, Judith May. *Chaucer's Creation of Universal Professional Stereotypes in Five of the Canterbury Tales.* Drew University Dissertation. 1982. See also *DAI*, 43 (1982), 1140-A.
'Treating the *Second Nun's Tale*, the *Prioress's Tale*, the *Man of Law's Tale*, the *Clerk's Tale*, and the *Physician's Tale*, the dissertation first looks at the medieval stereotype [of each profession], then analyzes each professional's portrait in the *General Prologue* and, finally, examines each tale to determine how the professional stereotyping of the narrator affects both his use of rhetoric and the manipulation of a common genre — the Saint's life' [from *DAI*; diss not seen].

165 Borenius, Tancred. 'The Iconography of St. Thomas of Canterbury.' *Archaeologia*, 79 (1929), 29–54.
Borenius provides information on the diffusion of Becket's legend and its artistic representations. See also his supplementary articles: 'Addenda to the Iconography of St. Thomas of Canterbury,' *Archaeologia*, 81 (1931), 19–32, and 'Some Further Aspects of the Iconography of St. Thomas of Canterbury,' *Archaeologia*, 83 (1933), 171–86. Cf lines 16–18.

166 ——. *St. Thomas Becket in Art.* London: Methuen, 1932.
Much background information on Becket's life and legend is included. Cf lines 16–18.

167 Bowden, Muriel. *A Reader's Guide to Geoffrey Chaucer.* New York: Farrar, Straus [1964]; New York: Noonday Press [1964, paperback]; London: Thames and Hudson, 1965.
Intended primarily for newcomers to the *CT*, in its comments on *GP* this

book reflects many of the materials assembled in Bowden's more detailed study (see **104**).

168 Boyce, Benjamin. *The Theophrastan Character in England to 1642*. Cambridge, MA: Harvard University Press, 1947; London: Oxford University Press, 1947.

GP 'is not a perfect example of the literature of Estates,' but shows 'connections with that kind of writing' (p 59). Chaucer's main classification is social and professional, rather than moral, though many of the portraits have 'a further moral classification' (p 60). As for the tradition of the Theophrastan Character, 'Chaucer's sketches are not Characters in verse. There is still too much *effictio*, too much of face, figure, and "array" in the manner recommended by the thirteenth-century *poetria*; and some pieces of exactitude such as the Wife's deafness, though they do not destroy the type, do not assist with it' (p 61). Thus 'Chaucer's method and his intention are not, on the whole, Theophrastan, but because of his psychological insight, his concreteness, and his scheme of social-moral types, the effect of the portraits is in some cases very similar' (p 61).

169 Brégy, Katherine. 'The Inclusiveness of Chaucer.' *CW*, 115 (1922), 304–13.

Chaucer is 'the poet of perpetual youth, of new beginnings, of vernal love and fresh enthusiasms' (p 304). Chaucer had sympathy 'for the most amazing variety of people' (p 309). He is tolerant of the Friar and the Monk, but 'he does not love the yellow-haired, eloquent, cynical Pardoner,' in whose portrait 'one sees a real abuse of the Church handled frankly, humanly' (p 311). His inclusiveness is thus not a thoughtless acceptance of all human traits.

170 Breslin, Carol Ann. *Justice and Law in Chaucer's Canterbury Tales*. Temple University Dissertation. 1978. See also *DAI*, 39 (1978), 2246-A.

Several of the pilgrims 'would have been associated directly or indirectly with the administration of justice (Knight, Reeve, Summoner, Man of Law, Franklin, and so on)' (p vi). In addition, the pilgrimage itself 'suggests the theme of justice' in both a moral and theological sense, and a secular sense (p 1). Individual pilgrims' connections to law and justice are considered in light of Chaucer's probable legal sources.

171 Brett-James, Norman G. *Introducing Chaucer*. London: Harrap, 1949.

This general book on Chaucer relates the treatment of town life, country life, and food in *GP* to contemporary conditions.

172 Brewer, D.S. *Chaucer*. London, Toronto, & New York: Longmans, Green, 1953. Men and Books Series. Second ed, with 'a slightly fuller bibliographi-

cal note' and minor revisions, 1960. Third ed, 'extensively revised and with additional material,' 1973.

In the chapter 'Prologue to the Canterbury Tales' (1953, pp 123–39), Brewer comments that the GP portraits are painted 'with the apparent simplicity of truly original genius' (p 132) and with 'concentrated brilliance' (p 133). The springtime opening is a conventional ingredient, but Chaucer's version, written in 'a modified "high style,"' is both 'spacious and precise' (p 132). The lack of a pattern in the descriptions, 'this very impression of casualness,' reflects the 'supreme art which conceals art' (p 133). The portraits are sharpened by a 'faint exaggeration' or by idealization, so that 'almost every person, whether good or bad, is said to be the perfect example of his or her kind' (p 135). The pilgrims are described according to their occupations, with overall reference to the concept of the three estates and the Christian ethics which that concept implied. Judged against these ethical standards, 'nearly every pilgrim' is seen to be 'ridiculous or self-seeking or wicked, or all of these' (p 136). Such a social and ethical background was 'part of Chaucer's mind' (p 138), but probably not a conscious part of his structure in writing the work. The mood of the portraits varies, with 'comic satire' (p 139) predominating — an attitude that tends to exclude the extremes of society. In GP 'we mainly see the middling people, and we see them from a slightly superior moral and social station' (p 139). The third edition's additional chapter also comments on GP, in particular discussing the meaning of honour and trouthe and other recurrent concepts, as well as the management of the Chaucerian persona.

173 ——. *Chaucer in His Time.* London: Thomas Nelson, 1963. Rpt London: Longman, 1973, 1977, 1980.

In this 'account of how life looked and felt around Chaucer' (Preface), GP is several times mentioned and used as illustrative material. Much information is provided on fourteenth-century domestic life, education, courtly culture, and so forth. GP 'unquestionably contains a good deal of satire of known individuals,' a satire that is 'personal rather than political, and never aimed at anybody really important' (p 200).

174 ——. 'Class Distinction in Chaucer.' *Spec,* 43 (1968), 290–305.

'Chaucer portrays not one class-system operative in society but three, different though overlapping, and ... none of these corresponds to the nineteenth-century concept of the upper, the middle, and the lower class' (p 290). These systems are: 1) the principle of rank or degree, whose image is a ladder, which allows for social mobility up and down rungs; 2) the concept of being — or not being — a member of the gentry, in contrast to the churls, a binary system in which *gentilesse* 'has become a moral ideal, a virtuous nobility of character independent of external social rank' (p 299); and 3) the traditional division of society into three estates or into Knights, Clergy, and Ploughmen, a system that Chaucer seems to use although he never refers explicitly to it. 'Those who are morally idealised are the Knight and his son the Squire; the Clerk of Oxford and the Parson; and the Ploughman and Yeoman. We obviously have here the three-fold functional division of society' (p 302). Anyone who does not fulfill the ideals of this third pattern or who falls outside it (and by Chaucer's time most people fell outside it) is liable to satire. The Franklin, for example, is not a fighting man, a cleric, or a ploughman, and 'is therefore lightly mocked or satirised' (p 303). The same is true of Chaucer himself, who as a literate layman could fit into the first two systems of class, but not into the third (the traditional) one, and who was therefore a 'new man,' which 'may have created in him a sense of insecurity, strain, loss, even desertion' (p 304).

175 ——. *Chaucer and His World.* London: Eyre Methuen, 1978.
Much background information and many illustrations pertinent to *GP* are included. 'The reference to living people in *The General Prologue*, indisputable in a few cases, highly probable in many more, does not deny the traditional literary structures in the portraits, but shows how Chaucer accepted them, partially broke them down, formed them anew' (p 199). There are many connections between *GP* and Chaucer's contemporary world: the historical Harry Bailly, for example, 'received what must be the most successful advertisement in the whole world's history for his already popular hotel' (p 202).

176 Bronson, Bertrand H. 'Chaucer's Art in Relation to His Audience.' In *Five Studies in Literature.* Berkeley, CA: University of California Press, 1940. University of California Publications in English, 8. Pp 1–54.
Chaucer writes with the awareness of a listening audience; his style shows a number of techniques appropriate for an author who is reading his poems aloud to an audience that includes personal acquaintances. Examples from *GP* are cited: the clarification of a term (lines 177–81), which 'seems to be due to the desire to have his audience with him in the least detail' (p 12); the habit of modesty that 'would assure us that what he says is merely his opinion' (p 22; see lines 82, 154–57, 183, 193, 284, 288, 385, 389, 454); and 'the natural overemphasis of the good raconteur' (p 24), so that the pilgrims are said to be 'the very best of their kind' (p 23). The most important person we meet in the poetry is Chaucer himself, and 'Chaucer's own physical presence' in reading it aloud (p 38) is ppppan important factor in the interpretation of the narrator's role.

177 ——. *In Search of Chaucer.* Toronto: University of Toronto Press, 1960; London: Oxford University Press; 1960. Rpt University of Toronto Press,

1963, 1967.

In the chapter 'So Full of Shapes' (1960, pp 3–33) and the chapter 'By Day' (pp 60–90), Bronson criticizes certain trends in modern criticism. As for the narrator's role, the 'schizoid notion of two Chaucers, so named, presented simultaneously, one a puppet, the other the living, speaking poet, with attitudes and intelligences radically different from each other's' (p 28), is not appropriate to Chaucer's situation as a poet writing for oral delivery. Thus 'nine-tenths of this talk' about the *persona* 'is misguided and palpably mistaken' (p 26). Chaucer establishes a 'preternatural sense of intimacy' with us, though he views the people around him with amused detachment: 'we are not deeply involved with them, nor does he ask us to be; but we are very personally involved with him, to our delight, and with his entire assistance' (p 67). He is the character 'who truly matters to us' (p 67). The people described in *GP* are so individualized that we might take them to be portraits of Chaucer's contemporaries, as Manly proposed (see **362**), but 'psychological and historical probability' (p 69) is against this thesis. It would have been personally risky for Chaucer to have recognizably depicted contemporary people, and awkward for him to attribute stories to them. Similarly, Kittredge's thesis that the tales exist for the sake of the pilgrims (see **317**) 'seems more than doubtful' (p 77). See also **588**.

178 Brooks, Harold F. *Chaucer's Pilgrims: The Artistic Order of the Portraits in the Prologue.* New York: Barnes & Noble, 1962.

Chaucer's art in *GP* includes changing the tone and the kinds of characterizing details. The portraits proceed in five groups, which are the military class, the regular clergy, the middle-class group, two 'characters of humble virtue,' and the 'churls and rascals' (p 12). Within the first group, there is a descending order of rank, relationship, and amount of individualization. Then begins a principle of contrast, for the Prioress, following upon the Yeoman, is very individualized, while he is only a type. Within this second group there is also a descending order of social standing and of morality. We are now prepared for the secular middle-class group, since the preceding religious personages have been 'increasingly secular-minded' (p 21). Within the middle-class group, 'As the Merchant stands first of the pilgrims from the world of business, so does the Clerk among those from the learned professions' (p 23). In social terms, the Serjeant holds the highest rank of the professional men and the Franklin of all these pilgrims, so that together 'they constitute the social peak, in the middle-class group, immediately following the moral peak, constituted by the Clerk' (p 25). The middle-class group also moves from the provinces toward London (the Guildsmen) and then away again (the Shipman). The Wife concludes the middle-class group as it began, 'with someone belonging to the world of trade and industry' (p 31). With the Wife we encounter the 'climax of humor' (p 33), which is followed by the portrait of the Parson, who provides a 'contrasting climax of virtue' (p 34), and by that of the Plowman, who represents the lowest point on the social scale as well as spiritual humility. The Plowman also provides social-class continuity — but moral contrast — to the last group, that of the churls and knaves, whose internal principle of organization is a sequence of 'increasing physical deformity' (p 44), except for the Manciple. We reach 'the nadir of the moral scale,' which is simultaneously 'the zenith of the satiric' (p 56), in the Pardoner's portrait. Thus Chaucer's method is to include a number of different emphases, types of connections, means of contrast, etc, in a 'structure partly defined by climaxes' (p 64), but interrelated in multiple ways.

179 Brown, Beatrice Daw. 'A Thirteenth-Century Chaucerian Analogue.' *MLN*, 52 (1937), 28–31.
A tale included in the *Dialogus Miraculorum* of Caesarius of Heisterbach, which may have been known to Chaucer, shows similarities to *GP*. In this analogue 'the riders are, like Chaucer's travellers, bound together by a common religious purpose, although they are not on pilgrimage' (p 28); the idea of discourse as entertainment is raised and the leader calls on a member of the group, who offers 'an apologetic disclaimer' (p 29) as a preface to his tale; the tale proceeds to attack another member of the group, whose reaction is mentioned. Cardinal Henricus, a character in this tale, resembles Chaucer's Monk: both are figures of authority, 'fond of good living and gay apparel,' and Henricus 'by implication' neglects the Church's rules, as the Monk does openly (p 30).

180 Brown, Carleton. 'The Man of Law's Headlink and the Prologue of the Canterbury Tales.' *SP*, 34 (1937), 8–35.
Brown argues that the Man of Law (not the Knight) was originally to have told the first tale, which would have been *Mel*. In what is now the prologue to *MLT*, the personality of the Host resembles the Host's characterization in *GP*. That passage would naturally follow upon *GP* — which originally ended, in Brown's reconstruction of Chaucer's original plan, at line 826. The 'more facetious traits in the Host's character' (p 26) might have been added later. The writing of the *CT* was a process involving repeated revisions. *GP* (to line 826) was written early. It was subsequently modified to lead into the *KnT* once Chaucer decided that the Knight, rather than the Man of Law, should begin the series. In summary, 'Chaucer's earlier arrangement seems to have been: the General Prologue (lines 1–826), followed by the Man of Law's head-link with the Tale of Melibeus, followed in turn (according to the large majority of mss) by the Squire's Tale and the Franklin's' (p 33).

181 Brown, Paul Alonzo. *The Development of the Legend of Thomas Becket.*
University of Pennsylvania Dissertation, 1930. Dir. Clarence G. Child.
Philadelphia, PA: [no publisher indicated], 1930.
The growth of the Becket legend is examined in detail. Brown summarizes
the various versions of the tale that Becket's mother was a Saracen princess,
the legends of his life and martyrdom, local traditions, prophecies assciated
with him, etc. Cf lines 16–18.

182 Buckmaster, Elisabeth Marie. *'Caught in Remembrance': Chaucer and the
Art of Memory.* University of Delaware Dissertation. 1981. Dir. W. Bruce
Finnie. See also *DAI*, 42 (1981), 2136-A.
In the chapter '*The Canterbury Tales:* Memory Images and Places of the
Pilgrimage Frame' (pp 45–58), Buckmaster examines 'the role of artificial
memory' (p 45) and memory traditions in rhetorical texts insofar as they
illuminate the framework of *CT.* 'In the context of the memory tradition,
the individual portraits function as corporeal similitudes of a cross-section
of fourteenth-century English society' (p 46). The pilgrims 'can be seen
as *imagines agentes,* containing the tales that are to be told' (p 46). The
Knight's portrait 'is a good example of the way in which Chaucer uses
class and profession as mnemonic signs' (p 48). The pilgrimage setting 'is
an *aide-memoire*' (p 53).

183 Buermann, Theodore Barry. *Chaucer's 'Book of Genesis' in the Canterbury
Tales: The Biblical Schema of the First Fragment.* University of Illinois Dissertation. 1967. See also *DA*, 28 (1968), 5009–5010-A.
After establishing Chaucer's knowledge of the Bible and its commentators,
Buermann proposes a Biblical series according to which Creation and Paradise are reflected in *GP*, Cain and Abel in *KnT*, Noah's Flood in *MilT*, and
Sodom and Gomorrha in *RvT*. The springtime opening of *GP* 'corresponds
to the opening of the Bible — namely, the creation of the world,' while 'the
pilgrims' brief stay at the Tabard is a figure for man's brief stay in another
place of comfort and pleasure, the Garden of Eden. Chaucer's character
portraits and occasional naming of the brief inhabitants of that inn may
then correspond to Adam's naming the animals in Paradise ... And leaving the inn may signify mankind's leaving Eden on its pilgrimage' (p 34).
April 15 was the traditional day of Creation. The order of the images in
the springtime opening (rain, plant life, etc) corresponds to the Biblical
days of Creation. Line 830 echoes Genesis 1:5, where evening similarly is
mentioned before morning. As early as the twelfth century, Paradise was
described as 'an inn in which Adam was but a very brief guest' (p 107). The
Host is analogous to the serpent in Paradise. His surname, Bailly, is connected to the Devil in *FrT*, where the Devil calls himself a *bailly* (III.1396).
'The General Prologue, then, with its unique and select arrangement of its

"reverdie" opening and with its theme of pilgrimage suggests the creation of the world and Mankind's expulsion from the "inn" of Paradise on the pilgrimage of the ages' (p 88). What 'probably represents for Chaucer the fall of mankind' is 'the pilgrims' unanimous and precipitate consent to a sensually pleasurable religious journey' to the shrine (p 88).

184 Burchfield, Robert. 'Realms and Approximations: Sources of Chaucer's Power.' *E&S*, New Series 35 (1982), 1–13.
Chaucer sometimes observed reality 'with minute care' (p 5), but at other times he was 'much less evidently concerned with visual confirmation of the objects all around him than with the approximations to reality which made up the normal poetic kit of a poet of the fourteenth century' (p 6). See **669, 1093**.

185 Burgess, Anthony. 'Whan that Aprille... ' *Horizon*, 13, #2 (1971), 45–59.
This illustrated overview of *GP* and the rest of *CT* is intended for a general audience.

186 Burlin, Robert B. *Chaucerian Fiction*. Princeton, NJ: Princeton University Press, 1977.
CT is examined among Chaucer's 'psychological fictions' (p ix). Occasional comments on *GP* are included, usually correlating the pilgrims' *GP* portraits to their later behavior. On the Merchant, Man of Law, and Franklin, Burlin comments that 'a certain coolness descends on these portraits; the narrator gives little sense of the human personalities that animate this merchant, lawyer, and professional host and officeholder' (p 195). These pilgrims 'anticipate a capitalistic society' and are 'almost obsessively conscious of the risks of their professions' (p 195). Correspondingly, in the *FranT* the 'nagging concern for *gentilesse*, for rank and postition, may be seen as but another variety of dissatisfaction with things as they are' (p 207).

187 Burrow, J.A. *Ricardian Poetry: Chaucer, Gower, Langland, and the Gawain Poet*. New Haven, CN: Yale University Press, 1971; London: Routledge & Kegan Paul, 1971.
The work of Chaucer and his contemporaries shares characteristics of style that entitle their era to be regarded as, 'in something like the full literary sense, a period' (p 141). *GP*, in which Chaucer displays his 'intensive manner,' is a 'veritable *locus classicus* of sustained superlative' (p 17). The effect is 'simple and minstrelesque, even "salesman-like,"' although we tend to view the narrator's enthusiasm with 'a harmonic overtone of irony' (p 18). Some of Chaucer's stock phrases show the use of doublets 'with an ironic twist' (p 20), as in the *symple and coy* of line 119 or the *war and wys* of lines 309–10. On the Host, see **1355**.

188 Cannon, Thomas F., Jr. *Chaucer's Pilgrims as Artists.* University of Virginia Dissertation. 1973. See also *DAI*, 34 (1974), 4190–4191-A.

Cannon draws upon the concept of the *populus peregrinus*, the community unified to promote common profit, as developed by Gregory the Great and Augustine. 'In the *populus peregrinus*, common profit is advanced by charity; in the fellowship of the Canterbury pilgrims, common profit is advanced by art' (p 52). 'The narrative contest in which the pilgrims participate requires that each become an artist for a time and direct whatever talent he has to the profit of his fellows' (p 55). A 'tale of "sentence" and "solaas" benefits the audience as well as the author — the audience is instructed and delighted, the author wins the game and the feast. Cast in such a role, an artist serves his own interests by serving those of others' (p 56). The narrator himself functions as the first of these artists, for the prologue, strictly speaking, occupies only the first 18 lines, after which the narrator begins his tale, telling the story of his joining the pilgrims' fellowship and coming to know them. Thus 'what emerges from the portrait is not an illumination of the pilgrim, as in the Ellesmere manuscript, but a picture of the narrator learning about the pilgrim' (p 9). The narrator describes the pilgrims as they themselves would, or did; thus, for instance, we learn the Friar's own sense of his self-worth (see line 251). The narrator finds each pilgrim attractive in one way or another. 'It is finally this openness and good will which urges audience acceptance amd assent, and which establishes the point of view of the narrator as morally and aesthetically true' (p 36). Examinations of individual portraits are included.

189 Casiddu, M. *La struttura del Prologo di Chaucer. Per una lettura semiologica del testo.* London: Sassari, 1981.

Not seen. Listed in *ChauR*, 17 (1982–1983), p 269.

190 Cazamian, Louis. *The Development of English Humor.* New York: Macmillan, 1930. Rpt (with new sections) Durham, NC: Duke University Press, 1952.

In the chapter 'Chaucer's Humor' (1930, pp 100–29), Cazamian suggests that there is a humorous intent behind the catalogues or repetitive series of names in the Physician's portrait, where 'a sense of mechanical and funny exaggeration' is achieved (p 122), and in the Knight's list of battles, which may be mocking 'the most approved style of the romances, in which the palm of valor is won, with unfailing ease, by one hero after another' (p 123). In the Parson's and Plowman's portraits the humor 'resides in the sheer idealism of such descriptions ... to set up such figures as living facts is an irony in itself' (pp 123–24).

191 Chalk, Edwin S. 'Chaucer Allusions.' *N&Q*, 169 (1935), 241.
Chalk reports 'a newly-discovered record of an official visit to Dartmouth by Geoffrey Chaucer. This goes to show that the Prologue of the Canterbury Tales sticks to the facts.'

192 Chamberlain, David. 'Musical Signs and Symbols in Chaucer: Convention and Originality.' In *Signs and Symbols in Chaucer's Poetry*. Ed. John P. Hermann and John J. Burke, Jr. University, AL: University of Alabama Press, 1981. Pp 43–80.
Chamberlain examines the conventional and the original uses of musical imagery. In *GP* 'an abundance of musical details of varying originality are all signs for inner folly or vice' (p 55). In lines 9–11, the music of the *smale foweles* is 'a music only of physical nature' (p 55). 'With varying degrees of obviousness, all other music in the Prologue is a sign of the fleshly rather than the spiritual orientation of the pilgrims' (p 55). The Prioress sings in her nose, but, by implication, not in her heart. The Pardoner sings in church for greed, on pilgrimage for lechery. The Monk's bells suggest pride and lechery; the Friar's singing, hypocrisy; the Squire's, frivolity and erotic interests. 'The Miller's bagpipe, like the melody of the little birds, is a sign that tends to characterize the music of the pilgrims as a whole' (p 55). *CT* as a whole 'has a significant musical frame, creating a contrast between the "melodye" of physical desire at the beginning and the "melodye" of spiritual joy at the end of the work' (p 79).

193 Chesterton, Gilbert Keith. *Chaucer.* London: Faber and Faber, 1932. Rpt 1934; new ed 1948; second ed 1959; paperbound 1962.
'The Prologue of *The Canterbury Tales* is the Prologue of Modern Fiction' (1962, p 15). Chaucer was proud to use the works of previous poets, but was also 'one of the most original men who ever lived. There had never been anything like the lively realism of the ride to Canterbury done or dreamed of in our literature before' (p 34). Chaucer chooses details carefully; the 'Prologue is, among other things, a medieval picture' that uses what others might consider to be 'trifles' to enable us to see, 'as clearly as a child sees the figures in a toy theatre, the Yeoman in his green coat and hood ... the Wife of Bath with her scarlet stockings ... the Squire with his long sleeves' (etc, p 63). Chaucer's descriptions are both imaginative and realistic, for 'he was imagining what he saw' (p 63). Chaucer's partisanship of causes should not be overestimated. In the Friar-Summoner contrast, 'I have myself a dark suspicion that Chaucer was writing a poem, and especially telling a story; and that to him as an artist the vivid and coloured figures of the Summoner and the Friar were of much more importance than the interests they represented in ecclesiastical law' (p 53). The Knight's battles are 'apparently deliberately remote' and he himself 'comes from the ends of

the earth,' as 'the ghost of a grander Europe,' a figure 'of larger make or framework than the rest' who 'throws a sort of giant shadow on the coloured crowd; a shadow almost of shame' (p 68). The Prioress conveys 'a delicately mingled atmosphere of refinement and fuss' (p 200). The Monk's portrait is 'a protest against the decline of monastic discipline,' not against monasticism itself (p 254), for Chaucer is no Protestant.

CT as a whole 'takes on the character of a Novel' in which 'the stories exist to tell us something about the story-tellers' (p 171) and the 'prolonged comedy which we call the Prologue' is 'made of much stronger material than the tales which it carries; the narrative is quite superior to the narratives' (p 164). Chaucer's scale of values is two-fold. On one level 'he has an impulsive movement to applaud what he does not approve' (p 271), as if impudence or eccentricity pleased him. In this spirit he seems to regard the Summoner's and Shipman's evils, which in the Shipman's case include murder (line 400), as mere 'trifles' (p 272) that do not interfere with his geniality or amusement. Thus he 'set up, as part of the structure of his own mind, a sort of lower and larger stage, for all mankind, on which anything could happen without seriously hurting anybody; and an upper stage which he kept almost deliberately separate, on which walked the angels of the justice and the mercy and the omniscience of God' (pp 272-3).

194 Chute, Marchette. *Geoffrey Chaucer of England.* New York: Dutton, 1946; London: Hale, 1951. Rpt London: Souvenir Press, 1977.
GP is briefly discussed in this general study of Chaucer, who is seen as ignoring or rejecting the traditions of his time. 'He did not set out to be moral,' or 'even entertaining,' but instead 'to be accurate' (1977, pp 248). Chaucer 'threw the whole book of rules overboard in his Prologue' (p 249) — refusing to obey, for instance, the regulations about orderly descriptions. On the Pardoner, see **1302.**

195 ——. 'On the Pleasure of Meeting Chaucer.' *EJ*, 45 (1956), 373–80, 394.
General remarks on *GP* are included in this appreciation. Chaucer's portraits are viewed as the product of a realist's rebellion against tradition: 'It was clear to the theorists who taught the art of writing that no poet should permit himself to stray away from the general and allegorical to the personal and precise. Real people had no place in fourteenth-century poetry until Chaucer put them there' (p 374). Chaucer could see each of the pilgrims 'as clearly as though they actually stood before him, and he lavished on them the exact, glowing reality of a Flemish portraitist' (p 378).

196 Clawson, W.H. 'The Framework of The Canterbury Tales.' *UTQ*, 20 (1950-1951), 137–54. Rpt in *Chaucer: Modern Essays in Criticism*, ed. Edward C. Wagenknecht (New York: Oxford University Press, 1959), pp 3–22.

After reviewing examples of frame-tales — *The Thousand and One Nights, Seven Sages, Fables of Bidpai, Disciplina Clericalis, Confessio Amantis,* Ovid's Daughters of King Minyas episode, Boccaccio's *Filocolo* and *Ameto* — Clawson compares the use of the framework in the *Decameron* to that in the *Canterbury Tales*. As for the question of whether Chaucer knew Boccaccio's story collection, 'his indebtedness to it must at most be regarded as not proven' (1951, p 140). Sercambi's *Novelle*, which depicts storytelling while a company of travelers journeys to different places, is also briefly compared. The distinctive features of *GP* include 1) a method of characterization that presents each pilgrim as an individual, as a representative of a social class, and as a universal type of character; 2) an effect of spontaneity that is achieved by the use of apparently haphazard detail; 3) the role of the Host as leader; and 4) the quarrels, disputes, and confessions which will develop further in later parts of the text. Although Chaucer is remarkable for his realism, at the end 'the Canterbury pilgrimage becomes symbolic' (p 154).

197 Clements, Robert J., and Joseph Gibaldi. *Anatomy of the Novella: The European Tale Collection from Boccaccio and Chaucer to Cervantes.* New York: New York University Press, 1977.
Brief references to Chaucer are included in this study of the European story-collections; the varieties of frames (here called cornices) used by a range of other writers are discussed.

198 Coghill, Nevill. *The Poet Chaucer.* London and New York: Geoffrey Cumberlege for Oxford University Press, 1949. The Home University Library of Modern Knowledge, 185. General Editors, Gilbert Murray et al. Rpt 1950 (with reading list), 1955, 1960 (with corrections), 1961, 1964. 2nd ed, London and New York: Oxford University Press, 1967. Oxford Paperbacks University Series. General Editors, Michael Abercrombie and A.D. Woozley. Parts rpt in *Chaucer and His Contemporaries,* ed. Helaine Newstead (New York: Fawcett, 1968), pp 164–73.
In the chapter 'The Prologue to the Canterbury Tales' (1961, pp 113–26), Coghill comments that in *GP* 'Experience had wedded Authority, and perhaps achieved sovereignty in the marriage' (p 113). 'The result was a new sort of poetical truth, the creation of a poetry of fact' and 'a new way of looking at people' (p 114). Chaucer painted a 'National Portrait Gallery' (p 115), one in which hierarchy is present 'though in a deliberately disordered chain' (p 116). 'A quizzical but affirmative delight in the created world, an eye for the immediate image and an ear for the natural music of speech gathered their forces in Chaucer to express in *The Prologue* his long experience of the daily dealings of men and women' (p 126). The effect is to enable every reader to 'open a Chaucerian eye on the world' (p 126).

199 ——. *Geoffrey Chaucer*. London: Longmans, Green, for the British Council and the National Book League, 1956. Writers and Their Work, No. 79. Rpt with revised bibliography, 1959, 1962, 1965. Rpt in *British Writers and Their Work No. 1* (Lincoln, NE: University of Nebraska Press, 1963), pp 1–68.

GP is briefly discussed in the chapter 'Men and Women' (1956, pp 48–63). Coghill points out that works on rhetoric, medicine, and astrology influenced Chaucer's portraiture; he reviews the rhetoricians' statements on *descriptio* and relates them to Chaucer's technique in the *GP* portraits. In describing the Wife, for example, 'Chaucer has worked his miracle by remembering his Cicero' (p 51) — virtually all of Cicero's eleven attributes for describing a person are included, along with characteristics corresponding to the precepts of Geoffrey of Vinsauf. The Prioress's portrait shows the influence of Matthew of Vendôme; the Franklin's, Reeve's, and Pardoner's portraits reflect 'the medical approach to character' (p 53). Chaucer's artistic eye, which 'altered everything' and 'knew what to look for' in Experience, was instructed by Authority (p 49).

200 Coleman, Janet. *Medieval Readers and Writers, 1350–1400*. New York: Columbia University Press, 1981. British edition: *English Literature in History, 1350–1400: Medieval Readers and Writers*. London: Hutchinson, 1981. Series Editor, Raymond Williams.

GP is briefly examined in the chapter 'Vernacular Literacy and Lay Education' (pp 18–57). The style and form of the portraits in *GP* were partially influenced by literary traditions, but for '*what* Chaucer tells us about his pilgrims, rather than *how* he tells us, contemporary society was his model more consistently than literary genres' (p 47). The idealized portraits of the Parson, Knight, and Plowman, representing the three estates, reflect older, traditional ideas. 'But by weighting his humanizing descriptions in favour of the very fully represented second and third estates, rounding them out with virtues and vices that were both typical of certain professions and particular to certain individuals, be they fictional or based on real-life models, he created a mobile society, rejecting the static ideal of fixed estates' (p 47). Much background information is provided about late-medieval literacy, memory, education, complaint-literature, preaching, the literary *compilatio*, the Wycliffite movement, etc.

201 Connolly, Terence L., S.J. *An Introduction to Chaucer and Langland (A Corrective of Long's History of English Literature)*. New York: Fordham University Press, 1925.

The chapter 'Chaucer' (pp 59–82) examines several *GP* portraits from the perspective that 'Chaucer was Catholic to the core' (p 82), not an early Protestant. The portraits of the Monk, Friar, Summoner, and Pardoner depict abuses, but 'Chaucer did not conclude the degeneration of all from the remissness of a few' (p 68). The idealized portraits — such as that of the Plowman, who is said to work *For Cristes sake* (line 537) — reflect Chaucer's Catholicism. The Prioress, 'as depicted by Chaucer, is distinguished for her nicety of external deportment no less than for her sensitiveness' (p 76). There is 'nothing in the text' to support Coulton's characterization of the Prioress and the Second Nun as being ' "like a pair of aristocratic pussy-cats" ' (p 77; cf **204**).

202 Corsa, Helen Storm. *Chaucer: Poet of Mirth and Morality*. Notre Dame, IN: University of Notre Dame Press, 1964.
In the chapter 'Modes of Comedy in the First Fragment' (pp 73–120), Corsa analyzes *GP* as comic. The role of chance or happenstance is recognized in such lines as 19 (*Bifil that*), 25 (*by aventure*), and 844 (*by aventure, or sort, or cas*). The narrator-observer maintains both commitment, as a member of the fellowship; and detachment, as a reporter. His combined attitude 'precludes satire or cynicism,' being 'more affectionate than critical, more amused than bitter' (p 76). The portraits depict each pilgrim's attempt to maintain an equilibrium — *not* between appearance and reality, for in Chaucer's view 'the accidents of things do not contradict their essences' (p 78); but instead between 'what the pilgrim is and what he senses, or has sensed, he should be' (p 78). Both the Knight at the beginning of the portrait series and the Pardoner at the end are, in their opposite ways, 'exactly what they appear to be' (p 79), while in between each pilgrim 'has a position within a moral spectrum' (p 81). The pattern of the three estates serves as a general grouping, though Chaucer's awareness of diversity goes beyond that pattern. The game-concept provides 'an ordered world in which the erratic can be contained, in which the agonistic impulses can be profitably used' (p 93). The Host is creator, umpire, and participant in the game, whose central rule is 'that mirth prevail' (p 95).

203 Cosman, Madeleine Pelner. *Famous Feasts: Medieval Cookery and Ceremony*. New York: Braziller, 1977.
Background information is provided about such topics as food and social class, food and sin, and food and sex, with illustrations from contemporary manuscripts and occasional brief comments on *GP*. 'For both the ecclesiastical and secular figures, gastronomy demonstrates social standing and personal sensibility' (p 104). Since a free supper at the Host's inn is the prize for the best tale, 'the tavern more than the shrine of St. Thomas of Canterbury is the architectural frame for all the later Tales' (p 105).

204 Coulton, George Gordon. *Chaucer and His England*. London: Methuen, 1908. 3rd ed, New York: Dutton, 1921; 4th ed, Methuen, 1927; 5th ed,

Methuen & Dutton, 1937; 8th ed, Dutton, 1950. Rpt New York: Russell and Russell, 1957. Rpt with new bibliography by T.W. Craik, 1963.

The dramatic qualities of *GP* are stressed in the chapter 'Canterbury Tales — The Dramatic Personae' (1963, pp 120–32). Nowhere else in medieval literature is there such a 'wonderful gallery of finished portraits,' based on 'the living men day by day, each in his simplest and most striking characteristics' (p 126), with their variety being 'as probable in nature as it is artistically effective' (p 126). Madame Eglantyne and her accompanying nun are 'like a pair of aristocratic pussy-cats on a drawing-room hearthrug' (p 129). [In objection to this characterization, see **201**.] The Prioress's 'pardonable luxuries of a fastidious nature' (which Chaucer describes in his 'most delicate irony') are set in contrast to the 'grosser indiscipline of the Monk' (p 129). The Parson and Clerk 'go far to redeem the Church' (p 130) from the irreligious ways of the Friar, Summoner, and Pardoner. Chaucer has an 'infallible eye' for the 'touch which makes a portrait live,' as in the Franklin's beard, the Shipman's difficulty in riding, the Wife's deafness, etc (p 130). Much background information is provided about medieval warfare, marriage, households, and so forth.

205 Courtney, Neil. 'Chaucer's Poetic Vision.' *CR*, 8 (1965), 129–40.

Courtney examines the portraits of the Knight, the Parson, the Miller, and the Pardoner, as well as considering the management of time in the opening eighteen lines of *GP* and discussing the extent to which Chaucer is properly called a realist. The Knight is 'essentially a simple man, of somewhat inflexible, formal dignity' (p 135). The Parson's description 'is really nothing but an objectified sermon, a series of Christian exempla' (p 135); the Miller 'has all the immediacy and dramatic realism for which Chaucer is celebrated' (p 136). As for the Pardoner, 'Nature in him is blighted, not blessed,' and perhaps it is finally 'self-ignorance, at a deeper level than his naked self-knowledge, which lies at the base of his deprivation' (p 138).

206 Cummings, Hubertis M. *The Indebtedness of Chaucer's Works to the Italian Works of Boccaccio (A Review and Summary)*. Menasha, WI: George Banta, 1916. University of Cincinnati Studies, 10, pt. 2. Rpt New York: Phaeton Press, 1967.

Cummings reviews opinion on Chaucer's use of Boccaccio's *Decameron* (and his *Ameto*) for the tale-telling framework. He argues against such influence, finding the evidence 'almost unvaryingly negative ... we cannot safely postulate any theory that the *Decamerone* was of any help whatsoever to Chaucer' in *CT* (1967, p 198). The book is based upon Cummings' dissertation, *Chaucer's Indebtedness to Boccaccio in Troilus and Criseyde and the Knight's Tale,* Princeton University, 1914. In reply, see **353**.

207 Cunningham, J.V. 'The Literary Form of the Prologue to the *Canterbury Tales.*' *MP*, 49 (1951-1952), 173–81. Rpt as 'Convention as Structure: The Prologue to the Canterbury Tales,' in J.V. Cunningham, *Tradition and Poetic Structure* (Denver: Allan Swallow, 1960), pp 59–75.

The fact that no exact antecedent for *GP* has been identified has led scholars to conclude that Chaucer here broke from tradition and turned directly to reality instead. However, 'what a writer finds in real life is to a large extent what his literary tradition enables him to see and to handle' (1952, p 173), and *GP* does indeed belong to a literary tradition. 'The literary form to which the Prologue to the *Canterbury Tales* belongs and of which it is a special realization is the form of the dream-vision prologue in the tradition of the *Romance of the Rose*' and associated poems (p 174). The typical important elements of the dream-vision prologue are that 1) the poem is set in a given time of year, usually in May, and this setting often leads to a description of the season; 2) the author, who is a character in the poem, comes to a place where he sees a company of people or a series of portraits on a wall, etc; 3) these people or images are described; 4) one of these people, or another character, initiates the remaining action of the work. The principle of development of Fragment A of *CT* (a consideration of courtly love, interrupted by the lower social orders and by strife among the churls) resembles the pattern of the *PF*, which is also written in this dream-vision tradition. Furthermore, 'the technical features of the portraits in the Canterbury Prologue have exact analogues in the portraits' of the *Romance of the Rose* (p 181). In both cases the portraits show a similar range of lengths and a nearly identical average length; the portraits are given in succession, with minimal transition; the series of portraits is briefly introduced in terms deriving from 'the medieval arts of poetry' (p 180); the method of description permits 'not only objective presentation and analysis but also author's comment' and sharp, realistic detail (p 181); some of the characters so described later interact, and the author who describes them also interacts with them. Thus *GP* develops rather than abandons Chaucer's earlier literary models; its 'originality lay in the application to fresh material of the old method' that Chaucer had used in several previous works (p 181). Cf **147, 287, 386.**

208 Curry, Walter Clyde. *The Middle English Ideal of Personal Beauty; as Found in the Metrical Romances, Chronicles, and Legends of the XIII, XIV, and XV Centuries.* Baltimore: J.H. Furst, 1916. Rpt New York: AMS Press, 1972.

Though not focussed on *GP*, this study supplies analogues for many of the physical traits assigned to the pilgrims. Sections are provided about hair, beards, the forehead, eyebrows, eyes, etc, down to legs and feet, with many contemporary sources cited to establish the criteria of beauty and the connotation of specific characteristics such as gray eyes (cf line 152), *stepe* eyes (cf line 201), a ruddy complexion (cf line 333), a lisping voice (cf line 264), and so forth. The book is based on Curry's dissertation of the same title, Stanford University, 1915.

209 ——. *Chaucer and the Mediaeval Sciences.* New York and London: Oxford University Press, 1926. Rpt 1942; 2nd ed (with bibliography), New York: Barnes & Noble, 1960.

Several chapters pertinent to *GP* are included. They are based on Curry's journal articles, as indicated below, but with some revision. For the chapter on the Physician (1926, pp 3–36), cf Curry, **1118**. On the Summoner and Cook (pp 37–53), cf Curry, **1268** and **1086**. On the Pardoner (pp 54–70), cf Curry, **1304**. On the Reeve and the Miller (pp 71–90), cf Curry, **1208**. On the Wife of Bath (pp 91–118), cf Curry, **1140**; the chapter as presented here is reprinted in *Chaucer: Modern Essays in Criticism*, ed. Edward Wagenknecht (New York: Oxford University Press, 1959), pp 166–87. In reply to Curry, see **271**. Cf **810, 1273**.

210 David, Alfred. *The Strumpet Muse: Art and Morals in Chaucer's Poetry.* Bloomington, IN, and London: Indiana University Press, 1976.

In the chapter 'Portrait of the Christian Community' (pp 52–76), David comments that much in *GP* 'harks back to the past' (p 53): its structure is indebted to the *Roman de la Rose*; the pilgrims are types; many details derive from books. Nevertheless, 'the scene in the General Prologue makes a radical break with Chaucer's earlier poetry' (p 54). After lines 1–11, which are written in the conventional high style, 'the ideal landscape of romance gives way to the medieval world' (p 54) in which the pilgrims 'are questers, but they are Englishmen and for the most part common folk' (p 55). 'The pilgrims are members of a single body,' a Christian society, 'and the health of that body is the subject of the Prologue' (p 56). We are shown 'that the body is sick' (p 56). Details are chosen to convey value judgments and we are invited to discriminate among the pilgrims, although the enthusiastic narrator does not. The ideal portraits of the Knight, Parson, and Plowman, representing the three estates, define the concept of *worth* in its best sense; Chaucer's use of that term elsewhere raises questions about contemporary values and the portraits are thus 'an essay in "worthiness" ' (p 58). The narrator's apology, with his claim that he is telling the story because it is truly what happened, departs from the usual viewpoint that stories are worth telling because of their lessons. 'The only comparable instance in the Middle Ages where a series of stories is justified simply by the fact that someone told them is Boccaccio's *Decameron*' (p 75). The Host, Chaucer's surrogate, offers the conventional literary criteria of *sentence* and *solaas* (line 798), but his manner and his words tell us that *solaas*, which will shorten our way on the journey, is his primary motive. 'Inadvertently the Host has described the purpose of Chaucer's new art' (p 76).

211 Delasanta, Rodney. 'The Horsemen of the *Canterbury Tales*.' *ChauR*, 3 (1968-1969), 29–36.

The pilgrims can be categorized into 1) a group of those who are overly proud riders or whose horses indicate their pridefulness: the Monk, Merchant, Summoner, Pardoner, Reeve, Wife; 2) a group whose horses are modest, or modestly arrayed: the Clerk, Nun's Priest, Plowman, Knight, and by extension Parson; and 3) a group censured for 'miserable horsemanship' (p 31): the Cook, Miller, Shipman, and later the Canon. In describing his 'rider-pilgrims Chaucer is alluding to a Biblical event' (p 32), Christ's entering Jerusalem on a donkey: a humble beast exalts the rider, while a proud beast has the opposite effect. Chaucer's world 'is peopled with many pilgrims of little faith whose primary concern is with what they shall eat and drink, what they shall put on, and indeed how they shall ride to their destiny. Chaucer's method was to remind them that their Master's own glorious destiny was achieved on a donkey and with a splendid unconcern for raiment' (p 35). Well-known Scriptural passages, such as Luke 19:35–6, suffice to supply the Biblical bases of Chaucer's imagery about horses, horsemanship, and clothing.

212 Denholm-Young, N. *The Country Gentry in the Fourteenth Century*. Oxford: Clarendon Press, 1969.

The chapter 'The Ranks of Society' (pp 1–40) discusses franklins in the context of knights, squires, and yeomen. The only difference between franklins and squires at this time 'was that the franklins, yeomen, bowmen, or free tenants did not aspire to become knights,' as the squires did (p 25). Details about individual families, using information from rolls of arms, are presented.

213 Dent, Anthony. 'Chaucer and the Horse.' *PLPLS-LHS*, 9 (1959-1962), 1–12.

The vocabulary pertaining to horses — the meaning of palfrey, courser, rouncy, etc — is explained, as are details of color, horseshoes, harness, and various other aspects of horsemanship. Dent includes notes on the Ellesmere illustrations of the horses ridden by the Knight (his horse's pictured brand may suggest that it comes from Germany), the Squire, the Prioress and Second Nun, the Merchant, the Cook, the Shipman, the Wife, the Reeve, the Summoner, and the Pardoner.

214 ——. 'Fair Burgesses.' *HT*, 11 (1961), 753–9.

Chaucer's pilgrims all belong within the middle class. They are 'typical of society' in the Southwest and Midlands of England (p 754), but not the whole country. 'His most northerly pilgrim is Osewold the Reeve from Norfolk, and his most westerly is the Shipman, master of the barge *Maudelayne*, registered at Dartmouth' (p 755). Dent considers the proportions of society represented by the pilgrims' ranks and professions. For example, the regular clergy and their attendants represent 24 percent of the group. 'It is not improbable that such people really did represent almost a quarter of the middle section of English society in Chaucer's day' (p 758). On the Plowman, see **1197**.

215 ——, and Daphne Machin Goodall. *The Foals of Epona: A History of British Ponies from the Bronze Age to Yesterday.* London: Galley Press, 1962.
Several of the horses said to be ridden by the pilgrims in *GP* are discussed. The Host later remarks that the Nun's Priest rides a jade, and in doing so unconsciously echoes an Old Norse proverb about not being ashamed of riding a poor horse, or not being ashamed of poverty. The Monk's palfrey was the traditional mount for churchmen. The Cook's capul may have been hired from the Tabard's stables, for the Cook would not normally keep a horse of his own. Giving the Shipman a rouncy was 'a stroke of malicious humour on the jobmaster's part' (p 116), since a rouncy trotted, while a pacer or an ambler would have been more comfortable for someone not accustomed to riding. The Plowman's mare may have been one of his own ploughing team, since in the southern counties plough-oxen were displaced by mares. The Reeve's mare is called a *stot*, which may have meant a good (though not expensive) horse; its name, 'Scot,' was a common farmer's name for a horse 'and was bestowed on the best horse in the yard' (p 117). Harry Bailly would have kept 'a mixed establishment of hackneys, palfreys, capuls, and rouncies' (p 120). Comments are also made on the Ellesmere illustrator's depiction of the pilgrims' horses.

216 De Sélincourt, Aubrey. *Six Great Poets: Chaucer, Pope, Wordsworth, Shelley, Tennyson, the Brownings.* London: Hamish Hamilton, 1956.
In the chapter 'Chaucer,' pp 9–39, De Sélincourt points out that Chaucer characterizes his pilgrims by means of significant detail and vivid imagery, but that many writers use those techniques. The special 'weapon in his armoury' is his humor, which 'allows him to sketch a character in the round without any ulterior motive, for the sheer pleasure ... of seeing him for what he is' (p 30). Chaucer shows neither anger nor satiric intent, but instead a 'serene and sunny irony' or humor that appears in brief flashes (p 31). 'Chaucer was not interested in perfection; he was interested in imperfection, which is much the same as saying that he was interested in human character' (p 32). Even the *parfit* Knight 'begins subtly to change his aspect upon a longer acquaintance' (p 32). The Parson is the only pilgrim

whom Chaucer describes without 'the almost unquenchable twinkle in his eye' (p 32).

17 Diekstra, F.N.M. *Chaucer's Quizzical Mode of Exemplification.* Nijmegen: Dekker and Van de Vegt, 1974.

'Chaucer exploited his sense of the incongruous in a variety of ironical techniques' (p 6), the most familiar of which is the *GP* technique of ostensible praise that turns into its opposite — as in the treatment of the Prioress' conscience, the Friar's courtesy, and the Monk's manliness, which come to be seen as 'very questionable virtues' (p 6).

18 DiMarco, Vincent J. 'Chaucer, Walter Sibile, and the Composition of the General Prologue.' *RBPH*, 56 (1978), 650–62.

DiMarco offers arguments to support the traditional dating of *GP* as 1388 or shortly afterward. The reference to Middleburgh (lines 276–7) points to 1386–88. As for Cook's suggestion that the Knight's Baltic expeditions reflect those of Henry, Earl of Derby, who returned to London in 1393, which would suggest a later date for at least this part of the *GP* (see **673**), DiMarco proposes a different connection through which Chaucer might have learned of the Teutonic Order and its Baltic activities: Walter Sibile, one of the three Englishmen who in 1388 negotiated a treaty between England and the Teutonic Order, had been 'Chaucer's former direct subordinate as collector of the petty subsidy' (p 655). Thus 'the allusion to the Teutonic Order in the portrait of the Knight can best be explained through reference to a former associate of the poet' (p 659). The tone of immediacy in the allusion, as well as 'the recent history of the Middleburg staple, the course of the war with France in the late 80's, and the fact that the impact and relevance of such events would soon naturally dissipate' all point to 1388 or not long afterwards as the date of composition of *GP* (pp 659–60).

19 Dodd, William George. *Courtly Love in Chaucer and Gower.* Boston: Ginn and Co, 1913. Harvard Studies in English, 1. Rpt Gloucester, MA: Peter Smith, 1959.

In the section 'The Prologue' (pp 232–4), several pilgrims are briefly examined in terms of courtly love. The Knight's virtues correspond to those of courtly lovers — which is not unexpected, since knights, when young, were supposed to be lovers, and most courtly lovers were knights. The Squire 'meets all the requirements with regard to character, behavior, dress, and accomplishments, which the god put before his lover in the *Romance of the Rose*' (p 233). The Prioress's motto and the Monk's love-knot (though 'neither of these characters was a lover') demonstrate 'the prevalence of love ideas at this time' (p 234).

220 Donaldson, E. Talbot. 'Chaucer in the Twentieth Century: Presidential Address to the New Chaucer Society, 1979.' *SAC*, 2 (1980), 7–13.
It is sometimes impossible to resolve Chaucer's meanings because he intended to depict the paradoxical nature of human beings. 'It seems to me that great poetry like Chaucer's or Shakespeare's recognizes mystery — reveals its existence — rather than trying to resolve it' (p 12). For example, the 'fact seems to be that there is good evidence that the Pardoner is and is not homosexual, and you may read him either way you please, with perfect confidence that you are probably wrong' (p 9).

221 Drucker, Trudy. 'Some Medical Allusions in *The Canterbury Tales*.' *NYSJM*, 68 (February 1, 1968), 444–47.
Chaucer's pilgrims journey to the shrine of the martyr who has helped them when they were sick. 'Thus a history of illness or disability is inferred about all of the pilgrims, and in most cases there is some major or minor disease or deformity still present' (p 444). It would 'not be unreasonable to suppose that the journey to Canterbury is being undertaken as much in expectation of present aid as in gratitude for past favors' (p 444). The Summoner suffers from a dermatosis that is probably venereal in origin. The Pardoner is clearly identified as a eunuch. The Host suffers from overindulgence in drink, and when affected emotionally by the Physician's tale he is aware of the heartbeat that accompanies stress. The Cook's ulcer 'secretes a white exudate' (p 445), while the Wife's red hue, large hips, etc, are 'compatible with the mild chronic hypertension that is found so frequently in overnourished matrons of agreeable disposition' (p 445).

222 Du Boulay, F.R.H. 'The Historical Chaucer.' In *Writers and Their Background: Geoffrey Chaucer*. Ed. Derek Brewer. London: Bell, 1974. Pp 33–57.

Du Boulay discusses the historical importance of travel. Just as Chaucer's contemporaries did a great deal of travelling, so, of the Canterbury pilgrims, 'at least thirteen not counting Chaucer himself were regular travellers by profession or taste' (p 34). The Knight and Squire had travelled in war; the Monk 'coursed over the countryside with a string of hunters'; in the Friar's order it was necessary to travel 'for study, preaching and organized begging'; the Merchant's business trips were commonplace; etc (p 34).

223 Duncan, Edgar Hill. 'Narrator's Points of View in the Portrait-sketches, Prologue to the *Canterbury Tales*.' In *Essays in Honor of Walter Clyde Curry*. Nashville, TN: Vanderbilt University Press, 1954. Pp 77–101.
Changes in point of view constitute a main formal device in *GP*. In the portrait of the Knight, for example, the first thirty lines are presented

'from the Narrator's omniscient point of view,' but the last six lines 'are strictly limited to the Narrator's point of view in the dramatic situation' (p 78). Other examples of changes of perspective in the portraits are noted. Chaucer's use of this device is somewhat similar to Guillaume de Lorris's use of it in the allegorical *Roman de la Rose*, but in *GP* 'generalizations must be supported by particulars, actions given some local habitation,' in a modification of the device as 'demanded by reality' (p 87). Chaucer's use of the conventional device also 'involved his revolt from it' — he used it on new materials, drawn from various aspects of experience, and for a new purpose, the 'representation of life' (p 107).

224 Dunleavy, Gareth W. 'Natural Law as Chaucer's Ethical Absolute.' *TWA*, 52 (1963), 177–78.
Chaucer knew and used the concept of natural law (*lawe of kinde*), a permanent and universal system of right action. In *GP* several reflections of natural law appear. The Friar and Summoner should be governed by canon law, 'a form of positive law that incorporates natural law idealism' (p 185), yet they flout its principles. The Summoner's duty is to administer canonical justice on the basis of the same laws that ought to apply to the Friar, but he is unethical and corrupt. To the Sergeant, law is 'chiefly decision, statute, and case,' and he uses it to earn status and money for himself (p 186). The Franklin 'exhibits openhanded hospitality in the oldest natural law tradition' and has legal learning that he uses for his tasks as *shirreve* and *contour*, but he 'does not seem the type to hold himself strictly to natural law ideas' (p 186). The Parson adheres to law as he should, as do the Knight and Plowman. At a time when the man-made laws of chivalry are becoming obsolete, the Knight adheres to concepts of natural law — to *trouthe* and *honour* in the sense of 'honorable dealing' (p 186). To Chaucer, *lawe of kinde* was a 'counter-balance to the extremes of materialism and covetousness reached by certain members of the Canterbury party and their contemporaries' (p 187).

225 Edmunds, E.W. *Chaucer and His Poetry*. London: Harrap, 1914.
Lines 1–18 are used as the basis of a short treatment of Chaucer's language (pp 21–22). The portrait series, regarded as a 'catalogue of dramatis personae' (p 126), is discussed (pp 126–43). For example, the Prioress's portrait is 'one of Chaucer's happiest and most humorous ... a continuous smile' (p 130). The Monk, though degenerate, is 'not a complete libertine' (p 131); 'by a mixture of description, incident, and humour the whole man is brought out' (p 133). The Friar 'is drawn with a frankly satirical pen' (p 133) as a man 'steeped to the soul in sleek hypocrisy' (p 134). The Reeve is 'a repulsive person, prosperous and pitiless,' whose tucked-up garment

and position at the end of the group 'reveal his mean suspicious nature' (p 140).

226 Ekroni, Aviv. 'Sippurei Canterbury.' [Canterbury Tales.] *Moznayim*, 52 (1981), 429–30.
Ekroni comments briefly on the secular and religious motivations for going on pilgrimage, the springtime setting, the combination of local and universal themes, and the presence in *GP* of details that will become important later in *CT*.

227 Eliason, Norman E. *The Language of Chaucer's Poetry: An Appraisal of the Verse, Style, and Structure.* Copenhagen: Rosenkilde and Bagger, 1972. Anglistica, 17.
Comments are provided on many lines of *GP*. On lines 1–2, the scansion is discussed (*Aprill* is regarded as disyllabic). On lines 1–18, 'the sound rather than the sense is all that matters' (p 17). On lines 1–100, the frequent double rhymes enhance 'the trueness of the riming' (p 43). On line 12, the stress of *than* is considered. On line 17, this is the only mention of the pilgrimage's destination; Chaucer 'never speaks of St.Thomas and his shrine again' and the journey 'might just as well have been a flight from a London Plague or a sight-seeing trip to Bath' (p 234). On lines 19–27, this passage initiates the casual style, 'disarmingly simple' in its verse-craft (p 23). On lines 93–100, their 'jam-packed information' (p 18) offers a contrast to lines 1–18, which contain little information; this later passage is the more typical. On line 77, a *pulled hen* would be an eviscerated one, distasteful because 'its freshness was dubious' (p 100). On line 214, *noble post* is not a pun. On lines 264–5, whether the Friar lisps 'because he thinks it sounds good or is afflicted with it because he is a pansy is problematic' (p 35). On line 306, Chaucer's praise of the Clerk's brevity is part of his distaste for excess, including verbosity. On lines 321–2, the 'sudden thrust' technique is used (p 89). On lines 369–76, Chaucer's Guildsmen may represent the enterprising provincial people who came to London and whose difference of speech would have been noticeable. On line 556, *erys* may be a pun on *ars*. On line 715, one of Chaucer's 'painfully clear transitions' (p 144) begins here (cf line 35), although at other times he is not always explicit in making transitions. On lines 725–46, the 'tongue-in-cheek' (p 110) apology shows that he did not really expect his audience to be offended. Eliason accepts the viewpoint of Kirby (see **124**) that to see the portraits as reflecting historical models is nonsense. Chaucer's descriptive technique in the portraits is static, presenting action as either past (eg, the Knight's career) or potential (eg, the Squire is able to compose songs) rather than as occurring at the moment. Many other issues relating to *GP* are considered. They include the persona of the narrator, the vagueness of Harry

Bailly's rules for storytelling, the differences between Chaucer's framework and those in other frame-tale collections, the suitability of particular tales to their tellers, and technical aspects of the verse (eg, the accentuation or placement of the caesura in specific lines and the characteristics of different levels of style).

228 ——. 'Personal Names in the *Canterbury Tales.' Names*, 21 (1973), 137–52.
Eliason briefly comments on *Eglentyne* — a 'flowery name' that is 'applied with gentle irony to the prioress' (p 143); on *Herry Bailly* — Chaucer knew him, or knew of him, as the actual Southwark innkeeper, and presumably 'was either having fun with an old friend or scoring off an old enemy' (p 144); and on *Huberd* the Friar — the name is not likely to be a pun. Most of the pilgrims are unnamed, being designated instead by title (Knight, Squire, etc), and even those who do have names are usually referred to by title. Perhaps Chaucer wished to avoid tedium; had he included a name in each portrait, 'the result would have been a tedious sameness' (p 151). Furthermore, the use of titles rather than names helps to prevent confusion and is therefore 'structurally defensible' (p 152). The main reason for the pilgrims' general anonymity, however, is stylistic. Chaucer wanted 'a style suggesting nonchalance on his part so that whatever he failed to tidy up properly would seem not to matter,' a style promising pleasure, not 'a finicky concern over trifles like names' (p 152). The nonchalant style is of course only seemingly careless. In reality the way Chaucer used names 'conceals but also reveals the careful attention he gave them' (p 152).

229 Elliott, Ralph W.V. *Chaucer's Prologue to the Canterbury Tales*. Oxford: Blackwell, 1960; New York: Barnes & Noble, 1963. Notes on English Literature. General Editor, John Harvey.
This guide for undergraduate students discusses the occasion, plan, and date of *GP*, the clerical pilgrims, the lay pilgrims, *GP* as a means of understanding medieval life, and Chaucer's language and artistry.

230 Emerson, Oliver Farrar. 'Some Notes on Chaucer and Some Conjectures.' *PQ*, 2 (1923), p 81–96. Rpt in *Chaucer Essays and Studies: A Selection from the Writings of Oliver Farrar Emerson, 1860–1927* (Cleveland, OH: Western Reserve University Press, 1929, and rpt Freeport, NY: Books for Libraries Press, 1970), pp 378–404.
Emerson proposes that the *GP* portraits are divided into intentional groups: (1) an upperclass group—Knight, Squire, and Yeoman; (2) a church group—Prioress, Nun-Chaplain, Priest(s), Monk, and Friar; (3) 'something like a professional class'—Merchant, Clerk, Serjeant of the Law, and Franklin; (4) a guildsmen's group—the five Guildsmen and their Cook; (5) 'a sort of provincial group'—Shipman, Doctor, Wife, Parson, and Plowman; and (6)

'a miscellaneous group'—Reeve, Miller, Summoner, Pardoner, Manciple, and Narrator (1923, p 90). For Emerson's comments on *preestes thre* and the total number of pilgrims, see **777**.

231 Engelhardt, George J. 'The Lay Pilgrims of the *Canterbury Tales*: A Study in Ethology.' *MS*, 36 (1974), 278–330.

GP includes an assortment of characters who represent good and characters who represent evil. Medieval schoolboys were taught to describe a character according to a set of attributes, central among which would be the person's *habitus* or 'habitual choice of virtue or vice' (p 281). Chaucer's 'mixed ethologue,' constructed in this way, is 'appropriate to the mixed congregation of true and false Christians' (p 284).

The Knight's end or *telos* is that of the *miles Christi*, the soldier of Christ who fights pagans and schismatics externally and spiritual enemies within. The Squire is advancing towards the perfection of his father. 'The Yeoman is the perfect servant' (p 292), in contrast to the pilgrimage's false servants. His arrows recall the glories of earlier English victories; his forester's skills evoke 'the solid skills of ancient folk-heroes' (p 293); 'nowhere else in the *Canterbury Tales* does Chaucer express such nostalgia for the past' (p 293). The Miller resembles the comic demon of morality-plays. The Miller and Reeve, 'variants on the generic ethos of the false servant' (p 309), are differentiated from each other by their relative ages, much as the Knight and Squire are: 'youth and maturity distinguish the two warriors; maturity and old age the villeins' (p 309). The Serjeant is a mercenary of language, suited to 'the age of the false Christian, the hypocrite' (p 312), for he sells his tongue for gain. He and the Manciple are described without physical detail, which signifies 'the cover of impersonality behind which the lawyers exploit the law and the Manciple exploits the lawyers' (p 316). The Merchant is 'playing the pilgrim' to avoid his debts (p 318); later, in the end-links, he will fabricate a story about an unhappy marriage — which exists only in his imagination — to 'dissimulate the actual motive for this pilgrimage' (p 318). The Shipman as a mariner is superior to the Merchant, for mariners could cheat merchants, even as merchants cheated their customers. Like the Wife, the Franklin places felicity in bodily delight. 'Both Alice and the Franklin are antiphrastically named — Alice from *alicia* because her reason prefers illusion to truth, and the Franklin from *franchise* because his spirit confuses prodigality with liberality' (p 325). The Physician pretends to be a Doctor, which should mean a teacher, but he is a mere craftsman who exploits his trade for profit.

232 ——. 'The Ecclesiastical Pilgrims of the *Canterbury Tales*: A Study in Ethology.' *MS*, 37 (1975), 287–315.

GP is 'an ethologue that reflects the medieval mixed congregation' of 'those perfect in ethos and those defective in ethos' (p 287). The Clerk 'embodies the ethos of a perfect clerk' (p 287). The Prioress, who has entered her convent through the wealth or influence of her family, is a feminine version of the *praelatus puer*, the 'instant priest or boy prelate' (p 291) who is not spiritually prepared for the position he holds. She is not attracted to men and her motto does not signify carnal love. Her oath by St Loy indicates her litigious nature; her name of Eglantyne suggests the *esglantiers*, the spiny plant of the *Roman de la Rose*. The Monk too represents the *praelatus puer*. Like the Prioress, he 'has comfortably withdrawn from the world the better to enjoy the world' (p 300). He is also *argos* (functionless), since he has the ability to be an abbot but 'is content with the sinecure of outrider' (p 302). In this sense he is opposite to the Host, who as *periergos* (overdoer) assumes functions beyond his abilities. The Host also fantasizes: he 'parades the faults of his wife' (p 303), but in reality she may have been quite blameless. The Friar is a 'huckster' (p 304), a 'self-serving prodigal' reminiscent of Judas (p 305), while his enemy the Summoner 'reverts to the simoniacal servant of Eliseus, the leprous Giezi' (p 306). The Pardoner 'has consummated his idolatry with sodomy' (p 307). Many details of the portraits are annotated in Christian terms. Both the good and the evil components of this mixed ethologue can be used for conversion to God.

33 Enkvist, Nils Erik. *Geoffrey Chaucer*. Stockholm: Natur och Kultur, 1964. Världsförfattare. General Editor, Annie Löfstedt.
In Chapter 7 (pp 53–67), Enkvist comments briefly on the springtime opening and on the portraits of the Knight, Squire, Yeoman, Prioress, Monk, Summoner, Pardoner, and Parson. The portraits reflect both good-natured tolerance and a considerable amount of irony, bordering on social satire. Chaucer's genius is shown by his satisfying both the timeless demand for credible individualism and the contemporary medieval demand for psychological universality ('Det är igen betecknande för Chaucers geni att han uppfyller bade det tidlösa kravet påtrovärdig individualisering och samtidens krav påpsykologisk allmängiltighet,' p 66).

34 Erskine, John. *The Delight of Great Books*. Indianapolis: Bobbs Merrill, 1928; London: Eveleigh Nash & Grayson, 1928.
An overview of the pilgrims is included in the general chapter 'The Canterbury Tales' (pp 33–49). Erskine divides the pilgrims into groups, comments briefly on the ambiguity of the Prioress's portrait, sees the Shipman as a 'sardonic person' who may be undertaking the pilgrimage for absolution after 'some recent profitable murder' at sea (p 40), and indicates that 'this society, so far as we have had our glimpse of it, rests on the knight and his son, on the parson and his brother the plowman, rather than on the

prosperous guild members, or the rich merchant, lawyer and householder' (p 42).

235 Evans, Elizabeth Cornelia. 'Roman Descriptions of Personal Appearance in History and Biography.' *HSCP*, 46 (1935), p 43–84.
Although *GP* is not discussed, this study of 'description as a device of characterization' in Latin literature (p 44) provides background on physiognomical doctrines in the ancient world and on classical portrait-writing. In Suetonius, for example, the physical appearance of the evil emperor Caligula 'is especially associated with the disagreeable features of the panther and the goat' (p 67; cf the Pardoner, line 688, on the goat). Many Latin descriptions of individuals seem to have been influenced by 'the laws for the interpretation of character from personal appearance which the physiognomists had carefully laid down' (p 74). Appendices provide lists of iconistic descriptions in Roman writings.

236 Evans, Gillian. *Chaucer*. Glasgow and London: Blackie, 1977. Authors in Their Age Series. General Editors, Anthony Adams and Esmor Jones.
In this general guide to Chaucer and his time, *GP* is briefly discussed. Background material on such subjects as Chaucer's London, the various categories of the clergy, astrology and concepts of the universe, medical practice, medieval rhetoric, etc, is included.

237 Everett, Dorothy. 'Chaucer's Good Ear.' *RES*, 23 (1947), 201–8. Rpt in Dorothy Everett, *Essays on Middle English Literature*, ed. Patricia Kean (Oxford: Clarendon Press, 1955), pp 139–48.
Everett comments on the alliteration in line 504 (noting the possible 'echoes of religious writing' in lines such as this, p 202), and on Chaucer's attentiveness to qualities of voices — as in the details about the Friar's lisp (lines 264–65) and the Prioress's singing (lines 122–23).

238 Ewald, Wilhelm. *Der Humor in Chaucers Canterbury Tales*. Halle: Niemeyer, 1911. Studien zur Englischen Philologie, 45.
Many different kinds of humor are present in the *CT* — subjective humor, objective humor, humorous allusions, and several kinds of stylistic humor in the narrower sense, such as the ironic use of stock phrases. Examples are cited, including many words, lines, or sections of *GP*, with comments on the direction, effect, and category of the humor. Ewald discusses individual words used ironically, among them some — *noble, worthy,* and *gentil* — occurring in *GP*. Chaucer has the perspective of a humorist and draws upon a considerable variety of comic devices. The study is based upon Ewald's dissertation, *Der Humor in Chaucers Canterbury Tales*, Georg-August-Universität (Göttingen), 1911, Dir. Lorenz Morsbach; excerpts

were printed under the same title at Halle: Karras, 1911, in addition to full publication in the Studien zur Englischen Philologie series listed at the beginning of this entry.

239 Fansler, Dean Spruill. *Chaucer and the Roman de la Rose.* New York: Columbia University Press, 1914. Columbia University Studies in English and Comparative Literature.

Fansler points out similarities between the *Roman de la Rose* and lines 5–6, 70–72, 90, 99–100, 127–35, 152, 177, 182, 253–55, 256, 281–82, 404, 431–32, 461, 475–76, 675, 701–4, 725–42, and 781 of *GP*. The book is based on Fansler's dissertation of the same title, Columbia University, 1913.

240 Farnham, Willard E. 'England's Discovery of the Decameron.' *PMLA*, 39 (1924), 123–39.

The available evidence about the early circulation of the *Decameron* suggests that it was not well known. No Englishman is known to have possessed a copy before 1414. Hence it is not surprising that Chaucer apparently did not encounter this work. In reply, see **353**.

241 Ferrie, Antoine. *Religion et gens d'église chez G. Chaucer.* University of Toulouse Dissertation. 1977. Dir. V. Dupont.

This is a massive (over 800-page) study that includes discussions of the Prioress, Second Nun, Nun's Priest, Monk, Friar, Pardoner, Summoner, and Parson (drawing for these pilgrims on later sections of *CT* as well as on *GP*). For the clerical pilgrims, Ferrie provides the most comprehensive group overview, to about 1970, since that given in Bowden's second edition (**104**). The dissertation is avowedly a work of synthesis ('un travail de synthèse,' p 12). Information on pilgrimage, the liturgy, preaching, Chaucer's religion, and a general conclusion and extensive bibliography are included, as well as sections on individual pilgrims. The overall approach is to examine Chaucer in view of contemporary history ('à étudier la réalité historique parallèlement au texte de Chaucer,' p 629), and a great many contemporary sources and parallels are cited. However, Chaucer is seen as a poet, not as a social historian in any modern sense, since for literary purposes he has altered many aspects of reality. In the *GP* portraits he satirizes as well as depicts, taking pleasure in emphasizing the eccentricities of the degenerate or parasitic clergy, but he nevertheless accepts his era and its Church as he found them ('il a simplement accepté son siècle et, avec son siècle, l'Eglise telle qu'il l'a trouvée,' p 663). Thus he achieved his own equilibrium and serenity ('son équilibre et sa sérénité,' p 663). For comments on individual passages, see **779, 1271**.

242 Finlayson, John. 'The Satiric Mode and the Parson's Tale.' *ChauR*, 6 (1971–1972), 94–116.

The comic-satiric effect of *GP* consists not in the establishment of a single moral perspective (as in *Piers Plowman*), but in a 'deliberate variation of tone and intention' in which the moral norm remains implicit (p 98). 'The *General Prologue* cannot be said to contain a direct moral voice: the creation of the plain, guileless, humble narrator forces the reader to become the moralist, to assign the *significatio*,' for the narrator does not have 'the status of an unequivocal voice of truth,' and 'where he makes simple judgments, they are almost always banal and wrong' (p 99). The fact that the idealized portraits are not grouped together, but interspersed with the others, is a way of suggesting that 'this world is a curious *mélange* of folly, vice, and virtue and that, while there are ideals readily available, the color and variety of life not infrequently reside in ... human folly' (p 105).

243 Finucane, Ronald C. *Miracles and Pilgrims: Popular Beliefs in Medieval England*. London: Dent, 1977; Totowa, NJ: Rowman and Littlefield, 1977. Background information on relics, miraculous cures, concepts of health and sickness, etc., is provided. Medieval records of (alleged) cures at English shrines are examined to document various aspects of popular practice and belief, including the expectations associated with the Canterbury pilgrimage in particular and the social classes and locations from which the pilgrims came.

244 Fisher, John H. 'Chaucer's Horses.' *SAQ*, 60 (1961), 71–79. Horses 'served as status symbols and touchstones of taste and character, much as automobiles do today' (p 71). The Knight's horse, plain in array, and the humble mount of the Plowman are in contrast to the showy Monk's horses. The Reeve, the Cook, and the Shipman 'all appear to be riding horses of an inferior sort' (p 73). The Shipman's rouncy would be 'lower in scale than courser and higher than hackney' (p 74). However, 'the use of horses merely for additional details of characterization is a fairly superfluous device' (p 75). A 'more profound' device involves the 'metaphoric transfer to the horse of some significant characteristic of the rider' (p 76), in order to broaden or deepen the portrait. In the Clerk's portrait, his horse, like himself, is lean, although the shared quality 'may be little more than a reinforcement' here (p 76). In the Wife's portrait, where her 'helpless ambler' is identified with her 'hapless husbands' (p 76), Chaucer is making use of a recurrent equine metaphor.

245 ——. 'Chaucer's Last Revision of the *Canterbury Tales*.' *MLR*, 67 (1972), 241–51. When the Knight is chosen for the first tale (line 845), the series is begun on a secular note. 'Since almost all lists of the estates in the Middle Ages begin with the clergy, and since saintliness was in the fourteenth century still

regarded as superior to either chivalry or gentilesse' (p 247), the choice of the Knight, rather than a cleric, to initiate the storytelling would have been significant to the contemporary audience. Fisher argues that 'Fragments I to V, from the General Prologue in its present form to the Franklin's Tale, represent a wholesale revision that Chaucer was engaged in at the time of his death,' while the rest of *CT* 'represents an earlier stage of composition before dramatic interplay had emerged in Chaucer's mind as a fundamental characteristic of the collection' (p 243).

246 Fisher, William Nobles. *Play and Perspective in the Canterbury Tales.* University of California (Santa Barbara) Dissertation. 1975. Dir. Frank C. Gardiner. See also *DAI*, 36 (1976), 7435-A.

In the chapter 'The Movement of Tales and Tellers' (pp 59–74), Fisher briefly examines the portraits of the Knight ('It is utterly impossible that he could have fought in all of the campaigns mentioned,' p 63), the Squire (he is 'both the provider for the aged and the usurper who will take the place of the aged,' p 63), the Prioress (her sentimental attitude toward pain in animals answers the 'necessarily bellicose world-view of the knight,' p 71), the Monk, the Friar, the Merchant, and the Clerk. The chapter 'The Quest for "Trouthe" ' (pp 75–101) examines Chaucer's uses of that term. On the Host, see **1359**.

247 Flügel, Ewald. 'Gower's Mirour de l'omme und Chaucer's Prolog.' *Anglia*, 24 (1901), 437–508.

Flügel presents many similarities between *GP* and the *Miroir de l'homme*, a long French poem by Chaucer's contemporary Gower. The *GP* lines for which parallels are found are 53, 60, 62, 70, 165–66, 172–73, 179, 186, 189, 193, 200–3, 206, 209, 211–12, 217–18, 222, 224, 233, 242, 252–55, 258, 261–66, 270, 275, 276, 278, 280, 282, 285, 290, 297, 299, 307, 309, 314, 317–18, 323, 328, 425, 477, 481, 486–87, 495, 497, 500, 504, 507, 510–12, 514, 529, 639, 650, 657–58, and 817. Parallels to works other than Gower's — such as the *Roman de la Rose*, the Benedictine Rule, Wycliffite texts, and poems by Machaut and Deschamps — are also presented for comparison. Flügel's purpose is not to argue that the specific citations presented here are necessarily the sources of Chaucer's phrasing, but instead to supply analogues (sometimes several pages for one *GP* line or passage) in what is one of the more comprehensive collections of such material. Overall, the comparisons show that Chaucer practices masterly restraint in his satire.

248 Foreville, Raymonde. *Le Jubilé de Saint Thomas Becket du XIIIe au XVe siècle (1220–1470).* Bibliothèque générale de l'Ecole practique des hautes-études, 6th section. Paris: S.E.V.P.E.N., 1958.

Foreville describes the development of the Canterbury pilgrimage after

Becket's death, emphasizing the tradition of holding special commemorations in jubilee years (there was a jubilee in 1370, the bicentennial of Becket's death). Cf lines 16–18.

249 Friedman, John Block. 'Another Look at Chaucer and the Physiognomists.' *SP*, 78 (1981), 138–52.

In addition to the 'humours' physiognomy that has been dealt with by Curry (see **209**) and others, Friedman points out that Chaucer would have been familiar with the traditions of affective physiognomy: a 'literary vocabulary of emotion' (p 139) in which the character's face reveals emotion by movements of the eyes, changes in color of the complexion, etc. The *GP* portraits tend to rely on humoural types, 'whereas affective physiognomy is used of aristocratic figures with more complicated inner lives' (p 149; Criseyde is an example).

250 Fyler, John M. *Chaucer and Ovid*. New Haven, CN, and London: Yale University Press, 1979.

The Ovidian qualities of *GP* are briefly discussed in the chapter 'Order and Energy in the Canterbury Tales' (pp 148–63). The 'Ovidian conflict of *ratio* and *impetus*' — order and energy, or stasis and flux — 'is the central structuring principle in Chaucer's poetry, as much as it is in Ovid's' (p 149). In *GP*, the 'catalogue of characters itself shows that confusion is close at hand even when order is being asserted most carefully' (p 151). For example, 'the first six pilgrims, in groups of three,' are linked 'with a clarity of logic that afterward vanished' in 'the morass that follows' — a section in which 'we are forced to search out the narrator's principles of order by retracing his subjective associations of significant detail' (p 151). In *GP* Chaucer has portrayed 'a society in a state of flux: institutions decay; people change their social class, as the anonymous, interchangeable guildsmen hope to do' (p 152). Lines 3187–97 of the *NPT* 'read almost as if the Nun's Priest were parodying the opening of the *General Prologue*' (p 160). Ovidian influence has also contributed to the character of the untrustworthy or inadequate narrator.

251 Gallo, Ernest. 'Matthew of Vendôme: Introductory Treatise on the Art of Poetry.' *PAPS*, 118 (1974), 51–92.

'Medieval poetics and medieval poetry are both based upon rhetoric' (p 54). 'For Matthew of Vendôme, the chief occupation of poetry is description; further, to describe means to reveal the essential characteristics, the properties, of the subject' (p 55). The Squire's portrait includes the rhetorical commonplaces (*topoi*) of rank, quality, age, physical attributes, deeds, place, time, motive, feeling, acquired disposition, pursuit, and office. There are standard lists of characteristics to describe various types of people. 'The purpose of description then is a *manifestatio*, a demonstration, a declaration of the nature of some person: and that person will be a type, not an individual .... The Reeve's skinny legs may seem an individual trait; but they are a sign of his cowardice, for the Reeve is a type of the "lowly man who rises high"' (pp 56-7). Poetry was expected to remain true both to traditional understandings of human nature and to literary precedent, and such poems would provide no surprises. 'The pleasure of reading poems of this kind is the pleasure of recognition, not discovery' (p 56).

A translation of Matthew of Vendôme's *Introductory Treatise on the Art of Poetry* is included.

252 Gardner, John. *The Poetry of Chaucer*. Carbondale, IL: Southern Illinois University Press, 1977; London: Feffer & Simons, 1977.
GP is analyzed in the chapters 'To Canterbury, and Beyond' (pp 216–26) and 'Fragment I' (pp 227–62). Gardner argues that the portraits are ordered by the 'scheme of the tripartite soul — rational, irascible, concupiscent' (pp 228–29). The Knight 'is a figure, in short, of the rational man' (p 233), the Squire's goals are those of the irascible and concupiscent souls, and the Yeoman 'is associated with the concupiscent or vegetative soul' (p 234). The next triad of pilgrims again develops the tripartite scheme, but with complications. 'The Prioress, as a governess, should be identified, like the Knight, with the rational soul; but here something's gone amiss' (p 234). The Monk is a figure of flawed irascibility; inappropriately, he behaves like a knight. The Friar shows 'a sinfully perverted' (p 235) emphasis on the lowest faculties; his portrait involves several sexual puns (*cost*, line 213; *post*, line 214; *ferthyng*, line 255). The tripartite scheme is now expanded: the Merchant, Cook, and Man of Law are all three associated with the rational soul, etc. Gardner continues to relate the pilgrims — more or less — to the tripartite scheme. For his comments on the Host, see **1361**.

- Review by Lee W. Patterson, 'Writing about Writing: the Case of Chaucer,' *UTQ*, 48 (1978–1979), 263–82: Patterson finds Gardner's book 'deficient in every respect' (p 264). The pattern of the tripartite soul is 'a vaguely suggestive taxonomy that survives only by its bland avoidance of detail' (p 267).

253 Gebhart, Emile. 'Merry Old England.' *Gaulois*, April 23, 1907, p 1.
Despite the proverbial concept of 'merry old England,' Gebhart notes that in reality the fourteenth century was hardly a merry time. Yet a joyous spirit is to be found in Chaucer, if not in historical events. Chaucer received the plan for his work from Boccaccio's *Decameron*, but improved upon it. His great invention is the portrait series, each figure of which is the effigy of a moral temperament ('Chaque figure du *Prologue* est l'effigie d'un

tempérament moral'). He avoids the grotesque in favor of the comic impulse ('pas une grimace, ni une difformité ridicule; Chaucer ne vise point à la caricature; il a le sens nécessairement mesuré et discret du comique, et le grotesque n'est point pour le séduire'). The world amused him; he found the appearance and actions of his fellows diverting and did not feel anger, bitterness, or sadness ('la contemplation du monde l'amusait; il jugeait divertissants les visages et les actes quotidiens de ses semblables et n'en ressentait ni colère, ni amertume, ni tristesse'). He expressed a light irony ('une ironie légère'), rather than sharply attacking, and is remarkable for his cheerful imagination, seasoned with malice and joviality ('Cette allégresse de l'imagination, assaisonnée de malice et du bonhomie').

254 Gerould, Gordon Hall. *Chaucerian Essays*. Princeton, NJ: Princeton University Press, 1952; London: Oxford University Press, 1952. Portions rpt in *Critics on Chaucer*, ed. Sheila Sullivan (London: Allen and Unwin, 1970), pp 129–32.

Gerould comments on several of the *GP* details that have occasioned difficulty in interpretation. Various theories about the Prioress's oath are reviewed. There may have been a cult of St Loy at court or at St Leonard's, but the oath 'remains a puzzle' (p 16). The Monk's reference to St Maurus (line 173) is also a puzzle, since there seems to be no evidence that this saint was connected with establishing any monastic rule. The passage on the Summoner's garland and cake (lines 666–8) may have been an addition to make the Summoner constitute the *ale-stake* referred to in the Pardoner's prologue: Gerould proposes that the pilgrims do not enter an inn at that point; instead, the Pardoner simply breaks off a piece of his companion's loaf and takes a drink of ale. This later scene explains the Summoner's great cake of bread in *GP*, for why would he carry 'such a grotesque and inconvenient object except to serve the Pardoner for precisely this reference?' (p 57). As for the Pardoner, perhaps Chaucer meant him 'to be sexually abnormal in one way or another, but did not bother to be specific' (p 60). His small voice (line 688) is hard to reconcile with his later acccount of his preaching. After Chaucer wrote *GP*, his idea of the Pardoner may have changed. For comments on the Franklin, see Gerould, **1048**, revised and reprinted here on pp 33–54.

255 Getty, Agnes K. 'The Mediaeval-Modern Conflict in Chaucer's Poetry.' *PMLA*, 47 (1932), 385–402.

Comparing Chaucer's descriptive technique with the medieval convention of 'the detailed description' (p 385), Getty finds that in *GP* detailed description is indeed present, but 'possesses a vivid, three-dimensional quality' not typical of the convention: it 'approximates word sculpture in contrast to bas reliefs and pastoral prints' (p 401).

256 Gibbons, F.L., and D.C. Perkins. *Chaucer's General Prologue*. Walton-on-Thames, Surrey: Celtic Revision Aids, 1981.
This brief guide is intended for students preparing for examinations.

257 Giles, Edith. 'The Prologue to Chaucer's Canterbury Tales.' *JE*, March 30, 1911, pp 349, 354; April 6, 1911, pp 379, 384; April 13, 1911, pp 411–12.
This three-part article is a brief general discussion of Chaucer's life, times, and *GP*; it is much indebted to Skeat's edition (3).

258 Gillmeister, Heiner. *Discrecioun: Chaucer und der Via Regia*. Bonn: Bouvier Verlag Herbert Grundmann, 1972. Studien zur Englischen Literatur, 8.
In a chapter on Chaucer's revisions (pp 160–94), Gillmeister considers the problem of the *preestes thre* (line 164) and the total number of pilgrims in the group. He proposes that in an earlier version of *GP*, the so-called church group was composed of the Prioress, the nun accompanying her, and three members of different orders: a Benedictine monk, a begging friar, and a canon with his servant ('Die sogenannte "church-group" setzte sich also in einer frühen Fassung der Tales aus der Priorin, der Ordensschwester in ihrer Begleitung und drei Mitgliedern verschiedener Orden zusammen: einem Benediktiner, einem Bettelmönch und einem Kanonikus mit seinem Diener,' p 192). Although line 269 now indicates that the Friar is named Huberd, in the earlier stage of *GP* it may have been the Canon's Yeoman who was given that name. Chaucer subsequently canceled the *GP* portraits of the Canon and his Yeoman, which brought the number of pilgrims back to the correct total, intending later to add a portrait for a single nun's priest. This viewpoint that the Canon and his Yeoman were originally included in *GP* is supported, Gillmeister argues, by the improbability of Chaucer's adding two wholly new pilgrims later, and giving one of them a long two-part tale, when other pilgrims from *GP* were still waiting for a chance to tell their stories ('Dass unser Chorherr und sein Spannmann überhaupt ein Porträt im *Allgemeinen Prolog* besessen haben müssen, legt allein schon die Überlegung nahe, dass Chaucer schwerlich zwei gänzlich neue Pilger in die Welt gesetzt und einen davon mit einer zweiteiligen, langen Geschichte ausgestattet haben wird, wo doch andere, im Prolog längstens vorgestellte Pilger noch auf ihr Stichwort warten,' p 192).

259 Green, Eugene. 'The Voices of the Pilgrims in the *General Prologue* to the *Canterbury Tales*.' *Style*, 9 (1975), 55–81.
GP 'suggests the quality of remembered talk' (p 55), but it is not necessary to assume that Chaucer was writing from personal experience or historical individuals. Many of his stylistic patterns here are developments from his earlier works or from antecedent literary traditions. Important quali-

ties of style that convey the impression of individual voices (the narrator's or those of the other pilgrims) include the use of hyperbole, the naming of places, the impulse to report speech, the tendency to experiment with syntax (paratactic, hypotactic, etc), the reporting of the narrator's own reactions to speech, the careful development of catalogues, and the mention of attitudes and opinions. If we listen in one way, we hear primarily the narrator's voice; if we listen in another, we hear the voices of the individual pilgrims. However, *GP* 'discourages such a double form of listening; it advances the illusion of a colloquy, all voices blended together in "felaweshipe" ' (p 78). The illusion is that of 'a diverse humanity joined in common purpose' (p 78). In creating this illusion, Chaucer is advancing upon the portraiture of his earlier works. His 'portrait series, from the translation of the *Romaunt of the Rose* on, steadily draws away from the allegoric to arrive at the human,' reworking the antecedent conventions 'to accommodate somewhat different customs and modes of speech' (p 78).

260 Griffith, Richard R. *A Critical Study Guide to Chaucer's The Canterbury Tales.* Totowa, NJ: Littlefield, Adams & Co. in association with Educational Research Associates, 1968.
The chapter 'Comprehensive Summary: the General Prologue' (pp 22–67) includes brief comments on such topics as the pilgrimage frame, the narrator's voice, the institution of chivalry, and the status of women, along with short interpretive summaries of each portrait. The section 'Chaucer's Characters: A Guide to Analysis' (pp 143–47) provides 'a brief review of the outstanding features of each portrait' (p 143).

261 Grose, M.W. *Chaucer.* London: Evans Brothers, 1967; New York: Arco, 1967. Literature in Perspective Series. Rpt 1969.
In this general introduction to Chaucer, Grose notes that *GP* can be seen as using the pattern of the conventional love-vision, beginning at the point where the dreamer starts to tell his dream. Some of the portraits 'seem almost to leap out of the page' (1967, p 137). Because the details follow no set order, they have an eye-witness effect, and because personal details (eg, the Wife's deafness) are included, the pilgrims can represent 'an individual typical of a class' (p 128) rather than simply being types. Symbolically, the pilgrimage setting suggests love, divine and natural.

262 Grossman, Judith S. *Convention and Innovation: Two Essays on Style in the Canterbury Tales.* Brandeis University Dissertation. 1968. See also *DA*, 29 (1969), 2709–2710-A.
'The specific intention in discussing the *General Prologue* is to reconsider the relation of the portrait series to medieval traditions of portraiture ... [Chaucer's] basic conceptual innovation in the *Prologue* was the extension

of the privilege of literary representation beyond the class of the noble, fair, and brave, and the complementary class of the wicked and deformed. Taking the courtly *effictio* as his initial model, Chaucer moves towards a more comprehensive account of persons. His chief sylistic innovation, from the Prioress's portrait onward, is the mingling and dove-tailing together of traditional languages of praise and blame within a single portrait, confounding the moral categories in the interests of human multiplicity and of the objective centre; and what has seemed to some a spontaneous disorder in the descriptions is here interpreted in terms of the ironic alternation of opposed traditions of representation' [from *DA*; diss not seen].

263 ——. 'The Correction of a Descriptive Schema: Some "Buts" in Barbour and Chaucer.' *SAC*, 1 (1979), 41–54.
Grossman finds that in *GP* the device of beginning a line 'with an emphatic "But" is a noticeable mark of style' (pp 50–1). Chaucer's 'consciousness of a departure from the expected, the schematic pattern, is registered by the use of the conjunction "but" at the point of departure from, or return to the pattern' (p 50). In the Prioress's portrait, after lines 137–41 — which present details that 'approximate to courtesy-book models of behavior appropriate to a lady' — the *but* in line 142 'marks a shift of focus to the inner moral dimension' (p 51). 'The effect of equivocation which the portrait gives surely results from the superimposing of one established schema on another and then a third on that' (p 52). Grossman discusses the use of *but* 'to ward off a rival schema' (Clerk, line 297); 'to retreat from or counteract a severely negative schema' (Monk, line 182, and Shipman, line 401); and 'to indicate a shift from the definition of the ideal to its embodiment in a specific physical context' (Knight, line 73).

264 Guerin, Richard Stephen. *The Canterbury Tales and Il Decamerone*. University of Colorado Dissertation. 1966. Dir. Donald C. Baker. See also *DA*, 28 (1967), 1396-A.
Guerin reviews the evidence for Chaucer's use of the *Decameron*, arguing that we should not discard the possibility. Though 'seemingly no tangible proof exists for a theory of a direct relationship between the *Canterbury Tales* and *Il Decamerone*, when all of the tentative evidence for such a theory is seen as a whole, and not as isolated instances of possible similarity, the view that Chaucer positively could not have known the *Hundred Tales* seems untenable' (pp 273–74). The chapter 'The Frame-Story' (pp 253–69) refers briefly to similarities between *GP* and the *Decameron*'s frame.

265 Guilford, E.L. *Travellers and Travelling in the Middle Ages*. London: Sheldon Press, 1924. New York: Macmillan, 1924. Texts for Students, 38.

Brief extracts from medieval travel accounts, documents mentioning pilgrimage, wills, and so forth, are collected here.

266 Hadow, Grace E. *Chaucer and His Times*. London: Williams and Norgate, 1914; New York: Holt, 1914. Home University Library of Modern Knowledge.
Comments on *GP* are included in this general book. Chaucer knows how to depict the commonplace aspects of life and includes several such people among the pilgrims; 'the remarkable thing about them is that they are so ordinary and yet so interesting' (p 123). 'The Prioress is very much what a fourteenth-century Cressida would have been if her friends had placed her in a convent instead of finding her a husband' (p 136). In his portraiture Chaucer shows 'how trifles may reflect personality' when he mentions the Monk's fur-edged sleeves and other details (p 185).

267 Hall, D.J. *English Mediaeval Pilgrimage*. London: Routledge and Kegan Paul, 1965; Bath, England: Cedric Chivers, 1973.
Hall's discussions of pilgrimage, the medieval mind, and Thomas Becket, as well as many other details throughout, provide background to Chaucer's pilgrimage setting.

268 Halliday, F.E. *Chaucer and His World*. London: Thames and Hudson, 1968.
A selection of the places, objects, activities, etc, mentioned in *GP* is included in this primarily pictorial overview.

269 Hanning, Robert W. 'Uses of Names in Medieval Literature.' *Names*, 16 (1968), 325–38.
In this general overview of medieval concepts of names (eg, Isidore's *Etymologiae* is briefly discussed), Hanning briefly comments on Chaucer's use of names, such as the Prioress's name of Eglantyne. 'Chaucer's control over names is too consummate to be typical, and his mixing of learned, courtly, and bourgeois literary conventions is also unique' (p 328).

270 ——. 'The Theme of Art and Life in Chaucer's Poetry.' In *Geoffrey Chaucer, A Collection of Original Articles*. Ed. George D. Economou. New York: McGraw-Hill, 1975. Contemporary Studies in Literature. General Editors, Eugene Ehrlich and Daniel Murphy. Pp 15–36.
Within the *CT*, 'two opposite, polar impulses are vigorously working' — one towards a self-effacing and mimetic concept of art, the other towards an awareness of the artist as the organizer of experience (p 23). The springtime energies of the pilgrims, removing them from normal routines, lead them to form new associations and orders among themselves; 'the *ordering*

impulse that creates society anew at the Tabard Inn provides the material for the *representational* impulse of the narrator' (p 25). The portraits 'give the simultaneous impression of reproducing life untouched and of constantly ordering it in accord with a variety of systems and perspectives' (p 25). The narrator, one of the two 'artists-in-residence' on the pilgrimage (p 27), offers through his apology (lines 725–46) 'a radical manifesto that art must be true to life, not bowdlerized, overly selective, or fictional' (p 26). The other artistic voice is that of the Host, who embodies the principles of ordering and organizing language; his plan is a 'manifesto of artistic order' (p 27). Both viewpoints are presented with ambiguity. Thus *GP* initiates a 'debate about art's relationship to life,' a debate which is continued in later parts of the work (p 28).

271 Hanson, Thomas Bradley. *Stylized Man: The Poetic Use of Physiognomy in Chaucer's Canterbury Tales.* University of Wisconsin Dissertation. 1970. Dir. Chauncey Wood and Robert K. Presson. See also *DAI*, 31 (1970), 1278-A
'Chapter III examines the physiognomies of eleven of the pilgrims in Chaucer's *General Prologue.* The characters are grouped according to their social class, and it is observed that Chaucer employs varying amounts of physiognomic detail for diverse poetic effects. He may use a single physical detail to complement a character otherwise described, as with the Knight, or he may use abundant detail to reveal complexities of character that lie beneath the surface, as with the Monk. Chapter IV discusses the pilgrims grouped at the end of the *General Prologue* — the Miller, Reeve, Summoner, and Pardoner — and Harry Bailly, since Chaucer employs as much physical detail for these as for all the other characters combined. Again, the physiognomic significance of each detail is examined for its poetic effect; this provides the basis for a discussion of Curry's conclusions in *Chaucer and the Medieval Sciences* [see 209]. In most instances Curry's procedures prove to be misleading and his interpretations of the churls inaccurate' [from *DAI*; dissertation not seen].

272 Harig, Sister Mary Laboure, S.N.D. *A Study of the Literary Garden Tradition and Chaucer.* Case Western Reserve University Dissertation. 1971. See also *DAI*, 32 (1972), 4565-A.
An examination of garden imagery in *GP* is included. Overall, 'Chaucer's perceptions were found to be highly conditioned by the literary and iconographic tradition which he inherited' [from *DAI*; diss not seen].

273 Haselmayer, Louis August, Jr. *Chaucer and Medieval Verse Portraiture.* Yale University Dissertation. 1937. See also *DAI*, 31 (1970), 2344-A.
The background of the formal portrait in classical Latin literature, me-

dieval rhetoric, medieval Latin poetry, Old French poetry, and Middle English poetry exclusive of Chaucer is presented, with extensive collections of examples. Chaucer's portraits (in various works) are divided into 'two types, learned and realistic. The learned portraits consist of all those in the minor poems, and a few from the *Canterbury Tales*, while the realistic portraits include those in the *General Prologue* and some from the *Tales*' (p 218). Each *GP* portrait is examined in terms of the antecedent rhetorical and literary traditions. 'The *Prologue* portraits stand out in brilliant and vivid colors, the greatest exception to the entire tradition of medieval verse portraiture, as well as its most magnificent aesthetic culmination' (p 382).

274 Haskell, Ann S. 'The Golden Ambiguity of the *Canterbury Tales*.' *ER*, 1 (1971), 1–9.
Just as *amor* encompasses 'the entire spectrum of life, from the heavenly to the earthly to the profane' (p 11), the ambiguous image of gold can represent 'a spectrum of meaning ranging from *cupiditas* to *caritas*' (p 2). In the Prioress's portrait, the ambiguous gold brooch of line 160 is foreshadowed by the earlier reference to St Loy the goldsmith (line 120). In the Monk's gold pin (lines 196–7), the conflict between his love of the world and his duty to love God is represented. The Physician's special love for gold in medications (lines 443–44) shows 'the ultimate in cupidity' — the love of material things 'perhaps even at the expense of another's very life' (p 4); but the Parson's reference to gold, in the following portrait (line 500), represents 'the opposite pole,' charity (p 4). The Miller's association with gold in the reference to his golden thumb (line 562) is continued in his tale. 'The love/gold references' function as an 'extended pun' (p 8) that exploits the ambiguous relationship between love and gold.

275 Heath, Sidney. *Pilgrim Life in the Middle Ages*. London: Unwin, 1911. Rpt Port Washington, NY: Kennikat Press, 1971. Rev as *In the Steps of the Pilgrims*, London: Rich and Cowan [1950].
Much background information about English pilgrimages is provided. Chaucer's pilgrims as described in *GP* are very briefly mentioned. The revision includes new appendix material on the Black Prince at Canterbury.

276 Héraucourt, Will. *Die Wertwelt Chaucers, Die Wertwelt einer Zeitwende*. Heidelberg: Winter, 1939. Kulturgeschichtliche Bibliothek, neue Folge, dritte Reihe, 1.
Some hundred lines from *GP* are cited in this study of Chaucer's value system, which is presented in terms of four cardinal virtues: wisdom (Klugheit), justice (Gerechtigkeit), valor (Tapferkeit), and moderation (Mass). Word-by-word analyses of Chaucer's vocabulary compare his use of terms in *GP* (*trouthe, chivalrye, worthy, simple* and *coy*, etc) with the use of these terms

elsewhere in his works. The book is based on Héraucourt's dissertation of the same title, Marburg, 1936.

277 Higdon, David Leon. 'Diverse Melodies in Chaucer's "General Prologue." '
Crit, 14 (1972), 97–108.
Musical imagery helps to establish the design of *GP*. Augustine, Boethius, Cassiodorus, Isidore, and others had set out theories of music and a discord-concord dichotomy that Chaucer may well have used. Three types of relationship between music and pilgrims are evident in the portraits. Pilgrims associated with song, dance, and harmony are the Squire, Prioress, Monk, Friar, and perhaps the Wife, Yeoman, and Serjeant; 'their music indicates the discrepancy between what they are and what they should be' (p 101). Pilgrims associated with noise, loudness, and discord are 'the unholy trio' of the Miller, Summoner, and Pardoner (p 104). Pilgrims not associated with any external music are the Knight, Clerk, Parson, and Plowman. Reflecting Jerome's instruction to ' "Sing to God, not with the voice, but with the heart" ' (p 107), in these portraits the absence of external music represents the presence of internal music. Thus 'the idealized foursome actually emerge as the most skillful musicians on the pilgrimage' (p 107). Music, like other metaphors, can be read as good or evil according to the context, and the three treatments of music in *GP* 'remain unresolved, unharmonized, in a hierarchy of tensions' (p 108) — as is repeatedly found in the Gothic art of juxtaposition.

278 Higgs, Elton D. 'The Old Order and the "Newe World" in the General Prologue to the *Canterbury Tales*.' *HLQ*, 45 (1982), 155–73.
Higgs offers 'a detailed exposition of the structural integrity of the tripartite division of the pilgrims introduced by Howard' (see **287, 288**). Each of the idealized pilgrims who begins a section — the Knight, the Clerk, and the Parson/Plowman pair — 'has a particular kind of virtue which is set against a corresponding type of vice in the pilgrims who follow in that section'; themes and characters are incrementally developed in the three sections; and Chaucer's idealization of the Old Order reflects 'his admiration for a degree of dedication to the "commune profit," which he considered more vital to an ordered society than the keeping of social distinctions' (pp 157-8). The portraits of the idealized pilgrims 'are progressively more remote from the center of society' (p 158). Correspondingly, the concluding pilgrim in each group — Merchant, Wife, Pardoner — becomes more openly disruptive of the Old Order; later these three pilgrims confess to circumstances that are 'progressively more threatening to social order' (p 166). The focus changes from noble behavior and reputation in Group I, to learning and knowledge in Group II, to attitudes toward being a servant in Group III. The idealized pilgrims who begin each section 'bring us by degrees from

the virtues of the body, to the virtues of the mind, to the virtues of the soul,' while their counterparts who end each section 'constitute the major gradations in a concomitant crescendo of vice' (p 170). 'These patterns reflect Chaucer's concern with the possible consequences of the emerging economic and social individualism of his day' (p 170).

279 Hill, Granville Syndor. *The Hagiographic Narrators of Geoffrey Chaucer's Canterbury Tales: The Second Nun, the Man of Law, the Prioress.* Rice University Dissertation. 1977. See also *DAI* 38 (1977), 1409-A.
The 'rhetoric of the narrator's intrusions is analyzed in terms of the speakers' professions and their portraits in the *General Prologue*' [from *DAI*; diss not seen].

280 Hinckley, Henry Barrett. *Notes on Chaucer: A Commentary on the Prolog and Six Canterbury Tales.* Northampton, MA: Nonotuck Press, 1907.
The extensive treatment of *GP* begins with an overview of other frame-tales (Gower's *Confessio Amantis*, Boccaccio's *Decameron*, and Sercambi's *Novelle*). Hinckley comments that Chaucer's 'compact picture of society' is a 'consummate masterpiece' (p 3), with which only the *Iliad*, Book 18 (the description of Achilles's shield), can compare. A great many individual lines are then annotated; a few only are noted here. On line 91, Hinckley supports the viewpoint that the Squire is whistling, not playing the flute. On line 120, to swear by St Loy may mean not to swear at all. On lines 124–26, it is 'barely possible' (p 11) that the Prioress's portrait reflects Mary Suharde, prioress of St Leonard's nunnery at Stratford. On line 159, *gauded* pertains to ornamented beads for saying prayers that begin with *gaudete* or *gaudia*. On line 162, the Prioress probably interpreted *Amor* religiously. On line 173, the Monk is a Benedictine. On lines 179–81, *recchelees* means 'careless, lax, negligent, slack' (p 15). On lines 212–13, probably all that is meant is that the Friar would marry runaway couples without charging them. On line 278, the Merchant's activities in exchanging money are evidently illegal, as is his *chevyssaunce* (line 282). On line 334, the Gospel account of dipping the sop at the Last Supper is pertinent. On line 364, the guild is not a craft or religious guild, but 'a town gild or gild-merchant' (p 27). On line 372, *alderman* should be taken to mean not a guild officer, but a municipal officer. On line 390, the Shipman's *rouncy* is not a common hackney but a 'great, strong horse' (p 30), perhaps a war-horse, which he rides uneasily. On line 468, *gat-tothed* may imply either that the Wife's teeth are set far apart, or that she is 'goat-toothed,' ie, lascivious (p 38). On line 526, *spiced conscience* means 'extraordinary complaisance,' so that lines 525–26 together imply that 'he did not pompously exact deference from others, neither did he lay flattering unctions to their souls,' or that 'he was neither

a snob nor a toady' (p 40). On line 664, *girles* means both young men and young women. On line 668, the cake was probably obtained by blackmail. On line 670, since line 692 locates the Pardoner not in London but between Berwick and Ware, it is possible that *Rouncivalle* indicates some place other than (as is usually thought) the hospital of St Mary Rouncyvalle in London: perhaps the Priory at Rouncevaux in Navarre had more than one cell in Britain. On line 675, the Pardoner, as a Dominican friar, should have shaven his crown. See **743**.

281 ——. 'The Framing-Tale.' *MLN*, 49 (1934), 69–80.
The framing-tale or 'boxed tale' is a very ancient form. Examples include the 'Westcar Papyrus' of ancient Egypt; Indian tale collections, one of which, the *Hitopadesha*, 'occasionally presents a story within a story within a story within a story' (p 70); and Homer's *Odyssey*, which also uses embedded narratives. However, it does not seem probable that Chaucer knew Boccaccio's *Decameron*, or in fact any of the specific 'boxed tales' described here. Chaucer's artistic innovation, within the general type, consists in the differentiation of the narrators' personalities and the adaptation of the tales to them.

282 Hira, Toshinori. 'Chaucer's Gentry in the Historical Background.' In *Nakayama Kyoju Kanreki Kinen Ei Bei Bungaku Ronso. (Essays in English and American Literature in Commemoration of Professor Takejiro Nakayama's Sixty-First Birthday.)* Tokyo: Shohakusha, 1961. Pp 31–44.
Hira briefly examines each of the pilgrims who might belong to the category of the gentry, both those who are of gentle birth in the traditional sense and those who are the 'new men' (p 36) — men whose rise can be correlated with the changing social and economic conditions in the fourteenth century.

283 ——. 'Chaucer's Framing Device of the Canterbury Tales.' *NDKK*, 16 (1975), 79–91, and 17 (1977), 107–19.
Not seen; listed in *A Bibliography of Publications on Medieval English Language and Literature in Japan* (Tokyo: Center for Medieval Studies, Tokyo University, 1983), p 143, #8.

284 Hoffman, Arthur W. 'Chaucer's Prologue to Pilgrimage: The Two Voices.' *ELH*, 21 (1954), 1–16. Rpt in *Chaucer: Modern Essays in Criticism*, ed. Edward C. Wagenknecht (New York: Oxford University Press, 1959), pp 30–45; in *Discussions of the Canterbury Tales*, ed. Charles A. Owen, Jr. (Boston: Heath, 1961), pp 9–17; and in *Chaucer: The Canterbury Tales, a Casebook*, ed. J.J. Anderson (London: Macmillan, 1974), pp 105–20.
Acknowledging general agreement that the portraits in *GP* form a unity,

Hoffman considers some of the 'aesthetically important internal relation-ships' (1954, p 2) that help to constitute that unity. The springtime open-ing of *GP* depicts a progression, for it moves from broad generalities to English specifications, and from *amor* in its natural, secular form to *amor dei*. Thus two views of pilgrimage are established. The physical vitality of the season restores the dry earth; the supernatural vitality represented by the saint restores health to sick humanity. Variations on the meanings of love occur throughout, with 'the theme of restorative power' (p 15) closely related to that of love. 'The pilgrims are represented as affected by a variety of destructive and restorative kinds of love' (p 16). Even the Summoner and Pardoner, with their 'appalling personal deficiency,' can suggest by contrast 'the summoning and pardoning' that are ideally associated with pilgrimage (p 16). In addition to this thematic form of unity, with its two kinds of love, a double view is evident within many of the portraits (eg, within that of the Prioress), and in sequences or groups of portraits (eg, in the Knight-Squire sequence, the Prioress-Monk-Friar sequence, and the Pardoner-Summoner sequence). The thematic and structural techniques can be combined. When the Summoner, 'the type of sexual unrestraint,' sings a love-song with the impotent Pardoner, they are structurally linked as a pair. Their song that acknowledges the absence of love 'is a superb dramatic irony' (p 12), for it suggests the love of God, which they ought to be experiencing. Cf **386, 475, 700.**

285 Hoffman, Richard L. *Ovid and the Canterbury Tales*. Philadelphia, PA: University of Pennsylvania, 1966; London: Oxford University Press, 1966. Portions rpt in Hoffman, **122,** pp 52–80.

In the chapters 'Ovid and the Structure and Theme of *The Canterbury Tales*' (1966, pp 1–20) and 'Ovidian Allusions in *The Canterbury Tales* — General Prologue' (pp 23–28), Hoffman argues that Chaucer continued to use Ovid in this stage of his poetic development. Among the passages show-ing Ovidian influence are lines 5–7, on Zephyrus, which may be a Golden Age image that balances the image of the scales of justice in the Parson's Prologue; lines 127–36, on the Prioress's manners, which are derived di-rectly from the *Roman de la Rose*, but indirectly from Ovid; lines 191–92, on the Monk's hunting, which imply sexual pursuit; and lines 475–76, on the Wife's *remedies of love* and *the olde daunce*. In addition to such instances of specific indebtedness, 'Chaucer like Ovid usually fits the tale to the teller' (p 7). He also uses the Ovidian 'device of telling tales in a competition governed by a judge who will reward the winner' (p 10). In the unifying theme of love, Chaucer may have been influenced by Ovid's treatment of the two Venuses, whose characteristics suggest the later Augustinian di-vision between *caritas* and *cupiditas*. The book is based upon Hoffman's dissertation, *Ovid and the Canterbury Tales*, Princeton University, 1964; abstract in *DA*, 25 (1965), 5280.

286 Holley, Linda Tarte. *Chaucer and the Function of the Word*. Tulane University Dissertation. 1975. Dir. Robert Geiger Cook. See also *DAI*, 36 (1976), 8075-A.
'In spite of his reason, ordinary man's word does not reliably represent either thought or deed. This alienation of thought and speech in the ordinary man is apparent in the General Prologue,' where often 'the pilgrims' words are merely external qualities that have little connection with substance. The exceptions to this unreliable utilization of the word are the three portraits recognized as "ideals": The Knight, the Clerk, and the Parson. The harmony of thought, word, and deed is realized in these characters and offers a striking contrast to the alienation of thought, word, and deed in the other portraits' [from *DAI*; diss not seen].

287 Howard, Donald R. '*The Canterbury Tales:* Memory and Form.' *ELH*, 38 (1971), 319–28. Rpt with revisions in *The Idea of the Canterbury Tales* (**288**), pp 139–58.
In *GP* we are '*not* in the inn, and *not* on the road, but in the realm of memory, of story, of empathy, even of fantasy' (1971, p 319). In the *CT* as a whole 'the essential principle of form' is 'a controlled lapse from one remembered world into another remembered world,' a 'regression by successive steps into the past and the unreal' (p 320). *GP* is structured according to medieval concepts of the trained or artificial memory. The portraits 'are arranged in associations easiest to remember, associations of class, alliance, and dependency endemic to medieval society' (p 322). The principles of order include the three estates, subdivided into natural associations of travelling companions. If the descriptions of the Prioress and her companions, and of the Guildsmen and their Cook, are each counted as one portrait, and if the Host is included, 'the portraits of the General Prologue can then be seen arranged symmetrically into three groups of seven, each headed by an ideal portrait' (p 324; for further discussion of Howard's three groups of seven, see **142** and **279**). The resulting shape 'resembles the artificial order imposed on words and images as an aid to memory' (p 324). *GP* forms a '*vade mecum* which we must carry with us as we proceed into the tales' (p 325). As a presentation of 'things remembered' (p 325), it shows us the things of this world. As a pilgrimage narrative, it finds its true analogues in other pilgrimage narratives. *GP* shares with the dream-vision poems, as Cunningham has shown (**207**), a 'quality of inner, remembered experience,' but here memory replaces dream as a 'principle of form' (p 327). There is 'a pervasive sense of obsolescence, the passing of experience into memory' (p 328), with old ideals in decline

and old things or events recalled (eg, the Prioress 'wears a medallion of some forgotten occasion,' p 328). At the end of the *CT*, however, Chaucer instead embraces 'the world he believed existed beyond memory' (p 328). In reply, see Robertson, **429**.

288 ——. *The Idea of the Canterbury Tales.* Berkeley: University of California Press, 1976. Paperback edition, 1978.

GP is discussed in the chapter 'The General Prologue' (1978, pp 139–58) and in other sections. *CT* is interpreted as being '*unfinished but complete*' (p 1). Within the outer form of the framework lies the inner form of the tales. (The plan laid out in *GP*, calling for more than a hundred tales, is the Host's, not necessarily Chaucer's.) The main discussion of *GP*, emphasizing the function of memory as form, is a revised and expanded version of Howard, **287**. Many other references to *GP* occur. The flower image that is part of the springtime opening (line 4) implies both transience and order. Chaucer mingles past and present verb tenses, with the present tense representing 'the moment of participation, the moment when a thing that *was* is passed from one brain to another in the mutual act of communication' (p 82). *GP* suggests the traditional three estates concept of society, but describes instead 'a variegated and mobile set of social distinctions' (p 94) as Chaucer shows the contrast between obsolescent concepts and the more complex reality of his world. The Knight, for instance, is 'an obsolescent hero' (p 94). The Prioress, Monk, and Friar are depicted 'against a past implied or stated in the portrait itself' (p 99). To the extent that the Plowman 'can be thought a reality rather than an ideal, he would indeed have seemed an anachronism' (p 102). Even the middle-class pilgrims are concerned with the past. 'Ideals are in the past, actuality in the narrative "now" ' (p 115). The idealized portraits conclude with a *sententia* or general statement, the others 'with a particular detail or a piquant phrase' (p 115).

- Review by Alastair Fowler, 'Patterns of Pilgrimage,' *TLS*, November 12, 1976, pp 1410–12: 'Professor Howard is surely right in seeing the General Prologue as a highly ordered structure' (p 1411). The central pilgrim, structurally, is the Franklin. Fowler accepts Howard's emphasis on memory. The interlace pattern, however, may be less useful than other structural principles, which are 'more regularly accretive, more firmly schematic' (p 1411).

- Review by Lee W. Patterson, 'Writing about Writing: The Case of Chaucer,' *UTQ*, 48 (1978–1979), 263–82: Patterson is unconvinced by Howard's concept of *CT* as an act of memory and by Howard's correlation of the *flour* (see line 4) to window-imagery; 'the reader who returns to the General Prologue after this magical mystery tour of Gothic culture ... is bound to be a little disappointed with mere Chaucer' (p 270).

289 ——. *Writers and Pilgrims: Medieval Pilgrimage Narratives and Their Posterity.* Berkeley: University of California Press, 1980.
Howard examines *CT* in the context of medieval pilgrimage narratives. There exist, for instance, 'some 526 accounts' of the Jerusalem pilgrimage (p 17). Comments on *GP* are included in the chapter 'Chaucer' (pp 77–103). *CT* 'as a fictional piece of travel literature' (p 77) opens in *GP* with references to 'the Jerusalem pilgrimage, the prototype of pilgrimages' (p 79), but presents instead 'the local, national pilgrimage to Canterbury' (p 79; see lines 13–14, which suggest foreign pilgrimage; lines 15–18, the English pilgrimage). In qualities such as its 'self-awareness' (p 83) and its preoccupation with language and verisimilitude, *CT* differs from typical pilgrimage narratives. For example, before the tales begin, at lines 725–36 the narrator 'makes the most outrageous truth-claim imaginable, that he can *remember* them all verbatim' (p 88). Chaucer's whole management of the narrator is quite different from what is customary in the pilgrimage accounts.

290 Howard, Edwin J. *Geoffrey Chaucer.* New York: Twayne, 1964. Rpt London: Macmillan, 1976, Griffin Author Series.
In the chapter 'The Canterbury Tales' (pp 118–89), Howard comments that the opening passage, in the 'high style,' is succeeded by Chaucer's 'usual comfortable style' (1964, p 120). The pilgrims represent not a cross section of Chaucer's whole society, but more accurately 'a cross section of middle-class society' (p 121). The pilgrims are made 'outstanding,' rather than ordinary (p 121). Chaucer has been said to abstain from moral judgment, but his method of allowing readers to form their own conclusions is more effective than 'a shrill outcrying against abuses' would have been (p 122).

291 Hoyt, Douglas Henry. *Thematic Word-Play in Chaucer's Canterbury Tales.* Saint Louis University Dissertation. 1973. See also *DAI*, 35 (1974), 2941-A.
The importance of play, apparent in the overall events of the pilgrimage, in the storytelling contest, and within individual tales, can also 'be seen to exist within the confines of a single word, or in the repetition of the same word in succeeding situtations' (p iv). The background to Chaucer's sense of word-play is explained through a review of the school-texts and other sources he would have known. In the opening of *GP*, 'Chaucer purposely chooses many words that, while operating on a literal level, convey at least secondarily a sense of human personality or divine life' (p 157; examples include *droughte* and *vein*, lines 2 and 3). Word-play in *GP* is concentrated

in the springtime setting; in the narrator's reportorial statements (*resoun*, line 37; *condicioun*, line 38; etc); and in the portraits that are ambiguous. By examining the word-play 'we can see the possibility that the Knight is not so superior to the others as has been generally affirmed, that his vision too has room for clarification, and that he, like the others, is somewhat tainted and in need of pilgrimage' (p 186). Similarly, in the Squire's portrait 'a few ambiguous adjectives and images throw the picture a little out of focus' (p 188). Other pilgrims are similarly examined. 'As a result of the high degree of ambiguous narration' in *GP* (p 238), Chaucer seems to have intended to arouse or establish several responses in his audience: 1) an awareness of both hierarchical order and variety; 2) 'mixed reactions' to most of the pilgrims (p 238); 3) 'a certain ambivalence of attitude, a suspension of final judgment' (p 239); 4) an understanding of the narrator's equivocal role as 'somehow symptomatic of the moral sickness pervading this pilgrimage world, where ambiguity and word-play are keynotes of a world of blurred human desires, motives, and moral standards' (p 239); and 5) the desire to resolve this flawed condition.

292 Hughes, Geoffrey. 'Gold and Iron: Semantic Change and Social Change in Chaucer's Prologue.' *Standpunte*, 137 (1978), 1–11.
Chaucer was well aware of linguistic change; he showed in *GP* that crucial terms representing value-concepts have different implications in different contexts, reflecting both social change and individual usage. His time saw 'the growth of an acquisitive, competitive, profit-oriented ethos occasioned by the labour shortages caused in turn by the Black Death' (p 6). The concept of profit was being altered, from common or public profit to private or individual profit. Terms such as *bisynesse* and *winne* were also undergoing change. '*Bisynesse* thus stands—together with *profit* and *winne*—at an ethical and semantic crossroads. They can pass down the way of true fellowship, of harmonious *caritas*; or down that of false fellowship, of alienating, competitive *cupiditas* .... Chaucer created in the ideally charitable and "profitable" representatives of the Three Estates essentially simple, limited "goode men" who appear, ironically, rather uninteresting figures, without "character" or "personality." ... He showed the "gold" of the clergy rusting into interestingly unnatural shapes as its currency became debased, and the "iren" of the Third Estate becoming eroded as it became gilded' (p 10). Throughout *GP* 'Chaucer shows in his deployment of nonce-words, key-words, status terms and moral terms, that character and language are inseparable, that words and values change as societies change, that the only true value attaches to virtue, which must be sought beyond the flux of words, since terms of value are particularly vulnerable to change in the hands of the ambitious' (p 11). On the Manciple, see **1235**.

293 Hulbert, J.R. '*The Canterbury Tales* and Their Narrators.' *SP*, 45 (1948), 565–77.

Responding to Kittredge's thesis that the tales express their narrator's personalities (see 317), Hulbert stresses the 'diversity in kind and amount of appropriateness of the tales to their narrators' (p 577). In some tales, the suitability is only that of matching the pilgrims' social class as identified in *GP*; in others, incongruities exist 'that might have been removed on revision'; in still others, there is full suitability of tale to teller in (as Kittredge proposed) 'dramatic situations' (p 577). Thus the relationship between the *GP* portraits and the rest of the *CT* is variable, perhaps reflecting Chaucer's changes of plan as he wrote.

294 ——. 'Chaucer's Pilgrims.' *PMLA*, 64 (1949), 823–28. Rpt in *Chaucer: Modern Essays in Criticism*, ed. Edward C. Wagenknecht (New York: Oxford University Press, 1959), pp 23–29.

Agreeing with Manly's viewpoint that certain pilgrims represent historical individuals (see 362), Hulbert acknowledges that 'probably we shall never know the full extent of Chaucer's individual references' (1949, p 825). Even when Chaucer seems to be writing in general or typical terms, he may have had specific individuals in mind. The Knight's career is not a typical or composite one, for he has fought only in religious wars; it is probably based on the career of 'a single knight known to Chaucer' (p 826). The Monk's portrait too may have been drawn from life. An important aspect of Chaucer's success in *GP* is the variety in the portraits: they may 'be entirely general,' or they 'may join realistic details to typical statements,' or they may involve satire or humor, or they 'may be made more serious by suggestion of moral disapproval' (p 827), and so forth. The variety itself is one of Chaucer's achievements.

295 Huppé, Bernard F. *A Reading of the Canterbury Tales*. Binghamton: State University of New York, 1964.

In the chapter 'The General Prologue' (pp 13–48), Huppé finds that 'The structure of the *Prologue* is largely rhetorical; that is, it is framed on the narrator's descriptive catalog and supported by contrastive and incremental repetition' (p 43). Because pilgrimage was associated with springtime (as in Berchorius's *Reductorium morale*), the mention of pilgrimage rather than love in line 12 is not 'an anticlimax after all, but a logical — if unexpected — sequel to the picture of Spring as an annual restatement of God's creative love' (p 18). The portraits show 'a scale of values from the ideal of the true pilgrim to the corruptness of the false pilgrim' (p 30). For the Knight Chaucer 'employs the device of the key word,' *worthy* (p 31; lines 43, 47, 50, 64, 68). The Squire's portrait 'develops the technique of using one portrait as a foil to another' (p 33). There is a 'failure in symmetry' (p 39) in that Chaucer provides ideal embodiments of the Active Life (Knight and Plowman) and the Prelatical Life (Parson), but not of the Contemplative Life (the Clerk is a contemplative only because he is not yet a priest). Huppé discusses such aspects as repetition and contrastive repetition; the fact that the end of *GP* 'becomes entirely dramatic' (p 43), rather than rhetorical; and Hammond's suggestion (**120**, p 254) that the final group of pilgrims was an addition. For Huppé's comments on the Friar and the narrator, see **929, 1345**.

- Review by John Lawlor, *RES*, New Series 17 (1966), 304–6: Lawlor objects to the 'root-assumption' that 'secular literature is to be treated on the same footing as divine' (p 305).

- Review by Albert C. Baugh, *ES*, 48 (1967), 435–38: Baugh sees many 'good things' in the book 'with which few are likely to quarrel' (p 438), though he questions whether it is 'a safe guide for the uninitiated' (p 437).

296 Hussey, Maurice. *Chaucer's World: A Pictorial Companion*. Cambridge, England: Cambridge University Press, 1967.
Many places, objects, activities, etc, mentioned in *GP* are depicted. There are discussions of each pilgrim or group of pilgrims, as well as background information on (for example) the zodiac, the four humors, the roads and villages of England, illness and plague, the Seven Deadly Sins, and agricultural life at the time.

297 —, A.C. Spearing, and James Winny. *An Introduction to Chaucer*. Cambridge, England: Cambridge University Press, 1965.
Background information — for example, on lawyers, representatives of the church (monks, friars, nuns, parsons, pardoners, summoners), pilgrimage, scientific concepts, and language — is included, often with reference to *GP* examples. An appendix briefly discusses the terms *clerk, corage, curteys, honest, nature, vertu,* and *worthy,* along with other terms (such as *gentillesse* and *pitee*) that are indirectly related to *GP* (see pp 185–90).

298 Hussey, S.S. *Chaucer: An Introduction*. London: Methuen, 1971. 2nd ed., 1981.
The section 'Plan and *General Prologue*' (pp 99–126) examines *GP*. 'Chaucer is clearly trying to give the illusion of pilgrimage rather than a completely realistic description' (1971, p 105). The pilgrims are presented in groups; the first such group consists of the Knight, Squire, and Yeoman. A range of attitudes is evident in the second group: 'with the Prioress Chaucer had been tolerant; with the Monk satirical but, in part, under-

standing;with the Friar he shows a complete lack of sympathy' (p 108). Next follows a middle-class group characterized by their attitudes towards material possessions, and then a small group of two idealized figures, the Parson and the Plowman. Chaucer humorously includes himself with the group of 'thieves and rascals' at the end (p 112). The 'apparently random impressions' (p 114) that compose the portraits perhaps represent the way in which an observer notices people, or may be intended to show the capabilities of Chaucer the pilgrim. *GP* blends 'realistic reporting and literary convention' (p 116). Chaucer the pilgrim supplies 'surface impression,' while Chaucer the author supplies irony (p 117).

299 Hutton, William Holden. *Thomas Becket, Archbishop of Canterbury.* London: Pitman, 1910. New enlarged ed., Cambridge: Cambridge University Press, 1926.
Although it does not extend to the fourteenth-century veneration of Becket, this general biography provides many details about his career.

300 Huxley, Aldous. *On the Margin.* London: Chatto & Windus, 1923; New York: George Doran, [1923].
In the chapter 'Chaucer' (pp 194–218), Huxley points out that 'Chaucer does not protest, he accepts' (p 196). Where Langland is appalled at the conditions of the times, Chaucer is a detached spectator who finds human behavior amusing. He 'has the power of getting into someone else's character,' and the *GP* sketches, 'in which the effects are almost entirely produced by the description of external physical features,' exemplify his abilities in 'three-dimensional drawing' (p 212). The chapter is also included in Huxley's *Essays New and Old* (New York: H.W. Wilson, 1932), pp 249–72.

301 Ida, Yoshiharu. 'The Prologue to the Canterbury Tales Ni Okeru Kaigasei. Engekisei To Montaju Shuho Ni Tsuite.' [Picturesqueness, Dramatic Qualities, and Montage Method in the Prologue to the Canterbury Tales.] *Volcano,* 1 (1965), 25–36.
Not seen; listed in *A Bibliography of Publications on Medieval English Language and Literature in Japan* (Tokyo: Center for Medieval Studies, Tokyo University, 1983) p 144, #3.

302 Iijima, Ikuzo. *Langland and Chaucer: A Study of the Two Types of Genius in English Poetry.* Boston: Four Seas Publishers, 1925.
In the chapter 'Geoffrey Chaucer' (pp 81–121), Iijima briefly discusses *GP* as 'a perfect genre picture' in which Chaucer represents 'almost all classes' of fourteenth-century England and demonstrates 'his marvelously keen sense of observation to the last detail' (pp 111–12).

303 *Illustrations of Chaucer's England.* Ed. Dorothy Hughes. Preface by A.W. Pollard. London: Longmans, Green, 1918.

Hughes prints excerpts from contemporary documents pertaining to 1) the Hundred Years' War, including material on the Crusade of 1383, which is sometimes associated with the Squire; 2) social conditions, including instructions to innkeepers and others for maintaining the peace; 3) ecclesiastical affairs, including references to Wycliffe; and 4) political and constitutional events, including the Peasants' Revolt.

304 Ito, Eiko. 'The Treatment of "Degree" in the General Prologue to the Canterbury Tales.' *KJDR*, 20, 2 (1973), 1–15.

Not seen; listed in *A Bibliography of Publications on Medieval English Language and Literature in Japan* (Tokyo: Center for Medieval Studies, Tokyo University, 1983), p 144, #7.

305 Jack, Adolphus Alfred. *A Commentary on the Poetry of Chaucer and Spenser.* Glasgow: Maclehose and Jackson, 1920; London: Macmillan, 1920.

In the chapter 'Chaucer' (pp 22–116), Jack views *GP* as a panorama of type-characters who also depict medieval realities. Chaucer's attitude is one of 'easy morality, a middle view' (p 86), or 'the natural cynicism of middle life' (p 87). None of the characters is wholly ideal. The Knight is 'a prosaic knight, like a retired general today — a gentleman, but with no foolishness of romance' (p 87). Chaucer 'disliked the professional religious people' and his temper 'was definitely anti-ecclesiastical' (p 88), although it is the representatives of the Church, not the Church itself, that he is attacking. On the storytelling plan, see **1365**.

306 Jaunzems, John. *Unifying Patterns in the Canterbury Tales.* University of Toronto Dissertation. 1972. Dir. G. Zekulin. See also *DAI*, 34 (1974), 5105–5106-A.

In the section 'The General Prologue' (pp 34–61), Jaunzems discusses the subdivisions of *GP*, briefly comments on individual portraits, and suggests that 'the groundwork is laid in the portraits for a narrative that is essentially episodic, rather than for one that is unified by a strong plot ... Chaucer establishes a flexible, inclusive society where eccentric, compulsive, threatening, and even downright repellent characters are ranged side by side with normal, rational, and pious citizens' (pp 45–6). The characterization of so many of the pilgrims as superlative emphasizes the fictional basis of *GP*, for 'surely no one ever supposed that Chaucer actually went on a pilgrimage where so many individual paragons happened to be gathered together' (p 49). In many of the portraits the pilgrim's 'specific superlativeness comes into alignment with the specific love or desire and thus forms a distinctive unity of personality' (p 56). *GP* 'implies a twofold formal cause' — pilgrimage and storytelling — and thus 'analysis should remain alert to didactic and mimetic dimensions simultaneously' (p 61).

307 Jenks, Tudor. *In the Days of Chaucer*. Introduction by Hamilton Wright Mabie. New York: Barnes, 1904; London: Authors' Syndicate, 1904.

Jenks's comments on *GP* emphasize its freshness and its realism. 'The first lines of the Prologue affect one as does the dawn of day in early spring' (p 175). The historical existence of Harry Bailly and the Tabard Inn are pointed out (pp 180–81). In the *CT* 'we come face to face with men and women of five hundred years ago, and know them as if we had mounted into the saddle and gone on the pilgrimage ourselves ... We are even conscious that the pilgrims are more real than the personages in their stories, though these do not lack distinctness' (pp 202–3). Chaucer's art of portraiture is superior to that of Longfellow, as Jenks shows through brief comparisons between the Parson's portrait and the portrait of Longfellow's theologian (from the 'Tales of a Wayside Inn'), and between the Host's portrait and that of Longfellow's landlord. 'Only in Shakespeare will better portrait-painting be found' (p 206). The *GP* pilgrims are presented in groups: those representing chivalry, the Church, the professionals, and the business and trade occupations.

308 Jennings, Margaret, C.S.J. 'Chaucer's Beards.' *Archiv*, 215 (1978), 362–68.

The attitudes towards beards in medieval physiognomy and in historical sources are explained. The beards in *GP* are significant: 'if one had only the poet's depiction of the beard to work with, one might arrive at a fair analysis of the characters called Franklyn, Merchant, Reeve, Summoner, Pardoner, and Miller' (p 365). The Franklin's beard indicates his 'cordiality, sincerity, and friendliness' (p 366); the Merchant's, his attention to fashion, but perhaps also 'the forkedness of his business deals' (p 366); the Reeve's, his status as an underling and his hypocrisy; the Summoner's, his syphillitic condition and unattractive character; the Miller's, his 'strong and disreputable' nature (p 367); the Pardoner's, his sexual abnormality. The manuscript portraits of Chaucer himself, depicting him with a full, neat beard of chestnut, grey, or white color, suggest a range of positive qualities.

309 Jones, H.S.V. 'The Plan of the "Canterbury Tales." ' *MP*, 13 (1915-1916), 45–48.

GP is 'a vivid realization in skillfully dramatic combination of that form of social satire which is specifically designated the *États du monde*' (p 45). Earlier examples of estates-satire literature are reviewed, along with works showing 'anticipations' of Chaucer's 'narrative adaptation of that type' (p

46). In the *Roman de carité*, for example, the poet visits 'the estates of the world instead of traveling in their company'; his destination is 'the uncertain abode of Charity' (p 46). *Piers Plowman* is the nearest analogue to Chaucer's combination of the pilgrimage setting with 'vividly described pilgrims' (p 47).

310 Jordan, Robert M. 'Chaucer's Sense of Illusion: Roadside Drama Reconsidered.' *ELH*, 29 (1962), 19–33.
To interpret *CT* as a 'roadside drama' (in the Kittredge tradition, see **317**), is only partially satisfactory, for 'the unity of the poem is less "organic" than mechanic' (p 19). Chaucer's sense of illusion is more complicated than the roadside-drama theory permits. The illusion of realism is supported by lines 725–36, the mock apology. However, given the distinction between the poet and the narrator — 'the poet is making a joke,' while 'the reporter is earnestly expounding the obvious' (p 20) — even as Chaucer 'protests his fidelity to fact he has ensnared us in fiction' (p 22). Rather than looking for historical antecedents of the pilgrims, as if each of them were an organic unity, we should (on the analogy of concepts from painting) allow for their existence as 'mechanic' or composite entities (p 19) in which the juxtaposition of divergent ingredients is intended. (Jordan's viewpoints on *GP* are also incorporated in **311**.)

311 ——. *Chaucer and the Shape of Creation: The Aesthetic Possibilities of Inorganic Structure*. Cambridge, MA: Harvard University Press, 1967; London: Oxford University Press, 1967. Portions rpt in *Critics on Chaucer*, ed. Sheila Sullivan (London: Allen & Unwin, 1970), pp 38–41.
In the chapter 'The Canterbury Tales: Concepts of Unity' (pp 111–31), Jordan rejects the 'roadside drama' viewpoint (see Kittredge, **317**; Lumiansky, **348**; and, in somewhat different version, Baldwin, **148**) as being inadequate to deal with 'the subtle play of human relationships between ourselves and the lively-minded poet' (p 123) or with Chaucer's complex sense of illusion. Chaucer repeatedly 'calls attention to the boundaries of the fiction' (p 125) and it is therefore inappropriate to see his work as organically unified and internally consistent. Its structure is inorganic. For Chaucer 'illusion itself is often the subject and is *ipso facto* limited' (p 125). In *GP* 'mankind is anatomized in the pilgrim-types and synthesized in the idea of pilgrimage' (p 238).

- Review by Richard L. Hoffman, *Spec*, 44 (1969), 468–71: Hoffman questions Jordan's basic concept of inorganic form, which he says leaves 'the disquieting suspicions 1) that the theories seem good but are not tested in practice, and 2) that some of the critical observations appear sound and illuminating but do not serve clinically to illustrate the theories' (p 469).

- Review by Francis Lee Utley, *MLQ*, 30 (1969), 284–91: although Jordan is said to be moving 'down the dangerous path toward a synthesis of the arts' (p 285), the book is praised for 'fresh solutions to problems both about the individual tales and the personae' (p 288), and it makes the case for inorganic structure well.

312 Jusserand, J.J. *English Wayfaring Life in the Middle Ages.* Trans. Lucy Toulmin Smith. 2nd ed. London: T. Fisher Unwin, 1920. Rpt 1921, 1925 (3rd ed.), 1929, 1931 (London: Ernest Benn), 1950 (4th ed., Benn).
Much background information about roads, bridges, travelers of all sorts, safety on journeys, pilgrimage routes, etc, is supplied, along with (in the 2nd and 3rd editions) appendices on such varied subjects as popular songs and ecclesiastical documents pertaining to English pardoners. (The 4th ed. omits the appendices and many of the illustrations.) Of special importance to *GP* are comments on the Canterbury pilgrimage, on statutes affecting the clothing of ecclesiastics, and on pardoners and other social types and officials. On pardoners, cf Williams, **1338**.

313 Kane, George. *The Liberating Truth: The Concept of Integrity in Chaucer's Writings.* London: Athlone Press, 1980. John Coffin Memorial Lecture (University of London, 11 May 1979).
Chaucer is 'primarily concerned with morality, the matter of goodness or badness of human behavior' (p 6), and one of his major moral preoccupations is *trouthe*, or integrity. The modern 'notion of a conflict between artist and moralist in later fourteenth-century England' is fallacious and anachronistic (p 13). Many of the pilgrims correspond to the moral system of the estates-satire tradition. We are meant to see them not as 'charmingly quaint genre representations' but as 'intensely dramatic realizations of various kinds of moral deficiency, of inharmonious personalities, exposed the more sharply to criticism by the vividness of their realization' (p 13). Chaucer uses the device of the 'allusion evocative of moral criticism' (p 15). For example, the Monk's question, 'How shall the world be served?' (line 187), echoes the maxims *Si quis amat Christum mundum non diligit istum* and *Quis liberabit* ? (p 15). Chaucer's discrepancies recall moral principles by contrast, as when the narrator praises the Monk's appearance as handsome and then depicts him as 'a grotesque figure bald as a coot, sweating profusely, grossly fat and with bulging eyes' (p 16). The appearance of a discrepancy awakens the reader's responsibility for moral evaluation, though Chaucer himself does not typically 'attach a moral label' (p 16).

314 Kanno, Masahiko. 'Chaucer no Hyogen no Bimyosa — Futatsu no Shiten.'
[Subtlety in Chaucer's Expression — a Dual View.] *EEK*, 29 (1979), 54–68.
Kanno examines Chaucer's techniques of characterization in comparison to
those of Gower. Chaucer uses metaphors and similes, such as the Friar's
white neck, or words with multiple meanings, such as the Monk's *venerie*, to
produce characterizations that are more subtle, complicated, and humorous
than those of Gower. (An English summary is included.)

315 Kean, P.M. *Chaucer and the Making of English Poetry*. Vol 2, *The Art of
Narrative*. London and Boston: Routledge & Kegan Paul, 1972.
GP is examined in the context of Chaucerian comedy (pp 78–83). Chaucer
presents the portraits through cumulative lists of details in which each
item helps to distinguish the pilgrims from one another. His basic style for
comedy is 'the simple style' (p 80). He typically uses a 'simple, paratactic structure so as to allow detail to pile upon detail' in those sections of
GP where 'we are left to supply our own assessment, guided by the narrator's hidden skill in timing and placing' (p 81). The occasional 'longer,
consecutive or periodic sentences, which do indicate a definite attitude to
the matter in hand, stand out sharply in contrast' (p 82). The 'calculated
emergences' and 'equally calculated withdrawals' of the narrator 'convey a
great part of the comedy,' and, 'if we identify ourselves with anyone, it is
with the half-glimpsed narrator' (p 80).

316 Kittredge, George Lyman. 'Chaucer's Discussion of Marriage.' *MP*, 9
(1911-1912), 435–67. Rpt in *Chaucer: Modern Essays in Criticism*, ed.
Edward C. Wagenknecht (New York: Oxford University Press, 1959), pp
188–215.
This important essay on the concept of a 'Marriage Group' of tales includes multiple (though brief) references to the *GP* descriptions of those
pilgrims — the Wife, Clerk, Merchant, Squire, Franklin, and Host — whom
Kittredge sees as participating in Chaucer's discussion of marriage.

317 ——. *Chaucer and His Poetry*. Cambridge, MA: Harvard University Press,
1915; London: Oxford University Press, 1915. Rpt 1946. Anniversary
ed with introduction by B.J. Whiting, Cambridge, MA: Harvard University Press, 1970. Portions rpt in *Discussions of the Canterbury Tales*, ed.
Charles A. Owen, Jr. (Boston: Heath, 1961), pp 33–36.
The chapter 'The Canterbury Tales — I' (1915, pp 146–80) presents Kittredge's thesis that the work resembles a drama. 'Chaucer was quite as
interested in the Pilgrims themselves as in their several narratives' (p 153).
He has created a 'Human Comedy' (p 154). From *GP* alone, we might
make the error of regarding the pilgrims as types, but *GP* is in fact 'not
merely a prologue: it is the first act, which sets the personages in motion'

and shows them moving 'by virtue of their inherent vitality' (p 155). Structurally, 'the Pilgrims do not exist for the sake of the stories, but *vice versa*' (p 155). The Pilgrims are motivated by both religious and social impulses, as the Host realizes (line 772). Chaucer's inclusion of himself in the group of pilgrims leads us to conclude 'that they are as real as he is' (p 161). The Host is the 'dynamic agent' (p 161), though the Knight is the actual ruler of the group. The Prioress is 'delicately portrayed' and 'sympathetically conceived' (p 175); Chaucer does not intend to poke fun at her. The sociable figure of Chaucer in *GP* is 'the real Chaucer' — he is silent later simply because he has decided 'to play the part of a listener' and is concentrating on what is taking place (p 184). In reply to Kittredge, see **293, 310, 331, 359, 1306**; cf **348**.

- Review by John L. Lowes, *MLN*, 31 (1916), 316–18: the book is 'a vital and luminous and comprehensive interpretation of Chaucer and his art' (p 317), which illuminates 'the whole field by an unsurpassed knowledge of the period, turned to account by a critical faculty which is here essentially creative' (p 318).

- Review by Thomas A. Knott, *MP*, 14 (1916-1917), 61–64: Knott offers general praise, but also a caution: 'it might be well to call attention to the danger that lies in the frequent use of the terms "dramatic," and "drama" ' (p 63), since the *CT* is not, in fact, a drama.

318 Kleinstück, Johannes Walter. *Chaucers Stellung in der Mittelalterlichen Literatur*. Hamburg: Cram, de Gruyter, 1956. Britannica et Americana (English Seminar of the University of Hamburg), Neue Folge, Band 1.
In what is said to be a slightly revised version of his 1954 thesis, Kleinstück presents European analogues to several *GP* passages, including parts of the descriptions of the Knight, Squire, Prioress, Friar, and Summoner. Provençal as well as the more common French examples of the general literary tradition are included.

319 Knapp, Daniel. 'The Relyk of a Seint: A Gloss on Chaucer's Pilgrimage.' *ELH*, 39 (1972), 1–26.
Although Chaucer's narrator seems to be undertaking the Canterbury pilgrimage for the first time, along with the other pilgrims, presumably Chaucer himself knew what they would find at St Thomas's shrine (cf lines 16–18) if they were to arrive there. (The *Peregrinatio Religionis Ergo* of Erasmus, which describes the shrine early in the sixteenth century, should be added to other historical sources that record its appearance.) We need to ask how Chaucer would have felt about some of the more grotesque aspects of the customary climax to the Canterbury pilgrimage—including venerating and kissing relics, among them Becket's hair breeches (cf the Host's remarks to

the Pardoner about breeches, after the *PardT*). In addition, Chaucer must have noted the contrast between the wealth displayed at Becket's shrine and the Christian ideals of poverty and avoidance of display. Thus the end-point of the Canterbury journey is in substantial thematic contrast to the goal of the spiritual journey. Despite the stated *GP* plan to travel to Canterbury, 'there seems to me very little doubt that Chaucer never intended to end his pilgrimage at Canterbury, and may well have never intended even to let his pilgrims approach the shrine too closely or linger there to venerate the relics of the Saint' (p 25). Arrival at the shrine could not be a climactic moment of piety or grandeur when—presented with Becket's breeches—we are likely to remember the Host's comment to the Pardoner, or Absolon's kiss, or sick Thomas's gift to the friar. 'Better never to arrive at all, than to arrive like that' (p 26). However, Chaucer is not to be regarded as a heretic or a reformer, but simply as having 'the kind of observant, independent, thoughtful mind' (p 20) that we associate with him in other contexts.

320 Knight, Stephen. 'Chaucer — a Modern Writer?' *Balcony*, 2 (1965), 37–43. Under the influence of the fourteenth-century philosophical shift from Realism (not to be equated with modern realism or other modern literary terms) to Nominalism, Chaucer 'starts to abandon the medieval method of presenting characters as being each an example of a type, and begins to show us characters who are single and individual' (p 37). Philosophical Realism implied that to understand a person it was more important to know the type to which he belonged, 'the universal ideas which were in him' (p 40), than to perceive his physical appearance or behavioral idiosyncracies. Nominalism, however, which shifted the emphasis towards sense-impressions rather than universal ideas, encouraged a writer to concentrate on individualized traits. Chaucer's characterization in *GP* shows a mixture of traditional type-characters who are not physically visualized — the idealized figures of the Knight, the Parson, and the Plowman — along with a more modern treatment of the villainous characters as 'naturalistic symbols' (p 42), ie, as individuals whose physical details make them wholly credible and to whom 'we instantly feel a reaction' (p 41).

321 ——. *The Poetry of the Canterbury Tales.* Sydney: Angus and Robertson, 1973.
Knight examines such aspects of Chaucerian poetics as diction, syntax, word-order, enjambment, metrical features, rhetoric, levels of style, and imagery. The chapter 'The General Prologue' (pp 3–18) analyzes the springtime opening (lines 1–18); in its last couplet, with its *riche* rhyme, the passage's 'two themes,' which are 'the rich beauty of the world and man's rational movement towards holiness, are brought together' (p 6). The variations of style in the individual portraits contribute to characterization.

Throughout *GP* 'Chaucer never lets his style fall into a rut; the poetry, as much as the wit, is mobile and supple and even here, when he is arranging the mechanics of the pilgrimage, the style remains varied and interesting' (p 18). Chaucer's 'poetic modulation' avoids boredom and 'often actually suggests to us what the poet wants us to think or feel' (p 18).

322 ——. *Rymyng Craftily: Meaning in Chaucer's Poetry*. Sydney, Australia, and London: Angus and Robertson, 1973.
Although *GP* itself is not analyzed, the appendix (pp 236–42) on the Figures of Style offers a clarification of rhetorical terms — from *adjunctio* to *transitio* — sometimes used in analyses of *GP*'s indebtedness to the medieval rhetorical traditions.

323 Knowles, David. *Thomas Becket*. London: A.&C. Black, 1970; Stanford: Stanford University Press, 1971.
This detailed critical biography of Becket provides background information on his life and on his conflict with King Henry II. The book does not deal with the development of Becket's legend in later centuries, or with the traditions of the Canterbury pilgrimage to his shrine.

324 Koellreutter, Maria. *Das Privatleben in England nach den Dichtungen von Chaucer, Gower, und Langland*. University of Zürich Dissertation. 1908. Dir. Th. Vetter. Published Halle: Ehrhardt Karras, 1908.
Private life is considered under such categories as housing or accommodations, clothing, family living, meals, etc; examples drawn from *GP* are briefly commented upon.

325 Kohl, Stephan. *Wissenschaft und Dichtung bei Chaucer: Dargestellt hauptsächlich am Beispiel der Medizin*. Giessen University Dissertation, 1972. Published Frankfurt am Main: Akademische Verlagsgesellschaft, 1973. Studienreihe Humanitas, Studien zur Anglistik.
Kohl assesses Chaucer's knowledge of science and his attitudes towards it, concentrating on medicine. Chaucer's use of medical information suggests moral values, for his details about the pilgrims' physiognomy, diet, and diseases reflect moral conditions and coincide with other information given about the pilgrims ('Die moralische Bedeutung der medizinischen Beschreibung stimmt stets mit den Informationen überein, die in anderer Form über die Charaktere gegeben werden,' p 371). The *GP* portraits of the pilgrims to whom Chaucer gave medical traits are examined. Their descriptions show a moral realism that differentiates itself from naturalism because of its structured surface, and differentiates itself from allegory because of its realistic surface ('Dieser "moralische Realismus" unterscheidet sich durch die *gestaltete* Oberfläche des Lebens von einer naturalistischen

Schreibweise, durch die Zeichnung einer "realistischen" Oberfläche von allegorischer Einkleidung,' pp 327–28). Citations from other texts elucidate the moral connotations of the realistic physical details used here. Chaucer's interest in medicine was not that of a scientist, but that of a poet who strove for 'realism' ('Chaucers Interesse an der Medizin war nicht das des Wissenschaftlers, sondern das des Dichters, der sich um "Realismus" bemühte,' p 377).

326 Kökeritz, Helge. 'Rhetorical Word-Play in Chaucer.' *PMLA*, 69 (1954), 937–52.

Three kinds of word-play known to medieval writers are discussed: 1) *traductio*, or 'juggling homonyms or multiple meanings of the same word' (p 940); 2) *adnominatio*, or 'reproducing almost the same word or name' while 'changing only its quantity' or a letter or two (p 940); and 3) *significatio*, or playing on meanings in a way corresponding to 'our double-entendre' (p 941). There is some confusion in terminology among the rhetoricians. Word-play of these types was fashionable in the French poetry that Chaucer used as his models. The rhymes of lines 17–18, 745–46, and 319–20 are examples of *rime riche*, a variety of *traductio*; the word-play on *philosophre* (line 297) is a *significatio*.

327 Korten, Hertha. *Chaucers literarische Beziehungen zu Boccaccio: Die künstlerische Konzeption der Canterbury Tales und das Lolliusproblem*. Englisches Seminar der Universität Rostock, Akademische Preisschrift, 1919. Rostock: Hinstorff, 1920.

Korten examines the resemblances between *GP* (and other parts of the *CT* framework) and Boccaccio's plan for the *Decameron*, reviewing previous work and concluding that Chaucer did use the *Decameron*: Chaucer's masterpiece shows his debt to Boccaccio. In a critique of Morsbach (**381**) and Tatlock (**471**), Korten finds Morsbach's argument to be essentially on the right track, but not Tatlock's ('Morsbachs Artikel, wenn auch methodisch nicht überzeugend, doch sachlich auf dem rechten Wege war, während Tatlock's Abhandlung methodisch wohl fundiert, in dem sachlichen Ziel, der Widerlegung von Morsbachs Ergebnis, trotzdem sich nicht behaupten konnte,' pp 46–47).

328 Laguardia, Eric. 'Figural Imitation in English Renaissance Poetry.' In *Actes du IVe Congrès de l'Association Internationale de Littérature Comparée, Fribourg 1964*. Ed. François Jost. The Hague: Mouton, 1966. Pp 844–54.

GP shows a 'double perspective on history,' facing 'backwards by means of the Knight and Squire into the chivalric world in which a vast formalism dictates and therefore precedes experience; backwards to a certain extent into the absolute design of the Christian myth through the ecclesiastical figures ... and forward by means of secular figures such as the Wife of Bath for whom experience certainly precedes absolutes' (pp 846–7).

329 Lanham, Richard A. 'Game, Play, and High Seriousness in Chaucer's Poetry.' *ES*, 48 (1967), 1–24.

It is appropriate to interpret the *Canterbury Tales* in light of modern games-theory. Chaucer saw 'society as a game and us as merely players,' and thus he 'could not hold human personality with that ultimate seriousness Arnold required' (p 24). The journey is both pilgrimage and game; the pilgrims tend to forget pilgrimage in favor of game; we also 'are meant to vacillate between the two' (p 10). Chaucer 'enforces a ground rule, not of levity only, but of a certain kind of both levity and seriousness, by having an innkeeper appoint himself games-master' (p 10).

330 Lawler, Traugott. *The One and the Many in The Canterbury Tales*. Hamden, CT: Archon, 1980.

Lawler studies the complementary relationship 'between unity and diversity, oneness and multiplicity,' in *CT* (p 15). This relationship is evident in the description of the pilgrims as *a compaignye of sondry folk* (lines 24–25), which calls attention both to the group, and to the fact that this group consists of a collection of individuals. The pilgrims belong to several kinds of groupings, as well as to this *compaignye*; 'as we read the General Prologue we are forced to notice how many general, unifying categories lie just beneath their individuality: not only profession but sex, social class, family, lay or religious status, wealth, dress, and many others' (p 15). In the opening sentence of *GP*, despite the overall movement from general to particular, 'the chief stress is on the general, on common, unifying factors', and 'the syntax holds the diversity within a larger unity' (pp 16–17). As for the specific details that follow in the portraits, such as details about clothing, 'generality lurks even here,' for much of the clothing points towards the pilgrims' profession or status (p 34). Chaucer did not need to give so much emphasis to profession, but 'the profession dominates each description' and finally 'this emphasis ... obliterates rather than makes distinctions' (p 35). See also 1184 and 1369.

331 Lawlor, John. *Chaucer*. London: Hutchinson, 1968; New York: Harper, 1969.

In the chapter 'Tales and Tellers: The Canterbury Tales (1)' (1969, pp 105–39), Lawlor questions the 'dramatic theory' (see Kittredge, 317, and Lumiansky, 348): 'But should we not ask whether the whole impulse to link the narrator of a tale with the Pilgrim characterised in the General Prologue, and to see the characterisation as extended and deepened in the end-link and narrator's prologue, is of any real utility?' (p 137). The Wife's and Pardoner's tales 'unarguably complement and extend what was said of their narrators in the General Prologue' (pp 138–9). However, in other cases the usefulness of this approach is 'minimal' (p 137).

332 Lawrence, William Witherle. *Chaucer and the Canterbury Tales.* New York: Columbia University Press, 1950; London: Oxford University Press, 1950. Rpt 1951. Rpt New York: Biblo and Tannen, 1969.
In the chapter 'Realism and Artifice' (1950, pp 24–63), Lawrence cautions that the realism of *CT* 'must not deceive us into forgetting its artificial elements' (p 41). We need not seek a specific literary source for Chaucer's basic plan, since pilgrimage, accompanied by storytelling, was common enough in Chaucer's time. However, literary sources and conventions are indeed present in *GP*, beginning with the first lines: 'the springtime opening was a hackneyed device' (p 41). We are asked to accept many conventions, such as people speaking in verse, that are unrealistic outside literary traditions. The pilgrims do not represent the whole of society, but were selected according to Chaucer's 'desires as an artist, to exhibit varied and picturesque types, suitable for the telling of his tales' (p 49). The aim in *GP* is to present 'an effect of unstudied realism' (p 57). However, the pilgrims are not based on historical models. The descriptions '*seem* to be portraits, but actually are not' (p 50); they are composites of various ingredients rather than pictures drawn from life.

333 Leana, Joyce Fitzpatrick. *Chaucer the Word-Master: the House of Fame and the Canterbury Tales.* Columbia University Dissertation. 1974. See also *DAI*, 35 (1974), 1049-A.
Leana examines Chaucer's relationship to the 'ecphrastic tradition' and sees *GP* as an example of the 'figured wall' device (p 61). In *GP*, as in *HF*, where the 'figured wall' also occurs, we find 'synasthetic aspects and the spectator's alternation of the roles of artist/non-artist' (p 61). The distance between narrator and poet while the portraits are being presented is also considered for the *Divine Comedy* and the *Romance of the Rose*; in addition, the tradition involves Ovid's *Metamorphoses*.

334 Legouis, Émile. *Geoffroy Chaucer.* Paris: Bloud, 1910. Les Grands écrivains étrangers. English Translation *Geoffrey Chaucer.* Trans. L. Lailavoix. London: Dent, 1913; NY: Dutton, 1913; rpt New York: Russell & Russell, 1961.
This general book on Chaucer includes extensive comments on *GP*. The pilgrims' ideas — conventional enough as ideas — are made to emanate from people of different temperaments and to demonstrate the prejudices of different classes or ways of life. Therefore, familiar ideas are given a new

and dramatic function ('emploi dramatique,' 1910, p 137). The pilgrims are treated in different ways. Some are described primarily in terms of their professions. Others are given a symbolic significance — the Squire signifies Youth, the Plowman Charity, the Wife the essential satiric view of Woman. Their relationships to the contemporary world also differ. The Knight, rather than seeming up-to-date, might just as well have followed St Louis on crusade, and the Oxford Clerk is only intermittently part of his contemporary world. In the treatment of the flawed clerics, a distant glimmer of Renaissance or Reformation attitudes can be discerned ('une aube incertaine de Renaissance ou de Réforme, on ne sait au juste, blanchit très loin à l'horizon,' p 143). The tales are designed to supplement the *GP* portraits ('les contes ont été pour Chaucer un moyen d'achever le portrait de ses pèlerins,' p 234). The art of portraiture involves a pretended negligence, an appearance of simplicity. Chaucer as narrator adopts the guise of a simple chronicler, giving the effect of a direct transcription of ordinary life ('une transcription directe de la vie commune,' p 138).

The English translation by Lailavoix replaces Legouis's preface with a longer preface summarizing Chaucer's reception in France. It also adds an appendix of Legouis's translations of Chaucer selections into French and an index. Cf **158**.

- Review by G.C. Macaulay, *MLR*, 6 (1911), 532–33: Legouis 'does full justice to Chaucer as the first dramatic realist in the literature of modern Europe, rightly regarding his portraiture of the pilgrims in the Prologue and in the conversations upon the road, and his comic presentation of contemporary life ... as the most original production of his genius' (p 532).

- Review by Martha Hale Shackford, *MLN*, 27 (1912), 119–21: 'Unquestionably this is the best general study of Chaucer yet published' (p 119); 'especially in the discussion of the *Prologue* to *The Canterbury Tales* M. Legouis has made a most important contribution' (p 120).

335 Leitch, L.M. 'Sentence and Solaas: The Function of the Hosts in the *Canterbury Tales*.' *ChauR*, 17 (1982–1983), 5–20.
Chaucer depicts the artist as being responsible to the audience. In *GP* he shows an awareness of the audience by his 'abundance of direct addresses to his readers' and his 'marked concern for the reader's approval' (p 7). At the end of *CT* the Parson replaces Harry Bailly as host. 'The antithetical natures of these two figures are clearly outlined in the *General Prologue*' (p 16). However, in *GP* there is also 'a single image which effectively links the two figures,' the image of the flock of people gathered together by a guide (p 17); see lines 822–24, 495–96, and 503–4. Similarly, at the end of

CT the Tabard Inn of *GP*, with its atmosphere of festivity (cf *solaas*), is replaced by the celestial city (cf *sentence*).

336 Lenaghan, R.T. 'Chaucer's *General Prologue* as History and Literature.' *CSSH*, 12 (1970), 73–82.
Both *GP* and a sociologist's model of society are 'representative fictions' (p 73). The predominant pattern of organization in *GP* is not the traditional three estates, but, instead, occupational labels. The pilgrims are perceived according to whether they derive their income from 1) land, or 2) service, trade, manufacture, etc. The pilgrims in the second category tend to be competitive and insecure, but at least at the lower social levels they have 'a free, sometimes boisterous conviviality' (p 78). The Friar, Summoner, and Pardoner live 'by their wits under economic pressure' (p 78) and are thus grouped with pilgrims such as the Shipman, Miller, and Manciple. 'The basic fact of life in the society of the *General Prologue* is economic struggle' (p 79). Those who escape this struggle are primarily the land-related wealthy, and a division of society into 'hustlers and gentlemen' results (p 80). The narrator's own position may be meant to be the same as Chaucer's, that of a civil servant to whom the landholders may have looked far more secure than he himself felt; 'both the distortion and the accuracy of Chaucer's social description are plausible for a civil servant' (p 82). The distortion is primarily the implication given that landholders were neither sexually active nor economically competitive.

337 Leyerle, John. 'Thematic Interlace in *The Canterbury Tales*.' *E&S*, New Series 29 (1976), 107–21.
Leyerle argues that the structure of *CT* involves not simply the linear sequence suggested by Harry Bailly at the end of *GP*, with pilgrims telling their tales one after the other; but instead a pattern of complex interlace, in which four thematic threads 'all have their beginnings in the General Prologue and their endings in the Parson's Tale' (p 109). The *Forma Praedicandi* of Robert Basevorn describes techniques belonging to 'the tradition of the medieval poetics of interlace' (p 110). In *CT* the four thematic threads concern (1) sexuality, including courtship, marriage, adultery; (2) food and drink; (3) gold, money, wealth; and (4) death. These themes, furthermore, are related to each other—for example, the plan of the Host, that the pilgrims should return to the Tabard and pay for another supper there, connects the theme of food and drink to that of expenditure. 'The labyrinthine interconnections of threads defy full elucidation, so complex are the contrasts, juxtapositions, parallels, and tensions' (p 121). On the Host, see **1370**; on the Plowman, **1200**.

338 Lindahl, Carl. *Chaucer the Storyteller: Folkloric Patterns in the Canterbury Tales.* Indiana University Dissertation. 1980. See also *DAI*, 41 (1981), 5204-A.

Chaucer's artistic background has usually been sought in literary traditions. However, in addition to elite traditions he also participated in folk culture. *CT* 'is a folkloric document in two senses: first, as a realistic depiction of storytelling in the Middle Ages; second, as a poem which — whether or not it was read aloud — was strongly influenced by certain rules of folk oral delivery' (p 3). While the elite culture may be shared impersonally, folk culture depends upon direct communication. The Miller's 'talent for smashing doors with his head' (p 20; see lines 550–51) offers an example of Chaucer's reference to folk entertainments; an antecedent literary parallel occurs in the romance of *Havelock*, but it would be absurd to assume that Chaucer 'based his description of the Miller on a silent reading of Havelock' when all 'he had to do was watch and listen to find his models' (p 20). The pilgrimage setting in *GP* 'is not only suitable, but ideal, for the type of entertainment described by Chaucer' (p 35).

339 Linthicum, M. Channing. ' "Faldyng" and "Medlee." ' *JEGP*, 34 (1935), 39–41.

Chaucer's comments on the pilgrims' clothing show 'the wide range of woolen and worsted cloths then worn in England' (p 39). The scarlet cloth of the Wife was the most expensive kind. The Plowman must have worn russet or blanket, since a statute of 1364 limited plowmen to those types of cloth. The Shipman's *faldyng* (line 391) was 'a soft, woolen, colored cloth' (p 39). The Man of Law's *medlee* (line 328) was 'a cloth made of wools which had been dyed and mingled before being spun into yarn' (p 40). Evidently it was not used by a class above that of the knights, and was usually trimmed with one of the less expensive kinds of fur. Contemporary documents referring to falding and medley are cited.

340 Loomis, Roger S. 'Was Chaucer a Laodicean?' In *Essays and Studies in Honor of Carleton Brown*. New York: New York University Press, 1940; London: Humphrey Milford, 1940. Pp 129–48. Rpt Freeport, NY: Books for Libraries Press, 1969. Rpt in *Chaucer Criticism*, 1, ed. Richard J. Schoeck and Jerome Taylor (Notre Dame and London: University of Notre Dame Press, 1960; 10th printing 1978), pp 291–310.

Loomis argues that in *GP* 'the scales are weighted in favor of the supporters of Wyclif and against the classes who opposed him' (1940, p 138). Details in the portraits of the idealized Knight, Clerk, and Parson are cited to support this view. [On the Knight, see **712** in reply.] *GP* contains only 'three wholly ideal portraits; of these one is plainly sketched in accordance with Wyclif's ideas, and the other two represent members of classes known to be sympathetic to his program' (p 145). Similarly, the three pilgrims who are made 'morally repulsive' (p 145) — the Friar, Summoner, and Pardoner — represent groups or practices that the Wycliffite literature condemned. Chaucer was 'no martyr for any cause' (p 148), but there cannot be 'much doubt as to where Chaucer's sympathies lay' (p 146).

341 Looten, C. 'Les portraits de Chaucer: leurs origines.' *RLC*, 7 (1927), 397–438.
Realistic, ideal, and symbolic portrait-traditions in classical and medieval literature are reviewed. Boethius, Martianus Capella, Alain de Lille, Guillaume de Lorris, Jean de Meun, Ordericus Vitalis, Benoît de Sainte-Maure, and Chrétien de Troyes are among the writers whose portraiture is examined. Chaucer may have been influenced, in devising the portraits of *GP*, by the continental realistic tradition. However, from the time it occurred to him to infuse his portraits with traits drawn from life, he became a master of portraiture ('A partir du jour où Chaucer eut l'idée d'infuser dans ses portraits les éléments vécus que lui fournissait une pénétrante et assidue observation de ses semblables, il fut le maître que nous admirons à si juste titre,' p 434). The portraits are life-like because they contain nothing conventional, for Chaucer sees, first and exclusively, the individual — such a knight, such a monk, such a prioress, etc, in particular ('Si les portraits des *Tales* sont vivants, c'est justement qu'ils n'ont rien de conventionnel ... Chaucer voit d'abord et exclusivement l'individu, tel chevalier, tel moine, telle prieure, etc, en particulier,' p 435). If he also captures the general type, it is unconsciously, because through grasping the individual he touches upon the indelible basis of the species ('s'il atteint au type et s'élève au général, c'est inconsciemment, parce qu'à force de s'attacher à l'individu il touche au fond indélébile de l'espèce,' p 436). Art begins by revealing the individual ('l'art commence à la révélation de l'individu,' p 436), while generalities are the province of philosophy, and Chaucer's genius consists in having seized upon this truth ('la génie en Chaucer est d'avoir saisi cette vérité,' p 436). This article is incorporated in Looten's book (342), pp 98–157.

342 ——. *Chaucer, ses modèles, ses sources, sa religion.* Lille: Économat des facultés catholiques, 1931. Mémoires et travaux publiés par des professeurs des facultés catholiques de Lille, 38.
In the chapter 'Chaucer et Boccace (Suite)' (pp 73–98), Looten reviews the question of *GP*'s debt to the *Decameron*, finding that the analogies constitute positive evidence ('les analogies entre les deux oeuvres ... sont un fait positif, devant lequel toute hypothèse adverse pâlit,' p 81). Chaucer's handling of the framework is superior to Boccaccio's, but he might not have handled it so well if he had not known the *Decameron*. The chapter 'Origine

des Portraits et des Descriptions' (pp 98–157) incorporates Looten's article (**341**). On the Parson, see **1185**.

343 Lowes, John Livingston. 'Illustrations of Chaucer, Drawn Chiefly from Deschamps.' *RomR*, 2 (1911), 113–28.
Several passages in Deschamps' *Miroir de Mariage* show similarities to passages in *GP*, though Lowes does not claim that the *Miroir* is necessarily Chaucer's source. The Friar's rounded gown (line 263) may have some relation to garments mentioned in the *Miroir*; the Wife's *wandring by the weye* (line 476) 'receives abundant illustration' in the *Miroir* (p 120); the Clerk's having spent a long time in the study of logic, without receiving a benefice, resembles a passage in the *Miroir* on the lengthy and expensive clerical education of sons.

344 ——. 'Chaucer and the Seven Deadly Sins.' *PMLA*, 30 (1915), 237–371.
Criticizing Tupper's concept of an architectonic use of the Seven Deadly Sins (see **482**), Lowes argues that Tupper has misinterpreted the medieval understanding of the Sins' taxonomy. No fixed system but instead 'a maze' of subcategories (p 250) existed. Discord, for example, is listed in different sources as a branch of Pride, Wrath, Envy, Avarice, and Gluttony. Thus even if a pilgrim can be proven to belong to one such subcategory, an assignment to one of the Seven Sins is not thereby determined. Virtually any instance of sin (or its antitype, virtue) 'could qualify as an *exemplum* of some branch or other of the Seven Deadly Sins' (p 258), so that unless an explicit label is given, the medieval audience would not have known which category the author meant to illustrate. Furthermore, at this point in his development as a writer Chaucer would not have 'reverted from the glorious liberty he had attained, to the more or less schematic tendencies of his earlier period' (p 370).

345 ——. *Convention and Revolt in Poetry.* London: Constable, 1919. 2nd ed. 1930. Rpt 1938.
Chaucer's originality involves the adaptation of existing literary conventions. The springtime opening of *GP* gives 'a spirited turn to a jaded commonplace' to produce a passage that is 'flawlessly organic' (1938, p 76). The portrait of the Prioress, which depicts 'the engagingly imperfect submergence of the feminine in the ecclesiastical,' was accomplished by 'a daring yet consummately adroit transference of conventions' (p 41). *Simple* and *coy*, as stock terms of courtly poetry, signal in this context the 'clash between the woman and the nun' (p 42) — as do the passage on the Prioress's manners, which is taken from the *Roman de la Rose*, and the passage on her physical appearance, which includes the standard details for describing a courtly lady. A final transfer of convention in her

portrait is her motto. The depiction of the Prioress uses 'the hovering of the conventions between their two environments' as a means of conveying 'the wavering of the Prioress's spirit between her two worlds' (p 45). (For Lowes's more detailed analysis of the Prioress's portrait, see **814**.)

346 ——. *Geoffrey Chaucer: Lectures Delivered in 1932 on the William J. Cooper Foundation in Swarthmore College*. Oxford: Clarendon Press, 1934. Rpt 1944, 1946, 1949, 1961, 1964. American edition, with title *Geoffrey Chaucer and the Development of His Genius*, Boston: Houghton-Mifflin, 1934. Rpt Bloomington, IN: Indiana University Press, 1958.

Parts of the chapter 'The Human Comedy' (1964, pp 160–99) relate most directly to *GP*, though occasional comments on the portraits appear elsewhere. *GP* is 'a new thing in the world' (p 161). Chaucer knew the portraits of Benoît's *Roman de Troie*, but those 'follow in benumbing iteration a set formula' (p 160), while *GP* is a 'singularly *modern* thing' (p 160) in its ability to convey 'the emergence of a character, step by step, through a succession of concrete details which fall in the end into perspective and reveal a person' (p 161). Chaucer perhaps had living persons in mind when creating the portraits, but he goes beyond realism to 'strike the delicate balance between the *character*, in the technical, Theophrastian sense of the word, and the *individual* — a balance which preserves at once the typical qualities of the one and the human idiosyncracies of the other' (p 163). For example, though Chaucer may have had John Hawley in mind when he depicted the Shipman, 'the Shipman assuredly has ceased to be John Hawley. He is the incarnation of the type to which John Hawley, and a score of his congeners, belonged' (p 163). In addition to being a prologue, *GP* is an integral section of the whole work, which was conceived as a drama, with the Host as Chaucer's chorus. 'The Prologue gives us the *tellers* — statically, in their potentialities,' while as *CT* continues 'the static becomes dynamic' (p 163).

347 Loxton, Howard. *Pilgrimage to Canterbury*. London: David Charles, 1978; Totowa, NJ: Rowman and Littlefield, 1978.

Becket's life and martyrdom are described, and information is provided on Canterbury Cathedral, the surrounding town, medieval sites that Chaucer's pilgrims might have seen on the roads from London to Canterbury, etc.

348 Lumiansky, R.M. *Of Sondry Folk: The Dramatic Principle in the Canterbury Tales*. Austin: University of Texas Press, 1955.

Lumiansky presents detailed examinations of each pilgrim who tells a story, developing the viewpoint of Kittredge (**317**) that the structure of *CT* is dramatic. The first sentence of *GP* 'skillfully introduces the human element into the idea of a pilgrimage' (p 18). In lines 19–27, Chaucer 'rapidly gives here the answers to all the necessary questions' (p 19) and continues the combination of motives by mentioning the narrator's devout heart, but also depicting his interest in social fellowship. In the portraits, Chaucer uses two 'technical devices' (p 20): a conversational style and 'a combination of the expected and the unexpected' (p 22). With the Host's speech (the first words spoken by someone other than the narrator) 'the curtain rises, and the action begins' (p 25). The company is at first indifferent or even somewhat suspicious of him. However, after his second speech, finding that 'his idea involves neither annoyance nor expense' (p 26), the pilgrims 'now bend over backwards in agreeing to Harry's proposal and to his leadership of the pilgrimage' (p 26). After the individual chapters, Lumiansky divides the pilgrims into: 1) a group in which there is a simple suiting of tale to teller; 2) a group in which this suitability is accompanied by 'an externally motivated dramatic situation' (p 247); and 3) a group in which the first two factors are accompanied by 'internally motivated and extended self-revelation of which the teller is not fully aware' (p 248). For comments on specific pilgrims, see **695, 891, 967, 1024, 1098, 1371.**

- Review by William W. Lawrence, *Spec*, 31 (1956), 179–82: 'The general procedure in the volume before us, if not too far pressed, seems entirely justifiable' (p 180).

- Review by John Lawlor, *RES*, New Series 8 (1957), 181–83: Lawlor finds some of Lumiansky's 'suppositions' to be 'merely fanciful,' comments on 'the disregard of the text,' and says that 'curious judgements result' from Lumiansky's applications of the pilgrims' characters, as he has determined them, to their tales (p 182). Cf **331.**

349 ——. 'Benoit's Portraits and Chaucer's General Prologue.' *JEGP*, 55 (1956), 431–38.

The *Roman de Troie* of Benoît de Sainte-Maure includes a collection of thirty-one portraits. The literary techniques there may have suggested to Chaucer his own treatment of the portraits in *GP*. The similarities include 'individualizing by a combination of physical and temperamental traits; structural grouping of portraits; inclusion within a sketch of material which matches later behavior by the personage; personal comment by the Narrator; and some similarity in detail between [Benoit's] Hector-Troilus and [Chaucer's] Knight-Squire pairs' (p 438). There is also an overall structural similarity since both collections of portraits consist of two main sections that are framed by an initial statement of the plan by the narrator, a transitional statement between the two sections, and a summarizing remark at the end. Lumiansky does not assert, however, that Benoit's portraits are a full model for Chaucer's, since there are also differences: all of Benoit's portraits describe people of one station, he does not include their past experiences, and his narrator's comments do not show 'the realistic prejudice' (p 438) of Chaucer's narrator. Nevertheless, it is likely that Chaucer was indebted to Benoît and that these differences are the result of Chaucer's 'own genius' (p 438).

350 ——. 'Chaucer's Retraction and the Degree of Completeness of the *Canterbury Tales.*' *TSE*, 6 (1956), 5–13.
Several of the pilgrims presented in *GP* lack tales. Lumiansky suggests that 'since the assignment of tales in the body of the book is primarily a matter of suiting the story and a given Pilgrim's individualizing traits, we can easily see why Chaucer may have postponed and finally avoided providing stories' for the Guildsmen, the Yeoman, and the Plowman, all of whom are presented as 'type sketches' without individualization. Those pilgrims would have presented Chaucer 'with the most difficult problem in assignment of suitable narratives' (p 10). Chaucer's plan may have evolved from the original arrangement that each pilgrim would tell four tales, to a later understanding that each rank or *degree* in the company — not necessarily each pilgrim — would have a tale. 'Chaucer probably intended to revise the Host's speech in the General Prologue so as to remove mention of the four tales by each Pilgrim and of a return trip, and the Knight's comment so as to do away with the reference to the final supper' (pp 10–11). Alternatively, Chaucer may have intended the *GP* scheme as a reflection of the Host's over-ambitious nature, later to be deflated, rather than as a guide to his own plans for the storytelling process.

351 Lyons, Clifford P. *A Study on the Framework of The Canterbury Tales.* John Hopkins University Dissertation. 1933 (?).
Not seen; listed in James F. Willard, *Progress of Medieval Studies in the United States of America*, 11 (1933), 53.

352 McCabe, John Donald. *The Comic in the Poetry of Chaucer: Congruence of 'Sentence' and 'Solaas.'* University of Minnesota Dissertation. 1968. See also *DAI*, 30 (1969), 285-A.
McCabe offers occasional comments on *GP*. The allusion in lines 741–42, on words being cousin to the deed, 'is clearly to the *Consolation of Philosophy* (Bk. III, Pr. 12),' where Lady Philosophy refers to Plato's statement as part of a discourse on God's governance of the world (p 64). This passage suggests that 'the questions that Chaucer confronts within the *Canterbury Tales* and in his other poems are similar to the questions that Lady Philosophy considers in the *Consolation*' (p 65). The pilgrims gathered together (line 824) are a community that 'manifests the essential orientation of creation towards a final end' (p 66). Between men who show

excesses of game and earnest there exists the *eutrapolos*, the moderate and balanced man whose 'characteristic virtue is liberality' (p 118). The Miller, 'unable to evince a proper reverence or seriousness about anything' (p 119), represents the excess of play, the Reeve represents its deficiency, and the Knight the balanced man. According to the *Tractatus coislinianus*, 'the characters of comedy are the buffoon, the imposter and the ironical man' (p 121). Fragment A (I) of *CT*, with its tales of the Knight, Miller, and Reeve, seems to reflect that principle, except that the *GP* portrait of the Knight does not portray in him 'an ironic self-reflection upon the limitations of the values that he upholds' (p 121), for he takes his chivalric values fully seriously. 'To the extent that the Knight falls short of the demanding self-knowledge of humility, we may question to what extent he exemplifies the virtues of the Christian *eutrapolos*' (p 122), but in all other respects he illustrates the liberal, well-bred, balanced individual. On the narrator, see 630.

353 McGrady, Donald. 'Chaucer and the *Decameron* Reconsidered.' *ChauR*, 12 (1977–1978), 1–26.
McGrady reviews previous work on this topic, especially pointing out what he sees as weaknesses in the studies of Cummings (206) and Farnham (240). His evidence shows that 'the *Decameron* was widely imitated in Italy, and certainly well known in other countries, during Chaucer's lifetime, despite declarations to the contrary' (p 7). McGrady argues for 'the direct indebtedness' of the *CT* to the *Decameron* in several of the tales, though the framework shows 'only a secondary use of Boccaccio' (p 14).

354 ——. 'Were Sercambi's *Novelle* Known from the Middle Ages On?' *Italica*, 57 (1980), 3–18.
There are notable similarities between Sercambi's narrative frame in the *Novelle* and Chaucer's in the *GP*. It seems reasonable to suppose that Sercambi's work circulated in manuscript form. Chaucer 'could have read and copied parts of the 1374 *Novelliero*' — an early version of the *Novelle* — 'as early as his trip to Italy in 1378 and imitated it when writing the stories of his own pilgrims' (p 14).

355 McKenna, Sister M. Bonaventure. 'Liturgy of the Canterbury Tales.' *CER*, 35 (1937), 474–80.
Sister McKenna briefly points out the references to church observances in lines 17, 158–59, 218–19, 377, 450, 709, 710.

356 McPeek, James A.S. 'Chaucer and the Goliards.' *Spec*, 26 (1951), 332–36.
Chaucer may have known two works from the tradition of Goliardic satire: the *Apocalypsis Goliae Episcopi* and *Magister Golias de quodam abbate*.

'Both satires are remarkable for their uncompromising condemnation of corruption in the clergy' (p 332). The sketch of the archdeacon in the *Apocalypsis* resembles the portrait of the Summoner in *GP*, while a parson depicted in the *Apocalypsis* 'is the antithesis of Chaucer's idealized figure' of the Parson in *GP* (p 334). The abbot in *Magister Golias*, who becomes indignant if his food is not well spiced, shares that trait with Chaucer's Franklin (see lines 351–52); furthermore, the eyes of that abbot are compared to planets, as the eyes of Chaucer's Friar are compared to stars (lines 267–68). Thus these Goliardic satires may have suggested several characteristics that Chaucer used in *GP*—or, if a source-relationship cannot be proven, these satires serve at least as analogues.

357 Maclaine, Allan H. *The Student's Comprehensive Guide to The Canterbury Tales*. Great Neck, NY: Barron's Educational Series, 1964.
The chapter on *GP* (pp 11–42) provides one-sentence digests of critical studies, summaries of portraits (eg, a three-sentence summary of the Prioress's portrait, p 18), glosses for difficult words, and annotations of individual lines.

358 Malone, Kemp. 'Style and Structure in the Prologue to the *Canterbury Tales*.' *ELH*, 13 (1946), 38–45. Expanded in 359.
After beginning *GP* in the traditional 'high style,' with line 18 Chaucer shifts to the informal, personalized style, reinforced by the use of personal pronouns, that he prefers. An aspect of the informal style is its 'carelessness, its intentional failure to provide for everything' (p 44). Some 'disorder' is necessary to achieve the 'easy, conversational effect' (p 44). In addition, 'Chaucer was not the man to worry overmuch about loose ends' — such as the missing portrait of the Second Nun — or to always 'make things neat and tidy' (p 43). The *GP* portraits are structured in two parts. These parts are divided by lines 542–44, a passage that reassures the reader about 'how much more of this kind of thing he may expect before the story proper is resumed' (p 42). Within each part, Chaucer presents some of the pilgrims in groups — five groups in the longer first part, one in the second part. The Knight, Squire, and Yeoman form 'a household group' (p 42). The Prioress and her companions form another kind of household; she is accompanied by her priests because 'a dignitary of the prioress's importance and sex could hardly be represented as traveling alone' (p 42). The other groups in the first part are the Man of Law and the Franklin; the Guildsmen and their Cook; and the Parson and Plowman. No two groupings 'are exactly alike in method of linkage' (p 43). Their variety contributes to the overall effect.

359 ——. *Chapters on Chaucer*. Baltimore: John Hopkins Press, 1951; London: Oxford University Press, 1951. Portions rpt in *Discussions of the Canter-*

bury Tales, ed. Charles A. Owen, Jr. (Boston: Heath, 1961), pp 28–32.

GP is examined in 'The General Prologue' (pp 144–62) and 'The Canterbury Pilgrims' (pp 162–234). In addition to 'their status as pilgrims to the shrine of Thomas Becket,' the pilgrims share three characteristics: they are part of a fellowship, they are English, and they are commoners (p 163). In most cases there is only one example of any occupation, but the Prioress's group includes two nuns and three priests, while both a Guildsman and the Reeve are carpenters. Thus 'Chaucer's general scheme forbade duplication, but he felt free to depart from this scheme' (p 166). 'He was willing to be reasonably systematic, but not rigorously so,' and this 'easygoing technic' is characteristic of his art (p 166). The pilgrims do not represent their occupations in any average or ordinary way, having been made superlative 'for *literary* reasons' (p 167). Chaucer makes them too good to be true — and in so doing he is following the literary expectations of his day. The Knight, for example, is described and labeled as a perfect knight (not necessarily a perfect man). The other pilgrims' perfections also stay in or near 'the orbit of their respective occupations' (p 173) and to that extent they are in fact typical. Even the worldly clerics are not misfits in their professions, for their very success shows that they have chosen the right careers for their personalities: the Pardoner 'is the ideal pardoner, if one may speak of ideals in such a connection' (p 177). Nevertheless, the Friar and Pardoner are depicted as 'wicked, vicious clerics,' for whom 'there is no excuse, no saving grace' (p 185). Malone rejects the theory that the pilgrims are based on real-life models (see Manly, **362**), arguing that the pilgrims 'have no reality apart from the poem in which they appear' (p 186). He also rejects the theory that the tales exist in order to characterize the pilgrims (see Kittredge, **317**). The discussion here includes an expanded version of Malone, **358**, and an expanded version of Malone, **1372**.

359a ——. 'The Works of Chaucer.' In *Literary Masterpieces of the Western World*. Ed. Francis H. Horn. Baltimore: Johns Hopkins Press, 1953. Pp 107–25.

GP is briefly discussed in this general chapter on Chaucer. 'Nearly all the pilgrims are perfect examples of their kind, though in some cases the kind is bad. The pardoner, for instance, is a scoundrel, but the most plausible and successful scoundrel that ever sold pardons, and the monk is a perfect example of clerical worldliness....By using extreme examples [Chaucer] secured more interest, a greater dramatic quality, than would be possible with ordinary humdrum average–type figures' (p 118).

360 Mandel, Jerome. 'Other Voices in the "Canterbury Tales." ' *Crit*, 19 (1977), 338–49.

In addition to making artistic use of the voices of the narrator, at times in *GP* Chaucer presents the voice of one or another character, 'using that character's diction, syntax, and style, without acknowledging the fact in the usual way' (p 340). In lines 184–88, we hear the Monk's voice; in lines 225–32 and 246–47, we hear the Friar's; and in lines 500–6, we hear the Parson's. Chaucer read his poems aloud. In that circumstance 'no problems of voice occur' since the speaker's 'changes of tone or pitch or timbre' (p 348) can identify the different voices to be heard.

361 Manly, J.M. 'Chaucer and the Rhetoricians.' *PBA*, 12 (1926), 95–113. Also printed separately, London: Humphrey Milford, 1926. Wharton Lecture on English Poetry, 17. Rpt in *Chaucer Criticism, I*, ed. Richard Schoeck and Jerome Taylor (Notre Dame, IN: University of Notre Dame Press, 1960), pp 268–90.
Manly argues that 'Chaucer was familiar with the rhetorical theories of his time, that he had studied the text-books and carefully weighed the doctrines' (*PBA*, p 98). The concepts and authorities of medieval rhetoric are reviewed. The doctrine consists of three main divisions: '1) arrangement or organization; 2) amplification and abbreviation; 3) style and its ornaments' (p 99). Chaucer 'came more and more to make only a dramatic use of these rhetorical elements, that is, to put them into the mouths of his *dramatis personae* and to use only such as might fittingly be uttered by them' (p 110).

362 ——. *Some New Light on Chaucer: Lectures Delivered at the Lowell Institute.* New York: Holt, 1926; London: Bell, 1926. Rpt New York: Peter Smith, 1952.
227zIn this 'collection of suggestions of a more or less speculative character' (1926, p ix), Manly proposes historical individuals as models for some of the Canterbury pilgrims. Although the pilgrims certainly 'illustrate English life and manners,' they do not represent 'an exhaustive survey of fourteenth century society' (p 71). 'Chaucer's personal interests and prejudices' and his range of acquaintances — rather than a comprehensive social principle — may have determined the membership of the group (p 73). See, on the Host, **1373**; the Reeve and Miller, **1249**; the Friar, **935**; the Pardoner, **1317**; the Serjeant and Franklin, **1026**; the Shipman and Merchant, **1101**; the Prioress and her priest, **823**; the Wife, **1150**; and the Cook, **1090**. Other pilgrims too have individualizing traits suggesting that they were drawn from contemporary models 'who either belonged to Chaucer's circle of acquaintances or had chanced to catch his observant eye' (p 260). Cf **696** on the Knight.

• Review by H.S.V. Jones, *JEGP*, 27 (1928), 555–57: Jones characterizes the historical identifications of the pilgrims as 'wavering outlines of ingenious conjecture' (p 557).

- Review by James F. Royster, *MLN*, 42 (1927), 251–56: Royster commends Manly's caution in regarding his identifications as tentative and calls the use of the historical method 'sane and reserved' (p 255).

- See **1029**.

363 Mann, Jill. *Chaucer and Medieval Estates Satire: The Literature of Social Classes and the General Prologue to the Canterbury Tales*. New York and London: Cambridge University Press, 1973.

GP is an example of estates literature: 'the form of the estates genre and the form of the *Prologue* are one and the same' (p 4). The emphasis on the pilgrims' occupations serves to 'ensure our sense of the estate' to which they belong (p 10); 'the features of the Canterbury pilgrims are overwhelmingly those which were traditionally associated with their estates' (p 15). The Monk and Friar are associated with the anti-clerical tradition; the Parson, Plowman, and Clerk with estates ideals; the Serjeant of Law, Doctor of Physic, Merchant, and Guildsmen with professional types; the Knight, Squire, and Wife with the independent traditions of chivalry and anti-feminism; the Prioress and Summoner with descriptive traditions; and the Pardoner, Franklin, Miller, and Reeve with scientific concepts. The Cook, Shipman, Yeoman, and Manciple seem to be 'new creations' as types (p 168). Chaucer's use of the estates genre is not wholly conventional. Rather, it encourages us to perceive the pilgrims as individuals through the techniques of eliciting contrary responses, making us uncertain of the 'facts,' incorporating the pilgrims' personal experiences to prevent us from taking them as 'eternal abstractions,' and involving the pilgrims' own points of view (p 189). By omitting mention of the victims or effects of the pilgrims' actions, Chaucer leads us to see their behavior from their own viewpoints: the narrator 'constantly identifies with the pilgrim's point of view' (p 194). The ambiguities and uncertainties, the omission of the victim, and the mixed reactions 'add up to Chaucer's *consistent removal of the possibility of moral judgement*' (p 197). The result is a relativist ethic of this world; incompatible things are shown to coexist. Furthermore, *GP* 'proves to be a poem about work,' one in which 'work as a social experience conditions personality' (p 202). In an excursus, the rhetorical *descriptio* form, the Seven Deadly Sins convention, and the physiological tradition are considered to have influenced *GP*. Mann suggests that Chaucer had read Gower's and Langland's works. Appendices list the estates as given in a range of estates satires. The book is based upon Mann's dissertation, *Chaucer and Medieval Estates Satire: Art and Tradition in the Prologue to the Canterbury Tales*, Cambridge University, 1972. For comments on specific pilgrims see **698, 748, 826, 895, 937, 1027, 1056, 1091, 1102, 1151, 1188, 1218, 1236, 1250, 1282,** and **1318.**

- Review by S.S. Hussey, *MLR*, 70 (1975), 387–88: 'Estates literature, as a genre, clearly formed part of the foundations of the *General Prologue*, but it will not quite take the load which Dr. Mann expects it to bear' (p 388). The evidence is strongest for the Monk, the Friar, and the Knight, weakest for the Franklin and the Miller.

364 Manzalaoui, Mahmoud. 'Chaucer and Science.' In *Writers and Their Background: Geoffrey Chaucer*. Ed. Derek Brewer. London: Bell, 1974; Athens, OH: Ohio University Press, 1975. Pp 224–61 (in 1975 ed.).
Science 'provides an objective correlative to the inward characteristics' of Chaucer's personages, as in 'the physiognomical descriptions of the pilgrims in the *General Prologue*' (p 228). There 'we have salient characteristics revealed through build of body, voice, or, more particularly, the features of the head and face, most especially of the eyes. Usually the characteristics are faults or bad inclinations, as we see in the descriptions of the Monk, the Friar, the Wife of Bath, the Miller, Summoner, and Pardoner' (p 259). The Prioress's portrait is satiric; the Franklin's combines physiognomic characteristics 'with details from the doctrine of humours' (p 259).

365 Markert, Emil. *Chaucers Canterbury-Pilger und ihre Tracht*. Julius-Maximilians-Universität Dissertation (Wurzbürg). 1911. Dir. O.L. Jiriczek. Published Würzburg: Drössler, 1911.
Details of the pilgrims' costumes are analyzed against the historical and literary background. Contemporary complaints against showy sleeves are cited with reference to the Squire's gown, examples of green garments are presented with reference to the Yeoman, and so forth.

366 Marks, Jason. *Tales from Chaucer as Projections of their Tellers' Needs*. New York University Dissertation. 1971. Dir. Charles N. Schirone. See also *DAI*, 32 (1971), 1480-A.
Using 'the technique of thematic apperception, devised by Henry A. Murray and Christiana Morgan in 1935' (p i), Marks analyzes the personalities of six pilgrims chosen according to a 'random sampling method' (p x) — the Knight, Man of Law, Chaucer (narrator), Pardoner, Clerk, and Second Nun. For example: 'Advanced research suggested that the Man of Law was an anal personality type' (p 23).

367 Martin, Dorothy. *A First Book About Chaucer*. London: Routledge, 1929. General remarks about *GP* are included in this presentation for young readers.

368 Martin, Loy D. 'History and Form in the General Prologue to the *Canterbury Tales*,' *ELH*, 45 (1978), 1–17.

The underlying form of *GP* is 'the rhetorical catalogue of types' (p 2), which Chaucer had used earlier in the dream-vision poems. In *GP* Chaucer 'expands the catalogue technique to signify a profound if brief and partial departure from ordinary life' (p 4): the pilgrims are people who temporarily depart from their usual locations and occupations. For example, the Parson, who normally remains with his parish (lines 507–13), has left it, and the Wife joins the pilgrimage 'at a time when she is not a wife' (p 10). The 'insistence on displacement from home, the introduction of pilgrimage as a special (though predictable) event, and the breadth of social representation among the pilgrims' are related to 'concrete social ambiguities and tensions' (p 12). The 'expanded catalogue' and the contest of *GP* 'embrace social change at one level — the interaction among members of separate classes — while resisting the more ominous implications of that change at another level — the mutual human destructiveness inherent in economic competition' (p 14). In *GP*, the consequences of losing in the competition are trivial, since the cost of the winner's dinner will be divided among all the other pilgrims. Members of different social groups can relate to one another, but are not tempted to injure each other. Thus the pilgrimage 'prefigures the celestial pilgrimage' but also 're-evaluates the daily lives of its participants' (p 15).

369 Masui, Michio. *Chaucer Kenkyu*. [Studies in Chaucer.] Tokyo: Kenkyusha, 1962.

A brief overview of *GP* is provided within the discussion of the *CT* (see especially pp 164–68). Other parts of the book also refer to *GP* — in considering, for example, word order, speech patterns, and rhetoric. A review of Chaucer research, with occasional mention of *GP*, is provided (pp 275–330).

370 ——. 'Chaucer No Sozoryoku Ni Tsuite, Josetsu 1.' [About Chaucer's Imagination, Prologue 1.] *EEK*, 12 (1965), 1–16.

Not seen; listed in *A Bibliography of Publications on Medieval English Language and Literature in Japan* (Tokyo: Center for Medieval Studies, Tokyo University, 1983), p 125, #2.

371 Mehl, Dieter. *Geoffrey Chaucer: Eine Einführung in seine erzählenden Dichtungen*. Berlin: Erich Schmidt, 1973. Grundlagen der Anglistik und Amerikanistik, 7. General Editors, Rudolf Sühnel and Dieter Riesner.

In the chapter 'The Canterbury Tales — Der Prolog' (pp 133–48), Mehl analyzes the springtime opening, pointing out the variety of traditions and implications incorporated in it. The first eighteen lines provide a spiritual point of departure, suggesting both the general and the particular, the worldly and the religious, and thus awakening in the reader the most diverse expectations, keeping open multiple possible impulses ('Innerhalb von achtzehn Zeilen ist ein geistiger Ausgangspunkt geschaffen, der Allgemeines und Spezielles, Weltliches und Religiöses anklingen lässt und daher im Leser die verschiedensten Erwartungen weckt, ihn für eine Vielfalt möglicher Anregungen offenhält,' p 134). Chaucer uses and modifies established rhetorical devices and traditional motifs. The sequence of the portraits does not fully follow rank or status, but demonstrates inherent resemblances, contrasts, and ideas. For example, the juxtaposition of the Parson and Plowman is based not on their social positions in a feudal hierarchy, but on their perfection as embodiments of an active Christianity. Similarly, their brotherhood is important not as a biographical statement, but as an illustration of their inner kinship. The representative or typical aspect of the pilgrims is more important than the liveliness of individual details ('dieser typische Aspekt für das Verständnis des Textes sehr viel wichtiger ist als die Lebendigkeit der Details,' p 136), though the typical and the individual elements complement each other. The Knight's portrait, for instance, reads as if it were based on the career of a contemporary person, but its purpose is certainly not exhausted by the small audience that would understand the specific reference, for the Knight is also a superlatively courtly example of a well-defined way of life ('ein ins Vorbildliche überhöhter Vertreter einer ganz bestimmten Lebensform,' p 137). The narrator's situation is too complex to be described by a simple division between a naive narrator and an omniscient author — the narrator himself is often ironic ('Der Erzähler selbst ist oft ironisch,' p 145). *GP* and the other parts of the *CT* framework depict a heterogeneous group of people and a multiplicity of human endeavors and insights.

372 Merlo, Carolyn. 'Chaucer's "Brown" and Medieval Color Symbolism.' *CLAJ*, 25 (1981), 225–26.
The Monk's horse is brown (line 207). 'Here, besides the realistic description of the horse as brown are the symbolic implications of brown suggesting humility and impoverishment which reflect ironically on the self-satisfied, well-fed Monk' (p 226). The Shipman's brown hue (line 394) may suggest his villainy or rascality. The Yeoman has a brown face (line 109); brown 'is frequently ascribed to characters of the lower classes' (p 226).

373 Metlitzki, Dorothee. *The Matter of Araby in Medieval England*. New Haven, CN: Yale University Press, 1977.
Chaucer is mentioned only rarely in this study, but it provides useful background information on topics such as the attitude toward Saracens in literary works of Chaucer's time (cf the Knight's battles in Islamic countries); the knowledge of Arabic learning in England (cf the Physician's medical

authorities); the function of works such as the *Disciplina clericalis*, a collection of framed tales, in transmitting Arabic literary motifs to the European vernacular traditions; and so forth. Metlitzki suggests that the Islamic paradise, depicted as the Land of Cocayne, was associated in European thinking with a Western Mediterranean location of Finisterre, or land's end—a location that was 'diametrically opposed to the biblical Eden' (p 213; cf the fact that the Shipman knows all the havens *Fro Gootlond to the cape of Fynystere*, line 408).

74 Meyer, Emil. *Die Charakterzeichnung bei Chaucer*. Halle: Niemeyer, 1913. Studien zur Englischen Philologie, 48.

The portraits of *GP*, among Chaucer's other characterizations, are given short analyses according to social categories. For example, the Knight is considered within Meyer's section on Chaucer's knightly characters; he is through and through a knight, but also a man ('Er ist durch und durch Ritter, aber nicht bloss Ritter, sondern darüber hinaus auch Mensch,' p 40). Comparisons are drawn, within or across categories. Except for the love-motif, for instance, the Franklin resembles the knight January of the Merchant's Tale. Chaucer's technique of characterization produces realistic, vigorous people ('wirkliche, lebenskräftige Menschen,' p 159). The study is based upon Meyer's dissertation of the same title, Georg-August-Universität (Göttingen), 1913, Dir. Lorenz Morsbach; excerpts were printed under the same title at Halle: Karras, 1913, in addition to the full publication listed at the beginning of this entry.

75 Minnis, A.J. 'The Influence of Academic Prologues on the Prologues and Literary Attitudes of Late-Medieval English Writers.' *MS*, 43 (1981), 342–83.

Minnis describes the kinds of prologues that by Chaucer's time had become conventional in academic writing. They were also used in vernacular literature. These academic prologues 'provided Gower with models for the composition of his own prolegomena' (p 374). 'By contrast, Geoffrey Chaucer did not employ any of the traditional prologue-paradigms, although many of his literary attitudes seem to have been influenced by academic literary theory' (p 374). In the intellectual climate of academic literary theory, a writer could justify his procedure by appealing to a Scriptural model, as Chaucer does in lines 739–40. Minnis notes in passing that in Jean de Meun's *apologia* for the *Roman de la Rose*, there are 'many striking parallels with Chaucer's General Prologue' (p 381).

76 Mohl, Ruth. *The Three Estates in Medieval and Renaissance Literature*. New York: Columbia University Press, 1933.

Although Chaucer was 'thoroughly familiar with the earlier literature of estates' and also with the estates literature of his own time, *GP* is not, strictly speaking, 'a piece of literature of estates' (p 103). Much background material on medieval concepts of social class is included.

377 Montgomery, Franz. 'The Musical Instruments in "The Canterbury Tales." ' *MusQ*, 17 (1931), 439–48.
Chaucer's descriptions of musical instruments provide useful information for the history of English music. In his time polyphony was being developed. In *GP*, 'which is perhaps the least derivative of his works, we may be reasonably sure that he describes only the people and customs of England,' and his details about music can be taken as representing 'with considerable accuracy the musical instruments in use in his day' (p 439). The types of instruments mentioned in *GP* are briefly reviewed. On the Squire, see **728**.

378 Morgan, Gerald. 'The Universality of the Portraits in the *General Prologue* to the *Canterbury Tales.*' *ES*, 58 (1977), 481–93.
The common opinion that the *GP* portraits are both 'individual and typical' (p 481) is mistaken. Chaucer is not depicting individuals. In all but two cases, the pilgrims have no personal names; they are designated by the names of types. Even where personal names occur — Madame Eglantyne the Prioress, Hubert the Friar — these names have a 'generalising force' (p 482). We should not take these names as individualizing the pilgrims, any more than the name Scot individualizes the Reeve's horse. 'None of us, I take it, is in any danger of mistaking the Reeve's horse for an individual' (p 482). All of the portraits, as Mann has pointed out (see **363**), are organized according to the conception of social estates. The moral and physiological traditions, as well as the estates tradition, 'point to the medieval habit of thinking in generic and not individual terms' (p 486). The many physical details included in *GP* — the Knight's campaigns, the Wife's residence near Bath and her clothing and deafness, the Prioress's elegance and beauty, etc. — 'do not exist for their own sake,' as if to individualize the characterizations, but instead 'have been determined by the general conception' (p 489). All of the pilgrims 'are ideal in the sense that they are archetypal' (p 490), with each achieving the perfection of that particular type. (The Miller is perfectly dishonest, as the Knight is perfectly valorous.) Chaucer, as a medieval poet, is 'characteristically concerned with the generic' (p 490). He writes according to the concepts of 'philosophical realism' (p 491), which stressed the importance of universals and of 'the idea' (p 490) in a work of art.

379 ——. 'The Design of the *General Prologue* to the *Canterbury Tales,*' *ES*, 59 (1978), 481–98.

The aesthetic expectation that there must be narrative unity and the sociological expectation that Chaucer must have depicted a 'middle class' have both interfered with the proper interpretation of *GP*. Donaldson and others have postulated a pervasive *persona* to create narrative unity, but 'the figure that Professor Donaldson describes is largely a product of his own imagination' (p 482; see Donaldson, **596**). Analyses of Chaucer's 'middle-class' pilgrims have been made, but the text 'is innocent of a single allusion' to such a class (p 483). The portraits are, however, indeed organized in terms of social class: Chaucer's claim that he has *not* 'set folk in hir degree' (line 744), which is a rhetorical *diminutio*, implies that indeed 'the portraits are correctly disposed in accordance with social rank' (p 484).

The underlying principle, the concept of the three estates, is treated from the secular viewpoint, for Chaucer begins with a Knight rather than with a Cleric. The group of the gentles extends from the Knight all the way through the Franklin. Then the portraits of the Guildsmen, Shipman, Physician, and Wife 'form a coherent grouping of those who are highest in rank among the commons' (p 495). In the portraits of the Parson and Plowman, 'the influence of the estates conception is once again apparent,' as this pair 'is symbolic of the harmony that should exist between the clerical and the labouring estates' (p 495). The bottom of the social scale is occupied by the churls, beginning with the Reeve. The Miller's wart suggests his brutishness, which 'places him outside the pale of civilised society' (p 496), while the derivation of *manciple* from *mancipium*, 'slave,' is part of Chaucer's irony. The sequence of the *GP* portraits represents a 'systematic social and not a moral declension,' although moral concepts are present also: 'generosity is seen to be characteristic of the gentils, materialism of the bourgeoisie and dishonesty of the churls' (p 497).

380 ——. 'Rhetorical Perspectives in the *General Prologue* to the *Canterbury Tales*.' *ES*, 62 (1981), 411–22.
To appreciate the art of *GP* means to understand 'the literary genre to which it belongs and the kind of work with which as a consequence it is most fitly compared' (p 420). *GP* includes the ridicule of vanity, but it is nevertheless comic rather than satiric, for it depicts 'the representation of virtue as well as vice' (p 416). The virtuous figures 'have a primary and not a secondary value; they are to be appreciated in and for themselves' (p 416). The irony within *GP* depends more on 'the centrality of the tradition of rhetorical description' (the Prioress's portrait is rhetorically analyzed as an example) than on any dualism between the narrator and the poet. Morgan questions Donaldson's presentation (see **596**) of the narrator's naiveté and bourgeois values. 'Indeed the view of the fictional pilgrim as a member of the "middle class" is based on no fictional evidence whatsoever' (p 415).

Overall, *GP* 'is to be seen not in terms of satire but of comedy' (p 420). The portraits imply 'neither naturalism nor a concern for individuality' (p 421). Chaucer 'has fashioned true poetic types' (p 422), not individuals, showing 'the ironic detachment of the moralist who can view the failings of man in the light of the love of God' (p 422).

381 Morsbach, Lorenz. 'Chaucers Plan der *Canterbury Tales* und Boccaccios *Decamerone.*' *ESt*, 42 (1910), 43–52.
Morsbach argues that Chaucer knew the *Decameron*, given four similarities in the basic plans of the two story collections: 1) the stories are told by a group or company, not by one or more separate persons; 2) an external circumstance — in Boccaccio the plague, in Chaucer the pilgrimage — joins the members of the group together; 3) the stories are bound by links between them; 4) the members of the group are under the control of an 'authority' — in Boccaccio the daily king or queen, in Chaucer the Host. These and other traits show that the *CT* plan, as presented in *GP* and fulfilled afterwards, was influenced by the *Decameron* ('der plan von Chaucers *Canterbury Tales* nicht ohne einfluss des *Decamerone* herangereift ist,' p 47). However, Chaucer's originality is evident in the motivation of pilgrimage and in the personality of the Host, who is the central figure and who, in rebuking or encouraging, plays the role of a chorus in the pilgrimage drama ('Der wirt ist nun einmal der mittelpunkt des ganzen, und indem er tadelt oder aufmuntert, spielt er gleichsam die rolle des antiken chors in dem munteren vielseitigen drama der Canterbury-pilgerfahrt,' p 51). Cf **327, 382, 1349**.

382 ——. 'Chaucers Canterbury Tales und das Decamerone.' *NNPL*, 1 (1934-1937), 49–70. Nachrichten von der Gesellschaft der Wissenschaften zu Göttingen, Philologisch-Historische Klasse, Neue Folge, Fachgruppe 4.
Morsbach supplements his earlier argument (**381**) that the plan of *CT*, including *GP* as a framework, is indebted to the *Decameron*. Cf **327, 1349**.

383 Mroczkowski, Przemysław. *Opowieści Kanterberyjskie na tle Epoki.* Lublin: Towarzystwo Naukowe Katolickiego Uniwersytetu Lubelskiego, 1956.
In what is said to be a combined sociological and formalistic approach to *CT*, the *GP* portraits are seen as consisting of details representing either the past or the present, along with individual or class traits. Chaucer may have worked inductively, starting from a concrete individual he had met; or deductively, starting from the general idea of a social class. When the reader's previous idea of the social class or the psychological type is confirmed by the details provided, there occurs the pleasure of recognition. Chaucer's humor ranges from aggressiveness (lines 184–88, Monk) to bitterness (lines 253–55, Friar) to indirectness (lines 507–10, Parson); he freely uses the convention of authorial omniscience.

384 Murphy, James J. 'A New Look at Chaucer and the Rhetoricians.' *RES*, New Series 15 (1964), 1–20. Portions rpt in *Critics on Chaucer*, ed. Sheila Sullivan (London: Allen and Unwin, 1970), pp 31–38.

Murphy questions the historical basis for assuming that Chaucer had an extensive familiarity with formal rhetoric. There is very little evidence for a native English rhetorical tradition. As for acquaintance with continental works, Chaucer's references to rhetorical terminology show that he 'possessed only a very general concept of rhetoric' (p 8). He seems to 'reveal a layman's consciousness of greater and less complexity in styles, without a rhetorician's technical knowledge of fine distinctions' (p 11). His knowledge of *figurae* may come from 'grammatical works or French models' (p 20). His allusion to Geoffrey of Vinsauf 'can be traced to Trivet' (p 20). Our investigations of his style should consider his broad verbal training, rather than assuming an extensive debt to the rhetoricians in particular.

385 ——. *Rhetoric in the Middle Ages: A History of Rhetorical Theory from St. Augustine to the Renaissance.* Berkeley: University of California Press, 1974.

GP is not discussed, but the chapter '*Ars poetriae*: Preceptive Grammar, or the Rhetoric of Verse-Writing' (pp 135–39) describes the treatises of Matthew of Vendôme, Geoffrey of Vinsauf, and other rhetorical theorists; and the appendix on 'Figures of Diction and of Thought' (pp 365–74) provides brief definitions of many of the technical terms used in rhetorical analyses.

386 Muscatine, Charles. *Chaucer and the French Tradition: A Study in Style and Meaning.* Berkeley and Los Angeles: University of California Press, 1957; London: Cambridge University Press, 1957. Rpt (paperback), with brief bibliographical additions, 1965; 6th printing, 1969.

In contesting 'a number of characteristically post-Victorian assumptions' about Chaucer, this analysis aims 'to explore his stylistic heritage,' emphasizing the usefulness of literary convention 'as a potentially powerful tool, not as something to be avoided or rebelled against, or even necessarily to be remoulded' (1957, p 1). *GP* is discussed in the chapter 'The Canterbury Tales' (pp 166–243). Muscatine accepts the viewpoint of Cunningham (see 207) that the dream-vision tradition underlies the form of *GP*, in conjunction with the interpretation of Hoffman (see 284), which shows the purposeful way in which traditional elements are used to create a double view of the framework's pilgrimage. 'Chaucer's use of the seasonal description and the portrait series — both of them conventional devices of romance and rhetoric — is part, then, of an artistic synthesis, and has nothing either of mechanical habit or gratuitous invention about it' (p 170). Given the formal portrait tradition, which implied 'an ideal ordering of experience,' Chaucer has pulled 'the traits out of their formulated, uniplanar arrangement' and has abandoned 'the reasoned sequence' technique of earlier portrait series (p 170). His version includes what naturalistic critics now see as realism, but 'also the tension, detail against form, observed nature against formulated order, that supports his deepest meaning' (p 171).

387 ——. '*The Canterbury Tales*: Style of the Man and Style of the Work.' In *Chaucer and Chaucerians: Critical Studies in Middle English Literature*. Ed. D.S. Brewer. London: Nelson, 1966; University, AL: University of Alabama Press, 1966. Pp 88–113. Rpt London: Nelson (Nelson's Paperback Series), 1970.

GP examples help to illustrate 'Chaucer's basic quality of insouciance and naturalness' (1970, p 90). His 'predilection for making lists of things' is also evident from *GP* (see lines 429–34 and 629–31). In fact, in 'a certain sense' the *GP* portrait-series itself 'has the form of a catalogue' and 'the individual portraits are themselves composed of catalogues of traits' (p 95). However, 'against the stasis and formality implied by the catalogue form' many of the portraits also create a 'complex characterization' and display 'potential energy' (p 95). They are 'based on the *effictio* of medieval rhetoric,' but with the 'complexity of structure' that is 'Chaucer's great innovation' (p 96). Chaucer's imagery, which can be 'so expressive as to have almost symbolic force,' enables him to catch economically the qualities of female sovereignty in the Wife, animalism in the Miller (p 97). On the Prioress, see **832**.

388 Nakao, Yoshiyuki. 'The Canterbury Tales No General Prologue Ni Okeru Hiyu No Yoho — Jinbutsu Tono Kanren Ni Oite.' [The Use of Metaphors in Characterization in the General Prologue to the Canterbury Tales.] *Phoenix*, 16 (1980), 3–23.

Not seen; listed in *A Bibliography of Publications on Medieval English Language and Literature in Japan* (Tokyo: Center for Medieval Studies, Tokyo University, 1983), p 146, #13.

389 Naunin, Traugott. *Der Einfluss der mittelalterlichen Rhetorik auf Chaucers Dichtung*. Friedrich-Wilhelms-Universität Dissertation (Bonn). 1929. Dir. W.F. Schirmer. Published Grossenhain: Plasnick, 1929.

Naunin reviews medieval rhetorical concepts and collects examples of Chaucer's use of *digressio, descriptio*, etc, including instances from *GP*. Lines 229–30 involve *sententia*, lines 177–80 a proverb, lines 715–24 *transitio*, and so forth.

390 Neuse, Richard. 'The Knight: The First Mover in Chaucer's Human Comedy.' *UTQ*, 31 (1961-1962), 299–315.

In *GP* as a whole, the concept of *caritas* 'in a general way forms the backdrop' for the 'endless metamorphoses of human love that we find in the

Canterbury pilgrims' (p 310). In *GP* 'each pilgrim is ruled by a specific *eros*,' varying from selfish love to selfless love; but all of them 'participate, however obscurely, in the transcendent-immanent love of the Creator for his creation' (p 310), since each type of love is capable of being converted into heavenly love. The goal of the pilgrimage is not to eradicate human love but to purify it. In coming together at the Tabard, the pilgrims 're-enact the fundamental rite on which all community life is based: the being together of people in "sociability" ' (p 311). The static portraits of *GP* are 'a momentary illusion' (p 312): the pilgrims progressively unfold their characters on the road to Canterbury, which is 'the stage on which the *dramatis personae* act out their natures' (p 312). See **701**.

91 Nevo, Ruth. 'Chaucer: Motive and Mask in the "General Prologue."' *MLR*, 58 (1963), 1–9.
It is incorrect to interpret *GP* as a general portrait-gallery or a miscellany. A 'persistent criterion of selection' operates upon the information we are given: 'there is no portrait which does not take its orientation from an attitude to money or from dealings with money' (p 2). The concept of Mammon 'provides the dynamic of the *Prologue*' and serves as 'the master key to its design' (p 3). The sequence of pilgrims moves from the members of the land-owning aristocracy, to the members of 'the great propertied religious houses and orders' (p 5), to the well-to-do or potentially well-to-do, to members of the lower middle class, to those who are of peasant origin, and finally to the parasites. This pattern is 'a clear, socio-economic ranking based on an analysis of the origins of income' (p 6). The Mammon theme is used to link socio-economic realities to moral values. 'Every character passes, or does not pass, the test of worldliness' (p 7). Chaucer's mask of the innocent narrator who takes the pilgrims 'at their face-value, the value they put upon themselves' (p 9), is used in order to unmask them. Chaucer's own viewpoint is one of tolerance based upon 'a profound and equable conviction of human frailty' (p 7), which is not the same as moral leniency. *GP* offers a combination of 'an acutely original analysis of a society in which commerce is just emerging from feudalism, and the disciplined vision of a tolerant but uncompromising moral sensibility' (p 4).

92 Newbolt, Henry. 'The Poetry of Chaucer.' *EngRev*, 15 (1913), 170–89.
Chaucer's 'truth to nature,' his 'power of exhibiting the universal in the particular,' is briefly described (p 171). Some of the pilgrims (eg, the Physician) represent modern types whom we immediately recognize. Even those who are at first sight not familiar to us possess as their 'principle part' a 'definite element of humanity,' although their names and occupations may have changed between Chaucer's time and ours (p 171).

393 Nicholson, Peter. 'The Two Versions of Sercambi's *Novelle*.' *Italica*, 53 (1976), 201–13.

Replying to Sinicropi (**453**) and to Pratt and Young (**410**), Nicholson reviews the evidence on the question of whether Sercambi's *Novelle* existed at a date early enough to have influenced *GP*. An eighteenth-century note and letter seem to refer to a version of the *Novelle* in which a group of men and women told tales on a journey through Tuscany, but the evidence for (or against) the existence of such a version before 1400 is inconclusive. All that we know is that in the eighteenth century 'the Baroni family of Lucca owned a manuscript of Sercambi's work which might have been different from the one we now have. Unless and until that manuscript or a better description of it is found, we can tell very little about what it contained' (p 212). Given the present state of our knowledge, the question of Sercambi's influence upon Chaucer cannot be satisfactorily resolved.

394 Norris, Robert. *Costume and Fashion, II: Senlac to Bosworth, 1066–1485*. London and Toronto: Dent, 1927; New York: Dutton, 1927.

The costumes of several of the pilgrims, and of pertinent individuals or social groups in this time, are depicted and explained. Some descriptions of accoutrements for horses are also included.

395 Norton-Smith, John. *Geoffrey Chaucer*. London: Routledge & Kegan Paul, 1974.

Chaucer's style in *GP* is discussed from a rhetorical perspective. The 'brisk, rapid velocity of the verse and the general procedural directness' are part of the initial impression given by *GP* (p 109). The 'extremely clear' *dispositio* (p 112) consists of *chronographia* and *praepositio* (lines 1–42), *ethopoeia* (lines 43–714), a transitional epitome (lines 715–23), *excusatio* (lines 724–46), and *narratio* (lines 747–858). The rhetorical characteristics of the portraiture are examined. Unexpected details or 'particularizing "surprises" tend initially to appear at the very end of the portrait' (p 116); examples include the descriptions of the Yeoman, Monk, Friar, and Cook. In the apology (lines 725–46), the 'key note of this passage would seem to lie in the persistent repetition of concessive clauses' (p 119).

396 Owen, Charles A., Jr. 'Morality as a Comic Motif in the Canterbury Tales.' *CE*, 16 (1954-1955), 226–32.

The *GP* portraits provided Chaucer with 'a continuing challenge in the depiction of moral traits' (p 288). The characters are presented 'in the comic perspective of an uncritical acceptance and enthusiasm,' with the narrator's 'fatuity of comment' encouraging the pilgrims' revelations (p 228). Chaucer relies upon 'the sharp eye and the sharp ear, but not the sharp tongue,' for 'accuracy of observation is the real essential in presenting moral value' (p 288). Chaucer often expresses morality in 'the single physical detail that epitomizes the moral posture of the pilgrim' (p 229), such as the Squire's embroidery, the Yeoman's weapons, the Prioress's large forehead and frame, the Shipman's dagger, the Wife's deafness, the Summoner's diseased skin, and so forth. The pilgrims are 'blissfully unaware that they carry these signs about with them,' but they nevertheless 'wear and speak and act and are their morality constantly' (p 229). It is this insight that gives the portraits 'their organic unity and their life' (p 229).

397 ——. 'The Development of the *Canterbury Tales.*' *JEGP*, 57 (1958), 449–76.

Chaucer probably began *GP* towards 1387, but 'reworked and added to the *Prologue* as his conception of the *Canterbury Tales* evolved' (p 454). The couplet (lines 163–4) in which the Prioress's chaplain and priest(s) are mentioned, but not described, 'is proof positive that the *Prologue* was not complete at Chaucer's death' (p 454). Rather than initially setting out an ambitious *GP* plan for four tales per pilgrim (see lines 793–4) and later reducing this plan to a smaller scope, as is usually thought, Chaucer may instead have expanded the project as he worked, in which case the *GP* plan could have been a late revision.

398 ——. 'The Earliest Plan of the Canterbury Tales.' *MS*, 21 (1959), 202–10.
GP was worked on at various times and 'was never finished' (p 207). 'Apparently the General Prologue grew with the work, some of the portraits preceding the tales of the pilgrims, others being composed after the tales were assigned to pilgrims, and finally, in at least one case, the Knight, both tale and portrait being composed before the happy inspiration that brought them into conjunction' (p 207). In the earliest version of *GP*, the Host suggested 'a single tale for each pilgrim' — not the present four tales, which represent 'an expansion of the design' (p 208) made when Chaucer incorporated the *KnT* and wrote the other tales of the first fragment.

399 ——. 'The Twenty-Nine Pilgrims and the Three Priests.' *MLN*, 76 (1961), 392–97.
Owen suggests that in Chaucer's first version of *GP*, written perhaps between 1387 and 1388, there were portraits of fourteen pilgrims and a joint portrait of the five Guildsmen. The Prioress's accompanying nun and three priests were simply mentioned, not described — except that the priests were given names. Following what is now line 164, there may have been a line such as 'Cleped Sir John, Sir Piers, and Sir Huberd' (p 396). In about 1396, Chaucer substituted the Monk and the Friar for two of these priests. He composed their portraits, using the name 'Huberd' for the Friar since it provided a rhyme for *berd* at the beginning of the Merchant's portrait (line 270). He left line 164 to be modified later, when he would be writing portraits for the Second Nun and the remaining Nun's Priest, but — perhaps

because of 'a sudden and incapacitating illness' (p 395) — he never made that further change. During this second period he also wrote portraits for the five churls, who were originally merely listed (see lines 542–44); probably at this time he added lines 35–42. Thus Chaucer's first plan included — counting the narrator — twenty-nine pilgrims (see line 24), some described, others just mentioned; his second plan, after replacing two of the priests by the Monk and Friar, would still have totalled twenty-nine.

400 ——. *Pilgrimage and Story-telling in the Canterbury Tales: The Dialectic of 'Ernest and Game.'* Norman, OK: University of Oklahoma Press, 1977.
GP is discussed in the chapters 'The Development of the Canterbury Tales' (pp 10–47) and 'The Meaning of Chaucer's Prologue and Its Art' (pp 48–86). *GP* was composed during 'the whole period of Chaucer's work on the *Canterbury Tales*, has a number of inconsistencies, and shows evidence of being incomplete' (p 41). Owen identifies components attributable to two main periods of work on *GP*, 1387?–1388 and ca. 1396. 'Originally the portraits were to start with the Knight and end with the Parson and his brother the Plowman,' with, in between, a 'moderate range of characters' (p 45). The Monk and Friar were inserted later, along with portraits for the five churls at the end. After these additions 'the society is far less firmly established,' more threatened, the outcome 'not predetermined' (p 46). The contest for the supper and the proposal that each pilgrim will tell four tales are probably 'late changes in Chaucer's plan' (p 33). Owen discusses the individual portraits. 'The art of the Prologue makes possible all that follows. It establishes the groundwork of character, the sense of a community, the impression of a literal actuality, and the potential of polysemous meaning that the game of storytelling may release' (p 85).

401 ——. 'The Alternative Reading of the *Canterbury Tales*: Chaucer's Text and the Early Manuscripts.' *PMLA*, 97 (1982), 237–50.
At Chaucer's death, *CT* consisted of 'a collection of fragments reflecting different stages of his plan for the work as a whole' (p 246). It was the third stage of Chaucer's plan that 'multiplied the number of tales, made the storytelling a contest, and arranged a new ending, the supper at the Tabard with the Host choosing the pilgrim who has told the best stories and the other pilgrims paying for the winner's meal' (p 247).

402 Owst, G.R. *Preaching in Medieval England: An Introduction to Sermon Manuscripts of the Period 1350–1450.* Cambridge: Cambridge University Press, 1926.
Background material on monks, friars, other ecclesiastics, customs of preaching, and sermon literature is presented.

403 ——. *Literature and Pulpit in Medieval England.* Cambridge: Cambridge University Press, 1933; New York: Macmillan, 1933. Rpt 1961.

This fundamental study refers several times to the *GP* portraits. Responding to Manly's view that some of the pilgrims represent historical individuals (see **362**), Owst replies that they are 'thoroughly representative and even commonplace' ingredients of sermon-literature (1933, p 230).

404 Parr, Roger Phillip. *The Rhetorical Tradition and Chaucer's Narrative Technique*. University of Toronto Dissertation. 1956. Dir. F.H. Anderson.
After surveying the classical and medieval rhetorical traditions, Parr examines Chaucer's beginnings and endings (*dispositio*), means of development (*amplificatio*), and figures of ornamentation. Occasional references to *GP* occur: 'The Prologue is linked intimately with the rest of the work by the clever repetition of words and phrases' (p 212); 'All of the portraits in the General Prologue are teasers, in a sense,' for they offer suggestions that make us want to know more (p 254); the rhyme at lines 17–18 is an example of *traductio* (p 326); etc. Chaucer uses rhetoric 'to a marked degree,' in late as well as early works (p 375).

405 ——. 'Chaucer's Art of Portraiture.' *SMC*, 4 (1974), 428–36.
Parr analyzes Chaucer's use of rhetorical techniques in the portraits, concentrating on the two devices of *effictio* (physical description) and *notatio* (description of moral qualities or character) as evident in the portraits of the Knight, the Prioress, and the Monk. In the Knight's portrait, for example, there are thirty lines of *notatio*, six of *effictio*; the devices of *traductio* and *superlatio*, as well as *distributio* and *conclusio*, also are used in a way that makes the inner character of the Knight, rather than his external appearance, predominate.

406 Patch, Howard R. 'Characters in Medieval Literature,' *MLN*, 40 (1925), 1–14.
The form of Chaucer's portraits — 'extensive but very compact summaries of descriptive detail and of traits of character, in which the use of what is concrete and realistic is striking' (p 3) — was known previously in treatises on the vices and virtues, and in allegories. In the treatises and the allegories, it would have been necessary to 'list the qualities and traits' as well as to 'reflect real life' (p 5) in order to depict the personality type in a way that reinforced a moral idea. Thus 'the descriptions of personified Avarice, Envy, Sloth, and the like, anticipate Chaucer's portraits' (p 5). Examples are cited from moral treatises and from allegorical texts. Gower's sketch of Vainglory, for example, shows some similarities to the portrait of the Squire. Chaucer's pilgrims tend to be more individualized than the characters depicted in the treatises or allegories, but they retain 'that element of the typical' (p 13) as well.

407 ——. *On Rereading Chaucer*. Cambridge, MA: Harvard University Press, 1939. 4th printing 1967.

In a general chapter, 'The Canterbury Tales' (pp 154–85), Patch comments briefly on most of the portraits. 'The pilgrims whom Chaucer seems to find most admirable are touched with a fine simplicity — the Clerk, the Parson, and the Plowman: which, we quickly add, is not to say that necessarily he liked them best' (p 155). In describing the Friar, Chaucer 'does not forget, be it noticed, to record the sin; but he likes the sinner' (p 160); in fact 'Chaucer likes everybody in due measure, except perhaps the Pardoner' (p 160). His emphasis on the ongoing process of human life enables him to be more tolerant than Dante, 'because no final judgment is involved ... There is little room for the whimsical or tentative in the *Inferno* or the *Paradiso*. But much jesting is possible on the road to Canterbury,' for Chaucer knows that most of his characters 'have another chance' (p 185). On the Pardoner, cf Duino, **1306**.

408 —. 'The Individual and The Type in Medieval Literature.' In *The McAuley Lectures, First Series, 1953-1959*. Preface by Anton C. Pegis. West Hartford, CN: Saint Joseph College, 1961. Pp 25–41.
Patch argues that medieval literature presents individual characters, not only types. Yet the background to the *GP* portraits includes 'the early treatises on vice and virtue, where they tell us what the avaricious man, the glutton, the slothful, and other sinners are like, all of them most realistically done' (p 38). In the allegories, the techniques of characterization have advanced even further: 'the allegories, in the way they deal with the vices, come down to earth sufficiently to prepare the way for characters like the Monk and the Friar and even the Prioress and the Merchant' (p 38). Patch's lecture, published here, was given in the series 'Christian Humanism in Letters' at Saint Joseph College in 1954.

409 Pison, Thomas. 'Liminality in *The Canterbury Tales.*' *Genre*, 10 (1977), 157–71.
Chaucer's pilgrims 'must all adapt to a novel social situation' (p 157), that of being on pilgrimage. In anthropological terms their transitional situation — they have left their ordinary lives behind, but have not yet arrived at the shrine — represents the middle or liminal phase of a rite of passage. In this phase there is an emphasis on *communitas*, a state in which they 'assimilate divergence of both person and opinion' (p 161) and enjoy freedom from normal social and structural restrictions. The Host performs the function of a 'ritual elder' or 'master of revels' (p 162). Chaucer's own social role was liminal, that of an 'artist who placed himself at the interstices of the social grid,' but he eventually entered the subsequent state of reaggregation in accepting 'the values of his adopted class' (p 170). In *CT* as a whole, it is the Parson who 'repudiates the random chaos of liminality' (p 170) that is depicted in *GP* and reaffirms the old truths. Nevertheless, the effect of

'the unfamiliar *communitas* of marginality' persists (p 171).

410 Pratt, Robert A., and Karl Young. 'The Literary Framework of the Canterbury Tales.' In *Sources and Analogues of Chaucer's Canterbury Tales.* Ed. W.F. Bryan and Germaine Dempster. London: Routledge & Kegan Paul, 1941. Pp 1–81. Rpt 1958.

Before Chaucer wrote *CT*, he was familiar with both the concept of frame-stories in literature and 'the device of a pilgrimage as a narrative framework' in actual life (1941, p 2). He 'could have conceived his design through his own observation' (p 2), but an examination of other literary works helps to disclose, 'by contrast, those aspects of Chaucer's art which are unmistakably his own' (p 3). Brief descriptions are provided of a range of frame-tales, including the *Fables of Bidpai*, the *Seven Sages*, the *Arabian Nights*, the *Disciplina Clericalis*, the daughters-of-Minyas section of Ovid's *Metamorphoses*, Gower's *Confessio amantis*, Boccaccio's *Ameto*, *Filocolo*, and *Decameron*, and especially Sercambi's *Novelle* (parts of this last are edited here). Cf **393, 507**.

The tradition of literary portraits in medieval poetry was based partly on classical Latin models and partly on the rhetoricians' precepts. Most such portraits do not much resemble those of *GP*. 'Perhaps the only comparable grouping of personal descriptions' occurs in the *Roman de Troie* of Benoît de Sainte-Maure and related Troy-texts, but even these portraits are 'much too limited in social variety and in realistic detail' to have served as the model for Chaucer's 'miscellaneous company of vivid and living personalities' (p 5). No source or fully appropriate analogue of his portrait-series is known.

411 Presson, Robert K. 'The Aesthetic of Chaucer's Art of Contrast.' *EM*, 15 (1964), 9–23.

'The antithesis, although primarily a device of emphasis, is clearly an indication of the way Chaucer saw experience' (p 23). Examples of several kinds of contrasts within *GP* are included.

412 Preston, Raymond. *Chaucer.* New York: Sheed and Ward, 1952. Rpt New York: Humanities Press, 1961; New York: Greenwood Press, 1969.

In the chapter 'Canterbury Prologue' (1952, pp 149–79), Preston comments that the opening of *GP*, 'like decoration in stone, is both "natural" and "conventional" ' (pp 151–52). In the portraits Chaucer 'throws out conventional compliments to see whether they stick' (p 153). Each of the portraits is examined. The design of *GP*, which looks haphazard, is not; 'there is an effective order of persons' and 'an effective order of detail in each character' (p 154). The portraits are composites of many kinds of information and viewpoints, with the observer 'constantly varying his distance and angle of vision, so as to produce more than two dimensions' (p 154). Chaucer's objectivity is based on self-knowledge: 'in order to understand the Prioress, Chaucer had first to know himself. And it is because he so neatly avoided both self-satisfaction and self-pity that we are left thinking how beautifully he has caught the object' (p 159).

413 Purdie, A.B. 'Canterbury Pilgrims.' *CW*, 94 (1912), 627–39.
The pilgrimage is imaginatively recreated.

414 Quiller-Couch, Arthur T. *The Age of Chaucer*. London and Toronto: Dent, 1926.
The pilgrims' *GP* portraits are briefly reviewed in this general book. Contemporary texts are cited to explain aspects of fourteenth-century life.

415 Quinn, Esther C. 'Religion in Chaucer's Canterbury Tales: A Study in Language and Structure.' In *Geoffrey Chaucer, A Collection of Original Articles*. Ed. George D. Economou. New York: McGraw-Hill, 1975. Contemporary Studies in Literature. General Editors, Eugene Ehrlich and Daniel Murphy. Pp 55–73.
The pilgrims' 'easy acceptance' of the Host's plan serves as a reminder 'of humanity's susceptibility to being led and misled' (p 59). It is the Host who 'sets the holiday mood' (p 60). The Prioress, Monk, and Friar all fail, in different ways, to live up to their vows; 'the Prioress is evasive, the Monk is defiant, the Friar misuses his office' (p 63). The Summoner and Pardoner are minor officials, and are corrupt, but 'it is part of Chaucer's irony that their names suggest the mighty powers of summoning to the divine tribunal and pardoning before the ultimate judge' (p 65). The Parson functions 'as a reminder of what constitutes true Christianity in contrast to so much that is inadequate and false' (p 66).

416 Rajna, Pio. 'Le Origini della novella narrata dal "Frankeleyn" nei Canterbury Tales del Chaucer.' *Romania*, 32 (1903), 204–67.
Chaucer may have observed from life certain aspects of the tale-telling contest, such as the practice of telling stories to shorten the journey (lines 793–4), but there are also fundamentally unrealistic aspects, such as the idea that one person's voice could be heard by a company of about thirty people as they rode along. Literary models, as well as the observation of reality, influenced Chaucer's work. Two components of *GP* are paralleled in the *Decameron* more strongly than in other analogues. One is the concept of agreeing in advance that each narrator will tell multiple tales (ten each in the *Decameron*; four each in *GP*, see lines 792–97). The second similarity concerns the role assumed by the Host. This idea of the creation of a sovereign — to whom the group simply assents, with surprising docility, when he sets out his requirements (lines 812–20) — draws upon the installation of the king and queen among the *Decameron's* storytellers ('Chè il concetto di quella curiosa creazione di un signore, dove il popolo non fa se

non consentire, e, meravigliosamente docile, all'assenso accompagna perfino le preghiere, presuppone, oso dire, il libero e spontaneo insediamento dei re e delle regine del Decameròn,' p 253). Rajna does not doubt Chaucer's knowledge of the *Decameron*, and the conception of *CT* can be seen as going back to it ('Sicchè il Chaucer conobbe — non posso dubitarne — il *Decameròn*, e al *Decameròn* è da riportare la concezione dei *Canterbury Tales*,' p 253).

417 Raleigh, Sir Walter A. 'On Chaucer.' In *On Writing and Writers: Being Extracts from his Notebooks*. Selected and ed. by George Gordon. London: E. Arnold, 1926. Pp 103–19.
'Anything on a large or generous scale, such as the housekeeping of the Franklin ("It snewed in his hous of mete and drinke" [line 345]), or the marriages of the Wife of Bath, arouses Chaucer's sympathy. He loves a rogue, so that the rogue be high-spirited and clever at his trade, and not a whey-faced, bloodless rascal' (p 112).

418 Reidy, John. 'Grouping of Pilgrims in the General Prologue to *The Canterbury Tales*.' *MichA*, 47 (1962), 595–603.
Chaucer begins *GP* with the Knight, Squire, and Yeoman to gain 'the initial goodwill of the audience towards a new kind of poem' (p 596), for this group reflects the predispositions of his courtly audience. The second group (Prioress, Monk, and Friar) introduces a satirical tone. The third group (Merchant, Man of Law, Franklin, and Clerk) is unified by the Clerk, 'on whom the group pivots' (p 600). The fourth group (the Guildmen) provides a bridge to more humble functions. The fifth group (Cook, Shipman, Doctor, Wife, Parson, and Plowman) consists of people 'engaged in some practical, nonadministrative type of work' (p 601); the section ends with the model Parson and Plowman, who with the model Knight represent the traditional three estates. After this point, which 'might have been an effective ending,' there follows a sixth group, the 'rogues' gallery' (p 602) of Reeve, Miller, Summoner, Pardoner, and Manciple, whose common characteristic is swindling. Overall, Chaucer arranged the groups 'for the literary purposes of manipulating his audience and for setting up different satirical standards, as well as for dealing with the pilgrims roughly in accordance with their status or function' (p 603). Different 'bridges of association' link each group to the next — except for the last group, where the abrupt break is 'a means of controlling the audience's attitude towards it' (p 603).

419 Reinecke, George F. 'Speculation, Intention, and the Teaching of Chaucer.' In *The Learned and the Lewed: Studies in Chaucer and Medieval Literature* [in Honor of Bartlett Jere Whiting]. Ed. Larry Benson. Cambridge, MA: Harvard University Press, 1974. Harvard English Studies, 5. Pp 81–93.

Reinecke considers that certain parts of *GP* represent work in progess, not a final text. What should be offered to students at lines 163–65 is line 163 as usually given, line 164 through the word *chapeleyne*, and then a full-line lacuna to suggest a break in the text before what is now line 165. That would constitute 'a text frankly imperfect and surely Chaucer's' (p 84). The missing portrait of the Second Nun is, like other cruxes, a sign of work in progess, for 'Chaucer could no more have fully developed all the pilgrims by one act of his imagination than he could have written all the tales simultaneously' (p 84). Similarly, the Guildsmen are not individuated, as would be required for 'that later interaction of pilgrims in link and tale which is the hallmark' of *CT* (p 85), and after *GP* they do not reappear anywhere. Nevertheless, they are 'Chaucer's own creatures,' and should be accepted as genuine, though 'Chaucer quite possibly intended to drop them from his finished work and may have hesitated only because he would have had to find a new reason for the presence on pilgrimage of his highly characterized Cook' (p 85).

420 Reiss, Edmund. 'The Pilgrimage Narrative and the *Canterbury Tales*.' *SP*, 67 (1970), 295–305.
CT should be seen in the context of other pilgrimage narratives, although it differs from them in several ways. 'It makes concrete the usual allegorical figures of the pilgrimage' (p 299); 'it fragments the usual Everyman-type journeyer into thirty or so characters, thus allowing for an even greater audience involvement' (p 300) than is typical. Because of these changes, most of the characters 'do not strike us essentially as pilgrims,' although they are indeed 'varieties of true and false seekers' (p 300) and to some extent represent the various sins that need to be purged. Those who are false seekers (the Miller, Friar, Summoner, and Pardoner, for example) seem to be on pilgrimage 'not to Jerusalem but to Babylon, worldly city of sin and allegorical figure of Hell' (p 300). The real pilgrim is the audience, whom the work supplies with an occasion for making a personal internal pilgrimage. See also **644**.

421 ——. 'Chaucer's Parodies of Love.' In *Chaucer the Love Poet*. Ed. Jerome Mitchell and William Provost. Athens, GA: University of Georgia Press, 1973. Pp 27–44.
Parody summons up the image of the ideal, as well as making fun of the actual. 'In seeing the inadequacies of Friar Huberd, we necessarily call up the ideal of friars' (p 27). Similarly, the Wife's portrait parodies the ideal of the Virgin Mary. As 'the Virgin was famous for weaving the cloth without a seam' (p 28), so the Wife is a weaver; Mary was called the Virgin but was not barren, while Alisoun is called the Wife but is without offspring; the kinds of love that they represent are ironically different. The Host is

'a parody of the Christian concept of Host, man's proper spiritual food' (p 28), and the primarily earthly pilgrimage suggests the ideal one by contrast.

The 'Discussion' section of this symposium volume, pp 91–106, also includes brief comments on *GP* — eg, reservations about Reiss's thesis, the suggestion that the Pardoner's song echoes the Song of Songs, and a consideration of humor in the Franklin's portrait.

422 Rhodes, James Francis. *Pilgrimage: Chaucer's Earnest Game.* Fordham University Dissertation. 1974. Dir. Joseph E. Grennan. See also *DAI*, 35 (1974), 1669-A.

Rhodes approaches pilgrimage 'in its cultural setting as another example of the earnest/game *topos*' (p 11). The etymology and functions of pilgrimage, with its sacred and secular aspects, are discussed. 'Before and even during Chaucer's lifetime there are indications that *play* and *game* were reaching to acquire independent existence from *earnest*' (p 26). Harry Bailly's proposal is 'the central game in the poem' and he himself 'is always predisposed to play' (pp 99–100). He 'makes no pretense of riding along with the pilgrims as a fellow pilgrim' (p 101), for his interest is wholly in the game. Despite its secular purpose, the game supports certain aspects of the sacred pilgrimage. For example, 'the levelling of social class distinctions by the game promotes the ideal of *compaignye*, or an approximation of the Christian ideal of *felaweshipe*' (p 103).

423 Richardson, Janette. *Blameth Nat Me: A Study of Imagery in Chaucer's Fabliaux.* The Hague and Paris: Mouton, 1970.

Chaucer's portraits (except for those of the Parson and the Manciple) combine *effictio*, or visual portraiture, with *notatio*, or statements about character. 'Unlike either the traditional *effictio* or *notatio*, the details in Chaucer's portraits are specific and unique,' chosen to 'suggest the essence of the pilgrim's personality' (p 67). Various devices of irony are involved, including 1) ironic figurative comparisons (eg, the Monk's bridle jingles like a chapel bell, line 171; the Friar is a noble post, line 214) and 2) the later recurrence of *GP* details elsewhere (eg, in the Friar's and Summoner's tales.) 'The portraits of the pilgrims, then, illustrate Chaucer's creation of irony through imagery, and his adaptation of a stylized rhetorical-poetic device to suit his own purposes' (p 72).

424 Rickert, Edith, compiler. *Chaucer's World.* Ed. Clair C. Olson and Martin M. Crow. Illustrations selected by Margaret Rickert. London: Geoffrey Cumberledge for Oxford University Press, 1948; New York: Columbia University Press, 1948.

A great many contemporary sources are used to document various aspects of fourteeth-century life. Of special relevance to *GP* are the sections on careers, travel (including pilgrimage), war, the rich and the poor, and religion (including devotional guilds). To give one example of the diverse and detailed materials represented here, there is a list of expenses for two boys sent to school by Gilbert Maghfeld, who has been suggested as the historical basis for the portrait of the Merchant (pp 112–14). See also **425**.

425 ——. *Life in Mediaeval Times: Extracts from Contemporary Writings from 'Chaucer's World' by Edith Rickert*. Illustrated by Celia Young. Maidstone College of Art (privately printed), 1950 (?).
This short book consists of illustrated selections from Rickert, **424**.

426 Ridley, Florence H. 'Questions without Answers—Yet or Ever? New Critical Modes and Chaucer.' *ChauR*, 16 (1981–1982), 101–06.
Ridley argues that Chaucer leaves questions unanswered in order to involve the reader in the process of creativity. Several of these questions pertain to *GP*: 'Does the Prioress's motto ... refer to Christian charity or secular concupiscence? Is the Friar's bestowing of doweries an act of openhanded generosity, or an attempt to hide the result of his dalliance with village maidens? Which way are we to take the ambiguous comments on the Man of Law .... Is he wise? Is he busy? Or does he only appear to be so? And what about the Merchant? .... Is he prosperous, or a bankrupt whose plight is as yet undetected? As teachers of Chaucer know full well, the questions in the *General Prologue* alone are many, multifaceted, and deliberate' (pp 103–04).

427 Robertson, D.W., Jr. *A Preface to Chaucer: Studies in Medieval Perspectives*. Princeton, NJ: Princeton University Press, 1962; London: Oxford University Press, 1962. 5th printing 1969. Rev ed. 1970.
Robertson emphasizes the allegorical nature of medieval literature and visual art: they are 'intended to lead the mind toward something beyond' (1962, p 137). *GP* shows Chaucer's use of iconographic detail in characterization. The Miller 'is the very picture of *discordia*' (p 243). Similarly, 'the various attributes of the prioress all point in one direction: she is a peculiarly striking exemplar of false courtesy,' nourished by 'excessive tenderness with respect to the flesh, or, in other words, by sentimentality' (pp 246–7). Chaucer's details in her portrait 'have no "dramatic" function,' for we do not see her eating or hear her speaking French; 'they serve only to enforce an idea' (p 247). Like the Prioress's portrait, the Monk's description 'reflects the technique of the grotesque,' for his habit suggests the principles of monasticism but his nature is that of 'a deliberate cultivator of the world and the flesh' (p 256). His *venerie* (line 166) and the references to horses in his portrait have sexual overtones; however, the point is not simply that he is lecherous (which would be a sin of the flesh), but that he is inconstant (which is a sin of the spirit). The Wife of Bath's five husbands, along with other details, 'suggest that the wife's marital condition may be

an iconographic device' referring to the Samaritan woman of the Bible, who also had five husbands (p 320). The *GP* characters, despite their verisimilitude, are intended to represent ideas such as these, and 'are in no sense "realistic" ' (p 247). The Host's mention of *sentence* (line 798) would lead Chaucer's audience 'quite naturally to look for *sentence* in the tales as well as for more superficial attractions' — although the Host himself 'is deaf to the *sentence* of what he hears' (p 365).

- Review by R.E. Kaske, 'Chaucer and Medieval Allegory,' *ELH*, 30 (1963), 175–92: Robertson's 'comments on the "iconographical" features of the General Prologue' are said to 'all ring generally true' (p 179), although Kaske interprets details of the Prioress's portrait differently (see **799**) and disagrees with some other specific points. Kaske accepts the book's basic approach and praises 'the richness of learning and the complexity of suggestion,' associating the work with other 'great original studies' (p 192).

- Review by Brinley Rhys, *SR*, 72 (1964), 335–41: Rhys criticizes what he sees as a tendency to view complex matters 'as either black or white' (p 341) and objects to Robertson's historical-allegorical approach.

- See **475**.

428 ——. *Chaucer's London*. New York: John Wiley, 1968. New Dimensions in History: Historical Cities. Series Editor, Norman F. Cantor.
Much information about London's customs, places, offices and officials, etc, is included. The Knight, Clerk, Parson, and Plowman would have reminded Chaucer's audience of the ideals associated with Becket, while the 'low characters were forceful reminders of the decay of the community as a whole' (p 218). The Friar is not meant to be either typical or realistic, but to serve as 'a vivid exemplar of mendicant weaknesses described in Chaucer's imaginative variation on a series of conventional themes' (p 195). The Guildsmen are 'exemplifications of a common weakness of the small businessman' (p 81). The Monk's portrait is 'an exaggerated picture of the inconstancy to which some monks were subject' (p 116). Robertson makes similar comments about other pilgrims. Overall, he argues that Chaucer's characters are not to be regarded as ' "personalities" or as "realistic" reflections of the times,' but instead as 'exemplifications of the ideals and foibles of members of various "degrees" in his society' (p 117).

429 ——. 'Chaucer Criticism.' *M&H*, New Series 8 (1977), 252–55.
Responding to Howard (**287**), Robertson takes issue with the viewpoint that the pilgrims represent a cross-section of English society, since 'there are many gaps' and 'the problem of why Chaucer selected the groups he did has never been faced squarely; it has simply been obscured by a convenient

generalization' (p 254). Similarly, although the pilgrims are said to be types, 'if this means that they are "typical," it is an absurdity' (p 254). The viewpoint that the portraits 'fall into "mnemonic groups" ' is found to be based on 'a rather obscure argument' (p 253) and an absence of familiarity with medieval memory-systems.

430 ——. 'Some Disputed Chaucerian Terminology.' *Spec*, 52 (1977), 571–81. Rpt in Robertson's *Studies in Medieval Culture* (Princeton: Princeton University Press, 1980), pp 291–301.
Evidence about fourteenth-century agrarian life indicates that 'Chaucer was not, in any modern sense of the word, "class conscious." He judged his characters on the basis of their moral qualities and on their abilities to contribute to the coherence of community life with self-restraint and industry' (1977, p 580). In the Reeve's portrait 'Chaucer is not attacking reeves, but is demonstrating or exemplifying the weakness to which unscrupulous as distinct from inefficient reeves might be especially prone' (p 575). Similarly, the Plowman 'is not meant to be either a "typical" plowman or an "individual," but a statement of ideals, just as the picture of the Reeve is a picture of the failure of ideals' (p 576). The Yeoman is 'a manorial servant, a "yeoman" by virtue of the fact that his industry and efficiency in faithful service have made him a man above his fellows' (p 579). His bow and arrows 'may be a reminder of the triumphs of English archers in the field' (p 579).

431 ——. 'Chaucer and the "Commune Profit": the Manor.' *Mediaevalia*, 6 (1980) [Special Volume in Honor of Bernard F. Huppé], 239–59.
GP includes several pilgrims associated with the manorial system. The Yeoman is 'clearly a manorial servant, though we are not given very much information about him' (p 249). The Franklin's 'expensive Epicurean tastes and his ostentation mark him as a self-seeking enemy of the old order' (p 249). The Franklin and the Wife — who may be 'an essentially rural character' — are 'amusing caricatures of persons whose views are dominated by a spirit of enterprising self-interest' (p 249). The Miller's sword, speech, and wrestling 'make him a striking if exaggerated exemplar of the contentiousness that plagued agrarian communities after 1349' (p 249). The Reeve is intended 'to exemplify the worst qualities of reeves who have no real fidelity either to their lords or to their communties' (p 250). The Parson and Plowman, presumably both peasants, show a concern for others that is in contrast to many contemporary examples of peasant behavior. 'Generally speaking, the loyalty of Chaucer's characters and their interest in community obligations were matters that would have registered at once in the minds of his audience' (p 250).

432 Robinson, Ian. *Chaucer and the English Tradition.* London: Cambridge University Press, 1972.

In the chapter 'Chaucer's Pure Poetry: I, The General Prologue' (pp 86–91), Robinson proposes that in *GP* 'the seriousness and the liveliness, properly understood, are the recto and verso of the same leaf' (p 86). Their double presence does not mean that Chaucer is tolerant, as he has been called, for 'Chaucer is not tolerant. He sees the grim things as straight as Dante; he shows their grimness (which is to be intolerant of them) and finds them funny nevertheless' (p 86). The Friar is depraved and the Summoner and Pardoner are horrifying, yet they are 'desperately funny' at the same time (p 87). Chaucer sees things, 'including the horrible and the mean,' as they are, and gives us 'the pure poetic joy of recognizing the truth' (p 90). *GP* is 'Chaucer's pure poetry' in the sense of being 'as near as he comes to doing everything at once' (p 90). As such it is 'the centre, and the other works, straining a little towards each other, meet in it' (p 91).

433 Rodax, Yvonne. *The Real and the Ideal in the Novella of Italy, France, and England.* Chapel Hill, NC: University of North Carolina Press, 1968. University of North Carolina Studies in Comparative Literature, 44.

Chaucer presents 'the illusion of real life' in *GP* 'by working in two directions: *outward*, from the abstract concept or prototype represented by each personage, and *inward*, from the material world in which he has securely anchored each one as an individual' (p 26).

434 Rogers, P. Burwell. 'The Names of the Canterbury Pilgrims.' *Names*, 16 (1968), 339–46.

'Chaucer was not particularly concerned about giving names to the pilgrims. They were ordinary people representing a cross-section of society' (p 346) and most of the names Chaucer chooses are quite ordinary ones. The Prioress's name, whether 'inspired by the name of the wild flower or by the name of a heroine of romance' (p 339), fits her personality. The Friar's name might perhaps have been influenced by 'the rise of something like a cult of St Hubert (c. 656–728), Bishop of Liège and patron of huntsmen' (p 341), or, as Muscatine suggests (**939**), by the Renart tradition. The Merchant is distinguished by being the only *GP* pilgrim about whom Chaucer remarks that he does not know his name. The other names of the pilgrims — eg, the Wife's name Alice or Alisoun — are also briefly considered.

435 Rogers, William Elford. 'Individualization of Language in the Canterbury Frame Story.' *AnM*, 15 (1974), 74–108.

The pilgrims' individualized styles of language in their end-links tend to fit their *GP* portraits. The percentage of Romance- and Latin-based words shows that, in general, 'churls speak as churls' while 'the pilgrims of higher educational level reflect their station in their speech' (p 79). On this measure, Chaucer the pilgrim falls at the middle, making him '*inconspicuous* — exactly what we should expect' (p 79). The Man of Law's concern with language (see lines 312–13 and 325–26) is evident in his prologue; 'through the rhetoric he assigns him Chaucer reinforces the notion that the Man of Law "semed bisier than he was" ' (p 83; see line 322). The Franklin's excessively high diction coincides with his mixture of 'social pretensions, genial hospitality, and affable "gentillesse" ' (p 80). The Prioress's speech is 'impassioned, but gently, and her utterance is from the beginning more clearly controlled' (p 83), which suits her *GP* portrait with its mention of courtly cheer and dignified manner (lines 139–41). The Clerk's syntax 'reinforces the impression that he is a man who would "gladly teche" ' (p 84; see line 308). The Reeve's imagery is 'appropriate to a man whose livelihood is the management of the physical objects of a farm' (p 87). The Host's speechmannerisms suggest his imperiousness and his 'foremost concern, that all the pilgrims be merry' (p 89); in his first *GP* speech (lines 761–83) he uses the terms *myrie* or *myrthe* five times, and he is said to be a merry man (line 757) who spoke of mirth (line 759) — thus his own language agrees with what the narrator says about him. The Pardoner's language shows a 'comparative poverty of concrete, homely imagery, of figurative language in general, and of proverbial sayings,' which 'reinforces the impression of his character' (p 90) as given in *GP*.

436 Root, Robert K. *The Poetry of Chaucer*. Boston: Houghton, 1906. Rev ed., 1922. Rpt 1934; and rpt New York: Peter Smith, 1950.
GP is briefly examined in the chapter 'The Canterbury Tales, Group A' (1950, pp 151–80). 'It is by their successful blending of the individual with the typical that the portraits of Chaucer's Prologue attain to so high a degree of effectiveness' (p 161). The details Chaucer includes 'nearly always *suggest* at once the individual and the type' (p 161). While the individualization gives the work 'its dramatic realism and lifelikeness,' the universality makes *GP* (and the whole work) 'a compendium of human life' (pp 161–2). The Wife represents 'certain of the primary instincts of woman,' for example, while the Prioress represents 'the conventional as opposed to the natural' type of woman (p 161). Since the pilgrims are on vacation, rather than being engaged in their usual tasks, 'it is their essential humanity which is emphasized; each is measured by the absolute standards of manhood' (p 162).

437 Rosenberg, Bruce A. 'The Oral Performance of Chaucer's Poetry: Situation and Medium.' *FForum*, 13 (1980), 224–37.
The oral delivery of Chaucer's works should caution us against assuming that every repetition would have been noticed by his audience, or must have

been intended as a device of parallelism. Many repetitions may represent only conventional ways of saying things. Eg, in line 99 Chaucer calls the Squire *curteis*, *lowely*, and *servysable*; in line 250 he calls the Friar *curteis* and *lowely of servyse*; but Chaucer is probably simply describing 'a situation, idea, or trait in conventional language ... It seems unlikely that an aural audience would recall these phrases, uttered as they were several minutes apart' (p 234). Therefore we should not interpret the verbal similarity as necessarily linking the two portraits with each other.

438 Rowland, Beryl. *Blind Beasts: Chaucer's Animal World*. Kent, OH: Kent State University Press, 1971.

The animal imagery in *GP* is discussed repeatedly in this study. A few examples concern the hare (lines 191, 684), the mouse (lines 144–45), birds such as the swan (lines 205–6 — with the possibility that the poultry-loving Monk is later to be identified with the fox of *NPT*), the sheep (lines 416, etc), the wolf (line 513), and the ape (line 706). As for horses, the Ellesmere manuscript's illustrations, as well as its text, are considered in assessing how the different kinds of horses function to characterize the pilgrims. The Shipman's rouncy, for example, was an impressive-looking horse, but would have had a hard gait unsuited to an inexperienced rider. The Monk's palfrey, with its bells, suggests his worldliness. In general, Chaucer uses conventional, traditional ideas about animals. Often 'the animal embodies the least attractive qualities of man' (p 167). Seen through 'the double vision of the Gothic world,' the 'unlicensed vitality' of animal life is 'a quality simultaneously attractive and repellant' (p 167). The book is based on Rowland's dissertation, *Blynde Bestes, Aspects of Chaucer's Animal World*, University of British Columbia, 1962.

439 ——. '*Pronuntiatio* and its Effect on Chaucer's Audience.' *SAC*, 4 (1982), 33–51.

'Chaucer's personal presence' while reciting his works 'made the reaction of the audience different from our own' (p 51). For example, because we do not know how the portrait of the Prioress was recited 'we can delight in the ambiguities,' but the text 'must have been less flexible to that contemporary audience' because Chaucer's mode of delivery would have clarified the interpretation (p 46). Lines 725–42 express 'a direct concern with problems of oral delivery' (p 44) and refer to 'the speech, not the writing, of the highest authority' (p 45). In transmitting the speech and facial expressions of his characters as he recited, Chaucer was conforming to the advice on *pronuntiatio*, or oral interpretation, given by the rhetoricians.

440 Ruggiers, Paul G. 'The Form of the Canterbury Tales: Respice Fines.' *CE*, 17 (1955-1956), 439–43.

GP resembles the *visio* form used by Dante, and like Dante 'Chaucer makes the journey himself' (p 440). However, unlike Dante 'Chaucer merges himself with a crowd, one of their number, as though humanity were too complex to be reduced to a type and he too diffident to define it' (p 440). The portraits constitute 'a living picture-gallery of medieval humanity' — 'an array of men and women who twitch and mutter while their creator holds them still for a moment within a traditional frame of medieval characterization' (p 440).

441 Rutledge, Sheryl P. 'Chaucer's Zodiac of Tales.' *Costerus*, 9 (1973), 117–43.

'The cyclical progression inherent in the arrangement of the figures of the zodiac' gave Chaucer 'a ready model of the natural flow of existence,' and 'this astrological pattern' has served as 'the hidden motif of *The Canterbury Tales*' (p 117). The first twelve lines of *GP* create 'an image of the first sign of the zodiac' (p 121) — then thought to be Aries, for the month in which the world was created. The section containing the portraits, however, 'occurs within the dominion of Taurus, the second sign' (p 120). The seventeenth-century writer William Lilly associates Taurus with '"the poverty or wealth of the people," a theme which Chaucer is known to have incorporated in his tales on a spiritual level' (p 120). In addition, as Wood has pointed out (see **662**), the Noah story provided an antecedent for a journey beginning in mid-April. It is perhaps for these reasons that Chaucer, although evoking Aries, sets the time of the journey in Taurus instead, progressing in the second section of *GP* from Aries, which is past, to Taurus, in 'the literary present' (p 121).

442 Saito, Shunichi. 'Chaucer's Method of Description in the Prologue to the Canterbury Tales and his Common Touch.' *KJDD*, 16 (1978), 223–33.

Not seen; listed in *A Bibliography of Publications on Medieval English Language and Literature in Japan* (Tokyo: Center for Medieval Studies, Tokyo University, 1983), p 148, #12.

443 Salter, Elizabeth, and Derek Pearsall. 'Chaucer's Realism.' In *English Poetry*. [Ed. Alan Sinfield.] London: Sussex Publications, 1976. Sussex Books, Questions in Literature. Pp 36–51.

In an edited dialogue, Salter and Pearsall discuss the range of realism in *GP*. The interpretation of certain portraits requires an accurate understanding of historical data. The Reeve's hair style, for example, was becoming more fashionable and marks him as 'very much a man of the future,' while the Squire's hair style 'is probably slightly more traditional' (Salter, p 38; cf lines 81, 589–90). *GP* shows degrees of realism, ranging from the accurate depiction of actual life to idealization. Sometimes a 'detail which has the arbitrariness of complete realism' (Pearsall, p 41) may also convey an ironic meaning, as with the Cook's *mormal* (line 386). The sequence of portraits, which seems to reflect the 'haphazardness of life,' is similarly 'intended to enhance our sense of the judgments that are being made under the surface. For instance, the Clerk is sandwiched between the Man of Law and the Merchant so that you get a stronger sense of the stringency and austerity of the Clerk's character' (Pearsall, p 42).

444 Saunders, John. *Chaucer's Canterbury Tales, Annotated and Accented, with Illustrations of English Life in Chaucer's Time.* New and revised edition. London: Dent, 1904.

The discussion of *GP* (pp 5–169) is divided into commentaries on the Tabard Inn and then on the pilgrims arranged into four groups: Chivalry, Religion, Professional Men, and Trade and Commerce. Extensive background information, some of it anecdotal, is provided. For instance, in the section on the Franklin (who is included in the category of Trade and Commerce) Saunders comments on Saint Julian, on the meaning of *contour* (line 359) and *vavasour* (line 360), and on the domestic economy and agricultural operations of manor-houses.

445 Schaar, Claes. *The Golden Mirror: Studies in Chaucer's Descriptive Technique and Its Literary Background.* Lund: Gleerup, 1955. Skrifter Utgivna av Kungl. Humanistiska Vetenskapssamfundet i Lund, 54. Rpt with index, 1967.

GP is discussed in several sections of the long chapter 'The Portraits' (1955, pp 167–367). The descriptions can be grouped into categories according to their techniques. In a few portraits, only one type of description is used; the Yeoman's portrait is wholly 'objective,' while the Cook, Manciple, and Parson 'are described exclusively with regard to their professions' (p 211). In the remaining portraits more than one descriptive approach is used. In some, concrete description is not stressed, being 'relegated to the end of the paragraphs,' while 'the character, profession, status, and habits' are of predominant interest (p 211) — the portraits of the Knight, Prioress, Monk, Friar, Man of Law, Physician, and Plowman belong in this category. In other cases, 'more stress is laid on the outward appearance of the figures' (p 211) — as with the Squire, Merchant, Clerk, Franklin, Guildsmen, Shipman, Wife, Miller, Reeve, Summoner, Pardoner. The medieval audience was 'used to the fact that descriptions of inward qualities dealt mainly with noble characters, but that concrete description was almost the only possibility in portraits of the other, less dignified and exalted *dramatis personae*' (p 330). Chaucer 'to some extent allowed this [traditional] distinction to influence his different ways of portraying the pilgrims' (p 333). Furthermore, concrete descriptions seem more common in Middle English poetry than in continental works. Chaucer 'seems to have developed to the full what may perhaps best be regarded as a traditional tendency' in

English poetry (p 325). Many aspects of this extensive study are indirectly applicable to *GP*. See also **446**.

446 ——. 'A Postscript to Chaucer Studies.' *ES*, 42 (1961), 153–56.
Schaar defends his earlier analysis (**445**) of Chaucer's portraiture.

447 Schinnagel, Margret. *Schmuck als Lebensäusserung in den Werken Chaucers.* Friedrich-Wilhelm-Universität Dissertation (Breslau). 1936. Dir. Dr. Matthes and Dr. Meissner. Published Würzburg: Triltsch, 1938.
Aspects of the pilgrims' personal appearance and adornment are briefly discussed. For example, under the category of long hair the Pardoner's hair and other instances are collected; under the category of girdles the Franklin's *gipser*, which hangs at his girdle (line 357), is mentioned; and so forth.

448 Schirmer, W.F. 'Boccaccios Werke als Quelle G. Chaucers.' *GRM*, 12 (1924), 288–305.
The similarities and differences in Chaucer's and Boccaccio's uses of the framework are indicated. Despite the resemblances, Chaucer's literary qualities are quite different from Boccaccio's. His genius was not shaped upon Boccaccio's, his way was not Boccaccio's, and he would have pursued it without Boccaccio. Therefore the whole question of substantive influence takes on only a subordinate significance. ('Chaucers dichterisches Genie ist durch Boccaccio nicht umgeformt worden, und da sein Weg nicht der Boccaccios war, wäre er ihn auch ohne Boccaccio gegangen. Damit nimmt aber die ganze Frage der stofflichen Beeinflussung eine untergeordnete Bedeutung an,' p 305).

449 Sedgwick, H.D. *Dan Chaucer: An Introduction to the Poet, his Poetry and his Times.* New York: Bobbs-Merrill, 1934.
In this general book, Sedgwick describes the Tabard, divides the pilgrims into Sympathetic and Unsympathetic categories, and briefly reviews the characteristics of each one. The Prioress, Host, and Monk are classed among the Sympathetic pilgrims; the Franklin, Shipman, Serjeant, Physician, and Merchant among the Unsympathetic pilgrims. The Wife 'stands in a category by herself' (p 238).

450 Sekimoto, Eiichi. 'Chaucer No Egaita Josei — Madame Eglentyne To Wife of Bath.' [Chaucer's Women — Madame Eglentyne and the Wife of Bath.] *SDB* 1, 1 (1953), 34–46.
Not seen; listed in *A Bibliography of Publications on Medieval English Language and Literature in Japan* (Tokyo: Center for Medieval Studies, Tokyo University, 1983), p 150, #12.

451 Shelly, Percy Van Dyke. *The Living Chaucer.* Philadelphia: University of Pennsylvania Press, 1940; London: Humphrey Milford, 1940. Rpt New

York: Russell & Russell, 1968.

In the chapter 'The Canterbury Tales: I' (1940, pp 194–241), Shelly lays emphasis on the originality of *GP* — 'it is the first thing of its kind in all literature' (p 194); on its breadth as 'a gallery of portraits' (p 195); and on its descriptive realism — 'the *Prologue* is a triumph of realism, and Chaucer's realistic method here is essentially descriptive, not dramatic' (p 195). Chaucer tends to accumulate facts. *GP*, as 'one of the most matter-of-fact compositions in the world,' shows the power of 'the sense of fact' and 'is one of the supreme examples of intensity in art' (p 197). The facts recorded in *GP* are drawn from life. The portraits are saved from monotony by Chaucer's zest (to him the world is never dull or insipid) and by his humor and satire. His fiction that everything stated in *GP* comes from the narrator's observation is sometimes ignored as he invokes instead the conventional omniscience of storytellers. *GP* is static, its portraits 'still-life,' and 'it gains its chief interest and importance from what follows, from the tales and links which put the pilgrims in action' (p 204).

452 Shilkett, Carol Lee. *'Chaucerian Realism': A Study of Mimesis in the Canterbury Pilgrimage.* Michigan State University Dissertation. 1972. See also *DAI*, 33 (1973), 5141-A.

The chapter 'The Pilgrims' (pp 18–113) examines each of the *GP* portraits in terms of the theory of Max Dvorak, who suggests that Gothic art 'aims to move from *imperfectum* to *perfectum* through *similitudo* — the process of mimesis' and that as figures approach perfection 'the more simplified, and less individualized,' they will be (p 18). Thus the 'portrait gallery at the Tabard Inn contains a variety of classes and varying levels of *imperfectum* and *perfectum*' (p 19). The inclusion of *realia* (external details) does not in itself produce an impression of complete realism and life-like personality. 'In many ways the characters governed by *realia* seem most realistic to the modern critic ... Yet they lack the character development which comes, most often, from the use and variation of conventions' (p 103). The most vivid pilgrims show both mimetic, external traits and 'satiric conventions indicative of certain personality traits' (p 103). An appendix (pp 108–9) offers a statistical tabulation of descriptive details, with an overall 'mimetic ranking' of the portraits: the Monk and Friar are at the top of the list, the Plowman and Parson at the bottom. 'The figures which are most lifelike are those portrayed in their transcience, in their faults. The least realistic are portrayed simply, in terms which stress their universality, not their individuality' (p 106).

453 Sinicropi, Giovanni, ed. *Giovanni Sercambi: Novelle.* Scrittori d'Italia, 251. Bari: Gius, Laterza & Figli, 1972.

Sercambi's *Novelle* has been proposed as a model for the *GP* framework.

Sinicropi argues, however, that the journey described in the *Novelle* cannot have been begun before 1399 or 1400 ('Ci sembra perciò evidente che la raccolta delle *Novelle* non poté essere iniziata prima dell'anno 1399 o 1400,' p 785n). The idea that Sercambi's work influenced Chaucer's is an impossibility, since Chaucer finished his collection in about 1385–1387 ('Cosa impossibile, dato che l'autore inglese, com'è noto, finiva di scrivere la sua raccolta nel 1385–87,' p 785n). This item incorporates the viewpoints expressed in Sinicropi's article, 'Per la Datazione delle Novelle del Sercambi,' *GSLI*, 141 (1964), 548–56. In reply, see Nicholson, **393**.

454 Sklute, Larry. 'Catalogue Form and Catalogue Style in the General Prologue of the *Canterbury Tales*.' *SN*, 52 (1980), 35–46.
The *GP* portraits use the traditional techniques of the literary catalogue and the rhetorical *descriptio*, but are more dynamic. Chaucer achieves this dynamic effect by several means. He emphasizes people's actions: 'We know what kinds of people these are by what they do' (p 39). He uses conjunctions in unusual ways. He recognizes the possibility of individual psychological motivation, as well as symbolic meanings; for example, the Prioress's combination of details 'produces a psychological picture of a woman whose frustrations lead her perhaps to over-eat' as well as 'to over-sentimentalize her charity' (p 41). He combines incongruous elements 'so that moral evaluation must remain inconclusive' (p 42). Chaucer also intertwines the portraits through repeated words (such as *worthy*) or echoing sets of lines (lines 99 and 250, 72 and 422, etc), thereby establishing 'an ironic dynamism between characters' (p 44). In addition, he uses the double-entendre, which 'conflates into one line or few the alternating or competing qualities which fill the catalogue form of each portrait' (p 45). In *GP* Chaucer has thus created 'a most unusual and complex form of description, at once traditionally and morally symbolic yet capable of energetic and psychologically mimetic development' (p 45). The characters 'rest in a middle state, a state between the static, the exemplary, and the dynamic, even the mimetic' (p 46). Like the narrator, they are ' "redy to wenden" ' on pilgrimage (p 46), with various possibilities of further development open to them.

455 Slaughter, Eugene Edward. *Virtue According to Love — in Chaucer*. New York: Bookman Associates, 1957. Bookman Monograph Series for Modern Language Studies.
Slaughter provides an analysis of medieval concepts of love and virtue, both religious and earthly. One pole of love is charity, the other cupidity; whether a desire is seen as good or bad depends on the system of virtue being applied. In the section on *GP* (pp 231–34), Slaughter briefly lists for each pilgrim the systems of loves and virtues represented and the particular

virtues, vices, and sins exemplified. The entry on the Franklin, for example, reads 'Systems represented: Religio-philosophical. Virtues: Largess (hospitality). Vices and sins: Gluttony' (p 233). The book is based on Slaughter's dissertation, *Love and the Virtues and Vices in Chaucer,* Vanderbilt University, 1946 — a condensed version of which was published in a private edition, Nashville, TN: Joint University Libraries, 1946.

456 [Smyth, Eleanor C.] *An Essay on Chaucer Chiefly on the Prologue to the Canterbury Tales, Together with some Criticisms on our Earliest Great Poet, by Competent Modern Writers. By the Author of Sir Rowland Hill, K.C.B., Etc. The Story of a Great Reform.* [Bexhill-on-Sea, England, 1924.]

In this 23-page pamphlet, brief comments by earlier critics such as Tuckwell (see **481**) are cited, and aspects of the pilgrimage framework and the portraits are appreciated. For example: 'April, Chaucer tells us, with its sweet showers, the drought of March had pierced to the root, and by the second half of that month of alternate smiles and tears was speeding towards May, a season for out-door expeditions and visits to favourite shrines' (p 10). The author's name and the publication data (given above) appear at the end of the text, not on the title page.

457 Snell, F.J. *The Age of Chaucer.* Intro. J.W. Hales. London: Bell, 1901.

GP is summarized. Chaucer may have been indebted to other frame-tales, but his work 'is individual in the sense that it is strongly dramatic' (p 195).

458 Speirs, John. 'Chaucer (II): The Canterbury Tales.' *Scrutiny,* 11 (1942–1943), 189–211; continued in *Scrutiny,* 12 (1943–1944), 35–57.

Chaucer's 'profounder seriousness' is to be discovered, 'where perhaps [Matthew] Arnold least thought of looking for it, at the basis of the great *Prologue*' (p 195). The ecclesiastical portraits in particular demonstrate Chaucer's criticism of life. These portraits are examined, along with comments on other pilgrims and on the tales. A sample: the Prioress's portrait 'presents us an elegant lady rather than a nun' (p 197); in the Monk's portrait 'the irony is founded on a corresponding, if less ambiguous, contrast between his grosser worldliness and sacred profession' (p 197). The importance of the imagery in the portraits is emphasized. On the Pardoner, for instance, Speirs comments that 'once again, if the similes were removed, the character would lose its distinctness' (p 201). Some of this discussion is incorporated in Speirs, **459.**

459 ——. *Chaucer the Maker.* London: Faber and Faber, 1951. Rev ed. 1960; paperback ed. 1964.

In the chapter 'The Prologue' (1964, pp 99–121), Speirs contrasts the celebratory springtime opening — 'poetry that is liberated from conventional diction' (p 100) — and the opening section of T.S. Eliot's *The Waste Land.* 'The *personae* are first presented in the great Prologue with a vividness not attained before in English, even by Chaucer, and seldom since' (p 97). In the portraits 'the art is as much in what is left unsaid as in what is said; and what is said consists in the simple juxtaposition of statements which it is left to the audience to know how to relate' (p 104). An 'inner beauty of life' (p 103) is shared by the Knight, Parson, and Plowman. The Prioress shows 'the most delicately poised irony' (p 104), while the irony directed at the Monk and Friar is stronger. In the ecclesiastical portraits 'the art is in seeing exactly what each is in relation to what each ought to be; an art of exact contemplation but not in a void' (pp 103–4). The pilgrims representing the secular occupations reflect the Seven Deadly Sins. 'Gluttony underlies the Frankeleyn, Avarice the Doctour of Phisyk' (p 112). The portrait of the Wife, 'most vivid of all the secular figures' (p 115), combines the comedy of the sins with a comedy of social types. The Summoner and the Pardoner are so degraded that 'they scarcely belong to the human community' (p 117). 'What composes the Prologue is exceptionally an awareness of ... distinct persons who, entering in a succession, combine into an impression of a people, the English people' (p 102).

460 Spencer, Brian. *Chaucer's London* [exhibit catalogue]. London: London Museum, 1972.
Several items pertinent to *GP* — eg, the effigy of a franklin, images of knights and squires, and pilgrimage souvenirs — are depicted and explained in this catalogue.

461 Spencer, William. 'Are Chaucer's Pilgrims Keyed to the Zodiac?' *ChauR*, 4 (1969-1970), 147–70.
'The twelvefold pattern of signs and planets' is the 'hidden ground plan of the *General Prologue*' (p 149). This pattern consists of the signs of the zodiac combined with the planets thought to rule them. The Knight represents Aries and Mars; Mars stood for war, Aries for beginnings. The Squire represents Taurus and Venus; Venus stood for love and youth, and the sun is in Taurus in May. The Yeoman represents Gemini and Mercury; Mercury stood for servants and intelligence and was associated with the peacock. The Prioress represents Cancer and the Moon. Cancer stood for femininity, mobility, virginal frigidity or coolness, and humidity, as in weeping. The Moon was both mother — the Prioress 'is a kind of mother-figure' (p 153) in her office — and virgin; the Moon as Diana was depicted with dogs. The Monk represents Leo and the Sun; the Monk's face shines like the Sun, which was said to incline people towards corpulence, hunting, gold, etc; the Lion too hunts. The Friar represents Virgo and Mercury; when ill-positioned, Mercury stood for fraudulent eloquence or for imperfections of speech. The Merchant represents Libra and Venus; Libra suggests weight and money; Venus's beauty and elegance are apparent in the Mer-

chant's appearance. The Clerk represents Scorpio and Mars; as 'Scorpio is the negative mansion of Mars' (p 157), the Clerk shows asceticism, plainness of garb, and a tendency towards silence. The Man of Law represents Sagittarius and Jupiter; Jupiter stood for the law. The Franklin represents Capricorn and Saturn; Saturn was associated with old age, eating, and cold. The Guildsmen's group represents Aquarius and Saturn, which stood for 'friendly association' (p 160); the Cook may have been suggested by Aquarius the water-carrier. The Shipman represents Pisces and Jupiter, who stood for a seafaring life involving battles and deceit.

A second cycle of the zodiac, incomplete and more conjectural, now begins. Briefly: the Doctor represents Aries/Mars; the Wife, Taurus/Venus/Mars; the Parson, Gemini/Mercury; the Plowman, Cancer/Moon; the Miller, Leo/Sun; the Manciple, Virgo/Mercury; the Reeve, Libra/Venus; the Summoner, Scorpio/Mars; and the Pardoner, Sagittarius/Jupiter. Chaucer's intention 'was to shape his *General Prologue* into a microcosm of the universe, to create a human pageant matching the pageant in the heavens' (p 169).

462 Stanley, Arthur P. *Historical Memorials of Canterbury*. 10th ed. London: Murray, 1904 [1st ed. 1854]. New ed. for Everyman's Library, London: Dent, 1906; New York: Dutton [1906].
Many details about Becket's murder, the shrine at Canterbury in Chaucer's time, and medieval pilgrimages are provided.

463 Steadman, John M. 'Chaucer's Thirty Pilgrims and Activa Vita.' *Neophil*, 45 (1961), 224–30.
The number thirty that is implied by *GP* — Chaucer the pilgrim plus the twenty-nine *sondry folk* (see lines 24–25) — may have been chosen because of 'the conventional medieval conception of thirty as symbolic of the active life and the married state' (p 227). The ideals of *activa vita* pertain not only to the secular pilgrims, but also to 'those who profess the contemplative and mixed lives' (p 226). Marriage is an important subject in the work as a whole, and the concepts of practicing moral virtue and performing good works, which are central to the ideal *activa vita*, are given recurrent emphasis. Two previous frame-tales that Chaucer knew, Dante's *Purgatorio* and Boccaccio's *Ameto*, had included symbols of *activa vita*. The symbolic value of the number thirty is directly related to the basic pilgrimage motif of the poem, since *activa vita* was associated specifically with journeying.

464 Stevens, Michael. 'The General Prologue.' In *Chaucer's Major Tales*. Ed. Michael Hoy and Michael Stevens. London: Bailey, 1969; Toronto: Clarke, Irwin, 1969. Pp 1–22.
In this guide for students, recent criticism is reviewed and major topics — eg, the pilgrimage setting, the suitability of tales to tellers, the rhetorical

influences on Chaucer's style, the multiple voices, the groupings of pilgrims, and the presence of both variety and unity — are briefly discussed.

465 Stokoe, William C., Jr. 'Structure and Intention in the First Fragment of *The Canterbury Tales.*' *UTQ*, 21 (1951-1952), 120–27.

Stokoe argues that Chaucer unites Fragment I of *CT* through dramatic conflict among the characters. He prepares us for conflict by warning 'the reader in the General Prologue that there are violent contrasts in this company of pilgrims' (p 123). Concentrating on the *MilT* as a response to the *KnT*, Stokoe proposes that 'the contrast between the Knight's and Miller's ways of treating stories about two men in love with the same woman gives the first fragment its essential structure' (p 127). The characterizations in *GP* have prepared the audience for this 'clash of attitudes' and personalities (p 127).

466 Strahan, Speer. 'The Largeness of Chaucer.' *CER*, 31 (1933), 395–411.

Strahan defends Chaucer against charges of immorality or of anti-clericalism. Chaucer was less sharply critical of clerics than were other medieval writers. His nuns 'are patterns of delicacy and good behavior. The Prioress's French, her dogs, her table manners, and her brooch with its *Amor super omnia* are beautiful humanizing traits' (p 406).

467 Sumption, Jonathan. *Pilgrimage: An Image of Medieval Religion.* London: Faber & Faber, 1975.

GP is not discussed in any detail, but a wealth of information about medieval pilgrimage routes, expenses, shrines, customs, etc, is included. For example, the discussion of pilgrimage as medicine for the sick is pertinent to lines 17–18 (see pp 73–97).

468 Swart, J. 'The Construction of Chaucer's *General Prologue.*' *Neophil*, 38 (1954), 127–36.

GP as a whole consists of 'a brief introduction, a long pageant of characters, and a kind of epilogue,' with the central 'procession of pilgrims' being twice interrupted or divided by a group — first by the Guildsmen, second by the 'hardened sinners,' who also appear initially as one group. Within the first division of portraits, the Knight-Squire-Yeoman sequence partly parallels that of the Prioress-Monk-Friar: the Knight can be compared to the Prioress, the Squire to the Monk, the Yeoman to the Friar. In the Merchant-Clerk-Man of Law group, the middle figure stands out by his lack of worldliness; in the Shipman-Physician-Wife group, the middle figure stands out by his learning. The general trend of the first division of *GP*, despite exceptions, 'is one of a decrease of personal and social welfare' (p 134). The Parson and Plowman mark a turning point between this division and that of the sinners. Chaucer's own presence in the latter group was meant 'as a joke with serious implications' (p 129). The Host represents the audience. Overall, 'here is no studied disorder, but a well laid-out whole' (p 136).

469 Taitt, Peter S. *Incubus and Ideal: Ecclesiastical Figures in Chaucer and Langland*. Salzburg: Institut für Englische Sprache und Literatur, Universität Salzburg, 1975. Salzburg Studies in English Literature, Elizabethan & Renaissance Studies, 44.

In the chapter 'Chaucer's Figures' (pp 4–83), Taitt reviews the *GP* portraits of the Friar, Summoner, Clerk, Pardoner, Monk, Prioress, and Parson, pointing out in his conclusion that 'Chaucer's method of characterisation concentrates our interest on the person satirised, while Langland's method concentrates on the abuses which it is concerned to reveal' (p 192). The Monk's portrait is dominated by metaphors of food and hunting; that of the Friar is dominated by wantonness. Similarly, the Summoner is associated with the idea of lechery, the Clerk with learning and virtue, the Pardoner with theft and deceit, the Prioress with matters of external appearance, and the Parson with love of one's neighbor (he is, 'in a limited sense, modelled on Christ in the gospels,' p 69).

470 Tatlock, J.S.P. *The Development and Chronology of Chaucer's Works*. London: Kegan Paul, Trench, Trübner, & Co., 1907. Chaucer Society, Second Series, 37. Rpt Gloucester, MA: Peter Smith, 1963.

In the chapter 'The General Prologue' (pp 142–50), previous viewpoints about the date of *GP* are reviewed. Tatlock points out that lines 276–77, which mention the ports of Middleburgh and Orwell, refer to the period between late 1383 (or early 1384) and 1388, since only during that period was Middleburgh the staple port for wool and similar products. The most probable date of composition of this passage, and presumably of *GP* as a whole, is 1387–1388. The Squire's military experience, which would have been in the 1383 expedition in Flanders, supports this dating. For political reasons it is not likely that Chaucer would have alluded to that campaign for his Squire much later than 1387; thus lines 85–87 on the Squire provide confirmation that 'at least the first part of the *Prologue* was written in 1387' (p 150). Furthermore, Chaucer's service as justice of the peace and as knight of the shire in 1385–1386 would make his mention of those offices in the Franklin's portrait (lines 355–56) 'especially natural' at this time (p 150).

471 ——. 'Boccaccio and the Plan of Chaucer's *Canterbury Tales*.' *Anglia*, 37 (1913), 69–117.

In contrast to Morsbach (**381**), who argued that Chaucer was influenced by the *Decameron*, Tatlock points out what he sees as more significant parallels between the *CT* and two of Boccaccio's other works, the *Filocolo* and *Ameto*. *Filocolo*, which we know Chaucer used in *TC*, includes an episode in which a group of speakers make short presentations; one person suggests the plan, appoints the speakers, and acts as judge, like Chaucer's Host in *GP*. While this episode may not have been 'the chief exemplar of the *Canterbury Tales*, it can hardly have been entirely absent' from Chaucer's mind (p 80). In addition, Boccaccio's *Ameto* includes a set of narratives related by members of a company who gather at a temple for a religious observance in April; their narratives are connected by links; the group has a head who appoints the speakers; the members of the party are fully described, one at a time, at the outset; there is a singing-contest, which is paralleled in the *Canterbury Tales* by the storytelling competition; the narratives are amorous confessions, as are some of those in *CT*; there are verbal similarities to *GP*. Overall, the resemblances to the *Decameron* are less close than those to the *Filocolo* and *Ameto*. In reply, see Korten, **327**.

472 ——. 'Chaucer and Wyclif.' *MP*, 14 (1916-1917), 257–68.

'If we find passages in the *Canterbury Tales* agreeing strikingly with certain of Wyclif's most emphatic opinions not often found elsewhere, it is an acceptable conjecture that Chaucer here shows his influence' (p 67). Two such passages showing Wycliffe's influence in *GP* are line 486, where the idealized Parson does not wish to have people excommunicated for non-payment of tithes; and lines 653–5, in the Summoner's portrait, where 'Chaucer seems to speak lightly and skeptically of both excommunication and absolution' (p 69). Such lines show 'an attitude of doubt toward the power of the keys as commonly understood in Chaucer's day' (p 70). The abuses related to excommunication are one of Wycliffe's main subjects, and the 'height of Wyclif's attack on the power of the keys came only some half-dozen years before the date when Chaucer probably wrote the *Prolog*' (p 72). Further *GP* passages that may show Wycliffe's influence are lines 649–51, on blackmail for concubinage; lines 259–63, on the garb of friars; and lines 235–7, on the friars' singing and playing to attract women. 'The question is not of Chaucer having been a Lollard' (p 67), since he was not a person given to martyrdom, but he certainly knew Wycliffe's views, would have sympathized with some of them, and apparently reflected these opinions in *GP*.

473 ——. *The Mind and Art of Chaucer.* [Ed. Germaine Dempster and Sanford B. Meech.] Syracuse, N.Y.: Syracuse University Press, 1950. Rpt NY: Gordian, 1966.

GP is discussed in the chapter 'The Canterbury Tales' (1950, pp 88–101). Although Chaucer's knowledge of the *Decameron* is not proven, 'it is incredible' that he did not hear of and see it, and Boccaccio is the writer to whom Chaucer owes most 'in congeniality and manner' (p 90). However, it is not necessary to identify a single model for *CT*. The opening of *GP* describes 'neither wild nor parklike nature, but workaday actual England,' which is 'the only fitting background' for the people of *GP* (p 92). The pilgrims, mostly middle-class, are 'vivid types' (p 92), although they sometimes also include atypical traits. The spirit of the portraits is 'rationalistic; Chaucer is becoming fully his essential self, realistic, not romantic' (p 92). The descriptions accordingly tend to be condensed and epigrammatic, with recurrent use of the 'Ovidian closed and balanced couplet' (p 93). The lifelike Host is 'a good toast-master and a crafty manager' who proposes his program of entertainment only after the bill has been paid (p 93).

474 Tedeschi, Svetko. 'Some Recent Opinions about the Possible Influence of Boccaccio's "Decameron" on Chaucer's "Canterbury Tales." ' *SRAZ*, No. 33–6 (1972–1973), 849–72.
Opinion on whether *GP* was influenced by the framework of the *Decameron* is reviewed. Tedeschi agrees with earlier writers who have *not* seen evidence of such influence.

475 Thompson, A. Hamilton. *The English Clergy and Their Organization in the Later Middle Ages.* Oxford: Clarendon Press, 1947.
Chaucer's clerical figures are occasionally mentioned in this broad study. Regarding the Parson, for example, we are warned against seeing him as a wholly ideal (unreal) figure: 'if we accept the Monk and the Prioress, two very respectable people, or the less reputable Friar as types of their several vocations, it would be unfair to assume that the Parson is presented to us as a rare example of a saint' — nor should we 'read into the Parson's simple orthodoxy the reforming zeal of the innovator' (p 101). Many details about ecclesiastical organization, institutions, customs, terminology, and people (eg, William of Clowne) are provided.

476 Thompson, Meredith. 'Current and Recurrent Fallacies in Chaucer Criticism.' In *Essays in American and English Literature Presented to Bruce Robert McElderry, Jr.* Ed. Max F. Schulz, William D. Templeman, and Charles R. Metzger. Athens, OH: Ohio University Press, [1967]. Pp 141–64.
Thompson finds that the analysis of *GP* by Hoffman (284) illustrates the fallacies of 'unwarranted schematic forcing,' 'unwarranted elaboration,' and 'unwarranted implication of ideas' (p 150). The approach of Robertson (427) is considered to involve 'the most exaggerated kind of allegorical fallacy' (p 153). Miller's interpretation of the Pardoner (1321) exemplifies the 'rationalistic fallacy' (p 158). Chaucer 'does not always need such elaborate interpreting, nor has benefited from much of it' (p 164).

477 Thompson, W.H. *Chaucer and His Times.* Foreword by W.L. Andrews. London: A. Brown, 1936.

Brief remarks on *GP* are included in this general sketch of Chaucer's life, times, and writings. In *GP* 'like a master dramatist he draws up the curtain, and we are at once in vital touch with the life of five centuries ago' (p 57).

478 Thundy, Zacharias P. 'Significance of Pilgrimage in Chaucer's *Canterbury Tales.' LHY*, 20 (1979), 64–77.
Chaucer, in choosing the pilgrimage setting, 'dissociated himself from Wycliffites' (p 67), since Wycliffe and his followers preached against pilgrimages. The opening of *GP* shows the synthesis or interpenetration of 'the secular and the sacred, nature and grace, earnest and game, reason and revelation, human love and divine love' (p 69).

479 Tisdale, Charles Pressley Roberts. *The Medieval Pilgrimage and its Use in The Canterbury Tales.* Princeton University Dissertation. 1969. See also *DAI*, 30 (1970), 4958-A.
After considering the significance of pilgrimage, especially the role of penance, Tisdale examines *GP*. The opening lines 'not only look to penance as the primary function of pilgrimage' (p 175), but also foreshadow the Parson's image that likens penitence to a tree (X. 110–15). The pilgrims at the Tabard Inn ought to be in a state of contrition, having made their confessions and being about to undertake the journey as satisfaction for their sins. However, many of them 'do not have that ideal goal in mind which the "Spring Song" and the Parson inspire' (p 183). The contrast between the portraits of the Parson and the Pardoner suggests the range from spiritual to worldly uses of pilgrimage. *GP* 'contains beneath its veil a profound statement about the pilgrimage of this life ... It anticipates the [Parson's] transparent statement of the single criterion necessary to a rewarding end, the repentance of all sinful wanderers' (p 189).

480 Tornwall, William Allen. *Studies in Chaucer's Imagery.* Louisiana State University Dissertation. 1956. Dir. Thomas A. Kirby. See also *DA*, 16 (1956), 1676.
Tornwall includes a chapter on 'The Imagery in Chaucer's Portraits' and shows that 'although his images characteristically contain a mixture of subject matter,' in *GP* the materials used for images 'are appreciably influenced by the character' of the work [from *DA*; diss not seen].

481 Tuckwell, Rev. W. *Chaucer.* London: Bell, 1904. Bell's Miniature Series of Great Writers.
GP is briefly examined in the chapter 'The Canterbury Tales' (pp 43–77). In *GP* Chaucer shows himself to be 'the most perfect story-teller in all literature' (p 49), describing the pilgrims so clearly that we see them all distinctly. 'In a single line, sometimes even by a single word, the verisimilitude is ineffaceably fixed' (p 50). 'Nor can we fail, I think, to observe the large catholicity of his portraits; each a type contemporary with time,

not a transcript from a single century; their traits essential, not provincial, or temporary, or casual' (p 53). Few character-painters have attained 'this universality of presentment' (pp 53–54). We also 'marvel at the naturalness and simplicity of his diction' (p 54), which cannot 'be sampled by detached sentences,' since 'the charm lies in the continuous flow' (p 54).

482 Tupper, Frederick. 'Chaucer and the Seven Deadly Sins.' *PMLA*, 29 (1914), 93–128.
An 'architectonic use' (p 97) of the Seven Deadly Sins is proposed. In the tales the Physician is concerned with Lechery, the Pardoner with Avarice and Gluttony, the Second Nun with Sloth, the Wife with Pride, the Manciple with Wrath, and the Man of Law with Envy. (The Friar's and Summoner's performances illustrate other aspects of Wrath.) The portraits of several of these pilgrims illustrate the sins that their tales will condemn, although this relationship may become apparent only later than *GP*. The 'device of the sins apparently came to the poet late,' since *GP* does not include 'certain of the Vice characteristics upon which so much stress is laid' in the end-links (p 117). On the sins-thesis (though not especially on *GP*) see also Tupper, 'Chaucer's Sinners and Sins,' *JEGP*, 15 (1916), 56–106. In reply, see Lowes, **344**, and Duino, **1306**.

483 ——. 'The Quarrels of the Canterbury Pilgrims.' *JEGP*, 14 (1915), 256–70.
The chief quarrels among the pilgrims represent clashes between classes, rather than individuals. The pairs of Friar and Summoner, Manciple and Cook, and Miller and Reeve would have been recognized in *GP* as representations of hostile classes or occupations. Contemporary regulations intended to curb the abuses of cooks are reviewed, along with other backgound materials. The quarrels of each pair later in *CT* are consistent with the traditions of class enmity drawn upon in *GP*. The combination of characters who represent vices and virtues, and characters who represent social classes or types, reflects a 'natural alliance between morality and class-satire' (p 256). Such a combination is evident elsewhere in medieval literature and was fully appropriate to Chaucer's time. 'Our generation, babbling of Chaucer's artistry and perversely closing its eyes to a moral intent so frequently clear to view, is quite as far away from the fourteenth-century mind, as the men of the Middle Ages, who moralized the *Metamorphoses* and allegorized the *Æneid*, were alien to the classical genius' (p 261). See also **1258**.

484 ——. *Types of Society in Medieval Literature*. New York: Holt, 1926. Brown University, The Colver Lectures, 1926.
Several discussions of *GP* are included. The pilgrims are '*individualized conventions*' (p 16); we prize them for their individualism, but the medieval audience would have prized them more for their typicality. 'Chaucer

is to us a great portrait-painter; to his own time a dextrous expositor or generalizer' (p 17). The pilgrims show similarities to the conventional understandings of human types, such as those that are described in the moralized *Chess Book* (the *Liber de Moribus Hominum et Officiis Nobilium*). For example, the antithesis between *worthy* and *wis* (line 68) corresponds to the *Chess Book*'s viewpoint that wisdom is the most important trait for a knight. Chaucer's Plowman resembles the *Chess Book*'s 'laborer of the earth' (p 41). The Merchant, Physician, and Host too show conventional features found in works such as the *Chess Book*. The quarrels between the Miller and the Reeve, the Friar and the Summoner, and the Cook and the Manciple are traditional quarrels between the occupations they represent. The convention of the Seven Deadly Sins is also used in *GP*.

485 ——. 'Chaucer and the Cambridge Edition.' *JEGP*, 39 (1940), 503–26.
Tupper defends his earlier viewpoint that some of the pilgrims illustrate the Seven Deadly Sins (see **482–484**) against what he sees as Robinson's inadequate acceptance of that concept in his edition (**42**). On the Wife, see **1168**.

486 Ullmann, Ingeborg M. *Der Erzähler der Canterbury Tales: Das Literarische Werk in seiner kommunikativen Funktion.* Bern: Herbert Lang, 1973. Europäische Hochschulschriften, Angelsachsische Sprache und Literatur, 15.
Using semiotic theories of language as communication, Ullmann considers earlier frame-tales; reviews modern criticism, especially analyses of the dramatic quality of *GP* and the *CT* as a whole; and discusses the springtime opening (lines 1–18) in detail, providing a stylistic diagram and a structural profile for the process of communication between writer and audience.

487 Ussery, Huling Eakin. *Chaucer's Pilgrims: Three Studies in the Real and the Ideal.* University of Michigan Dissertation. 1963. See also *DA*, 24 (1963), 2491.
'The Monk is probably either the Benedictine or Cistercian head of a dependent cell ... He is primarily a realistic figure, and particular elements of "irony" and "satire" in Chaucer's description are often overemphasized.' The Clerk is 'seemingly an eminent Oxford logician between thirty and fifty years of age....' Five contemporary logicians are suggested as historical models. The Clerk is depicted as a 'blend of the real and the ideal.' The Physician 'is almost certainly a cleric who looks to the church for his greatest preferment.' Previous historical identifications are rejected, but 'five possible models' are suggested. The Physician's portrait is 'primarily realistic' and its 'ironic and "satiric" elements have been unjustly exaggerated' [from *DA*; diss not seen]. Cf Ussery, **909, 1002, 1003, 1131**.

488 Van Dyke, Henry. *The Man Behind the Book: Essays in Understanding.* New York: Charles Scribner's Sons, 1929.

In the chapter 'The Morning Star' (pp 3-26), Van Dyke praises GP as 'a wonderful portrait-gallery of Chaucer's England. Each of these persons stands out distinctly in his habit as he lived' (p 19).

489 Wagenknecht, Edward C. *The Personality of Chaucer.* Norman, OK: University of Oklahoma Press, 1968. Rpt 1969.

Many references to GP occur in this 'psychographic' study of Chaucer's habits, background, interests, and attitudes. One example: 'Most Chaucer critics seem to be of the opinion that Chaucer liked the Monk but disliked the Friar ... To me, on the other hand, nothing seems clearer than that Chaucer liked the Prioress but disliked both the men' (1969, p 121).

490 Walter, Gertrud. *Grundtypen der Erzähl- und Darstellungstechnik bei Chaucer.* Ludwig-Maximilians-Universität Dissertation (Munich). 1964. Dir. W. Clemen and F. Wölcken. Published Munich: Schön, 1964.

The technique of character-description in GP is briefly considered. Chaucer's artful brevity, which permits the audience to fill out the details of the portraits, is noted ('Der Anteil an rein deskriptiven Einzelzügen ist überraschend gering, doch treffend gewählt, so völlig in den Dienst der humoristisch-ironischen Charakterisierung gestellt, dass sich die Phantasie des Lesers aus diesen Anknüpfungspunkten ein voll gerundetes Bild der dargestellten Person ausmalen kann,' p 45).

491 Ward, H. Snowden, and C.M.B. Ward. *The Canterbury Pilgrimages.* London: Adam and Charles Black, 1904.

The portraits are briefly discussed, with some emphasis on Becket's influence. On the Knight, it is suggested that 'the fact that St Thomas of Canterbury had been taken as the patron saint of Acre caused Chaucer to connect this pilgrim knight with the body founded in that city,' ie, the Teutonic Order (p 158; see lines 52-53). See also **860**.

492 Watt, Francis. *Canterbury Pilgrims and Their Ways.* New York: Dodd, Mead, and Co., 1917.

In this general book about Thomas Becket, Canterbury pilgrimages, different possible routes, etc, Watt includes occasional remarks about CT and GP. Chaucer's realism is noted: 'what he saw he could place before his readers' so that 'the very man or woman rises before your eyes' (p 77). To Chaucer the inn or tavern 'was a little globe where he studied in miniature the aspects of the great world' (p 79).

493 Welch, Jane Toomey. *Chaucer's Low Seriousness: A Study of Ironic Structure in the 'Canterbury Tales.'* Syracuse University Dissertation. 1978. See also *DAI*, 39 (1978), 3569-A.

Brief studies of the Manciple, Squire, Franklin, Man of Law, Physician, Prioress, Second Nun, and Clerk in *GP* are included. The statement that the Physician was *grounded in astronomye* (line 414), for example, is ironic since it links the earth (ground) with heavenly concerns (astronomy); the juxtaposition of the contrasting terms deflates the Physician's seriousness. Because the Clerk is said to be *sownynge in moral vertu* (line 307), in contrastive echo of the remark that the previous pilgrim, the Merchant, was *sownynge alwey th'encrees of his wynnyng* (line 275), both pilgrims are characterized: the verbal similarity makes the Merchant seem shadier, the Clerk more virtuous. Chaucer's irony in *GP* initiates an ironic tone for the *CT* as a whole.

494 Whiting, Bartlett Jere. *Chaucer's Use of Proverbs.* Cambridge, MA: Harvard University Press, 1934. Harvard Studies in Comparative Philology and Literature, 11.
Proverbial material in *GP* is briefly examined (pp 76–77). The only proverb included in *GP* concerns the Miller's gold thumb (line 563). 'There are, however, seven sententious remarks' (p 76). They concern the Prioress's motto (line 162), the Friar's *purchas* and *rente* (line 256), the Physician's small study of the Bible (line 438), the Parson's comparison of rusted gold to a corrupted priest (lines 500–4), the Summoner's jay that says 'Watte' (lines 642–43), the narrator's quotation from Plato (lines 741–42), and the Host's wondering whether *even-song and morwe-song accorde* (line 830).

495 Whitmore, Sister Mary Ernestine. *Medieval English Domestic Life and Amusements in the Works of Chaucer.* Washington, DC: Catholic University of America, 1937.
Many topics pertinent to *GP* are touched upon in this survey of Chaucer's references to houses and furnishings, gardens, meals and table manners, dress and adornment, and sports and pastimes. For example, it is suggested that the Knight may have begun the board in Prussia (lines 52–3), though he was not of the highest rank in society, because 'etiquette seems to have required that strangers be accorded special privileges' (p 122). The red and light blue of the Physician's gown (line 439) 'seem to have been a usual combination' of colors (p 149). The Plowman, the most simply dressed of the pilgrims, wears a tabard whose material and color are not mentioned (line 541); it was probably 'a nondescript garment such as only the poorer classes' would have worn (p 153). Most of the pilgrims are briefly mentioned. The book is a published version of the author's dissertation of the same title, Catholic University, 1937, Dir. Speer Strahan.

496 Whittock, Trevor. *A Reading of the Canterbury Tales.* Cambridge: Cambridge University Press, 1968.
GP is permeated by a 'harmony between the spiritual and the mundane'

(p 44). The opening passage both conveys the freshness of spring and 'portrays the essence of this key moment in the Christian year' (p 45). The portrait of spring is a shared and public one, not a private experience. It emphasizes the harmony of the different components and the shared commonality of springtime's affirmation. The movement from 'the large affirmation and joy' of the opening to 'the ordinary and mundane world of the Tabard Inn' entails no conflict (p 47), but illustrates Chaucer's 'inclusive understanding which links great and small, high and low matters' (p 48). Similarly, within each of the portraits Chaucer depicts not only the pilgrim's appearance, social status, and other worldly concerns, but also spiritual state. Chaucer the pilgrim cannot really know their spiritual condition (only God can), and his limitations of knowledge 'are delicately stressed' (p 49). However, Chaucer does uncover their condition through such techniques as 'apparently "realistic" details [that] are actually symbolic' (p 50), as in the Knight's clothing; contrasts between pilgrims, as in the Knight-Squire pair; and omissions of information, as in the Yeoman's emphasis upon his trees, craft, and weapons. By the absence of other details, Chaucer shows the limitations of the Yeoman's life. Similarly, the tales too reveal the pilgrims' 'spiritual *being*' as well as their characters (p 53). The three key figures in *GP* are Thomas Becket, the 'foolish pilgrim, Chaucer, who so embodies the fallibility of human awareness,' and 'the grand secular figure of the Host' (p 52).

497 Wilkins, Nigel. *Music in the Age of Chaucer.* Chaucer Studies, I. Cambridge, England: D.S. Brewer, 1979; Totowa, NJ: Rowman and Littlefield, 1979.

Chaucer's references to music are collected in the chapter 'Chaucer' (pp 111–24). 'Chaucer was certainly no practising musician,' but his works inform us 'about the place and nature of music in the society of his time' (p 111). In *GP*, 'his portrait of a young squire such as he himself must have been ... shows us the ideal' (p 111), which corresponds to the Household Book of Edward IV in suggesting that squires were expected to pipe, harp, or sing. 'The small harp, so often represented in contemporary miniatures, was played with particular zest by Chaucer's Friar' (p 114). The bagpipe played by the Miller is a 'really rustic out-of-doors instrument' (p 116). Other brief comments on Chaucer's musical references are provided, along with much information about English, French, and Italian music in the fourteenth century.

498 Williams, George. *A New View of Chaucer.* Durham, NC: Duke University Press, 1965.

As Manly (362) suggested, Chaucer's portraits may reflect specific people or events with which he was familiar. Previous identifications for the

Knight, Prioress, Serjeant of Law, Franklin, Guildsmen, and Reeve are discussed. Williams argues throughout for identifications based on Chaucer's connections with figures at court, especially with John of Gaunt. In addition to specific identifications, Chaucer's portraits of churchmen, both good and evil, 'are precisely the sort that John of Gaunt and the people surrounding him would have heartily approved' (p 154).

499 Willy, Margaret. *Life Was Their Cry*. London: Evans, 1950.
Comments on the *GP* characters are included in a general appreciation of Chaucer's life and works. Chaucer's 'unqualified acceptance of humanity enabled him to enjoy it without reserve' (p 39). While Langland and Gower used people to convey moral concepts, Chaucer created them and allowed them to act on their own.

500 Wilson, P.W. 'He Was a Veray Parfit Gentil Poet.' *NYTM*, May 12, 1940, pp 8, 19.
The pilgrims 'are delineated with colorful exactitude ... Chaucer was not content to call a spade a spade. He looked at the dirt that had gathered on its rough metal. The perfect gentle knight had fought with great renown in fifteen mortal battles, but these exploits did not alter the fact that his jerkin of fustian was all begrimed' (p 19).

501 Wilson, S. Gordon. *With the Pilgrims to Canterbury, and The History of the Hospital of Saint Thomas*. London: Society for Promoting Christian Knowledge, 1934.
This general book on Canterbury and pilgrimages provides background to *GP*, which is recapitulated in the form of a dialogue emphasizing the Host's role.

502 Wimsatt, James I. *Allegory and Mirror: Tradition and Structure in Middle English Literature*. New York: Pegasus, 1970. Pegasus Backgrounds in English Literature.
In the chapter 'The Mirror of Society: Chaucer's Canterbury Tales' (pp 163–89), Wimsatt comments that the 'very center of the work, its keystone, is the General Prologue' (p 163). By including one member of each category — one Knight, one Squire, etc — *GP* 'betrays Chaucer's intention of mirroring society' (p 165), for this pattern would not describe any actual pilgrimage group. In his division of society, Chaucer used the estates-literature tradition, adopting all three of its forms of characterization: 1) characters 'who represent the ideal'; 2) characters 'who have debased the ideal'; and 3) typical figures 'who possess the skills and faults natural to their ways of life' (p 170). The Knight, Clerk, Parson, and Plowman exemplify the ideal; the Monk, Friar, Summoner, Pardoner, Miller, Reeve, and Manciple exemplify the debasement of ideals; the remaining pilgrims exemplify not ethical concepts but social types. The Prioress and the Wife

between them 'divide the estate of women' (p 171). The mirror of society presented in *GP* is later expanded by the addition of more characters and the further development of those who were introduced in the initial portrait series.

503 Wolpers, Theodor. *Bürgerliches bei Chaucer.* Göttingen: Vandenhoeck & Ruprecht, 1980. [Originally published in *Über Bürger, Stadt und städtische Literatur im Spätmittelalter*, Abhandlungen der Akademie der Wissenschaften in Göttingen, Philologische-Historische Klasse, Third Series, 121 (1980?).] Wolpers uses part of *GP* to show the bourgeois characteristics of Chaucer's work: he 'analyses suprapersonal formalizations in Chaucer's work which can be traced back to the imaginative cast of mind and habits of thought of the late-medieval burgher' [from the review by Karl Heinz Göller, *SAC*, 4 (1982), pp 190–93; quotation p 190 — item not seen].

504 Woo, Constance, and William Matthews. 'The Spiritual Purpose of the Canterbury Tales.' *Comitatus*, 1 (1970), 85–109.
Woo's part of this essay (pp 85–97) points out themes essential to the spiritual meaning of *CT*. 'These themes, body versus soul, ideal versus real, are most evident in the portraits of the *General Prologue*' (p 86). 'The Prioress, the Monk, the Friar, the Pardoner are all ecclesiastics, and one expects a certain amount of religious detail in their depiction. But each portrait is characterized by either the absence of such detail or the perversion of it' (p 89). The Parson 'is the only religious man among the pilgrims who brings together the real and the ideal' (p 89). Matthews's part of the essay (pp 97–end) reviews the narratives told by the non-ecclesiastical pilgrims and comments very briefly on their *GP* portraits.

505 Woolf, Rosemary. 'Chaucer as a Satirist in the General Prologue to the Canterbury Tales.' *CritQ*, 1 (1959), 150–57.
GP shows the intentional use of a persona: it is not Chaucer the poet but 'Chaucer the easily-impressed pilgrim who so indiscriminately praises the characters, sharing with them through an obtuse innocence the immoral premises from which they speak' (p 152). Occasionally Chaucer the poet uses a different satirical method and 'speaks outright in his own voice, making a pointed exposure,' but usually 'the ironic voice of Chaucer the satirist' is heard 'behind the blank wall of obtuseness of Chaucer the pilgrim' (p 153). The idealized descriptions correspond to the traditions of satire, in which an ideal standard was included: Chaucer's virtuous pilgrims 'imply a censure of the rest' (p 155). It is incorrect to see Chaucer the poet as aloof, or to think that he 'loved his satirised characters despite or including their faults,' though his tone shows a 'specious mildness' (p 155). Chaucer's knowledge of the classical satirists is not proven, although resemblances exist to the satirical techniques of Juvenal, Horace, and Ovid. He 'sees

himself as a poet in the classical tradition,' and behind the disguise of Chaucer the pilgrim 'is the truly personal tone of the satirist, which is quite un-medieval' (p 156).

506 Wurtele, Douglas. 'Some Uses of Physiognomical Lore in Chaucer's *Canterbury Tales*.' *ChauR*, 17 (1982–1983), 130–41.

The physiognomical details in the portraits 'come not from random and folklorish notions but from the authority of several *physiognomica*' (p 132). They represent 'a mode of popular wisdom' (p 133). Their insertion into the portraits is due to the narrator, who is defined by this descriptive technique as 'a fellow evidently versed in the wisdom to be acquired from studying those physical details upon which the physiognomists base their predictions about human behavior' (p 134). Some of the details are used inconsistently or confusingly. 'Perhaps the Pilgrim-observer is presented as a man impressed by this form of wisdom and keen to display it, while, perhaps, doing so selectively. Yet the author may be viewing its inconsistencies if not skeptically, then at least ironically' (p 136). Traits from the Miller's, Reeve's, and Pardoner's portraits are discussed. Chaucer may 'regard with some skepticism the physiognomists' theories along with their absurd system of animal analogy. At the same time, he would know well that common observers, like the gentlefolk on his fictive pilgrimage, might not be skeptical at all' (p 140).

507 Young, Karl. 'The Plan of the *Canterbury Tales*.' In *Anniversary Papers by Colleagues and Pupils of George Lyman Kittredge*. [Ed. F.N. Robinson, E.S. Sheldon, and W.A. Neilson.] Boston and London: Ginn, 1913. Pp 405–17.

Young proposes that Sercambi's *Novelle*, written about a decade before *CT*, provides closer resemblances to Chaucer's storytelling plan than does Boccaccio's *Decameron*. Like Chaucer in *GP*, Sercambi presents a mixed group of pilgrims and a leader who is elected after suggesting that the group should have such a leader (see lines 777–79). Although in the *Novelle* the leader tells all the stories, he does call on the other travelers for 'other sorts of recitation' (p 413), so that 'the share of other pilgrims in the general entertaining suggests, remotely at least, the distribution of tales' among different tellers in Chaucer's plan (p 414; see lines 781–95). During his Italian journeys of 1373 and 1378 Chaucer 'had a fair opportunity for hearing about Sercambi and his work,' which provides 'the most likely of all *literary* sources' of *CT* (p 417). Cf **393, 410, 453**.

508 Zacher, Christian. *Curiosity and Pilgrimage: the Literature of Discovery in Fourteenth-Century England*. Baltimore and London: Johns Hopkins University Press, 1976.

Zacher examines late medieval attitudes toward travel. By Chaucer's time, pilgrimage had become 'largely an outlet for *curiositas*, no longer a strictly solemn spiritual exercise' (p 88). The chapter 'Curiosity and the Instability of Pilgrimage' (pp 87–129) briefly comments on *GP*. Although at the beginning of *GP* there is an air of *felaweshipe* (lines 26, 32), the fellowship of the pilgrims is finally hollow, for it is not based on true Christian *amicitia*. Chaucer emphasizes the pilgrims' 'willingness to make a game and contest out of the pilgrimage' and to form their unity on the basis not of piety, but of a competitive pact (p 88). Most of the portraits show that the ideals of pilgrimage are being blurred or compromised. Nearly all of the pilgrims 'are characterized by their attitudes toward travel and wandering' (p 93). There are contrasts, for example, between the Knight's proper travels as an ideal crusader and the Monk's improper wandering: 'One pursues infidels, the other rabbits' (p 94). Several of the ecclesiastics are 'wanderers by nature, stricken by restlessness' — 'extraterritorial vagrants' who constitute 'emblems of curiosity' rather than of piety (p 94). The pilgrimage group displays a preoccupation with economic issues and shows inherent tendencies towards disorder. The tale-telling contract, 'a spiritually impertinent kind of sworn pact,' fails to stabilize the company (p 100).

509 Zanco, Aurelio. *Chaucer e il suo mondo*. Turin: Petrini, 1955.
In the chapter 'Il Prologo' (pp 152–65), Zanco briefly comments on the differences between Chaucer's frame and those of other frame-tales, on the dramatic vitality of the pilgrims, on antecedent examples of portraiture such as the portraits in the *Roman de la Rose*, and on the use of conventions such as the springtime opening. Chaucer's portraiture shows that he seems to dislike mediocrity, flatness, or homogeneity ('sembra odiare il livellamento, l'omogeneità'); merely conventional or generic figures are rare ('Rare sono veramente le figure generiche'); instead, his dramatic tendency uses individualizing traits as a means of access to human nature (p 156).

Part 4: Language, Metrics, and Studies of the Manuscripts or Early Editions

Additional comments on the manuscripts are included in some of the editions (see Index, under 'manuscripts'). Items **19**, **25**, **79**, **92**, **93**, and **94** in the Editions section are reproductions of manuscripts or early editions.

510 Bateson, F.W. 'Could Chaucer Spell?' *EIC*, 25 (1975), 2–24.
'The scribe or supervisor of the Ellesmere *MS* was an excessive syllable-counter' (p 16). To that person is due the *-e* on *Aprille* (line 1), as Ellesmere spells it, and also the *-e* on *halfe* (line 8). The 'decasyllabic supervisor' (p 16) supplied the extra *-e*'s in order to reach a regular syllable-count. 'With the realization that Ellesmere is an edited and emended text the almost canonical authority attributed to it recently must collapse' (p 17).

511 Bauer, Gero. *Studien zum System und Gebrauch der 'Tempora' in der Sprache Chaucers und Gowers.* Vienna: Braumüller, 1970. Wiener Beiträge zur Englischen Philologie, 73.
Occasional examples from *GP* are included in this study of verb tenses.

512 Baum, Paull F. 'Chaucer's Puns.' *PMLA*, 71 (1956), 225–46.
A general discussion of puns is followed by an annotated list. Items that apply to *GP* are *burdoun* (Summoner, line 673), *charity* (Wife, line 452), *chevyssaunce* (Merchant, line 282), *clause* (narrator, line 715), *complection* (Franklin, line 333), *conscience* (Prioress, line 142), *cordial* (Physician, line 443), *crowned* (Prioress, line 161), *dress* (Yeoman, line 106), *grey* (Prioress, line 152, and Reeve, line 616), *grope* (Summoner, line 644), *harlot* (Summoner, line 647), *philosophre* (Clerk, line 297), *pinch* (Merchant, line 326), *point* (Monk, line 200, and narrator, line 790), *pricking* (Monk, line 191),

purchasing (Friar, line 256, and Man of Law, lines 318, 320), *sooth* (Merchant, line 283), *space* (narrator, line 35; Squire, line 87; Monk, line 176), *vein* (narrator, line 3), *venery* (Monk, line 166), and *without* (Wife, line 461). In reply on *burdoun*, see **1260**.

513 ——. 'Chaucer's Puns: A Supplementary List.' *PMLA*, 73 (1958), 167–70.
Puns are suggested on *gaude grene* (Prioress, line 159), *gold thumb* (Miller, line 563), *goliardeys* (Miller, line 560), *Rouncivale* (Pardoner, line 670), *wandering by the way* (Wife, line 467), and *wanton* (Friar, line 208). In addition, a pun on *ful* (in the later remarks of the Host to the Monk, line VII.1932) reflects the Monk's *GP* portrait.

514 ——. *Chaucer's Verse.* Durham, NC: Duke University Press, 1961.
In comparison to Chaucer's *Pity*, lines 1–100 of *GP* are used 'as a specimen of his later and most mature versification' (p 13). Baum considers stress, spondaic and trochaic effects, the final -*e*, hiatus and elision, etc. Lines 1–18 are analyzed as 'one of Chaucer's most studied and carefully composed passages,' consisting of 'two balanced parts,' lines 1–11 and 12–18, each of which has subsidiary parts (p 80). 'It should go without saying that throughout this opening paragraph Chaucer is poetic, following a long tradition, and is in no sense realistic' (p 83). The March drought, the nightingales, Zephirus, etc, are 'ornaments laid on to warn us that none of this springtime is really real but part of the larger comedy to follow' (p 83). These lines are followed by a change of style into 'friendly engaging casualness' (p 84).

515 Berndt, Rolf. *Einführung in das Studium des Mittelenglischen unter Zugrundelegung des Prologs der 'Canterbury Tales.'* Halle: Niemeyer, 1960.
Intended primarily as an explanation of Middle English phonology, this study presents *GP* as a sample, using the Manly-Rickert text (**49**). A phonetic transcription, a glossary, and a general survey of Chaucer's life and work are included.

516 Beschorner, Franz. *Verbale Reime bei Chaucer.* Halle: Niemeyer, 1920. Studien zur Englischen Philologie, 60.
In this partial publication of Beschorner's dissertation of the same title, Göttingen, 1920, instances of verbs at the rhyme in *GP* are counted as 157 (p 31). Chaucer had an extraordinary tendency for making such rhymes ('Die Tendenz, Verbformen zu reimen, ist bei Ch. ausserordentlich stark,' p 1).

517 Biggins, Dennis. 'Chaucer's Metrical Lines: Some Internal Evidence.' *Parergon*, 17 (1977), 17–24.

Using the first 100 lines of *GP* as his sample, Biggins argues that statistically most of them fall into one or another type of iambic pentameter pattern: 'iambicality has the numbers' (p 24).

518 Blake, N.F. 'The Relationship between the Hengwrt and the Ellesmere Manuscripts of the "Canterbury Tales." ' *E&S*, New Series 32 (1979), 1–18. Blake argues that the Hengwrt ms 'was the first published text' of the *CT* and that the Ellesmere ms was based upon it. At Chaucer's death he left only one copy of the work, 'more fragmentary than we previously imagined' (p 17).

519 ——. 'On Editing the *Canterbury Tales*.' In *Medieval Studies for J.A.W. Bennett*. Ed. P.L. Heyworth. Oxford: Clarendon Press, 1981. Pp 101–20. Blake reviews several persistent manuscript problems and argues that the Hengwrt ms was copied from an exemplar consisting of 'Chaucer's own fragments' (p 116); at that point there was only one text from which the scribes worked — Chaucer's own copy — but emendations were then made as multiple copies were written out.

520 Brusendorff, Aage. *The Chaucer Tradition*. London: Oxford University Press, 1925; Copenhagen: Branner, 1925. Occasional comments on *GP* are included in this general study of the Chaucer text and mss. On line 13, the punctuation is discussed; on line 120, the Prioress's oath was probably chosen simply for the rhyme; on lines 124–26, the statement about the Prioress's French is ironic; on line 179, *rechelees* is correct; on line 202, it is the Monk's head (not eyes) that steamed, and the meaning is ' "That steamed as a furnace does when a piece of lead is put into it" ' (p 480); on the added (?) couplet at lines 252a–b, these lines lack authority; on lines 256 and 705–6, Chaucer is using the English *Romance of the Rose*; on lines 396–97, what is meant is that the Shipman has captured foreign ships while their owners slept. Other brief remarks on *GP* occur (see Brusendorff's Index A).

- Review by Howard R. Patch, *MP*, 25 (1928-1929), 361–66: 'Dr. Brusendorff attacks all the main tenets in the field, and finds many of them impossible ... the chief impression he leaves is that of being liberally destructive' (p 365).

- Review by Ernest Kuhl, *MLN*, 41 (1926), 402–6: Kuhl finds the book to be 'one of the most important studies in recent years,' with 'fresh contributions' appearing 'on nearly every page' (p 402). 'It is hardly an exaggeration to say that Dr. Brusendorff sets new standards in Chaucerian research' (p 403).

- Review by Robert K. Root, *JEGP*, 26 (1927), 258–62: Root warns against the book's 'inaccuracies and unwarranted assumptions,' though he finds that it includes valuable material (p 262).

521 Buck, Howard. 'Chaucer's Use of Feminine Rhyme.' *MP*, 26 (1928-1929), 13–14.
'In Chaucer, the feminine rhyme is at the very least upon an equal footing with the masculine' (p 13). In *GP* 'the proportion is 380 lines with masculine endings to 480 with feminine' (p 13). The feminine rhymes cause a change in rhythm from the iamb to the anapest or dactyl. They also show 'a marked tendency' not only to occur in single couplets but also 'to form in clusters' (p 13).

522 Burnley, David. 'Inflexion in Chaucer's Adjectives.' *NM*, 83 (1982), 169–77.
Occasional examples from *GP* are included in this study of Chaucer's final -*e* on adjectives. The scribe's practice is found to be more correct in the Hengwrt than in the Ellesmere ms.

523 Caldwell, Robert A. 'The Scribe of the Chaucer MS, Cambridge University Library Gg.4.27.' *MLQ*, 5 (1944), 33–44.
The peculiar scribal errors in this copy, including several in *GP*, might be explained by the hypothesis that the scribe was Dutch-speaking. [This article reports part of Caldwell's dissertation, *Linguistic Peculiarities of the Cambridge University Library Manuscript Gg.4.27*, University of Chicago, 1938 — not seen.]

524 'The Cardigan Chaucer.' *TLS*, March 19, 1925, p 207.
The sale of a Chaucer manuscript is announced; ms variants in lines 185, 189, 192, and 231 are listed.

525 Christophersen, Paul. 'The Scansion of Two Lines in Chaucer.' *ES*, 45, Supplement (1964), 146–50.
Lines 49 and 173 'are usually felt to be awkward' in scansion (p 146). Christophersen argues that both can be read as regular lines. In line 49, he proposes that *cristendom* was disyllabic (as in Lydgate's spelling *crysdome*). In line 173, he proposes that *Seint Maure* was pronounced with a heavier stress on *Seint* than on *Maure* (as in the modern version of the name, ie *Seymour*). Chaucer's verse does not necessarily show 'a uniform jog-trot' (p 150) kind of regularity, but possibilities for regularity should be adequately considered before lines are regarded as irregular, or before the assumption that Chaucer is using a five-stress iambic pentameter line is rejected as outmoded.

526 Cloyd, Manie G. 'Chaucer's Romance Element.' *PQ*, 11 (1932), 89–91.
This study tests the supposition that in *GP*, 'which is recognized as almost entirely original' (p 89), Chaucer's percentage of Romance-language words would be less than in a work such as *SNT*, which is closely dependent on a Latin source. However, a statistical analysis of the words in *GP*, *SNT*, and also *KnT* and *MLT* shows that 'Chaucer used the same percentage of words of Romance origin when writing independently as when taking the material from a Romance source' (p 91).

527 Crow, Martin Michael. *Scribal Habits: Illustrated in the Paris Manuscript of Chaucer's Canterbury Tales.* University of Chicago Dissertation, 1935. Sections were published as 'Corrections in the Paris Manuscript of Chaucer's *Canterbury Tales*,' *SE*, 15 (1935), 5–18; and as 'Unique Variants in the Paris Manuscript of Chaucer's *Canterbury Tales*,' *SE*, 16 (1936), 17–41. Those two chapters were also printed in pamphlet form as *Corrections and Unique Variants in the Paris Manuscript of Chaucer's Canterbury Tales* (Chicago, IL: University of Chicago Libraries, private edition [1937?]).
GP examples of correction, of attempted 'improvement' of the text, etc, in this manuscript are mentioned. The work of both the scribe and the owner can be separately established.

528 Dempster, Germaine. 'Manly's Conception of the Early History of the *Canterbury Tales*.' *PMLA*, 61 (1946), 379–415.
The Manly-Rickert edition of *CT* (**49**) does not always make explicit Manly's underlying concept of the Chaucer text and its transmission. Dempster pulls together the indications that Manly provided — often in scattered notes or comments — about the state of *CT* at Chaucer's death, the relative value of different mss, and so forth. The Ellesmere ms is, 'in Gen. Pro and in eight tales, the sole extant representative of its genetic group' in Manly's classification (pp 397–8).

529 Donaldson, E. Talbot. 'The Manuscripts of Chaucer's Works and Their Use.' In *Writers and Their Background: Geoffrey Chaucer.* Ed. Derek Brewer. London: Bell, 1974. Pp 85–108.
Examples from *GP* are included in this discussion of the problems of punctuation, meter, etc, presented by the Chaucer mss. The lines briefly examined are 3, 5, 7, 8, 10, 12, 14, 17, 19, 52, 77, 152, 169–76, 459–60.

530 ——. 'Some Readings in the *Canterbury Tales*.' In *Medieval Studies in Honor of Lillian Herlands Hornstein.* Ed. Jess B. Bessinger, Jr., and Robert R. Raymo. New York: New York University Press, 1976. Pp 99–110.
In line 60, the proper reading is likely to be *aryue* (*ariue*) — not, as Donaldson earlier thought (see **63**), *armee*. [On *aryue/armee*, cf **684**, **697**,

709.] Lines 252a–b, sometimes regarded as an interpolation, are genuine. Lines 637–38, which some mss lack, are not due to authorial revision, but were missed in those mss because of a scribal error in copying; they have the same textual status as the surrounding lines.

531 ——. 'Adventures with the Adversative Conjunction in the General Prologue to the *Canterbury Tales*, or, What's before the But?' In *So meny people, longages, and tonges: Philological Essays in Scots and Medieval English Presented to Angus McIntosh*. Ed. Michael Benskin and M.L. Samuels. Edinburgh: Benskin and Samuels, 1981. Pp 355–66, 413.

Donaldson studies the 37 examples of the adversative *but* in *GP*, seeing about a third of them as belonging to the 'inherently logical, rather uninteresting kind' (p 355), and the rest as showing various illogical, but more interesting, responses of the narrator. On the narrator's reaction to the Pardoner, see **1305**.

532 Doyle, A.I. and M.B. Parkes. 'The Production of Copies of the *Canterbury Tales* and the *Confessio Amantis* in the Early Fifteenth Century.' In *Medieval Scribes, Manuscripts and Libraries: Essays Presented to N.R. Ker*. Ed. M.B. Parkes and Andrew G. Watson. London: Scolar Press, 1978. Pp 163–203.

The differences between the Ellesmere and the Hengwrt mss of *CT* are reviewed in this detailed study of early fifteenth-century book production as seen in several mss of Chaucer's works and other texts. Doyle and Parkes propose that Hengwrt and Ellesmere were copied by the same scribe, though from different exemplars, and that 'Ellesmere's exemplar had been prepared by an editor' (p 186). In both mss running titles have been provided by the scribe who wrote the text or by another scribe — except for *GP*. The Ellesmere copy presents the *CT* as a *compilatio*. It 'emphasizes the importance of the pilgrims as a major factor in the work ... and connects the tales with the General Prologue' (p 191). 'An intelligent person has thus developed the potential of Chaucer's unfinished material into a conventional form' (pp 191–92).

533 Duke, Elizabeth Anne Foster. *Evolution of the Text of Chaucer's Canterbury Tales: 1477–1775*. University of Iowa Dissertation. 1968. Dir. Robert R. Howren. See also *DA*, 29 (1969), 3971-A.

GP is used as the sample on which to assess editorial practices. Chapters are included on the editions of Caxton, Pynson, Wynkyn de Worde, Thynne, Speght, Urry, and Tyrwhitt. Variations in the printing of *GP* are discussed.

534 Everett, Dorothy. 'Another Collation of the Ellesmere Manuscript of the *Canterbury Tales*.' *MÆ*, 1 (1932), 42–55.

Everett identifies 19 *GP* errors — beginning with the *-e* on *Aprill(e)* of line 1 — which Furnivall made in transcribing the Ellesmere ms and which have influenced the editions of Skeat (3) and the Globe editors (4), as well as studies of Chaucer's language.

535 Everett, Virginia Thornton. *A Study of the Scribal Editing in Twelve MSS of the Canterbury Tales.* University of Chicago Dissertation. 1940.
Examples from *GP* are included in this study of three kinds of scribes: popularizing scribes who were making commercial copies; correcting scribes who were interested in censoring or (as they saw it) improving the text; and amateur scribes who were copying at least partially for aesthetic reasons. The scribe of Harley 7333, for example, edited the Prioress's portrait: he removed the detail about her small mouth (line 153), which he apparently found 'inappropriate, at least if one were to believe a medieval physiognomist,' and made her mouth *measurable* instead (p 70). Lines 134, 189, 329, 342, 357, 372, and 726 were altered by more than one scribe studied; religious terms or phrases were altered at lines 479, 590, and 699. The mss studied are Harley 7334, Helmingham, Cambridge University Library Ii.3.26, Harley 7333, Hatton Donat.1, New College (Oxford) D 314, Northumberland, Rawlinson Poetry 149, Royal 17.D.xv, College of Physicians 13, Glasgow, and Trinity College (Oxford) 49.

536 Fifield, Merle. *Theoretical Techniques for the Analysis of Variety in Chaucer's Metrical Stress.* Muncie, IN: Ball State University, 1973. Ball State Monograph #23 (Publications in English #17).
Using generative linguistics to study Chaucer's stress patterns, Fifield suggests that lines 1–4 might have been read as a sentence, with the *whan* of line 5 marking the pause; or that lines 1 and 2 may have been read as a sentence, with the *and* of line 3 marking a new start. 'Sentence by the Chaucerian concept may, in particular contexts, mean unified idea or image, instead of a surface noun phrase plus verb phrase' (p 33).

537 Gaylord, Alan T. 'Scanning the Prosodists: An Essay in Metacriticism.' *ChauR*, 11 (1976–1977), 22–82.
This study of Chaucer's verse discusses several passages from *GP* — lines 17–18, 45–46, 68, 183–84, 249–50, 290–96, 425–26, 443–44, 467–68, 500, 635, 661–62, 782, 841, 853–54, and 857–58. Gaylord reviews the different theories that have been offered to describe Chaucerian prosody. One of the main problems is that we have no clearly authoritative line established by Chaucer himself: '*There is no such thing as Chaucer's own line.* There are only scribal versions of it' (p 27). Directions in which future examinations of Chaucer's prosody should develop are suggested.

538 Halle, Morris, and Samuel Jay Keyser. 'Chaucer and the Study of Prosody.'
CE, 28 (1966-1967), 187-219.
GP examples are included in this examination of stress and other characteristics of meter; the lines briefly discussed or categorized are 1 [mislabelled
17], 2, 5, 15, 16, 20, 22, 27, 112, 122, 190, 260, 293, 294, 343, 350, 364,
421, 445, 491, 500, 545, 662, 764. For a dissenting view, though not based
on *GP*, see Dudley L. Hascall, 'Some Contributions to the Halle-Keyser
Theory of Prosody,' *CE*, 30 (1968-1969), 357-65. See also Wimsatt, **583**.

539 Hammond, Eleanor Prescott. 'On the Order of the Canterbury Tales: Caxton's Two Editions.' *MP*, 3 (1905-1906), 159-78.
Sections from *GP* are used to assess the relationship between Caxton's first
edition of *CT* and his second edition. For instance, Caxton I includes an
additional line between (in the usual numbering) lines 163 and 164; it does
not include the couplet at lines 252a-b; other differences between the first
and second editions are noted. Caxton II was based on Caxton I ('its resemblance to Caxton I is so strong that we cannot think the later print set
up independently of the earlier,' p 176). However, Caxton II was corrected
according to a different ms than the one that had served for Caxton I.
The ms used for Caxton II, 'while deriving, as regards arrangement, from
the same archetype as the debased and careless Caxton I, was copied at a
somewhat later date' (p 177).

540 Hart, James Paxton. *Thomas Tyrwhitt (1730-1786) as Annotator and
Glossarist of Fragment A of The Canterbury Tales, and His Editorial Relations.* University of Pennsylvania Dissertation. 1971. Dir. Robert A. Pratt.
See also *DAI*, 32 (1971), 2056-A.
Tyrwhitt is shown to have had a major influence on editorial traditions of
glossing and annotation. A table identifying the correspondences in annotation in a number of editions — those of Speght (1602), Urry (1721),
Morell (1737), Tyrwhitt (1775), Wright (1847), Skeat (1894), and Robinson
(1957) — is included (pp 67-72). Hart provides detailed discussions of the
annotations those editors provide to the following lines: 1, 57, 85, 209, 282,
310, 359, 360, 390, 391, 433, 468, 526, 560, and 661. On the Knight, see
686.

541 Hoya, Katusuzo. 'Latin and French Loan Words in the "General Prologue"
to the *Canterbury Tales*.' *Memoirs*, 30 (1979), 39-51.
Not seen; according to *SAC*, 3 (1981), 201, this is a 'complete list of the
Latin and French loan words in *GP*, including proper nouns.'

542 Joerden, Otto. *Das Verhältnis von Wort-, Satz- und Versakzent in Chaucers
Canterbury Tales.* Halle: Niemeyer, 1914. Studien zur Englischen Philologie, 55. General Editor, Lorenz Morsbach.

Examples from *GP* are included in this study of Chaucer's versification, which is divided into categories, such as lines in which the accent of the words or sentences coincides with the accent of the verse, and lines in which it does not. The book is based upon Joerden's dissertation of the same title, Georg-August-Universität (Göttingen), 1914; also printed under the same title at Halle: Karras, 1914.

543 Kerkof, Jelle. *Studies in the Language of Geoffrey Chaucer.* Leidse Germanistische en Anglistische Reeks van de Rijksuniversiteit te Leiden, V. Leiden: E.J. Brill and Leiden University Press, 1982. 2nd ed., rev. and enlarged. [1st ed., 1966, not seen.]
Examples from *GP* are frequently cited in this general study of Chaucer's verbs, nouns, pronouns, articles, adjectives, adverbs, numerals, interjections, conjunctions, and patterns of 'conversion' (use of an adjective as a noun, etc.)

544 Kharenko, M.F. 'Spivvidnoshennya zalozshenogo ta pervinnogo elementiv u slovniku 'Kenterberiis'kikh opovidan' Dzh. Chosera.' [The Proportion of Borrowed and Native Elements in the Vocabulary of Chaucer's Canterbury Tales.] *Inozemna*, no. 11 (1967), 23–30.
Kharenko tabulates 303 words in *GP*, of which 45 are classified as foreign or borrowed, 258 as native. Repetitions of words are also examined: native words are repeated more frequently than are borrowed words.

545 Kilgour, Margaret. 'The Manuscript Source of Caxton's Second Edition of the *Canterbury Tales.*' *PMLA*, 44 (1929), 186–201.
A comparison of *GP* variants supports the thesis that there is 'a very close connection' betweeen Caxton's second edition of *CT* and British Library Additional Ms 35286 (p 201).

546 Koch, John. *A Detailed Comparison of the Eight Manuscripts of Chaucer's Canterbury Tales as Completely Printed in the Publications of the Chaucer Society.* London: Kegan Paul, Trench, Trübner and Co, and Oxford University Press, 1913. Chaucer Society Publications, 2nd Series 47 (1913).
The *GP* variants for eight major mss, with comparisons to other mss, are listed. [This compilation was superseded by Manly-Rickert, **49.**]

547 ——. 'Textkritische Bemerkungen zu Chaucers Canterbury Tales.' *ESt*, 47 (1913), 338–414.
Koch annotates lines 16–22, 60, 140, 164, 179–81, 217, 234, 257–58, 260, 363, 491, 512, 514, 520, 686, 791, 829–30. His emphasis is on examining manuscript variants in order to establish the best reading of these lines or to clarify their pronunciation.

548 Kökeritz, Helge. *A Guide to Chaucer's Pronunciation*. Stockholm: Almqvist and Wiksell, 1954; New Haven, CN: Whitlock, 1954. Rpt 1961. Rpt with revised preface, New York: Holt, Rinehart, and Winston, 1962.
Phonetic transcripts of four passages from *GP* — lines 1–42, 118–62, 285–308, and 477–500 — are provided.

549 Kolinsky, Muriel. 'Pronouns of Address and the Status of Pilgrims in the *Canterbury Tales*.' *PLL*, 3 (Supplement, special issue ed. by John Gardner and Nicholas Joose, Summer 1967), 40–48.
Chaucer used the polite pronoun *ye* and the familiar pronoun *thou* intentionally: 'the choice made of *ye* or *thou* in each speech addressed to a pilgrim by the Host is closely correlated with the order in which that pilgrim appears in the *General Prologue* and hence with his social status' (p 40). Thus 'Chaucer respected rank, both when he ordered the portraits in the *General Prologue* and when he selected the Host's choice of the pronouns of address' (p 48).

550 McCormick, William, with the assistance of Janet Heseltine. *The Manuscripts of Chaucer's Canterbury Tales, a Critical Description of Their Contents*. Oxford: Clarendon Press, 1933.
The contents of 57 complete or virtually complete copies of *CT* (including Caxton's first and second printed editions) and 28 defective mss are described. Details such as the presence of the additional couplet after line 252, changes of handwriting, missing leaves, scribal rubrics, etc, are noted. According to the rubrics, *GP* was considered to be *the prolog* (p 22), *prologus* (pp 138, 512), *the prolog of this boke* (pp 156, 180, 284, 336, 388, 474, 484), *the prologe of the Kneytis tale* (p 200), *the prolog of the tales of Caunterbury* (p 224), *prologus fabularum Cantuar* (p 274), or *the proheme of all the tal* (p 312).

551 Macek, Dora. 'A Draft for the Analysis of Verbal Periphrases in the "Canterbury Tales."' *SRAZ*, No. 33–6 (1972–1973), 695–708.
GP is taken as the sample for this preliminary computerized analysis of periphrastic verb forms in *CT*. Data are provided for such indicators as the general frequency of periphrastic forms and the frequency of periphrases using particular auxiliary verbs (*be, have, can, may*, etc).

552 Manly, John M., and Edith Rickert, eds. *The Text of the Canterbury Tales Studied on the Basis of All Known Manuscripts*. 1940. See **49**.
The groupings of mss for *GP* are explained in vol 2, pp 78–96. *GP* appears in 50 mss: it is complete or nearly so in 27; incomplete at the beginning in 21; fragmentary in 2, of which 1 is 'negligible because written from a poor memory' (2:78). Of the 49 significant copies, 43 derive from 'the same

common ancestor' (2:78). This ancestral copy, now lost, represented not a final version prepared for publication, but instead 'the stage of development the text had then reached'; this copy was 'intended to serve as a basis for further work' (2:95). For example, in this copy line 164 did not extend beyond the word *chapeleyne*, rather than mentioning the three priests, who are a 'manifest absurdity' (2:95) due to someone else's effort to complete the line. Similarly, on the margin of this 'incompleted working-copy' (2:95) Chaucer may have written the couplet 252 a–b, without clearly indicating whether it was to be included or not.

The individual mss identified here are described in detail in vol 1, pp 20–544. Two of the most important are the Ellesmere ms, which many modern editors have followed [see this bibliography's section on Editions, above], and the Hengwrt ms, which has been chosen as the basis for the Variorum Chaucer series in progress. On Ellesmere, see here 1:148–59; 'an intelligent person, who was certainly not Chaucer, worked over the text' when this ms was copied (1:150). On Hengwrt, see here 1:266–83; this copy shows 'great freedom from accidental errors' and 'entire freedom from editorial variants,' and is therefore 'of the highest importance' (1:276).

553 Masui, Michio. *The Structure of Chaucer's Rime Words.* Tokyo: Kenkyusha, 1964.
The rhymes of *GP* are discussed in this overall study of Chaucerian rhymewords. For example, under the topic of rhymes with proper names, Masui comments on the metrical mastery achieved in Chaucer's rhyming of the medical authorities in the Physician's portrait (lines 429–34) and on the contrast in the rhyme of *Beneit* and *streit* in the Monk's portrait (lines 173–74). The alternation of masculine and feminine rhymes in the Prioress's portrait produces 'a very happy harmony' of the two kinds (p 233). Many other aspects of rhyme are examined.

554 Mersand, Joseph. *Chaucer's Romance Vocabulary.* Brooklyn, NY: Comet, 1937. Rpt New York: Kennikat, 1968.
Mersand evaluates previous work and discusses Chaucer's Romance-language vocabulary in detail. *GP* includes 48 Romance-background words being used for the first time in the English language (1937, p 54). Statistics on various characteristics — on the percentage of Romance words in *GP*, on the average number of Romance words per line, etc — are provided (pp 76, 87, 99, 124, 129, 132). It is sometimes thought that Chaucer uses Romance words primarily when he is working from a Romance-language source, but in *GP* he has an abundant Romance vocabulary too: though *GP* 'is shorter by 298 lines than the *Clerk's Tale*, it has seventy more Romance words' (p 80).

555 Moorman, Charles. 'Computing Housman's Fleas: A Statistical Analysis of Manly's Landmark Manuscripts in the General Prologue to the Canterbury Tales.' *ALLCJ*, 3 (1982), 15–35.
Moorman uses a computerized statistical analysis to examine the relationships among *GP* manuscripts. The results substantiate the findings of Manly-Rickert (**49**) that ms groups *c* and *d* are inseparable in *GP*. 'To a lesser extent the data also confirms Manly's statement that groups *a* and *b* are "independent and constant" ' in *GP* (p 17). Graphs and tables representing the statistical analysis are included.

556 Muscatine, Charles. *The Book of Geoffrey Chaucer: An Account of the Publication of Geoffrey Chaucer's Works from the Fifteenth Century to Modern Times*. San Francisco: Book Club of California, 1963.
Several references to *GP* occur in this history of printed Chaucer editions. For example, lines 1–18 as they appeared in Thynne's edition (1532) are cited to show how Chaucer's meter was presented at that time. Reproductions of sections of *GP*, or illustrations of *GP*, from several notable editions are included.

557 Nathan, Norman. 'Pronouns of Address in the Canterbury Tales.' *MS*, 21 (1959), 193–201.
The use of *ye* and *thou* in *GP* is correct, according to the usage of the time. The 'pronouns addressed to the reader(s)' are not included in this survey (p 193).

558 Ness, Lynn, and Caroline Duncan-Rose. 'A Syntactic Correlate of Style Switching in the *Canterbury Tales*.' In *Papers from the Third International Conference on Historical Linguistics*. Ed. J. Peter Maher, Allan R. Bomhard, and E.F. Konrad Koerner. Amsterdam: Benjamins, 1982. Amsterdam Studies in the Theory and History of Linguistic Science, Series IV: Current Issues in Linguistic Theory, 13. Pp 293–322.
Chaucer's shifts from preterit tense to present, and back again, are a reflection of his ability to exploit 'to the utmost the total linguistic competence of his audience' (p 306), since changes of tense formed part of the audience's *Sprachgefühl* — ie, its 'feel for the rightness of a linguistic form in its total cultural context' (p 293). Most of *GP* consists of the category of language called External Narration, though some sections (such as lines 35–42) consist of External Direct Discourse. Lines 82, 389, and 659 represent a change of category from External Narration to External Direct Discourse, and their verb forms are not properly regarded as examples of tense switching. Only one clear instance of tense switching because of rhyme occurs (line 588). The other changes of verb tense reflect appropriate changes of content or perspective. For example, lines 1–18 'describe regularly recurring events.

These lines are in the present tense. In lines 19 through the first half of 34, the poet begins the description of the events of one particular spring in the past. These lines are in the preterit. Similes, metaphors, and proverbs are in the present' (p 311).

559 Nishizawa, Takao. 'Canterbury Tales (Prologue): Usage of "Were" and "Wolde," from the Viewpoint of Mood and Tense.' *OGD*, 3 (1976), 40–56. Not seen; listed in *A Bibliography of Publications on Medieval English Language and Literature in Japan* (Tokyo: Center for Medieval Studies, Tokyo University, 1983), p 147, #4.

560 Owen, Charles A., Jr. 'Thy Drasty Rhyming ... ' *SP*, 63 (1966), 533–64. Chaucer typically avoids regarding the rhymed couplet as 'a distinct unit of meaning,' favoring 'a kind of verse paragraph' instead (p 555). However, he occasionally shows 'a pointed use of the couplet,' as in lines 307–8 on the Clerk and lines 321–22 on the Man of Law, though he more frequently presents a 'striking "sentence" ' within one line, as in line 72 on the Knight, line 92 on the Squire, and line 251 on the Friar (p 555). In lines 97–98, 'the sound pattern serves as an artificial embellishment of the patent hyperbole' about the Squire's loving (p 556). 'Satiric reinforcement of meaning by rhyme occurs repeatedly' in *GP* (p 557). Examples include lines 167–68, 177–78, and 181–84, on the Monk, and lines 633–38, on the Summoner. 'Most striking of all, because confined to the rhyme word alone, is the satire in the lines on the Prioress's emotional life' (p 558; see lines 142–44, with the rhyme *pitous/mous*). Other special rhyme-choices occur in lines 133–35 on the Prioress; lines 213–14 and 243–50 on the Friar; and lines 499–504, 523–24, and 527–28 on the Parson.

561 Peters, Robert A. *Chaucer's Language.* Bellingham, WA: Western Washington University, 1980. Journal of English Linguistics, Occasional Monographs 1.
This student guidebook includes a phonetic transcription of lines 1–100 and of lines 285–308, along with general statements about Chaucer's language.

562 Piper, Edwin Ford. 'The Miniatures of the Ellesmere Chaucer.' *PQ*, 3 (1924), 241–56 and 8 pages of unpaginated plates.
Piper regards the Ellesmere miniatures as 'characterizations of Chaucer's pilgrims' (p 241) that successfully capture 'Chaucer's stark realism, his vigorous interpretation of man and horse' (p 256). Cf **25, 572, 575, 580.**

563 Pyle, Fitzroy. *English Heroic Line-Structure from Chaucer to Wyatt.* University of Dublin Dissertation. 1933.
Chaucer's concept of versification is related to his overall attitudes. We 'know Chaucer for a man with a genial and tolerant outlook: the Shipman

can be a blackguard and yet "a good felawe". He was attracted more by the rich variety of life than by the colourless uniformity of abstract types characteristic of medieval allegory and romance ... One would expect that as in his portraiture so in his metre, while there was no danger of his losing sight of the type, it would be the variations upon the type ... that would be of most interest to him' (p 91). Line 1 of *GP* is one of several 'nine-syllabled lines which seem especially designed to produce an effect of directness' (p 97). Instances of catalexis (line 384), the epic caesura (lines 148, 491, 514, 829), and other metrical variations are noted.

564 Ramsey, Roy Vance. 'The Hengwrt and Ellesmere Manuscripts of *The Canterbury Tales.*' *SB*, 35 (1982), 133–54.
Ramsey argues that, contrary to the usual opinion which attributes the copying of both mss to the same scribe, 'Hengwrt and Ellesmere were copied by different scribes with different habits of registering certain accidentals, different habits of proofing finished copy, and different habits of registering substantive readings' (p 133). Graphic and graphemic contrasts for ten characteristics (eg, single vowel/double vowel) in *GP* are recorded.

565 Robinson, Ian. *Chaucer's Prosody: A Study of the Middle English Verse Tradition.* London: Cambridge University Press, 1971.
Many examples from *GP* are included in this examination of Chaucer's rhythm, meter, terminology, use of final -*e*, stress patterns, and so forth. 'Below the high style but above the low come things like the descriptions in the General Prologue' (p 164). The Manciple's portrait is analyzed as a sample, using the punctuation given in the Ellesmere ms (p 164). Lines 1–42 are prosodically marked in detail (pp 169–71) to show how the various elements of versification 'co-operate to express the life of the poetry' (p 169).

566 Roscow, G[regory] H. *Syntax and Style in Chaucer's Poetry.* Cambridge, England: D.S. Brewer, 1981; Totowa, NJ: Rowman & Littlefield, 1981. Chaucer Studies, 6.
More than 50 lines from *GP* (listed in an index) are cited in this study of Chaucer's language, with chapters on word-order, idiomatic usage, pleonasm, ellipsis, relative clauses, and co-ordination and parataxis. For example, the 'front-shifting of a predicate adjective qualifying the subject of a sentence is a very common feature of Chaucer's descriptive verse,' as in lines 93, 99, 250, 290, 312, 332, 458, 468, and 479 (p 15).

567 Salter, Elizabeth, and Derek Pearsall. 'Pictorial Illustration of Late Medieval Poetic Texts: the Role of the Frontispiece or Prefatory Picture.' In *Medieval Iconography and Narrative: A Symposium.* Ed. Flemming G. Andersen, Esther Nyholm, Marianne Powell, and Flemming Talbo Stubkjaer.

Odense: Odense University Press, 1980. Pp 100–23.

The paintings of the pilgrims in the Ellesmere manuscript reflect 'a careful and deliberate attempt to underline the meaning of the poem and enhance its appeal ... The artist, or the supervisor who gave him his instructions, shows himself responsive to the concrete and detailed texture of Chaucer's realism' (p 105). It is incorrect to suppose that an awareness of the dramatic nature of *CT* is a modern discovery, for the placement of the illustrations in this manuscript — not at the pilgrims' descriptions in *GP* but at each pilgrim's tale — 'shows a recognition of the dramatic structure of the Canterbury Tales as a whole ... within a year or two of Chaucer's death, the importance of the dramatic principle, of the existence of the Tales as narrations by dramatically conceived characters, was very fully recognised' (p 105).

568 Sampson, Gloria Marie Paulik. *Social Systems and Lexical Features: Pronominal Usage in the Canterbury Tales.* University of Michigan Dissertation. 1969. Dir. James W. Downer. *DAI*, 31 (1970), 747-A.

'This study presents a sociolinguistic analysis of the second-person singular pronouns' in *CT*. 'All pilgrims ... are assigned status positions in the context of a model which views society in terms of Social, Kinship, and Ideational Domains' [from *DAI*; diss not seen].

569 Sanders, Barry Roy. *Doubles-Entendres in the Canterbury Tales.* University of Southern California Dissertation. 1967. Dir. Prof. Mahl. See also *DAI*, 28 (1967), 1058-A.

Although earlier critics underestimated Chaucer's word-play or examined it only incompletely, it forms a significant part of his language. In the rhetorical tradition, what we call a double-entendre would have been called a *significatio per ambiguum*. Sanders identifies and explains examples of this figure throughout the *CT*. There are 38 instances in *GP* (*inspired*, line 6; *ryde*, line 94; *gay*, lines 111 and 113; *coy*, line 119; etc). On the Yeoman, see **749**.

570 Sasaki, Fumio. 'General Prologue To "and." ' [The General Prologue and the Word 'and.'] *CDBK*, 5, 1 (1970), 51–80.

Not seen; listed in *A Bibliography of Publications on Medieval English Language and Literature in Japan* (Tokyo: Center for Medieval Studies, Tokyo University, 1983), p 149, #11.

571 ——. 'General Prologue to Goi.' [Vocabulary of the General Prologue.] *CDBK*, 5, 2 (1970), 55–84.

Not seen; listed in *A Bibliography of Publications on Medieval English Language and Literature in Japan* (Tokyo: Center for Medieval Studies, Tokyo University, 1983), p 149, #12.

572 Schulz, Herbert C. *The Ellesmere Manuscript of Chaucer's Canterbury Tales.* San Marino, CA: Huntington Library, 1966.
The Ellesmere portraits of the pilgrims are reproduced in color (see also **25**, **562**, **575**, and **580**). Schulz supplies a description of the ms. 'One of the most notable features of the paintings is the care exercised by the artists in following, as closely as conditions would permit, the descriptions of the Pilgrims given by Chaucer in his General Prologue' (p 3).

573 Southworth, James G. *Verses of Cadence: An Introduction to the Prosody of Chaucer and his Followers.* Oxford: Blackwell, 1954.
The placement of the caesura (according to the Hengwrt ms) and other aspects of prosody are discussed for several passages in *GP*. See also **574**.

574 ——. *The Prosody of Chaucer and His Followers: Supplementary Chapters to Verses of Cadence.* Oxford: Blackwell, 1962.
Southworth uses *GP* as evidence that Chaucer did not write iambic pentameter (pp 55–57). Manuscript punctuation, particularly the use of the *virga* sign, indicates other kinds of readings. 'It is true that if one disregards the position of the virga hundreds of lines in the *Prologue* alone can be forced into the iambic pentameter line. If, however, the reader observes the intonational pattern at these junctures ... the pattern changes' (p 55). Cf **573**.

575 Stemmler, Theo, ed. *The Ellesmere Miniatures of the Canterbury Pilgrims.* Mannheim: English Department (Medieval Section) of the University of Mannheim, 1976. 2nd ed. 1977. 3rd ed. 1979. Poetria Mediaevalis, 2.
Excellent-quality reproductions of the miniatures from the Ellesmere ms are presented here. (The accompanying text of *GP* is somewhat modernized.) Stammler's introduction discusses the similarities between the miniatures and the verbal portraits of *GP*. Cf **25, 562, 572, 580**.

576 Tani, Koji. 'Chaucer *Prologue* Yogo no Oboegaki.' [The Terminology of Chaucer's *Prologue*.] *ERon*, 5 (1969), 102–10.
Not seen; listed in *A Bibliography of Publications on Medieval English Language and Literature in Japan* (Tokyo: Center for Medieval Studies, Tokyo University, 1983), p 153, #5.

577 Tatlock, John S.P. *The Harleian Manuscript 7334 and Revision of the Canterbury Tales.* London: Kegan Paul, Trench, Trübner, and Henry Frowde, 1909. Chaucer Society, Second Series, 41.
The variant readings of manuscript Harley 7334 are discussed. They imply not simply error, but revision — a revision made by 'some devoted student of Chaucer' who, after the poet's death, 'undertook to improve the text of

the *Canterbury Tales*' (p 32). *GP* passages supporting the theory of revision are the Harley versions of lines 175, 179, 196, 241, 253, 305, 307, 338, 363, 371, 377, 407, 415, 452, 485, 514, 516, 520, 527-28, 540, 583, 604, 612, 617, 663, 741, 752, 764, 778, 782, 799, 803, and 876.

578 Tatsumi, Shinya. '*Canterbury Monogatari* No Joshi No Eigobunkei.' [English Patterns in the Prologue to the Canterbury Tales.] *OSDR*, 26–27 (1968), 300–20.

Not seen; listed in *A Bibliography of Publications on Medieval English Language and Literature in Japan* (Tokyo: Center for Medieval Studies, Tokyo University, 1983), p 153, #6.

579 Ten Brink, Bernhard. *The Language and Metre of Chaucer.* 2nd ed., rev by Frederich Kluge. Trans. by M. Bentinck Smith. London and New York: Macmillan, 1901.

Many examples from *GP* are cited in this general study of Chaucer's language and versification. Lines commented upon include 6, 13, 16, 17, 28, 32, 37, 40, 47, 49, 59, 65, 74, 80, 93, 94, 122, 130, 134, 135, 140, 149, 170, 176, 180, 183, 192, 193, 194, 203, 215, 260, 274, 281, 298, 349, 386, 491, 523, 553, 617, 658, 661, 665, 711, 716, 733, 864, 848, 870. (This list is not exhaustive. Many words are cited without line-references, and there is no index by work.) Special aspects such as elision, run-on couplets, and stress are discussed.

580 Thorpe, James. *A Noble Heritage: the Ellesmere Manuscript of Chaucer's Canterbury Tales.* San Marino, CA: Huntington Library, 1974.

The Ellesmere miniatures of the pilgrims are reproduced (see also **25, 562, 572,** and **575**). Thorpe describes the manuscript and comments on the suitability of the illustrations to the text. 'The artists must have read the tales with care — or been given exact instructions by some knowledgeable person — because the details they use in depicting the pilgrims are in keeping with Chaucer's description of them' (p 9).

581 Wild, Friedrich. *Die Sprachlichen Eigentümlichkeiten der wichtigeren Chaucer-Handschriften und die Sprache Chaucers.* Vienna and Leipzig: Braumüller, 1915. Wiener Beiträge zur Englischen Philologie, 44.

A modification of Wild's dissertation *Die Sprache Chaucers und das Ellesmere-Manuskript*, Vienna, 1909, this study examines various words (listed at the end) as recorded in different mss in order to assess Chaucer's linguistic practice. For example, *Caunterbury* may have been pronounced with effectively three syllables (lines 16, 22, 801), since the mss suggest that metrically a four-syllabic pronunciation was not Chaucer's usual form ('metrisch viersilbiges Caúnterbúry nicht Chaucers gewöhnliche Form war,' p 55).

582 Wimsatt, W.K., Jr. 'One Relation of Rhyme to Reason: Alexander Pope.'
MLQ, 5 (1944), 323–38. Rpt in W.K. Wimsatt, Jr., *The Verbal Icon* (Lexington, KY: University of Kentucky Press, 1954), pp 153–66; rpt 1967.
Wimsatt compares Chaucer's handling of couplet-rhyme to Pope's. In the
GP portraits 'a kind of loose parallel often prevails for ten or twenty lines,
as one feature of a pilgrim after another is enumerated. The sense is continuous, in that the couplets tend to be incomplete, but the lines are all
members of a parallel bundle' (1944, p 331). The Yeoman's portrait illustrates this tendency. Several of its rhymes — *thriftily/yemanly* (lines 105–
6), *bracer/bokeler* (lines 111–12), *grene/kene* (lines 103–4), *sheene/grene*
(lines 115–16) — are considered to be 'tame rhymes because the same
parts of speech are used in closely parallel functions' (p 331); such rhymes
represent 'minimum rhyme, only one step away from homoeoteleuton' (p
332).

583 —. 'The Rule and the Norm: Halle and Keyser on Chaucer's Meter.'
CE, 31 (1969–1970), 774–88. Rpt in p*Literary Style: A Symposium*, ed.
Seymour Chatman (London and New York: Oxford University Press, 1971),
pp 197–215 and see pp 215–20 for additional discussion.
Several lines in *GP* are examined in reply to the metrical analysis of Halle
and Keyser (**538**): lines 2, 5, 20, 63, 136, 195, 294, 343, 358, 445, 542, 545,
564, 617, 629, 634, 635, 662, 703.

Part 5: The Springtime Setting, the Narrator, and the Gathering at the Tabard

See the Introduction, pp xxxii–xxxiii above, for a brief summary of the criticism on this section of the *General Prologue*, and see the Index for further references.

584 Baldwin, Ralph. *The Unity of the Canterbury Tales.* 1955. See **148**.
Baldwin analyzes the rhetoric of lines 1–42. Lines 1–11 'are a type of *reverdie'* or spring-song (p 20); Nigel Wirecker's preface to his *Tractatus* is among the many analogues. 'But it is noteworthy that Chaucer alone made his *reverdie* the groundsong for a pilgrimage' (p 24), even though springtime was traditionally the time of Christian as well as natural renewal.

585 Baum, Paull F. 'Canterbury Tales A 24.' *MLN*, 69 (1954), 551–52.
One solution to the problem of *wel nyne and twenty* (line 24), which has caused difficulty since twenty-nine is *not* the total number of pilgrims, is to assume that the Squire was a later insertion. Without him there are indeed twenty-nine pilgrims who arrive at the Tabard. Alternatively, Chaucer may have first written 'wel five and twenty' or 'wel four and twenty,' prior to adding the last five pilgrims. The Reeve, Miller, Summoner, Pardoner, and Manciple may have been later additions, as suggested by Hammond (**120**), p 254. Chaucer would then have changed the number to 'nyne and twenty' — correctly, if the first version had said 'four and twenty' and the Squire had not yet been included; mistakenly, if the first version were 'five and twenty,' or if the Squire were already present.

586 Blake, N.F., ed. *The Canterbury Tales by Geoffrey Chaucer. Edited from the Hengwrt Manuscript.* 1980. See **95**.

Blake comments on lines 1–18: 'This is the traditional Spring opening recommended for poems by medieval manuals of poetry' (p 29). Chaucer uses syntactical parallelism as a mean of heightening the style. On line 2, 'it is because the Spring theme is Mediterranean in origin that March is presented as a dry month' (p 29). The astronomical details of the dating in this passage 'may have been intended to suggest a general, rather than a specific, time' (p 29).

587 Bloomfield, Morton W. 'The Gloomy Chaucer.' In *Veins of Humor.* Ed. Harry Levin. Cambridge: Harvard University Press, 1972. Harvard English Studies, 3. Pp 57–68.
Though not directly about *GP*, this discussion of the Chaucerian narrator — 'Chaucer's portrayal of himself, the person who may or may not be Chaucer but who certainly bears some relation to the real man' (p 61) — is pertinent to the subjects of the ironic persona and of Chaucer's humor.

588 Bronson, Bertrand H. *In Search of Chaucer.* 1960, 1963, 1967. See **177.**
The opening lines of *GP* are remarkable since they contain 'not a single visual image,' yet they convey 'a profound realization of the stir and meaning of Spring's re-birth — of April to the end of time' (1967, p 18).

589 Burlin, Robert B. ' "Voice" in the *Canterbury Tales*' [letter in *Forum* section]. *PMLA*, 95 (1980), 880–81.
Responding to Leicester, **626**, Burlin finds that Leicester's argument is 'slippery' (p 880) and that it leaves us with two Chaucers in any case — one tied to the fiction, the second comprehending 'all the "voices," the "incomplete" one of the Prologue' (p 880) as well as those of the tales. In addition, Burlin finds Leicester's use of the 'textuality' concept (p 880) to be inappropriate. For Leicester's further reply, see **1347.**

590 Cook, Albert Stanburrough. 'Chauceriana I.' *RomR*, 8 (1917), 210–26.
What exactly is meant by the *licour* of line 3? If Chaucer's source here is Petrarch's Sonnet 9, then 'it would appear that it is the water of the sweet showers that, distilled through the alembic of the soil, becomes charged with generative vigor' (p 225). A correspondence between Petrarch's terms *vertù* and *fioretti* and Chaucer's terms *vertu* and *flour* (line 4) makes it more probable that Chaucer was indeed using Petrarch's sonnet at this point.

591 ——. 'Chaucerian Papers, I.' *TCA*, 23 (1919), 5–63.
Cook provides a collection of classical antecedents for the springtime opening of lines 1–11 — citations from Aeschylus, Euripides, Lucretius, Vergil, Columella, Petronius, the *Pervigilium Veneris*, and Horace. A passage from Vergil's *Georgics* is closest: 'not only are individual Chaucerian words and

phrases accounted for' there, but 'the general thought of the whole eleven lines, with the exception of 8, 10, 11, is to be found in the Virgilian passage' (p 10). A detailed analysis of lines 1–11 is presented. On *droghte* (line 2), for example, Cook cites an English proverb on the rarity of dry weather in March, suggests that the drought 'seems like a literary reminiscence of more tropic conditions' (p 11), and offers, alternatively, that *droghte* might mean 'a caked condition of the soil, due, not to heat, but to cold' (p 11). (See **614** in reply on the drought.) On line 5, Cook suggests that Chaucer 'may have had in mind' a twelfth-century French poem, 'La Dame de Fayel' (p 22). Line 11 is indebted to Lucretius. See also **1085, 1178.**

592 Cummings, Hubertis. 'Chaucer's Prologue, 1–7.' *MLN*, 37 (1922), 86–90.
Two passages in Boethius' *Consolation* show similarities to the opening lines of *GP* — similarities that are closer than those in Boccaccio's *Filocolo*, which Lowes proposed as an analogue (see **627**). Book I, metrum 5, lines 18–22, and Book II, metrum 3, lines 5–8, of the *Consolation* provide precedent for the concept of 'the breath of Zephyr as a thing which brought back life *in* or *into* the leaves of the vernal season' (p 87). Furthermore, the words 'mites ... frondes' in the first of these passages may underlie Chaucer's phrase *tendre croppes* (line 7).

593 Daley, A. Stuart. 'Chaucer's "Droghte of March" in Medieval Farm Lore.' *ChauR*, 4 (1969-1970), 171–79.
Despite previous arguments that the *droghte of March* (line 2) is a metaphor or a literary reminiscence, Daley proposes that the phrase is meant in its common, literal meaning and that a dry spell in March 'was in fact a recognized feature of March weather and agriculture in a number of regions of the island of Britain' (p 172). Medieval agricultural treatises refer to the dry time of March and correlate it with specific agricultural tasks. In the context of *GP*, the following ideas are intended: 1) the important March dry spell has occurred, bringing with it proper conditions for initiating the springtime agricultural tasks; 2) 'the germinating rain and gentle breeze' (p 178) of April have now arrived, in orderly manner; and 3) 'the balance of wet and dry' (p 178) implies a good yield later in the year. Thus the opening couplet of *GP* sets a scene 'firmly in the spring agricultural sequence' (p 179). The subsequent lines, which expand the implications and suggest 'natural harmony under divine dispensation' (p 179), resemble Isaiah 55:10-2, where images of rain, seed, sowing, budding, joy, and other agricultural and emotional concepts are presented. Chaucer's setting thus 'manifests a fresh, recreated world of promise' (p 179).

594 Danby, John F. 'Eighteen Lines of Chaucer's "Prologue".' *CritQ*, 2 (1960), 28–32.

The opening lines of *GP* are discussed in terms of 'energy dynamically released and yet easily kept in hand' (p 29), an etymological sensitivity to words (*licour, vertu, inspired, corages*), the interpenetration of human and natural worlds, the generalized vocabulary (different from eighteenth-century abstractions), and the suggestion that Chaucer expresses 'the common civilisation' (p 30). 'Chaucer is not a satirist' (p 31). In his depiction of the Prioress, for example, he does not intend for us to read her in either/or terms and to pass judgment against her. 'His irony is an irony of sympathy — a sympathy that includes both judge and victim, both writer and reader' (p 31).

595 Derocquigny, J. 'Notes sur Chaucer.' *RevG*, 6 (1910), 203-6.
French parallels are cited for the phrase *of which* (line 4). See also **717, 874, 1198, 1209, 1357.**

596 Donaldson, E. Talbot. 'Chaucer the Pilgrim.' *PMLA*, 69 (1954), 928-36.
Rpt in *Chaucer Criticism*, ed. Richard J. Schoeck and Jerome Taylor (Notre Dame and London: Univ. of Notre Dame Press, 1960; 10th printing 1978), pp 1-13; in *Discussions of the Canterbury Tales*, ed. Charles A. Owen, Jr. (Boston: Heath, 1961), pp 18-24; in *Speaking of Chaucer*, by E. Talbot Donaldson (London: Athlone Press; New York: W.W. Norton, 1970), pp 1-12; and in *Chaucer, The Canterbury Tales: A Casebook*, ed. J.J. Anderson (London: Macmillan, 1974), pp 93-104. Cf **597.**
The Chaucerian narrator has been interpreted as a naive, simple fellow, and, in the other direction, as a 'highly urbane, literal-historical' person who set out to accurately record every detail about a group of people who existed in real life (1954, p 929). Neither of these interpretations is satisfactory. The narrator is usually 'acutely unaware of the significance of what he sees, no matter how sharply he sees it' (p 929). This narrator-pilgrim, with his 'uncertain sense of values,' is 'merely an average man, or mankind,' whose judgment is faulty. He belongs in the literary tradition exemplified by Long Will of *Piers Plowman*, the protagonist of *Pearl*, the protagonist of Gower's *Confessio Amantis*, the teller of Chaucer's *TC*, and the pilgrim-Dante of the *Divine Comedy*, who is 'perhaps the immediate original of these other first-person pilgrims' (p 934). Chaucer's narrator in *GP* is thus part of the 'very old — and very new — tradition of the fallible first person singular' (p 934). This device of the *persona* is used to 'present a vision of the social world imposed on one of the moral world' (p 934). It creates an opportunity to disclose 'a world in which humanity is prevented by its own myopia, the myopia of the describer, from seeing what the dazzlingly attractive externals of life really represent' (p 935). The *persona* also has a comic function; Chaucer's audience would have been delighted by the similarities and dissimilarities between Chaucer the man — reading aloud

to that audience — and Chaucer the pilgrim. 'The constant interplay of these two Chaucers must have produced an exquisite and most ingratiating humor' (p 936).

Donaldson then argues that there are, in fact, three Chaucers. Just as Chaucer the pilgrim liked the Prioress very much, Chaucer the man (who got on well with people) would have liked her too. 'But the third entity, Chaucer the poet, operates in a realm which is above and subsumes those in which Chaucer the man and Chaucer the pilgrim have their being. In this realm prioresses may be simultaneously evaluated as marvelously amiable ladies and as prioresses' (p 936). The poet somehow makes both points of view harmonious in 'that double vision that is his ironical essence' (p 936). The result is an inseparable whole; we cannot always determine which attitude is meant to have the last word.

In reply, see **379, 380, 632**.

597 —, ed. *Chaucer's Poetry: An Anthology for the Modern Reader.* 1958, 1975. See **63**.

In line 11, Nature is capitalized (representing the personification). Chaucer's first sentence says not only that people want to go on pilgrimage in the spring, but also that 'the spring, which engenders thoughts of love, makes people want to go on pilgrimages, during which they will see the world, in order to perform an act of piety' (1975, p 1037). This mixture of diverse motivations suggests that 'the divine love that revives the dead world annually is large enough to countenance the whole paradox of man's nature' (p 1037). Donaldson's comments on Chaucer the pilgrim here are similar to those in his essay, **596**.

598 Donner, Morton. 'Chaucer and His Narrators: The Poet's Place in his Poems.' *WHR*, 27 (1973), 189–95.

Chaucer's use of the first-person narrator shows a balance between subjectivity and objectivity: Chaucer 'uses a first-person narrator who is involved in the narrative, thus implying subjectivity,' but 'the apparent aim of Chaucer's narrative poems is objectivity, since they concern ideas, people, and events that the narrator ostensibly presents as described for their own sake' (p 190). Thus 'Chaucer narrates subjectively through the medium of "I" but objectively by de-emphasizing the role of "I" ' (p 190). In *GP* and elsewhere in the *CT*, 'the narrator of the pilgrimage and the poet Chaucer, known to the Man of Law as he is to Chaucer's audience, are not one and the same person' (p 193). The narrator 'must be some other man, as nameless as the Knight and the Pardoner' (p 194). Because the narrator has been distinguished from the poet, the poet has been established as objectively outside the poem. In Chaucer's 'most satisfactory fusion of subjectivity and objectivity' (p 195), he himself is both outside the poem and within it.

599 Eade, J.C. ' "We ben to lewed or to slowe": Chaucer's Astronomy and Audience Participation.' *SAC*, 4 (1982), 53–85.
Chaucer expected his audience to understand astronomical allusions. In the opening lines of *GP*, for instance, the audience is expected to recognize, by the precision of the phrasing, that the *halve cours* of the sun (line 8) was the second half of the course, 'just as they are expected to know who/what "Zephirus" is, and that the "Tabard" is a hostelry' (p 57; cf lines 5 and 20).

600 Eckhardt, Caroline D. 'The Number of Chaucer's Pilgrims: A Review and Reappraisal.' *YES*, 5 (1975), 1–18. Rpt in *Essays in the Numerical Criticism of Medieval Literature*, ed. Caroline D. Eckhardt (Lewisburg, PA: Bucknell University Press, 1980), pp 156–84.
Previous discussions of the discrepancy between the announced *nyne and twenty* pilgrims (line 24) and the actual number have argued, to put these viewpoints into general terms, either 1) that the phrase *nyne and twenty* is an error of Chaucer's or a scribe's; or 2) that there are indeed exactly twenty-nine pilgrims if we interpret certain lines in *GP* in unusual ways; or 3) that someone else has tampered with Chaucer's text. Arguments along these lines are rejected in favor of seeing the discrepancy as part of Chaucer's intention. He has made his narrator miscount as one of the many examples of the narrator's fallible and hasty judgment. The actual number of pilgrims who arrive in the *compaignye* of line 24 is thirty; the final number of pilgrims in *CT*, thirty-three, represents the number of years of Jesus's life. Chaucer's structural use of this number may be indebted to Dante's *Commedia*, or to other medieval works in which the numbers thirty-three and thirty-four 'were used as a means of suggesting some relationship between a literary work and Christian idealism' (1975, p 16). The narrator's inaccurate count in *GP* thus helps to characterize him and is related to larger structural and thematic principles.

601 Elbow, Peter. *Oppositions in Chaucer*. Middletown, CN: Wesleyan University Press, 1975.
GP is briefly discussed in Elbow's essay 'Irony Relinquished' (pp 131–42). At its beginning, *GP* offers 'a genial resolution of a whole set of oppositions: secular/religious; physical/spiritual; sexual/holy' (p 131). The opening lines 'resolve the widest spectrum of events into one profound springing of transcendent life-giving juice,' although *CT* as a whole, concluding with *ParsT*, 'ends by denying this synthesis' (p 132).

602 Elliott, Ralph W.V. *Chaucer's English*. London: Deutsch, 1974.
The opening passage (lines 1–18) is, except for its length, 'characteristic of much of Chaucer's style, with its astronomical reference and its classical allusion, its generous use of adjectives, mostly premodifying but occasionally

postmodifying, [and] its tendency to mingle common, homely words with some more learned ones, like the rare and in the thirteen-eighties relatively novel word *inspired*' (p 68; cf line 6). See also **1342**.

03 Enkvist, Nils Erik. *The Seasons of the Year: Chapters on a Motif from Beowulf to the Shepherd's Calendar*. Copenhagen: Ejnar Munksgaards Forlag, 1957. Societas Scientiarum Fennica, Commentationes Humanarum Litterarum, 22.

Enkvist endorses the viewpoint of Tuve (see **657**) that Chaucer draws upon a complex tradition of springtime descriptions, not upon a single literary source; and that within the tradition he prefers scientific images rather than images of courtly love. 'This is, of course, wholly in keeping with the realistic, unromantic tone of the Prologue' (p 113).

04 Evans, Robert O. 'Whan that Aprill(e)?' *N&Q*, New Series 4 (1957), 234–37.

Although earlier editors have rendered the beginning of the first line of *GP* as *Whan that Aprille*, indicating that *Aprille* is to be pronounced as trisyllabic, with the accent on the second syllable, Manly (see **49**?) begins the line as *Whan that Aprill* and argues that *Aprill* was *not* meant to be read as trisyllabic. According to Evans, however, the mss do not provide 'sufficient evidence' (p 237) about Chaucer's metrical practice to support Manly's version. 'As there is no conclusive textual evidence, I submit that there is a strong possibility, even a probability,' that the line is 'a regular decasyllable, perhaps with a trochaic substitution in the first foot' (p 237) — which reinstates the earlier reading.

05 Everett, Dorothy. 'Some Reflections on Chaucer's "Art Poetical."' [Sir Israel Gollancz Memorial Lecture.] *PBA*, 36 (1950), 131–54. Rpt in Dorothy Everett, *Essays on Middle English Literature*, ed. Patricia Kean (Oxford: Clarendon Press, 1955; rpt 1959), pp 149–74, and in *Chaucer's Mind and Art*, ed. A. C. Cawley (Edinburgh & London: Oliver and Boyd, 1969), pp 99–124.

The opening of *GP* illustrates — as do earlier Chaucerian works — the use of traditional rhetorical techniques to present an *idea*. This passage combines a number of devices that are described in the rhetorical treatises; the *idea* that it establishes is the nature of the revivifying springtime. Chaucer's disclaimers of the colors of rhetoric 'suggest a consciousness on his part, perhaps even an acute consciousness, of the kind of thing they disclaim' (1950, p 132).

06 Farina, Peter M. 'The Twenty-Nine Again: Another Count of Chaucer's Pilgrims.' *LangQ*, 9 (1971), 29–32.

Farina reviews opinion on the problem of line 24, where Chaucer says that twenty-nine pilgrims arrive in a company although there seem to be thirty plus the narrator. Farina proposes that the narrator be included in the count, which is meant to represent the size of the company within the Tabard Inn — not the size of the arriving group, for 'it would be unrealistic to assume that the nine-and-twenty arrived all together at the inn' (p 29). Secondly, line 164, which reads 'That was hir chapeleyne and Preestes thre,' should be amended to read 'Ther was hir chapeleyne and Preestes thre.' The Prioress and the Second Nun are accompanied by their chaplain (a priest), while the 'Preestes thre' are the Monk, the Friar, and the Parson. By these adjustments, Farina proposes, the company totals twenty-nine.

607 Fineman, Joel. 'The Structure of Allegorical Desire.' In *Selected Papers from the English Institute, 1979–1980*. Ed. Stephen J. Greenblatt. Baltimore and London: Johns Hopkins University Press, 1981. Pp 26–60.

Fineman's analysis draws upon Jacobson's linguistic theories and the psychoanalytic principles of Freud and Lacan. In lines 1–2 occur the two primary syllables of human speech: 'there in the intersection of *A*pril and *Ma*rch we have also the juncture of /pa/ and /ma/' (p 44). 'With the piercing of March by April, then, the allegorical structure thus enunciated has already lost its center and thereby discovered a project: to re-cover the loss dis-covered by the structure of language and of literature' (p 44). In this situation 'the structurality of the text holds out the promise of a meaning that it will also perpetually defer, an image of hermeneutic totality martyred and sacralized by and as the poetical' (p 45). Fineman also includes an extended note on the problem of 'the way a traditionally female April is made to fecundate a traditionally male March' (p 29).

608 Fisher, John H. 'Chaucer's Use of "Swete" and "Swote."' *JEGP*, 50 (1951), 326–31.

Chaucer's word *swote* or *soote* — (line 1) — means 'fragrant or gentle,' rather than 'sweet.' Overall, Chaucer uses *swete* to refer to taste (and secondarily to such concepts as charm and dearness), *swote* to refer to smell (and secondarily to blandness and gentleness).

609 ——, ed. *The Complete Poetry and Prose of Geoffrey Chaucer*. 1977. See **91**.

The order of ideas in lines 1–18 'slants our thinking subliminally' towards the traditional hierarchy of value, 'from inanimate matter, through vegetable, animal, and man, up to God' (p 6). Concepts of hierarchy are evident elsewhere too.

610 Galway, Margaret. 'Whan That Aprille ... ' *TLS*, October 6, 1950, p 629.

Just as Dante 'gave his symbolic pilgrimage an "ideal" date in the past,' so Chaucer may be alluding, in the opening lines of *GP*, to April 11 as the date on which Holy Week began in the year that Richard II was born (1367) and also in the first springtime that Richard was king (1378). 'Chaucer's primary allusion seems to be to 1378, with a glancing allusion to 1367.' The imagery of drought, showers, etc, is appropriate to the spiritual aspects of Lent and Easter. *GP* prepares us for a poem that will discuss 'the means to the good life, especially the art of maintaining "felaweship."'

611 Garbáty, Thomas J. 'The Degradation of Chaucer's "Geffrey."' *PMLA*, 89 (1974), 97–104.
The narrator in *GP* must be discussed in relation to the narrators in Chaucer's other works, for there is 'a continuum of the pose' (p 97). Despite the common characteristics — the pose is of someone loveless, chubby, bookish, introspective, and intellectually imperceptive or dull — we must not expect complete consistency, for the pose 'interests Chaucer only intermittently' (p 98). In *GP*, 'Chaucer slips here and there' (p 103). Overall, Chaucer decreased the perceptive abilities of his narrators, leading to a progressive degradation of the persona.

612 Goffin, R.C. 'Chaucer and "Reason."' *MLR*, 21 (1926), 13–18.
The word *resoun* (line 37) represents the rhetoricians' concept of *ordo* as rule or decorum. A reference to *ordo* would be expected in the opening section of a medieval work, 'for this "part" of rhetoric was recognized as applying there with particular force' (p 16). It would be 'in right Chaucerian vein' for the poet to 'justify his Imagination from the book of Authority' (p 14).

613 Hankins, John E. 'Chaucer and the *Pervigilium Veneris*.' *MLN*, 49 (1934), 80–83.
The *Pervigilium Veneris*, a Latin poem of the second century AD, celebrates an April festival of Venus. Some of its lines resemble the opening section of *GP*. From similarities between the *Pervigilium* and passages in Chaucer's *PF*, it seems probable that he knew that Latin poem. The *Pervigilium* should thus be considered among the other probable sources for Chaucer's springtime description. See **658** in reply.

614 Hart, James A. '"The Droghte of March": A Common Misunderstanding.' *TSLL*, 4 (1962–1963), 525–29.
Although Cook (see **591**) and others have regarded the March drought (line 2) as a literary ingredient reflecting Mediterranean climates, on the grounds that in England March is not a dry month, meteorological data show that in London and Kent 'February and March are the driest months' (p 526), while April is 'on the whole a wetter month than March' (p 527). No clear

pattern of a drought in March emerges from Mediterranean data, or from the classical writers whose literary tradition is supposedly being followed. Thus 'the opening lines of the General Prologue make use of a natural occurrence' (p 529) in eastern England, rather than ironically referring to a literary tradition.

615 Heidtmann, Peter Wallace. *The Chaucerian Narrator*. University of Wisconsin Dissertation. 1965. Dir. Helen C. White. See also *DA* 25 (1965), 5905–6.
'The Chaucerian narrator is a composite whose characteristics may be derived from an examination of the individual narrators that appear in the poet's works. The basic characteristic of all these narrating figures is naiveté or dull-mindedness, thereby making Chaucer's pose the traditional one of the slyly comic writer ... The pilgrim-reporter performs admirably the role given him in the *General Prologue*, and then, except for the *Thopas* interlude, abandons the stage almost entirely in deference to the other characters' [from *DA*; diss not seen].

616 Hodgson, Phyllis, ed. *Chaucer: General Prologue [to] The Canterbury Tales*. 1969. See **80**.
The proposal to describe each pilgrim according to appearance, dress, etc (see lines 35–42), which would have been 'firmly in the rhetorical tradition,' is a joke, since the precision of that announced scheme 'serves to emphasize the actual disorder which ensues' (p 15).

617 Holloway, Julia Bolton. 'Medieval Liturgical Drama, the *Commedia*, *Piers Plowman*, and *The Canterbury Tales*.' *ABR*, 32 (1981), 114–21.
The medieval tradition of the *Officium Peregrinorum* plays may have influenced Chaucer. In these plays, based on Luke 24, two pilgrims (one of whom is Luke) tell tales while journeying to Emmaus; they are joined by Christ, whom they do not recognize. The plays show 'Christ, who is Truth, veritas, himself paradoxically as a lying, fable-telling pilgrim, thereby yoking lie and truth,' and thus 'Chaucer, because of Luke xxiv and the *Officium Peregrinorum*, could justify' his 'lying, yet truthful, pilgrim poetry' (p 117). Furthermore, Luke as pilgrim is shown with the book that he will write and is depicted as a fool, slow to believe. Similar characteristics are attributed to Chaucer's narrator. 'All three poets, Dante, Langland, and Chaucer, mirror Luke in placing themselves within their pilgrim poems as foolish poets questing the Truth, who tell and hear tales told while on a journey' (p 117).

618 Howard, Donald R. 'Chaucer the Man.' *PMLA*, 80 (1965), 337–43. Rpt in *Chaucer's Mind and Art*, ed. A.C. Cawley (Edinburgh and London: Oliver

& Boyd, 1969), pp 31–45.

In *GP* the narrator is a 'returned traveller,' which explains his 'air of omniscience' — returned travellers often report not only facts but also 'gossip and surmises' (1965, p 341). The personality of this narrator is that of 'an exaggerated bourgeois type — uncritical, affable, admiring the rich and powerful, even impressed with successful thievery' (p 342). In his tendency to see the good side of his companions, the narrator 'plays a kind of Holy Fool who stumbles into Christian charity unawares' (p 343). We are enabled to see both that there is evil beneath good appearances, and that there is good beneath evil.

619 ——, ed. , with the assistance of James Dean. *Geoffrey Chaucer: The Canterbury Tales; A Selection*. 1969. See **81**.
Analyzing the narrator, Howard remarks that in the persona of the 'pilgrim-observer,' it is 'as if the poet has put on a mask—the mask of the fool' (p xii). Chaucer does not use the persona to condemn people, though the praise of characters such as the Monk is ironic. The 'pilgrim-observer is a kind of holy fool, and his generous, affable acceptance of everyone is a figure of Christian charity,' which leads us to disapprove of abuses but not to reject individuals (p xiii).

620 Hyams, C. Barry, and Karl H. Reichert. 'The Month of April in English Poetry.' *NS*, New Series 6 (1957), 522–28.
A dialogue between 'T.' and 'P.' (teacher and pupil) is used to make basic comparisons between the springtime opening of *GP* and T.S. Eliot's use of the April motif.

621 Keenan, Hugh T. 'A Curious Correspondence: *Canterbury Tales* A 24–25, Mirk's *Festial*, and Becket's Martyrdom.' *AN&Q*, 16 (1978), 66–67.
The number twenty-nine (line 24) may be intended as an allusion to Thomas Becket, whose saint's day is December 29. The saint may further be linked to the phrase *of sondry folk* (line 25), since in John Mirk's *Festial* — a sermon-collection 'nearly contemporary with the poem' — the saint's name is equated with 'alle mon' (p 66). In addition, in this work Becket is praised for serving the king, serving God, and dying meekly. This description of the saint 'sounds curiously like an outline for the first figure described, the Knight' (p 66), who serves secular authority in battle, is devoted to Christianity, and shows meekness.

622 Kellogg, A.L. 'Chaucer's Self-Portrait and Dante's.' *M Æ*, 29 (1960), 119–20. Rpt in Alfred L. Kellogg, *Chaucer, Langland, Arthur* (New Brunswick, NJ: Rutgers University Press, 1972), pp 353–55.
Chaucer and Dante show a 'remarkably similar use of what might be called

the dual first-person singular' (1960, p 119). Just as in the *Divine Comedy* there is a distinction between Dante the author and Dante the Pilgrim, so Chaucer's self-portrait is double, and is indebted to Dante's. When the Host addresses the downward-looking Chaucer in the Prologue to *Th*, he uses language very similar to that of *Purgatorio* xix, 40–53. The Host as guide resembles Vergil, guide of Dante the Pilgrim. This connection is useful in resolving 'the supposed contradiction between the gregarious Chaucer of the *General Prologue* and the aloof Chaucer of *Sir Thopas*' (p 119). In the gregarious Chaucer at the Tabard, Chaucer the author represents 'a fictive creation whose function, like that of Dante's Pilgrim, is to live in the moment and see only the moment' (p 120). In the Prologue to *Th*, however, Chaucer is 'showing himself to us as the artist, the withdrawn intelligence which does not exist from moment to moment, but encompasses the whole fabric of its work' (p 120).

623 Kimpel, Ben. 'The Narrator of the *Canterbury Tales*.' *ELH*, 20 (1953), 77–86.
Chaucer's narrator in *GP* has been interpreted as a gregarious person, oddly at variance with the unsociable narrator of *Th*. However, in *GP* the fact that the narrator speaks with each of the pilgrims is simply a necessity of Chaucer's plan, for the narrator must 'know enough about the pilgrims to describe them' (p 79). He is *not* presented as being unusually genial or gregarious. He does make brief comments in response to some of the pilgrims, but 'these one-line comments tell us very little about the narrator' (p 80), and 'it is unlikely that Chaucer was conscious of whether such brief remarks were his own comments or the narrator's' (p 81). Neither was Chaucer 'concerned with preserving his narrator's point of view' (p 80), since the narrator at times seems to be omniscient. Overall, it does not seem that 'the narrator in the Prologue is a more important personage than is necessary for the narration, or that his personality is very vividly sketched' (p 82). Furthermore, 'there is no proof that the narrator in the *Canterbury Tales* is in any sense Chaucer' (p 86). In fact, the narrator 'is not a definite enough personality to prove anything' (p 86).

624 Knott, Thomas A. 'A Bit of Chaucer Mythology.' *MP*, 8 (1910–1911), 135–39.
The viewpoint that the narrator is characterized inconsistently — as a gregarious person in *GP*, but a reticent person in the Prologue to *Th* — rests on a misunderstanding. The first couplet of the Prologue to *Th* shows that the whole company is in a sober mood; Chaucer is merely 'in the same emotional condition as all the rest of the pilgrims' (p 138). The Host's jesting 'aims to bring Chaucer to his merry self again' (p 138). The poet is

here recording an emotional response to the preceding tale, not creating a whole personality that is at variance with the *GP* portrayal.

625 Knox, Norman. 'The Satiric Pattern of *The Canterbury Tales*.' In *Six Satirists*. [Ed. Beekman W. Cottrell, David P. Demarest, Jr., and John A. Hart.] Pittsburgh, PA: Carnegie Institute of Technology, 1965. Carnegie Series in English, 9. Pp 17–34.

The ironic narrator of *GP* is one of the elements that bring unity to *CT*. The narrator initially seems to be so 'obviously candid,' lacking 'the self-consciousness to distort and color things,' that we give full trust to him (p 26), but the Prioress's portrait creates 'a hint of doubt' (p 27). In the Monk's portrait the irony increases. 'Honest as our guide seems to be, we begin to suspect him of gullibility, and the further we read the stronger our suspicion becomes' (p 28). *GP* thus establishes a critical perspective for the entire *CT*: 'by the time we end the Prologue, our suspicions are aroused by every incongruity, we are hounds sniffing after the slightest scent of a quarry. Thus Chaucer, by lighting a fire under our critical faculties, illuminates the whole world of the *Canterbury Tales*' (p 29).

626 Leicester, H. Marshall, Jr. 'The Art of Impersonation: A General Prologue to the *Canterbury Tales*.' *PMLA*, 95 (1980), 213–24.

Leicester argues against the tendency of recent critics to postulate a divided narrator — to divide the narrator into the pilgrim and the poet behind the pilgrim. The speaker is created by the text, not the other way around. Hence 'there is nobody there,' for 'there is only the text' (p 221). The personality of the pilgrims is not wholly given in advance in *GP*, but must be completed from the tale. Thus 'it is the tale that specifies the portrait, not the other way around' (p 218). As for the speaker of *GP*, he is a sophisticated personality who deliberately denies us an exact sense of himself, 'who is not telling us, any more than he told the Monk, his whole mind in plain terms' (p 220). Since 'the reality of characters is a function of their mystery' — the impression that there is more to them than we can know — the speaker is 'present as uncomprehended' (p 220).

The poem is written as 'a literary imitation of oral performance' (p 221), not as a drama. 'There is no pilgrimage, there are no pilgrims' (p 221). What exists is '*the speaker of the poem*,' who is involved in a 'continual attempt, continually repeated, to see from another's point of view, to stretch and extend the self by learning to speak in the voices of others' (p 221). The indeterminant quality of the speaker relates to one of the principal themes of *GP*, 'the insufficiency of traditional social and moral classifying schemes — estates, hierarchies, and the like — to deal with the complexity of individuals and their relations' (p 221). The voice of *GP* 'is a prologal voice, a voice that is only beginning to speak,' and it is only through an understanding of the rest of the work that this 'self-constructing voice' might be comprehended (p 222). The final aspect of the speaker's 'art of impersonation' is 'to impersonate himself, to create himself as fully as he can in his work' (p 222). (In reply see Burlin, **589**, and, in answer again, Leicester, **1347**). On the Physician, see **1123**.

627 Lowes, John Livingston. 'The *Franklin's Tale*, the *Teseide*, and the *Filocolo.*' *MP*, 15 (1917-1918), 689–728.
Lines 1–7 show that 'Chaucer seems definitely to have recalled the phraseology' of Boccaccio's *Filocolo* (p 707). The resemblances between Chaucer's springtime imagery and sections II.238 and II.239 of the *Filocolo* are 'too close to be readily accounted for as mere coincidence' (p 707). In reply, see **592**.

628 ——. 'The Art of Geoffrey Chaucer: Sir Israel Gollancz Memorial Lecture.' *PBA*, 16 (1930), 297–326. Rpt in *SatR*, 7 (1930–1931), 937–39, in a shortened version against which Lowes protested in *SatR*, 8 (1931–1932), 46.
The opening passage of *GP* — Chaucer's 'exquisite *ave atque vale*' to the preceding poetic tradition — represents 'the continuity, through steadily maturing powers, of Chaucer's art' (1930, p 326).

629 Lumiansky, Robert M. 'The Meaning of Chaucer's Prologue to "Sir Thopas."' *PQ*, 26 (1947), 313–20.
The depiction of Chaucer in the Prologue to *Th* — where he is ironic in mood, planning to expose Harry Bailly's poor sense of literature — 'is in no way inconsistent with the highly sociable and slyly ironic qualities' (p 320) attributed to the affable narrator of *GP*.

630 McCabe, John Donald. *The Comic in the Poetry of Chaucer: Congruence of 'Sentence' and 'Solaas.'* 1968. See **352**.
The narrator shows traits associated with 'the prophet of the Hebraic tradition' (p 100), such as the trait of passivity: the pilgrim-narrator did not either anticipate or invite the company, though he becomes a participant and observer. Similarly, 'the prophet cannot control what he sees; he simply sees what he sees, and what he sees is something that (at least interiorly) happens to him' rather than being something brought about by his active instigation (p 101). The Hebrew tradition also provides precedent for the viewpoint that play and contemplation can constitute a single process.

631 Magoun, F.P., Jr. '*Canterbury Tales* A 11.' *MLN*, 70 (1955), 399.
The word *Nature* should be capitalized here: Chaucer is thinking of the personified concept. In *GP*, Nature is said to incite the birds to mate (line 11); similarly, in *PF* Nature's 'interest in the sex-life of birds is unbounded.'

Given the parallel, and the fact that 'Chaucer evidently thought of Natura as virtually the patron saint of birds,' the personification — rather than the weaker concept spelled without a capital letter — is appropriate for *GP*.

32 Major, John M. 'The Personality of Chaucer the Pilgrim.' *PMLA*, 75 (1960), 160–62.

In a critique of Donaldson (**596**), Major argues that it is difficult to see the narrator of *GP* as a 'fully conceived human being with a distinct personality the opposite of Chaucer's own,' given the inconsistencies of the *GP* persona (p 160). The narrator would have to be a 'complete fool' (p 161) not to realize the contradictory sets of values expressed in *GP*. The persona is not that of a fool, but that of a narrator who speaks in '*conscious* irony' (p 161) and who has an outlook 'almost indistinguishable from Chaucer's own' (p 162). Unless we see Chaucer the pilgrim as 'a marvelously alert, ironic, facetious master of every situation,' we are misreading the text (p 162).

33 'The Borough of Southwark.' In *The Victoria History of the County of Surrey*, 4. Ed. H.E. Malden. London: Constable & Company, Ltd., 1912. Pp 125–62.

Pages 127–29 within the section on Southwark contain references to the Tabard Inn (see line 20). The Tabard was evidently part of the property of the Abbot of Hyde at the dissolution of the monasteries in the sixteenth century and probably belonged to that abbot from 1306 onward. A portion of the inn was reserved for his use, but 'a great part' of the building 'was an inn in the modern sense' (p 127).

34 Manly, John M., and Edith Rickert, eds. *The Text of the Canterbury Tales Studied on the Basis of All Known Manuscripts*. 1940. See **49**.

The word *Aprille* (line 1) should not be read as a trisyllable; the line 'obviously begins with a falling or trochaic rhythm' (vol 3, p 421).

35 Maynard, Theodore. 'Chaucer's Literary Development.' *CW*, 138 (October 1933), 65–75.

Brief remarks on Chaucer's appreciation of springtime and of birdsong are included in this general overview of his career.

36 Mehl, Dieter. 'Erscheinungsformen des Erzählers in Chaucers "Canterbury Tales." ' In *Chaucer und seine Zeit: Symposium für Walter F. Schirmer*. Ed. Arno Esch. Tübingen: Niemeyer, 1968. Buchreihe der Anglia, 14. Pp 189–206.

Arguing that it is a mistake to analyze the narrator according to modern theories of psychological consistency, Mehl cautions against interpretations that depict the narrator as wholly untrustworthy, naive, or ironic. In the first 120 lines the narrator shows no symptoms of a dulled or limited comprehension ('in den ersten 120 Zeilen keinerlei Symptome einer beschränkten Auffassungsgabe verrät,' p 192). In the portrait-series the question of the narrator's untrustworthiness occurs in only specific locations, and it is an impermissable overestimation of these instances to assume that the narrator is naive and credulous throughout GP ('es bedeutet doch wohl eine unzulässige Überbewertung dieser Stellen, wenn man von ihnen aus für den ganzen Prolog einen naiv-gutgläubigen Erzähler annimmt,' p 193). On the contrary, the narrator tends to establish an atmosphere of private understanding and intimacy between himself and the reader, which is much more effective than the persona of a naive pilgrim could be ('schafft der Erzähler eine Atmosphäre des geheimen Einverständnisses und der Vertrautheit zwischen sich und dem Leser, die sehr viel wirkungsvoller ist als es eine einfältige Pilgerfigur sein könnte,' p 193). The narrator, who withholds judgment, is characteristically not untrustworthy but instead relatively vague and indeterminable ('verhältnismässig vage und unbestimmbar,' p 196).

637 Myers, A[lexander] R[eginald]. London in the Age of Chaucer. Norman, OK: University of Oklahoma Press, 1972. Centers of Civilization Series, 31. Many details about fourteenth-century London are provided. The Tabard Inn (see line 20) was among the taverns 'regarded as very respectable,' though some other Southwark inns 'were notorious as brothels' (p 202).

638 Nitzsche, J.C. 'Creation in Genesis and Nature in Chaucer's General Prologue 1–18.' PLL, 14 (1978), 459–64.
The opening lines of GP show a 'specific thematic and structural indebtedness' to the 'hexameral creation of the cosmos and its inhabitants in the Book of Genesis' (p 459). The first day of the world, according to Aelfric, was March 15; Chaucer's April pilgrimage allows 'time enough after the Fall' (p 460). More important is the correspondence in the 'sequence of ideas and images' (p 460). Chaucer uses Nature, rather than God directly, as the agent of (re)creation, since his scene takes place after the Fall; his concept of Nature is drawn from Alain de Lille and is more fully expressed in PF. Just as the first day of Creation involved the separation of light from dark, so in GP Nature begins by separating 'the season of light, spring, from that of dark, winter' (p 461), for April has succeeded March. The second day of Creation involved spatial separation and 'commerce between the natural world and the supernatural one' (p 462); Chaucer shows communication between 'the lower aerial region below the moon and the earth,' as the showers descend and 'the waters above join the waters below,' the moisture in the plants (p 462). The third day of Creation produced plant

life; Chaucer mentions roots, flowers, etc. The fourth day created the sun, moon, and stars; Chaucer mentions the sun. The fifth day's birds of the air are represented by the small birds who sing all night. The 'allusion to folk and palmers seeking pilgrimage' functions as 'a synecdoche for the creation of mankind on the sixth day' (p 462).

The second section of *GP* (lines 12–18) presents a 'human chain of being' (p 463) in identifying human types. Professional pilgrims move outward to seek shrines in strange lands, while the Canterbury pilgrims move from many places inward toward the fixed point at Canterbury. These two motions correspond to two motives and two types of human nature. Thus early in *GP* Chaucer has depicted 'the difficulties of man in understanding and coping with the regeneration of his nature in a postlapsarian world continually regenerating itself in opposition to chaos, death, nothingness — a proper prolegomenon to the specific examples provided in the *General Prologue* and the *Tales* themselves' (p 464).

639 Peck, Russell Albert. *Number Symbolism and the Idea of Order in the Works of Geoffrey Chaucer.* Indiana University Dissertation. 1963. Dir. Robert Mitchner. See also *DA*, 24 (1964), 2894–95.

Chaucer indicates that *wel nyne and twenty* pilgrims 'set out from the Tabard Inn' (line 24; p 200). 'Whether there were actually *twenty-nine* or not is less significant than the fact that Chaucer uses the number as a sign, or measure, of the pilgrims. *Twenty-nine* is a number of imperfection, inadequacy, or sin' (p 201); the associations of this number mark the pilgrims as they begin their journey to the shrine.

640 ——. 'Number Symbolism in the Prologue to Chaucer's *Parson's Tale.*' *ES*, 48 (1967), 205–15.

The number twenty-nine is mentioned both in *GP* (line 24) and in the Prologue to *ParsT* (X.4). Peck suggests that 'the number at the beginning of the poem not only forms a harmonious link with the number at the end of the poem, but that both numbers function as metaphors of the spiritual welfare of the pilgrims in the company' (p 206). Twenty-nine indicates 'imperfection, concupiscence, and spiritual decrepitude,' according to medieval number theory; it is thus 'an apt emblem for the pilgrims' (p 207).

641 Pollard, Alfred W., et al., eds. *The Works of Geoffrey Chaucer.* 1898. See 4.

Pollard marks the opening phrase for pronunciation as *Whán that Aprílle* (line 1) and capitalizes *Nature* (line 11), implying the personification (p 1).

642 Prins, A.A. 'The Dating in the *Canterbury Tales.*' In *Chaucer and Middle English Studies in Honour of Rossell Hope Robbins.* Ed. Beryl Rowland.

London: Allen & Unwin, 1974. Pp 342–47.
The dating implied by the opening lines of GP has been seen as inconsistent with the dating implied by the Prologue to the MLT. However, the discrepancy disappears if in GP we take Chaucer to be referring not to the terrestrial or astrological zodiac of the ninth sphere, but instead to the stellar zodiac of the eighth sphere. (A passage in the FranT shows that Chaucer was familiar with the stellar zodiac.)

643 Rea, John A. 'An Old French Analogue to General Prologue 1–18.' PQ, 46 (1967), 128–30.
Chaucer may have been acquainted with Adenet le Roi's Berte aus Grans Pies, the opening passage of which (like the opening of GP) combines the motifs of pilgrimage and springtime, along with framing a narrative. Verbal similarities are also present. Chaucer probably drew on another work by this author when he wrote SqT; a fourteenth-century English ms of Berte exists. It is thus 'a tempting hypothesis' (p 130) that Chaucer used Berte.

644 Reiss, Edmund. 'The Pilgrimage Narrative and the Canterbury Tales.' 1970. See 420.
The pilgrimage begins in GP at 'the Babylon-like Tabard Inn — next to the Bell, a Southwark brothel'; it ends proceeding to 'the Jerusalem-like holy place of Canterbury' (p 301). Both the near-beginning of the text (GP) and its near-end (the prologue to ParsT) refer to the number twenty-nine, which in medieval number symbolism suggested 'the approach to perfection,' a concept appropriate for pilgrimage (p 304).

645 ——. 'Chaucer's Thematic Particulars.' In Signs and Symbols in Chaucer's Poetry. Ed. John P. Hermann and John J. Burke, Jr. University, AL: University of Alabama Press, 1981. Pp 26–42.
The number twenty-nine, occurring at line 24 and also in the Parson's prologue, is 'less a realistic detail than a thematic particular' (p 28). 'As a numerological equivalent to the approach to salvation and/or perfection, it gives a spiritual dimension, even a cosmic sense, to the journey at hand' (p 28). See also 841, 1159.

646 Robinson, F.N., ed. The Works of Geoffrey Chaucer. 1957. See 42.
In line 11, nature should perhaps be capitalized. 'Chaucer may have had in mind the familiar conception of the goddess Nature,' which he uses in PF (p 651).

647 Rudat, Wolfgang E.H. 'Heresy and Springtime Ritual: Biblical and Classical Allusions in the Canterbury Tales.' RBPH, 54 (1976), 823–36.
The opening lines of GP 'imitate, among other sources, a passage in the

Second Georgic, where Virgil describes the spring rain in terms of a sexual union between Jupiter alias Aether, and Earth' (p 824). As Ross (see **130**) has indicated, *corage* can have sexual connotations; 'the centripetal vectors of Chaucer's allusion suggest — especially in view of the *corages/pilgrimages* rhyme — that the pilgrimage to Canterbury, touched off by the witnessing of the sexual union between April and March, is as sexually motivated as the singing of the birds' (p 826). The pilgrim Chaucer, who mentions his own *corage* (line 22), shares this motivation. Chaucer also seems to be using Vergil's *Third Georgic*, 'which describes how in spring Zephirus has with his wind the same impregnating effect as raining Jupiter' (p 832). The 'allusion to the miraculous impregnating power of Zephirus becomes operative in Chaucer's satiric portrayal of the Prioress' (p 833). There is an implication that 'without giving up her celibacy and without an act of fornication, the Prioress could conceive a child from Zephirus' (p 833) — an idea that parodies Mary's impregnation by the holy spirit. In certain passages of the *CT* 'Chaucer is downright heretical and therefore has good reasons for his *retracciouns*' (p 823).

648 ——. 'The *Canterbury Tales*: Anxiety Release and Wish Fulfillment.' *AI*, 35 (1978), 407–18.
The term *corage* (lines 11 and 22) includes a sexual connotation. 'The pilgrimage to Canterbury then is, among other things, an attempt to sublimate the sex drive' (p 408). Lines 1–2 allude to Vergil's Second *Georgic*, which describes the springtime impregnation of Earth by Jupiter. 'Chaucer imitates the causal sequence in Virgil to suggest that the union between April and March stimulates not only the animal world but also humans whose behavior is governed by their libido, which is channeled into conversation' (p 409).

649 Ruggiers, Paul G. *The Art of Canterbury Tales.* Madison, Milwaukee, and London: University of Wisconsin Press, 1965. Rpt 1967. Portions rpt in *Critics on Chaucer*, ed. Sheila Sullivan (London: Allen and Unwin, 1970), pp 111–14.
In the Chapter 'The Narrator' (1965, pp 16–41), Ruggiers comments that the narrator's 'persistent innocence' in *GP* 'leads to a simpleton's appreciation of the pilgrims without regard to a common standard of morality, a yielding to the essential humanity of his companions, a sense of being overwhelmed by their worth, and success, and obvious talents' (p 17). This 'remarkable reporter' is Chaucer's 'slyest joke' (p 18). The narrator's persona is more consistently maintained in *GP* than elsewhere in *CT* — but even in *GP* the apology at the end assumes knowledge of the whole *CT*, 'a foresight that can be only the poet's' (p 18). On the Summoner, see **1290**; on the Pardoner, **1329**.

650 Schildgen, Brenda D. *The Conflict Between Art and Morality in Two Fourteenth-Century Poets: Juan Ruiz and Geoffrey Chaucer*. Indiana University Dissertation. 1972. Dir. L. Beltrán. See also *DAI*, 33 (1973), 4362-A.
Since Chaucer intended to depict the reality of his times, both *caritas* and *cupiditas* had to be represented. Schildgen's section on the narrator (pp 152-68) briefly considers his attitude toward each of the pilgrims as shown in the details of the portraits. The narrator shows conventional and worldly prejudices, 'bourgeois and secular tendencies' (p 160), innocence and naivete. He generally assesses what he sees according to social, not moral, grounds; thus 'he lauds the Prioress, the Monk and the Friar because he is influenced by their impressive appearance or social class' and 'is less kind to the pilgrims from the working classes' (p 164). He represents 'an ordinary, secular, and rather simple man with fairly bourgeois values; his social bias shows his *cupiditas* quite clearly as indeed his unfailing ability to single out the ideal in the Parson, the Plowman, the Knight and the Clerk demonstrates his *caritas*' (pp 165-66). The narrator thus 'creates ambivalence towards *caritas-cupiditas*' (p 166). On the Summoner, see **1291**.

651 Schmidt, A.V.C., ed. *Geoffrey Chaucer: The General Prologue to the Canterbury Tales and the Canon's Yeoman's Prologue and Tale*. 1974. See **89**.
In lines 1-4, 'the basic metaphor here is a sexual one: April is seen as "impregnating" March in order to bring forth from the barren winter earth the vegetation of spring ... "Shoures" (line 1) had the meaning both of "rainshowers" and of "showers" of falling missiles or weapons. This military metaphor is present here in a subdued way ... the "wound" experienced by the last winter month is a "wound" of love, bringing at once death (of the old) and a new life' (p 123). In line 11, a personification of Nature may be intended.

652 Skeat, Walter W., ed. *The Complete Works of Geoffrey Chaucer, Edited from Numerous Manuscripts*. 1894-1897. See **3**.
Aprille (line 1) is trisyllabic (vol 5, p xxiv). The springtime opening shows similarities to Guido delle Colonne's *Historia Troiae* and Vincent of Beauvais's *Speculum naturale*.

653 Spitzer, Leo. *Classical and Christian Ideas of World Harmony: Prologomena to an Interpretation of the Word 'Stimmung.'* Ed. Anna Granville Hatcher. Preface by Réne Wellek. Baltimore: Johns Hopkins Press, 1963. Distributed in England by Oxford University Press, London.
Spitzer briefly discusses music and harmony in *GP* (pp 179-80). Religious worship is related to music, including to bird song. Chaucer's *Natureingang*

depicts a harmonious world, of which the birds' music (see line 9) forms a part. The small birds of line 9 may be nightingales. The nightingale, 'symbol of love-inspired song' (p 179), can — with its open eyes (line 10) — function as a symbol of loving vigilance. Elsewhere the nightingale is 'the musician of God' (p 180). Chaucer's springtime prelude (lines 1–11) offers an 'image of world harmony — here appropriate because the theme of the pilgrimage itself was inspired by the idea of love' (p 179).

654 Spraycar, Rudy S. 'The Prologue to the *General Prologue*: Chaucer's Statement about Nature in the Opening Lines of the "Canterbury Tales." ' *NM*, 81 (1980), 143–49.

Lines 1–11 of *GP*, written in the high style, are a *Natureingang* emphasizing the venereal activities of springtime, but lines 12–18, written in the plain style, emphasize the spiritual exercise of pilgrimage instead. The first eighteen lines, which constitute a *sententia*, make 'a general statement about life' and are 'rhetorically and temporally separate' from the rest of the work (p 145). Therefore, the date they imply need not agree with any dates mentioned elsewhere. These lines indicate a date 'near the first of April,' with Chaucer's emphasis on Aries and April stressing 'nature's venereal aspects' (p 145); *Nature* (line 11) should probably be capitalized, representing the goddess Natura. The 'when ... then' structure of the opening passage can be read as a logical argument — as if it were 'a series of "whereases" followed by a "therefore" ' (p 147). In logical terms, the activities of the lower creatures are a series of premises, with our reaction being 'a conclusion to be drawn from those premises' (p 148) if we use our reasoning abilities to read the book of Nature correctly. Of all creatures, 'only man can draw a conclusion from the book of Nature' (p 149): the conclusion should be that 'pilgrimage is necessary for the regeneration of his soul' (p 142).

655 Taylor, Paul B. 'The Canon's Yeoman's Breath: Emanations of a Metaphor.' *ES*, 60 (1979), 380–88.

Lines 1–18 of *GP*, which Taylor calls the Invocation, allude to 'the Christian scriptural tradition of creation and grace' (p 380). Zephirus's action in inspiring the crops reflects 'God's gift of life to man' (p 380) at Creation and also the gift of grace to Noah when God stilled the rains with his breath. 'Appropriately Chaucer has the procession leave the Tabard on the morning of 17 April, the biblical date for the start of the Flood rains' (p 380). Both the vegetation of springtime and the procession of the pilgrims are 'visible — or public — features of a privy and invisible force of God, which Chaucer represents by Zephirus, the west wind' (p 380). But while the natural world manifests God's power, in many of the pilgrims 'the ideal is too high, the practice too low' (p 381). The breath of God, 'authority for the allegorical pilgrimage' (p 381), is thus demeaned by the characters of some of the pilgrims. 'Chaucer's most explicit parody of Divine creation is carried by his images of breath, wind and odour, all of which suggest and yet oppose the sweetness of Zephirus' (p 381). Such parodies of the *GP* metaphor are found in the *MilT*, the Summoner's Prologue and *SumT*, and the Canon's Yeoman's Prologue and *CYT*.

656 ——. 'The Alchemy of Spring in Chaucer's *General Prologue.*' *ChauR*, 17 (1982–1983), 1–4.

GP 'opens with a metaphor of alchemy' that conjoins 'nature with spirit' (p 3). *Zephirus* (line 5) suggests 'a breath of life that seasonally rehearses Divine creation' (p 1), while *licour* (line 3) represents 'the *aqua vitae* upon which the breath of life moves' (p 1), 'an image of the primal waters of life, the *logoi spermatikoi* of the pilgrimage itself,' and 'a mysterious model for generation of spirit and knowledge' (p 3). Later in *CT* there are other themes of 'purifying transformations' and the pilgrimage itself rehearses 'the ultimate transformation of matter to spirit, which is the *ultimate* goal of alchemy as well' (p 3).

657 Tuve, Rosemond. *Seasons and Months: Studies in a Tradition of Middle English Poetry.* Paris: Librairie universitaire, 1933. Rpt Folcraft, PA: Folcroft Library Editions, 1971; Cambridge, England: D. S. Brewer, 1974.

References to the seasons and the months constituted 'a formal, obligatory and complex convention characteristic of Middle English literature' (1933, p 3). The convention is represented in several different strains or varieties. The opening of *GP* seems especially indebted to the semi-scientific material on the seasons included in treatises such as the *Secreta Secretorum*, which was 'one of the most influential books of the Middle Ages' (p 50) and which shows 'striking similarities' to *GP* (p 47). Other sources also show such similarities, 'but the *Secreta Secretorum* is at least a very likely place for [Chaucer] to have seen many details combined which he also combined in his description' (p 55). On the Squire, see **735**. Cf **603**.

658 ——. 'Spring in Chaucer and Before Him.' *MLN*, 52 (1937), 9–16.

Tuve is here partly responding to the suggestion of Hankins (**613**) that the *Pervigilium Veneris* was a source for the springtime opening of *GP*. Tuve argues that while Chaucer may have known the *Pervigilium Veneris*, it is inappropriate to claim any single source, since Chaucer was 'consciously following a long-standing and complicated tradition' (p 9) of which the Latin poem is only one example. The typical scientific description of spring in treatises such as the *Secreta Secretorum* and the *De natura rerum* includes dating by the zodiac, the movement of the humours through the roots into the tops of trees and herbs, the blowing of the wind, the inclination of birds toward love, and Nature's impulsion to procreate. Although the *Per-*

vigilium Veneris indeed praises Venus as bringer of showers, goddess of fertility, etc, 'this figure in one guise or another, often in almost exactly that which Chaucer gives her, embodies the most constantly recurring emphasis within the tradition of seasons-description' (p 11); sometimes she is Nature, sometimes Venus, etc. Similarly, 'traditional associations' (p 15) would have favored an April setting. Thus Chaucer's 'sources and models were innumerable, what he makes of them is new and his own' (p 16).

659 Whitbread, L. 'Six Chaucer Notes.' *NM*, 79 (1978), 41–43.
It is suggested that the opening lines of *GP* may echo a passage from Catullus. See also **1036, 1171, 1228, 1294.**

660 Willard, Rudolph. 'Chaucer's "Holt and Heeth." ' *AS*, 22 (1947), 196–98.
The formula *holt and heeth* (line 6) creates a contrast 'between the treed, wooded, forested terrain, the holt, and the open, likewise vegetation-mantled land, the heath,' both of which are natural elements responding 'to the influences of April, Zephyrus, and the young sun' (p 198). The word *holt* should not be glossed 'plantation,' since — at least to American audiences — a plantation implies something quite different from natural woodlands.

661 Wood, Chauncey Derby. *Chaucer's Use of Astrology for Poetic Imagery.* Princeton University Dissertation. 1963. See also *DA*, 25 (1964), 2970.
'Chapter X has an investigation of the astrological image of the sun in Taurus that opens the *Prologue*, and I suggest that the imagery leads us to a consideration of Noah's flood. The departure of the pilgrims on the day of the departure of Noah' is discussed [from *DA*; diss not seen; cf **662**].

662 ——. 'The April Date as a Structural Device in *The Canterbury Tales*.' *MLQ*, 25 (1964), 259–71.
The mid-April date implied for Chaucer's pilgrimage (lines 1–12) finds precedent in the journey of Noah on the ark, which would have been understood as beginning on April 17. 'The coincidence of the departure of the Canterbury pilgrims with the date of the departure of Noah's ark furnishes us with a precise and not unlikely rationale for Chaucer's choice of a specific month and day for the beginning of his poem' (p 265). Realism does not provide a sufficient explanation of the date, for 'there is no historical evidence to show that a majority of pilgrims went on their journeys in the spring, and, indeed, the major pilgrimages to Canterbury were undertaken in December and July' (p 266). The opening description, with its mention of April and rain and journeying, was intended to make the audience recall the Biblical flood. The parallel with Noah suggests symbolic associations: the flood 'is a two-sided symbol that is ideal for Chaucer's purposes, for the flood was sent to punish sin, and yet the event itself figures forth the

way of salvation, through the ark for Noah and through baptism and the other sacraments for the individual Christian' (p 268). The theme of the flood is further developed in *MilT*. Furthermore, 'Noah escaped punishment through God's grace (Genesis 6:8), and the Parson concludes Chaucer's group of tales with a sermon on how that grace may be achieved' (p 270). (This article is incorporated into Wood's book, *Chaucer and the Country of the Stars: Poetic Uses of Astrological Imagery*, Princeton: Princeton University Press, 1970; see esp. pp 162–72.) Cf **661**.

❧ Part 6: The Knight

See the Introduction, p xxxiii above, for a brief summary of criticism on
the Knight, and see the Index for further references.

663 Andersen, Wallis May. *Rhetoric and Poetics in the Canterbury Tales: the
Knight, the Squire, and the Franklin.* 1979. See **145**.
The Knight's *GP* portrait contains details that only later become understood as hints of the imperfections in his character. In *GP* it is 'possible
that there is irony in the size of the list of sieges the Knight is avowed
to have participated in ... One might argue that going on his pilgrimage
without cleaning up first does not mean he is pious so much as it is a way
of flaunting his experience in battle. Or one might take the reference to
his tunic and mail being "al bismotered" [line 76] as emblematic of his
character ... Yet it is hard to find in simply the portrait convincing proof
that the Knight is not an ideal character. Only when one looks at the *Tale*
is it possible to find foreshadowings of the Knight's character flaws in his
portrait' (pp 81–82).

664 Barber, Richard. *The Knight and Chivalry.* London: Longman Group,
1970; London: Sphere Books, 1974.
Much background information pertinent to Chaucer's Knight — for example, information on warfare, the Teutonic Order, and medieval attitudes
towards chivalry — is presented.

665 Beidler, Peter G. 'Chaucer's "Knight's Tale" and its Teller.' *EngR*, 18, 4
(1968), 54–60.
The Knight has a sense of humor; he is not wholly solemn. The tone of
levity evident in parts of *KnT* is appropriate to his *GP* description. He
tells his story to amuse as well as to instruct the other pilgrims. Indeed, he
could have told that particular story only with some irony, since his own

plainness of array is in contrast to the richness of array in the tale, and his 'real battles against real and deadly enemies' are in contrast to the chivalric 'games' of the tale (pp 58–9). Thus 'he would be amused by the artificiality of the typical romantic tale' and 'would assume a tone of irony as he told some of the more unrealistic parts of his romance' (p 58). His response to being assigned the first tale (lines 853–54, 857) indicates that 'a cheerful knight is about to begin what he considers to be a game' (p 59).

666 Bowden, Muriel. *A Commentary on the General Prologue to the Canterbury Tales.* 1948. See **104**.
Chaucer's Knight personifies chivalric ideals, but is also 'flesh and blood' (p 44), although the evidence is too scanty to permit firm identification with a specific historical model. Chaucer was not a reformer and would have shared the 'almost undivided' opinion of his time (p 67) in approving holy wars. The chivalric vocabulary of the portrait is discussed in comparison to Watriquet de Couvin's description of his patron, whom Chaucer might well have known. The Knight's campaigns are reviewed. See the chapter 'The Perfect Knight' (pp 44–73, supplementary notes on pp 318–19).

667 Brewer, D.S. 'Honour in Chaucer.' *E&S*, New Series 26 (1973), 1–19.
The implications of Chaucer's term *honour* and related words — especially *trouthe* — are discussed (the Knight himself is not the subject).

668 Bryant, Frank E. 'Did Boccaccio Suggest the Character of Chaucer's Knight?' *MLN*, 17 (1902), 235–36.
Stanza 40 of Book VI of Boccaccio's *Teseide* describes a warrior, King Evander, as arriving in Athens grimy from his arms and sweat (cf the fact that the Knight's clothes are stained from his armor—lines 75–76); as judged to be valorous by all, although his appearance was not beautiful (cf the fact that the Knight is worthy and wise, though not gay–lines 68, 74); and as being humble in manner and polite to all people (cf the Knight's meek bearing and courteous speech to inferiors—lines 69–71). In Bryant's view these resemblances do not seem 'due to mere chance' (p 236). 'The *Knight's Tale* is itself the story of the *Teseide* .... what is more natural than to suppose that Chaucer might have taken the essential traits of this personage [from the *Teseide*] as the nucleus around which to build up his own character of the Knight?' (p 236).

669 Burchfield, Robert. 'Realms and Approximations: Sources of Chaucer's Power.' 1982. See **184**.
Most of the names of the Knight's battles 'seem (and were meant to sound) romantically distant and remote,' like places 'unimaginably removed from the banks of the Thames' (p 9).

670 Camden, Carroll, Jr. 'Chauceriana.' *MLN*, 47 (1932), 360–62.
   Worthy (line 43 and later occurrences) seems to have different connotations
   depending upon the context, with the general meaning of ' "able," "fit,"
   "suitable," "having such qualities as to be deserving of or adapted to some
   specified thing" ' (p 360). See also **980, 1044**.

671 Coghill, Nevill. *Chaucer's Idea of What is Noble*. London: Oxford University Press, 1971. Presidential Address to the English Association, 1971.
   Chaucer's concepts of nobility and *gentilesse* are examined in relation to the
   ideas of Aristotle, the New Testament, Boethius, Ramon Lull, Guillaume
   de Lorris, Dante, and Langland. It is a mistake to see the Knight's portrait as 'romantic hankering' for an outmoded ideal (p 9). The standards
   he represents are pervasive ideals, not mere nostalgia. Neither should the
   'absolutely pin-pointed realism of the Knight's history and appearance' be
   ignored (p 9). To us it may seem unrealistic that the Knight has fought in
   Lithuania, but 'it was a sober fact that young knights were sent to Lithuania
   to gain military experience' (p 9). Henry Bolingbroke went there in 1390,
   not long after Chaucer's portrait of the Knight was written. Chaucer's
   careful accuracy in factual matters 'gives a kind of guarantee that we can
   trust him in spiritual matters too' (p 9). The Knight's virtues of Chivalry,
   Truth, Honour, Freedom, and Courtesy are examined.

672 Cook, Albert Stanburrough. 'Beginning the Board in Prussia.' *JEGP*, 14
   (1915), 375–88.
   The meaning of Chaucer's statement that the Knight began the board in
   Prussia (lines 52–53) is clarified by two contemporary descriptions of the
   'table of honor' ceremony that the Teutonic Order periodically held. Only
   a small number of distinguished foreign knights — perhaps from ten to
   fourteen — would be chosen to participate.

673 ——. 'The Historical Background of Chaucer's Knight.' *TCA*, 20 (1916),
   161–240. Rpt as book, *The Historical Background of Chaucer's Knight*,
   New York: Haskell House, 1966.
   Cook presents a detailed study of the career of Henry, Earl of Derby (the
   future Henry IV), and of Chaucer's connections to him and his family.
   Cook suggests that Chaucer witnessed Henry's entry into London on July
   5, 1393, recording his impressions in the *KnT*. The statements in *GP* about
   the Knight's having *reysed in lettowe* (line 54) and about the Teutonic table of honor (lines 52–53) were modelled upon the Earl of Derby's career;
   therefore, at least those parts of *GP* were written no earlier than the summer of 1393. The Knight's expeditions in the South reflect the career of
   an earlier Henry, who was also Earl of Derby (this one was the father of
   Blanche of Lancaster, and the grandfather of the Earl of Derby who be-

came Henry IV). Chaucer's Knight thus praises both the then-current Earl of Derby and that Earl's grandfather. Excerpts from contemporary reports of both sets of military expeditions are included. (See **217** in reply.)

674 ——. 'Two Notes on Chaucer.' *MLN*, 31 (1916), 441–42.
The fact that Chaucer's 'Lyeys' (line 58) was in Lesser Armenia supports the interpretation of 'Ermony' in *Anel* as Armenia.

675 DiMarco, Vincent Joseph. *Literary and Historical Researches Respecting Chaucer's Knight and Squire.* University of Pennsylvania Dissertation. 1972. Dir. Robert A. Pratt. See also *DAI*, 33 (1972), 1677-A.
DiMarco offers a reappraisal of the Knight and the Squire, presenting the Knight as more ambiguous or negative than critics have usually done, and the Squire as more sophisticated. The meaning of each key term in the Knight's portrait (*trouthe, honour, fredom, curteisie*), in both earlier and fourteenth-century contexts, is discussed. For the Knight's military campaigns, DiMarco presents detailed historical summaries, beginning several centuries prior to Chaucer's time, so that we can understand 'the facts known and assumptions shared by the fourteenth century poet and his audience' (p 263). Much of this information puts the Knight in a rather unfavorable light, or sets him among unattractive companions. The Lyas campaign, for example (see line 58), 'was at best lackluster and, at worst, a dismal failure' (p 275). Similarly, 'it is difficult to avoid the conclusion that the Knight, who apparently persists in the Lithuanian campaigns while many other European knights have been dissuaded, is clearly in the company of the most ruthless and materialistic of adventurers' (p 320; see line 54).

676 Donaldson, E. Talbot, ed. *Chaucer's Poetry: An Anthology for the Modern Reader.* 1958, 1975. See **63**.
For Chaucer, the idealized Knight 'resolves one of the oldest antitheses in Western thought, the one that is supposed to exist between the valiant warrior and the sage counselor' (1975, p 1043), for the Knight is both brave and wise. His battles are not the futile political struggles of the Hundred Years' War, but holy wars in defense of Christendom.

677 Ebner, Dean. 'Chaucer's Precarious Knight.' In *Imagination and the Spirit: Essays in Literature and the Christian Faith Presented to Clyde S. Kilby.* Ed. Charles A. Huttar. Grand Rapids, MI: Eerdmans, 1971. Pp 87–100.
The 'Knight's position on fortune's fickle wheel is indeed precarious' (p 92). The *GP* portrait establishes his 'preference for worldly wealth and power' (p 93). Line 72 does not mean that the Knight is very perfect, or shows gentle behavior, but that he is a true (*verray*) knight whose 'noble birth is

of a perfect quality' (*parfit gentil*; p 94). He is famous and honored (line 50). He takes an extra horse with him on the pilgrimage because 'he is used to travelling in a manner appropriate to his high station in life' (p 94). He allows the Squire 'to remain dressed in a manner befitting his occupation as a court dandy' (p 94). The portrait 'indicates neither a renunciation of worldly goods nor unusual piety' (p 94). The Knight is a successful man who is close enough to the top of Fortune's wheel 'to sense what a plunge into adversity would mean' (p 95). Hence his later interruption of the Monk's Tale is appropriate.

678 Edsall, Donna Marie. *Chaucer and the Chivalric Tradition.* Ohio University Dissertation. 1981. Dir. R. Vance Ramsey. See also *DAI*, 42 (1981), 2663-A.
Background information about medieval warfare is summarized. Edsall regards ironic interpretations of Chaucer's references to warfare as inappropriate, for 'Chaucer's audience approved of war and tournaments and enjoyed hearing about them even at the same time as they were interested in sermons against these things' (p 4). 'Chaucer wrote in agreement with those whose patronage supported him, and probably agreed with them himself' (pp 4–5). Recent critical opinion on the portraits of the Knight and the Squire is reviewed in the section 'Chaucer's Knight' (pp 74–80). Edsall finds both portraits favorable.

679 Engel, Claire-Elaine. 'Les Croisades du Chevalier.' *RSH*, New Series, 120 (1965), 577–85.
The Knight's battles are reviewed, with emphasis on their resemblance, in the earlier campaigns, to the career of Henry, Earl of Derby. Chaucer may have heard about the campaigns in Asia Minor from Sir Richard Scrope. *Tramyssene* (line 62) may be Termessos, near Sattalia. The Knight's last battle, at Alexandria, took place in 1365; the pilgrimage seems to take place in 1387; the Knight's activities in the interim are not explained. After Alexandria he disappears until the moment when, having returned to his country, he departs on the Canterbury pilgrimage. His portrait depicts not only the character of the perfect knight, but also the thirst for distant and exotic adventures, the quest for new settings and landscapes, the call of unknown territories ('la soif de l'aventure lointaine, exotique, la quête de nouveaux cadres et de nouveaux paysages, l'appel des régions inconnues,' p 585).

680 Ethel, Garland. 'Horse or Horses: A Chaucerian Textual Problem.' *MLN*, 75 (1960), 97–101.
In line 74, 'His hors were goode, but he was nat gay,' the verb *were* is intended not as 'the indicative but as the subjunctive 3rd person singu-

lar preterit' (p 99). There is only one horse, since with the verb taken as subjunctive the subject *hors* can be singular. Thus the line means that although the Knight's horse is good, it is not ostentatiously arrayed. The Parson later criticizes ostentation in the equipment of horses, and the Monk's horse is said to be in 'greet estaat' (line 203). That the Knight's horse is *not* proudly arrayed supports his own simplicity in dress, for he wears a gypon 'Al bismotered with his habergeon' (line 76). The relative plainness of the horse also enhances the Knight's moral stature, since he adheres to the Church's warnings against prideful displays of riding equipment. (In reply, see French, **683**.)

681 Fichte, Joerg O. 'Man's Free Will and the Poet's Choice: The Creation of Artistic Order in Chaucer's Knight's Tale.' *Anglia*, 93 (1975), 335–60.
Fichte regards the Knight as 'an ideal representative of his social class,' one who could be regarded as personifying the quality of worthiness (p 335). Both fortitude and wisdom, the two traditional heroic virtues, are attributed to the Knight. His military career demonstrates his fortitude; his tale will demonstrate his wisdom. 'The Knight's moral excellence, his experience, and his authority add weight to his pronouncements and thus make him the ideal mouthpiece for Chaucer, the poet' (p 338). At a time when chivalry was in decline, Chaucer, like Deschamps, reasserts the chivalric ideal.

682 Fink, Z.S. 'Another Knight Ther Was.' *PQ*, 17 (1938), 321–30.
The fifteenth-century career of the German knight Jörg von Ehingen shows strong similarities to that of the Knight of *GP*. Chaucer's portrait is a plausible account of a wandering knight's prowess, and we can minimize, 'rather than emphasiz[e], the element of idealization in Chaucer's knight' (p 330). Given the fact that (as Manly showed, **696**) the Knight's career resembles the campaigns of two Scrope knights, and that (as Cook showed, **673**) it also resembles the campaigns of two earls of Derby, and now that it additionally resembles the campaigns of this German knight, perhaps numerous knights had careers of this sort. Therefore it is 'probably futile' (p 330) to propose specific originals for Chaucer's Knight.

683 French, W.H. 'General Prologue 74: Horse or Horses?' *MLN*, 76 (1961), 293–95.
In reply to Ethel (see **680**), who interprets line 74 to mean that only one horse is present — a horse that may be good but that lacks gay trappings — French argues that the form of the adjective *goode*, with its plural final -*e*, 'guarantees that "hors" also had the plural form' (p 295). Although scribes sometimes introduced inorganic -*e*'s, Chaucer's poetic system 'permitted him to add the vowel to adjectives only in weak positions, the vocative,

and the plural (attributive or predicate)' (p 294). Thus it is the plural horses that are good, and it is the Knight who is not gay.

684 Görlach, Manfred. ' "Canterbury Tales" Prologue, 60: The Knight's Army.' *N&Q*, New Series 20 (1973), 363–65.

The *GP* manuscripts show uncertainty as to whether the proper reading for line 60 is 'many a noble *armee*' or 'many a noble *ariue*'; the meter does not decide the issue either. Neither term is well represented in Middle English. The prose legend of *Alban* (ca. 1438) offers a parallel situation: in different copies Julius Caesar is said to have made 'an armee,' 'a ryue,' 'arivan,' 'an ariuau,' 'a Ryuage,' and 'a shippyng' (p 364). Thus *ariue* (a ryue) 'could have been an English word in the early fifteenth century' (p 365). *Armee* was a new word in French in about 1400, having been adopted from the Italian. The growing popularity of *armee* may have led scribes to substitute it for the difficult *ariue*. However, Chaucer himself could have encountered *armee* in Italy and introduced it into English. Cf **530, 697, 709.**

685 Górski, Karol. 'The Teutonic Order in Prussia.' *M&H*, 17 (1966), 20–37.

Though *GP* is not discussed, much information is provided about the activities of the Teutonic Order in Prussia (cf lines 52–53).

686 Hart, James Paxton. *Thomas Tyrwhitt (1730–1786) as Annotator and Glossarist of Fragment A of The Canterbury Tales, and His Editorial Relations.* 1971. See **540.**

Hart points out that Tyrwhitt suggested, in 1775, that the Knight was modeled upon Matheu de Gourney, which 'considerably deflates Manly's claim' to be the first to use the biographical-model approach to the pilgrims (p 27; for Manly, see **362** and **696**).

687 Hatton, Thomas Jenison. *The Canterbury Tales and Late Fourteenth Century Chivalry: Literary Stylization and Historical Idealism.* University of Nebraska Dissertation. 1966. Dir. Paul A. Olsen. See also *DA*, 27 (1966), 456-A.

To establish the ideal of chivalry in Chaucer's period, Hatton examines the works of Froissart, Geoffrey de Charny, Philip of Mézières, and other writers. Key concepts associated with the Knight — *worthy, wise, fredom, trouthe*, etc — 'combine to form the fourteenth century ideal of chivalric character' (p 41). The religious ideals of chivalry are represented by the Knight's wars in defense of the Church and by his presence on the pilgrimage. The Squire's portrait, however, emphasizes secular loving. Chaucer here 'presents us with a picture of the wrong kind of lover, the knight who has become enthralled by concupiscent love and who, although superficially attractive, nevertheless represents a serious departure from the chivalric ideal represented by the Knight' (p 95). The Knight embodies the precepts of Geoffrey de Charny and other writers, but the Squire 'embodies many of the complaints of these writers' (p 185).

688 ——. 'Chaucer's Crusading Knight, A Slanted Ideal.' *ChauR*, 3 (1968-1969), 77–87.

Chaucer's portrait of the Knight is an idealization, but rather than representing a *general* ideal of knighthood, it is slanted to reflect the political program of the French theorist Philip de Mézières, which was well known at the English court towards the end of the fourteenth century. All the Knight's battles are between Christians and pagans. This emphasis on crusading is not part of most other presentations of the chivalric ideal, but it corresponds exactly to the proposals of de Mézières, who called upon the kings of England and France to cease the strife between them (the Hundred Years' War), to join forces with his own Order of the Passion of Jesus Christ, and to protect Christianity against the infidel. De Mézières specifically commended the Mediterranean battles of Peter of Lusignan (in which Chaucer's Knight took part) and thought that campaigns against the Moors in Spain (in which the Knight also took part) were equal in spiritual benefit to campaigns in the Holy Land. Chaucer's audience 'could hardly fail to see the program of the Order of the Passion reflected in the Knight's portrait' (p 86).

689 Jones, Terry. *Chaucer's Knight, The Portrait of a Medieval Mercenary*. London: Weidenfeld and Nicolson, 1980; Baton Rouge, LA: Louisiana State University Press, 1980.

Jones's thesis is that the Knight is not an ideal character, but the opposite. Chapter 3, pp 31–140 (notes on pp 244–78), is a detailed analysis of the Knight's portrait in *GP*. According to Jones, the Knight is a mercenary soldier; he has participated in merciless massacres; he has served Christian and heathen alike; his personality is 'homicidal' (p 85). Furthermore, 'he has never once fought for his own country — and that in an age when England stood in almost continuous peril' (p 94). 'In short, the Knight's career has not been that of a responsible member of the knightly class, nor even of a dedicated militant Christian, but of a self-serving itinerant mercenary, and this would have been quite obvious to Chaucer's contemporary readers' (p 100). The Knight is 'a shabby mercenary without morals or scruples — the typical product of an age which saw war turned into a business' (p 140).

- Review by J. A. Burrow, 'The Imparfit Knight,' *TLS*, February 15, 1980, p 163: Burrow believes Jones's 'hypothesis to be mistaken,' for Jones's evidence is 'outshone' by 'the great battery of moral terms which Chaucer turns on at the beginning of the portrait,' terms that are 'not dimmed' by Jones's criticisms. However, Jones is correct 'to reject as too bland and insipid the conventional account of the Knight' as a wholly idealized figure. According to Burrow, the Knight *does* participate in England's political wars: his 'foreign adventures are additional to fighting in the Hundred Year's War,' given the force of *thereto* and the meaning of *lordes* in lines 47–48. See also Lester, **693** and **694**.

690 Kahrl, Stanley J. 'Introduction.' In *The Holy War*. Ed. Thomas Patrick Murphy. Fifth Conference on Medieval and Renaissance Studies, Ohio State University, 1974. Columbus, OH: Ohio State University Press, 1976. Pp 1–8.

By Chaucer's time, the religious idealism earlier associated with the crusades had mostly shifted into other directions. Philip de Mézières, in seeking participants for the campaign of 1365, was an anachronism. 'Chaucer's Knight too is an anachronism .... The Knight himself portrays laconically the ambiguities of a Crusade in his description of Theseus's campaign against Thebes' (p 2).

691 Kaske, R.E. 'The Knight's Interruption of the *Monk's Tale*.' *ELH*, 24 (1957), 249–68.

Kaske elaborates on Schofield's suggestion (**706**) that the Knight's later interruption of the Monk uses the paired contrasts established between the two pilgrims in *GP*. The two pilgrims' portraits in *GP* 'are virtually antitypes' (p 252), with the Monk representing softness in living, the Knight austerity; the Monk having no real achievements, the Knight impressive achievements; the Monk being brusque and outspoken in manner, the Knight reserved. Beyond these specific traits, the two pilgrims represent 'the two great Christian ideals of chivalry and monasticism, the Knight the unlikely fulfillment of his ideal as the Monk is the too-likely negation of his' (p 253). The Knight typifies the Active Life, the Monk the Contemplative Life. They also represent the two highest of the three estates, feudalism and the Church. Furthermore, Chaucer uses the idea of the hunting monk 'as a kind of comic imitation of knighthood' and develops the Monk's *GP* portrait 'as a subtle though fairly thoroughgoing parody on that of the Knight' (p 254).

692 King, Francis, and Bruce Steele, eds. *Selections from Geoffrey Chaucer's The Canterbury Tales*. 1969. See **82**.

Does Chaucer depict the Knight 'with the same unsmiling idealism that he gives the Parson and his brother? There is at least room for doubt' about the Knight, because of the contrast between the ideal figure and the contemporary context into which he is set (p 340). Thus 'the vivid reality of the world in which he is placed makes him something of a melancholy anachronism, even perhaps slightly comic. He is a figure from an attractively simple imaginary world who just does not fit the complex, awkward world we know' (p 340).

693 Lester, G.A. 'Chaucer's Knight and the Earl of Warwick.' *N&Q*, New Series 28 (1981), 200–2.

Arguing against the thesis of Jones (**689**), which questions the good reputation of the Knight, Lester describes a fifteenth-century work known as the *Warwick Pageant*. While later than Chaucer, this text describes knightly exploits similar to the Knight's and shows that they were regarded as noble and chivalrous. Thus the *Pageant* 'goes a long way in undermining the "ironic" interpretation of Chaucer's Knight' (p 202). Cf **694**.

694 ——. 'Chaucer's Knight and the Medieval Tournament.' *Neophil*, 66 (1982), 460–68.

Jones's study of the Knight (**689**) does not, according to Lester, give an accurate presentation of the 'form and function of tournaments and other feats of arms in Chaucer's time' (p 460). The Knight's participation in contests of arms (lines 61–62) refers to the formal duel, in which the death of the loser was the normal outcome, not to sporting tournaments. Chaucer 'thus chose to depict the Knight as a successful participant' in what was regarded as ' "the grettist dede that may be in armes" ' (p 463), according to the formulary of Thomas of Woodstock, who was Duke of Gloucester and Constable of England in Chaucer's time. Jones is 'wildly wrong' (p 463) in seeing the Knight as homicidal for killing his foe in the lists. Cf **693**.

695 Lumiansky, R.M. *Of Sondry Folk: The Dramatic Principle in the Canterbury Tales.* 1955. See **348**.

The unexpected ingredient of the Knight's portrait, signalled by the phrase *And though* (line 68), is that he is 'notable for courteous conduct and piety, and these are not qualities regularly found in professional military men of any age' (p 33). Lumiansky's comments on the Knight incorporate his article 'Chaucer's Philosophical Knight,' *TSE*, 3 (1952), 47–58.

696 Manly, John Matthews. 'A Knight Ther Was.' *Transactions of the American Philological Association*, 38 (1907), 89–107. Rpt in *Chaucer: Modern Essays in Criticism*, ed. Edward C. Wagenknecht (New York: Oxford University Press, 1959), pp 46–59.

The Knight's battles, all of them against the infidel and 'on the very confines of the civilized world' (1907, p 90), were in almost all cases campaigns 'sufficiently brilliant or long-continued to furnish matter for wonder and admiration for many long years' (p 91). They fall into three groups: the struggle against the Moors in Spain; the campaigns connected with Pierre de Lusignan and the capture of Alexandria; and the expeditions of the Teutonic Order. The Knight may have just returned from one of the Teutonic campaigns, since he has joined the pilgrims in London, which means that he did not land from overseas at any port in Kent but 'perhaps at some northern port lying nearer to Prussia' (p 103). Details of the Knight's battles are provided. He 'was probably between sixty and sixty-five' at the time of the pilgrimage, he 'began his military career in the early forties while Chaucer was still an infant' (p 104), and he may represent 'one or more men' (104) whose careers approximate the information given for the Knight in *GP*. A dispute between the Scrope and Grosvenor families has preserved the records of several fourteenth-century knights with careers of that sort. 'Not only in details, but in its entirety, the career which Chaucer ascribes to his "gentil knight" is that which actually fell to the lot of more than one of his contemporaries and acquaintances' (p 107). Thus 'Chaucer was painting no picture of fancy, but giving us a figure at once realistic and typical of the noble and adventurous idealists of his day' (p 107).

697 ——, and Edith Rickert, eds. *The Text of the Canterbury Tales Studied on the Basis of All Known Manuscripts*. 1940. See **49**.
In line 60, *armee* is the correct reading; in French it is 'the usual word for an invading army by land or sea' (vol 3, p 421). (Cf **530, 684, 709**.)

698 Mann, Jill. *Chaucer and Medieval Estates Satire*. 1973. See **363**.
'The Knight and the Squire are representatives of chivalry, but in different aspects. The Knight is a "worthy man," the Squire a "lovyere and a lusty bachelere." The difference does not merely derive from their individual personalities, nor even from their difference in age; it reflects differing aspects of the ideal of chivalry itself' (p 106). The Knight's armour-stained garment and extensive battles show that he 'follows primarily the ascetic crusading ideal' in particular (p 114). It is left unclear whether his aim is to convert the heathen or to exterminate them; his role 'is merely to fight, win, and move on .... he is a professional specialist, and the relevance of his profession to the lives of the rest [of the pilgrims] is not made clear' (p 115). As for the fact that the Squire is the Knight's son, 'the blood-relationship between the individuals seems to derive from a connection between two estates' (p 115). The Squire's emphasis upon loving remains 'enigmatic,' since his passion could be 'aroused in the course of a lustful *affaire*, or a noble attachment' (p 117). Within *GP*, 'admiration of the Knight's ascetic ideal of chivalry does not mean ... rejection of that of his son' (p 120).

699 Mitchell, Charles. 'The Worthiness of Chaucer's Knight.' *MLQ*, 25 (1964), 66–75.

The terms of praise applied to the Knight — terms such as *worthy* (lines 43, 64, 68) — are ambiguous, especially in light of the use of those terms in other portraits. The Knight has fought 'almost excessively' (p 68) and may be serving his own ego in striving for reputation. The *verray parfit* Knight (line 72), like the *verray parfit* Physician (line 422), is 'perfect in his profession, but imperfect as a man' (p 70). The pilgrims whose portraits follow the Knight's 'externalize three facets of his character: the Squire points up the Knight's commitment to chivalric ideals; the Yeoman brings out the Knight's martial efficiency in slaughtering the enemy; the Prioress demonstrates the dainty exercise of courtly manners' (p 72). The meaning of *curteys* degenerates as we move from Knight (cf line 46) to Squire (line 99) to Prioress (cf line 132), and 'even in the Knight's courtliness there is a gesture of the merely mannered' (p 72). Similarly, the Squire bears resemblances to the Friar, who is also said to be *curteys* and *lowely* (line 250), and the vanity of the Friar's service suggests a similar element of vanity in the service of the others. Thomas Becket had made a transition 'from knighthood to sainthood,' and the fact that *GP* begins with the Knight as he travels towards Becket's shrine 'suggests the distance which separates courtly and spiritual perfection' (p 73). All of the pilgrims 'are tainted,' and all 'have limitations, but we are told that *Amor vincit omnia*' (p 75).

700 Moorman, Charles. 'The Philosophical Knights of *The Canterbury Tales*.' *SAQ*, 64 (1965), 87–99. Rpt with changes in Charles Moorman, *A Knyght There Was: The Evolution of the Knight in Literature* (Lexington, KY: University of Kentucky Press, 1967), pp 76–95.

The Knight in *GP* should be read in the context of actual fourteenth-century chivalry. Chaucer is reasserting the reality of the chivalric ideal; his Knight 'is an idealized reality' (1965, p 92). The two voices of love, in Hoffman's terms (see **284**), 'call conjointly throughout the General Prologue, in the relation of Knight and Squire to each other and to their code, in the tension between courtly and ecclesiastical values in the Prioress, in the brotherhood of the Parson and Plowman, in the lechery of the Friar, the vanity of the Monk, the austerity of the Clerk, the Epicureanism of the Franklin, the greed of the Physician, the sensuality of the Wife of Bath' (p 93–94). In *WBT* we see 'the historical reality in the process of becoming the ideal of the General Prologue; transformed by an understanding of the nature of gentilesse, bully here yields before our eyes to philosopher' (p 97). The Knight comes to represent 'a new concept of chivalry for a new age,' a chivalry 'ready to stand in the midst of the new mercantilism as a symbol of the conservative, middle-class values that Chaucer everywhere praises' (p 99).

701 Neuse, Richard. 'The Knight: The First Mover in Chaucer's Human Comedy.' 1962. See **390**.
KnT shows the Knight 'in an unbuttoned, holiday mood' (p 300). This does not contradict the GP portrait, however, for the method of GP is to present the pilgrims as 'concrete universals' (p 301), while their personalities will become more evident later. Thus the Knight's portrait in GP 'gives us not so much an abstract chivalric ideal as clues for understanding a character conceived in its human complexity' (p 301). The comic outlook of his tale requires the qualities that his GP portrait identifies, worthiness and wisdom (line 68), and the tale deals with the themes that concern him. Part of the Knight's audience is his son; 'their portraits suggest two stages of the chivalric life' (p 313).

702 Olson, Paul A. 'Chaucer's Epic Statement and the Political Milieu of the Late Fourteenth Century.' Mediaevalia, 5 (1979), 62–87.
The Knight's battles represent multiple contemporary political perspectives — including those of Richard II as well as those of the opposition party. 'Chaucer carefully presents the perfect Knight as fighting in crusades which Richard favored and in those Henry and Gloucester favored' (p 68).

703 Palmer, David Andrew. Chaucer and the Nature of Chivalric Ideas. McMaster University Dissertation. 1976. See also DAI, 37 (1977), 6507-8-A.
Palmer proposes that chivalric ideals were culturally significant beyond the 'comparatively modest significance of actual knights and knighthood.' Chaucer's knights 'do not reflect contemporary social realities but rather this broader symbolic potential.' The Knight of GP is 'mainly an emblem of right spiritual orientation rather than an endorsement of specifically knightly duties or contemporary crusade projects. The traditional polarity between love-service and Christian knighthood underlies the portraits of the Knight and the Squire' [from DAI; diss not seen].

704 Robinson, F.N., ed. The Works of Geoffrey Chaucer. 1957. See **42**.
'Chaucer presents in the Knight a completely ideal figure. Although chivalry in the fourteenth century was in its decline and had a very sordid side, Chaucer has wholly refrained from satirizing the institution. It has been suggested, indeed, that in this very ideal presentation the keenest satire was concealed. But it may be doubted if such was Chaucer's intention' (p 652).

705 Schlauch, Margaret. 'King Arthur in the Baltic Towns.' BBSIA, 11 (1959), 75–80.

A number of Baltic towns, including Danzig, had organizations — called Brotherhoods of King Arthur — that perpetuated chivalric customs and standards, although the activities of these groups ranged beyond those of aristocratic clubs to include mercantile and religious functions. On a higher social level, Danzig was also the location of the Teutonic Knights' ceremony of the table of honor, a ceremony indirectly influenced by the concept of King Arthur's Round Table. English visitors to the region — including Henry Hotspur (who traveled there in 1392), John of Gaunt's natural son John Beaufort (1394), and Henry Bolingbroke, later Henry IV (1390–91 and 1392–93) — 'were in a position to report that chivalrous practices in memory of King Arthur were being kept alive there by two organizations of two differing social types' (p 80). Thus Chaucer, 'listening to such reports, would have had more than one reason for envisaging the Baltic area as an appropriate scene for his Knight's adventurings' (p 80).

706 Schofield, William Henry. *Chivalry in English Literature: Chaucer, Malory, Spenser, and Shakespeare.* Cambridge, MA: Harvard University, 1912; London: Frowde, 1912. Harvard Studies in Comparative Literature, 2.
The Knight is discussed in the chapter 'Chaucer,' pp 11–72. The list of his campaigns 'might have occurred to anyone as the most suitable for an errant warrior' (p 30). The portrait may be indebted to a poem by Machaut. The chivalric standards attributed to the Knight 'resemble closely those used by Watriquet de Couvin to describe his patron,' the Constable of France (p 31), and the Knight's characterization thereby gains in realism, since an actual person was described in the same chivalric way. The Knight's plain array is set in contrast to the display of the Monk. Moreover, Chaucer's 'portrait of the ideal Knight resembles in fundamental nature his portrait of the ideal Parson' (p 35). The Knight is 'nobly meek' and 'Christ-like in his behaviour to his fellows' (p 36). Cf **691**.

707 Sedgwick, W.B. 'Satalye (Chaucer, *C.T. Prol.* 58).' *RES*, 2 (1926), 346.
The Knight is said to have been at *Satalye* (line 58). 'Satalye is clearly Attalia, the modern Adalia'; the initial *S* is a survival of a Greek preposition.

708 Skeat, Walter W., ed. *The Complete Works of Geoffrey Chaucer, Edited from Numerous Manuscripts.* 1894–1897. See **3**.
Analogous passages from Gower's *Confessio Amantis* and the romance *Sir Beves of Hamptoun* support the interpretation of line 52 as meaning 'He had been placed at the head of the dais, or table of state' (vol 5, p 6). The correct reading in line 60 must be *aryve*, since *armee* 'gives no good sense' (5:8). In line 54, Satalye is Attalia (Adalia) in Asia Minor. In line 74, *hors* is plural, representing the Knight's three horses: 'one for himself, one for his son, and one for the yeoman' (5:8).

709 ——. *The Eight-Text Edition of the Canterbury Tales, with Remarks upon the Classification of the Manuscripts and upon the Harleian Manuscript 7334.* London: Kegan Paul, Trench, Trübner and Co, and Oxford University Press, 1909. Chaucer Society Publications, 2nd Series 43.

In the section 'On the Word *Arivee* in the General Prologue' (pp 55–57), Skeat argues that in line 60 the correct reading is not *armee* but *aryvee* — a word that accords better with the preposition *at* and is attested in fourteenth-century French. Cf **530, 684, 697**.

710 Sledd, James. 'The *Clerk's Tale*: the Monsters and the Critics.' *MP*, 51 (1953-1954), 73–82.

Sledd reports having once pointed out — in the spirit of parodying certain 'oversimple assumptions' among Chaucer critics (p 82) — that the Squire, who is twenty years old in April 1387, must have been conceived in July 1366, when 'the Knight was in the Middle East' (p 82). His parody, based on 'the consequences of these facts,' was apparently taken seriously by the editors of a journal to which he sent it (p 82).

711 Stevens, William D. 'The "Gipoun" of Chaucer's Knight.' *MLN*, 18 (1903), 140–41.

Contemporary evidence about the *gypon* (see line 75) indicates that it was worn over—not, as sometimes assumed, underneath—a knight's armor. The *gypon* of Chaucer's Knight is nevertheless said to be discolored from his armor. This makes sense if we picture the *gypon*, a snug-fitting white outer garment, as showing 'rust stains from the iron beneath, after a long campaign; and, as it was sleeveless, it was exposed, especially on the sides, to contact with the sleeves of the habergeon, which might also effect a "bismotering"' (p 141).

712 Stillwell, Gardiner, and Henry J. Webb. 'Chaucer's Knight and the Hundred Years' War.' *MLN*, 59 (1944), 45–47.

This article disputes the viewpoint of Loomis (**340**) that the Knight's portrait indicates hostility to the Hundred Year's War. The Knight and Squire go to war together. Therefore, Chaucer has simply avoided repetition by not listing the Squire's military place-names in the Knight's portrait too; they are covered, for the Knight, by saying that he has fought in Christendom. Furthermore, Chaucer's omission of details, or the discrepancy between a portrait and reality, should not be equated with social criticism. If that concept were valid, we would have to conclude, for example, that Chaucer is hostile to the real peasantry, since the idealized Plowman is at variance with the typical peasants of Chaucer's time. (Part of this note is further developed in Stillwell's longer discussion, see **1202**.)

Part 7: The Squire

See the Introduction, p xxxiii above, for a brief summary of criticism on the Squire, and see the Index for further references.

713 Baum, Paull Franklin. 'Notes on Chaucer.' *MLN*, 32 (1917), 376–77.
The Squire's description in *GP* shows him to be a young man of considerable experience — 'a merry young gallant,' 'an ardent lover' (p 376), a practiced person who has been to war, knows how to dress, can comport himself well, and so forth. He is 'no timid inexperienced youth' (p 376). Therefore, his later modesty about his tale is to be taken as an expression of 'his naturally courteous manner' (p 376), not as an indication of any actual apology for some lack of ability on his part.

714 Bowden, Muriel. *A Commentary on the General Prologue to the Canterbury Tales.* 1948. See 104.
The Squire, who 'speaks to youth in youth's language' (p 74), may be a 'smiling reminiscence of young Geoffrey himself' (p 74). Although his short coat would have been condemned by the preachers, the Squire has 'our, as well as the poet's, indulgent approval of his gay young spirits' (p 81). His campaign was probably selected mostly for its convenient date; given his age, 'the campaign of 1383 is exactly right for the Squire' (p 83). The chapter on the Squire (and the Yeoman) is on pp 74–91 (supplementary notes in the 2nd ed., pp 319–20).

715 Brown, Carleton. 'The Squire and the Number of the Canterbury Pilgrims.' *MLN*, 49 (1934), 216–22.
Although the narrator in *GP* says that 'nyne and twenty' pilgrims arrived (line 24), there are thirty. Whether we count three priests or only one (and there is evidence for all three being present), the number does not total twenty-nine. Brown here proposes that the Squire was a later addition to

GP. His career is 'oddly dissociated both in time and place from the military excursions of the Knight' (p 221). It is probable that the Yeoman (who is mentioned at the conclusion of the Squire's portrait) was meant to accompany the Knight; with the Squire's description removed, the 'connection is perfect' (p 221) between the Knight and the Yeoman. Thus in Chaucer's '*original plan* there would be exactly twenty-nine pilgrims' (p 222). When Chaucer later added the Squire, he simply neglected to change his total number.

716 ——. 'Author's Revision in the *Canterbury Tales*.' *PMLA*, 57 (1942), 29–50.
The Squire's military campaigns (lines 79–80) include the so-called Crusade in Flanders led by Henry le Dispenser, Bishop of Norwich. This crusade was much criticized by Wycliffe, who wrote a tract against it. In addition, 'when the Bishop returned to England after his inglorious campaign he was received with reproaches by John of Gaunt' (p 37). The Squire has thus participated in a military venture opposed by the Lollards, which would influence his behavior towards 'the Lollard parson' (p 37).

717 Derocquigny, J. 'Notes sur Chaucer.' 1910. See **595**.
The phrase *of evene lengthe* (line 83), or its equivalent, is associated with physical beauty in French sources.

718 Fehrenbach, Robert J. 'The Gown of Chaucer's Squire.' *ELN*, 15 (1977–1978), 4–7.
The Squire's 'courtepy is red and white because the colors are associated with chivalry, with the knighthood to which this young probationer aspires' (p 5). The Squire 'is not merely a quasi-allegorical figure representing youth and spring; he is an individualized character, slightly humorous as a fashionable fellow slavishly following all the dictates of a culture composed of crystallized conventions,' including 'attire that is not only extravagantly faddish, but is also, by its colors, associated with his chivalric profession' (p 7).

719 Fleming, John V. 'Chaucer's Squire, the "Roman de la Rose," and the "Romaunt." ' *N&Q*, New Series 14 (1967), 48–49.
Chaucer's lines on the Squire's riding, jousting, dancing, etc (lines 94–96) echo a passage from the *Roman de la Rose*. In the *Roman* this passage is unfavorable: the God of Love tells Amant how to display his abilities in the context of *fol amour*, foolish love. Chaucer's audience, therefore, 'would have viewed the seeming praise of the Squire in an ironical light' (p 49). The *Roman* passage does not mention poetry-making, but a reference to songs is found in its English translation, the *Romaunt*. It is possible that

the translator of the *Romaunt* recalled Chaucer's description of the Squire and therefore added this trait to those he found in his French text.

720 Gaylord, Alan. 'A85-88: Chaucer's Squire and the Glorious Campaign.' *MichA*, 45 (1960), 341–61.

The *chyvachie* in which the Squire has participated (lines 85–88), in all probability the Crusade of 1383, suggests a historical context that is 'uncomplimentary and ultimately satirical in regard to the Squire' (p 343). This expedition, part of the Hundred Years' War, was 'a disgrace to a Christian nation,' a military failure, and a cause of 'public revulsion' after its conclusion (p 343). Nevertheless, Chaucer's aim is not to condemn the Squire. His portrait is a stereotype, 'an echo of the past,' 'a virtual archetype of the fashionable young lover' depicted in the *Roman de la Rose* (p 357). The reference to his *chyvachie* is 'the one harsh reality that disturbs an otherwise placid idealization of a character' (p 358). Chaucer's implication is that although the aristocracy 'still liked to pretend it could get back to the good old days of chivalry' (p 358), the modern reality is quite different. The Knight, being older, may have been present in the earlier glorious victories, but the career for which the Squire is preparing now consists of campaigns like the Crusade of 1383. Cf **736**.

721 Goodrich, W.J. 'Chauceriana.' *N&Q*, 109 (1904), 121–24.

The Clerk's portrait is not likely to contain autobiographical references, but the Squire's is. Like the young Chaucer, the Squire writes poetry; other similarities are proposed. Overall, 'it is altogether a tempting assumption that we have here a portrait, sufficiently disguised to preserve artistic illusion, of Chaucer when he was "a lusty bachelor" "as fresh as is the month of May" ' (p 124). Lines 89–90, usually taken to refer to the Squire's garments, apply to his complexion instead. See also **788, 1344**.

722 Haller, Robert S. 'Chaucer's *Squire's Tale* and the Uses of Rhetoric.' *MP*, 62 (1964-1965), 285–95.

The Squire is 'the only poet' among the pilgrims (p 286; cf line 95). The ability to write poetry would be appropriate to the Squire's training and status, not only as part of his courtly manners but also as a skill 'required in diplomatic correspondence, should he ever hold high office' (p 286). He would have studied from the same sources that Chaucer knew — Geoffrey of Vinsauf, Matthew of Vendôme, Peter of Riga, etc. The similarity between the Squire and the figure of Youth in the *Parlement of the Three Ages* is suggested. On the Franklin, see **1049**.

723 Hatton, Thomas J. 'Thematic Relationships between Chaucer's Squire's Portrait and Tale and the Knight's Portrait and Tale.' *SMC*, 4 (1974),

452–58.
The Squire's portrait is 'built around his condition of *lover*' (p 453), which is, in Baldwin's terms, the *radix trait* or central characteristic of the description (see **148**, p 49, although Baldwin takes the Squire's *radix trait* to be youth). 'While the Knight's love is based on the spiritual values of chivalry, the Squire's is a "hot" love based on the attractions of the flesh' (p 454). Medieval warnings against this kind of love among knights or squires are reviewed. Nevertheless, in the portrait 'Chaucer's satire remains characteristically gentle' (p 456). The Squire's indulgence in undisciplined love, evident in the portrait, is mirrored in his tale. Although he is young, at the age of twenty he is old enough to assume adult responsibilities (as Richard II claimed of himself at that age). Thus 'through the Squire and his tale, Chaucer may be gently hinting to the knights of the court ... that it is time to return to the values represented by his perfect knight' (p 458).

724 Hinckley, Henry Barrett. 'Chauceriana.' *MP*, 14 (1916–1917), 317–18.
Annotating line 82, Hinckley presents parallels to Chaucer's phrase *I gesse*. Cf **886, 927, 1276**.

725 Kahrl, Stanley J. 'Chaucer's *Squire's Tale* and the Decline of Chivalry.' *ChauR* 7 (1972–1973), 194–209.
The Squire's military career, like his tale, shows evidence of the decline of chivalry in Chaucer's time. 'If the Knight was one of the last of the *defensores fidei*, his son was certainly cast in the mold of one of the "new men" of the court of Richard II' (p 208). The Squire's crusade (see lines 85–86) was a 'miserable affair,' with the participants recruited for it 'consisting largely of London apprentices and others of the same sort' (p 208).

726 Kuhl, Ernest P., and Henry J. Webb. 'Chaucer's Squire.' *ELH*, 6 (1939), 282–84.
The Squire's humility and obedience are emphasized by the reference to his carving (line 100), which also 'shows that the Squire was being honored by his father' (p 282). Contemporary documents indicate that carving or serving at table was a duty required of squires and also an honor performed by persons of high rank. The couplet at lines 99–100 'forms a fitting climax' to the portrait of the Squire, who 'is in the great tradition, worthy to follow in the footsteps of his father' the Knight (p 284).

727 Mead, William Edward. *The English Medieval Feast*. Boston: Houghton, 1931. Rpt 1967.
The Squire, in carving before his father (see line 100), 'occupied a post of distinction' (1931, p 149) since carving was an honor, not a menial service. It required strength, dexterity, and conformity to 'recognized conventions, infraction of which brought unkind comment' (p 149). See also **1057**.

728 Montgomery, Franz. 'The Musical Instruments in "The Canterbury Tales." '
1931. See **377**.
The Squire is said to be *floytinge* (line 91): 'since Chaucer elsewhere mentions the flute, it seems reasonable to believe that the Squire was really a musician' (p 441).

729 Orme, Nicholas. 'Chaucer and Education.' *ChauR*, 16 (1981-1982), 38–59.
Chaucer presents the Squire as an ideal aristocratic pupil. Though fourteenth-century aristocratic education would have included 'religion and morality, war and athletics, and literary and cultural pursuits,' the omission of the first pair from the Squire's portrait is 'probably without significance,' arising from 'Chaucer's strategy of dividing the qualities of the ideal aristocrat among the Knight, the Squire, and the Franklin, the religious and moral material being given to the Knight' (p 43). The portrait presents the Squire as being well-trained as a warrior, athlete, and cultured young man. However, the completely ideal aristocrat is the older man, the Knight. On the Clerk, see **993**.

730 Owen, Charles A., Jr. 'A Certain Nombre of Conclusions: the Nature and Nurture of Children in Chaucer.' *ChauR*, 16 (1981-1982), 60–75.
The Squire and the Knight show mutual respect. The contrast between them 'belongs to their respective ages rather than to any fundamental dissonance' (p 63). They share their military orientation, their courteous manners, and a 'mutual forbearance' that 'makes the archetypes of generation gap and oedipal feeling irrelevant' (p 64).

731 Pearsall, D.A. 'The Squire as Story-Teller.' *UTQ*, 34 (1964–1965), 82–92.
The Squire is meant to be seen as 'a very young, young man,' the youngest member of a pilgrimage group whose other members 'are almost without exception all middle-aged or at least mature (like Chaucer)' (p 82). Thus the Squire is 'a young man among his elders,' who are 'men of substance' or, in the case of the Reeve and Miller and Summoner, men who 'have about them a kind of confidence and toughness' (p 83). Chaucer is being realistic here, 'since incentive and opportunity combined to make the pilgrimage a predominantly middle-aged as well as a middle-class pastime' (p 83). The self-assurance of the bourgeois pilgrims also reflects the economic realities of Chaucer's time.

732 Prins, A.A. 'Two Notes to the Prologue of Chaucer's Canterbury Tales.'
ES, 30 (1949), 42–44, 83–86.
The phrase *in chyvachie* in the Squire's portrait (line 85) derives from a French phrase which means either military service, or a raid or expedition. In this case, the difference between the two meanings would not be very great. On the Monk, see **901**.

733 Stewart, George R., Jr. 'The Meaning of '*Bacheler*' in Middle English.' *PQ*, 13 (1934), 40–47.

The word *bacheler* had several meanings: (1) a knight-bachelor, ie, a knight who was not a knight-banneret; (2) an unmarried man — a rare meaning; and (3) in a general sense, a young man. Chaucer applies the term *lusty bacheler* to the Squire (line 80), the knight in the Wife's Tale (line III.883), and Phoebus in the Manciple's Tale (line IX.107). In applying the same term to these three characters, Chaucer 'was thinking neither of their marital felicity nor of their martial advancement, but simply of their being young men' (p 47). In any case, the word does *not* mean an aspirant to knighthood, though it is sometimes glossed that way.

734 Tristram, Philippa. *Figures of Life and Death in Medieval English Literature*. London: Paul Elek, 1976.

Occasional comments on *GP* are included in this study of youth, age, mortality, etc. Chaucer does not uncritically idealize the young. The Squire, who is 'Chaucer's personification of Youth,' is shown to be 'culpably, not ideally, romantic,' though it is not easy to say exactly how he falls short of the ideal (p 27). The portrait is 'two edged: the Squire, like some people, is too consciously set in the mould of fashion; yet his virtues, whilst less than absolute, are more than mere affectation' (p 28).

735 Tuve, Rosemond. *Seasons and Months: Studies in a Tradition of Middle English Poetry*. 1933. See **657**.

The Squire's portrait may be indebted to visual depictions of the months and their occupations. In books of hours, May is often represented as a youth who has curly yellow hair, wears a short gown with wide sleeves (sometimes embroidered), and rides a horse. 'Perhaps Chaucer's squire was "as fresh" as a very particular "month of May" ' that the poet had been seen depicted in such a manuscript illustration (p 187).

736 Wood, Chauncey. 'The Significance of Jousting and Dancing as Attributes of Chaucer's Squire.' *ES*, 52 (1971), 116–18.

Chaucer's basic source for the Squire's portrait, as others have recognized, is a passage in the *Roman de la Rose*. Chaucer's version, however, connects jousting with dancing (line 96). In the *Livre de seyntz medicines* of Henry of Lancaster — father of the duchess Blanche, whom *BD* commemorates — jousting and dancing 'are yoked together and placed under the inspiration of lechery' as activities that are not intrinsically bad, but 'can be seriously abused' (p 117). The contrast between the Knight and the Squire is enhanced, since the Knight's portrait links jousting with holy wars, the Squire's with 'social amusements' (p 118). In the *Livre de seyntz medicines* there is also a contrast between an older and a younger attitude. Given the definite influence of the *Roman* and the possible influence of the *Livre* on the *GP* passage, Chaucer's intention was probably 'to put the young Squire's "hotte" loving in an unpraiseworthy light'; similarly, as Gaylord (see **720**) has shown, the Squire's military exploits strike a 'very sour note' in the portrait (p 118).

❧ Part 8: The Yeoman

See the Introduction, p xxxiii above, for a brief summary of criticism on the Yeoman, and see the Index for further references.

737 Birney, Earle. 'The Squire's Yeoman.' *REL*, 1 (1960), 9–18.
The Yeoman's portrait has been regarded as completely lacking in social criticism, personal satire, or humor. Nevertheless, all of those qualities may be present as part of Chaucer's 'quiet and sunny irony of exaggeration' (p 17), for the Yeoman is decked out, 'as it were, for parade' (p 12), with many of his accoutrements more decorative than functional. He serves the Squire, not the Knight, and 'the habiliments of this Yeoman are exactly those with which the Squire would furnish him when he selected him as his personal attendant' (p 13). The Yeoman is elaborately provided with arms, as if he were dressing up in 'peace-time display' (p 12). His dagger is decorated, his bracer studded or painted, etc. His short haircut may have been meant to suggest 'military spruceness' (p 14). Peacock-feathered arrows are more likely to have been prized for display than for actual use: 'there are no references to the use of such arrows in any accounts of medieval fighting' (p 15), though there are references to their use 'as a sumptuous present' or as part of 'the tackle of pageantry' (p 15). The Yeoman's portrait has functional significance as 'an illuminating pendant to the Squire's' (p 17), since it is the Squire who has arranged for his companion to appear this way. It is also 'a study of a recognisable type,' the overly showy and somewhat impractical 'parade-ground guardsman,' in modern terms (p 17). See **747** in reply.

738 Cawley, A.C. 'Chaucer's Summoner, the Friar's Summoner, and the *Friar's Tale.*' *PLPLS-LSH*, 8 (1956-1959), 173–80.
As a link between the *FrT* and *GP*, the devil of the *FrT*, who is disguised as a Yeoman, is given 'dress and accoutrements' that are 'remarkably like

those of the Yeoman in the *General Prologue*' (p 177). On the Summoner, see **1267**.

739 Donaldson, E. Talbot, ed. *Chaucer's Poetry: An Anthology for the Modern Reader.* 1958, 1975. See **63**.
The Yeoman is neat, efficient, and careful about his equipment. 'The portrait of the Yeoman carries into the lower-class milieu the sense of purposeful order that we associate with the Knight he serves' (1975, p 1044).

740 Dove, Mary. 'The Criticism of Medieval Literature: A Sermon and an *Exemplum.*' *CR*, 21 (1979), 36–44.
In the Yeoman, Chaucer depicts a figure contrasting to the Squire. The last line of the portrait 'is disquietingly different' (p 40), with a falling rhythm and an irresolute close that should alert us to problematic aspects of the characterization. The portrait embodies a tension 'between blandly naif approbation and menace's cutting edge' (p 41). The Yeoman's advancing age is suggested by several details of the description: the green-and-brown earth colors, the autumn-nut comparison, even the Christopher medal, whose image shows 'an old man weighed down by the Christ-child' (p 43). Thus the Yeoman is perceived as 'an old man weighed down by death-dealing weapons, sharpened for the kill' (p 43). His horn suggests Judgment Day. 'The autumn-Yeoman mirrors in himself the Fall, but he also mirrors the consummation of the fallen world and the harvest of souls' (p 43).

741 Emerson, O.F. 'Chaucer and Medieval Hunting.' *RomR*, 13 (1922), 115–50. Rpt in *Chaucer Essays and Studies: A Selection from the Writings of Oliver Farrar Emerson, 1860–1927* (Cleveland, OH: Western Reserve University Press, 1929, and rpt Freeport, NY: Books for Libraries Press, 1970), pp 320–77.
The Yeoman is an under-forester; the term *forster* (line 117) 'was nearly equivalent to modern *game-keeper*' (p 122). See also **878, 1046**.

742 Herben, Stephen J., Jr. 'Arms and Armor in Chaucer.' *Spec*, 12 (1937), 475–87.
In this general treatment of fourteenth-century armaments and Chaucer's references to them, *GP* examples are mentioned — especially the portrait of the Yeoman, who is the most heavily armed pilgrim: 'there seems to be a suggestion of the enthusiast in Chaucer's three successive references to arrows' (p 485).

743 Hinkley, Henry Barrett. 'Chauceriana.' 1916–1917. See **280**.
Annotating line 110, Hinckley points out that the equivalent of *woodcraft* may be implied in the *Roman de Troie*.

744 Holt, J.C. 'The Origins and Audience of the Ballads of Robin Hood.' *PP*,
18 (1960), 89–110.

Considering the social status and implications of the category of 'yeoman,'
Holt remarks that 'The succession of yeoman, squire, knight seems to have
been commonly accepted at this time, and is indeed implied by Chaucer's
Prologue' (p 100). The fact that Chaucer's Yeoman is a forester recalls 'one
of the earliest sources for the word yeoman'—the twelfth-century *Pseudo-
Cnut de Foresta*, where '"yongermen" appear as foresters' (p 100). Foresters
seem traditionally to have been associated with the imagery of bows and
arrows. In the Robin Hood legend, for example, 'Robin's most famous
weapons, his bow and arrows, were at once the tools and insignia of the
local foresters which distinguished them from other baillifs, and which appeared as their characteristic accoutrement on their tombs' (p 101—cf lines
104–08 on the Yeoman's bow and arrows).

Holt's article associates yeomen with the gentry, not the peasantry. In
reply, see Maurice Keen, 'Robin Hood—Peasant or Gentleman?' *PP*, 19
(1961), 7–15; Keen suggests that 'we cannot take words such as yeoman . . .
as implying sharp definitions of social status' (p 13). In turn, Holt's next
response, 'Robin Hood: Some Comments,' *PP*, 19 (1961), 16–18, proposes
that Keen 'thinks of yeomen as the upper crust of the peasantry, I as the
lower ranks of the gentry and as men in official status. On this point we
are both right' (p 17).

745 Kelly, Henry Ansgar. 'Chaucer's Arts and Our Arts.' In *New Perspectives
in Chaucer Criticism*. Ed. Donald M. Rose. Norman, OK: Pilgrim, 1981.
Pp 107–20.

Chaucer, in contrast to Spenser, has very few unrealistic portraits. 'In
the General Prologue the only character who is overladen with emblems is
the one described pilgrim whom Chaucer failed to interview, namely, the
Yeoman. It seems clear that Chaucer did not speak with him at all, if we
can take his awareness of the man's expertise in woodcraft as supplied by
omniscience; for he has to guess that he is a forester. It is an easy guess,
however, for he is dressed for the hunt (the Knight must simply have told
him to get his gear and move out, without bothering to say that they were
going on pilgrimage). But even if he were in the forest, one would think
that he could hardly move, what with his sheaf of arrows, mighty bow,
bracer, sword, buckler, dagger, Christopher, horn, and baldric' (p 118).

746 Krappe, Edith Smith. 'A Note on Chaucer's Yeoman.' *MLN*, 43 (1928),
176–77.

Two references to peacock-arrows (cf line 104) are presented: in a London
will of 1361, an apothecary bequeathes to his kinsmen some arrows with

peacock-feathers; in a tale of the *Mabinogion* cycle, two blond young men are said to carry peacock-feathered arrows.

747 Malarkey, Stoddard. 'Chaucer's Yeoman Again.' *CE*, 24 (1962-1963), 289–90, 295.

In reply to the argument of Birney (see **737**) that the Yeoman is accompanying the Squire, Malarkey re-asserts the view that the Yeoman is accompanying the Knight. The *Book of the Ordre of Chyvalry*, printed by Caxton, indicates that a knight should be attended, but describes a squire as riding alone. Thus the Knight needs an attendant, for he would not 'travel in a manner that might bring shame on himself or his class,' while the Squire does not need an attendant and would not be likely 'to assume a position of elegance and pomp that would exceed that of his revered sire' (p 290). One explanation for this group's disparity in dress is that, although they have been traveling together, the Knight in the hazard of campaigning might have vowed to undertake an immediate pilgrimage on his safe return, while the Squire and and Yeoman, who have not made such a vow, are 'in more of a holiday mood' (p 295) and have therefore adorned themselves more than the Knight has.

748 Mann, Jill. *Chaucer and Medieval Estates Satire.* 1973. See **363**.

'No yeoman appear[s] in estates literature before Chaucer,' but the Yeoman is nevertheless a recognizable professional type (p 172). We respond positively to the portrait because of the Yeoman's physical attractiveness. 'As our judgement on the Pardoner and the Summoner is determined largely by their revolting looks, so our favourable attitude to the Yeoman is produced by his colorful neatness. To show us this more clearly, the portrait is devoid of ironic touches and ambiguities' (p 172).

749 Saunders, Barry Roy. *Doubles-Entendres in The Canterbury Tales.* 1967. See **569**.

In the Yeoman's portrait the meaning of *gay* — not only 'bright and lovely' but also 'showily dressed' — indicates that he 'appears to be a fop' (p 13); similarly, his *pecok* arrows (line 104) suggest the connotation of the peacock as 'a symbol of vainglory' (p 13—cf lines 111, 113).

750 Schmidt, A.V.C., ed. *Geoffrey Chaucer: The General Prologue to the Canterbury Tales and the Canon's Yeoman's Prologue and Tale.* 1974. See **89**.

'The image of the Yeoman clad in green conveys an impression of full summer after the springtime image of the Squire which precedes. This is reinforced by the detail of his *brown visage* (line 109) — either a naturally dark complexion or, more likely, tanned by the summer sun in his mainly outdoor existence (cf the Shipman, line 394)' (p 130).

751 Skeat, Walter W., ed. *The Complete Works of Geoffrey Chaucer, Edited from Numerous Manuscripts.* 1894–1897. See **3**.

The Yeoman is accompanying the Squire; *he* (line 101) refers to the Squire. Nevertheless, 'both the squire and the squire's man were necessarily servants to the knight' (vol 5, p 11).

752 Test, George A. 'Archers' Feathers in Chaucer and Ascham.' *AN&Q*, 2 (1964), 67–68.

Ascham's derogatory opinion of peacock arrows 'seems to cast an uneasy shadow across the otherwise idealized portrait of the Yeoman' (p 67). A number of modern works on archery show that peacock feathers are well regarded. Robert P. Elmer's analysis suggests that Ascham may have had in mind the tail feathers, while it is the wing feathers which are used for arrows. Apparently 'Ascham was indeed wrong in this instance' and 'Chaucer's unerring eye for detail did not fail him' (p 68).

Part 9: The Prioress and her Companions

See the Introduction, p xxxiii–xxxiv above, for a brief summary of criticism on the Prioress, the Second Nun, and the three (?) Priests. See the Index for further references.

753 Baugh, Albert C. 'Fifty Years of Chaucer Scholarship.' 1951. See **101**.
The Prioress may have been modelled on Madam Argentine of St Leonard's, as Manly thought (see **823**), even though Manly later withdrew this suggestion (**824**) because Madam Argentine never became Prioress. Baugh refuses 'to accept the withdrawal' of this identification (p 670), since Chaucer could well have used Argentine as his model and simply promoted her to Prioress for literary purposes.

754 Bowden, Muriel. *A Commentary on the General Prologue to the Canterbury Tales.* 1948. See **104**.
The Prioress, a 'gracious gentlewoman' who 'probably began life as a dowerless daughter' (p 92), is given a portrait that is 'satiric, though it is also gentle and understanding' (p 93). Her name, oath, physical description, manners, dress, and brooch are discussed. In her vanities and her pets she is 'shown to be the eternal feminine' (p 98); we 'smile indulgently' (p 99) over her concern for her dogs. Chaucer includes 'a touch of sterner criticism' (p 99), however, when he indicates that her charity and pity are limited to animals. She is not accurately seen as a female parallel of the Monk, since her deviations from proper conduct are in the direction of elegance and refinement, while those of the Monk represent 'gross self-indulgence' (revised ed., p 321).

755 Bowles, Patrick. 'Chaucer's *General Prologue.*' *Expl*, 35 (1976–1977), 5–6.
The Prioress drinks from a communal cup: *hir* in line 134 should be understood as 'the' or 'their,' not as 'her.' Thus it is appropriate for her to wipe her mouth clean, as a thirteenth-century French poem explains, in order not to leave unwelcome food particles in the cup that will be passed to the next person.

756 Boyd, Beverly. 'Chaucer's Prioress: her Green Gauds.' *MLQ*, 11 (1950), 404–16.
The Prioress's green gauds (line 159) are usually interpreted as being green beads used for saying *Pater nosters*, separating the coral beads used for saying *Ave Marias*. However, the history of the rosary shows no evidence that in Chaucer's time the *Ave Marias* were separated by *Pater nosters* in that way. More likely to be correct for the customs of the time would be the interpretation that the Prioress's gauds were 'ornamented markers to facilitate counting' (p 413), or that they 'denoted some practice in connection with the five joys of the Virgin — perhaps anthems, perhaps meditations, perhaps both' (p 416).

757 ——. *Chaucer and the Liturgy.* Philadelphia: Dorrance, 1967.
Comments on several *GP* pilgrims are included, as well as background information (for example, how to read an ecclesiastical calendar). The Prioress's oath by St Loy (line 120) may be due to considerations of rhyme; Chaucer may have used the saints' lists in the calendars as 'a thesaurus of rimes' (p 41). The Prioress has 'a markedly liturgical orientation' (p 60), which Chaucer makes fun of since its basis is not virtue but sentimentality. Although it has been said that the Prioress would not have sung the divine service on the journey, so that the narrator must be drawing upon something other than observation in line 122, Boyd observes that in medieval times the service was sung more widely than now, that the company of pilgrims may well have heard it, and, therefore, that in alluding to it 'Chaucer was dealing with a familiar institution, not with something understood only by those who had special connections with convents' (p 62). On the Parson, see **1177.**

758 Braddy, Haldeen. 'Chaucerian Minutiae.' *MLN*, 58 (1943), 18–23.
Commenting on the Prioress's 'crowned A' (line 161), Braddy notes that 'a crowned letter as a contemporary royal emblem was hardly unconventional' (p 20); eg, a crowned A was used as an emblem for Queen Anne. However, that situation is 'inapplicable to the Prioress' (p 20), who is not royal and whose name begins with E, not A. The scribe Shirley's use of the crowned A in his own motto, or his statement of ownership, is also discussed.

759 Brennan, Dom Maynard J., O.S.B. 'Speaking of the Prioress.' *MLQ*, 10 (1949), 451–57.
The Prioress's smile (line 119) should be associated with the Benedictine tradition of mild and silent laughter; in that context it is a quite appropriate form of behavior. It is probable that she sang 'with a decided nasal twang that was entirely in harmony with, and the result of, her consciousness of French after the *schole of Stratford atte Bowe*' (p 456). Her portrayal is intended, as part of Chaucer's 'art of comedy' (p 456), to stand in contrast to the Monk's and to the Parson's. Both she and the Parson 'are first and foremost cast in a religious mold; but they have diverse ideas on what is compatible with their spiritual life' (p 456). As a prioress, Madame Eglantyne may be second in authority after her abbess, or, if her community has no abbess, first in authority herself. In her case, as in the other portraits, Chaucer 'simply refuses to paint a common, ordinary, and nondistinctive character'; she is a 'Prioress par excellence' (p 457). It is risky to judge spirituality on the basis of external information. 'The Prioress was such a compound of courtly manners and quaint habits that a judgment is especially temerarious in her case' (p 457).

760 Brewer, D.S. 'The Ideal of Feminine Beauty in Medieval Literature, Especially "Harley Lyrics," Chaucer, and Some Elizabethans.' *MLR*, 50 (1955), 257–69.
The traditional manner of describing feminine beauty, from the fifth century onward, is reviewed. Chaucer shows his use of the convention in his portraits of the Duchess Blanche, Criseyde, and (in parody) Alison in *MilT*. 'In the General Prologue, the Prioress's appearance is also of the conventional type,' although the usual list of attributes is not completed (p 268).

761 Brosnahan, Leger. 'The Authenticity of *and preestes thre*.' *ChauR*, 16 (1981-1982), 293–310.
Brosnahan argues that although the phrase *and preestes thre* (line 164) existed in the common original of all extant *GP* mss, it did not exist in Chaucer's own version and is a 'scribal patch' (p 308). The 'multiple disruptions' (p 300) created by its presence disappear if it is removed. The phrase disrupts the announced plan of describing the status, qualities, rank, and clothing of each pilgrim; it causes a conflict over the number of pilgrims; it cuts off the portrait of the Second Nun and leaves us without a portrait of the Nun's Priest. Other 'disruptions' too are discussed. The suppression of the phrase, on the other hand, contributes to 'a tighter and more consistent text' (p 307). Overall, 'the uniformity with which the effects of suppressing the half-line improve, tighten, and make more consistent the text is impressive and persuasive of the fact that *and preestes thre* is not Chaucer's' (p 308).

762 Brown, Emerson, Jr. 'Chaucer and the European Literary Tradition.' In
   Geoffrey Chaucer: A Collection of Original Articles. Ed. George Economou.
   New York: McGraw Hill, 1976. Pp 37-54.
   The indebtedness of the Prioress's portrait to the *Roman de la Rose* was
   meant to be recognized by Chaucer's audience. 'This passage is not sim-
   ply a borrowing from another literary work but an allusion to it. All of
   Chaucer's borrowings may be, in effect, allusions' (p 48).

763 Brumble, H. David, III. 'Chaucer's *General Prologue: Canterbury Tales.*'
   Expl, 37 (1978-1979), 45.
   The Prioress's concern for trapped mice (lines 142-45) should be interpreted
   according to the medieval allegorization of the mouse as the devil caught by
   Christ's sacrifice. Her *conscience* aligns her 'with the dark power caught
   in the trap which Christ's flesh had baited.' The detail about mice is
   'further evidence that we should not be taken in by the Prioress's attempts
   to conceive of herself as an innocent child'; that self-characterization is a
   means of avoiding her proper responsibilities.

764 Cawley, A.C. 'A Note on Chaucer's Prioress and Criseyde.' *MLR*, 43
   (1948), 74-77.
   The Prioress and Criseyde share several descriptive traits. Their external
   resemblances, however, are less important than their sharing of 'the same
   skeletal pattern of character — tenderness of heart and instability of temperament' (p 77). For example, Criseyde is 'inconstant in her earthly love;
   the Prioress is hardly more constant in her heavenly love' (p 76). Both
   'belong to the same type of feminine character' (p 77).

765 Clark, Thomas Blake. 'Forehead of Chaucer's Prioress.' *PQ*, 9 (1930),
   312-14.
   Chaucer tells us first that the Prioress's forehead is large (lines 154-55) and
   afterwards that she is not undergrown (line 156). The first of these pieces
   of information, according to contemporary physiognomical beliefs, would
   imply 'dullness and foolishness, stupidity and slowness' (p 314), qualities
   that seem incongruent with the presentation of her as attractive. However,
   the second piece of information shifts our attention towards 'the meaning of
   a broad forehead which is not out of proportion to the remaining features
   and to the body' (p 314). In this context, contemporary opinion of a broad
   forehead was quite favorable, associating it with 'great virtue, wisdom, and
   magnanimity' (p 314), as well as physical attractiveness. Thus the portrait
   of the Prioress is consistent.

766 Cohen, Maurice. 'Chaucer's Prioress and Her Tale: A Study of Anal Character and Anti-Semitism.' *PsychQ*, 31 (1962), 232-49.

The Prioress's portrait is discussed in terms of reaction-formations and 'Freud's formulations on the sadomasochistic, sexually ambiguous characteristics of anal eroticism' (p 232). Her brooch, for example (line 160), is 'a singularly appropriate anal-erotic token' (p 234). Her dogs (lines 147–50) involve 'a sexual innuendo' (p 234); they 'stand not only for children but for children about to be sacrificed' (p 240). Her wiping of her upper lip (line 133) hints 'at her equation of mouth and anus' (p 238).

767 Copland, R.A. 'A Line from Chaucer's Prologue to the Canterbury Tales.' *N&Q*, New Series 17 (1970), 45–46.
In line 136, although it is usually thought that the Prioress reached after her meat, the word *raughte* could come from a verb meaning ' "to clear the throat, spit, hawk," ' or ' "to eructate, belch" ' (p 46). Thus the line is to be rendered ' "Decorously after her meal she belched" ' (p 46) — which is bathetic since one would expect that after meat the Prioress would say grace. (Cf Cutts, 768, and Drennan, 773.)

768 Cutts, John P. 'Madame Eglentyne's Saint Loy.' *StHum*, 7, 2 (1979), 34–38.
Cutts suggests that the Prioress is a large woman, that she 'reaches' after her meat in the sense of burping, that her name implies 'the country rose not the court rose, the country bumpkin who is struggling so hard' in order to 'upgrade herself' (p 35), and that Chaucer describes her with fascinated admiration. Her *St Loy* (see line 120) represents St Louis as well as St Eligius. Her concern for small creatures 'stems from her basic country upbringing' (p 35). (Cf Copland, 767, and Drennan, 773.)

769 David, Alfred. 'An ABC to the Style of the Prioress.' In *Acts of Interpretation: The Text in Its Contexts, 700–1600: Essays on Medieval and Renaissance Literature in Honor of E. Talbot Donaldson*. Ed. Mary J. Carruthers and Elizabeth D. Kirk. Norman, OK: Pilgrim, 1982. Pp 147–57.
The Prioress's portrait 'has a feeling of constraint, of a talent thwarted by its confinement to the cloister. That is the basis of both the amusement and the sympathy the reader feels for the Prioress' (pp 154–55). Her courtesy and her tears are 'complementary aspects of her style' and she 'anticipates the heroines of the sentimental novel' (p 154). 'The life of a prioress is like a string of beads or pearls. Madame Eglentyne's endeavor is to make that string shine brightly' in her daily singing of the office and in the ritual of eating and drinking: the 'ordinary meal is celebrated as meticulously as the mass' (p 154). Her qualities of style are correlated to those implied by Chaucer's depiction of the Virgin in the *ABC*: 'she, too, is a woman of style' (p 154). 'The stylistic analogies between *An ABC* and the portrait and tale of the prioress suggest ... the emergence of a new religious and

literary sensibility that increasingly finds aesthetic satisfaction in religious experience' (p 157).

770 Davies, R.T. 'Chaucer's Madame Eglantine.' *MLN*, 67 (1952), 400–2.
Davies here replies to Kuhl, **809**, who argued that the Prioress's name Eglantyne has religious associations. Kuhl had cited as evidence a passage from *Mandeville's Travels* that refers to the use of the *Eglentier*, a kind of plant, in crowning Christ. Davies points out that Kuhl's citation of the passage is incomplete. The omitted lines make it clear that the crown Christ wore on the cross is *not* the one made of *Eglentier*, but another, the crown of thorns. Thus Kuhl's evidence is not satisfactory. More important as a clue to the implications of the Prioress's romantic name is the fact that, as Manly (**823**) pointed out, Elizabeth of Hainault left in her will a bequest for a nun with the strongly romantic name of 'Idoine.'

771 Donaldson, E. Talbot. *Speaking of Chaucer.* London: Athlone Press; New York: W. W. Norton, 1970.
The chapter 'The Masculine Narrator and Four Women of Style' (pp 46–64) discusses the Prioress. The Prioress's portrait is an example of Chaucer's ability to 'create complexity with his basically simple style — or rather, with a style that might better be called deceptively simple' (p 61). The narrator tries to describe the Prioress as a nun, but ends up describing her, 'in all delighted honesty, as a romance heroine, thereby accomplishing, without using one satiric word, a double satire, on himself as a man as well as on her as a nun' (p 62). As for the three priests, editors should not remove them. Line 164 is 'one of those great rarities in the *Canterbury Tales*, a line with no manuscript variants' (p 62). While she should not 'be going to Canterbury in the company of three priests,' as a 'romance heroine' she does exactly that (p 63). 'I'm afraid that the three priests are a part of the prioress's character, and while it may be courteous of scholars to try to relieve her of moral responsibility for them, it is untrue to that simple, trustworthy narrator, Geoffrey Chaucer' (pp 63–64).

772 ——. 'Gallic Flies in Chaucer's English Word Web.' In *New Perspectives in Chaucer Criticism.* Ed. Donald M. Rose. Norman, OK: Pilgrim, 1981. Pp 193–202.
The Prioress's portrait shows the use of French constructions. It is only natural that she, as a 'French-speaking charmer,' should 'bring to the triumphant fore the Gallic in her infatuated portraitist' (p 195). Line 146 shows the use of a partitive *of*, like the French *de*: the phrase *Of smale houndes hadde she* resembles the French pattern, *De (or des) petits chiens avait elle.* Similarly, the *But* of line 154 'is surely the exclamatory *mais*' of

French idiom, 'for in the harmony of the Prioress's beauty there is simply no place for an adversative' (p 195).

773 Drennan, C.M. 'Chaucer's Prioress, "C.T.," Prol. 136: "Ful Semely After Hir Mete She Raughte." ' *N&Q*, 129 (1914), 365.
Drennan proposes that the word *raughte* (line 136) means not 'reached,' as it is usually understood, but instead 'retched' or 'spit.' 'One would be inclined to think that this little Rabelaisian touch has more of the true Chaucerian ring than the tame anticlimax of "She reached for her meat in seemly wise." ' (Cf Copland, **767**, and Cutts, **768**.)

774 Dunn, Charles W., ed. *A Chaucer Reader: Selections from the Canterbury Tales.* 1952. See **57**.
'Chaucer does not attempt to individualize *all* the characters in the *Prologue*,' and this technique may be purposeful (p 7). 'The Prioress's discreet companions, the Nun and the three Priests, are not described at all, although it has often been suggested that Chaucer intended ultimately to provide portraits of them; but their very silence, even if it supplies no positive information about their own characters, emphasizes the dominating character of their superior' (p 7; see lines 163–64).

775 Eckhardt, Caroline D. ' "Canterbury Tales" D.1554: "caples thre." ' *N&Q*, New Series 20 (1973), 283–84.
Lehmann (**811**) proposed that the phrase *preestes thre* (line 164) might refer to one priest, with *thre* being a numeral summarizing the whole group rather than modifying *preestes* only; and that line 1554 in *FrT*, ending with *caples thre*, shows the same construction. Eckhardt replies that no such summarizing numeral is used in *FrT*: the *caples thre* there are simply three horses and, similarly, the *preestes thre* of *GP* must mean three priests.

776 Eliason, Norman E. 'Chaucer's Second Nun?' *MLQ*, 3 (1942), 9–16.
The couplet that refers to the Second Nun (lines 163–64) is, according to Eliason, probably a non-Chaucerian interpolation based on a misunderstanding of manuscript rubrics. The rubric for *SNT* may have originally indicated that this tale was the second tale of the nun, ie, the second tale of the Prioress — not, as is usually thought, the tale of the Second Nun. An early confusion on this point would have led to the addition of lines 163–64. Thus it is suggested that in Chaucer's own version of *GP* no Second Nun (or *preestes thre*) existed.

777 Emerson, Oliver Farrar. 'Some Notes on Chaucer and Some Conjectures.' 1923. See **230**.
The narrator states that there are twenty-nine pilgrims (see line 24). Emerson proposes that the *preestes thre* (line 164) are the Nun's Priest, the

Monk, and the Friar. If the narrator is also counted in the pilgrimage group at this point, the total will be twenty-nine. In accordance with his plan to include a hundred and twenty tales in all, Chaucer intended from the beginning to introduce the Canon's Yeoman later, as the thirtieth pilgrim.

778 Evans, W.O. '"Cortaysye" in Middle English.' *MS*, 29 (1967), 143–57.
A survey of the uses of *cortaysye* in Middle English suggests that the word often has connotations of religious virtue and that 'it is by no means synonymous with courtly love' (p 157—*GP* is not discussed, but cf line 132).

779 Ferrie, Antoine. *Religion et gens d'église chez G. Chaucer*. 1977. See 241.
The Prioress's dogs do not accompany her on the pilgrimage; they are reported from conversation ('Chaucer en parle par oui-dire,' p 50). As F.S. Ellis pointed out [Chaucer's Prioress's "greatest oath,"' *Athenaeum*, No 3353, January 30, 1892, p 150], the Saint Loy by whom she swears (see line 120) could be St Lô, by whom Louis IX swore — as might have been known in England during the Hundred Years' War. However, St Eloi (Eligius) is more probable. The Prioress oscillates between opposite inclinations ('elle oscille sans cesse entre deux pôles contraires,' p 78); she exists somewhere in between the outer world and the convent ('à mi-chemin entre le monde et le couvent,' p 79). Nevertheless she conveys an impression of harmony and serenity ('une impression d'harmonie et de sérénité,' pp 78–9) and is able to maintain her unusual equilibrium ('une rare équilibre,' p 79). She represents a fusion, not a tension, of contraries.

780 Fischer, Walther. 'Die französischen Sprachkenntnisse von Chaucers Priorin.' In *Probleme der Englischen Sprache und Kultur, Festschrift für Johannes Hoops*. Ed. Wolfgang Keller. Heidelberg: Carl Winter, 1925. Pp 149–51.
Fischer argues that Chaucer's description of the Prioress's French pronunciation (lines 124–26) is meant as humorous criticism. About a century earlier than *GP*, an English nun apologized for what she called the false French of England ('Un faus françeis sai d'Angleterre,' p 151). By Chaucer's time the two kinds of French would have been even more differentiated. Madame Eglantyne's French would have aroused Chaucer's displeasure, since he was accustomed to the sound of continental French ('Madame Eglantine mit ihren anglofranzösischen Sprachkenntnissen tatsächlich das Missfallen des an kontinentalfranzösische Laute gewohnten Chaucer erweckte,' p 151).

781 Fisher, John Hurt. 'Embarrassment of Riches.' *CLAJ*, 7 (1963), 1–12.
In a brief analysis of the Prioress's portrait, Fisher remarks that its ambiguity 'rests upon the fact that Chaucer was in this portrait embarking upon a literary mode almost unknown in the Middle Ages — that is, criticism of

an *institution* rather than the typical criticism of an erring *individual'* (p 3). The portrait suggests the disillusionment that radical reformers, such as Wycliffe and Huss, were beginning to express.

782 Förster, Max. 'Chauceriana I.' *Archiv,* 132 (1914), 399–401.
Förster assembles evidence on the function of the nun-chaplain in late-medieval nunneries. Records of the visitations of several cloisters show that the chaplain's appointment rotated, rather than being permanently assigned to one nun, and that the duties included sleeping in the prioress's chamber and being personally attendant upon her. Thus we can easily understand why Chaucer's Prioress takes her nun-chaplain along on the pilgrimage (line 164).

783 Foster, Brian. 'Chaucer's "Sëynt Loy": An Anglo-French Pun?' *N&Q,* New Series 15 (1968), 244–45.
The Prioress's oath (see line 120) may refer to St Eligius, patron of black-smiths and carriers, as has been thought. However, the name is also a pun on the French word *loi* in its meaning of 'licence' or 'permission' (p 245). In effect, the Prioress is swearing by 'St Permission' or 'St Do-as-you-like' (p 245).

784 Frank, Mary Hardy Long. *The Prioress and the Puys: A Study of the Cult of the Virgin and the Medieval Puys in Relation to Chaucer's Prioress and her Tale.* University of Colorado Dissertation. 1970. Dir. Donald C. Baker. See also *DAI,* 31 (1970), 2874-5-A.
'Chaucer is generally supposed to be mocking, more or less gently, the discrepancies in his Prioress between the worldliness of her appearance and demeanor and the unworldliness demanded by her profession .... The study attempts first to show that her Tale complements the Prioress described in the Prologue, that the style and substance of that description are as Marian as they are courtly, that indeed the medieval cult of the Virgin popularly did not distinguish between courtly and celestial love but instead delighted in the ambiguity. Even in her frailties the Prioress is seen as the Virgin's devoted handmaiden' [from *DAI*; diss not seen, cf **785**].

785 ——. 'Chaucer's Prioress and the Blessed Virgin.' *ChauR,* 13 (1978–1979), 346–62.
Frank defends the Prioress against charges of inappropriate courtly world-liness and instead associates details of her portrait with the Virgin Mary. The phrase *simple and coy* (line 119) and near-equivalent phrases occur in poems addressed to Mary. The eglantine flower (line 121) 'was, like many another flower, a common symbol for the Virgin' (p 349). St Eloy, by whom she swears (line 120), was 'pleasing in the sight of the Virgin' (p 349); St

Thomas, whose shrine she is going to see, was said to have been several times visited by the Virgin and had other associations with her. As for the Prioress's beauty, adornment, and care for her cleanliness, these too were characteristics of the medieval depiction of Mary. Both Mary and her handmaiden the Prioress, 'Chaucer saw, were stereotypically feminine — whimsical, capricious, emotional, irrational, unconventional' (p 359). In this behavior, Mary's motives 'were great and pure, and surely those of her handmaiden, who in everything else mirrors her Mistress, are no less' (p 360). Cf **784**.

786 Friedman, John Block. 'The Prioress's Beads "Of Smal Coral." ' *MÆ*, 39 (1970), 301–5.

In the Middle Ages, coral was thought to protect people against demons and evil spirits, as well as against the manifestations of their activities — lightning, storms, etc. Coral was thus a suitable gem for travelers, who might be exposed to the hazards of such evil influences on their journeys. As lapidaries and wills demonstrate, coral rosary beads were widely used by members of the wealthier classes, especially while they were pilgrims and travelers. The Prioress may have chosen the coral rosary because 'it seemed one of the attributes of the aristocratic world she fancied' (p 303), but she may also have chosen it for more pious reasons. In her tale she correctly associates the emerald with chastity and the ruby with martyrdom. Thus she may also have known about the symbolic protective value of coral. Given both possibilities, 'the coral rosary is as ambiguous in meaning as the motto on the ornament which hangs from it' (p 304).

787 Gaylord, Alan T. 'The Unconquered Tale of the Prioress.' *MichA*, 47 (1962), 613–36.

Both the Prioress's portrait and her tale reveal 'a delicate but nonetheless devastating satire' (p 615), which in *GP* is conveyed largely by the arrangement or context of the details. Since Madame Eglantyne is a prioress, she must be evaluated according to her responsibilities for her flock. She and the Parson are the two pilgrims explicitly charged with others' spiritual welfare. The Parson's attention to his duties predominates, but for her this is not so. Her smiling calls attention to courtliness; her oath (she should not be swearing at all) 'continues that falling away from the expected direction' (p 619). Some of the details about her appearance become 'decidedly acidulous' (p 619) since she is probably not a young, dainty person, but a middle-aged woman of considerable size. Her concept of courtesy, like that of the Squire, is described partly in terms of the *Roman de la Rose*. However, Chaucer does not intend a specific association between the Prioress and La Vieille, the old whore of the *Roman*: 'he does not need to intimate that she is a bad woman; it is enough to intimate that she is not a good Prioress' (p 621). Her table manners show that 'she imitates not the court of the new Jerusalem but of Babylon' (pp 621–2). The passage on her conscience is bathos. Her brooch, which involves 'the strongest irony' (p 623), indicates that she can represent charity on an ornament, but does not understand it. Her description, which is 'associated more with an aesthetic than an ascetic point of view,' constitutes 'a criticism of life or a part of life' (p 624).

788 Goodrich, W.J. 'Chauceriana.' 1904. See 721.
Lines 124–26, despite the opinion of Skeat (see 851) that they are straightforward, contain sly humor at the Prioress's inferior French.

789 Hamilton, Marie Padgett. 'The Convent of Chaucer's Prioress and her Priests.' In *Philologica: The Malone Anniversary Studies*. Ed. Thomas A. Kirby and Henry Bosley Woolf. Baltimore: Johns Hopkins Press, 1949. Pp 179–90.
The three priests of line 164 should be accepted as such, not reduced to one. The arguments against the presence of all three are unconvincing. 'An escort of only one man for the two nuns would have been at variance with monastic custom and the sense of decorum' of the Prioress (p 190). St Leonard's was not a small or insignificant religious house; a retinue of three priests would not have been inappropriate for its status. Chaucer 'could have found no thriftier way' (p 190) to indicate the size of the house, as well as the Prioress's sense of authority and dignity, than by including the *preestes thre*.

790 Hammond, Eleanor Prescott. 'Ashmole 59 and Other Shirley Manuscripts.' *Anglia*, 30 (1907), 320–48.
A letter resembling a 'crowned A,' or 'a fusion of letters of the word *Amor*' (p 320), appears in two mss copied by the scribe Shirley. This symbol can be compared to the initial and motto on the Prioress's brooch (lines 161–62). Other such initials are also mentioned.

791 ——. 'Two Chaucer Cruces.' *MLN*, 22 (1907), 51–52.
A passage from Lydgate's *Virtue of the Mass* clarifies the connotations of St Loy, by whom the Prioress swears (line 120). Lydgate's reference to this saint — 'Seynte loye youre iournay schall preserue' — suggests that St Loy was suitable for a traveler to invoke. The Yeoman's St Christopher (line 115) also occurs in Lydgate's passage.

792 Harper, Gordon H. 'Chaucer's Big Prioress.' *PQ*, 12 (1933), 308–10.
Chaucer's Prioress 'was in fact fat. Chaucer's humor lies in the delayed disclosure of the Prioress's bulbous figure after he has carefully built up a picture of affected manners usually associated with daintiness' (p 308).

She has an unusually large forehead (line 155), the rest of her body is presumably in proportion to her forehead, and we are told that 'she was nat undergrowe' (line 156). To see her as a spinster of quite large physical size makes her a more humorous character.

793 Haskell, Ann S. *Essays on Chaucer's Saints.* The Hague and Paris: Mouton, 1976.
In the chapter 'The St Loy Oath Reconsidered' (pp 32–37), Haskell suggests that the allusions involved in the Prioress's oath (line 120) constitute 'a sort of iconographic acrostic' (p 36) that ironically comments on her behavior. St Loy was associated with three women saints — Bathilda, Gertrude, and Aurea — all of whom were abbesses or benefactors of Benedictine houses and were known for both courtliness and charity. Their legends coincide with many details in the Prioress's portrait (Gertrude was depicted with mice, for example; elsewhere mice sometimes represented the Jews). The Prioress might wish to vicariously participate in the courtly circle of these three saints, but unlike them she does not practice austerities or seek to alleviate human misery.

794 Helmeke, Theodor. *Beteuerungen und Verwünschungen bei Chaucer.* Christian-Albrechts-Universität Dissertation (Kiel). 1913. Dir. Dr. Holthausen. Published Kiel: Handorff, 1913.
The Prioress's oath is listed (without discussion) among others in the categories of oaths by saints, and oaths occurring at the rhyme.

795 Hemingway, Samuel B. 'Chaucer's Monk and Nun's Priest.' *MLN*, 31 (1916), 479–83.
The Monk reminds the Nun's Priest 'irresistibly of a sleek and pompous, well-groomed rooster' (p 480), which suggests the choice of the Chanticler tale. The Priest is meant to be understood as younger than the Monk and is 'unquestionably a gentleman — none but a gentleman could be in the retinue of Madam Eglantine' (p 480).

796 Hostia, Sister Mary. 'The Prioress and her Companion.' *CE*, 14 (1952–1953), 351–52.
Chaucer delineated the Prioress very carefully, but gave only 'a cursory line and a half to the Second Nun' in *GP* (p 351). This situation might have been intended to emphasize their similarity, 'implying that one was the counterpart of the other,' or alternatively it might have been intended to alert us to a 'fundamental dissimilarity' between them (p 351). Given that their tales show a strong contrast — between the worldliness, vanity, and insincerity of the Prioress's, and the more truly religious spirit of the Second Nun's — their *GP* treatment was evidently 'deliberately contrived

in such a way as to make the reader aware that fundamental differences existed between these two characters' (p 352).

797 Hunter-Blair, D. Oswald, O.S.B. 'Women Chaplains in Convents.' *N&Q*, 106 (1902), 324–25.
The office of the nun who served as chaplain should not be confused with that of the 'chaplain, or spiritual father, of the community,' for the *capellanissa*'s duties are 'of a purely ceremonial kind, and consist chiefly in attendance on the lady abbess in the choir on great festivals' (p 324).

798 Jacobs, Edward Craney. 'Further Biblical Allusions for Chaucer's Prioress.' *ChauR*, 15 (1980-1981), 151–54.
Developing the work of Knoepflmacher (**807**), Jacobs collects additional allusions that pertain to the difference between *amor* and *caritas* and to the wearing of gold. These passages 'heighten the ironical nuances of the Prioress' gold brooch and its motto "Amor vincit omnia"' (p 151).

799 Kaske, R.E. 'Chaucer and Medieval Allegory.' 1963. See **427** (review).
In this extended review-essay on Robertson's *Preface* (**427**), Kaske takes issue with Robertson's viewpoint that the Prioress's broad forehead indicates stupidity or indiscretion, interpreting it instead as part of the ideal of feminine beauty, suitable for a romance heroine but not for the Prioress. Kaske also sees a greater complexity in the word *conscience* (lines 142, 150). Our first understanding of the statement about the Prioress's *conscience* (lines 142-3), ' "But with regard to her conscience, she was so devout and so full of piety ... "' soon 'collapses hilariously' in the anticlimax about the mouse, and we then substitute a second understanding, 'But with regard to the sensitivity of her feelings, she was so tender-hearted and so full of emotional pity ... "' (p 185). The word *conscience* thus contains the two meanings sequentially. The Prioress herself has substituted sensitive feelings for true conscience, just as we do in reading this passage.

800 Kastner, V. 'Chaucer: "Prestes Thre" or "Prest Estré"?' *Athenaeum*, No 4087, February 24, 1906, pp 231–32.
The troublesome phrase *prestes thre* of line 164 should be emended to *prest estré*, which would mean 'a presbyter domesticus, what the French call an aumônier' (p 232). In addition, the preceding line is unsatisfactory metrically and should also be emended. The following version of lines 163–64 is suggested: 'A nonne and eke a prest with her hadd she, / Who was hir chapeleine and prest estre' (p 232).

801 Kelly, Edward H. 'By Mouth of Innocentz: The Prioress Vindicated.' *PLL*, 5 (1969), 362–74.
The Prioress's portrait shows her as having a penchant for things that are

small, petty, or helpless — a 'preoccupation with inconsequential diminutives' (p 364). She herself, however, is likely to be large and heavy-set. Her name 'connotes anything but delicacy in size or appearance' (p 365): the eglantine plant grows to be eight feet high and is 'tall, wide, and hardy' (p 365). The diminutives in the portrait function humorously in contrast to the large size of the Prioress's person. Her tale continues the suggestions of immaturity and the emphasis on things small. Her beads (line 159) are echoed by the 'similar color and gem imagery' of the tale (p 367); other characteristics of the *GP* portrait are also evident in the tale. The tone of the portrait is more appropriately considered comic than satiric, in view of the humorous contrast between smallness and largeness in the description.

802 Kiernan, Kevin S. 'The Art of the Descending Catalogue, and a Fresh Look at Alisoun.' *ChauR*, 10 (1975–1976), 1–16.
Kiernan reviews the rhetorical device of the descending catalogue, which describes a beautiful woman head-to-foot, and its variations. The Prioress's portrait emphasizes her mouth. The description 'simultaneously descends and reverts, from mouth to nose to mouth to fingers to breast to mouth' (p 9), as we watch her eat. 'The descent from face to body is subtle, and understandably prudent' (p 9), but the downward movement nevertheless makes the reader 'rather uncomfortable' (p 10) because Chaucer is applying a secular convention to a nun. On the Wife, see **1148**.

803 Kinney, Muriel. '*Vair* and Related Words: A Study in Semantics.' *RomR*, 10 (1919), 322–63.
Kinney suggests that Chaucer, in saying that the Prioress's eyes were grey as glass (line 152), may have intended a set of double meanings, for English glass of this period was poor in quality and had a muddy grey color, while Venetian glass and French glass were high in quality and had a more brilliant color. 'Now Chaucer loved nothing better than double meanings. One can imagine his smiling now, in whatever state he may be, at the war of words over his intentions as to the prioresse. Those of us who believe him to have been shyly poking fun at her may easily see a double meaning in his description of her eyes: they were grey as glass, that is, grey in the sense of a neutral tint mostly black-and-white blended, like the muddy English glass; or grey in the sense of *vair*, sparkling, colorful and bright, like the rare Venetian glass, or French *vitre*' (p 341).

804 Kiralis, Karl. 'William Blake as an Intellectual and Spiritual Guide to Chaucer's *Canterbury Pilgrims*.' *BlakeS*, 1 (1969), 139–90.
The Monk may come from an even higher social class than the Prioress, 'since he dresses even more expensively than she does' (p 158). The Prioress and the Knight may be attracted to each other. The Host, characterized

by 'basic shrewdness and general intelligence,' is able to see through 'the Prioress's ways of courtly love' (p 163). See also **1214**.

805 Kirby, Thomas A. 'The French of Chaucer's Prioress.' In *Studies for William A. Read*. Ed. Nathaniel M. Caffee and Thomas A. Kirby. University, LA: Louisiana State University Press, 1940. Pp 29–34.
Chaucer's comment on the Prioress's French (lines 124–26) 'need not be taken satirically' (p 32). Similarly, the nasality of her singing was simply the customary way of chanting the service; her behavior at table 'is typical of the conduct of any well-bred medieval lady'; and her clothing is just 'the usual dress of a Benedictine nun,' although she was indeed fastidious (p 33). Thus 'the Prioress's French, like her singing, her table manners, and her dress, may be satisfactorily explained and completely understood if taken quite literally and properly related to the actual state of affairs in later fourteenth-century England' (p 34).

806 Knight, S.T. ' "Almoost a Spanne Brood." ' *Neophil*, 52 (1968), 178–80.
The description of the Prioress's forehead as being 'almoost a spanne brood' (line 155) probably means that it is three to four inches *high* — rather than almost a hand-span *wide*, as is usually thought. The Middle English word *span* could indicate a measure of length equal to the breadth of the hand (ie, 3–4 inches), and the word *brood*, referring to the shorter of two dimensions, could, in speaking of the forehead, apply to its height. A high forehead would have been a fashionable mark of beauty. Thus Chaucer 'makes a sharply ironical point about the Prioress,' since her wimple is worn 'improperly high for the sake of a totally worldly fashion' (p 179). The narrator seems to explain her high forehead in terms of her overall size, for he remarks that she is 'nat undergrowe' (line 156), but his interpretation is 'a foolishly innocent explanation of a piece of description which is loaded with ironical malice' (p 179).

807 Knoepflmacher, U.C. 'Irony through Scriptural Allusion: A Note on Chaucer's Prioresse.' *ChauR*, 4 (1969-1970), 180–83.
Chaucer's comment that the Prioress wipes her upper lip clean of *grece* (lines 133–35) may involve a pun on the modern senses of *grease* and *grace*. He would have expected his audience to recall Matthew 23:25–26, where hypocrites are criticized for cleaning the outside of the cup while remaining unclean within. The nature of the Prioress's charity is clarified by Matthew 15:26–28, where Jesus first seems to reject the appeal for help made by a Canaanite mother, but then, when she tells him that the whelps also eat the crumbs that fall from their masters' table, he praises her faith and grants her a cure for her sick daughter. Just as Jesus at first seemed too exclusive in distributing his charity, the Prioress is too exclusive with hers:

in her tale 'her lack of charity towards "the cursed Jews" merely mirrors the Jews' own bias against the child,' and in *GP* her concern for her dogs is 'a perversion of the same charity the parable was meant to exemplify' (p 182). The Prioress, however, shares with the Canaanite mother a strongly emotional temperament, and 'like the Canaanite's daughter and like most of the pilgrims on the journey, the childlike Prioresse can be cured' (p 183). The Scriptural allusion thus softens the previous ironies. Cf **798**.

808 Kuhl, Ernest P. 'Notes on Chaucer's Prioress.' *PQ*, 2 (1923), 302–9.
Six notes concern the Prioress's portrait in *GP*. 1) The term *wastel* (line 147) meant 'for practical purposes the choicest bread' (p 303), a superior quality of wheat bread. It was apparently not sweetened and should not be equated with cake. 2) As for the Prioress's 'smale houndes' (line 146), records limiting the whereabouts of pets show that 'it was apparently not uncommon for nuns to have their dogs' (p 304). 3) In addition to the previously recognized functions of a female chaplain (line 164), it was her duty to attend the prioress at the prioress's installation, as a 1397 record from Barking Abbey shows. 4) As 'an illustration of the temptation from outside' the cloister (p 305) — with reference to the Prioress's brooch (line 160) — a 1397 injunction forbade the nuns of a Yorkshire prior to wear brooches, but in 1355–1356 a nun of Barking, who was perhaps a relative of Chaucer's, was willed jewelry. 5) The Stratford convent (line 125) was relatively poor, while Barking had long been connected with the court and its prioresses 'were of the aristocracy and royalty' (p 307). Thus the Prioress, coming from the undistinguished house, would naturally not have known Parisian French. 6) The Prioress of Barking, who was genuinely courtly, *would* know court manners and Parisian French. The nuns at Stratford might well wish to imitate their aristocratic neighbors. Thus a pun on *court* (line 140) may be intended: the Prioress may try to imitate the behavior not only of the court at Westminster, but also of the court at Barking Abbey.

809 ——. 'Chaucer's Madame Eglantine.' *MLN*, 60 (1945), 325–26.
A passage from Mandeville's *Travels* indicates, according to Kuhl, that the Prioress's name Eglantyne (line 121) may have Christian symbolic value. The passage as cited describes an episode in which Jesus was '*crouned with Eglentier*' and explains that we should therefore venerate this crown. (For a critique of Kuhl's use of this passage, see Davies, **770**.)

810 Lee, Dwight A. 'Chaucer's Prioress and Saint Venus.' *MSCS*, 3 (1968), 69–75.
At the Prioress's birth, 'the dominant planet in her horoscope was Venus' (p 69) and she therefore has a propensity for courtly love. Her characteristics correspond quite well to those that Curry (see **209**) identifies with the

children of Venus. Thus 'Chaucer's portrayal of the lady must have been universally recognized by his contemporaries as that of a child of Venus' (p 73). Chaucer does not indicate that she practices courtly love, only that by birth she inclines towards it. She is 'a woman who has committed her life to a role for which she is unsuited' (p 73). Chaucer treats this situation with predominant humor, although also with pathos.

811 Lehmann, W.P. 'A Rare Use of Numerals in Chaucer.' *MLN*, 67 (1952), 317–21.
German and French passages are presented to show the existence of an 'additive construction' (p 320) in which different items are included in a cumulative number stated towards the end of a line. In line 164, according to Lehmann, Chaucer 'counts the Nun, her Chaplain, and her Priest as three people' (p 320). Although *preestes* is plural in form, it refers to only one priest. Thus the phrase *preestes thre* means that the Prioress, the Second Nun, and the one Nun's Priest are being added up to total three. As evidence that Chaucer knew this 'additive constructive,' a passage from the *FrT* is cited. (See Spitzer, **853**, and Eckhardt, **775**, in reply.)

812 Livingston, Charles H. 'The Fabliau "Des Deux Anglois et de l'Anel." ' *PMLA*, 40 (1925), 217–24.
A thirteenth-century French tale in which a hungry Englishman wants to request *agnel* (lamb) to eat, but asks instead for *anel* (a young ass) and so eats donkey-meat, is cited to show 'the lack of esteem in which the French dialect spoken in England must have been held by the continentals' (p 218; see lines 124–26). Two later analogues are also presented, suggesting that 'the subject was a popular one' (p 224). (Cf Matske, **828**.)

813 Lowes, John Livingston. 'The Date of Chaucer's *Troilus and Criseyde*.' *PMLA*, 23 (1908), 285–306.
The Prioress's crowned *A* on her brooch (see line 161) is not related to the use of the crowned *A* as an emblem for Queen Anne (pp 290–91).

814 —. 'Simple and Coy: A Note on Fourteenth Century Poetic Diction.' *Anglia*, 33 (1910), 440–51.
Chaucer's entire description of the Prioress is 'steeped in reminiscences of the poetry of courtly love' (p 440) and thus 'suggests the delightfully imperfect submergence of the woman in the nun' (p 442). The terms *simple* and *coy* are conventional in courtly poetry, as is, in French, the combined phrase *simple et coi*. Many examples of these terms are cited, including instances from the poetry of Machaut, Froissart, Gower, and Deschamps. Thus Chaucer's statement that the Prioress's smiling is *symple and coy* (line 119) subtly suggests, as do many other traits of her characterization, the

'beloved "chere of court" ' (p 451) that she attempts to imitate (lines 139–
40). The connotations of other stock phrases of fourteenth-century poetic
diction might also be worthy of examination, since inadequate attention
has been given to Chaucer's 'individual use of conventional phraseology'
(p 442). French songs about 'bele Eglentine' (cf the Prioress's name, line
121) are cited, as are parallels for Chaucer's description of the Prioress's
physical features. See also 345.

815 ——. 'The Prioress's Oath.' *RomR*, 5 (1914), 368–85.
The Prioress's oath (line 120) is fully appropriate to her, for St Loy (Eligius)
'was at once, in a word, an artist and a courtier and a saint, a man of great
physical beauty, and a lover, in his earlier days, of personal adornment' (p
369). He was known for his craftsmanship as a goldsmith; the hymns to
St Loy usually stress 'his peculiar office of lending beauty to the symbols
of holiness' (p 373). The brooch on the Prioress's rosary (line 160) is,
in this sense, 'symbolic of the work of St Eligius' (p 375). The saint's
reputation for physical beauty, courtliness, and gentility makes him 'pretty
much all that the Prioress either was or "peyned hir" to be,' so that the
Prioress's swearing by this saint is 'one more characterizing touch' in this
'masterpiece of portraiture' (p 380). It is not necessary to suppose that
Chaucer planned this association by assembling St Loy's qualities, one by
one, as we now need to do. Since the saint's reputation would have been
'familiar knowledge' in his day, the choice was more likely to have been 'a
flash of inspiration' whereby the 'hovering associations' suddenly 'focussed,
precipitated themselves — or whatever figure one may use — in the poet's
mind' (p 380). Cf 859.

816 Lumiansky, R.M. 'The Nun's Priest in *The Canterbury Tales*.' *PMLA*, 68
(1953), 896–906.
Replying primarily to Sherbo (see 845), Lumiansky proposes that the Nun's
Priest was meant to be seen as 'scrawny, humble, and timid' (p 897).
Whether Chaucer meant for the Prioress to have three priests with her (see
line 164) cannot be established by citing contemporary documents, since
'Chaucer was not always controlled in his writing by a desire for historical
accuracy' (p 896).

817 Lynch, James J. 'The Prioress's Gems.' *MLN*, 57 (1942), 440–41.
In her tale the Prioress refers to three gems which have symbolic implications — the emerald (chastity), ruby (martyrdom), and pearl (perfection)
— 'all of which must have appealed strongly to the Prioress' (p 441). In
particular, chastity was the virtue that 'would most appeal to Chaucer's
Prioress as a professed nun' (p 440).

818 ——. 'The Prioress's Greatest Oath, Once More.' *MLN*, 72 (1957), 242–49.
Although the identification of the Prioress's *Seinte Loy* (line 120) with St
Eligius the goldsmith is generally accepted, Lynch proposes that St Eulalia,
not St Eligius, is meant. French place-names show much phonetic variation
for the name of Eulalia; 'the interpretation of the Prioress's "Seinte Loy"
as St Eulalia is phonetically possible' (p 247). There were two St Eulalias,
both of them young and virgin martyrs. Given the Prioress's later tale, it
would be appropriate for her to venerate a young martyr. The fact that
some mss show a final -*e* on *seint(e)* in line 120 suggests that Chaucer may
have used the form appropriate for a female saint. He could have known
of St Eulalia either through literary sources or through her cult, which
was established in parts of France through which he traveled. Interpreting
Seinte Loy as St Eulalia helps to restore decorum to the Prioress's *GP*
portrait.

819 McCarthy, Sister Brigetta, O.S.B. 'Chaucer's Pilgrim-Prioress.' *Bene-
dictineR*, 6 (1951), 38–40.
Sister McCarthy indicates that Chaucer's Prioress, who comes from the
Benedictine Abbey of Bromley, Middlesex, is described mostly in conventional terms. Chaucer made her 'too conscious of worldly gentility,' but 'it
is very obvious that he did respect her; otherwise he would not have assigned to her that heart-appealing tale that she related with deep sincerity'
(p 40).

820 McKnight, G.H. 'The French of Chaucer's Prioresse.' *MLN*, 19 (1904), 62.
The *Vie de Saint Thomas* (probably written in the twelfth century) differentiates between the French of France and that of England: the poet says
that his language is good because he was born in France. This passage
lends further support to the interpretation that Chaucer is indeed 'poking
fun at Anglo-French' in lines 124–6.

821 Madeleva, Sister M. [=Mary Evaline Wolff.] *Chaucer's Nuns and Other
Essays.* Foreword by B.H. Lehman. New York and London: Appleton,
1925.
The chapter 'Chaucer's Nuns' (pp 1–42) argues that the nuns of *CT* should
be considered from the perspective of a nun's experience, not from that of
secular criticism. (Cf **859**.) The Prioress's smiling is within the spirit of
the Benedictine Rule; her name may have hagiographical echoes. Her style
of singing the service would have been normal for the cloister. Her care
to avoid soiling her garments reflects a nun's proper respect for her habit,
while her seemliness in reaching for her food suggests self-control at meals,
and her gathering of leftover food for her dogs reflects ancient custom. Her
wimple implies not vanity, but duty; similarly, her beads would not have

seemed extravagant in her time. Her motto is 'the most typical motto that could have been engraved upon the brooch' and the brooch itself is a 'good, but not over-elaborate medal' of the sort used to remind the owner of religious concepts (pp 19–20). The Prioress is not a young woman still preoccupied with the world, but 'a woman a decade or more beyond middle age,' one who has been 'spiritually transformed by the rules and religious practices' of her chosen way of life and who 'can be in the world without being of it' (pp 21–22). Older nuns are more typically permitted to keep pets and would be more likely to show sympathy to mice. The Benedictine Rule includes provisions for traveling, though 'nothing but a very urgent spiritual quest could have induced [the Prioress and her companion] to leave their cloister and join so worldly and public an excursion' (p 27). Chaucer himself sees the Prioress and Second Nun 'chiefly from the outside,' and may therefore misinterpret them, but a 'more human' understanding is obtained by viewing them from within the characteristics of their own way of life instead (p 28). The chapter is reprinted in Sister M. Madeleva, *A Lost Language and Other Essays on Chaucer* (New York: Sheed and Ward, 1951), pp 31–60.

822 Manley, Francis. 'Chaucer's Rosary and Donne's Bracelet: Ambiguous Coral.' *MLN*, 74 (1959), 385–88.
The Prioress's coral rosary (lines 158–59), like the coral bracelet in one of John Donne's sonnets, draws upon the traditionally ambiguous associations of coral. On the one hand, it was thought that coral furnished protection against the devil; on the other hand, it gave entrance to love. Thus the Prioress's beads are 'as delicately ambiguous as everything else about her' (p 388). It is suitable for a bride of Christ to have a coral rosary, but since coral also signified earthly love, 'perhaps that explains why her beads are small and fine enough to please the gross eyes of the world' (p 388).

823 Manly, John Matthews. *Some New Light on Chaucer*. 1926. See 362.
In the chapter 'The Prioress and the Wife of Bath, the Second Nun and the Nuns' Priest' (pp 201–34), Manly suggests that the Prioress, who is associated with the Benedictine nunnery of St Leonard's, may be based upon the Madame Argentyn, nun, who is mentioned in the will of Elizabeth of Hainault. [For Manly's later change of opinion, see 824.] The Nun's Priest — there is only one, despite the *prestes thre* of line 164 — was the parish priest who served as confessor to the nuns, not a special priest of the nunnery. Cf 770.

824 ——. 'The Prioress of Stratford.' *TLS*, November 10, 1927, p 817.
Documents show that the fourteenth-century prioress Mary Syward sold a bird and a cage to one William Bartilmeer; this episode illustrates the

Prioress's fondness for pets. Mary Syward was probably the prioress of St Leonard's at Stratford at the time when Chaucer wrote the *CT*. Given this new evidence, Manly now regards as 'highly improbable' his earlier suggestion (see **823**) that Madame Eglantyne reflects the Domina Argentyn named in Elizabeth of Hainault's will. (In reply see Baugh, **753**.)

825 ——, and Edith Rickert, eds. *The Text of the Canterbury Tales Studied on the Basis of All Known Manuscripts.* 1940. See **49**.
Chaucer stopped in the middle of line 164, intending to supply the rest of the section later but not doing so. It was someone else's hand that added the three priests. 'That there were not three priests in the company of the Prioress seems quite certain' (vol 3, p 422).

826 Mann, Jill. *Chaucer and Medieval Estates Satire.* 1973. See **363**.
The Prioress's portrait reflects a 'tradition of translating the role of the courtly heroine into a religious sphere' (p 134). Earlier examples include the sermons of Guibert of Tournai and a long poem for nuns written by Gautier de Coincy. 'Both Guibert and Gautier see the nun not just as the bride of Christ, but as his *courtly* mistress' (p 136). In Chaucer's portrait the courtly imagery has been returned to its original secular context, for the '"curteisie" which the Prioress venerates is worldly, not spiritual .... And it is the use of the estates ideal which teaches us the relativist character of each pilgrim's values; "curteisie" is not an absolute, but an ideal that each pilgrim defines for himself' (p 137).

827 Masui, Michio. 'Chaucer's Tenderness and the Theme of Consolation.' *NM*, 73 (1972), 214–21.
Discussing Chaucer's tendency toward empathy, Masui finds that the description of the Prioress's *conscience* (see lines 143–50) shows 'how Chaucer's personal feeling ... works when he sees any object that "souneth into gentilesse"' (p 215).

828 Matske, John E. 'Some Examples of French as Spoken by Englishmen in Old French Literature.' *MP*, 3 (1905-1906), 47–60.
Matske collects examples of the kind of French found in England (see lines 124–26). One fabliau, for instance, concerns an Englishman's mispronunciation of *aignel* as *anel*: he is given donkey-meat, rather than lamb, for dinner. (Cf Livingston, **812**.)

829 Moore, Arthur K. 'The Eyen Greye of Chaucer's Prioress.' *PQ*, 26 (1947), 307–12.
The Prioress is said to have 'eyen greye as glas' (line 152). Whether the medieval term *greye* corresponds to modern 'blue' or 'gray' has been debated. Elsewhere Chaucer applies *grey* or *greye* to objects that we would call gray,

and he 'never associates eye-color with any object that is inevitably blue' (p 310). Therefore, the Prioress's eyes are indeed gray. Nevertheless, in medieval usage the term *greye* included a wider range of color than we would now expect — 'any shade between slate-gray and sky-blue' but with a predominant 'gray effect' (p 312).

830 Moorman, Charles. 'The Prioress as Pearly Queen.' *ChauR*, 13 (1978–1979), 25–33.

Moorman argues that the Prioress is not an aristocratic lady, but 'a woman who is by nature portly, good-natured, sentimental, motherly, and a trifle earthy, if not vulgar ... an East Londoner, a Cockney' (p 27). The word *countrefete* (line 139) epitomizes her portrait. She is 'a nun who foregoes her proper and appropriate demeanor of high sanctity in order to present an *assumed* "cheere of court" [lines 139–40] which she must strain to maintain' (p 27). Chaucer indicates her status partly by 'her pronunciation of French, which, like any serious social climber, she insists on speaking at every opportunity' (p 27), and which would have been influenced by her local dialect of English.

831 Mossé, Fernand. 'Chaucer et le "Métier" de l'Écrivain.' *EA*, 7 (1954), 394–401.

Mossé suggests that some of Chaucer's saints' names were probably chosen simply for the sake of the rhyme. The Prioress's *Seinte Loy*, for instance (line 120), probably enters the portrait only in order to rhyme with *coy* ('n'intervient là que pour rimer avec *coy*,' p 400).

832 Muscatine, Charles. 'The Canterbury Tales: Style of the Man and Style of the Work.' 1966. See **387**.

Chaucer's portraits show a complexity of structure, with the introduction of multiple 'systems of connotations' into the characterizations (p 96). 'Thus in the celebrated portrait of the Prioress we may roughly distinguish two groups of traits, compatible but not completely harmonious, one connoting religious sensibility and the other courtly delicacy. In this case the mere statement of the Prioress's occupation has such strong connotations that a large number of courtly traits can be played against it. Chaucer delights in finding traits that belong in both systems' of ideas (p 96), such as *conscience* (line 150).

833 Okada, Terutada. 'Meki No Shi Ni Okeru "ME" No Keiyoji ikko — "grey" = "blue"?' [Adjectives to Describe Eyes in Middle English — Does 'grey' = 'blue'?] *ND*, 29 (1981), 29–34.

Not seen; listed in *A Bibliography of Publications on Medieval English Language and Literature in Japan* (Tokyo: Center for Medieval Studies, Tokyo University, 1983), p 135, #12.

834 Olson, Clair C. 'Chaucer and the Music of the Fourteenth Century.' *Spec*, 16 (1941), 64–91.
Chaucer shows his 'roguish delight in humorous incongruity' (p 71) in lines 122–23, on the Prioress's singing, and in lines 672–74, on the Summoner's *bourdoun*. Chaucer was apparently not very interested in the theoretical or technical aspects of music.

835 Orr, John. *Old French and Modern English Idiom*. Oxford: Basil Blackwell, 1962.
'Chaucer's "ferthing of grece" [line 134] is a happy inspiration prompted by a misunderstanding of *maillettes*,' the word in his French source, the *Roman de la Rose* (p 9). In French there were two words *maille*, one meaning a small coin, the other meaning a spot; Chaucer understood the former, where the *Roman* intended the latter. (See Reid, **840**, in reply.)

836 Parker, David. 'Can We Trust the Wife of Bath?' *ChauR*, 4 (1969-1970), 90–98.
The pilgrims 'are all, to a varying degree, to be taken as individuals' (p 92). Irony requires 'that the reader see the figure against whom it is directed as an individual,' since one 'can't be revenged on an abstraction' (p 93). In the description of the Prioress's *conscience* (lines 142–50) the reader responds to two different judgments — 'that love of animals is a misdirection of Christian charity' and that 'love of animals is good' (p 93). The irony compels us 'to respond to the prioress as an individual' and to exercise complex judgment (p 93).

837 Pollard, Alfred W., et al, eds. *The Works of Geoffrey Chaucer*. 1898. See 4.
On the Prioress's oath at line 120, Pollard comments that 'St Eligius refused to take an oath which King Dagobert demanded of him, so perhaps this means the Prioress did not swear at all' (p 3).

838 Power, Eileen. *Medieval English Nunneries*. New York: Macmillan, 1922; Cambridge: Cambridge University Press, 1922. Rpt London: Hafner, 1964.
In *GP* Chaucer may have depicted 'the typical prioress' of his time (1922, p 8) — an aristocratic lady, perhaps religious, certainly courtly and worldly. Much information pertinent to the Prioress and the Second Nun is included (material on the routines of nunnery life, the activities of prioresses, animals kept as convent pets, nuns in literature, and so forth).

839 ——. *Medieval People*. London: Methuen, 1924. Rpt 9 times by 1950; 10th ed. with new chapter, 1963.
The chapter 'Madame Eglantyne, Chaucer's Prioress in Real Life' (1924, pp 85–110) provides background material from episcopal registers and other

sources, integrated into an account of what Madame Eglantyne's life as a prioress would have been like.

840 Reid, T.B.W. 'Chaucer's "Ferthing of Grece."' *N&Q*, New Series 11 (1964), 373-34.

The *ferthing* of grease that the Prioress is careful not to leave in her cup (lines 133-35) has been interpreted as reflecting a misunderstanding of a French term in the *Roman de la Rose*, Chaucer's source at this point (see **835**). However, the *Clef d'amors*, an adaptation of Ovid's *Ars amatoria*, refers to spots of grease by the names of small coins. Thus 'the association between the name of a small coin and a spot of grease on the surface of a liquid was obviously in existence in French before Chaucer's time' (p 374). The question of whether he might have taken it from the *Clef d'amors* is raised.

841 Reiss, Edmund. 'Chaucer's Thematic Particulars.' 1981. See **645**.

The reference to *preestes thre* (line 164) 'demonstrates vividly Chaucer's preference of theme over narrative. Functioning immediately as part of the Prioress' entourage, the three priests are the final touch in a portrait dominated by an imitation of the courtly; they, superfluous in number, comprise the incongruous retinue of a great lady who is making what seems to be more a progress than a pilgrimage' (p 27). When Chaucer later has a single priest tell a tale, neither he nor the audience is likely to have worried about the discrepancy. The detail functions thematically in one way in *GP* and is used differently later.

842 Ridley, Florence H. *The Prioress and the Critics*. Berkeley and Los Angeles: University of California Press, 1965; London: Cambridge University Press, 1965. University of California Publications, English Studies 30.

Ridley reviews previous commentary on the Prioress, pointing out that 'critical opinion as to whether the Prioress's behavior is appropriate for a nun seems hopelessly divided, with almost as much said for it as against it' (p 18). Ridley herself finds that the Prioress's *GP* characterization is 'indeed satiric, but only mildly so' (p 14). The original Benedictine Rule was strict, but it had become relaxed by Chaucer's time, so that the Prioress represents 'no extreme departure from contemporary Benedictine regulations' (p 19). Her portrait is meant to contrast with the Monk's, which is harsher. Unlike the Monk, the Prioress is not conscious of her failings: 'She does not try to justify her too human inclinations, I think, simply because she does not know that it is necessary. The misdirection in her spiritual life is there, but she fails to recognize it because she is "ful symple," having neither intelligence nor spiritual depth' (p 25). The portrait is not written in a way that invites us to strongly condemn her; some of the details 'appear amusing' but 'do not seem designed to transform her into a monster or a villain in any way comparable to the Friar or the Pardoner' (p 26).

843 Robinson, F.N., ed. *The Works of Geoffrey Chaucer*. 1957. See **42**.
In line 164, 'there is every reason to doubt the presence of more than one priest with the Prioress. Only one is mentioned later. It is altogether improbable that she would have been attended by three' (p 655).

844 Schoeck, Richard J. 'Chaucer's Prioress: Mercy and Tender Heart.' *Bridge*, 2 (1956), 239–55. Rpt in *Chaucer Criticism, 1*, ed. Richard J. Schoeck and Jerome Taylor (Notre Dame and London: Univ. of Notre Dame Press, 1960; 10th printing 1978), pp 245–58.
In the Prioress's portrait, Chaucer employed 'superbly controlled irony and devastating tact' to 'leave shadows of doubts, several kinds of uncertainty, and some strong implications' in the audience's mind (1956, p 245). Similarly, Chaucer possessed 'a clear-eyed recognition of the inhumanity of her Tale,' but rather than condemning it openly he showed that 'anti-Semitism could be viewed through the recognizable frame of such a woman as the Prioress, one who succumbed too easily to the worldly concern with things and manners, and whose charity was too much of this world' (p 255). Chaucer's attitude toward her is 'one of understanding pity' (p 255).

845 Sherbo, Arthur. 'Chaucer's Nun's Priest Again.' *PMLA*, 64 (1949), 236–46.
The Prioress probably belongs to a larger convent than the one at Stratford. Her three priests act 'both as attendants and as bodyguards' on the journey (p 245). The Nun's Priest, as we later find out, has the physical qualities that would make him a suitable bodyguard, though not a suitable confessor. He may be 'just one of a number of priests attached to a convent,' or 'a priest hired for the duration of the pilgrimage' to augment the Prioress's entourage (p 246). A contemporary account is cited to show that the Prioress might indeed be in danger during the pilgrimage journey and that it would therefore not be unnatural for her to want three priests for protection. In reply, see **816**.

846 Shibata, Shozo. 'Tretys and Fetys — A Chaucerian Note.' *TGD*, Series 2, 17, #3 (1966), 23–6.
Not seen; listed in *A Bibliography of Publications on Medieval English Language and Literature in Japan* (Tokyo: Center for Medieval Studies, Tokyo University, 1983), p 136, #5.

847 Shikii, Kumiko. 'Chaucer No Prioresse Saiko.' [Second Thoughts on Chaucer's Prioress.] *Soundings*, 7, #7 (1981), 11–24.

Not seen; listed in *A Bibliography of Publications on Medieval English Language and Literature in Japan* (Tokyo: Center for Medieval Studies, Tokyo University, 1983), p 151, #7.

848 Shimogasa, Tokuji. 'Middle English Adverbs of Affirming.' *EEK*, 25 (1980), 13–28.
In Chaucer's usage, the adverb *sikerly* (lines 137, 154) 'has an original proper meaning of affirming. It is not a mere embellishment or line-filler, we should think' (p 23).

849 Short, Ian. 'On Bilingualism in Anglo-Norman England.' *RP*, 33 (1979–1980), 467–79.
An anecdote in Walter Map's *De Nugis Curialium* (written in 1181–1192) serves as a 'precursor' of Chaucer's comment that the Prioress spoke *Frenssh ...After the scole of Stratford atte Bowe* (lines 124–26). In this anecdote, Walter objects to the anglicized French of Marlborough spoken by the Bishop of Lincoln, calling it *Gallicum Merleburgae*, or Marlborough-French. Other examples are collected to show that beginning in the mid- or late-twelfth century, there existed a tradition of distinguishing between insular and continental French; continental French was regarded as the preferable, high-status variety.

850 Simons, Rita Dandridge. 'The Prioress's Disobedience of the Benedictine Rule.' *CLAJ*, 12 (1968), 77–83.
The Prioress's misinterpretations or rejections of the Rule are reviewed.

851 Skeat, Walter W., ed. *The Complete Works of Geoffrey Chaucer, Edited from Numerous Manuscripts.* 1894–1897. See **3**.
Analogues to swearing by St Loy (Eligius) are supplied (see line 120). Skeat records the earlier viewpoint of Hales that such an oath was virtually 'no oath at all' (vol 5, p 14) since Eligius himself refused to swear. In any case, the Prioress's oath is 'a very mild one for those times' (5:14). In line 126, Chaucer intends no disparagement of her Anglo-French dialect. He 'merely states a *fact*' about her language and would have had 'no special reason for thinking *more highly*' of the Parisian accent than of the French used in his own country (5:15). (See **788** in reply.) An abbess, it is shown, might have had as many as five priests, as well as a chaplain; the difficulty with *preestes thre* (line 164) is not so much the multiple priests themselves as how to reconcile them with the twenty-nine of line 24.

852 Smith, Fred Manning. 'Chaucer's Prioress and Criseyde.' *WVUPP*, 6 (1949), 1–11.
'The twenty-one lines describing Criseyde and the forty-five lines describing the Prioress have so much in common that we are led to a conclusion that

consciously or unconsciously Chaucer was following the portrait of Criseyde in his description of the Prioress' (p 3). The phrase *slydynge of corage* used to describe Criseyde (*TC*, V.825) may have the same implications as the term *conscience* used to describe the Prioress (lines 142, 150): both women respond to the pain of the moment. Thus the Prioress responds to hurt mice, Criseyde first to the pain of Troilus and later to that of Diomede. The similarities suggest that 'in describing the Prioress, Chaucer may still have been under Criseyde's spell' (p 11).

853 Spitzer, Leo. 'And Prestes Three (*Cant. Tales*, Prol 164).' *MLN*, 67 (1952), 502–4.

Spitzer rejects the argument of Lehmann (**811**) as having been based on a misunderstanding of the Old French examples. Their grammatical structure is different from Chaucer's and has 'no bearing at all on the Chaucer passages' (p 503). However, Spitzer here proposes that if *prestes* (line 164) is taken not as a nominative plural, but instead as a genitive singular — 'the genitive of shape and arrangement' — then the meaning of *and prestes three* is ' "and (the) priest's three" ' (p 504), or the total of three that is achieved by the priest in the group consisting of the Prioress, the Second Nun, and himself. Hence only one priest is necessary to arrive at a total of three in this line. Cf **775**.

854 Starr, Herbert W. 'Oaths in Chaucer's Poems,' *WVUPP*, 4 (September 1943), 44–63.

The Prioress's and the Host's 'standards of intensity' about oaths would differ; to the host '*Seinte Loy* would be exceedingly mild,' yet to the Prioress '*Seinte Loy* is as strong as *Goddes blood* is to the Host' (p 50).

855 Steadman, John M. 'The Prioress's Dogs and Benedictine Discipline.' *MP*, 54 (1956-1957), 1–6.

In keeping dogs, Madame Eglantyne was either violating her convent's regulations, or else its rules were laxer than at some of the stricter houses of her order. The *rosted flessh* that she fed the dogs (line 147) may have been fowl, or may have been meat covered under a general dispensation that permitted the eating of flesh, but this too 'marked a departure from the standards of the stricter monasteries' (p 2). More important is Chaucer's treatment of the Prioress's charity and mercy, which are misdirected. 'Chaucer's ironic account of the Prioress's charitable activities' towards dogs or mice is apparently 'an indirect attack on contemporary neglect of the works of *misericordia* required by monastic rule' (p 5). The Prioress resembles the Monk, evidently, in finding the monastic rule old-fashioned and restrictive. Her faults are additionally important because she holds a position of authority, being 'partly responsible for enforcing the Benedictine Rule' (p 6). By depicting a prioress who is lax about the Rule, 'Chaucer has also implied that the Rule is no longer observed, in its pristine strictness at least, by those under her' (p 6).

856 ——. ' "Hir Gretteste Ooth": The Prioress, St Eligius, and St Godebertha.' *Neophil*, 43 (1959), 49–57.

The Prioress's greatest oath was *by Seinte Loy* (line 120), who is St Eligius. However, St Eligius himself did not swear — he refused to do so when requested. Therefore, in swearing by a saint who did not swear, Madame Eglantyne 'achieved the ultimate refinement' in swearing: 'an oath by St Loy was, in effect, the mildest conceivable expletive' (p 57). Eligius was also a suitable choice since he had been mentor of St Godebertha, whom he diverted from worldly love to spiritual love, using his own ring to pledge her to Christ. 'Having converted one protegée from secular wedlock to a mystical marriage with Christ, he might well assist another in spiritualizing and refining the "Love that conquers all things" ' (p 56). St Godebertha became a Benedictine abbess, just as Madame Eglantyne is prioress of a Benedictine house. The ring that St Eligius gave St Godebertha is paralleled by the Prioress's brooch, since both objects are personal ornaments usually associated with secular love, but here consecrated to a religious purpose. However, the genuine works of charity of St Eligius 'stand in striking opposition' to the Prioress's 'parody of the works of mercy' (p 57), so that her oath by the saint emphasizes the irony of Chaucer's treatment of her charitable nature.

857 ——. 'The Prioress's Brooch and St Leonard.' *ES*, 44 (1963), 350–53.

Chaucer's Prioress is presumably the prioress of the Benedictine nunnery of St Leonard's in Middlesex. St Leonard was known for freeing prisoners from bondage; secular love was often represented as a form of bondage. The Prioress's motto, *amor vincit omnia* (line 163), can mean both 'love conquers all' and 'love binds all' (p 352), since *vincit* can be a form of *vincio* (ie, bind and fetter) as well as a form of *vinco* (conquer). Chaucer is therefore 'exploiting an analogy between literary and hagiological tradition, between the lover's figurative bondage and the physical chains and fetters from which St Leonard liberated his votaries' (p 353). Any ironic contrast that may be intended between 'the sense of her motto and the meaning of her vocation' is heightened by the opposition between St Leonard's association with freedom from bondage and 'the suggestion of bondage inherent in the word *vincit*' (p 353).

858 Van Herk, A. 'Chauceriana.' *Neophil*, 2 (1917), 292–94.

Van Herk suggests that the nun-chaplain (line 164) is the female version of the *capellani*, who are not a special group of ecclesiastics, but only the least worldly of their servants — such as might serve a bishop or abbot in his sleeping quarters ('dan minder-wereldlijke of geestelijke kamerdienaars, die tot in het slaapvertrek getuigen zijn van het gedrag van den bisschop of abt en hem dienen,' p 294). On the Friar, see **953**.

859 Wainwright, Benjamin B. 'Chaucer's Prioress Again: An Interpretive Note.' *MLN*, 48 (1933), 34–37.

According to Lowes (**815**), St Eligius is the Prioress's favorite saint (see line 120) partly because he was known for physical beauty and other secular qualities; her brooch summarizes the subtle clash between her secular and her religious inclinations. This viewpoint has been attacked by Madeleva (**821**), who associates it with an inappropriately journalistic approach. Wainwright here defends journalism: 'Chaucer, like Addison, Steele, De Quincey, and Hazlitt centuries later, was in a sense a journalist, for he closely observed and vividly reported the doings and sayings of the travelers in his famous cavalcade' (p 36). Following the direction of Lowes's interpretation, Wainwright also suggests that the Prioress's motives in going on pilgrimage were 'mixed and that she succeeded in hiding the less lofty ones from herself' (p 36). As for St Eligius, 'unwittingly the nun admired the superb physique and handsome face of this versatile and attractive saint,' for whom 'unconsciously she had a very human affection' (p 36). Such an interpretation does not belittle the Prioress, 'but, on the contrary, by humanizing her it makes her dedication to the religious life more significant and perhaps more heroic' (p 37).

860 Ward, H. Snowden, and C.M.B. Ward. *The Canterbury Pilgrimages*. 1904. See **491**.

The Prioress's oath (line 120) may not be an oath at all, 'but rather an exclamation directed to her horse,' for horses would be urged on by the cry of 'Eloy!' since St Eloy was the patron of mule-drivers and horsemen (p 189).

861 Weissman, Hope Phyllis. 'Antifeminism and Chaucer's Characterization of Women.' In *Geoffrey Chaucer, A Collection of Original Articles*. Ed. George D. Economou. New York: McGraw-Hill, 1975. Contemporary Studies in Literature. Pp 93–110.

In his characterizations of the Prioress and the Wife, 'Chaucer confronts his audience with the New and Old Women in the form of living images' in order to emphasize 'the difficulty of self-realization in an environment which presses such images on human beings' (p 104). The Prioress, who is *nat undergrowe* (line 136), has a nature 'too big to be forced into images'; although she thinks, in her 'self-constriction,' that she is conforming to the

image of the New Woman as Mary, instead she is conforming to the image
of the courtly lady (p 104). On the Wife, see also **1169**.

862 Wentworth, Clarence L. 'The Prioress's Oath.' *RomR*, 27 (1936), 268–69.
The Prioress swears by St Loy (see line 120). St Loy was, in general, a
suitable saint for aristocratic devotees, since 'he had maintained the dignity and honors of his position, yet in secret he had practiced penance'
by wearing a hair shirt (p 269). However, St Loy was not really a wholly
suitable model for those who had chosen the religious life. The Prioress,
'vowed to a life of mortifications, used the example of the Saint to justify
her for the indulgence in little luxuries, trivial and harmless in themselves,
but contrary to the spirit of her religious vows' (p 269).

863 Witte, Stephen P. '*Muscipula Diaboli* and Chaucer's Portrait of the Prioress.' *PLL*, 13 (1977), 227–37.
The Prioress's charity is expressed in terms of mice (lines 143–5). Mice
were associated with drunkenness, which, as a form of gluttony, is in opposition to charity. In addition, the Augustinian metaphor of *muscipula
diaboli*, in which the cross of the Lord was seen as the devil's mousetrap,
would probably have been familiar to Chaucer, either through Augustine's
writings themselves or through the *Sentences* of Peter Lombard. Chaucer's
audience may well have seen the Prioress 'as manipulated, perhaps will-
ingly, in her sentiments and actions by Satan. If this is the case, then
the portrait Chaucer gives us of Madame Eglantyne must be regarded as
fraught, indeed, with condemning satire' (p 237).

864 Wood, Chauncey. 'Chaucer's Use of Signs in his Portrait of the Prioress.'
In *Signs and Symbols in Chaucer's Poetry*. Ed. John P. Hermann and John
J. Burke, Jr. University, AL: University of Alabama Press, 1981. Pp 81–
101.
'In the portrait of the Prioress there are signs that are apparently misunderstood, that are given in an unexpected order, unexpectedly qualified,
inaccurately or inadequately defined, or left out altogether in spite of high
expectations' (p 83). Wood examines 'this process of manipulation of the
signs and of the reader's responses' (p 83). Line 151, for example, which
mentions the Prioress's pleated wimple, combines two techniques: 'the inappropriate sign, a pleated as opposed to a plain wimple, and the unexpected
qualification' about the seemliness of the pleating (p 84). The reiteration of
the word *ful* (lines 119, 122, 123, 124, etc) 'overpraises the Prioress and creates a subtle and very entertaining irony' (p 90). Wood comments also on
the terms *conscience* (lines 142, 150), *reverence* (line 141), and *contrefete*
(line 139). The references to the Prioress's large forehead and considerable size imply corpulence, in contrast to the expectation that a nun would

be thin as a sign of spirituality. Her brooch 'seems surely to be worn in violation of precept' and, when we visualize the gold brooch attached to a green-and-coral rosary, the effect 'is to transform the normally spiritual into something that makes a primarily aesthetic appeal' (p 97). In general, 'every sign in the portrait of the Prioress points to her worldliness — the very antithesis of the essence of monasticism. And, as a nun who wants to be a fashionable lady she ends up being neither. She is nothing' (p 100). The affection felt towards her by modern critics is misguided, for Chaucer's goal in this portrait 'was not to arouse our affection but rather to inspire us in medieval fashion to "laugh her to scorn" ' (p 101).

865 Woolf, Virginia. *The Common Reader* [First Series]. New York: Harcourt, Brace 1925. 2nd ed. 1925; new ed. 1929. Rpt 1932, 1935.
Chaucer's characters demonstrate solidity, conviction, and an 'immense variety' that nevertheless shows, 'persisting underneath, one consistent type' (1929, p 26). Woolf cites lines 151–56 to illustrate Chaucer's concept of a young woman. This concept of personality 'has a stability which is only to be found where the poet has made up his mind about young women, of course, but also about the world they live in, its end, its nature, and his own crafts and technique, so that his mind is free to apply its force fully to its object' (p 27).

❧ Part 10: The Monk

See the Introduction, p xxxiv above, for a brief summary of criticism on the Monk, and see the Index for further references.

866 Beichner, Paul E., C.S.C. 'Daun Piers, Monk and Business Administrator.' *Spec*, 34 (1959), 611–19. Rpt in *Chaucer Criticism*, 1, ed. Richard J. Schoeck and Jerome Taylor (Notre Dame and London: University of Notre Dame Press, 1960; 10th printing 1978), pp 52–62.

Chaucer's Monk should be seen as a designated official of his monastery, not as a 'caustic caricature' (1959, p 619) of an ideal. Having decided to include a monastic character, Chaucer may have chosen an outrider because such a person would be more dramatically functional than, for example, a cloisterer, who 'would have been insipid fare' (p 611), or an abbot, who would have outranked all the others unless an earl or count were also included. An outrider was a monastic officer charged with supervising the house's external manors. Thus in being outside his monastery the Monk is obeying, not defying, his obligations. He is said to be a *kepere* of a cell (line 172), which may indicate that he is responsible for its property — not (as is usually thought) that he is a prior, responsible for spiritual leadership. In the Monk's worldly show, which includes his fine hunting-horse, Chaucer shows that 'he has succumbed to the occupational disease of those religious who deal with the worldly — worldliness' (p 619) and that he has acquired expensive tastes, as many a modern business administrator does. Nevertheless, he is a gentleman and a successful man of high position, not simply a negative example showing the abuses of monastic discipline.

867 Berndt, David E. 'Monastic *Acedia* and Chaucer's Characterization of Daun Piers.' *SP*, 68 (1971), 435–50.

The Monk's philosophical limitations have often been pointed out, but 'a more balanced interpretation' (p 436) of his condition would include the psychological aspects of *acedia* or sloth, a vice particularly identified with monks. 'Inordinate wandering,' such as the Monk exemplifies, 'is often mentioned as a characteristic effect of *acedia*' (p 437), as is an unwillingness to perform labor, along with a disinclination to study. The Monk himself argues that 'he is a "prikasour" *because* he cannot stand the monotony of the cell' (p 440). He is prone to disobedience and anger, which are among the effects of *acedia* identified in medieval sources. The Monk of *GP* and the Monk of the subsequent *MkT* section both share traits of *acedia*; the characterization is a unified one.

868 Boitani, Piero. *English Medieval Narrative in the Thirteenth and Four-teenth Centuries.* Trans. Joan Krakover Hall. Cambridge: Cambridge University Press, 1982.
Chaucer conveys information about pilgrims such as the Monk in an am-biguous way, so that as we react to the details he supplies we repeatedly wonder whether our assessments are correct. 'Thus the Monk, while he is a type, acquires the depth of a real individual through the reactions that Chaucer's presentation provokes in the reader. The key to Chaucer's mime-sis is, in short, a fiction in which the mimetic function is shifted from the object of the description (the pilgrim) to the subject of its perception (the reader)' (p 243).

869 Bressie, Ramona. ' "A governour Wily and Wis." ' *MLN*, 54 (1939), 477–90.
Bressie suggests, as a historical model for the Monk, the only hunting monk on record: William de Cloune, abbot of Leicester from 1345 to 1378, who was well known to Edward III and John of Gaunt. The information known about Cloune or his abbey corresponds to the *GP* portrait of the Monk. The Chapter of the Augustinian order, meeting at Leicester in 1346, passed a statute that hunting dogs (see line 190) should not be kept — but that if they were, they should not eat the food meant for the poor. By a papal dispensation during Cloune's time the Leicester monks were allowed to wear boots (line 203), which were normally forbidden. Like the Monk, Cloune evidently 'heeld after the new world' (line 176): in his time the abbey was 'notoriously Lollard' (p 484) and practiced a liberal, rather than a restrictive, interpretation of the Augustinian precepts. A symbol similar to the Monk's love-knot (line 195) appears in a medieval window from Leicester; it is possible that 'the Monk's pin may imply an interest in some religious fraternity such as the Corpus Christi guild at Leicester' (p 488). The abbey might have had its own swans. Chaucer may imply (line 206) 'that the Monk was fond of high festivities' (p 488), such as those at which roast swan would be served, and that he was often invited.

However, though the Monk of *GP* seems to be of Cloune's era, the more conventional Monk shown later in the *CT* suggests instead the attitude of Leicester abbey during the reign of Richard II, when the abbey reverted to the older ways that Cloune had let pass. If Chaucer had written the *GP* portrait as a satire on Cloune, and if the usual assumption of a date of 1387 or later for *GP* is correct, then the time had passed when such a satire would be best appreciated. Nevertheless, 'at court and in the household of Lancaster, for those who had hunted with the abbot' (p 490), Chaucer's Monk might recall Cloune. For a reply, see Tatlock, **907**, and, in defense, Bressie, **870**.

870 ——. 'Chaucer's Monk Again.' *MLN*, 56 (1941), 161–62.
In reply to comments by Tatlock (**907**), in which Bressie's earlier article (**869**) was criticized, Bressie here disputes Tatlock's association of the Monk with Westminster Abbey, states that Tatlock misrepresented her own thesis, and finds it more likely that the Monk was Augustinian than Benedictine.

871 Brown, Joella Owens. 'Chaucer's Daun Piers: One Monk or Two?' *Crit*, 6 (1964), 44–52.
Despite the apparent contrasts between the Monk's characterization in *GP* and in his own prologue and tale, he is being characterized consistently. The *GP* traits that show him to be preoccupied with food and hunting, for example, reappear in his tale.

872 Crawford, S.J. 'Chaucer and St Augustine.' *TLS*, November 13, 1930, p 942.
The text 'that seith that hunters beth nat hooly men' (line 178) is from Augustine, *De Civitate Dei*, 16:4. *GP* says that the Monk, in hunting, is breaking St Austin's rule; this passage in Augustine explains why hunters are not thought to be holy.

873 Delasanta, Rodney. 'Chaucer's General Prologue.' *Expl*, 38 (1979–1980), 39–40.
In lines 198–200, Chaucer refers to the Monk's shiny bald head and shiny face. This passage involves a Biblical parody. In Matthew 6:16–18, Jesus says that we should not fast as the hypocritical Pharisees do: they make a point of letting everyone know that they are fasting by disfiguring their faces and appearing to be sad, while the truly pious manner of fasting does not draw attention to itself. In fact, the fasting person is told to 'anoint thy head, and wash thy face' and thus to conceal the fact of fasting. 'Chaucer describes the Monk as contemptuous of fasting while remaining unwittingly faithful to the outward form of Jesus's imperative' (p 40), since the Monk's love of fine food produces the sweat and oil that make his skin shine. Thus 'the ointment of holiness has become the excreta of gluttony'

in this 'militantly carnal man for whom even the fast of the Pharisee is an unreachable ideal' (p 40).

874 Derocquigny, J. 'Notes sur Chaucer.' 1910. See **595**.

A parallel to the jingling bridle of lines 169–70 is found in *Huon de Bordeaux*. In line 172, *kepere of the celle* may mean not the head of an annex to the monastery, as it is usually understood, but instead simply the cellarer, the person in charge of store-houses or store-rooms. The Host seems to make this assumption when he later remarks, in the prologue to *MkT*, that the Monk must be an officer, a sexton, or a cellarer. Cf Farina, **879**.

875 Donovan, Mortimer J. 'Three Notes on Chaucerian Marine Life.' *PQ*, 31 (1952), 439–41.

The Monk dismisses the viewpoint that a *reccheless* monk (line 179) is like a fish out of water by declaring that text to be not worth an *oystre* (line 182). The word *oyster* may have been chosen as a convenient rhyme for *cloister* (line 181; the rhyme-pair also occurs in the *SumT*), but it has other values. Oysters, as a common item in a meatless diet, could imply 'a trifle or paltry nothing' (p 440). In addition, 'the monk may be recalling that a medieval monk out of his cloister is like an oyster with its shell open' (p 440) — unprotected and liable to be eaten. A passage from Alexander Neckam explains the allegory of the open-shelled oyster and the crab that preys upon it.

876 Eichler, Albert. 'Zu Chaucer, *Canterbury Tales*, *General Prologue*, l. 207.' *ESt*, 70 (1935-1936), 102–5.

The Monk's palfrey is said to be as brown as a berry — a rather puzzling (though commonplace) comparison, since most berries are not brown. Eichler considers this problem in some detail, proposing that it is the hawberry that is meant ('So ist denn mit einiger Sicherheit die Hagebutte als die "Beere" zu verstehen,' p 105), since as it ripens this berry shows brownish colors. He also points out that the colors brown and red seem to overlap in other natural contexts — as when someone refers to a 'red' cow, the color of which is reddish brown.

877 Emerson, Oliver Farrar. 'Some of Chaucer's Lines on the Monk.' *MP*, 1 (1903-1904), 105–15.

The text which the Monk rejects in lines 177–78 (the authority claiming that hunters are not holy men) is likely to have been a passage in the *Decretum* of Gratian, a work well known in Chaucer's time. In related sources 'the hunter is made a type of the devil and this is a common conception of medieval writers' (p 109). As for the disputed word *reccheless* (line 179), both Old English and Middle English examples show that it is a quite satisfactory term: it implies someone who neglects or violates duty, a transgressor. The reading should not be emended.

878 ——. 'Chaucer and Medieval Hunting.' 1922. See **741**.

In the Monk's portrait, *prikasour* (line 188) means a hunter, especially a hunter of the hare. Contemporary custom is reflected here, for the hare was highly valued as a game animal and greyhounds were used for hunting it (line 190).

879 Farina, Peter M. 'Two Notes on Chaucer.' *LangQ*, 10, 3–4 (1972), 23–26.

Farina proposes that line 172 means that the Monk was his monastery's cellarer, ie, the keeper of 'the store-room within the monastic walls' (p 23). Cf Deroquigny, **874**.

880 Fleming, John V. 'Daun Piers and Dom Pier: Waterless Fish and Unholy Hunters.' *ChauR*, 15 (1980-1981), 287–94.

The three main ideas — unholy hunters, cloisterless monks, and waterless fish — that Chaucer associates with each other in lines 177–82 are found, associated together, in the prologue to Peter Damian's *De divina omnipotentia*. Chaucer may have known this text, and by naming his monk Piers he may have been 'amusing himself and at least some of his readers by drawing attention through daun Piers to Dom Pier, an earlier and somewhat more reputable authority on "modern" monasticism' (p 292). Peter Damian, faced with the administrative responsibilities and worldly concerns of a bishop's appointment, resigned it to return to monastic solitude. Dante, in *Paradiso* 21.118–20 and 127–35, 'introduces Peter Damian precisely as a rebuke to "modern" churchmen' (p 292). Chaucer may have been following Dante's lead, for nearly all of Dante's imagery here reappears in the Monk's portrait — including the detail that Chaucer calls the Monk's horse a palfrey (line 207), a term that occurs in the Dante passage but is not Chaucer's typical word for a horse.

881 Garbáty, Thomas Jay. 'The Monk and the *Merchant's Tale*: An Aspect of Chaucer's Building Process in the *Canterbury Tales*.' *MP*, 67 (1969-1970), 18–24.

Garbáty develops Manly's brief suggestion (**35**) that the Monk was the original teller of *MerT*. This hypothesis includes a reading of the Monk's GP portrait in terms of sexual puns: *venerie* (line 166), *prikyng* (line 191), *pulled hen* (line 177), and *love-knotte* (line 197). The parallelism between the Prioress's and the Monk's portraits is pointed out: 'Chaucer shows that the Prioresse and the Monk are the female and male counterparts of the same religious type' (p 19). Thus 'where the Prioresse shows womanly weaknesses, the Monk exhibits very manly foibles' (p 19). Both portraits are part of a gradation of anti-clerical satire, based partly on sexual themes, that begins with the Prioress and extends — except for the Parson — through the Summoner. The Monk, 'where he fails as a fisher of men, is more successful as a hunter of frailer and more timid game' (p 20).

His personality in *GP* would have made him a suitable teller of the tale subsequently assigned to the Merchant.

882 Gillmeister, Heiner. 'Chaucers Mönch und die "Reule of Seint Maure or of Seint Beneit." ' *NM*, 69 (1968), 222–32.

The portrait of the Monk involves subtle but strong criticism through allusions to the Benedictine Rule. Oysters were included in monastic menus; the *pulled hen* of line 177 also represents a permitted food, since the Rule allowed the eating of fowl. Thus the Monk values the ascetic text (line 177) as hardly worth an ordinary meal. The implication of his loving swan 'best of any roost' (line 206) is that he probably ate roasted meats also and that his preference for swan comes from personal taste rather than respect for the Rule. An edict at the beginning of the fourteenth century had relaxed the regulation against monks' eating meat, but Chaucer is adhering to the Rule as stated and is more holy than the pope ('päpstlicher als der Papst,' p 225). The monk's steaming cranium (line 202) suggests the smoke of hell-fire. This highly metaphoric portrait would have vexed those who understood its allusions, principally the Benedictines themselves. Perhaps Chaucer's decision not to pursue this characterization, but later to make the Monk a moralizing tragedy-teller instead, was influenced by a violent response to the *GP* portrait from some powerful monk who felt himself personally attacked ('Vielleicht verdanken wir es einer mehr oder weniger heftigen Reaktion vonseiten des Ordens, oder gar eines mächtigen Ordensherrn, der sich persönlich angegriffen fühlte, dass der Dichter die im Allgemeinen Prolog einmal eingeschlagene Richtung nicht weiterverfolgt,' p 232).

883 Grennen, Joseph E. 'Chaucerian Portraiture: Medicine and the Monk.' *NM*, 69 (1968), 569–74.

The impression of psychological plausibility in Chaucer's portraits need not derive from historical models for his pilgrims, but can come from the ideas 'found in such sources as physiognomies, astrological manuals, and medical treatises' (p 570). (Much of this article is virtually identical with Grennen, **884**.)

884 ——. 'Chaucer's Monk: Baldness, Venery, and Embonpoint.' *AN&Q*, 6 (1968), 83–85.

The Monk's baldness suggests sexual activity — according to Pliny, prior to performing the works of Venus nobody becomes bald — as does the phrase that he 'lovede venerie' (line 166). In Latin treatises the word *venus* and its inflected forms regularly refer to sexual intercourse. The Monk's shiny or oily face and his plumpness (lines 199–200) should be read in the context of medical discussions of obesity, while his steaming head may refer to the medical theory that the head 'receives the vapors arising from decomposing food' (p 84). In refusing to study (though mental work was recommended for weight reduction) and in preferring a diet of rich foods, the Monk is rejecting the treatment that would be good for his health. He represents 'a monstrous distortion of a regimen of health' (p 85) and 'a kind of medical case history of a pampered body grown to obesity' (p 84). (Much of this article is virtually identical with Grennen, **883**.)

885 Hatton, Thomas J. 'Chaunticleer and the Monk.' *PLL*, 3 (Supplement, special issue ed. by John Gardner and Nicholas Joose, Summer 1967), 31–39.

The Monk is depicted as a false version of a knight. 'He has all the pleasures of temporal lordship without any of its responsibilities' (p 34). Where the Knight serves the world in battle and loves chivalric ideals, the Monk 'loves only himself' (p 34). The many echoes of the Monk's *GP* portrait in *NPT* function to link the Monk's spiritual condition to Chaunticler's situation: as Chaunticler finally saved himself, so the Monk too could still escape tragedy if he would 'recognize his peril' (p 39) and return to the principles that he ought to exemplify.

886 Hinckley, Henry Barrett. 'Chauceriana.' 1916–1917. See **724**.

The phrase *in good poynt* (line 200) appears also in the romance *Sir Ferumbras*.

887 Knowles, Dom David. *The Religious Orders in England, II: The End of the Middle Ages*. Cambridge: Cambridge University Press, 1955.

What is noticeable about Chaucer's portraits of the Monk and Friar, in contrast to clerical portraits by Wycliffe and Langland, is his 'moderation of tone' (p 111), yet 'the very absence of moral indignation serves only to deepen the melancholy impression given by his devastating satire' (p 112). The 'Monk and the Friar embody all the self-indulgence and versatile hypocrisy of their respective classes' (p 112). On the resemblance of the Monk to William Cloune or Clown (see Bressie, **869**), it is 'next to unthinkable that Chaucer, with his connexions with the Court circle, should not have known of Abbot Clown and his hunting, while it is even more inconceivable that his courtly readers, when they heard the lines of the *Prologue*, should not have been reminded of the prowess of the late abbot of Leicester' (p 366). The influence of literary sources on the portrait, however, 'must not be forgotten' (p 366).

On the Friar, see **933**.

888 Kruisinga, E. 'A New Chaucer Word.' *Athenaeum*, No 3918, November 29, 1902, pp 722–23.

Line 179 of *GP* reads 'Ne that a monk whan he is recchelees' (variant, 'cloysterlees'). Kruisinga argues that neither *recchelees* nor *cloysterlees* is correct. Since line 181 gives the explanation 'This is to seyn, a monk out of his cloystre,' we must discard *cloysterlees*, a word for which such an explanation would be superfluous. Since *recchelees* does not mean 'out of his cloystre,' that word is not suitable either. What apparently happened is that the correct reading, *reulelees*, was misread as *recchelees* by a scribe. 'It is true that "reulelees" does not occur in any M.E. text, but that is an argument in its favour, for if it had been common Chaucer would not have thought it necessary to explain it' (p 723).

889 Kuhl, E.P. 'Chaucer's Monk.' *MLN*, 55 (1940), 480.
Replying to two statements in Tatlock's article on the Monk (see 907), Kuhl argues that 1) the term *monk* could indeed be applied to an Augustinian canon; and that 2) Edward the Confessor, whose life the Monk says he can recount, was indeed a prominent saint throughout fourteenth-century England (not only or primarily at Westminster, as Tatlock suggested). In reply, see Tatlock, 908.

890 Lepley, Douglas Lee. *The Philosophic and Artistic Purposes of Chaucer's Monk's Tale*. Lehigh University Dissertation. 1978. See also *DAI*, 39 (1978), 1539-A.
Lepley's thesis, 'that the *Monk's Tale* is a respectable narrative,' requires a reconsideration of 'the appropriateness of this tale to the Monk.' His 'accomplishments and education show that he is worthy of a serious tale' [from *DAI*; diss not seen].

891 Lumiansky, R.M. *Of Sondry Folk: The Dramatic Principle in the Canterbury Tales*. 1955. See 348.
Some of the responsibility for the Monk's worldliness 'must rest upon the institution, the Church, which allotted to an individual who presumably had decided to withdraw from the world work which necessitated his taking an active part in the business of that world' (p 98). In the portrait 'no comment occurs here to indicate that he is licentious or otherwise guilty of sexual infractions of his rules' (p 98).

892 ——. 'Two Notes on the Canterbury Tales.' In *Studies in Language and Literature in Honour of Margaret Schlauch*. Ed. Mieczysław Brahmer, Stanisław Helsztyński, and Julian Krzyżanowski. Warsaw: PWN-Polish Scientific Publishers, 1966. Pp 227–32. Rpt New York: Russell & Russell, 1971.
In the explanation of the widow's eating habits at the beginning of *NPT*, Chaucer has created 'a dietary lecture' for the Monk (1966, p 230), whose *GP* portrait shows his concern for food — both at meals and in metaphor (he refers to a plucked hen and to an oyster; see lines 177, 182). Thus the Priest 'is commenting on the Monk's folly in his love of food' (p 232). See also 1055.

893 Macaulay, G.C. 'Notes on Chaucer.' *MLR*, 4 (1908), 14–19.
Macaulay defends the reading *recchelees* (line 179), with the meaning 'careless' or 'regardless of duty or obligation' (p 14). Examples are cited from *Piers Plowman* and the Rule of St Benet. See also **1187**.

894 Manly, John M., and Edith Rickert, eds. *The Text of the Canterbury Tales Studied on the Basis of All Known Manuscripts.* 1940. See **49**.
On line 179, 'the correctness of "recchelees" is not open even to suspicion' (vol 3, p 423).

895 Mann, Jill. *Chaucer and Medieval Estates Satire.* 1973. See **363**.
Many of the traits associated with the Monk—his gluttony, fine clothing and boots, horses and dogs, love of hunting, etc.—are traditional in descriptitons of clerics. However, Chaucer's 'method is frequently to remind us of traditional satire while discouraging or circumventing the moral judgements it aimed to elicit. And one way in which Chaucer circumvents moral judgement is to show us the Monk from his own point of view' (p 27). An effect of realism is thereby achieved. 'In Chaucer's portrait, the images are sensuously attractive, and faulty behaviour is presented from the point of view of its perpetrator, or can only be inferred from hints. And thus we have a sense of depth, of contradictory responses to the Monk, of not knowing him fully, of his having views of his own .... We become convinced that he does not exist simply on the level of theoretical moralizing ("what he ought to be" set against "what he is") but on the plane of real existence' (p 37).

896 Maynard, Theodore. 'Chaucer's Monk.' *Month* (London), February 1935, 165–68.
Although Chaucer's Monk is depicted in *GP* as a person preoccupied with hunting and good living, we later discover that he has quite a collection of literary materials in his cell. It is possible to see in the Monk's situation a 'personal tragedy' (p 166). Perhaps the Monk, when he was a young novice, was 'full of an enthusiasm for something besides horses and hounds and fat roasted swans' (p 168). It was evidently some time ago that the Monk was a serious student, but he remembers his Boethius, and despite his 'surrender to ease' he perhaps still venerates some teacher who served as 'an exemplar of Benedictine learning' (p 168).

897 Olsson, Kurt. 'Grammar, Manhood, and Tears: Chaucer's Monk.' *MP*, 76 (1978–1979), 1–17.
Olsson defends 'the coherence of Chaucer's entire presentation of daun Piers' (p 1). Details of the *GP* portrait are analyzed in terms of the personality later shown by the Monk in his prologue and tale. The Monk's hunting, for example, reflects the Christian imagery of the sacred hunt. 'The Monk is obviously excluded from this chase' (p 5). However, his

kind of hunting is 'congruous with the show of erudition, pedantry, and idle curiosity' in his tale's introduction, in view of Augustine's equation of attention to hare-hunting with *curiositas* or 'lust of the eyes' for worldly knowledge, including literary erudition (p 6).

898 Oruch, Jack B. 'Chaucer's Worldly Monk.' *Crit*, 8 (1966), 280–88.
The Monk's personality as portrayed in *GP* is consistent with his later tale. The tale's implication that people should 'avoid seeking positions of great authority' fits his own position, for he himself keeps 'a middle way in a minor clerical post,' where he is safe from women's deceits and can enjoy luxuries but need not fear the wheel of Fortune (p 288).

899 Peter, John. *Complaint and Satire in Early English Literature*. London: Oxford University Press, 1956.
Brief discussions of Chaucerian satire are included in this general study. The Monk's portrait is compared with Langland's depiction of Sloth in *Piers Plowman*. Langland 'presents a caricature, not a person,' but since the Monk 'is conceived in terms that allow for some of the intricacy of real life there is no necessity for Chaucer to simplify or stylize his appearance' (p 7).

900 Pollard, Alfred W., et al, eds. *The Works of Geoffrey Chaucer*. 1898. See 4.
On line 179, Pollard comments that neither reading, *reccheless* nor *cloysterles*, 'is satisfactory' (p 3).

901 Prins, A.A. 'Two Notes to the Prologue of Chaucer's Canterbury Tales.' 1949. See **732**.
Lines 173–76 in the Monk's portrait, whose structure and meaning have been somewhat difficult to explain, might be paraphrased as follows: 'The rule of St Maur or of St Benet, being somewhat old and strict (narrow), this same monk let old people (= thynges) go through, or, observe (= pace)' — that is, he 'left it for the monks of former times or perhaps also for old-fashioned monks in his own day' (p 84). The Monk himself, however, *heeld ... the space* (line 176) in the sense of taking 'the spacious world for his province, in accordance with more "modern" conceptions' (p 84). So interpreted, the passage involves an antithesis between the cloister and the 'space' of the wider world.

902 ——. [Reply to Visser.] *ES*, 30 (1949), 133–34.
In a brief note responding to Visser (see **910**), who was himself replying to an earlier article by Prins (see **901**), Prins here rejects Visser's interpretation of *pace* and Visser's proposed reading of lines 173–76.

903 Reiss, Edmund. 'The Symbolic Surface of the *Canterbury Tales*: The Monk's Portrait.' *ChauR*, 2 (1967–1968), 254–72; continued in *ChauR*,

3 (1968–1969), 12–28.

The Monk's portrait involves many symbolic references that identify his inner character. The term *venerie* (line 166) has sexual implications, as do *prikyng* and hunting the hare (line 191). The *space* (line 176) sought by the Monk suggests the spaciousness of this world. His clothing indicates both worldliness and sexuality; his pin recalls the Prioress's. He shines because he is 'exceptionally fleshy, sweaty, and greasy' (p 268), with the word *enoynt* (line 199) ironically referring to blessing or ordination. His oily face and burning eyes imply his overheated inner state; the *forneys* (line 202) also implies 'the punishment his sins are inflicting on him' (p 270). He represents the vices of *accidia*, *tristitia*, and especially pride. His eyes, prominent and rolling, represent 'evil and depravity of all kinds' (p 13). The swan that is his favorite roast (line 206) represents himself. Swans were associated with deceptive beauty and also with death-songs; the Monk too has an apparently healthy and attractive exterior but an unattractive interior personality, and his tale concerns death. As for his horse, the homophonic similarity between *bery* (line 207) and words for 'bier' (p 23) implies death, and the phrase *broun as a bery* is used by Chaucer 'to describe figures associated with the easy worldly life, a life that is false' (p 25). On the human level the Monk may 'nudge us into chuckling at his flaws,' but on the level of 'the pilgrimage from Babylon to Jerusalem' he is seen instead as a failure, a man whose 'underlying sinfulness glares forth as something monstrous and demonic' (p 27).

904 Rowland, Beryl. 'The Horse and Rider Figure in Chaucer's Works.' *UTQ*, 35 (1965–1966), 246–59.

The horse and rider image was traditionally interpreted to equate 'the horse with the body or with Woman, the evil repository of sex; the rider is the soul or Man' (p 246). Narratives of ghostly mounted huntsmen, of riders into hell, etc, are recurrent. The Monk's *prikyng* (line 191) may have sexual implications. The remark that the Monk is not pale like a ghost may reflect 'the tortured spirit in the hell-hunt which the Monk must ultimately become' (p 250).

905 Sequeira, Isaac. 'Clerical Satire in the Portrait of the Monk and the Prologue to *The Monk's Tale*.' In *Literary Studies: Homage to Dr. A. Sivaramasubramonia Aiyer*. Ed. K.P.K. Menon, M. Manuel, and K.A. Paniker. Trivandrum: Dr. A. Sivaramasubramonia Aiyer Memorial Committee, 1973. Pp 34–43.

The Monk's deviation from the monastic ideal is reviewed under seven headings: claustration, hunting, the Rule of St Benedict, monastic study, poverty, asceticism, and celibacy. It is clear that 'the Monk is in conscious and deliberate conflict with his monastic vows, and his profession' (p 43).

906 Skeat, Walter W., ed. *The Complete Works of Geoffrey Chaucer, Edited from Numerous Manuscripts.* 1894–1897. See **3**.

At line 179, *cloisterlees* is the preferable reading, rather than *recchelees*. Since *cloisterlees* is a coined word, 'Chaucer goes on to explain it in line 181' (vol 5, p 22).

907 Tatlock, John S.P. 'Chaucer's Monk.' *MLN*, 55 (1940), 350–54.

'Chaucer's Pilgrims are mostly vivid types' (p 350). Although Chaucer had a 'deep regard for the concrete' (p 350), the portraits do not primarily depict specific individuals. Certain traits may well have been drawn from people Chaucer knew, but 'the suggestion that The So-and-So *is* Such-and-Such would be almost always unprovable and also too exact' (p 350). The Monk, like the Friar, 'seems generic, not specialized' (p 351). He belongs to an important Benedictine house (though *GP* does not indicate which type); he is physically attractive; 'without ridicule he is also worldly' in garments and interests (p 351). But 'this is essentially all' (p 351). Chaucer 'really esteemed the man' (p 351), rather than regarding him with sarcasm. When the Monk speaks later he is 'substantially the same' (p 351). His mention of St Edward may suggest a connection with the Benedictine abbey of Westminster, where St Edward was prominently revered. As for the proposal of Bressie (see **869**) that the Monk was modelled on William de Cloune, the points of resemblance — that both were notable hunters of hares, were known to the court, and belonged to prosperous houses — are not unique; 'there were many such monks' (p 354). And if 'we should unwisely seek a single prototype for a Benedictine prior we need not accept an abbot of Augustinian canons' (p 354). In reply, see Kuhl, **889**. Cf **908**.

908 ——. 'Is Chaucer's Monk a Monk?' *MLN*, 56 (1941), 80.

Tatlock here defends 1) his earlier distinction (**907**) between a monk and a canon, and 2) his characterization of Edward the Confessor as 'not a specially prominent saint in the fourteenth century,' against the attack on these points made by Kuhl (**889**).

909 Ussery, Huling E. 'The Status of Chaucer's Monk: Clerical, Official, Social, and Moral.' *TSE*, 17 (1969), 1–30.

The Monk is probably a Benedictine. As *kepere of the celle* (line 172), he is likely to be in charge of an outlying house; he may or may not be a prior; in either case, he is responsible both for the administration of the property and for the spiritual welfare of the monks and lay persons in his authority. His designation as an *outridere* (line 166) does not mean that he fills that specific office, for no such office seems to have existed. In a general sense the term refers descriptively to any monk who rides out on business, and pejoratively to monks who roam. In this case 'the label referring to the Monk is primarily, though not entirely, a pejorative use of the general sense' (p 24). There should be no comma after *outridere*, since the meaning of the line is ' "A cloisterless monk who loved the hunt" ' (p 25). His titles *lord* and *prelaat* 'place him relatively high on the social scale' (p 29). The Monk is qualified for an abbacy, and might become an abbot. The portrait is 'essentially realistic' as well as 'ironic' (p 30). Although we are indeed shown the Monk's contrasts to the monastic ideal, it is not likely, 'reformers aside, that contemporary opinion would severely condemn him' (p 30). Chaucer's statement of approval of the Monk is usually taken as ironic, yet 'we are troubled by a faint doubt: perhaps Chaucer really did mean what he said. We feel that he liked the Monk, and we may well like him ourselves, as we like someone whose weaknesses we know well' (p 30). This mixed reaction is a tribute to 'the ring of truth in the description,' for 'when the eye penetrates into the heart of the matter, it discovers in the real an essential ambiguity' (p 30). Cf **487**.

910 Visser, F. Th. 'Chaucer's *This ilke monk leet olde thynges pace.*' *ES*, 30 (1949), 133.
Commenting on the interpretation of Prins (**901**), Visser proposes that *leet* (line 175) means 'to regard as, to reconsider.' The passage as a whole (lines 173–75) means that 'This monk regarded the rule of St Maur or of St Benet as a precept of old-fashioned people,' with *pace* meaning 'precept' and *things* regarded as a genitive plural meaning 'people's.' (For Prins's further reply, see **902**.)

911 Wailes, Stephen L. 'The Hunt of the Hare in "Das Häslein." ' *Seminar*, 5 (1969), 92–101.
The favorite sport of Chaucer's Monk, hunting the hare (lines 191–2), is to be understood in sexual terms. Similarly, in 'Das Häslein,' a German fabliau from the late thirteenth or early fourteenth century (as well as in other texts), the hare functions as a sexual symbol. This usage is well attested in classical and medieval sources.

912 White, Robert B., Jr. 'Chaucer's Daun Piers and the Rule of St Benedict: The Failure of an Ideal.' *JEGP*, 70 (1971), 13–30.
White's review of previous studies shows that the Monk 'has not been subjected to extensive adverse criticism' (p 13), yet he exemplifies 'the satiric consummation of all possible monastic faults' (p 15). The Monk violates all the essential requirements of Benedictine monasticism as established in the Rule and other sources: obedience, poverty, celibacy, labor, claustration, restricted diet, propertylessness. His description in *GP* is sometimes subtle — particularly in discussing his sexuality, where Chaucer uses indirect tactics, such as a series of sexual puns, to come 'as close as discretion will allow' (p 29). Yet the meaning is clear enough, as Harry Bailly's sexual references in the prologue to *MkT* show. The Monk's guilt is 'compounded

by the fact that it is conscious and deliberate' (p 29), for he knows the obligations that he chooses to ignore. Furthermore, as prior of an outlying cell he is responsible for guiding his brethren there, and his poor example is all the more damaging. He is thus not merely a typical monk, to be excused for a few failings because these were common in his time; to the contrary, he represents everything that a monk should not be. 'He has compromised all of his vows deliberately, and he has not only neglected his own soul but also has led the souls of others into spiritual danger' (p 30).

913 Willard, Rudolph. 'Chaucer's "Text That Seith That Hunters Ben Nat Hooly Men." ' *SE*, 26 (1947), 209–51.

The viewpoint that hunters are sinful men has a long tradition, which is here reviewed in detail. Medieval texts on related issues — such as attitudes towards the monks' keeping of hunting dogs, and the viewpoint that fishing is acceptable though hunting is not — are also presented.

⏻ Part 11: The Friar

See the Introduction, pp xxxiv–xxxv above, for a brief summary of criticism on the Friar, and see the Index for further references.

914 Bennett, Josephine Waters. 'The Mediaeval Loveday.' *Spec*, 33 (1958), 351–70.
The term *loveday* (line 258) could be applied to 'any meeting of contending parties for the purpose of settling their dispute,' including 'private settlements out of court,' 'regular cases of arbitration in which the court took an active interest,' and 'the settlement of all kinds of private and public quarrels' (p 361). Thus the assumption of Spargo, **947**, that *loveday* was a more restricted technical term is not accurate. In principle, the loveday was based upon Christian concepts of 'brotherly love and forgiveness' (p 362), but contemporary complaints accuse it of being 'even more open than the law courts to bribery, intimidation, and injustice' (p 364).

915 Besserman, Lawrence. 'Chaucer and the Pope of Double Worstede.' *ChauN*, 1,1 (1979), 15–16.
Lines 261–62, with their rhyme of *pope* to *semycope*, and lines 642–43, which include the 'comparison of the Pope to a popinjay,' reflect 'Chaucer's pointed anti-papal satire in the *GP*,' a satire aimed specifically at the rival claimants to the papacy (p 15).

916 Bloomfield, Morton W. 'The Magic of *In Principio*.' *MLN*, 70 (1955), 559–65.
The Friar's phrase '*In principio*' (line 254) referred to the first part of the Gospel of John. By the early Middle Ages the phrase was regarded 'as a highly efficacious remedy, along with such objects as the cross itself, against the ills of life' (p 564), especially those evils associated with demons. Thus when the Friar entered people's houses and uttered this formula, 'which

to superstitious folk helped to clear the air of the malignant forces which lay everywhere ready to strike' (p 565), he was providing them with what they would have seen as protection against harm. In this sense he 'not only begged, he also gave, according to the lights of many, some value for what he received' (p 565).

917 Bowden, Muriel. *A Commentary on the General Prologue to the Canterbury Tales*. 1948. See **104**.
The Friar is both one of the most typical and one of the most individualized of the pilgrims. Bowden reviews the orders of friars and the contemporary criticism directed at them, as well as summarizing opinion on the Friar's seductions of young women, his use of *In principio*, his participation in lovedays, his garments, his resemblance to the character False-Seeming in the *Roman de la Rose*, and the probability that he represents 'some actual contemporary' (p 139), perhaps one of the Beverley Franciscans.

918 Bowers, R.H. 'A Middle-English Poem on Lovedays.' *MLR*, 47 (1952), 374–75.
No full contemporary account of the procedures involved in a loveday is known (see lines 258–61). However, a fifteenth-century poem describes the virtues appropriate to the presiding official — virtues 'which would have amused a man of Friar Hubert's stripe' (p 375). It also discusses the evil of foreswearing oneself at a loveday and uses Pontius Pilate's poor behavior as a judge 'as a warning of how not to conduct lovedays' (p 375). The poem described here is edited by Heffernan, **926**.

919 Bruce, J. Douglas. 'Prologue to the Canterbury Tales.' *MLN*, 34 (1919), 118–19.
The statement that the Friar's *purchas* was better than his *rente* (line 256) is very similar to a locution in the *Romaunt of the Rose* ('My purchas is better than my rent'). In fact, this is a French proverbial expression. Chaucer may well have taken it from the *Roman de la Rose*, but 'he might also have picked up this proverbial phrase in the ordinary social intercourse of the time' (p 119).

920 Duncan, Edmonstoune. *The Story of Minstrelsy*. London: Walter Scott Publishing Co, 1907; New York: Scribner's, 1907. Rpt Detroit: Singing Tree Press, 1968.
Chaucer's references to music are collected with brief comments (1968, pp 230–40); the Friar's *rote* (line 236) 'was in all likelihood a form of hurdy-gurdy' (p 231).

921 Flügel, Ewald. 'Zu Chaucer's Prolog zu C.T.' *Anglia*, 23 (1901), 225–41.
Flügel provides background to clarify lines 218–20, on the Friar's being a

licentiate and claiming to have more power of confession than a curate. The decrees that gave the friars authority to hear confession, and the contemporary complaints against their abuse of this power, are summarized. In line 256, *rente* cannot mean a regular income, since as a friar he could not properly have an income for himself: whatever he received he was supposed to give to his order. *Rente* is the same as *ferme* (line 252b). Chaucer means that the Friar withheld a goodly part of the money he begged ('Der frere, will Chaucer sagen, behielt noch von seinem erbettelten ein schönes sümmschen,' p 233) to pay his expenses for fine knives, tavern costs, and women. Thus the *ferme* or *rente* that he gave the order was only part of the receipts; he kept the *purchaas* for himself. The whole arrangement violated the rule of St Francis, which rejected all such financial dealings. In line 252c, *haunt* means the special area in which the friar would beg. The practice of begging within a fixed limit was attacked in contemporary writings.

922 Förster, Max. 'Nochmals ae. *fregen* "Frage."' *Archiv*, 135 (1916), 399–401.
Two medieval systems for writing in code are described. Förster cites fifteenth-century English verses that use one of these codes to describe friars with knives who go around swyving men's wives (cf lines 233–34).

923 Frank, Robert Worth, Jr. 'Chaucer and the London Bell-Founders.' *MLN*, 68 (1953), 524–28.
Chaucer's remark that the Friar's semicope was 'rounded as a belle out of the presse' (line 263) may have been based on personal observation, for bell-founders worked and lived near Chaucer's house above Aldgate.

924 Greenlaw, Edwin A. 'A Note on Chaucer's *Prologue*.' *MLN*, 23 (1908), 142–44.
Chaucer says that the Friar's 'purchas was wel bettre than his rente' (line 256). The contrast between *purchas* and *rente* occurs elsewhere — for instance, in the *Roman de la Rose* and in one of the Towneley plays. The word *rente* indicates both a sum paid *by* another and a sum paid *to* another, and implies legal income; *purchas*, on the other hand, 'generally connotes practices of doubtful propriety' (p 144). Chaucer means that the Friar made more money 'by unjust and dishonorable practices than the sum allowed him by his superior amounted to' (p 144). Cf **932**.

925 Havely, N.R. 'Chaucer's Friar and Merchant.' *ChauR*, 13 (1978–1979), 337–45.
The Friar is the first of the *GP* pilgrims to be associated with mercantile or commercial imagery. He appears as 'a worthy harbinger of the Merchant' (p 337). Havely describes the traditional 'association and even identification

of mendicants with merchants' (p 340). Chaucer uses this tradition in the Friar's portrait 'in a way that makes neither tolerance nor indignation easy' (p 341).

926 Heffernan, Thomas J. 'A Middle English Poem on Lovedays.' *ChauR*, 10 (1975–1976), 172–85.
The poem edited here illustrates 'the abuses to which the practice of loveday making was susceptible in late fourteenth-century England' (p 176). As for Chaucer's Friar, it is not only his 'participation in the secular and easily manipulated loveday that exposes him but the manner of his meddling. Friar Huberd sits in judgment ' "lyk a maister or a pope" ' (p 176; lines 258–61). See also 918.

927 Hinckley, Henry Barrett. 'Chauceriana.' 1916–1917. See 724.
Lovedays, in which the Friar is said to participate (line 258), are presented as fraudulent in *Piers Plowman*. As for the Friar's lisping (line 264), in the *Roman de Troie* Hector is said to stammer.

928 Horton, Oze E. 'The Neck of Chaucer's Friar.' *MLN*, 48 (1933), 31–34.
Chaucer remarks that the Friar's neck was as white 'as the flour-de-lys' (line 238). Horton cites authorities to show that a soft or white neck was 'an indication of perversion' (p 33). Along with the Friar's lisp and twinkling eyes, this detail 'seems to point to a character of licentiousness and depravity of some sort in the Friar' (p 34).

929 Huppé, Bernard F. *A Reading of the Canterbury Tales*. 1964. See 295.
The Friar's *harping* (line 266) may contain 'a possible reminder of a contrasting imagery, of the harping of David in praise of God' (p 37).

930 Jeffrey, David Lyle. 'The Friar's Rent.' *JEGP*, 70 (1971), 600–6.
When Chaucer says of the Friar, 'His purchas was wel bettre than his rente' (line 256), he means to imply a contrast between the term *purchas*, which refers to begging or gaining profit for oneself; and the term *rente*, which for a cleric is service owed 'in the vineyard of the world or Church' (p 604), as in the medieval understanding of the vineyard parable (Matthew 21:33–41, etc). Therefore, *rente* in this line refers not to fixed or regular income, as has been thought, but instead to religious responsibilities. 'To say that the Friar's *purchase* is better than his *rente* is to say in no uncertain terms that he has reneged on his spiritual and prelatical homage responsibilities, and that in his fixation on worldly purchase he is in a state of spiritual idolatry and disobedience' (p 606).

931 Kennard, Joseph Spencer. *The Friar in Fiction, Sincerity in Art, and Other Essays*. New York: Brentano, 1923.

The chapter 'Some Friars in English Fiction' (pp 3–220) includes brief comments on the orders of friars in Chaucer's England and on the abuses practiced by the Friar, the Summoner, and the Pardoner.

932 Kittredge, G.L. 'Chaucer's *Prologue* 256.' *MLN*, 23 (1908), 200.
The *purchas* and *rente* contrast (line 256) probably reflects an Old French proverb. In addition to instances previously cited by others, Kittredge points out that this proverb occurs in Froissart's *Joli Buisson*. As Greenlaw (see 924) has shown, the proverb was popular in England.

933 Knowles, Dom David. *The Religious Orders in England, II.* 1955. See 887.
The Friar, who is a Minorite, exemplifies the typical abuses. Nevertheless Chaucer 'was conscious of no mission or desire to reform society' (p 114).

934 Law, Robert Adger. ' "In Principio." ' *PMLA*, 37 (1922), 208–15.
The Friar's phrase *In principio* (line 254) appears in non-Chaucerian writings in contexts showing that it referred to the beginning of the Gospel of John (rather than to Genesis). Just as the *Paternoster* meant the whole of the Lord's Prayer, so *In principio* meant the whole of John 1:1–14. These verses were regarded as being of special importance. For example, they were evidently written on amulets, used as a charm, and said after Mass. The Friar uses *In principio* not simply as a greeting, but 'probably as a "favorite devotion" ' (p 213) when he enters a widow's house.

935 Manly, John Matthews. *Some New Light on Chaucer.* 1926. See 362.
In the chapter 'The Summoner, the Friar and the Pardoner' (pp 102–30), Manly proposes that the Friar is modeled upon a Franciscan friar from Beverley in Holderness.

936 ——, and Edith Rickert, eds. *The Text of the Canterbury Tales Studied on the Basis of All Known Manuscripts.* 1940. See 49.
The additional couplet after line 252 (usually printed as lines 252a–b) is not included in most of the mss. The fact that these two lines are commonly omitted in the mss 'suggests that they were cancelled by Chaucer, probably as interrupting the flow of the narrative and adding little to the picture of the Friar' (vol 3, p 424).

937 Mann, Jill. *Chaucer and Medieval Estates Satire.* 1973. See 363.
Many traits of the Friar's characterization had already been assembled in the estates satire tradition, where friars were associated with lechery, avarice, etc., and depicted as 'a class that flatters and wheedles and yet at the same time is inspired by pride and a strong sense of status' (pp 53–54). Chaucer has modified this tradition by his 'constant use of ambivalent words which make it hard to subject the Friar to moral analysis' (p 54).

938 Mossé, F. 'Chaucer et la liturgie.' *RevG*, 14 (1923), 283–89.
In principio (line 254) refers not only to the opening verse of the Gospel of John, but to a more extended passage, the first fourteen verses of the Gospel ('*In principio* fait allusion non au premier, mais aux quatorze premiers versets du chapitre I de Saint Jean,' p 283). That passage was regarded with special veneration, as if it were a summary of the mysteries of the faith. On the Pardoner, see **1323**.

939 Muscatine, Charles. 'The Name of Chaucer's Friar.' *MLN*, 70 (1955), 169–72.
The Friar's name Huberd (line 269) may be 'an ironic literary allusion' (p 169) to Hubert the kite in the French *Renart* poems. Hubert the kite is, 'like Chaucer's friar, both cleric and confessor' (p 169); he is lewd, like the Friar. Both of the Huberts 'are somewhat at odds with other clergymen' (p 171) and interpret their office in a way that is comfortable for them. Furthermore, the kite as a bird was associated with rapacity and voluptuousness. Thus the tradition of Hubert the kite 'associates a cleric-confessor of dubious reputation with the name Hubert' (p 172). Chaucer used a version of the *Renart* tale in *NPT*, and the name Huberd 'could have been recognized by Chaucer's audience as a specific literary allusion' (p 172). It is possible that a personal allusion could be intended in addition (or instead), but 'I find it hard to imagine any personal reference that would not mar the delicate balances in this description between the individualizing and the typical, between championship and rascality' (p 172). The name can also create a link to the friar of *SumT*, 'where, as in the *Roman de Renart*, the evil confessor is cruelly deceived by his client' (p 172).

940 Mustanoja, Tauno. 'The Suggestive Use of Christian Names in Middle English Poetry.' In *Medieval Literature and Folklore Studies: Essays in Honor of Francis Lee Utley*. Ed. Jerome Mandel and Bruce A. Rosenberg. New Brunswick, NJ: Rutgers University Press, 1970. Pp 51–76.
Mustanoja suggests that the Friar's name Hubert (line 269), which is also the name of a magpie in *The Man in the Moon*, might involve a bird-allusion.

941 Pearcy, Roy J. 'The Marriage Costs of Chaucer's Friar.' *N&Q*, New Series 17 (1970), 124–25.
The thirteenth-century fabliau *Frere Denise* includes a friar who seduces a girl and then supplies a dowry for her marriage. This narrative provides 'a scheming friar, an innocent young woman, seduction, exposure, and the payment by the seducer of a dowry for the marriage of his victim as a form of reparation' (p 124). The fabliau helps to confirm the interpretation that

lines 212–13 of *GP* pertain to young women whom the Friar has himself seduced.

942 Pollard, Alfred W., et al, eds. *The Works of Geoffrey Chaucer*. 1898. See 4.
On *purchas* and *rente* (line 256), Pollard explains that the Friar 'earnt more than he received from fixed property: a proverbial phrase pointed here by the fact that of fixed property friars had none' (p 4).

943 Reiss, Edmund. 'Chaucer's Friar and the Man in the Moon.' *JEGP*, 62 (1963), 481–85.
The Friar's name, Huberd, may have been applied to the Man in the Moon, who according to legend was associated with Cain and with thievery. Thus Chaucer, 'by using this name for his Friar, may have been relating the thieving, Sabbath-breaking, Judas- and Cain-like Man to his thieving, hypocritical son of Cain, the Pilgrim-Friar' (p 484). To reinforce the connection, just before identifying the Friar's name (line 269) Chaucer mentions the stars (line 268), and it is 'an easy mental transition from the stars to the moon' (p 485). Chaucer apparently chose Huberd for the name of the Friar to initiate 'a chain of associations in the mind of his audience' (p 485) and to reveal the Friar's evil nature and the incongruity of the praise that is given him.

944 Richardson, Janette. 'Friar and Summoner: The Art of Balance.' *ChauR*, 9 (1974–1975), 227–36.
Comparison of the *GP* portraits of the Friar and Summoner 'reveals that although the two pilgrims are completely unlike in externals — that is to say in appearance and manners — they are nonetheless moral equals' (p 227). They exhibit the same vices, though in different forms. 'Because the Friar is a mendicant who has taken religious vows, his abuse of his profession is perhaps more self-destructive in spiritual terms than is the Summoner's even though its physical manifestations are less gross and vulgar' (p 288). The *GP* balance of 'external difference masking internal likeness' (p 229) is duplicated in their tales.

945 Shomura, Tetsuji. 'Chaucer No "Worthy" No Imi — Tokuni "This worthy lymytour" O Chusin Ni Shite.' [The Meaning of 'Worthy' in Chaucer, Especially in the Phrase 'This worthy lymytour.'] *KSR*, 31 (1970), 117–38.
Not seen; listed in *A Bibliography of Publications on Medieval English Language and Literature in Japan* (Tokyo: Center for Medieval Studies, Tokyo University, 1983), p 136, #13.

946 Skeat, Walter W., ed. *The Complete Works of Geoffrey Chaucer, Edited from Numerous Manuscripts*. 1894–1897. See 3.

The young women for whose marriages the Friar pays (see lines 212–3) are 'almost certainly' his concubines (vol 5, p 25).

947 Spargo, John Webster. 'Chaucer's Love-Days.' *Spec*, 15 (1940), 36–56.
The etymology of the legal term *lovedayes* (line 258) is not clear, but it probably came from ancient Scandinavian *lof*, which had the meaning of permission or license. The technical implication is that of permission to settle a dispute out of court (although the court retained the right to collect fees). By Chaucer's time this institution had become corrupt; for example, a 1329 proclamation of regulations to ensure the peace during the king's absence in France prohibited lovedays, along with other potentially troublesome meetings. Clerics were at first allowed to participate in the arbitration of disputes, but this permission was later limited to cases involving the poor. We know that the Friar does not serve the poor. 'That he should meddle in such a secular matter as a loveday, notably in a loveday between persons of substance, as implied,' is an integral component of his characterization as 'a clever, unscrupulous blackguard, contravening all the rules, great and small, of his order' (p 56). In reply, see Bennett, 914.

948 Szittya, Penn R. 'The Antifraternal Tradition in Middle English Literature.' *Spec*, 52 (1977), 287–313.
GP is not directly discussed, but Szittya describes the criticism of friars that had become conventional by Chaucer's time. Some of the charges leveled against the friars, such as the claim that they were proliferating, were demonstrably inaccurate. Szittya suggests that the antifraternal tradition was based on 'a perception which was not political, not empirical, not realistic, but fundamentally theological and symbolic' (p 313).

949 Szövérffy, Joseph. 'Chaucer's Friar and St Nicholas (Prologue 212).' *N&Q*, New Series 16 (1969), 166–67.
St Nicholas was said to have given gold to save impoverished young women from prostitution. 'Obviously, Chaucer wanted to contrast our Friar with St Nicholas who unselfishly provided a dowry for girls in danger of being sent to brothels' (p 167). Chaucer's Friar may also contribute marriage money, but the young women seem to be those whom he has himself seduced (lines 212–13).

950 Tatlock, John S.P. 'Notes on Chaucer: the Canterbury Tales.' *MLN*, 29 (1914), 140–44.
The phrase *In principio*, used by the Friar (line 254), was particularly reverenced and 'used in various ways, liturgical and superstitious' (p 141). Tatlock supplies examples, including instances showing its use as a charm against fever and as an aid to a demoniac.

951 —— . 'The Date of the *Troilus* and Minor Chauceriana.' *MLN*, 50 (1935), 277–96.

The order to which the Friar belongs is not clear. The friar within *SumT* is probably a Carmelite, but given 'such hints as there are' (p 290), the Friar in *GP* may have been Franciscan. St Francis was known for his service to lepers; in the Friar's disdain for lepers and other poor people (lines 242–7), 'it is natural to detect a sarcastic comparison between the Friar and his "father" St Francis' (p 291). Nevertheless, tending to lepers was not confined to any one group. The Ellesmere illustrator shows the Friar in garb suggesting a Dominican or Augustinian, 'but neither by any means perfectly' (p 291). The artist seems to have found that *GP* gave no specific indication and therefore 'portrays here the genus, not a species' (p 292). Correspondingly, Chaucer's own 'complete contempt for his friars allows us to suppose that he disregarded differences. He gives a composite picture. He had in mind the *genus Frater* rather than a species,' and though an individual historical friar would have to belong to a specific order, 'a friar in the imagination' does not (p 292). In the phrase *heeld ... the space* (line 176), *space* probably means 'course': the Latin *spatior* means to walk or go; other related words are cited (p 294).

952 Tillotson, Kathleen. 'The Friar's Lisp.' *TLS*, April 25, 1936, p 356.

A passage from Ovid's *Ars Amatoria* suggests that the habit of lisping 'is typical, though not of Friars.' Chaucer's comment on the Friar's lisping gains 'in innuendo' through this parallel, since Ovid is speaking of women. The parallel therefore increases 'the recurrent hints of the Friar's prowess in flirtation.'

953 Van Herk, A. 'Chauceriana.' 1917. See 858.

The phrase *In principio* (line 254), with which the widow seems to be familiar, was popular even before its official inclusion in the Mass. It served as a charm against bad weather or illness, as a means of exorcism, etc. It appears in this function in a Dutch play.

954 Whitesell, J. Edwin. 'Chaucer's Lisping Friar.' *MLN*, 71 (1956), 160–61.

The Friar of *GP* is said to lisp (line 264). The friar in *SumT* — which is directed at Friar Huberd — may also have a lisp or affectation of speech. Perhaps that friar's pronunciation of *ferthyng*, in the line 'What is a fer-thyng worth parted in twelve?' (*SumT*, III.1967), is to be understood as having suggested the joke played upon him. This link provides further evidence of Chaucer's 'dramatic skill in tying together descriptive items in the Prologue with events in the tales themselves' (p 161).

955 Williams, Arnold. 'Chaucer and the Friars.' *Spec*, 28 (1953), 499–513. Rpt in *Chaucer Criticism, 1*, ed. Richard J. Schoeck and Jerome Taylor (Notre

Dame: University of Notre Dame Press, 1960; 10th printing 1978), pp 63–83.
'Whenever Chaucer has occasion to mention Friars, we get the same characterization, of unextenuated hypocritical villany' [sic] (p 499). Chaucer is more critical of the friars than of other clerics. Friar Huberd's faults — his very successful begging, his avoidance of the poor, his cope (the friars' ostentatious clothing was condemned in a document of about 1340), his participation in secular affairs, his seeking out of women — reflect 'the most important of the charges made against the friars' by their leading attackers, charges that had been 'repeated in every generation' (p 513) for more than a century by Chaucer's time. In using this anti-mendicant tradition, 'Chaucer accepts and reflects the attitude of the secular party,' which 'must have dominated the thinking of the upper-class, governmental circles in which Chaucer moved' (p 513). Given this partisan orientation, 'we should no more take Chaucer's friars as representative of the mendicant orders as a whole than we take his parson as typical of the parochial clergy' (p 513).

956 —— . 'Two Notes on Chaucer's Friars.' *MP*, 54 (1956–1957), 117–20.
Discussing Chaucer's reference to Friar Huberd's fine cope (lines 262–63), Williams points out a contemporary controversy in which the cope was used 'specifically as an example of the extravagance of the friars' (p 118). Thus to mention the cope with this significance may have been 'a commonplace, well known to Chaucer and his readers' (p 118).

957 —— . 'The "Limitour" of Chaucer's Time and His "Limitacioun." ' *SP*, 57 (1960), 463–78.
Chaucer's Friar is said to be a *lymytour* (line 209). Williams indicates that the meaning of this term has not been clear. It is not accurate to say that a *lymytour* was a friar licensed to beg in a certain district, since friars were licensed to preach and hear confessions — not to beg. A detailed review of medieval records shows that the territory of a convent was divided into definite areas; 'the limitour is the friar assigned to one of these subdivisions of the territory,' with duties normally including 'preaching, hearing confessions, and begging' (p 478). His confessing and preaching were open to regulation by the bishop or archbishop. Chaucer's description of Friar Huberd accords with contemporary records except in lines 252a–252b, a couplet whose textual authority has been questioned. The statement there, that the limitour paid for his rights to his district, does not seem accurate. 'If Chaucer wrote and then canceled' this couplet, 'as most scholars believe, it may be that some informed person had called his attention to the inaccuracy' (p 478) — but this explanation is only a surmise.

958 ——. 'Relations between the Mendicant Friars and the Secular Clergy in England in the later Fourteenth Century.' *An M*, 1 (1960), 22–95.
Although *GP* is not directly discussed, many documents pertaining to the activities of friars as confessors, preachers, officiators at burials, etc. are presented, along with information that clarifies the financial and legal arrangements involved. The friars were often (though not universally) resented. 'Despite the fact that the mendicant orders were a hundred or more years old by the second half of the fourteenth century, a large section of opinion still regarded them as intruders' (p 92).

959 Young, Karl. 'A Note on Chaucer's Friar.' *MLN*, 50 (1935), 83–85.
A document of 1321, in which a vicar is charged with having failed to provide funds towards the marriage of a woman with whom he has had children, helps to clarify what Chaucer meant by the Friar's financial contributions to the marriages of young women (lines 212–13).

Part 12: The Merchant

See the Introduction, p xxxv above, for a brief summary of criticism on the Merchant, and see the Index for further references.

960 Bowden, Muriel. *A Commentary on the General Prologue to the Canterbury Tales.* 1948. See **104.**
   The Merchant may be a Stapler or an Adventurer, or both. He is 'typical of his class' (p 147). Given the resemblances between the historical Gilbert Maghfeld and the Merchant, it is 'tempting to jump to the conclusion that Maghfeld and the merchant' are the same (p 152). However, Chaucer would not be so imprudent as to identify him openly, for Maghfeld was an important man to whom many people owed money.

961 Brown, Emerson, Jr. 'Chaucer, the Merchant, and their Tale: Getting Beyond Old Controversies, Part II.' *ChauR*, 13 (1978–1979), 247–62.
   Brown associates the Merchant's views on marriage with Chaucer's own, and aspects of the Merchant's *GP* portrait with his later tale. Janus (cf January in the tale) was a patron of merchants and commercial transactions. Chaucer's audience might perhaps have recognized in the Merchant a real person with 'not only well-known financial troubles but also well-known marital troubles' (p 253). The *GP* portrait would then arouse questions that the tale resolves.

962 Cahn, Kenneth S. 'Chaucer's Merchants and the Foreign Exchange: An Introduction to Medieval Finance.' *SAC*, 2 (1980), 81–119.
   Much information about medieval financial dealings is presented. Cahn proposes that 'it is impossible to conclude — as many Chaucer scholars have — that the merchant was a usurer or any type of money lender. Contrary to most opinion, he did not deal profitably in monetary exchange by speculating, or in any other manner, legal or illegal' (p 81). Lines 278–82 indicate

that the Merchant is borrowing money; 'like other English merchants' he 'borrows English money by selling Flemish shields in exchange' (p 93). His choice of hat (line 272) is part of his need to 'simultaneously suggest that he is essentially a solid English citizen with some Flemish connections' (p 94). The 'buying and selling of shields was lawful' and these transactions 'were not considered usurious' (p 113). Because of the fluctuation of capital costs, it was necessary to choose the situation and time properly to avoid bankruptcy. 'Chaucer's merchant apparently borrowed and survived' (cf line 278, '*Wel* koude he in eschaunge sheeldes selle'). He 'was usually, if not always, in debt, but with considerable care he managed to keep that fact unknown and so, through credit, could function' (p 118). Because he needs to 'promote the impression of himself as a good credit risk, he always suggests that his profits are growing' (line 275) and takes pains 'to make certain that no one knows that he is in debt' (lines 278–80). As for his anonymity, it 'follows that the name of a merchant without capital is not and ought not to be known' (lines 283–84).

963 Crane, John Kenny. 'An Honest Debtor?: A Note on Chaucer's Merchant, Line A276.' *ELN*, 4 (1966-1967), 81–85.

Despite the viewpoint of Park, **969**, who defends the Merchant's honesty, 'the Merchant has probably committed every money-crime on the books' (p 82). He probably wants the sea kept clear of pirates 'for four formidable reasons: first, obviously, to protect his cargoes; second, to embezzle from the king's import taxes; third, to force the king into debt to him, usually usuriously; fourth, after banking the money from the previous three plans, to pirate on his own, now with little trouble at all' (p 83). In support of this interpretation Crane cites the Merchant's placement in *GP* between the Friar and the Clerk, both of whom 'are involved in thievery of one brand or another — the Friar sells penances, the Clerk steals book-money' (p 84). In addition, the Merchant's forked beard and motley clothing indicate Chaucer's ironic attitude toward him, which is part of the 'whole theme' of *GP*: 'reality is to be distinguished from appearance' (p 84). Finally, although 'the unnamed Merchant was *not* named Gilbert Maghfeld' (p 85), as an interpretation in the Manly tradition might have suggested (see **362**), nevertheless 'Chaucer's dealings with the notoriously-shady Maghfeld gave him, subconsciously at least, a model' for merchants as a class (p 85).

964 Donaldson, E.T., ed. *Chaucer's Poetry: An Anthology for the Modern Reader.* 1975. See **63**.

Given the high cost of borrowing funds, a merchant would tend to be 'particularly careful to hide his indebtedness from a prospective lender, lest the interest rates go up. Sometimes when his ships failed to dock on time he might have to leave town suddenly, in which case a pilgrimage would offer a good excuse for his departure' (1975, p 1049). Maintaining anonymity (see line 286) would also be prudent.

965 Johnson, Oscar E. 'Was Chaucer's Merchant in Debt? A Study in Chaucerian Syntax and Rhetoric.' *JEGP*, 52 (1953), 50–57.
Although the statement 'Ther wiste no wight that he was in dette' (line 280) has commonly been taken to mean that the Merchant *was* in debt and concealed this fact, Johnson argues that Chaucer means 'He was decidedly not in debt,' or 'He was anything but in debt' (p 51). A discussion of where Chaucer would have placed metrical stress when reading the line aloud, and of similar constructions in other parts of Chaucer's works, is offered to support this reading.

966 Knott, Thomas A. 'Chaucer's Anonymous Merchant.' *PQ*, 1 (1922), 1–16.
Chaucer's Merchant was not the equivalent of an ordinary modern tradesman, but 'a much more imposing personage' (p 1). The power of the English merchant class, the wool trade, the 'staple' towns, the system of taxation, the merchants' activities in foreign exchange and in lending money to the king, etc, are explained. Knott discusses the details of the Merchant's portrait in connection with fourteenth-century trading activities. For example, he proposes that the wool port on the Orewell that serves as the Merchant's home port must be Ipswich, not Harwich as is usually thought. The Merchant's motley costume is only customary; however, 'the words "bargain" and "chevisance" were in very bad repute in Chaucer's day' (p 12). The Merchant could have concealed his debts if he were one of the merchants who were 'deeply involved in the national finances' (p 14). As for the fact that the Merchant remains anonymous, Knott suggests that Chaucer, as 'friend and official associate of the greatest London merchants' (p 15), claims not to know the Merchant's name because he is 'a tactful writer' who would want to prevent his readers from leaping 'at a ready identification' (p 16) with a particular merchant whom he, and they, knew.

967 Lumiansky, R.M. *Of Sondry Folk: The Dramatic Principle in the Canterbury Tales.* 1955. See **348**.
'For some reason that will probably never be fully clear, Chaucer's sketch of the Merchant' shows 'such cautious disinterestedness and evident lack of sympathy that it stands unique among the series of portraits' (p 152). The Merchant's greatest social failing 'is that he is a terrible bore,' subjecting 'anyone who will listen to detailed accounts of his own business acumen' (p 152; see line 275).

968 Miller, F. 'The Middleburgh Staple, 1383–1388.' *CHJ*, 2 (1926), 63–66.
Details on the export of wool via Middleburgh (see line 277) are provided,

with statistics for the amount of wool exported between 1380 and 1390.
'The Middleburgh Staple was established wholly upon the initiative of the
merchants' (p 63), who wanted to use Middleburgh for export during certain years because unstable political relations with France made it risky to
continue using their usual port, Calais. When the danger of hostility from
France had passed, the merchants returned to using Calais. Extant records
show that Middleburgh was used most heavily in 1383–84, 1386–87, and
1387–88.

969 Park, B.A. 'The Character of Chaucer's Merchant.' *ELN*, 1 (1963-1964),
167–75.
Chaucer's Merchant has been misinterpreted as engaging in illegal business
affairs and being insolvent. A closer look at fourteenth-century economics
and law leads to a revision of his character. 'First, his selling of *écus* in
exchange is not illegal. Second, his manipulations of credit do not necessarily include loans at usury. Finally, his indebtedness does not imply his
insolvency' (p 167). He is not 'a man whose show of circumstance conceals a series of illegal, immoral, and insecure transactions,' as has been
thought, but instead 'a more realistic and less melodramatic' person, 'a
typical medieval man of affairs' (p 117). Lines 278, 282, and 280–82 (taken
as a sentence) are examined in detail. In reply, see **963**.

970 Rickert, Edith. 'Documents and Records: Extracts from a Fourteenth-
Century Account Book.' *MP*, 24 (1926–1927), 111–19 and 249–56.
The account book of Gilbert Maghfeld 'illustrates the life and business of
a great London merchant of the type described in Chaucer's *Prologue*' (p
112). Chaucer himself is mentioned in this document as having borrowed
money from Maghfeld. Many details of Maghfeld's career parallel the *GP*
description of the Merchant. Since Maghfeld was 'a familiar figure at court
and in the city' and 'a likely subject for satire,' he may be Chaucer's model
for this portrait (p 256). If so, Chaucer's refusal to state the Merchant's
name may reflect his own situation: perhaps he refrained from naming the
Merchant because of the possibility that he would need another *chevyssaunce* (line 282) from Maghfeld in the future.

971 Stillwell, Gardiner. 'Chaucer's "Sad" Merchant.' *RES*, 20 (1944), 1–18.
The usual character of the merchant in the fabliaux is examined in terms
of illustrating 'the philosophy of a middle-class breadwinner who hopes to
gain but is well aware of the dreadful possibility of failure' (p 3). Guild
records also show some of the same middle-class preoccupations.

972 ——. 'Chaucer's Merchant: No Debts?' *JEGP*, 57 (1958), 192–96.
Stillwell argues that line 280 is probably directed 'not so much to the Mer-

chant's actual financial status as to his *manner* of giving a certain impression of his status' (p 194). The Merchant is careful to foster the impression that he is prosperous. 'He has, in other words, a front to keep up' (p 195). In this quality he resembles the Lawyer, the Guildsmen, and the Physician, all of whom are middle-class characters described ironically. It is more ironic for Chaucer to refer to the Merchant's dignified front than simply to his prosperity itself. The line might therefore be paraphrased, 'If he was in debt, the spectator would certainly never know it!' (p 196). The behavior of the merchant in *ShT*, who explains to his wife that he must keep his financial status a secret and perhaps even pretend to be on pilgrimage, lends support to this interpretation of the Merchant's portrait in *GP*.

973 Stock, Lorraine Kochanske. 'The Meaning of *Chevyssaunce*: Complicated Word Play in Chaucer's *Shipman's Tale*.' *SSF*, 18 (1981), 245–49.
In *ShT*, the word *chevyssaunce* (VII.1519, 1537, 1581) implies both a business transaction and a strategem or device [cf line 282].

974 Thrupp, Sylvia L. *The Merchant Class of Medieval London, 1300–1500*. Chicago: University of Chicago Press, 1948. Rpt Ann Arbor, MI: University of Michigan Press, Ann Arbor Paperbacks, 1962.
Much information pertinent to the Merchant is included, as well as related material of many sorts: details on London guilds, the criteria that determined gentle rank, the fees paid to physicians, the relationships between the merchant class and the landed gentry, aldermanic families, standards of living, population estimates, and so forth.

975 Walker, A. Stanley. 'Note on Chaucer's *Prologue*.' *MLN*, 38 (1923), 314.
The Merchant's desire to have the sea kept safe between Middleburg and Orwell (lines 276–77) has been used to date *GP* between 1384 and 1388, since those were the years when the wool staple was located at Middleburg rather than at Calais. Walker proposes that notices in the Patent and Close Rolls can be used to date *GP* somewhat more narrowly, to 'the time when the plague of pirates was at its height, that is to say, between 1385 and 1386.'

⭐ Part 13: The Clerk

See the Introduction, p xxxv above, for a brief summary of criticism on the Clerk, and see the Index for further references.

976 Axelrod, Steven. 'The Wife of Bath and the Clerk.' *AnM*, 15 (1974), 109–24.

As part of the thesis that the Wife is interested in acquiring the Clerk as husband number six, Axelrod argues that the Clerk's portrait in *GP* has been misunderstood by critics who take the fallible narrator's interpretations as valid. In reality, the Clerk is 'not merely a cliché cleric' (p 113). 'This Clerk is no holy man; he is a scholar and an intellectual,' a 'witty, spirited, flawed and attractive human being' (p 113). Given the sexual motifs present in the opening lines of *GP*, his relationship to the Wife 'stems from concupiscent rather than irascible impulses' (p 114).

977 Beall, Chandler B. 'And Gladly Teche.' *ELN*, 13 (1975–1976), 85–86.

Line 308 may be indebted to Seneca's epistle to Lucilius, VI.4, a passage in which the 'learning, the teaching, and the joy thereof' are 'concisely put' (p 85).

978 Bennett, J.A.W. *Chaucer at Oxford and at Cambridge*. Oxford: Oxford University Press, 1974; Toronto: University of Toronto Press, 1974.

Why is the Clerk associated with Oxford (see line 285) rather than with Cambridge, the other English university of the time? Bennett suggests that there were more students (and readers of literature) at Oxford than at Cambridge, and that 'an Oxford scholar setting out on a pilgrimage would be likely to make for Saint Thomas's shrine,' while a Cambridge scholar 'would more naturally go to Walsingham, England's next most popular shrine,' instead (p 15). An appendix on 'Poor Scholars' (pp 117–19) reviews evidence on the poverty of university students. See also **1204, 1241.**

979 Bloomfield, Morton W. 'Middle English "Gladly", An Instance of Linguisticism.' *NM*, 63 (1962), 167–74.
Line 308 should be paraphrased as 'And he liked to learn and liked to teach,' with *gladly* having the force of 'like to' (p 174).

980 Camden, Carroll, Jr. 'Chauceriana.' 1932. See **670**.
Chaucer's intention in the phrase *moral vertu* (line 307) has been differently interpreted, but from the seven instances of the term *moral* in Chaucer's works 'it would seem that *moral* has much the same meaning in Chaucer' (p 361) as in modern English.

981 Chattergee, A.B., ed. *The Prologue to the Canterbury Tales (Chaucer)*. 1963. See **70**.
The Clerk's characterization shows him as having an inferiority complex. His poverty 'has made him diffident' and 'he has turned to books where he is not likely to face any competition from the rich' rather than to more public or worldly situations (pp xxix–xxx).

982 Fleming, John. 'Chaucer's Clerk and John of Salisbury.' *ELN*, 2 (1964-1965), 5–6.
Chaucer's famous statement about the Clerk, 'And gladly wolde he lerne and gladly teche' (line 308), may echo a passage in the *Policraticus* of John of Salisbury, which includes the words *ut doceatur aut doceat* in a description of true philosophers. Since Chaucer used the *Policraticus* in *PardT*, we know that he was familiar with this work. Chaucer would have agreed with John of Salisbury on the rarity of such ideal men. Cf **1006**.

983 Ginsberg, Warren. '"And Speketh so Pleyn": The Clerk's Tale and its Teller.' *Crit*, 20 (1978), 307–23.
Ginsberg finds the Clerk's characterization to be complex. In *GP* he 'is nearly, in fact, a walking litotes' (p 322; see lines 288–89 on his thinness). 'The Clerk, in sum, is *in transitu*; a young and eager man, in orders, who may become a preacher of note .... Beneath a modest yet severe front, he hides desire enough to engage and experience the world' (p 322).

984 Green, A. Wigfall. 'Chaucer's Clerks and the Mediaeval Scholarly Tradition as Represented by Richard de Bury's *Philobiblon*.' *ELH*, 18 (1951), 1–6.
Chaucer's Clerk in *GP* need not be based on any one individual or literary source. He represents a considerable medieval tradition about the ideal scholar. Although Chaucer probably did not meet Richard de Bury personally, Richard's *Philobiblon* is a useful expression of the general ideal. Like Chaucer's Clerk, Richard in *Philobiblon* stands for the veneration of books (Aristotle in particular), for impoverishing oneself if necessary in order to

buy books, etc. In addition, in 1330 Richard met Petrarch; Chaucer's Clerk too says that he — the Clerk, not Chaucer's narrator as others have thought — met Petrarch. Since the *Philobiblon* was written for an Oxford college, it may well have been familiar to those who knew the Oxford libraries well, and it is 'not impossible' (p 6) that Chaucer saw it.

985 Hulton, Samuel F. *The Clerk of Oxford in Fiction.* London: Methuen, 1909.

The Clerk is briefly discussed in a description (based largely on Chaucer) of fourteenth-century Oxford student life.

986 Jacob, E.F. 'English University Clerks in the Later Middle Ages: The Problem of Maintenance.' *BJRL*, 29 (1946), 304–25. Rev and rpt in E.F. Jacob, *Essays in the Conciliar Epoch*, 2nd ed. (Manchester: Manchester University Press, 1953)—not seen; and in that book's 3rd ed. (Manchester: Manchester University Press, 1963), pp 207–22.

Although Chaucer's Clerk is not discussed, Jacob presents information on the costs of education at the English universities and on the options available to impoverished clerks (cf lines 290–92 and 297–300 on the Clerk's poverty). Poverty among clerks studying at the universities was common; 'as a general rule, the clerk who wanted to stay beyond his fourth year had either to seek the help of a foundation, if he was not in one already, or to take Holy Orders and secure a benefice (and a dispensation to study) for his support' (1946, p 313). In the fourteenth century, the number of students at Oxford declined, partly because of the difficulty in securing benefices. Loan funds were sometimes established by individual benefactors; students receiving loans might have to deposit their books as collateral and the books could be sold off by the custodians of the funds if the loans were not repaid on time.

987 Jones, H.S.V. 'The Clerk of Oxenford.' *PMLA*, 27 (1912), 106–15.

The Clerk is said to spend on books and learning 'al that he myghte of his freendes hente' (line 299). This phrase does not mean, as others have thought, that he was a beggar. Only a very few extremely poor Oxford scholars were given licenses to beg. It is more likely that his income came from a 'chest' (p 110), a deposit of money similar to a later-day scholarship; or from the special collections on behalf of scholars taken up on St Scholastica's Day; or from a patron, such as a neighboring abbot or archdeacon — 'So habitual was this kind of patronage that a large proportion of University students must have been supported' by such arrangements (p 111). Although Chaucer did not assign the Clerk to any specific College at Oxford, perhaps he would have associated him with Merton, in view of such evidence as the presence of Chaucer's friend Strode there.

988 King, Francis, and Bruce Steele. *Selections from Geoffrey Chaucer's The Canterbury Tales.* 1969. See **82**.

Chaucer does not take the Clerk completely seriously, depicting him as being excessive in his devotion to learning; 'there is also a wry comment on the uselessness of all philosophy and on the comicality of the scholar who effects nothing in the practical world' (p 346). 'The thin figure on an emaciated horse, with his mind on higher things amid the bustle and vitality of the pilgrimage, is inevitably comic' (p 347).

989 Lea, Charles H. 'A Fourteenth-Century Book Lover.' *EngRev*, 44 (1927), 714–19.

Among the twenty books that the Clerk would have at his bed, it is suggested, might have beeen a copy of Richard de Bury's *Philobiblon*, the contents of which are described here. The Clerk 'would have heard of it, even if he had not been fortunate enough to see it' (p 714).

990 Longsworth, Robert. 'Chaucer's Clerk as Teacher.' In *The Learned and the Lewed: Studies in Chaucer and Medieval Literature* [in Honor of Bartlett Jere Whiting]. Cambridge, MA: Harvard University Press, 1974. Harvard English Studies, 5. Pp 61–66.

The Clerk is said to gladly teach (line 308). His use of his tale as an opportunity for instruction shows that his teaching 'is skillful and appropriately "sownynge in moral vertu"' (p 66; line 307), though 'Chaucer's tribute to the learned profession of teachers is not without overtones of amusement' (p 66).

991 Morse, J. Mitchell. 'Chaucer: A Meaning of "Philosophye."' *N&Q*, New Series 2 (1955), 11.

In line 295, the word *philosophye* probably means 'commentators and disciples.' This meaning is more likely than simply 'philosophy,' which in context would pad the line or produce an unsatisfactory overall sense.

992 —— . 'The Philosophy of the Clerk of Oxenford.' *MLQ*, 19 (1958), 3–20.

The Clerk's academic milieu at Oxford would have been affected by the main intellectual dilemma of his time, which was the controversy between the Nominalists and the Realists over the nature of universals, authority, and individualism. John Wycliffe was Master of Balliol College at Oxford between 1360 and 1381; other major figures in the controversy also taught at Oxford. 'The Clerk, then, breathed an atmosphere charged with individualism and incipient revolt' (p 14). We may infer that he originally intended to enter the Church, but that he has 'so fallen in love with logic' (p 15) that he has prolonged the study of this secular subject for its own sake. The Clerk's tale demonstrates his complex attitude towards the authority-vs–individualism debate; he is 'conducting an argument with himself' (p

15). Chaucer, though 'not a philosopher in any technical sense,' would probably have been 'aware of the main issues and the general drift' of the Oxford controversies (p 14), given his general alertness, his reading, and his connection with John of Gaunt.

993 Orme, Nicholas. 'Chaucer and Education.' 1981. See **729**.
Brief comments on the Clerk and on medieval university education are included.

994 Richardson, M.E. 'The Clerk of Oxenford.' *TLS*, May 5, 1932, p 331.
Waulthier Dissy, who is termed *jadys Clerk de Ozenford* in William Mowbray's will of 1391, is proposed as the model for Chaucer's Clerk. The Mowbray family was almost certainly known by Chaucer, given its connections with the Hollands, who were half-brothers to Richard II. (See also Richardson, **995**, and Turton, **1001**.)

995 — . 'The Clerk of Oxenford.' *TLS*, May 26, 1932, p 390.
Details about the life of Waulthier Dissy (see Richardson, **994**, and Turton, **1001**) are supplied. Dissy studied at Cambridge, not Oxford. He was confessor to John of Gaunt and appears in Gaunt's Registers as receiving payment for saying masses. That Dissy was noted for his learning and was paid to say masses makes him resemble Chaucer's Clerk, who concentrated on learning and who prayed for those who gave him funds to continue his studies (lines 301–2).

996 Schramm, Wilbur Lang. 'The Cost of Books in Chaucer's Time.' *MLN*, 48 (1933), 139–45.
Schramm reviews records that show the costs of parchment, scribal copying and illumination, and binding. Books were sold at widely varying prices, but in general they were extremely expensive. Exeter College, for example, built a new library in 1383, with the records showing that the cost of the building was no more than the amount that 'a very few books' (p 144) would have been worth. 'In the fourteenth century a book was treasure, capable of being pawned, often as valuable as a country estate' (p 144). Philosophical books such as those prized by the Clerk (lines 293–95) 'were not especially inexpensive' (p 145). The twenty volumes which the Clerk would like to have by his bed might well have been worth some sixty times his likely annual income.

997 Severs, J. Burke. 'Chaucer's Clerks.' In *Chaucer and Middle English Studies in Honour of Rossell Hope Robbins*. Ed. Beryl Rowland. London: Allen & Unwin, 1974. Pp 140–52.
The Clerk, rather than being, along with the Squire, the youngest of the pilgrims (as is sometimes thought), was probably a graduate student in

theology, and in his early thirties. 'He is an obviously learned and mature man' who has been at the university for 'a long time,' teaching there as well as pursuing his studies (p 149).

998 Simmonds, James D. ' "Hende Nicholas" and the Clerk.' *N&Q*, New Series 9 (1962), 446.

The similarities between Nicholas of the *MilT* and the Clerk of *GP* may have been intended to 'present the Miller as satirizing the Clerk as an individual, and, through him as representative of a type, clerks in general.' The Miller implies that clerks with a modest, sober, and apparently virtuous demeanor are really hypocrites.

999 Spearing, A.C. *Criticism and Medieval Poetry.* London: Edward Arnold, 1964; New York: Barnes & Noble, 1964. 2nd ed. 1972.

The Clerk is said to speak not one word more than necessary (line 304). 'The brevity of Chaucer's Clerk appears in an essentially moral context — it is part of his general abstemiousness, a Christian plainness analogous to the avoidance of rhyming and chiming urged upon the preacher by the *artes praedicandi*' (1972, p 166). His brevity is not 'conciseness for its own sake' as a rhetorical principle (p 166), but part of his overall characterization.

1000 Taylor, Jerome. *'Fraunceys Petrak* and the *Logyk* of Chaucer's Clerk.' In *Francis Petrarch, Six Centuries Later: A Symposium.* Chapel Hill, NC: University of North Carolina Department of Romance Languages, 1975; Chicago: Newberry Library, 1975. North Carolina Studies in the Romance Languages and Literatures, 3. Pp 364–83.

In *GP*, Chaucer's Clerk is shown to be a devotee of logic and of Aristotle, though in the prologue to his tale he is shown to be a devotee of Petrarch, who was a critic of scholastic logic and of Aristotelian ideas. However, these two characterizations of the Clerk are not in conflict. The Clerk is 'a devotee of logic in its broadest medieval sense,' not a scholastic 'dialectical quibbler' (p 378) of the sort to which Petrarch objected. Through the Clerk, Chaucer projects 'such views on philosophy, logic, poetry, and moral persuasion as Petrarch may be found to express directly' (p 367). Thus the Clerk 'is given the best of two only apparently conflicting worlds: the best of the world of Aristotle and "logic" as the Middle Ages and Petrarch would interpret these, and the best of the fabulous poetic world of Petrarch' as well (p 383).

1001 Turton, R.B. 'The Clerk of Oxenford.' *TLS*, May 19, 1932, p 368.

Responding to Richardson (**994**), this article corrects certain details pertaining to William Mowbray and his will. Slight skepticism of the identification of the Clerk with Waulthier Dissy is expressed, though without discussion. In reply again see Richardson (**995**).

1002 Ussery, Huling E. 'How Old is Chaucer's Clerk?' *TSE*, 15 (1967), 1–18.
Although the Clerk is often interpreted as a young college student, it is far
more probable 'that he is an eminent middle-aged scholar and logician' (p
18), probably between thirty and fifty years old. The word *clerk* is used by
Chaucer to refer to many eminent individuals (Aristotle, Plato, Augustine,
Boethius, etc); hence the term does not limit the Clerk's position to that of
a young student. It would not be likely for a young student to be called a
philosophre, or to have an extensive library, or to be teaching. The internal
chronology of the Clerk's statement that he heard his tale from Petrarch
means that the Clerk must be over thirty, since Petrarch died in 1374.
The 'maturity of his talk' (lines 304–7) 'would seem priggish in a young
man, appropriate in a mature man' (p 9). His position in *GP*, between the
Merchant and the Man of Law, indicates that he is likely to be eminent,
since the overall sequence of portraits proceeds from high to low social
status. His poverty is no obstacle to this interpretation, for 'a professional
scholarly concern with logic was an active hindrance to ecclesiastical and
worldy advancement' (p 14). He corresponds to the character of the ideal
clerk in Vincent of Beauvais's *De Eruditione Filiorum*, which may be one of
Chaucer's sources, but he also corresponds to reality. His portrait embodies
a 'perfect blending of real and ideal' traits (p 18). Cf **487**.

1003 —— . 'Fourteenth-Century English Logicians: Possible Models for Chaucer's Clerk.' *TSE*, 18 (1970), 1–15.
The careers of 36 fourteenth-century logicians in England are examined.
On the whole, these men were secular rather than regular clerics, were
affiliated with Oxford (especially with Merton College), and were not particularly successful in obtaining either secular offices or clerical benefices.
'Consequently, the fact that the Clerk has no benefice should not be taken
to imply that he is young, inept, or unworldly. It is entirely in accordance
with the professional study of logic during his time' (p 11). It is not necessarily to be assumed that the Clerk is in orders, for 'among logicians it was
usual to put off the taking of even minor orders until a benefice was assured'
or even afterwards (p 12). The Clerk is 'a mature Oxford scholar and logician, as prominent in his field as his flankers in the *General Prologue*, the
Merchant and Sergeant of the Law, were in their fields' (p 15). Five men
are suggested as possible or likely models for the portrait: Edward Upton,
Robert de Alyngton, John Chilmark, Robert Stonham, and Ralph Strode.
Cf **487**.

1004 Weisheipl, James A., O.P. 'Curriculum of the Faculty of Arts at Oxford in
the early Fourteenth Century.' *MS*, 26 (1964), 143–85.
Though *GP* itself is not discussed, much information pertinent to the

Clerk's experiences as an Oxford student is presented here. Weisheipl describes medieval methods of teaching, stages of university education (undergraduate, bachelor, master), books likely to be read in each part of the curriculum, etc. 'At Oxford the greatest emphasis was placed on the study of logic, which occupied about half of the actual curriculum' (p 169—cf line 286).

1005 Winney, James, ed. *The General Prologue to the Canterbury Tales by Geoffrey Chaucer.* 1965. See **73**.
The Clerk shares some characteristics of the Reeve's outward appearance and 'is treated in part as a comic figure' (p 38). He has beggared himself but has achieved no benefice (see line 293). 'His physical hollowness supplies an ironic comment on the worth of a pursuit which substitutes book-learning for an immediate personal experience of life' (p 38). The Clerk's 'underfed horse, and his own scarecrow appearance, reveal a man starved of contact with the great concourse of everyday human affairs' (p 98).

1006 Wood, Chauncey. 'Chaucer's Clerk and Chalcidius.' *ELN*, 4 (1966-1967), 166–72.
Wood acknowledges that Chaucer's description of the Clerk may be indebted to John of Salisbury's *Policraticus*, as Fleming (**982**) has shown. However, the passage on learning and teaching (line 308) is also paralleled in the *Roman de la Rose*, and both of these sources are indebted to Chalcidius's translation of Plato's *Timaeus*. Chalcidius 'broadened Plato's meaning enough so that Jean de Meun could discover the purposes of speech to be not only understanding and communication but also communication for the purpose of teaching others' (p 170). Chaucer's further modification was 'to make the power of speech into an active virtue' (p 170). In this characteristic the Clerk can be compared to the Parson, who is also a *clerk* (line 480) and who uses speech for charitable teaching. 'Chaucer himself was a kind of "Clerk," and it seems undeniable that his choice of the pilgrimage for the framework of the *Tales* was motivated by his desire to have characters use speech to one another so that he might teach and we might learn, just as the pilgrims instruct and learn (or do not instruct and do not learn)' (p 171).

✌ Part 14: The Serjeant at Law

See the Introduction, p xxxv above, for a brief summary of criticism on the Serjeant (Man of Law), and see the Index for further references.

1008 Baugh, Albert C. 'Chaucer's Serjeant of the Law and the Year Books.' In *Mélanges de Langue et de Littérature du Moyen Age et de la Renaissance offerts à Jean Frappier par ses collègues, ses élèves et ses amis.* Geneva: Droz, 1970. Publications Romanes et Françaises, 112. Vol 1, pp 65–76.
If Chaucer were proceeding strictly according to 'degree,' it would be the Serjeant of the Law, not the Knight, who would begin the sequence of portraits and tales, since the Serjeant is the pilgrim of most distinguished rank. The phrase *In termes* (line 323) has occasioned some difficulty in interpretation. When Chaucer tells us 'that the Man of Law *hadde in termes* cases and judgments going back to the Conqueror he is saying that this successful lawyer had a collection of those medieval law reports which we call the Year Books' (p 76).

1009 Beichner, Paul E., C.S.C. 'Chaucer's Man of Law and *Disparitas Cultus.*' *Spec,* 23 (1948), 70–75.
The Man of Law's knowledge of the legalities pertaining to *disparitas cultus* (difference of religion), which is displayed in his tale, is suitable to his *GP* portrait. Trained in civil law, he would have known canon law insofar as it affected civil law — as it would in a marriage of questionable legality from the Church's viewpoint, such as Constance's marriage to the Sultan in his tale.

1010 Bowden, Muriel. *A Commentary on the General Prologue to the Canterbury Tales.* 1948. See **104.**
Bowden reviews the functions of the Serjeant of the Law. He is 'a shrewd business man as well as a noted lawyer' (p 168); contemporary criticisms

of lawyers are compared to the details in the portrait. For Chaucer's audience, he 'could have been none other than the ever-clever and somewhat dubiously rich Thomas Pynchbek of Lincolnshire' (p 172).

1010 Browne, W[illia]m Hand. 'Notes on Chaucer's Astrology.' *MLN*, 23 (1908), 553–54.
The Man of Law's personality in *GP*, which shows him 'evidently at the top of his profession,' is suitable to his tale, which he tells 'as if he were pleading before a jury' (p 53). Cf **1020**.

1011 Coffin, R.C. 'Notes on Chaucer, II, In termes.' *MLR*, 18 (1923), 336–37.
Coffin suggests that the phrase *In termes* (line 323) means 'in legal jargon,' ie in Anglo-French or Latin law terminology (p 336).

1012 Cohen, Herman. *A History of the English Bar and Attornatus to 1450.* London: Sweet and Maxwell, 1929; Toronto: Carswell, 1929.
Chaucer's legal references in *GP* are considered from the viewpoint of English legal history. 'His view of the lawyers represents the prevailing view of the English people' (p 486). Chaucer was evidently not trained as a lawyer, 'but was conversant socially with legal circles' (p 488), judging from his familiarity with legal situations. His portrait of the Serjeant is 'the first finished picture of an English lawyer' (p 489); given the date, his choice of a serjeant to represent lawyers is expected. The mention of King William in the Serjeant's knowledge of statute and case-law 'seems to imply, correctly, that the popular view was that the forensic system of the day practically began with the coming of the Normans and not earlier' (p 492). The Serjeant is represented 'as belonging to the upper middle class' (p 492). What Chaucer does *not* mention in connection with the Serjeant is also of historical value: he does not mention the legal functions of *narrator, attornatus,* or *countour* in connection with his lawyer, although the Franklin is said to be a *countour.* Conspicuously absent in the Lawyer's portrait are the Inns. Those houses are mentioned instead in the Manciple's portrait — and Chaucer's treatment of the inn of court implies that at this time it was a residence, rather than a place of education. 'Perhaps, indeed, his silence confirms our belief that as yet there was no, certainly no developed, system of legal education' (p 497).

1013 David, Alfred. 'The Man of Law vs Chaucer: A Case in Poetics.' *PMLA*, 82 (1967), 217–25.
'The Sergeant of the Law is a man of appearances,' as lines 312–13 and 321–22 suggest (p 221). 'In his own life, we are led to suspect, he is perhaps neither so dignified nor so moral as he would like to appear' (p 221).

1014 Delasanta, Rodney. 'And of Great Reverence: Chaucer's Man of Law.' *ChauR*, 5 (1970–1971), 288–310.

The Serjeant's characterization in *GP* is supported by his later appearances in *CT*. Throughout, he is shown as 'being less than he pretends to be' (p 297). Though the *GP* narrator often seems uncritically enthusiastic about the pilgrims, he 'immediately hedges with the Man of Law,' for his cautionary phrase, *He semed swich* (line 313), implies that the narrator is not wholly certain. Delasanta finds that 'Manly's famous designation of Thomas Pynchbek as the biographical source of Chaucer's inspiration for the Man of Law is convincing' (p 306; see **1026**), but suggests that Biblical and Lollard components are probably present in the characterization too.

1015 Eliason, Mary. 'The Peasant and the Lawyer.' *SP*, 48 (1951), 506–26.

Chaucer has idealized the lowest aspects of society, presenting the Parson and Plowman as ideal Christians who offer the social remedy of 'love expressed through humble labor' (p 506). The Serjeant of the Law too could have been of such a background. Law-cases show that peasants used the courts to obtain the status of freemen. Some lawyers were themselves of humble origin (instances are noted) and thus 'in the lawyer the poor man of the third estate saw a living witness to the fact that men of energy and brains could prosper' (p 520). The Man of Law 'had a native ability that insured his success' (p 522), for he is not depicted as owing his position to dishonesty. He may retain 'a small core of insecurity that makes him hate poverty' (p 525) and strongly admire success. He may recognize in the Miller and Reeve 'the life that he had escaped when he left the farm,' while the Knight 'must have reminded him of all that he desired' (p 525). The Man of Law looks forward towards a future when 'all men could hope to prosper' (p 526).

1016 Farrell, Robert T. 'Chaucer's Man of Law and His Tale: The Eccentric Design.' In *J.R.R. Tolkien, Scholar and Storyteller, Essays in Memoriam*. Ed. Mary Salu and Robert T. Farrell. Ithaca, NY, and London: Cornell University Press, 1979. Pp 159–72.

The Man of Law is an impressive figure, 'rich and skilled in his profession,' though the 'element that strikes me as most obvious' in the portrait 'is *tension*' (p 164). In lines 312–13 and 321–12 'the surface of the character is twice lifted' and suspicion is aroused, though 'no specific cause for uneasiness is given' (pp 164–5). His tale too shows tension; it is 'a revelation of an acutely troubled intelligence' (p 172).

1017 Frost, George L. 'Chaucer's Man of Law at the Parvis.' *MLN*, 44 (1929), 496–501.

The Man of Law has often been 'at the parvys' (line 310). In contrast to the usual assumption that this phrase means the porch of St Paul's, where laywers met their clients, Manly (see **35**), in annotating this line, has suggested that it refers to the court of the Exchequer or to student sessions in the inns of court. Frost argues, against Manly, that the usual interpretation — St Paul's — is more likely to be correct. However, the exact location was evidently not an *outside* porch, but an area *inside* the building, at 'the pillars along the north aisle of St. Paul's' (p 500).

1018 Goffin, R.C. 'Notes on Chaucer.' *MLR*, 18 (1923), 336-37.
The phrase *in termes* (lines 323) apparently means ' "in legal jargon," ie in Anglo-French or Latin law phraseology' (p 336) — rather than, as Pollard suggests (see **4**), 'exactly, precisely,' which does not as satisfactorily 'bring out the obvious meaning' (p 337).

1019 Hamilton, Marie P. 'The Dramatic Suitability of "The Man of Law's Tale." ' In *Studies in Language and Literature in Honour of Margaret Schlauch*. Ed. Mieczysław Brahmer, Stanisław Helsztyński, and Julian Krzyżanowski. Warsaw: PWN-Polish Scientific Publishers, 1966. Pp 153-63. Rpt New York: Russell & Russell, 1971.
Examining 'the incongruity between the [Man of Law's] portrait in the General Prologue and the impression made by the Lawyer in his headlink and tale' (1966, p 153), Hamilton finds that the contrast has been exaggerated. Chaucer apparently modified his sources to make the tale more suitable to the Man of Law as depicted in *GP*. Aspects of the narrative style of the Man of Law — 'the rhetorical manner in which he punctuates the narrative with pleas, encomiums, apostrophes, and imprecations; his professional handling of the problem of *disparitas cultus*; his informed presentation of the trial of Constance' (p 163) — suggest a knowledge of legal precedent befitting the pilgrim of *GP*.

1020 Knowlton, Edgar C. 'Chaucer's Man of Law.' *JEGP*, 23 (1924), 83-93.
Despite doubts that have been raised about the suitability of the Man of Law to his tale, the tale *is* appropriate to his personality as depicted in *GP*. We need not assume that as a lawyer he would be sceptical of miracles, and we should indeed assume that as a lawyer he knew 'what would carry with his audience' (p 84). As Browne pointed out (see **1010**), the tale is told in a lawyer's manner, and there is no reason why the Man of Law should not have been interested in secular literature. It is possible that, within the narrative framework of *GP*, the Man of Law would have been known to Chaucer the pilgrim prior to the group's arrival at the Tabard, or that Chaucer made himself known to the Man of Law there. Thus the Man of Law's later comments about Chaucer the poet are based on his knowledge that the poet is part of the group.

1021 Lambkin, Martha Dampf. 'Chaucer's Man of Law As a Purchasour.' *Comitatus*, 1 (1970), 81–84.

Chaucer's uses of the term *purchase*, which are supported by other writers' examples, establish that illegal or improper financial transactions are meant. In the portrait of the Man of Law, Chaucer's use of *purchasour* (line 318) and *purchasyng* (line 320) may involve a *double-entendre* that adds the legal meaning of 'possession of land by means other than descent' (p 82) to this meaning of reprehensible transactions. There is 'a strong suspicion' that Chaucer has depicted the Man of Law as 'akin to a crook, albeit a socially and professionally prominent one' (p 84).

1022 Lewis, Robert Enzer. 'Chaucer's Artistic Use of Pope Innocent III's *De Miseria Humane Conditionis* in the Man of Law's Prologue and Tale.' *PMLA*, 81 (1966), 485–92.

In *GP* two of the most important features of the Man of Law's portrait are 'his present wealth' and 'his preoccupation with acquiring more' (p 486). This concern with wealth appears in his later apostrophe to poverty. If, as Manly thought (see **1026**), the Man of Law was modelled upon Thomas Pynchbek, then the praise of wealthy merchants in the Man of Law's headlink is quite suitable, since Pynchbek was a wealthy landowner. The *De Miseria*, source of the lines on poverty, is used to further develop 'the character of the Man of Law as presented in the General Prologue' (p 492).

1023 Loomis, Dorothy Bethurum. 'Constance and the Stars.' In *Chaucerian Problems and Perspectives: Essays Presented to Paul E. Beichner, C.S.C.* Ed. Edward Vasta and Zacharias P. Thundy. Notre Dame and London: University of Notre Dame Press, 1979. Pp 207–20.

Although 'Chaucer has done something to adjust the tale to the Man of Law,' the Constance story is *not* 'an especially appropriate one' for the pilgrim of *GP* (p 207). Neither the trial scene nor Chaucer's added rhetoric should be taken as demonstrating the teller's skill.

1024 Lumiansky, R.M. *Of Sondry Folk: The Dramatic Principle in the Canterbury Tales.* 1955. See **348**.

The Serjeant, who 'rood but hoomly in a medlee cote' (line 328), was dressed quite modestly for his station: 'Sergeants seem generally to have dressed more richly' (p 63). The Host, as an innkeeper, would have been accustomed to estimating people's status by their clothing, and the relative plainness of the Serjeant's garb in *GP* may explain why the Host later calls him simply a man of law, not a 8serjeant (see Prologue to *MLT*, II.33). Although Manly is correct that Pynchbek is a model for the Serjeant (see **1026**), 'this is not to say that the literary creation equals Pynchbek; it is to say, however, that there are humorous overtones in the literary sketch that

would have been meaningful to anyone who knew much about Pynchbek'
(p 63).

1025 McKenna, Isobel. 'The Making of a Fourteenth Century Sergeant of the
Lawe.' *RUO*, 45 (1975), 244–62.
The qualifications, responsibilities, selection procedures, and ceremonies
of the serjeants-at-law are reviewed. The serjeants felt a special respect
for Becket, who represented 'an intelligent man from the people who supported the separation of church and state' (p 250), a separation that facil-
itated the development of common law. It is therefore not surprising that
Chaucer's Serjeant, who in almost every characteristic 'corresponds to the
typical serjeant-at-law of the period' (p 261), is undertaking a pilgrimage
to the place of Becket's martyrdom. The short, parti-colored robe given to
the Serjeant in the Ellesmere manuscript's i8llustration 'would seem to be
an accurate representative of the traveling costume for his rank' (p 258).
'Modestly and correctly, the Serjeant is wearing informal dress, indicating
his rank as was required. Then, having told us of the Serjeant's skill and
accomplishments and proper apparel, Chaucer simply had nothing else to
add. This is a man totally committed to his place in the world, which was
the medieval ideal for the good life: he is the perfect Serjeant of the Law'
(p 260).

1026 Manly, John Matthews. *Some New Light on Chaucer*. 1926. See **362**.
In the chapter 'The Man of Law and the Franklin' (pp 131–68), Manly
suggests that the Serjeant may be modeled upon the historical Thomas
Pynchbek, whose career corresponds to that of Chaucer's pilgrim, and
whose name may be included, in punning fashion, in line 326. The Serjeant's companion, the Franklin, may be modeled upon John Bussy, who
li8ved near Pynchbek's home and held manors not far from the holdings of
Katherine Swynford, Chaucer's sister-in-law. Cf **1014**, **1022**, **1024**, **1029**,
1067.

1027 Mann, Jill. *Chaucer and Medieval Estates Satire*. 1973. See **363**.
'The concentration on means rather than ends in Chaucer's descriptions of
the professional skills of the pilgrims is clearly illustrated' by the portraits
of the Serjeant, Physician, Merchant, and Guildsmen—pilgrims who share
'the narrator's enthusiastic admiration for their professional qualififcations
and capabilities, but the social effects of their sometimes dubious practices
are left out of account' (p 86). Any awareness of their victims is omitted.
Having no clear information about the results of the Serjeant's activities,
we are forced to take him 'on the terms of his façade ... we do not know
what lies behind it. To suggest a front without giving away the reality is a
feat which Chaucer manages with dexterity' (pp 90–1). Similarly, 'we have

no *evidence* that the Doctor is a grasping charlatan, despite our suspicions' (p 98); with the Merchant too, 'the professional façade is the basis of our knowledge' (p 102); and 'the moral state of the Guildsmen is not something on which we're given evidence' (p 105).

1028 Norman, Arthur. 'The Man of Law's Tale.' In *Studies in Language, Literature and Culture of the Middle Ages and Later* [Festschrift for Rudolph Willard]. Ed. E. Bagby Atwood and Archibald A. Hill. Austin: University of Texas Press, 1969. Pp 312–23.

'Except for the eloquent prayers and the impassioned apostrophes by the narrator, the Man of Law's Tale never bombards the reader or listener with those grenade-bursts of details that assault us throughout the General Prolog' (p 322).

1029 Reed, A.W. Review of *Some New Light on Chaucer*, by John Matthews Manly (see **362, 1026**). *RES*, 4 (1928), 217–20.

Reed explains the phrase *In termes* (line 323): the Serjeant of the Law had a collection of cases in Year Books arranged according to the Hilary, Easter, Trinity, and Michaelmas *Terms*. In reply, see **1037**.

1030 Rickert, Edith. 'New Life Records of Chaucer—I.' *TLS*, September 27, 1928, p 684.

Contemporary writs indicate that Chaucer would have had 'mental associations hardly of a pleasant character with the name of Thomas Pynchebek,' whose 'career affords the closest parallel suggested as yet to that of Chaucer's Man-of-Law.'

1031 Scheps, Walter. 'Chaucer's Man of Law and the Tale of Constance.' *PMLA*, 89 (1974), 285–95.

'The Tale of Constance is intended to be an encomium upon the teller's profession'; it shows the rhetorical excesses of his training, which 'has enabled the Man of Law to attain his eminent position' (p 285). The *GP* portrait 'is certainly satirical' (p 286), especially in lines 312–13, 318–20, and 321–22, and probably also in line 327. The Man of Law's vanity is 'to some extent justifiable' since he has obtained an important position 'on the basis of his superiority to his colleagues' (p 286). His position brings him prestige, but is not necessarily lucrative, and he is concerned about wealth. He also takes pride in his learning. In the tale the Man of Law engages in 'professional idealization' or 'wish fulfillment' — it is a tale in which 'lawyer, victim, truth, and God are all on the same side' and are shown to prevail (p 292). Chaucer has used this narrative as 'primarily a vehicle for the revelation of the teller's character,' with 'everything we learn of the Man of Law in the General Prologue' being made 'dramatically present' within the tale (p 294).

1032 Skeat, Walter W., ed. *The Complete Works of Geoffrey Chaucer, Edited from Numerous Manuscripts.* 1894–1897. See **3**.

Skeat proposes that *In terms hadde he* (line 323) means that the Man of Law 'knew how to express in proper terms' his legal cases (vol 5, p 32).

1033 Sullivan, William L. 'Chaucer's Man of Law as a Literary Critic.' *MLN*, 68 (1953), 1–8.

In *GP* 'three features of the Man of Law's character are outstanding: first, his apparent wisdom and busyness; second, his concern with the acquisition of wealth; and third, his unusual memory' (p 2). In lines 312–13 and 321–22, 'Chaucer intimates that the Man of Law is *not* all he seemed to be' (p 2). This characterization is continued in the Man of Law's later prologue to his tale: we need not accept his comments on literature there as if he really *were* as wise as he seems, since in *GP* we have been warned that he is not.

1034 Warren, Edward H. 'Serjeants-at Law; the Order of the Coif.' *VLR*, 28 (1941–1942), 911–50.

Warren reviews the origin, functions, and decline of the serjeants-at-law, along with providing information about legal education, ceremonies, types of judges, etc. The number of practicing serjeants-at-law at one time was probably no more than about a dozen. During the long reign of Edward III, fifty-seven serjeants-at-law were created; during the reign of Richard II, twenty-one. Their identifying symbol of dress was the coif — a cloth head-covering, white or at least partly white, which was worn even in the presence of the king. They had very high status: 'Serjeants-at-law were awe-inspiring personages. They fed the Bench; they led the Bar; they were in an inner circle of the Great Men of the Realm' (pp 911–12).

1035 Wentersdorf, Karl P. 'The *termes* of Chaucer's Sergeant of the Law.' *SN*, 53 (1981), 269–74.

Lines 323–27 mean that the narrator reports that the Serjeant was familiar, through 'experience and study,' with 'all the hearings and judgments as far back as the Conquest,' so that he could use this learning *in termes* 'or during the court sessions' (p 274). This claim, which is 'patently absurd,' is used to help characterize the lawyer, and, 'in recording the Serjeant's self-laudatory hyperbole, Chaucer the artist is simply practising his customary irony' (p 274).

1036 Whitbread, L. 'Six Chaucer Notes.' 1978. See **659**.

Line 326 has been interpreted as containing a reference to Thomas Pynch-bek. Whitbread finds such a reference doubtful, in view of an analogous passage suggesting that to 'pinch at,' ie, to rebut, was a term with 'idiomatic status at least in the lawyers' talk of Chaucer's day' (p 41); thus no specific reference to any person need be intended.

1037 Wyatt, A.J. 'Chaucer's "In Termës." ' *RES*, 4 (1928), 439.

Wyatt reasserts the usual interpretation of line 323, in which the phrase *In termës* has been taken to mean that the Sergeant of the Law could use proper legal terminology. Wyatt rejects Reed's interpretation (that the Sergeant has a collection of Year Books arranged according to the law Terms of the Year; see **1029**).

❧ Part 15: The Franklin

See the Introduction, p xxxv above, for a brief summary of criticism on the Franklin, and see the Index for further references.

1038 Berger, Harry, Jr. 'The F-Fragment of the Canterbury Tales.' *ChauR*, 1 (1966–1967), 88–102 [Part I] and 135–56 [Part II].

The Squire's and Franklin's tales are discussed as being suitable to their tellers' *GP* descriptions. The Franklin's diet, which varies according to the seasons (see lines 347–48), shows that 'his innate tendency to self-indulgence is fitted into the wider frame of social and natural order. As a natural and sensual function eating is self-directed, but the Franklin has made it the basis of a social or ritual occasion . . . . even if we read his careful hospitality as a display of status which may reflect upward-mobile tendencies, it seems clear that this indulgence is also justified by his generosity' (p 139).

1039 Birney, Earle. 'The Franklin's "Sop in Wyn." ' *N&Q*, New Series 6 (1959), 345–47.

The Franklin's sop (line 334) should not necessarily be interpreted as a rich repast. Sometimes the sop in wine was only dried or toasted bread in spiced wine, and Langland uses *sop* to mean 'anything of small value' (p 346). The Franklin may choose it for practical reasons. In the *Awntyrs off Arthure* Sir Gawain is given a sop to strengthen him and clear his head. Medieval statements on health and diet recommend the sop in wine 'for salutary purposes' (p 346). Bryant (**1042**) noted the healthful characteristics of the sop in wine, but his picture of the Franklin as a temperate man is at variance with lines 343–44, which state that his house snowed with meat, drink, and dainties. The only other Chaucerian character to take a sop in wine, January of the *MerchT*, 'does so in the wake of manifold self-indulgence' (p 347). The Franklin's indulgences too 'might prompt him to begin the new day with something to purge his teeth and sharpen his sight and restore his digestion' (p 347). In fact, he might choose a spare breakfast to permit himself a keener appreciation of 'the supper to come' (p 347).

1040 Blenner-Hassett, Roland. 'Autobiographical Aspects of Chaucer's Franklin.' *Spec*, 28 (1953), 791–800.
The Franklin (in his *GP* portrait and in his tale) 'contains hints about Chaucer's own nature and training' (p 791) and can be seen as partially autobiographical. The Franklin accompanies the Man of Law because of shared interests; Chaucer too would have had legal concerns. Two of the offices held by the Franklin (lord of the sessions and knight of the shire) were offices that Chaucer held himself.

1041 Brewer, D.S. 'Chaucer and Chrétien and Arthurian Romance.' In *Chaucer and Middle English Studies in Honour of Rossell Hope Robbins*. Ed. Beryl Rowland. London: Allen and Unwin, 1974. Pp 255–59.
Frankis (**1047**), in suggesting that Chaucer's use of the word *vavasour* (line 360) was indebted to Chrétien de Troyes, knew of no other evidence that Chaucer used Chrétien's works. Brewer here suggests that a knowledge of Chrétien may also underlie the references to Lancelot in *NPT* (VIII. 3212) and *SqT* (V. 287); and that Chaucer's lost *Book of the Leoun* may have been a translation of Chrétien's *Yvain*.

1042 Bryant, Joseph Allen, Jr. 'The Diet of Chaucer's Franklin.' *MLN*, 63 (1948), 318–25.
The Franklin, though by no means a young man, seems to enjoy excellent health. Chaucer has given us part of the explanation in lines 347–48, where we are told that the Franklin changed his diet according to the seasons. Such a practice was recommended by the *Secreta Secretorum* and other sources. In addition, the specific foods mentioned as forming the Franklin's diet are those that medieval authorities would have recommended. According to contemporary theory, he should eat 'an abundance of firm, dry food; and this is precisely the kind of food Chaucer has prescribed for him' (p 323). The partridge, for example, was regarded as a dry bird, easily digested; bream and luce are drier than certain other fish; even the Franklin's morning sop in wine would have had 'drying qualities' (p 324). Chaucer's Physician 'would probably agree that the Franklin has taken satisfactory precautions to preserve the balance of elements which constitutes his natural endowment of good health' (p 324). He is well-supplied with the kind of food that he should eat, it is prepared healthfully, and he has cultivated a taste for the recommended foods and seasonings. Thus his care about his diet would seem to provide 'a reasonable explanation of the old man's unusual vigor' (p 325). In reply, see Birney, **1039**.

1043 Burlin, Robert B. 'The Art of Chaucer's Franklin.' *Neophil*, 51 (1967), 55–73. Rpt with revisions in *Chaucer: The Canterbury Tales, A Casebook*, ed. J.J. Anderson (London: Macmillan, 1974), pp 183–208.

The Franklin is socially insecure; he ranks with the landed gentry but is 'unsure of real gentility' (1967, p 57). Most of his *GP* portrait is devoted to his Epicurean behavior. The enthusiasm expressed for this materialism is the narrator's, not the author's. The Franklin's main concern is shown to be 'the splendid display of unsurpassed wealth and taste' (p 58). His companionship with the Serjeant of Law suggests some incongruity in the Franklin, though not the kind of deception found in the Serjeant himself. Overall, the portrait shows 'an otherwise sober, capable man of practical affairs who is innocently infatuated with an aristocratic performance which he can imitate but not quite fully understand' (p 59).

1044 Camden, Carroll, Jr. 'Chauceriana.' 1932. See **670**.

Chaucer says that the Franklin is *sangwyn* (line 333) and that he is generous, loves food, and seeks pleasure. 'Such a description is in accord with medieval conceptions of the sanguine humor' (p 360), judging from the *Secreta Secretorum* and other texts.

1045 Carruthers, Mary J. 'The Gentilesse of Chaucer's Franklin.' *Crit*, 23 (1981), 283–300.

The Franklin clearly holds the rank of gentleman. His emphasis on the table in his hall (lines 353–54) accords with an earlier ethic of sharing one's food, rather than dining apart. 'By maintaining the custom of the hall, Chaucer not only identifies the Franklin as generous but associates him with an antique social ideal no longer honored in an age of greed and rancour' (p 290). Earlier vavasours in literature 'represent hospitality, familial concern, honesty, unfailing generosity and the wisdom of ripe years' (p 292; for *vavasour* see line 360). However, this idealization 'is qualified by the nostalgia which clings unmistakably to these dear old dads' who 'appear as quaint, a bit too good to be true, and thus peripheral if helpful figures. That same nostalgia surrounds Chaucer's Franklin' (p 292).

1046 Emerson, O.F. 'Chaucer and Medieval Hunting.' 1922. See **741**.

The seasonal changes in the Franklin's diet (lines 347–48) were 'doubtless partly dependent on hunting' (p 143).

1047 Frankis, P.J. 'Chaucer's "Vavasour" and Chrétien de Troyes.' *N&Q*, New Series 15 (1968), 46–47.

Past discussions of Chaucer's word *vavasour*, applied to the Franklin (line 360), have left it still a problem. The word was not in common usage in England and its meaning by etymology, 'a vassal of vassals' (p 46), is not helpful here. It is probable that Chaucer is drawing upon Chrétien de Troyes, who in *Yvain* and in *Erec et Enide* presents a character who is called a *vavasor* and is notable for his hospitality; in *Erec* he is also white-haired and employs a cook. Thus the vavasour would have been, in a literary sense, 'a model of hospitality' (p 46). There is no other evidence that Chaucer knew Chrétien's poems. However, the French poet's work was available, as the Middle English poem *Ywain and Gawain*, dated to the first half of the fourteenth century and based on Chrétien's *Yvain*, indicates. See also **1041**.

1048 Gerould, Gordon Hall. 'The Social Status of Chaucer's Franklin.' *PMLA*, 41 (1926), 262–79. Rpt with revisions in Gerould, **254**, pp 33–54.
A study of medieval occurrences of the term *franklin* supports the viewpoint that Chaucer's Franklin belongs to the landed gentry. He travels with the Serjeant of Law; they are of the same rank and share common interests in the law; *sergeant* in fact was sometimes equated with *franklin*. The Franklin is certainly 'a gentleman by token of his election' to Parliament (p 273), if not in other ways. He is a wealthy man, 'notable in his shire' (p 273), 'of high position in his county' (274), and, as a *vavasour* (see line 360), he 'was a magnate, and a person of dignity' (p 276). Thus the Franklin should *not* be interpreted (as is sometimes done) as a parvenu, insecure about his background or his social status. In reply, see **1049**.

1049 Haller, Robert S. 'Chaucer's *Squire's Tale* and the Uses of Rhetoric.' 1965. See **722**.
Haller replies briefly to the viewpoint of Gerould (**1048**) that the Franklin belongs among those who are *gentil* by class.

1050 Hart, Walter Morris. 'The Franklin's Tale.' In *Haverford Essays: Studies in Modern Literature Prepared by Some Former Pupils of Professor Francis B. Gummere.* Haverford, PA: Haverford College [privately printed], 1909. Pp 185–234.
The Franklin's tale reflects the vavasour of *GP*, who is aware of his status, who combines 'delight in high living and high thinking,' and who would naturally express a 'sturdy middle-class morality' (p 186). The tale's descriptions of Aurelius and Arveragus resemble the portraits of the Squire and Knight of *GP*, but the *GP* versions are more vivid and concrete.

1051 Keenan, Hugh T. 'The General Prologue to the Canterbury Tales, Lines 345–346.' *NM*, 79 (1978), 36–40.
Chaucer's comment that the Franklin's house *snewed* with food (line 346) associates the Franklin's feast with the Mass. The miracle of the manna, which was presented in images of hoarfrost, sleet, and snow, was seen as

a figure or type of the Last Supper and the Eucharistic banquet of the saved. The manna was also said to take on the flavor of whatever food the eater desired; the Franklin's superlative feast similarly provides whatever dainties his guests can think of. 'Beside it, the Host's promised supper, the game for which all are contending, pales into insignificance' (p 39). What Chaucer intended by this metaphor is 'debatable,' depending on one's overall interpretation of the Franklin, but it is certain that 'the Franklin's feast becomes ambiguous through its Eucharistic shadows' (p 40).

052 King, Francis, and Bruce Steele, eds. *Selections from Geoffrey Chaucer's The Canterbury Tales.* 1969. See **82**.
The Franklin 'comes to seem an almost mythical figure, not of Appetite but of Abundance' (p 348). He accepts social responsibility as well as enjoying his wealth. 'It is ironic that, of all the pilgrims, only the ideal Parson and Ploughman and the Epicurean Franklin show active charity' (p 348).

053 Kuhl, Ernest P. 'Chaucer's Burgesses.' *TWA*, 18 (1916), 652–75.
Several Justices of the Peace owned property along the pilgrimage route between London and Canterbury. Chaucer may have observed, from life, the hospitality of the Franklin. Thomas Shardelowe is suggested as a possible candidate for a historical model behind the Franklin's portrait. See also **1076**.

054 Lumiansky, R.M. 'The Character and Performance of Chaucer's Franklin.' *UTQ*, 20 (1950-1951), 344–56.
In the Franklin's portrait Chaucer has depicted an Epicurean who is also able and industrious. 'It may be that the Franklin acts the part of St Julian in his country in an effort to imitate conduct he thinks suitable for great nobles, whose ranks he is eager to join,' for he is anxious for social advancement (p 347). He is an ambiguous character, with 'a double concern for the behaviour of the nobility, on the one hand, and for the everyday world, on the other' (p 356). In reply, see **1066**.

055 ——. 'Two Notes on the Canterbury Tales.' 1966. See **892**.
The *GP* contrast between the Franklin's and the Physician's attitudes towards food and money supports the viewpoint that the Physician's tale was meant to follow the Franklin's. Such a 'contrast in personal traits between successive story-tellers' (p 228) appears in the Miller-Reeve and Friar-Summoner pairs; Chaucer may well have intended the Franklin-Physician pair to tell successive tales also.

056 Mann, Jill. *Chaucer and Medieval Estates Satire.* 1973. See **363**.
'Franklins as a class do not figure in estates literature' (p 152), but three major aspects of the Franklin's portrait—'first, his character as gourmet

and host; secondly, his sanguine complexion; thirdly, his tenure of various public posts' (p 153)—are found in medieval satiric writings, often in association with various vices and forms of corruption. The *GP* portrait, however, omits any openly negative components. Where other writings associate a great love of food with gluttony, Chaucer invites us to 'admire the means, the superlative way in which the Franklin pursues a life-style, rather than the ends towards which it is directed' (p 158). Similarly, where other writings associate the holding of public office with extortion, bribery, and the oppression of the poor, Chaucer 'removes any hint of corruption or extortion from his account of the Franklin's public offices. They are presented merely as evidence for his status as a "worthy vavasour"' (p 159).

1057 Mead, William Edward. *The English Medieval Feast.* 1931. See **727**.
Four good effects of wine-sops (see line 334) are explained: they clean the teeth, sharpen the sight, complete the digestion, and reduce 'superfluous digestion' (1931, p 128).

1058 Miller, Robert P. 'The Epicurean Homily on Marriage by Chaucer's Franklin.' *Mediaevalia,* 6 (1980 — Special Volume in Honor of Bernard F. Huppé), 151–86.
The Franklin is said to be *Epicurus owene sone* and to regard *pleyn delit* as perfect felicity (lines 336–37). Miller examines the attitudes towards Epicureanism expressed by Boethius (whose *Consolation* 'is obviously Chaucer's *immediate* source for the terminology in the *General Prologue,*' p 154), John of Salisbury, and other authorities. The traditional medieval understanding of Epicureanism interpreted its endorsement of bodily comfort as emphasizing 'the appearance, rather than the essence, of peace and tranquillity: as rationalizing rather than reason. The substitution of *delit* based on temporizing with the state of fallen human nature for a *uoluptas* or *iucunditas* based on natural justice or rectitude of the will is consistently regarded as the characteristic Epicurean "error"' (p 179).

1059 Pearcy, Roy J. 'Chaucer's Franklin and the Literary Vavasour.' *ChauR,* 8 (1973-1974), 33–59.
The Franklin is said to be a 'worthy vavasour' (line 360). The literary traditions involving the vavasour are 1) that of the romances, in which the vavasour is a lesser aristocrat who lives in rural isolation and represents hospitality, general wisdom, and the trustworthiness befitting an older and settled person; and 2) that of the fabliaux, in which the vavasour no longer shares the chivalric value-system but has become materialistic and self-centered. The Franklin's behavior in his prologue and link suggests that he is 'the figural representative of an age wistfully asserting spiritual allegiance with an antique chivalric world whose values are rapidly becoming

anachronistic' (p 53). The Franklin's *GP* portrait reflects the romance tradition, but includes some details that suggest the fourteenth-century world, such as his public service and his companionship with the Serjeant of Law. These details imply 'a legalistic mind' (p 54) closer to the personality of a fabliau vavasour. The Franklin is a person who looks towards the past; the details about his 'complexion, eating habits, and dress suggest a desire to turn back the clock — to a more youthful time of life, or to an earlier period of society' (p 59).

.060 Prins, A.A. 'Further Notes on the Canterbury Tales.' *ES*, 32 (1951), 250–51.
Prins argues for the French origin of two rhyme-phrases in the Franklin's portrait, *in muwe* and *in stuwe* (lines 349–50). French examples are presented for comparison.

.061 Rickert, Edith. 'Thou Vache.' *MP*, 11 (1913-1914), 209–25.
To judge by his household effects, Sir Philip de la Vache, who is mentioned in Chaucer's lyric *Truth*, was apparently 'given to lavish hospitality' (p 225). Rickert suggests that Chaucer may have borrowed this feature for the Franklin's portrait. Vache is also associated with offices such as those which the Franklin held.

.062 Robertson, D.W., Jr. 'Chaucer's Franklin and his Tale.' *Costerus*, New Series 1 (1974), 1–26. Rpt in Robertson's *Essays in Medieval Culture* (Princeton, NJ: Princeton University Press, 1980), pp 273–90.
The Franklin (like the Serjeant) is an administrator of royal justice. 'That the Franklin is the Serjeant's companion does not suggest that he is a very trustworthy character' (1980, p 275), since Chaucer is clearly satirizing the Sergeant. Robertson reviews the responsibilities of the Franklin's offices — in which he may have enriched himself — and suggests that connivance between him and the Sergeant may be implied. The Franklin's Epicurean emphasis (lines 334–38) associates him unfavorably with January in *MerT*. 'If Chaucer had wished us to admire the Franklin, he would certainly have indicated some interest on his part in justice; instead he emphasizes a consuming desire for self-indulgence of a kind that only wealth can bring. ... as we see him riding along wearing a defiant dagger and a bag of silk suggestive of avarice hanging from his white girdle, any suspicions we may have about his exercise of his various offices are fully justified' (pp 278–9).

1063 Robinson, F.N. ed. *The Works of Geoffrey Chaucer.* 1957. See **42**.
Although the Franklin has been taken to be 'a kind of parvenu,' conscious of his inferiority to the gentles, this representation is not satisfactory. 'Certainly Chaucer's Franklin is described as a person of wealth and dignity;

his traveling companion is the Sergeant, a figure of consequence; and he held offices to which a man below the rank of gentleman was not ordinarily eligible' (p 659).

1064 Savage, Henry. ' "Seint Julian He Was." ' *MLN*, 58 (1943), 47–48.
The Franklin is said to be the *Seint Julian* of his country (line 340). A chronicle describing the hospitality of the Count of Savoy in 1386 refers to his house as the house of Saint Julian (*la maison Saint-Julien*), because of the availability of food to all comers. This phrase 'shows the currency in the later fourteenth century of the expression that a certain person was "a St Julian," or his house a "maison" or "hostel" of that saint' (p 47).

1065 Sleeth, Charles R. 'Astrology as a Bone of Contention Between the Man of Law and the Franklin.' *ChauN*, 1, 1 (1979), 20–21.
Sleeth interprets line 331 as meaning that the Franklin and the Man of Law 'undertook the pilgrimage together, which implies that they had been friends for some time' (p 20); later, in the spirit of old friends having an argument, in their tales they disagreed about astrology.

1066 Specht, Henrik. *Chaucer's Franklin in the Canterbury Tales: The Social and Literary Background of a Chaucerian Character.* Copenhagen: Akademisk Forlag, 1981. Publications of the Department of English, University of Copenhagen, Second Series, 10.
Critics such as Lumiansky (see 1054) tend to accept a historical model for the Franklin and to see him as being insecure in his social status. Specht argues, on the contrary, that 'Chaucer deliberately made the description of the Franklin so general, or representative, that his audience could be expected to associate the Franklin with no single individual, but rather with the esteemed members of the country gentry in general' (p 145). From about 1300 onward, only or primarily 'freeholders and landowners of much substance and high social status' were called franklins (p 179). According to literary and documentary evidence, they were 'associated with easy circumstances, large households, a grand scale of living, and a dominant position in their own locality' (p 180). The most important contemporary social distinction was that between the simple and the gentle classes. Chaucer's Franklin is 'almost conclusively' a member of the country gentry (p 180). As for a specific model, William de Spayne is as likely as other suggested models, but the fact that multiple candidates can be proposed supports the thesis that Chaucer intended the Franklin to be understood as a representative untitled gentleman, not any specific individual. The portrait is a positive one. The Franklin's excessive interest in food is a fault, but — according to both Boethius and the Parson — a venial one. And that fault is counterbalanced 'by an engaging *joie de vivre*, generosity,

and sense of responsibility' (p 153). The Franklin is not depicted as an insecure parvenu. Much legal, economic, and social documentation bearing upon the contemporary functions and status of franklins is presented.

1067 Wood-Legh, K.L. 'The Franklin.' *RES*, 4 (1928), 145–51.
In response to Manly's identification of the Franklin with John Bussy (see 1026), Wood-Legh replies that the details of Bussy's life do not wholly correspond to the Franklin's portrait. Furthermore, five knights who served with Chaucer in the Parliament of 1386 are better candidates, and one of them, Stephen de Hales, was connected with Thomas de Pynchbek, whom Manly sees as the model for the Serjeant of Law. However, the Franklin clearly has much in common with many other members of his class and 'may continue to be regarded as a type' (p 151), even if one particular person can be identified as the basis of the portrait.

☙ Part 16: The Guildsmen

See the Introduction, pp xxxv above on the Guildsmen (the Burgesses), and see the Index for further references.

1068 Camden, Carroll, Jr. 'Query on Chaucer's Burgesses.' *PQ*, 7 (1928), 314–17.

Chaucer's five Burgesses are described only briefly as a group and then do not reappear, either as tellers of tales or as pilgrims mentioned in endlinks. They may have been inserted by Chaucer 'as an after-thought, when the *Prologue* had been finished' (p 314) and the *Tales* were well underway. Their composite portrait was perhaps added after 1391, when the controversy between the victualling and the non-victualling guilds had died down. On such an assumption, 'we see how smoothly the *Prologue* runs on after the apparently irrelevant description' (p 316) of this group is deleted. The Cook, whose description currently follows that of the guildsmen, would instead accompany the Serjeant of Law and the Franklin. Those two pilgrims would 'naturally take along a cook' (p 315), while the guildsmen would probably not be able to afford one. 'Cooks were prohibitively expensive, often costing one hundred dollars for a single night' (p 316). The viewpoint that the Burgesses were a late addition is consistent with other opinions suggesting that *GP* portraits were added or revised.

1069 C[oulton], G.G. 'Minor Notices.' *MLR*, 12 (1917), 512.

In this brief note, Kuhl's thesis about Chaucer's Burgesses (see **1076**) is rejected as showing 'more industry than logic.'

1070 Fullerton, Ann B. 'The Five Craftsmen.' *MLN*, 61 (1946), 515–23.

Chaucer's Guildsmen cannot all belong to one trade guild, since they practice different crafts. They might come from a town having a guild-merchant, where all crafts were indeed associated in one guild, but it is more likely that they come from London, which had no guild of that type. They are members, therefore, of a local or parish guild, a fraternal organization based upon the locality or parish as a unit, rather than on occupation. Such fraternities, very common in London towards the end of the fourteenth century, wore liveries at official gatherings. The Guildsmen may have belonged to a fraternity connected with St Thomas of Canterbury in particular, since his shrine is the goal of the pilgrimage. A combined fraternity of St Thomas and *Salve Regina* existed in the parish of St Magnus. It would be a suitable guild for Chaucer's group, but we cannot be sure whether any such specific reference was intended. The function of the Guildsmen as citizens implies that *alderman* in this context (see line 372) means not the head officer of the guild, but a ward alderman; in this meaning all five Guildsmen could have been aldermen at once. In reply, see **1078**.

1071 Garbáty, Thomas Jay. 'Chaucer's Guildsmen and Their Fraternity.' *JEGP*, 59 (1960), 691–709.
Chaucer's Guildsmen belong to the clothing trades — with the exception of the Carpenter. His presence in the group helps to identify the particular type of parish guild to which they must have belonged: it must have been one with a strong, but not exclusive, representation from the clothing industry. The cloth tradesmen seem to have been concentrated in the Aldersgate Ward. A study of the guilds there indicates that the most likely one for Chaucer to have meant is the Guild of St Fabian and St Sebastian of St Botolph's Church, Aldersgate. This fraternity consisted substantially of members of the clothing trade, but carpenters and other tradesmen also belonged to it. The guild was of major importance and its members wore livery. Of the four men elected as aldermen in 1384, at least two (perhaps three) were members of this guild. Women could be members. The specific springtime meeting date of this guild, which was the Sunday after Easter, would have been April 14 in the year 1387, the most probable year for the pilgrimage as represented by Chaucer. This schedule would have left its members free to leave for a journey on April 17, the presumed start of the Canterbury pilgrimage. Chaucer, as controller of customs, would have been familiar with this prominent guild for clothworkers, since he was concerned with the wool trade.

1072 Goodall, Peter. 'Chaucer's "Burgesses" and the Aldermen of London.' *MÆ*, 50 (1981), 284–92.
Goodall replies to Kuhl (**1076**), who proposed that Chaucer has diplomatically avoided referring to either side of the feud between London's victualling and non-victualling guilds; Goodall argues that Kuhl's account of the guild controversy is not wholly correct. Furthermore, it is not likely that men from the guilds that Chaucer includes would have had any real

chance of becoming aldermen of London. The Guildsmen's array does not necessarily imply that they are very wealthy. Perhaps *alderman* (line 372) meant a guild office, rather than a municipal position, or perhaps Chaucer was not referring to London specifically. However, Goodall's preferred explanation is 'to accept that Chaucer was well aware that his guildsmen had no chance of becoming aldermen and to read the whole passage as a piece of irony' (p 290). The present status of their wives cannot be very high 'if such a meagre tribute as being called "madame" can give them so much pleasure' (p 290, see lines 374–78). The narrator's credulity here is part of that persona's characterization, for he apparently fails to see the discrepancy between the Guildsmen's status and their ambitions. 'In his attitudes towards the Guildsmen, especially in his ignorance of their real social standing, the hopelessness of their ambitions, and their inevitable exclusion from the powerful London middle class, the pilgrim Chaucer shows himself as more petty-bourgeois than bourgeois' (p 291).

1073 Herndon, Sarah. 'Chaucer's Five Gildsmen.' *FSUS*, 5 (1952), 33–44.
Detailed information is provided about the situation of the guilds in the years when Chaucer was presumably working on *GP*. He avoided including any craft associated with the London dispute between the victuallers and non-victuallers (a dispute over free trade vs. protectionism) during the 1380s. Similarly, the overall brevity of the Guildsmen's treatment may reflect Chaucer's caution in view of a 1388–1389 investigation of the guilds, when Parliament ordered them to file returns giving the details of their property, etc. Chaucer would certainly have known of the guild investigation. He may have written the Prologue around 1387, introducing the Guildsmen fairly briefly, and then have hesitated to develop them because he did not know what the outcome of the investigation would be. 'They did not interest him sufficiently for him to fill in the details and elaborate the characters after the crisis in gild affairs was past' (p 44).

1074 Kirby, Thomas A. 'The Haberdasher and his Companions.' *MLN*, 53 (1938), 504–5.
The Guildsmen should be regarded not as ordinary craftsmen, but as members of an 'incorporated livery company,' men of importance who 'belonged to the select group which was growing up within the gilds and which gradually took over their control' (p 505). The fact that they have brought the Cook with them makes more sense in this interpretation, since important men might bring a cook along, but ordinary workers would hardly do so. However, it is also possible that the Cook may be meant to accompany *all* the pilgrims, not just the preceding five listed — though Kirby does not think this is the likely interpretation.

1075 Kramer, Stella. *The English Craft Gilds: Studies in their Progress and Decline*. New York: Columbia University Press, 1927; London: Humphrey Milford, 1927.
Concentrating on the late-medieval amalgamation of trading (mercantile) and craft guilds, Kramer examines many guild records from Chaucer's period and later.

1076 Kuhl, Ernest P. 'Chaucer's Burgesses.' 1916. See **1053**.
Chaucer has chosen his Guildsmen in order to remain politically neutral. He does not mention any of the victualling guilds, which were prominent in London politics; nor does he mention any of the ten guilds that attacked Mayor Brembre (a victualler) in the Parliament of 1386, of which Chaucer was a member. 'In his selection of the burgesses, therefore, Chaucer the artist becomes Chaucer the diplomat' (p 655). *GP* was not written 'before the latter part of 1386' (p 658), ie, before the Parliamentary controversy whose participants Chaucer excludes. Many details are given about the guilds from which Chaucer did choose. Lines 369–72 refer to the abilities of Chaucer's Guildsmen to serve as municipal aldermen. The Host's bargain, according to which whoever disobeys him must bear everyone's costs, has precedent in an incident of 1382, when the mayor and aldermen agreed that the aldermen should wear special garments for the Feast of Pentecost; one alderman who disobeyed was required to give a dinner, at his cost, for all the others. London wills show guildsmen leaving to their heirs certain garments, knives, etc, that resemble those of Chaucer's Guildsmen. In reply, see **1069, 1072, 1081**.

1077 Lisca, Peter. 'Chaucer's Guildsmen and Their Cook.' *MLN*, 70 (1955), 321–24.
The portrait of the Guildsmen is 'done in the dry point of satire' and is 'one of Chaucer's most incisive' (p 321). Although the Knight rides in array that is plain, the Guildsmen wear fresh new livery and carry silver-decorated knives. This display must have amused the pilgrims, since 'ordinary tradesmen and craftsmen were forbidden the use of precious metals for such ornamentation' (p 321). When it is said that each of the Guildsmen was fit to be an alderman because (as we are next told) he had enough property and an ambitious wife, Chaucer is using the technique of a 'modifying context' (p 321) to convey his satiric intention, since it is doubtful that he would have considered property or a wife's ambitions to be the right qualifications for holding public office. As for the Cook, he may be the final satiric touch in Chaucer's portrait: given his mormal and what it implies, it is possible that — although the Guildsmen think he contributes to their high-class appearance — he has been discharged from other employment. Perhaps the Guildsmen have 'been able to engage him at a bargain' (p 323).

1078 McCutchan, J. Wilson. ' "A solempne and a Greet Fraternitee." ' *PMLA*,
74 (1959), 313–17.

Although it has been argued that the Guildsmen's fraternity is a local or
parish fraternity (see Unwin, **1082**, and Fullerton, **1070**), McCutchan here
proposes that Chaucer instead intended them to belong to a craft fraternity, such as the Drapers' Fraternity or Brotherhood of St Mary of Beth-
lehem. The Draper's Fraternity admitted members of other crafts (records
show that a weaver, a dyer, and two tailors belonged). This fraternity
was prosperous, was the dominant one among those representing the cloth
and textile industries, and was politically active. Its members were not
ordinary tradesmen or craftsmen, but wealthy and prominent individuals
who could certainly have afforded to hire a cook if they had wanted one.
Chaucer's portrait may indeed smile at their pretensions, but it is inappropriate to interpret his satire as being directed against a group of merely
typical guildsmen. 'Mentioning five nonvictualing crafts, four of which were
directly concerned with the clothing trade, and bringing them together "in
o lyveree" would almost surely have suggested the Drapers' Fraternity to
any Londoner' of this time (p 316).

1079 McKee, John. 'Chaucer's *Canterbury Tales, General Prologue.' Expl*, 32
(1973-1974), item 54.

Chaucer has described the Guildsmen by means of one group portrait,
rather than by individual portraits, in order to reflect their own 'middle-
class tendency to conformity.' His 'control of proportion' in other portraits
also (the Franklin's, the Knight's, and the Squire's) indicates the characteristics that are important to each pilgrim portrayed.

1080 Nathan, Norman. 'The Number of the Canterbury Pilgrims.' *MLN*, 67
(1952), 533–34.

It is normally assumed that there are five Guildsmen, two of whom are a
Weaver and a Dyer. However, at line 362 one manuscript reads *A webbe
dyer*, which indicates, according to Nathan, the existence of an occupation
called *webbe dyer*. In that case, there would be only four Guildsmen (one
of them would be the *webbe dyer*) and the total number of pilgrims in *GP*
would be, as line 24 says, twenty-nine.

1081 Trauschke, Ernst. 'Zu Chaucer.' *NS*, 37 (1929), 651–3.

Commenting on Kuhl (**1076**), Trauschke proposes that the carpenters may
indeed have had a guild before 1386, though Kuhl thought that they were
not organized until that date. In his choice of guildsmen Chaucer implies
that these five guilds, though not then represented in the aldermancy, included members as qualified as some from guilds that *were* represented —
and this implication constitutes a political allusion.

1082 Unwin, George. *The Gilds and Companies of London.* London: Methuen, 1908. Revised ed. 1925. 3rd ed. (London: Allen & Unwin), 1938, with revision of appendices. 4th ed., intro. by William F. Kahl, 1963.

Many details pertinent to the Guildsmen and to related subjects — such as specific London companies, medieval feasts, and religious observances — are provided. Cf 1078.

❦ Part 17: The Cook

See the Introduction, p xxxvi above, for a brief summary of criticism on the Cook, and see the Index for further references.

1083 Braddy, Haldeen. 'The Cook's Mormal and its Cure.' *MLQ*, 7 (1946), 265–67.

The Cook's *mormal* (line 386) is apparently 'an ulcer or a sore, not a cancer' (p 267). It seems to have been of the 'wet or running' type, which may give 'special point' to Chaucer's next statement, a comment on how well the Cook could prepare *blankmanger* (p 267).

1084 Cook, Albert Stanburrough. 'Miscellaneous Notes.' *MLN*, 33 (1918), 378–79.

The Cook has a *mormal* on his leg (see line 386). A passage cited from the *Manière de Langage*, 1396, describes a case in which a person has sustained an injury to the leg and fears that it will become a *mormal*, leading to his death, unless he rapidly receives a remedy.

1085 ——. 'Chaucerian Papers, I.' 1919. See **591**.

On line 386, Cook presents a passage from John Arderne's *Treatises*, which discusses a mormal on a patient's leg, as an analogue.

1086 Curry, Walter Clyde. 'Two Notes on Chaucer.' *MLN*, 36 (1921), 272–76.

The *mormal* on the shin of the Cook (line 386) is what medieval medical authorities call *malum mortuum*, 'a species of ulcerated, dry-scabbed apostema' (p 274) that may have caused the Cook continual itching. Medieval statements about the cause of the disease provide an understanding of the Cook's character. 'In addition to being a filthy person of low degree, he is doubtless such a thrifty soul that he devours all the tainted meats and spoiled victuals which he cannot put off on long-suffering pilgrims' (p 275).

His excessive drinking and his interest in dirty tales also fit the contemporary analyses of *malum mortuum*, which is associated with overeating, overindulgence in strong wine, personal uncleanliness, and relations with unclean women. Cf **209**.

1087 Hieatt, Constance B. ' "To boille the chiknes with the marybones": Hodge's Kitchen Revisited.' In *Chaucerian Problems and Perspectives: Essays Presented to Paul E. Beichner, C.S.C.* Ed. Edward Vasta and Zacharias P. Thundy. Notre Dame and London: University of Notre Dame Press, 1979. Pp 149–63.
Medieval recipes and ingredients for some of the Cook's culinary specialties are provided.

1088 Lyon, Earl D. 'Roger de Ware, Cook.' *MLN*, 52 (1937), 491–94.
Roger de Ware, model for Chaucer's Cook, 'was in no position to object to Chaucer's ugly picture of him,' since a London ward presentment shows that he was accused of being 'a common nightwalker' and that he confessed to the offense (p 494). Cf **1089, 1090, 1092**.

1089 ——. *Chaucer's Cook's Tale and its Background.* University of California Dissertation (Berkeley). 1938. Dir. John S.P. Tatlock.
Lyon examines the London cooks' trade, the organization of cooks into a guild, and other aspects of the Cook's background, along with presenting legal documents that show that Roger de Ware, a historical person, was a common nightwalker (disturber of the peace). Though Chaucer may be describing the traditional concept of a cook, 'and though he selected his details for their moral and social significance and their power to evoke a picture, in this one case surely ... he wrote with his eye on a single contemporary' (p 24). Cf **1088, 1090, 1092**.

1090 Manly, John Matthews. *Some New Light on Chaucer.* 1926. See **362**.
In the chapter 'The Others' (pp 253–65), Manly argues that the Cook is 'clearly individual' and suggests that perhaps some document will be found that mentions 'a London cook named Hogge of Ware, contemporary with Chaucer' (p 259; see **1089, 1092**).

1091 Mann, Jill. *Chaucer and Medieval Estates Satire.* 1973. See **363**.
'The Cook's portrait is almost entirely constructed on the basis of his estate. Chaucer assures us of his professional excellence' (p 168). Lists of foods and cooking procedures are common in gluttony-satire, and a cook appears in Gower's *Vox Clamantis*, but Chaucer's decision to include the Cook in *GP* may be due to *Piers Plowman*, the prologue of which ends with a picture of cooks and their knaves: 'we must see here also a stimulus from *Piers Plowman*' (p 169).

1092 Rickert, Edith. 'Chaucer's "Hodge of Ware." ' *TLS*, October 20, 1932, p 761.

Historical records demonstrate that there was a Roger Ware of London who was a cook in Chaucer's time. Thus Chaucer gave the Cook, as well as the Host, a real person's name (the Cook is named not in *GP* but at I.4336 and I.4345). Cf **1089, 1090**.

🐚 Part 18: The Shipman

See the Introduction, p xxxvi above, for a brief summary of criticism on the Shipman, and see the Index for further references.

1093 Burchfield, Robert. 'Realms and Approximations: Sources of Chaucer's Power.' 1982. See **184**.
Although the Canterbury pilgrims include a Shipman, and Chaucer himself repeatedly crossed the Channel, when he mentions the sea 'the vocabulary he uses is that of a landlubber' rather than that of 'closely observed detail' (p 7).

1094 Chatterjee, A.B., ed. *The Prologue to the Canterbury Tales (Chaucer)*. 1963. See **70**.
Line 406 provides a comic anti-climax in the Shipman's portrait. The 'reader knows that the Shipman has passed through many storms and is, perhaps, mentally prepared to have [a] description of one such storm. He is given one but the storm is shown not in its effect on his ship but as playing havoc with his beard. We have a glimpse of the brown, brawny shipman tossing in a frail ship, pulling desperately at ropes to save the ship and madly issuing out orders to his men — his long, thick, white beard all the while violently blowing in the wind and causing him as much trouble as the storm itself' (p xlv). It is the unexpectedness of this detail 'that has made the picture so vivid, suggestive and laughter-charged — one of the grandest anti-climaxes' in the English language (p xlv).

1095 Conrad, Bernard R. 'The Date of Chaucer's "Prologue." ' *N&Q*, 152 (1927), 385.
Lines 399–400, on the Shipman's fighting at sea, may refer to the naval battle of March, 1387, in which the English defeated a combined French, Flemish, and the Spanish fleet off Margate — and captured ships carrying

wine. This incident would support other arguments for 1387 as the date of *GP*.

1096 Donovan, Mortimer J. 'Chaucer's Shipman and the Integrity of His Cargo.' *MLR*, 50 (1955), 489–90.

As master of his ship, the Shipman is specifically responsible for its cargo. The laws of seagoing affairs (the 'Laws of Oleron') mention that a cargo of wine needs special supervision and that the shipmaster should look after it as if it were his own property. In the other direction, the merchant might give the shipmaster and his crew 'a gratuity in wine' (p 489) as a courtesy. In view of these regulations, Chaucer's Shipman 'is a worse offender than an ordinary seaman,' for 'he has violated the trust placed in him as an officer' (p 490) in stealing some of the wine that he carries as cargo. As for the gratuity, we can imagine either that he has found it insufficient, or that the merchants whose wine he has transported — assessing his character correctly — have concluded that 'on him *courtoisie* would be wasted' (p 490) and have not given him the gratuity at all. Cf **1106**.

1097 Galway, Margaret. 'Chaucer's Shipman in Real Life.' *MLR*, 34 (1939), 497–514.

Chaucer, in describing 'a shipmaster who was living in England and knew every creek in Spain' (p 499), may not have meant an Englishman. In fact, the Basque shipmaster John Piers, of Chaucer's time, 'is an exact counterpart of the Shipman' (p 499). John Piers' career is reviewed in detail. He captured a ship named the *Magdaleyn*, for example, in a notorious act of piracy (see line 410). To kill a captured ship's crew (as the Shipman evidently does) was regarded as part of 'the traditional cruelty' attributed to 'Spaniards' in general (p 500). The Shipman's costume 'is certainly not unlike' that of a Basque (p 501). Overall, the Shipman's portrait in *GP* 'reads like a review' of Piers' career and personality (p 513), and it is not likely that Chaucer would have written such a portrait — or that the courtly and other members of his audience would have listened to it — without seeing the resemblance.

1098 Lumiansky, R.M. *Of Sondry Folk: The Dramatic Principle in the Canterbury Tales.* 1955. See **348**.

'In some ways the Shipman's presence is the hardest to account for' among the pilgrims (p 71). He is surely not going to Canterbury to repent of his misdeeds, nor 'does a pilgrimage seem the kind of vacation the ship's captain would likely choose' (p 73). Nevertheless, he is 'a very likable person, who makes no bones about what he is,' and who is 'thoroughly competent' in his profession (p 73).

1099 Malone, Kemp. 'King Alfred's "Geats." ' *MLR*, 20 (1925), 1–11.
Chaucer's *Gootlond* (line 408) represents Jutland. Lines 407–8 imply that
the Shipman knew the havens 'from cape to cape,' much as 'from Hulle to
Cartage' (line 404) means 'from port to port' (p 6).

1100 ——. 'From Hulle to Cartage.' *MLN*, 45 (1930), 229–30.
In line 404, does *Cartage* refer to Carthage in Africa, or to Cartagena
(New Carthage) in Spain? It would be more likely for the Shipman to be
concerned with Cartagena than with Carthage, which had been 'destroyed
by the Arabs in the seventh century' (p 229). However, the Spanish city
is typically differentiated from the African city by an adjective, such as
nova. To establish that Chaucer could have intended Cartagena by his
single term *Cartage*, without an adjective, it is necessary to show that
some other authority referred to Cartagena in that way. A passage from
Orosius supplies the necessary precedent. 'If Orosius could use a simple
Carthago with reference to Cartagena, it seems reasonable to believe that
Chaucer could do the same thing' (p 230).

1101 Manly, John Matthews. *Some New Light on Chaucer*. 1926. See **362**.
In the chapter 'The Shipman and the Merchant' (pp 169–200), Manly considers whether the Shipman from Dartmouth might be modeled upon the
historical John Hawley, owner of the *Maudeleyne* (see line 410). However,
Hawley was 'too wealthy, distinguished, and perhaps too courtly' (p 178)
for the *GP* portrait, which is probably based on George Cowntree or on
Peter Risshenden, captain of the *Maudeleyne*. The Merchant is unnamed
because Chaucer did not tend to name 'any character of the upper or middle
classes that he treated satirically' (p 200).

1102 Mann, Jill. *Chaucer and Medieval Estates Satire*. 1973. See **363**.
The Shipman's portrait includes details traditionally asociated with sailors,
such as fraud, stealing, and a tendency to commit murder. In the *GP*
portrait, 'these typical features are presented from the point of view of
the Shipman,' who jokes about sending his enemies home by water and
expresses scorn for *conscience* (p 171; see lines 398, 400). 'The euphemism
to express murder, and the lack of distinction between excessive feeling
and any moral feeling at all, suggest the lack of clarity with which the
Shipman is aware of his own actions and moral assumptions. His point of
view dominates his portrait' (pp 171–72).

1103 Moore, Arthur K. ' "Somer" and "Lenten" as Terms for Spring.' *N&Q*,
194 (1949), 82–83.
Moore argues that the word *somer* (line 394, on the Shipman's complexion)
usually means 'spring,' although the entire time between February and the
autumnal equinox may be included.

1104 Robinson, F.N., ed. *The Works of Geoffrey Chaucer.* 1957. See 42.
Cartage, in line 404, probably represents 'one of the Spanish ports, Cartagena, or Cartaya, rather than the ancient Carthage' (p 661).

1105 Stillwell, Gardiner. 'Chaucer's Shipman and the "Shipman's Gild." ' N&Q, 192 (1947), 203–5.
Chaucer's portrait and the regulations of the Shipman's Guild of Lynn 'can profitably be set side by side' (p 205). The guild's ordinances seem to be an effort 'to hold down the boisterous spirits of "good fellows" who were not notable for scrupulously ethical conduct or for spiritual refinement' (p 203).

1106 Stobie, Margaret R. 'Chaucer's Shipman and the Wine.' *PMLA*, 64 (1949), 565–69.
The Laws of Oléron or Judgments of the Sea, a set of maritime laws established in the twelfth century, would have governed the Shipman's relations with his crew and also with the merchants whose goods he transported. These rules show that the shipmaster was required to provide drink for his crew. The merchant too was expected — but not required — to provide wine for the crew as a courtesy, when the ship was carrying wine. The 'courtesy wine' (p 568) would presumably be stored in a readily accessible place. It is this wine that the Shipman steals at night in order to save the expense of providing his normal allotment of drink to the crew. 'The courtesy wine would disappear with astonishing rapidity' (p 568), but it would be awkward for the merchant to complain since he was dependent upon the crew for the safe arrival of the ship and its freight. The comment 'Ful many a draughte of wyn had he ydrawe' (line 396) is meant to have literal force: the Shipman was presumably 'drawing off the next day's wine rations for the crew' (p 568). Cf 1096.

1107 White, Florence E. 'Chaucer's Shipman: John de Roches v. John Hawley.' *MP*, 26 (1928–1929), 249–55 and 379–84; continued in *MP*, 27 (1929–1930), 123–28.
Extensive documents pertaining to the legal dispute between John de Roches and John Hawley (the case lasted from 1393 to 1401) are presented here as 'a valuable cross-section view of the life of Chaucer's contemporaries,' especially useful for those 'who seek among Hawley's crew for the prototype of the shipman' (p 249).

❧ Part 19: The Physician

See the Introduction, p xxxvi above, for a brief summary of criticism on the Physician, and see the Index for further references.

1108 Aiken, Pauline. 'Vincent of Beauvais and the "Houres" of Chaucer's Physician.' *SP*, 53 (1956), 22–24.
Lines 415–16, concerning the Physician, read 'He kepte his pacient a ful greet deel / In houres by his magyk natureel.' Curry (**1118**) and others have assumed that the astrological hours are meant. However, Vincent of Beauvais, in the *Speculum Doctrinale*, repeatedly uses the term *horas* for the stages of development of a disease. Therefore, Chaucer's lines might be rendered ' "He took care of a patient *during the various stages of a disease* by means of natural magic — that is, by practices based on astrology" ' (p 24).

1109 Arnold, Richard A. 'Chaucer's Physician: The Teller and the Tale.' *RUO*, 51 (1981), 172–79.
'The Physician's Tale is generally not understood because neither is his portrait' (p 172). The portrait depicts the Physician as 'immensely learned, skillful in diagnosing and treating a patient's bodily ailments, a shrewd businessman, and finely dressed,' but also as 'avaricious and irreligious,' a man concerned with the flesh but not with the spirit (p 173). In the Physician's inner being Chaucer 'finds greed, deceit, and atheism' (p 178). These qualities are also evident in his tale. 'Together, the portrait and the tale become Chaucer's commentary on doctors of his time' (p 179). The Physician is 'an emblem of misdirected energies. Chaucer would say that the Physicians are necessary and their education is to be respected, but to sacrifice the spirit for the sake of knowledge of the flesh ... is too great a price to pay' (p 179).

1110 Bashford, H.H. 'Chaucer's Physician and his Forbears.' *NCent*, 104 (1928), 237–48.

A general overview of medical knowledge and practice in medieval England is followed by a summary of the careers of Gilbertus Anglicus and John Gaddesden, two English physicians included in the Physican's list of medical authorities (see line 434). John of Gaddesden, who was physician to Edward II and possibly to Edward III, and was known for his financial as well as medical concerns, might have suggested certain traits for Chaucer's portrait of the Physician in *GP*.

1111 Bassan, Maurice. 'Chaucer's "Cursed Monk," Constantinus Africanus.' *MS*, 24 (1962), 127–40.

Among the Physician's learned medical authorities, there appears the name of Constantine (line 433). In *MerT*, Constantine is referred to as a '"cursed monk" who appears to have written a nasty book containing (in part, one gathers) information about aphrodisiacs' (p 127; see *MerT* lines 1807–12). Bassan summarizes the life and works of Constantinus Africanus, who was an eleventh-century translator of Arabic medical works into Latin: 'his importance as one of the first great communicators of ancient and modern learning to Western Europe cannot be discounted' (p 132). A copy of his treatise *De coitu* seems to have been acquired by Merton College, Oxford, in the late fourteenth century.

1112 Bolduan, Nils W. 'Chaucer and Matters Medical.' *NEJM*, 208 (1933), 1365–68.

Chaucer's references to medicine are viewed as indicating the type of medical knowledge available to the educated class of his time. From the Physician's portrait alone, 'a picture of Medical Art in Chaucer's time might be drawn' (p 1367). The Physician is rather 'a composite picture of many medieval physicians, than that of any one individual' (p 1367). On the Pardoner, see **1300**.

1113 Bowden, Muriel. *A Commentary on the General Prologue to the Canterbury Tales.* 1948. See **104**.

The Physician is portrayed with 'considerable satire,' for his 'exaggerated proficiency' makes him 'too good to be true' (p 199). Chaucer 'must have esteemed some medical men,' and may have used John Arderne's ideal as a model, 'but his obvious recognition of the sins of many others' (p 211) among the physicians has made the Doctor reflect a class as well as an individual. The term *horas* (line 416) may involve a pun on both 'hours of the day,' the usual meaning, and 'stages of the disease' (revised ed., p 325).

1114 Branca, Geraldine Sesak. *Experience versus Authority: Chaucer's Physician and Fourteenth-Century Science.* University of Illinois Dissertation

(Urbana-Champaign). 1971. Dir. Richard H. Green. See also *DAI*, 32 (1972), 5731-A.

Branca interprets the Physician as representing the issue of Experience versus Authority in the scientific realm: medieval *physica*, 'a much broader area of study than simply medicine' (p 5), 'stressed the theoretical or speculative with little empirical or observational attendance to the particulars of matter' (p 6). *PhyT* is seen as an allegorical presentation of 'the relationship of science or nature to theology or faith,' with faith, in the person of Virginius, slaying nature, in the person of Virginia (p 10). In the chapter 'The Physician in the General Prologue' (pp 53–82), Branca analyzes the portrait in detail. The catalogue of authorities, while it establishes the Physician's theoretical training to supplement the earlier information that he is an expert practitioner, may also 'be intended as a parody of the Physician's theoretical background' since it is a 'breathless recitation of names without works' (p 57). Line 413, which mentions both *phisik* and *surgerye*, bridges the contemporary gap between those fields, for surgery was regarded as 'a low manual craft' (p 58). However, 'the moderns in the Physician's list of authorities, Bernard, Gilbert, and Gaddesden, were all surgeons' (p 63). 'With his surgical bias toward experience, and his knowledge of astrology and alchemy, Chaucer's Physician resembles Bacon's ideal physician' (p 72). He would have read the Bible as part of the required arts curriculum, but his 'study would lean more to the created present ... to the natural and demonstrable, in preference to the mystical and supernatural' (p 73). The portrait emphasizes his professional competence, but also depicts his materalism, and his reason for going on pilgrimage is not clear. 'Since it is no secret that he cares much for gold and little for the Bible, I do not think that we can contend that the Physician travels to Canterbury to deceive anyone concerning his piety. I think Chaucer wants us to wonder, however, what this materialistic Physician's spiritual vision might be' (p 76). The tale's later depiction of 'the dilemma of nature versus faith, experience versus authority' (p 105) suggests that 'faith is still the more powerful by reason of authority. Virginius slays Virginia and the Physician wends his way to Canterbury' to seek Becket's shrine (p 106).

115 Brown, Emerson, Jr. 'What is Chaucer Doing with the Physician and His Tale?' *PQ*, 60 (1981), 129–49.

The Physician's portrait emphasizes his ability to discover the causes of illness, an ability necessary to providing a cure (see lines 419 and 423–24). However, perhaps the narrator has been led to believe that the Physician is a good judge of causation when this is not the case. Subsequently 'the Physician as story teller reveals himself to be unable to apply a skill which is singled out in the General Prologue as essential to the process of healing,'

for he fails to deal clearly with causality in presenting Virginia's death
(p 137). Thus our 'suspicions' about the *GP* portrait 'are confirmed: the
Physician lacks an indispensable skill required to make people well' (p 137).
The tale resolves the ambiguity of the portrait. *CT* concerns, 'among other
things, humanity sick beyond its own capacities for healing and stumbling
towards a cure,' and it is good that the Physician and the others are moving
towards the shrine of the martyr who has aided the sick (see lines 17–18).

1116 Campbell, Donald. *Arabian Medicine and Its Influence on the Middle
Ages*, 1. London: Kegan Paul, Trench, Trübner & Co, 1926. Trübner's
Oriental Series. Rpt New York: Arno Press, 1973.
The authorities mentioned in the Physician's portrait show that 'the med-
ical profession of England during this era was thoroughly Arabized' (1973,
pp 198–99).

1117 Cosman, Madeleine Pelner. 'Medieval Medical Malpractice and Chaucer's
Physician.' *NYSJM*, 72 (1972), 2439–44.
Cosman defends the Physician against modern detractors: 'rather than a
figure of satire, condemnation, or amusement the physician is a splendid
representative of both medieval physician and medieval surgeon. An exemplary figure to whom Chaucer applies the same adjectives as the equally
exemplary Knight, he is "a verray, parfit pracktisour," a true and perfect
practitioner' (p 2439). The Physician has been said to show an 'illogical
unity between learning and superstition' since he is familiar with the major
medical treatises, but also practices astrology and magic (p 2439). However, in Chaucer's time the study of astrological influences represented an
effort 'to discover order amidst chaos, to emend the venerable pagan notions
to new purpose, to explain the otherwise inexplicable, and to align man's
mind and body with the great design of the universe'(p 2443). Edicts and
standards intended to prevent malpractice, along with malpractice suits,
are reviewed. A malpractice suit of 1424, in which three accused surgeons
were exonerated, shows that astrological influences were accepted as adequate reason for the failure of a first effort at treatment. The folding
manuscripts with astrological information, the revolving disks (*volvellae*)
used to facilitate calculations, and the bronze quadrants that physicians
took with them to treat patients are described.

1118 Curry, Walter Clyde. 'Chaucer's Doctor of Phisyk.' *PQ*, 4 (1925), 1–24.
Chaucer's Physician 'has no peer when it comes to *speaking* of physic and
of surgery' (p 1). Given the theory and practice of medieval medicine, a
doctor would have been familiar with astrology and with the concept of
the humours. (A sample medical case and its treatment are presented.) He
would know how to 'fortunen the ascendent / Of his ymages' (lines 417–

18), which meant how to prepare images — for example, a round metal seal to be laid on the patient's head. While this use of amulets and charms might be seen as mere Black Magic, if the physician could thus free a patient from fear and strengthen the desire to live, real improvement could result. As for Chaucer's Physician, he may not *really* know those medical treatises; he may be cooperating with the apothecary to cheat his patients; his small study of the Bible may show his intellectual arrogance — but we are not sure. 'In fact, we are not quite sure about anything in the Doctor's character. Chaucer has created him so' (p 24). It is the uncertainty, the 'human contradictoriness,' that 'lends a certain life-like complexity' (p 24) to the characterization. The Physician's character is 'second only to that of the Wife of Bath in complexity' (p 23). Cf **209, 1118.**

1119 Grennen, Joseph E.   *'Double-entendre* and the Doctour of Phisik.' *AN&Q,* 1 (1963), 131–32.
Although the phrase 'he was but esy of dispence' (line 441) is usually taken to mean that the Physician is slow to spend money, other meanings should be considered. One is that the Physician is moderate in prescribing (dispensing) medicines; another is that 'the doctor is to be admired for dispensing lenitive potions' (p 131), rather than the harsh ones such as those which Chaunticler dislikes (VII.3153–6). In superficially praising the Physician in this way, Chaucer is giving the portrait 'greater ironic point' (p 132).

1120 Hoffman, Richard L. 'Jephthah's Daughter and Chaucer's Virginia.' *ChauR,* 2 (1967–1968), 20–31.
The reference to Jephthah in the story of Virginia serves 'to demonstrate the Physician's ignorance of the Bible,' as implied in line 438. 'For had the Physician stolen enough time from his medical practice to study Judges XI, he would certainly not have made Virginia cite the case of Jephthah's daughter,' which is not really parallel to her own (p 25). The Physician's 'province, after all, is the body, not the mind or soul' (p 31). His interest in the Bible is even more modest than that in food (line 435). He is preoccupied with externals, such as his rich clothing: 'It is the clothing, after all, which shows' (p 31).

1121 Houseman, Percy A. 'Science in Chaucer.' *SM,* 38 (1934), 561–64.
Houseman remarks briefly that the Physician's 'partnership with the pharmacist is described in satirical vein' (p 562; see lines 425–28).

1122 Landrum, Grace W. 'Chaucer's Use of the Vulgate.' *PMLA,* 39 (1924), 75–100.
Mathew 4:4 may underlie lines 435–38 of *GP.* The Biblical passage, on 'the necessity of feeding upon the Word,' may explain 'the gap in thought'

(p 97) between line 437, which comments on the Physician's diet, and line 438, which mentions the Bible. We may assume that Chaucer knew the Vulgate directly.

1123 Leicester, H. Marshall, Jr. 'The Art of Impersonation: A General Prologue to the *Canterbury Tales.*' 1980. See **626**.

The statement that the Physician did not tend to study the Bible (line 438) might lead us to condemn him, but his tale shows him to be 'a man of irreproachable if conventional morality whose profession channels his reading into medical texts' and who 'uses such biblical knowledge as he has for pathetic effect at the expense of narrative consistency' (p 218).

1124 Morris, E.E. 'The Physician in Chaucer.' In *An English Miscellany Presented to Dr. Furnivall in Honour of his Seventy-Fifth Birthday.* [Ed. W.P. Ker, A.S. Napier, and Walter W. Skeat.] Oxford: Clarendon Press, 1901. Pp 338–46.

'No where is there such a moving and lifelike panorama of the various classes of bygone days as in Chaucer's *Prologue*' (p 338). Among the names of the Physician's authorities, the order 'is mainly historical — first the Greeks, then the Arabs, then the more modern men' (p 339; these authorities are reviewed). Morris reports the earlier suggestion of Norman Moore [in the *Dictionary of National Biography* entry on John of Gaddesden] that the Physician may be modelled upon Gaddesden. The medieval processes of medical diagnosis and prescription are explained.

1125 Nicholls, Albert G. 'Medicine in Chaucer's Day.' *DR*, 12 (1932), 218–30.

In the portrait of the Physician Chaucer has included 'an antithesis of ideals' — 'on the one hand, knowledge, skill and devotion; on the other, avarice and a desire to impress the laity' (p 219). The career of John of Gaddesden 'seems to correspond fairly well' (p 220) to Chaucer's portrait. The Physician has demonstrated bravery in not running away from the plague, for we are told that he kept what he earned in the pestilence. His education was 'the best of its kind' (p 224); he probably studied at one of the universities. Chaucer presumably had a reasonably good knowledge of medical concepts. At Dover and Canterbury, towns through which he must have traveled, there were important collections of medical manuscripts. Medieval concepts of the influence of the stars on health, of the humors, and of medical practice are reviewed. In England alone there were some seven hundred and fifty almshouses, hospitals, and lazar-houses for the sick. 'Despite his defects of character, Chaucer's "Doctour" may be taken as the representative of the better type of medical practitioner' (p 228), although the higher ideal may be seen in the career of John Mirfeld, physician and monk of Chaucer's time.

1126 O'Neill, Ynez Violé. 'Chaucer and Medicine.' *JAMA*, 208 (1969), 78–82.
O'Neill comments on the Physician's learning ('the poet credited the medical practitioner with an enormous amount of reading,' p 78) and on the
Summoner's disorder, which may correspond to the condition called *couper-
ose* in the *Chirugia magna* of Guy de Chauliac, written shortly after Chaucer's death.

1127 Regenos, Graydon W. 'The Doctor in Nigellus Wireker and Chaucer.' In
*Classical, Medieval, and Renaissance Studies in Honor of Berthold Louis
Ullman*. Ed. Charles Henderson, Jr. Rome: Edizioni di Storia e Letteratura, 1964. Vol 2, pp 41–46.
In depicting the Physician satirically, it seems 'altogether likely' that Chaucer 'at least had in mind the doctor of the *Speculum Stultorum*' of Nigellus
Wireker (p 41). In that work, a doctor named Galienus is at first shown as
having both professional integrity and religious faith. Later, when his patient — Brunellus the ass, who wants a longer tail — remains unreasonable,
Galienus is shown to be avaricious. 'In satirizing the avaricious tendencies
of the doctor, Nigellus and Chaucer are in perfect agreement' (p 46).

1128 Robbins, Rossel[l] Hope. 'The Physican's Authorities.' In *Studies in Lan-
guage and Literature in Honour of Margaret Schlauch*. Ed. Mieczysław
Brahmer, Stanisław Helsztyński, and Julian Krzyżanowski. Warsaw PWN-
Polish Scientific Publishers, 1966. Pp 335–Rpt New York: Russell and
Russell, 1971.
The list of authorities whose works the Physician knows (lines 429–34) is
sometimes said to have come from a literary source, the *Speculum majus* of
Vincent of Beauvais. However, the *Speculum*, which was compiled ca. 1260,
does not mention Chaucer's later authorities — Bernard, Gaddesden, and
Gilbert — or Rufus of Ephesus. A survey of medical rather than literary
manuscripts shows that 'Chaucer's list contains just those names that an
educated doctor of his day would have cited' (1966, p 341). The only rarely
occurring name is that of Rufus.

1129 Sullivan, Frank. 'Chaucer's Physician and Genesis XXXI:20.' *LAT*, December 31, 1948, p 9.
Not seen. According to the annotation in the MLA Bibliography for 1948
(*PMLA*, 64, May 1949, p 21), this notice points out that 'Moses used gold
in physic, but not cordially, as the Physician would have known had his
study been upon the Bible.'

1130 Tupper, Frederick. 'Chaucer's "Doctour of Phisik." ' *Nation*, 96 (1913),
640–41.
'The Doctor's "study was but little on the Bible," not because he is a typical
physician of any or every age, but because he is a fourteenth-century Arabist

and astrologer' (p 640). The Physician's devotion to Arabic authorities would have been associated by Chaucer's contemporaries with a neglect of Christianity: Petrarch accused a physician of preferring Averroes to Christ, and there are other such complaints. Similarly, astrology, which the Physician practices, is associated with infidelity to the faith.

1131 Ussery, Huling E. *Chaucer's Physician: Medicine and Literature in Four-teenth-Century England.* New Orleans, LA: Tulane University, 1971. A TSE Monograph, Tulane Studies in English 19.
Ussery argues that the Physician is a cleric, not a layman, and that he is, 'in his medical practices, as distinguished from his desire for gain, a learned, competent, and highly qualified practitioner' whose tale is 'exceptionally appropriate' to his characterization (p 2). The careers of eighty physicians of Chaucer's time, along with contemporary records about medical educa-tion, the distinctions between physicians and surgeons, and related topics, are reviewed. Ussery rejects the suggestion that the Physician is modeled upon John of Gaddesden, John of Arderne, or John Mandeville, proposing, as more likely models, William de Holme, Geoffrey de Melton, and John of Wyke; and, more likely yet, Louis Recouchez de Luce (physician to John of Gaunt and twice named in documents that also name Chaucer); and, most likely of all, John de Middleton (physician to Richard II and to Henry of Derby). The portrait is primarily realistic, not composed of stock or satirical attributes. 'The realism is modified by hyperbole, humor, and wit — and a single thrust of irony' in lines 443–44 (p 114). In this portrait, as in others, 'Chaucer is primarily concerned with revealing human nature; he observes morals and manners, body and array, not with intent to correct, but with intent to discover, to describe, and to illuminate. His mediaeval audience was doubtless pleased to feel understanding, enlightenment, and amusement; they were not moved to moral indignation' (p 117).

This monograph incorporates, in revised form, Ussery's article 'The Appropriateness of the Physician's Tale to Its Teller,' *MichA*, 50 (1965), 545–56. Cf also 487.

✎ Part 20: The Wife of Bath

See the Introduction, p xxxvi above, for a brief summary of criticism on the Wife, and see the Index for further references.

1132 Barnouw, A.J. 'The Prente of Seinte Venus Seel.' *Nation*, 103 (1916), 540.
The Wife is said to be *gat-tothed* (line 468). Women who were 'gap-toothed by nature were believed to be predestined for the office of love,' as is suggested by various superstitions and primitive practices that associate a gap in the teeth with sexuality.

1133 Biggins, [Dennis]. 'Chaucer's General Prologue, A 467.' *N&Q*, New Series, 7 (1960), 129–30.
The statement that the Wife 'koude muchel of wandrynge by the weye' (line 467) means that she 'was fully acquainted with the moral by-ways as well as with the pilgrim routes of the world' (p 129). The line should be read in conjunction with the subsequent one, where we learn that she is *gat-tothed* (line 468). In this case also, we are meant to perceive 'a typical Chaucerian irony in which an innocent meaning overlies a less innocent one' (p 129), since on one level the Wife's teeth imply simply that she will be fortunate and will travel, but on another level they imply lasciviousness. Other Chaucerian uses of the words *weye* and *wandrynge* are considered.

1134 ——. '"O Jankyn, Be Ye There?" ' In *Chaucer and Middle English Studies in Honour of Rossell Hope Robbins*. Ed. Beryl Rowland. London: Allen & Unwin, 1974. Pp 249–54.
Are we to see the Wife of Bath as a woman whose husband is alive, or as (again) a widow? Her 'flamboyant attire as described in the *General Prologue* hardly suggests a widow' (p 250). Nevertheless, 'the critic is forcibly thrown back on equivocation, doubts, and ambiguities' about her (p 252). The dissonances in her overall characterization 'may be Chaucer's

way of putting us on our guard against too readily accepting' the Wife's world 'at face value' (p 253).

1135 Blake, N.F. 'The Wife of Bath and her Tale.' *Leeds SE*, New Series 13 (1982), 42–53.
Although it has been suggested that the Wife's portrait was revised after the prologue to her tale was written, Blake rejects this viewpoint. 'In [*GP*] the Wife is a rich, jolly oversexed woman who must satisfy her desires either in or out of marriage. Her wealth and position give her the opportunity to indulge herself in this way. There is no reason, therefore, to suggest that this portrait was written after [the Wife of Bath's Prologue] or in any way influenced by the information given there' (p 47). The *GP* portrait seems to represent the first of four or more stages in the development of the Wife's characterization. Certain *GP* traits are changed or ignored later — in her prologue three of the five husbands are amalgamated, and her independence, travelling, and love of finery are not stressed. 'In other words the Wife of Bath is portrayed as two different types' (p 48). Some *GP* traits recur later, but others do not, because in *GP* 'Chaucer uses the theme of the satirised woman of estates literature,' while in her prologue the Wife's depiction draws instead upon 'the theme of the tyrant in its special form of the tyrannical wife' (p 48).

1136 Braddy, Haldeen. 'Chaucer, Alice Perrers, and Cecily Chaumpaigne.' *Spec*, 52 (1977), 906–11.
Braddy suggests that Alice Perrers, mistress of Edward III and 'the often mated stepmother of Cecilia, served as the living prototype of the often married Alice of Bath' (p 910).

1137 Christie, Sister Mary Joannes. *The Provenance of Chaucer's Self Portraits: The Pardoner and the Wife of Bath.* Fordham University Dissertation. 1958. Dir. Grover J. Cronin.
In the chapter 'The Wife of Bath's Portrait' (pp 232–74), Sister Christie reviews previous scholarship on the Wife (emphasizing her later performance rather than the portrait in *GP*) and considers 'rhetoric's share in the creation of the Wife of Bath' (p 252). Cicero had specified eleven qualities for characterization: *nomen, natura, victum, fortunam, habitum, affectionem, studia, consilia, facta, casus,* and *orationes*; in several of these categories of information, details about the Wife that are 'offered as key characteristics in the General Prologue' are subsequently 'picked up and expanded in her personal prologue where the revelation centers' (p 252). For example, *studia* (interests) and *consilia* (plans) are represented by husbands and journeying; *nomen* (name) is postponed for later identification, but *natura* (nature) 'is broadly and economically suggested' by the traits given in *GP*

(p 253). The 'Ciceronian outline may be regarded as a broad structural device supporting the character as it emerges in the General Prologue,' though there is 'no rigidity of application' of the outline, since in Chaucer's mature writing 'rhetoric was a technique, not a ball and chain' (p 255). On the Pardoner, see **1301**.

1138 Coder, Ralph Vernon. *Chaucer's Wife of Bath.* University of Iowa Dissertation. 1941. Dir. E.P. Kuhl.
Coder comments briefly on the Wife's portrait as depicting 'a new type of woman characteristic of the last years of Chaucer's period' (p 51). Her pride in her status, her haughtiness, and her excess of dress reflect the newly rich burghers' wives, a social class 'nonexistent before the late fourteenth century' (p 52). The references to Ypres and Ghent (line 448), which 'associate her with the conditions peculiar to the 1390's and later,' may indicate either national pride in English weaving, or else good-natured mockery of west-country cloth (p 57). As for her pilgrimages, perhaps she had accompanied her husbands on business trips.

1139 Cook, Albert S. 'Chaucer, *Prol.* 446.' *MLN*, 22 (1907), 126.
Information is provided on the medieval transport of pilgrims to the shrine of St James of Compostella, one of the places that the Wife of Bath has visited (see line 446).

1140 Curry, Walter Clyde. 'More About Chaucer's Wife of Bath.' *PMLA*, 37 (1922), 30–51.
The Wife's personality has been conceived with reference to medieval concepts of the influence of the stars. Thus 'the cause of Dame Alisoun's peculiarly contradictory character lies not in herself but in her stars; she is in no way responsible' (p 31). The good influence of her dominating planet, Venus, has been largely vitiated by the bad effect of Mars. For example, although Venus would have given her small, attractive teeth, because of the influence of Mars she has 'long, spike-like teeth, set far apart with gaps between' — she is *gat-tothed* (p 45, see line 468). Chaucer's portrait is pathetic, heroic, even tragic. The Wife's yearning for the better nature that should have been hers, except for the evil influence of Mars, is pathetic, while 'the struggle which has kept unmarred a bit of her original nature in the midst of sordid conditions of life and in the face of adverse circumstances is heroic' (p 50). Chaucer perhaps 'considered her his most tragic figure because — as is certainly the case — she is the most nearly completely human' (p 51). In creating her character, he set up a horoscope for her and then amused himself 'with the inevitable actions and emotions of his living creature,' who is depicted as 'a woman both blessed and cursed by the stars' (p 51). Cf **209**.

1141 Donaldson, E.T., ed. *Chaucer's Poetry: An Anthology for the Modern Reader.* 1958, 1975. See **63**.
The Wife, as a weaver, is 'an economically independent bourgeoise, a type that was becoming increasingly common in Chaucer's time. One ought not to forget, however, that Eve, the prototype of all women, was the weaver who spun while Adam dug the earth, and that the Wife of Bath in all respects takes after her first mother' (1975, p 1054).

1142 Fleissner, R.F. 'The Wife of Bath's Five.' *ChauR*, 8 (1973–1974), 128–32.
Chaucer's choice of *fyve* husbands for the Wife (line 460) was not determined simply by the need for a rhyme to *lyve* (line 459). 'The reason why the Wife of Bath had five husbands' may be 'that Chaucer recognized in the Pythagorean endorsement of *five* ... the symbol, not just of the flesh or earthly love, but of marriage' (p 129). Chaucer's familiarity with number lore is suggested by an indirect reference to the Golden Proportion in *KnT* and by his indebtedness to writers such as Dante, who used numerical patterning. The 'reference to five husbands reflects back on the interrelationship of heavenly and earthly love as revealed in the pentad and pentagonal symmetry' (p 130).

1143 Garbáty, Thomas Jay. 'Chaucer's Weaving Wife.' *JAF*, 81 (1968), 342–46.
Most discussions of *GP* interpret the pilgrims in terms of historical identifications, physiognomic studies, or medieval sterotypes. However, a pilgrim can also represent an archetype, a traditional figure widely represented in folklore. The Wife is 'the old bawd, the standard type of go-between' (p 342). Her direct antecedent is La Vieille in the *Roman de la Rose*, but her traits have a long tradition. Analogies are presented for several of her characteristics. For example, she is associated with weaving, like Frau Hölle, 'patron goddess of all spinning women' in German fairy-tales (p 345), and like many other such characters. The Wife as weaver belongs to an archetype that 'must go back to the oldest weavers who controlled the destiny of all men and who were more powerful even than the gods, the Parcae' (p 345). Chaucer would not have known this archetype as such; we cannot know whether he unconsciously drew together different traits he remembered from childhood stories, or unconsciously designed a composite figure that fits the archetype. Nevertheless, the 'archetype motif-figure' is clearly present and stands 'as a tremendous tribute to his craft' (p 346).

1144 Hawkins, Harriett. *Poetic Freedom and Poetic Truth: Chaucer, Shakespeare, Marlowe, Milton.* Oxford: Clarendon Press, 1976.
Chaucer knows what to leave to the imagination. The Wife makes a vivid impression, yet the only information given about her appearance concerns her red face, broad hips, teeth, hat, stockings, shoes, and spurs. Had

Chaucer completed all the visual details of her description — had he 'typed her for all eternity, as, say, a brunette' — we could not so easily 'recognize her anywhere and everywhere' and her effect would be much more limited (p 121).

1145 Hoffman, Richard L. 'The Wife of Bath as Student of Ovid.' *N&Q*, New Series 11 (1964), 287–88.

The Wife knew Ovid's *Remedia Amoris*, which she mentions explicitly (line 475), but she was probably a far more eager student of the *Ars Amatoria* — to which she is likely to be referring when she mentions *art* in line 476. Her *olde daunce* (also line 476) is a reference to the Dance of Lechery.

1146 ——. 'The Wife of Bath's Uncharitable Offerings.' *ELN*, 11 (1973–1974), 165–67.

In her insistence that she be the first to make an offering in church, and her resentment against any possible competitors (see lines 449–52), the Wife ignores the message of Matthew 5:23–24, a passage in which Christ tells those who would make an offering that they must first be reconciled with anyone whom they may have injured—in other words, that they must be in a proper condition of harmony with their fellows. To Chaucer's audience, the Wife's uncharitable attitude about her acts of charity would have been 'one more instance of her spiritual deafness to the words of Christ' (p 167).

1147 Kernan, Anne. 'The Archwife and the Eunuch.' *ELH*, 41 (1974), 1–25.

The later interchange between the Wife and the Pardoner is anticipated in *GP*. Both portraits show a concern with headgear (lines 470–71 and 680–83). Both mention the offertory of the Mass; 'both pilgrims view the offertory as an opportunity for their own advancement' (p 4; lines 449–52 and 710–13). Both pilgrims are widely travelled (lines 463–67; 671, 685–87). They are experienced pilgrims who 'undertake their pilgrimages for reasons other than religious' (p 4). Their travels 'may suggest a psychological aspect of these two restless and self-contradictory characters' (p 4).

1148 Kiernan, Kevin S. 'The Art of the Descending Catalogue, and a Fresh Look at Alisoun.' 1975–1976. See **802**.

The Wife's portrait, like the Prioress's, shows the 'deliberate misuse, or incongruous use' (p 10) of the technique of the descending catalog that describes a woman head-to-foot. The Wife is not the standard beautiful woman, but 'the great homely lady' (p 13). Here 'Chaucer uses the conventional descent from head to toe without being able to offer any conventional feminine delights,' and so produces a humorous catalogue that describes 'Alice's massive girth almost solely by implication' (p 13).

1149 Kittredge, G.L. 'Chauceriana.' *MP*, 7 (1909–1910), 465–83.
Lines 449–52, on the Wife's insistence that no one precede her at offering, are illustrated by a passage in Deschamps' *Miroir de Mariage*. See also 1280.

1150 Manly, John Matthews. *Some New Light on Chaucer*. 1926. See 362.
In the chapter 'The Prioress and the Wife of Bath, the Second Nun and the Nuns' Priest' (pp 201–34), Manly points out that in the parish of St Michael outside Bath, Alice was a common name. More than one recorded Alice from that parish 'rejoiced in three or more husbands' (p 234), though no evidence has been found of an Alice who had five. In reply, on the Wife's head-dress, see 1173.

1151 Mann, Jill. *Chaucer and Medieval Estates Satire*. 1973. See 363.
The estates-satire tradition recognized women as a separate class, with their duties and failings often depicted from the viewpoint of the male moralist. Associated with women in the estates tradition are sexuality, cloth-making as a profession, concern for precedence in church, irascibility, pride, love of pilgrimages, interest in items of apparel, etc. Traditionally, women were either beautiful, young, and able to carry on love affairs; or ugly, old, and interested in love but unable to practice it. 'The uniqueness of the Wife of Bath is that, although she has certain traits in common with the *vetulae* [old women], Chaucer presents her as attractive .... In the social ethic of the *Prologue*, what ensures our admiration for the Wife is that she is fun to be with' (pp 126–27).

1152 Masefield, John. *Chaucer: The Leslie Stephen Lecture Delivered at Cambridge 3 March 1931*. Cambridge: Cambridge University Press, 1931; New York: Macmillan, 1931.
The Wife may perhaps be 'a portrait of Mrs. Chaucer' (p 33).

1153 Parks, George B. *The English Traveller to Italy, I: The Middle Ages*. Rome: Edizione di Storia e Letteratura, 1954.
The Wife's 'three trips to Jerusalem are plainly meant to be ironical' (p 352; see line 463). 'I do not know of any Englishman who went there more than twice, if only because each journey was likely to take a whole year' (p 352).

1154 Plummer, John F. 'The Wife of Bath's Hat as Sexual Metaphor.' *ELN*, 18 (1980-1981), 89–90.
The Wife's broad hat (lines 470–71) is compared to a buckler or a small shield. This martial imagery is appropriate to her; for instance, she also wears sharp spurs. However, the buckler involves an additional sexual innuendo, as citations from other sources show. 'Chaucer does not actually say,

here, that the Wife is sexually aggressive, but the hat-buckler-pudendum image suggests as much' (p 90) and foreshadows the fuller revelation of her sexuality in her Prologue.

1155 Pratt, Robert A. 'The Development of the Wife of Bath.' In *Studies in Medieval Literature in Honor of Professor Albert Croll Baugh.* Ed. MacEdward Leach. Philadelphia: University of Pennsylvania Press, 1961; London: Oxford University Press, 1961.
Pratt suggests that the *GP* portrait of the Wife was revised by Chaucer as his conception of her changed. Her characteristics of being 'addicted to pilgrimages and punctilious about precedence at offerings' (p 57) may have been added to an earlier version of the portrait, after Chaucer decided to make her somewhat older and domineering. The Wife 'as first conceived by Chaucer' may have shown 'no hint of old age; of a man-hungry widow; of a wife-wielded whip of tribulation; or of many marriages' (p 49).

1156 Puhvel, Martin. 'The Wyf of Bath and Alice Kyteler — A Web of Parallelism.' *SN*, 53 (1981), 101–6.
The historical Dame Alice Kyteler of Kilkenny, Ireland, shares a number of characteristics with the Wife of Bath. Dame Alice was married at least four times (cf line 460); she was accused of magical practices involving the making of potions and ointments to arouse love (line 475). Although the charges of magic and satanic practices were made against Dame Alice in 1324, before Chaucer's lifetime, the case became quite notorious, and Chaucer as a 'well-informed courtier and man of public affairs' (p 104) might have known of it. Both Dame Alice and the Wife of Bath are 'unconventionally self-assertive and aggressive women in a male-dominated society' (p 105).

1157 Reid, David S. 'Crocodilian Humor: Chaucer's Wife of Bath.' *ChauR*, 4 (1969–1970), 73–89.
'The General Prologue is a sophisticated pantomime,' a 'masquerade of the world' in which 'the type figures, the Wife among them, are representative of the Estates of the Realm and of Christian pilgrims' (p 77). These stock figures 'are disguised as a crowd of people' and given traits that seem to individuate them, but, 'as in a dream allegory, those clues to what the persons are confront us enigmatically or transparently in the form of a mask' (p 77). The urbanity of *GP* 'privileges us to view the sorts and conditions of men as a spectacle or entertainment' (p 78). The Wife 'makes sense only in terms of burlesque and knockabout comedy' (p 79).

1158 Reisner, Thomas Andrew. 'The Wife of Bath's Dower: A Legal Interpretation.' *MP*, 71 (1973-1974), 301–2.
The Wife has had five husbands *at chirche door* (line 460). If, as editors

usually point out, medieval marriages customarily took place by the door of the church, why is it necessary to mention the location? Does it have some special significance here? Reisner proposes that the phrase refers, in legal terms, to dower *ad ostium ecclesiae*, a kind of dower granted by the husband on arriving at the church door for the marriage ceremony. This type of dower was financially advantageous to the woman. The Wife, 'shrewd and circumspect,' would have known this (p 302). 'Chaucer's emphasis on the specific condition upon which she entered her marriage alliances not only underscores her Venerean nature but also sheds a new and ironical light on her personality as a venal adventuress' (p 302).

1159 Reiss, Edmund. 'Chaucer's Thematic Particulars.' 1981. See **645**.
The Wife's portrait 'offers a wealth of details that, for all their vivid realism, function primarily as thematic particulars' (p 30). Her deafness suggests her distorted views. Her skill in cloth-making suggests the Virgin, who wove the cloth without seam. Her hat may imply her grossness, her interest in clothing, and, in conjunction with her spurs, her preparation for adventure. Additionally, 'the broad hat may also parody a well-known iconographical detail, the cardinal's hat of Saint Jerome' (p 31). Despite the Ellesmere picture in which the hat is black, Chaucer perhaps meant it to be red. In this perspective, the hat shows the Wife to be a ludicrous authority-figure, both knight *manqué* and clerk *manqué*.

1160 Robertson, D.W., Jr. ' "And for my land thus hastow mordred me?" Land Tenure, the Cloth Industry, and the Wife of Bath.' *ChauR*, 14 (1979-1980), 403-20.
The Wife of *biside Bathe* (line 445) has been assumed to come from the parish of St Michael's *juxta Bathon*, but Robertson argues that 'Chaucer's phrase could just as well imply any village near Bath or simply a birthplace' (p 409). 'It is probably quite safe to conclude that Chaucer meant his audience to think of the Wife of Bath as a rural clothier from the west country and quite possibly as a bondwoman' (p 415). Information about medieval systems of landholding and about clothiers is provided.

1161 ——. 'Simple Signs from Everyday Life in Chaucer.' In *Signs and Symbols in Chaucer's Poetry*. Ed. John P. Hermann and John J. Burke, Jr. University, AL: University of Alabama Press, 1981. Pp 12-26.
'Chaucer's technique of portraiture in the General Prologue reflects a medieval tendency to identify individuals in terms of attributes' (p 20). The tendency is apparent, for example, in the fact that images of St Peter were intended to be recognized by his keys; similarly, in everyday life a bailiff could be fined for not carrying his rod of office in the manorial court. The individual tales 'often elaborate the significance of the attributes mentioned

in the Prologue, serving, in effect, as additional attributes of the speakers' (p 21). The Wife, like the Monk, 'represents a new and distinctive feature of fourteenth-century life' (p 23). Robertson comments on her dress, on the contemporary cloth industry, and on women as weavers. 'We should imagine the Wife of Bath as the master of a shop, becoming wealthy through the labors of other women' (pp 23–24). Prosperous female masters 'caused some uneasiness among male masters of the trade' (p 24). 'No one in the audience would have failed to recognize the Wife as a greedy exploiter of female labor who could be expected to enjoy a sense of mastery over men as well as over women' (p 24). She typifies 'a new spirit of self-aggrandizement and a new kind of wealth that were disrupting traditional values cherished by Chaucer and most of his audience' (p 26); the cloth industry afforded a vivid illustration of this process.

1162 Shumaker, Wayne. 'Alisoun in Wander-Land: A Study in Chaucer's Mind and Literary Method.' *ELH*, 18 (1951), 77–89.
Chaucer is commonly regarded as an empirical or realistic artist, and therefore as modern. The Wife does indeed seem to be ' "real," not a type' (p 79), as vivid as if she were drawn from life, as she probably was. However, 'there is another and opposite side' (p 80) which is suggested by Chaucer's handling of the passage on her experiences as a pilgrim (lines 463–67). These lines make us curious to know more, but in her own Prologue the Wife refers only twice, and briefly, to her pilgrimages. Chaucer does not capitalize on 'the opportunities for realization of situation and incident' (p 87). This case is not unique, for Chaucer nowhere commits himself wholly 'to an exploration of the implications of personality' (p 88). Except 'by way of introduction in the General Prologue,' he does not 'keep the focus very long upon *men*,' for he has 'no really profound curiosity about the individual soul' (p 88). He would not have been satisfied to depict the Wife as an individual, for his 'strongest interest is in the general — in what is not (as it would have seemed to him) self-limiting and therefore trivial' (p 88). As a medieval writer, Chaucer finds the inner will of a character to be more important than the individual attitudes and habits.

1163 Silvia, D.S. 'The Wife of Bath's Marital State.' *N&Q*, New Series 14 (1967), 8–10.
Silvia argues that the Wife is not a widow. Her presence on the pilgrimage is indeed due to her search for a sixth husband, but Jankyn, her fifth husband, is still alive. Having lost interest in him, she is going on the pilgrimage to seek a replacement to have ready in advance.

1164 Storm, Melvin. 'Alisoun's Ear.' *MLQ*, 42 (1981), 219–26.
The Wife's deafness (see line 446), which is 'the most rhetorically promi-

nent detail' of her presentation (p 219), echoes 'a long patristic tradition of equating the ears and hearing with the apprehension of truth' (p 220). Deafness connotes understanding that is impeded — according to some commentators, wilfully so. Deafness in only one ear suggests the Old Testament, with God feared as Creator but not loved as Redeemer. Hearing with the left ear is taken to indicate a preoccupation with the present life and 'attention to pious works in this world' (p 224). This implication accords with the Wife's external acts of religious observation (see lines 449–52, 453–55, and 463–66). 'One need only contrast the portrait of the Prioress to see the relative prominence of such details in the Wife's descripton,' though the Wife's performance of these pious acts 'may stem more from worldly than from spiritual considerations' (p 225). The patristic tradition of deafness is applicable to her later prologue and tale, as well as to the *GP* portrait.

1165 Tatlock, John S.P. 'Puns in Chaucer.' In *Flügel Memorial Volume*. Stanford, CA: Stanford University, 1916. Leland Stanford Junior University Publications, University Series, 21. Pp 228–32.

'In Chaucer the pun is common' (p 229). *Withouten* (line 461) means both 'without' and 'besides.' Thus Chaucer 'leaves us guessing whether or not the Wife of Bath had lovers before she married' (p 229).

1166 Thundy, Zacharias P. 'Matheolus, Chaucer, and the Wife of Bath.' In *Chaucerian Problems and Perspectives: Essays Presented to Paul E. Beichner, C.S.C.* Ed. Edward Vasta and Zacharias P. Thundy. Notre Dame and London: University of Notre Dame Press, 1979. Pp 24–58.

The *GP* portrait of the Wife shows twenty-four parallels to the *Lamentationes* of Matheolus, a thirteenth-century Latin misogynous poem which existed also in a French translation by Jehan Le Fèvre, who added a refutation called *Le Livre de Leësce*. Among the parallels are the Wife's deafness (Matheolus), her weaving (*Leësce*), her insistence on precedence at the Offertory (Matheolus), her kerchiefs (Matheolus), and her knowledge of the remedies for love (Matheolus — in the sense of contraceptives). Given the fact that the Wife shows 'certain characteristics traditionally associated with men,' one might wonder whether Chaucer 'intended to caricature her also as a hermaphrodite' (p 47). However, 'there is no single viewpoint governing the physical and moral portrait of the Wife of Bath' (p 49).

1167 Tupper, Frederick. 'Saint Venus and the Canterbury Pilgrims.' *Nation*, 97 (1913), 354–56.

Chaucer's audience would have realized that 'Venus was the reigning star of pilgrimages' and that in addition 'she dominates the mid-April days of the Canterbury pilgrimage' (p 354). The Wife of Bath, who later explains that she is 'al Venerien,' is inevitably a pilgrim, but she is not the only one whom the goddess affects, for Venus presides over the entire pilgrimage and the subject of all of it is love. Although 'Chaucer nowhere in his Prologue explicitly indicates his controlling idea,' this purpose would have become 'speedily clear to the mediaeval readers,' who 'must have recognized the traditional domination of pilgrimages by Venus, and her "influence" upon the season of this very journey, and, forgetting Thomas à Becket for the nonce, must have reverently hailed the goddess as the patron saint of the Canterbury road' (p 356).

1168 ——. 'Chaucer and the Cambridge Edition.' 1940. See **485**.
The Wife's insistence on taking precedence at offerings (lines 449–52) and her 'extravagant array of clothing' (p 516) correspond to sermon-literature attacks upon the pride of women; she 'is the Proud Wife' (p 518). The Samarian woman with her five husbands, met beside a well, is likely to have been 'the literary ancestress' of the Wife from *besyde Bathe* (p 518; see line 445).

1169 Weissman, Hope Phyllis. 'Antifeminism and Chaucer's Characterization of Women.' 1975. See **861**.
The portrait of the Wife functions to establish her as 'an incarnation of the fabliau woman and more especially the Old Eve' (p 105). The portrait is also 'a parody of the Virtuous Woman (*mulier fortis*) of Proverbs 31' (p 105). The Wife's depiction as a 'mock knight,' her weaving, and her 'capitalist mentality' extended into 'the marriage industry' provide echoes of the Biblical passage (p 106). The Virtuous Woman's husband is said to be ' "known in the gates," ' while the Wife's 'parade of husbands, on the other hand, must have been notorious at the "gates," ' for she has been five times married at church door (p 106).

1170 ——. 'Why Chaucer's Wife is from Bath.' *ChauR*, 15 (1980-1981), 11–36.
The Wife is said to come from *biside Bathe* (line 445). Although this location suits her occupation as a weaver, it has other connotations too, for baths were 'connected fundamentally with the experience of the natural body and the expression of sexual impulses' (p 12). Baths were associated with sexual license or prostitution in the literary tradition of Ovid, Juvenal, Jerome, and Jean de Meun; in manuscript illustrations of bathhouses; and in medieval terminology, where *stew*, for example, meant both 'bath' and 'brothel.' In the other direction, the mineral waters at Bath, under the jurisdiction of the bishop, were associated with healing. Being 'controlled by the representatives of official culture,' they were 'the preserve, indeed the sacred precincts, of a patriarchal world' (p 25). Since she lives not *in* but *beside* Bath, the Wife 'has been banished from the patriarchal precincts' and has 'taken up her residence outside the magic circle in the antipathetic

Venerean stew' (p 25). Thus she exemplifies the official culture's banishment 'of the woman in her human fullness, of the human in the fullness of its flesh' (p 25).

1171 Whitbread, L. 'Six Chaucer Notes.' 1978. See **659**.
The redness of the Wife (see line 458) hints at what will later be made explicit — that the Wife is astrologically a Martian. The reference to her five husbands (line 460) perhaps reflects the prohibition on having more than five husbands in Jesus' statement to the Samarian Woman (John 4:17–18).

1172 Winny, James, ed. *The General Prologue to the Canterbury Tales by Geoffrey Chaucer.* 1965. See **73**.
The Wife 'represents mankind's uninhibited enjoyment of its natural appetites, of raucous companionship, of adventurous curiosity and of pride in its exploits and achievements.... A raw spirit of life bears her forward, jaunty and indestructible, like a cork on a stream' (p 109).

1173 Wretlind, Dale E. 'The Wife of Bath's Hat.' *MLN*, 63 (1948), 381–82.
The Wife wears a heavy head-dress, according to lines 454–55. Although Manly has indicated (**1150**) that such weighty head-gear had been out of style since mid-century, this is not the case. It was only after Anne of Bohemia arrived in England (she became queen in 1382) that the large or heavy head-dresses became popular. Thus the Wife 'was not thirty-five or more years out of style; she was, rather, very much in style in her choice of hats' (p 382).

⚙ Part 21: The Parson

See the Introduction, pp xxxvi–xxxvii above, for a brief summary of criticism on the Parson, and see the Index for further references.

1174 Bennett, H.S. *Life on the English Manor*. 1937. See **154**.
Background information about country priests is provided. The parish clergy was typically 'ill-trained, ill-educated' (1948 rpt, p 325), with priests often recruited from the peasant class and given only a minimal preparation for their pastoral duties. For the majority of them, 'a moderate ability to read and construe the Latin of the service books, and a knowledge of the Church services, gained by years of experience, was all their stock in trade' (pp 326–7). The country priest's stipend was often inadequate to his needs; he would participate in the agricultural economy of his village in order to support himself. Corruption among priests was common. Nevertheless, a capable and sincere priest, such as Chaucer's Parson, would have been 'a focus of all those forces making for good in the parish, and a constant warrior against evil and superstition.' (p 335).

1175 Biggins, D. 'A Chaucerian Crux: Spiced Conscience, *CT* I(A) 526, III(D) 435.' *ES*, 47 (1966), 169–80.
Previous interpretations of the phrase *spiced conscience*, which occurs in the Parson's portrait (line 526) and in the Wife of Bath's Prologue (III.435), are discussed. The phrase implies the concept that if spices are beaten or crushed, their fragrance will smell sweeter; metaphorically, it suggests 'a long-suffering sensibility, a heart that acquires fortitude from the patient acceptance of trials' (p 176). Line 526 means that the Parson 'did not affect a long-suffering sensibility that he did not really possess' (p 179).

1176 Bode, Edward L. 'The Source of Chaucer's "Rusted Gold." ' *MS*, 24 (1962), 369–70.

The image of rusted or tarnished gold is found in several places in the Bible. However, the specific application to the decadence of priests is a patristic interpretation. Therefore 'it appears preferable to assign a patristic source' (p 369) for the Parson's reference to this image (line 500). Chaucer might have found the idea in the writings of Gregory, which he used in the *ParsT*, but it is not necessary to identify a single source as long as the general patristic background is recognized.

1177 Boyd, Beverly. *Chaucer and the Liturgy.* 1967. See **757.**
Lines 527–28 imply that 'Chaucer did not like the current emphasis upon ritual that accompanied the widespread adoption of the Use of Sarum' (p 47).

1178 Cook, Albert S. 'Chaucerian Papers, I.' 1919. See **591.**
On lines 493–98 and 527–28, parallels in Bede's *Ecclesiastical History* and in the Bible are pointed out.

1179 Cowling, George H. *Chaucer.* London: Methuen, 1927.
'The Portrait of the poor Parson is a veritable triumph, for Chaucer has made a good man attractive for his own sake without the spice of an eccentricity or a weakness; and that is the hardest task in the whole art of fiction' (p 152).

1180 Fleming, John. 'The "Figure" of Chaucer's Good Parson and a Reprimand by Grosseteste.' *N&Q*, New Series 11 (1964), 167.
The Parson's figure of speech, 'if gold ruste, what shal iren do?' (line 500), has been traced to the *Roman de Carité* and ultimately to Lamentations 4:1 as glossed by Gregory [see Kittredge, 'Chaucer and the Roman de Carité,' *MLN*, 12 (1897), 113–15]. However, Fleming argues that nearer to Chaucer is the thirteenth-century bishop Robert Grosseteste, who also used this figure. The bishop 'was himself one of the most notable "good parsons" of the high Middle Ages in England.'

1181 Grennan, Eamon. 'Dual Characterization: A Note on Chaucer's Use of "But" in the Portrait of the Parson.' *ChauR*, 16 (1981-1982), 195–200.
The Parson's portrait includes eight occurrences of the word *but*. 'Such reiteration suggests a deliberate rhetorical strategy on the poet's part' (p 195). The conjunction is used to stress the Parson's 'physical and moral existence as an individual as distinct from his institutional function' (p 195). As for the narrator, his 'use of conjunctive phrases beginning in "but" repeatedly testifies to an enthusiasm for the modest priest which he wishes his audience to share' (p 198). '*We* learn by seeing the Narrator adjust his own awareness' and thus Chaucer's 'calculated rhetoric,' including the use of *but*, makes us participate, not merely be spectators (p 200).

1182 Ives, Doris V. 'A Man of Religion.' *MLR*, 27 (1932), 144–48.

The Parson's portrait reflects Lollard concepts and language, especially in the term *man ... of religioun* (line 477): ' "man of religion" applied to a secular priest, would have the significance 'Lollard" ' (p 145). The portrait points to Wycliffe himself. The Parson is a learned man and comes from a farming family, like Wycliffe. His character 'agrees well with the ideal of priesthood set forth in the Lollard writings' (p 145). It has been objected that Chaucer would not have sent Wycliffe on a pilgrimage, but the pilgrimage is 'only a literary device' (p 147) that should not be heavily stressed; it is possible that the Parson is going to Canterbury for some other reason, rather than as a pilgrim, or that Chaucer was 'unaware of the Lollard dislike of pilgrimages' (p 148). Furthermore, Wycliffe 'seems to have had a special reverence for St Thomas' (p 148). It would not have been dangerous for Chaucer to praise Wycliffe, since John of Gaunt, Chaucer's patron, was Wycliffe's protector.

1183 Kuhl, E.P. 'Chaucer and the Church.' *MLN*, 40 (1925), 321–38.

The Parson's portrait shares the viewpoints on the corruption of the clergy expressed in a remonstrance sent to the Pope by Richard II, John of Gaunt, and other leaders of the English court in 1390. The 'ideals of this perfect shepherd parallel the views set forth in the protest to Rome' (p 338). If *GP* were written in 1387, as is usually assumed, the connection between Chaucer's views and those of the remonstrance is not necessarily invalidated, since 'the petition of 1390 was merely the breaking forth of a long-smouldering fire' (p 338). In any case, there is no proof that all parts of *GP* were composed at the same time.

1184 Lawler, Traugott. *The One and the Many in the Canterbury Tales*. 1980. See **330**.

Both the Wife and the Parson are introduced by their sex, she as a good wife, he as a good man (see lines 445, 477). This kind of introduction invites us to see their portraits as 'complementary' (p 55). The rhetorical patterns in these protraits reinforce the two pilgrims' contrasts.

1185 Looten, C. *Chaucer, ses modèles, ses sources, sa religion*. 1931. See **342**.

In the chapter 'La Religion de Chaucer' (pp 215–43), Looten reviews opinion on whether the Parson's portrait reflects Wycliffite concepts, and argues against that interpretation: the Parson shows not an atom of the pride of Wycliffe and is certainly no Lollard ('Il n'y a en lui pas un atome de l'orgueil de Wyclif. ... Lollard, il ne l'est certainement pas,' pp 230–31).

1186 Lowes, John L. 'Chaucer and Li Renclus de Moiliens.' *PMLA*, 29 (1914), xxix.

The Parson's portrait may be indebted to the *Roman de Carité* of Renclus de Moiliens, which draws together a half-dozen conventional ingredients in an arrangement similar to Chaucer's. (This item is an abstract only, in the 'Proceedings for 1913' report published as an appendix to *PMLA*.)

1187 Macaulay, G.C. 'Notes on Chaucer.' 1908. See **893**.

The Parson's *spiced conscience* (line 526) means 'highly refined (or fastidious) feelings' (p 16). The passage as a whole (lines 525–27) indicates that 'He demanded no pomp or reverence, nor did he cultivate highly-refined feelings; but he taught the Gospel simply, and set an example by first following its rules himself' (p 16).

1188 Mann, Jill. *Chaucer and Medieval Estates Satire*. 1973. See **363**.

'The Parson is representative of what the estate of priesthood should be like. He possesses all the virtues which writers for centuries had associated with the pastoral ideal' (p 66). Yet his values are not necessarily to be applied to the other pilgrims. 'The absolute values of the Parson are temporarily made relative by being taken as absolute only *for him*' (p 67). The fact that the Plowman is the Parson's brother reflects the traditional linkage between the estates of priest and peasant; eg, the 'two ideals of priesthood and labour' are fused in the figure of Piers the Plowman (p 68), and it is possible that Langland's use of the plow as a symbol influenced Chaucer's decision to make his laborer specifically a plowman. Both the Parson and the Plowman seem isolated from the other travelers. 'The Parson does not seem to impinge on the other pilgrims, nor does the Ploughman' (p 73); their concept of idealized service is not widely operative in the society of *GP*. Similarly, the Clerk too represents an estates ideal, but one whose function in society remains somewhat unclear. 'In these three portraits of medieval estates ideals, Chaucer may almost be said to use the concept of the estate against itself. Starting from the usual theory of the estates, he throws into prominence the concept of specialised services for each class, and subtly undermines the concept of the interchange of such services which leads to social harmony .... The portraits of the Parson and the Ploughman are unusual in the *Prologue* in indicating the effects of the actions of each on the other; they are like actors playing in a different style from the rest of a cast, and if we are to ask what makes the production hang together, it is evident that it cannot be the principles on which they, but nobody else, are working' (p 85).

1189 Maxfield, Ezra Kempton. 'Chaucer and Religious Reform.' *PMLA*, 39 (1924), 64–74.

Although the Parson's portrait has been interpreted as heterodox, or as a portrait of Wycliffe, these viewpoints are not necessarily supported by the text. Has Chaucer 'committed himself to anything but a picture of a noble priest — one so old fashioned as to be sincere?' (p 73). It is inappropriate to regard Chaucer as a Wycliffian, or a Lollard, or a pre-Reformation protestant, on the basis of the Parson's idealized portrait — just as it would be inappropriate to 'maintain that he was a pagan because he keeps classical deities in certain of his poems' (p 74).

1190 Rex, Richard. ' "Spiced Conscience" in the *Canterbury Tales*.' *MP*, 80 (1982-1983), 53–54.
The Parson's *spiced conscience* (line 526) is in deliberate contrast to the Prioress's conscience: 'whatever the Prioress's conscience *is*, the Parson's is *not*' (p 53). In lines 142, 150, and 526, *conscience* 'does not refer to the moral faculty, but to affected emotion or exaggerated sensibility' (p 53). The verb *maken* (line 526) means 'to pretend.' Thus the Parson 'does not feign sensibility or concern for others; instead he demonstrates his charity with deeds' (p 53).

1191 Robinson, F.N. *The Works of Geoffrey Chaucer.* 1957. See **42**.
'The sketch of the Parson is an ideal portrait of a good parish priest,' not intended to represent specifically Wycliffe or his followers; the Parson does not hold 'some of the most distinguishing beliefs of the Lollard party' (pp 663–4).

1192 Rockwell, K.A. 'Canterbury Tales: General Prologue, 526, the Wife of Bath's Prologue, 435, "Spiced Conscience." ' *N&Q*, New Series 4 (1957), 84.
Rockwell proposes that in the Parson's portrait, '*spiced conscience* would mean a hot or peppery, easily aroused moral indignation, such as a wise parson cannot afford.'

1193 Tatlock, John S.P. '*Bretherhed* in Chaucer's *Prolog*.' *MLN*, 31 (1916), 139–42.
The Parson does not leave his parish behind 'with a bretherhed to ben withholde' (line 511) — as, by implication, some priests apparently did. The term *bretherhed*, which is simply a translation of *fraternitas*, signifies a guild. Medieval guild records repeatedly mention priests and chaplains. 'We are to understand, then, that the Parson would have been retained or engaged to give all or most of his time to the good of the gild members' (p 141). The pay would have been low, but the duties would have been correspondingly light. This kind of office would have attracted priests who rejected the heavier pastoral tasks of a country parish, such as the one that the Parson serves.

1194 Westlake, H.F. *The Parish Gilds of Mediaeval England.* London: Society
for Promoting Christian Knowledge, 1919; New York: MacMillan, 1919.
Lines 509-11 of *GP* — referring to a priest who goes to St Paul's in search
of chantry employment instead of staying at home with his parish — are
usually taken to mean that such a priest seeks a chantry assignment within
the cathedral itself. However, the cathedral and its vicinity were also a center for the hiring of priests for guild chantries, and Chaucer may have had
this kind of arrangement in mind (see p 48). Much information pertinent
to the Guildsmen, and to a lesser extent to other pilgrims such as the Wife
and the Pardoner, is also presented.

❧ Part 22: The Plowman

See the Introduction, p xxxvii above, for a brief summary of criticism on the Plowman, and see the Index for further references.

1195 Barney, Stephen A. 'The Plowshare of the Tongue: The Progress of a Symbol from the Bible to *Piers Plowman*.' *MS*, 35 (1973), 261–93.
GP itself is not discussed, but Barney describes the long tradition of medieval symbolism that associated agricultural labor with spiritual labor, and the plowman's activities with preaching. 'In medieval literature the hard heart is likened to an untilled field, the truth to be spread to seed, the virtue which follows from a life of faith to a fruitful tree, the act of spreading the word to sowing, the act of preparing the heart to receive the word to plowing. The plowshare is the preacher's tongue; the plow is the symbol of the penitential act; a farmer or ox is a symbol of a preacher' (p 276). This system of symbolic associations appeared in vernacular works such as *Piers Plowman* (which is roughly contemporary with *CT*) as well as in Latin writings.

1196 Coghill, Nevill. 'Two Notes on Piers Plowman.' *MÆ*, 4 (1935), 83–94.
The second of these notes, 'Chaucer's Debt to Langland' (pp 89–94), deals with *GP*. Coghill argues that Chaucer was familiar with *Piers Plowman* and that the Plowman's portrait in *GP* is indebted to that work: 'only the first and last lines of Chaucer's picture of the plowman are not paralleled in Langland; the differences are principally those of literary technique and of point of view; Chaucer is pretending to describe an objective person, secretly compounded from allegorical elements; he concentrates our attention on what he would have us think of as *actual*. Langland, who suggested the elements, keeps his plowman in the world of allegory and idea' (p 94).

1197 Dent, Anthony. 'Fair Burgesses.' 1961. See **214**.
Chaucer's Plowman represents one component of the middle class. His type of worker, who with an ox or a horse 'controlled the sole source of motive power,' should not be confused with 'the enormous mass of peasant labourers' (p 759): they would have worked by hand and would not have been able to go on pilgrimages.

1198 Derocquigny, J. 'Notes sur Chaucer.' 1910. See **595**.
Corroborating evidence is presented for the interpretation that riding upon a mare (see line 541) implies a lack of status.

1199 Horrell, Joe. 'Chaucer's Symbolic Plowman.' *Spec*, 14 (1939), 82–92. Rpt in *Chaucer Criticism, 1*, ed. Richard J. Schoeck and Jerome Taylor (Notre Dame: University of Notre Dame Press, 1960; 10th printing 1978), pp 84–97.
Chaucer's Plowman, 'his only perfect Christian among the lay pilgrims,' is not 'dim and uncharacterized' (1939, p 82), but represents several medieval traditions. Plowmen were among the first kinds of peasants to work for money as independent laborers; in the 1350 Statute of Laborers, the plowman 'is the only specific type of laborer mentioned' (p 83). The Peasants' Revolt enhanced the prestige of plowmen. In literature they were often handled contemptuously (eg, by Gower, who presents plowmen as lazy and avaricious), but Langland's Piers Plowman is an idealized figure. The specific tasks of threshing, diking, and delving mentioned in Chaucer's portrait were among the usual duties of plowmen, and by Chaucer's time the tabard was their usual dress. To ride a mare indicated humble station, humility, or even humiliation. Chaucer's Plowman was most likely a free laborer who owned property. In his honest payment of his tithes, in his willingness to work for poor people without payment, and especially in his 'parfit charite,' he represents a long medieval tradition that praised charity — towards one's fellow men and, according to Aquinas, principally towards God — as the highest of virtues. Thus Chaucer 'found in the Plowman an appropriate symbol' for several ideals (p 92).

1200 Leyerle, John. 'Thematic Interlace in *The Canterbury Tales*.' 1976. See **337**.
'The one unambiguously virtuous pilgrim concerned with food is the Ploughman, whose job is to grow crops for the rest of society. Nothing at all is said about his eating habits; here, as often, Chaucer's silences are significant' (p 114).

1201 Patch, Howard R. 'Chaucer and the Common People.' *JEGP*, 29 (1930), 376–84. Rpt (without documentation) in Patch's book *On Rereading Chau-*

cer (Cambridge, MA: Harvard University Press, 1939, 4th printing 1967), pp 187–94.

Chaucer's portrait of the Plowman, who represents 'the whole class of decent laboring-men' (930, p 383), is seen as part of the evidence for the poet's broad social sympathies. 'Gower and Langland give all the necessary evidence that they pitied the poor. Chaucer without sentimentality appears to have loved them' (p 384).

1202 Stillwell, Gardiner. 'Chaucer's Plowman and the Contemporary English Peasant.' *ELH*, 6 (1939), 285–90.

In the Plowman's portrait, Chaucer's 'evident affection for the ideal peasant suggests an antagonism toward the actual peasant,' for the portrait is very far removed from reality (p 285). In contrast to many peasants, the Plowman is economically contented and lives in peace. At the time of the Peasants' Revolt of 1381, Chaucer was 'connected with most of the principal groups against which the anger of the peasants was chiefly directed' (p 287). In the Parliament of 1381–1382, middle-class representatives joined the nobility in condemning the peasants' movement. Chaucer would have shared the general viewpoint of his class, as well as perhaps having personally been in danger when the rebels entered London through Aldgate, above which he lived. He did not need to openly indicate his opinion, since 'to portray an ideal Plowman is to express sufficient disapproval' of a reality that does not conform to that ideal (p 289). Chaucer was 're-expressing the conservative, medieval ideal of the proper order of society, that ideal according to which each individual had his God-given niche to fill' (p 290). This article incorporates the second section of Stillwell's dissertation, *Chaucer Studies: (1) The Political Meaning of the Tale of Melibee; (2) Chaucer's Plowman and the Contemporary English Peasant; (3) Important Analogues to the Manciple's Tale in the Ovide Moralisé and Machaut's Voir-Dit*, State University of Iowa, 1940. Cf **712**.

1203 White, Beatrice. 'Poet and Peasant.' In *The Reign of Richard II: Essays in Honour of May McKisack*. Ed. F.R.H. DuBoulay and Caroline M. Barron. London: Athlone Press, 1971; New York: Oxford University Press, 1971. Pp 58–74.

'Chaucer's Plowman, like his brother, the Parson, is altogether too good to be true' (p 67). In the manner of classical satire, Chaucer may have used 'a refinement of actuality to describe his "good" characters, in order to delineate his rascals and ruffians more clearly by contrast' (p 67). 'Or perhaps he was saying, "This is how the *rusticus*, the *villanus*, ought to behave. But just take a look round and you'll see for yourselves how it is", and by a double irony he was presenting the best so that the worst should be the more conspicuous' (p 67).

Part 23: The Transition and the Miller

See the Introduction, p xxxvii above, for a brief summary of the criticism on this section of the *General Prologue*, and see the Index for further references.

1204 Bennett, J.A.W. *Chaucer at Oxford and at Cambridge.* 1974. See **978**.
'The mill and its "services" epitomizes the economic and social life of the time' (p 7). An appendix on 'Mills and Milling' (pp 120–23) briefly reviews the characteristics and functions of medieval water-mills, and indicates the imagery and traditions often associated with millers.

1205 Biggins, Dennis. 'Sym(e)kyn / *simia*: The Ape in Chaucer's Millers.' *SP*, 65 (1968), 44–50.
The miller in the *RvT*, who is named Symkyn (a name that was perhaps pronounced trisyllabically, ie Symekyn), is given many ape-like characteristics. The name itself may involve a pun on *simus* (flat-nosed) and *simia* (ape). The ape-like traits include the round face, wide nose, large mouth, and — depending upon the exact meaning of Chaucer's word *piled* (line I.3935) — perhaps the hairless head, as is often shown on the apes depicted in manuscript illustrations. Symbolically, the ape was associated with lasciviousness, pride, drunkenness, and other bad characteristics. The Miller of *GP* shares many characteristics with the Reeve's Symkyn.

1206 Block, Edward A. 'Chaucer's Millers and Their Bagpipes.' *Spec*, 29 (1954), 239–43.
The Miller's bagpipe is useful as a realistic detail, since the bagpipe was a common rustic or folk instrument that would have been suitable to illustrate the Miller's description as 'a rough, crude country fellow' (p 240). The use of bagpipes on pilgrimages is also realistic, as is shown in a 1407 document

involving the Archbishop of Canterbury's defense of pilgrimages — and pilgrims' bagpipes. Furthermore, the bagpipe has symbolic value, for it represents gluttony and lechery, qualities that characterize the Miller of *GP* and also link him to the miller in *RvT* (that miller knows how to play the bagpipe too).

1207 Cowgill, Bruce Kent. *Chaucer and the Just Society: Conceptions of Natural Law and the Nobility in the Parliament of Fowls, the Knight's Tale, and the Portraits of the Miller and Reeve.* University of Nebraska Dissertation. 1970. Dir. John W. Robinson. See also *DAI*, 31 (1971), 5357-A.

According to medieval concepts of hierarchy, responsibility for the maintenance of social order and justice rested primarily with the nobility. Several aspects of *CT* are interpreted as a criticism of the nobility's failings. 'Chaucer's portraits of Robyn and Oswald function as caricatures of an erring nobility' (p 3), demonstrating, in a comic mode, what happens when fighting and administering justice are regarded as opportunities for personal gain rather than public service. The chapter 'Robyn and Oswald: Studies in Comic Satire' (pp 138–62) presents the Miller and Reeve as knight and administrator *manqué*. The Knight's and Miller's portraits show parallelism and contrast. For example, just as the opening lines in the Knight's portrait, which praise his worthiness, 'prepare us for the redemptive nature of the Knight's many battles,' so the opening lines in the Miller's portrait, which stress his physical prowess, precede the evidence that the Miller too 'has often "foughten" for his "feith" by wrestling and breaking down doors' (p 150). Line 558, which states that the Miller wore a sword, is given additional impact by the unexpected placement of this detail in the midst of physiognomic traits; it was illegal for a Miller to bear a sword — which helps to 'further sharpen his role as a "knight manqué"' (p 151). The Knight, 'by birth and demeanor the true leader' of the pilgrimage's society, is displaced in that function by the Miller, who rides at the head of the group. 'Taken compositely, thus, the various details in Robyn's characterization suggest a perversion of the noble ideal' (p 152). Similarly, the Reeve, whose rule is harsh and self-serving, represents a judge or administrator *manqué*.

1208 Curry, Walter Clyde. 'Chaucer's Reeve and Miller.' *PMLA*, 35 (1920), 189–209.

The Miller's face and stocky figure, according to medieval concepts of physiognomy, show that he is 'shameless, immodest, and loquacious,' as well as 'bold and easily angered' (p 198). His thick hair, coming low over his forehead, associates him with apes and with negative qualities such as fearfulness, servility, inner cowardice, etc. Therefore, 'for all his boasting, the Miller is still a bully, a coward at heart' (p 202). His large mouth identifies him as 'a glutton, a swaggerer, a sensualist, and an impious fornicator' (p

202). His wide nostrils show that he is given to anger, while his wart — depending on exactly where on the nose we are to understand it as placed — suggests a variety of uncomplimentary qualities, such as an inclination to 'filthy infamous luxury,' the tendency to sow discord, or 'envious hostility' towards others (p 208). Cf **209, 1244.**

1209 Derocquigny, J. 'Notes sur Chaucer.' 1910. See **595.**
Perhaps what lies behind the proverb about the golden thumb of millers (line 563) is their habit of measuring out quantity with their thumbs grasping the inside rim of the container, and thus bringing them the benefit of the volume of their thumb in the measure.

1210 Galway, Margaret. 'The History of Chaucer's Miller.' *N&Q*, 195 (1950), 486–88.
The Miller of *GP*, the knave Robyn of *MilT*, the miller of *RvT*, and the historical Robert or Robyn Grymbald all 'show a notable facility in fusing into one' person (p 488), who would have been known to Chaucer's courtly circle.

1211 Hart, Walter Morris. 'The Reeve's Tale: A Comparative Study of Chaucer's Narrative Art.' *PMLA*, 23 (1908), 1–44.
The Reeve's portrait of the miller Symkyn 'skilfully suggests, yet does not reproduce, the miller of the *General Prologue*' (p 11). Similarities in the details and in the overall techniques of portraiture of the two millers are presented.

1212 Jones, G[eorge]. Fenwick. 'Wittenwiler's *Becki* and the Medieval Bagpipe.' *JEGP*, 48 (1949), 209–28.
The social implications of the medieval bagpipe show that it was a rural, rude, or rustic instrument, suited to those of low status or bad character (such as Chaucer's Miller). Deschamps called the bagpipe the 'instrument des hommes bestiaulx,' for example (p 213), and many other instances of its low-life associations are presented. 'Possibly Chaucer himself was being satirical in having a bagpiper lead his ostensibly pious pilgrimage' (p 218).

1213 ——. 'Chaucer and the Medieval Miller.' *MLQ*, 16 (1955), 3–15.
Chaucer's Miller is not to be interpreted as the realistic portrait of a specific person; Chaucer 'did not intend to describe any particular miller, but rather to create a character embodying certain characteristics popularly attributed to the millers as a class' (p 3). Analogues from other literary references to millers (most of them from fifteenth-century German materials) show parallels for the following features of Chaucer's Miller: his red hair, coarse features, social ambitions, muscular body, vulgarity, drunkenness, stupidity, dishonesty, armaments, and associations with the Reeve. The miller within

RvT, modeled upon the Miller of GP, also fits this conventional pattern.

1214 Kiralis, Karl. 'William Blake as an Intellectual and Spiritual Guide to Chaucer's *Canterbury Pilgrims.*' 1969. See **804.**
The Miller need not be assumed to ride first of the group, since his bagpipe 'could be heard from anywhere, and perhaps even best toward the rear' (p 141), where Chaucer placed him in the GP sequence of portraits. The Plowman and the Miller form a contrasting pair, for the 'Plowman uses his strength for useful and benevolent purposes,' while 'the Miller exhibits his strength to the grandstand' (p 147) but benefits only himself.

1215 McCracken, Samuel. 'Chaucer's *Canterbury Tales*, A. 565–6.' *Expl*, 23 (1964-1965), item 55.
In the last couplet of the Miller's portrait, Chaucer is punning on *towne*, with the meanings 'town' and 'tune.' Thus the Miller, playing out of tune, brings the group out of town. A passage from the Towneley *Secunda Pastorum* play shows that the idiom 'out of tune' was known.

1216 Manly, John Matthews. 'Familia Goliae.' *MP*, 5 (1907-1908), 201–9.
Although GP is not discussed, the background information supplied here on the Goliardic tradition is pertinent to the description of the Miller, who is called a *goliardeys* (line 560).

1217 Mann, H. George. '*Canterbury Tales, Prologue*, Line 559.' *N&Q*, New Series 1 (1954), 37.
Mann's query seeks information to substantiate the viewpoint that line 559 reflects 'an old English or Dutch saying, proverb, or quotation.'

1218 Mann, Jill. *Chaucer and Medieval Estates Satire.* 1973. See **363.**
Millers are rare in estates satire, but a miller 'does appear in Langland, and as with the Summoner and the Pardoner, it seems to be the influence of *Piers Plowman* which has secured him a place in the *Prologue*' (p 160). The 'basis of the creation—the swaggering, story-telling, dishonest miller, who merges so easily with the outlines of the "goliardeys," the "ribaud" or the fox-like redhead—is a popular stereotype' (p 162), even though a few specific details of the portrait, such as the sword and buckler, the white tunic, and the blue hood, are not accounted for in earlier works.

1219 Owen, Charles A. 'One Robyn or Two.' *MLN*, 67 (1952), 336–38.
Replying to Pratt (**1220**), Owen argues against identifying the Miller of GP with the carpenter's knave of *MilT*. The fact that both the Miller and the carpenter's knave are named Robyn is 'probably accidental' (p 338). The Miller in GP is characterized by 'a noisy and aggressive outspokenness' (see

lines 560–61), so that if he were indeed recounting his own experiences, it seems unlikely that he 'would not tell us unequivocally of his part in the story' (p 337). On the Reeve, see **1253**.

1220 Pratt, Robert A. 'Was Robyn the Miller's Youth Misspent?' *MLN*, 59 (1944), 47–49.
The *GP* portrait of the Miller (who is later said to be named Robyn) and the description of the knave Robyn within *MilT* show similarities: both are said to be stout fellows capable of breaking down doors. Perhaps here, as in the Wife's and Canon's Yeoman's cases, 'a narrator was portrayed as recounting events in which he played an actual part' (p 49). If as a youth the Miller had himself been the knave Robyn and had worked for the Reeve, that past relationship would help to explain their present enmity. In reply, see Owen, **1219** and **1253**.

1221 ——. 'The Beard of Chaucer's Miller.' *N&Q*, 195 (1950), 568.
This query raises the question of whether 'the magnificent beard worn by Robyn the Miller' (lines 552–53) was exceptional, given another literary source that suggests that a clean-shaven face would be more convenient for a miller.

1222 Reiss, Edmund. 'Chaucer's Miller, Pilate, and the Devil.' *AnM*, 5 (1964), 21–25.
'Chaucer is not only giving general bestial and demonic characteristics to his Miller,' but also 'putting these traits to a consistent and specific use by metaphorically connecting the pilgrim with Pilate — a man apocryphally linked with millers — who was traditionally an agent of the devil. Such an association thus makes metaphorically functional many details in the Miller's portrait that have generally been thought to be realistic and nothing more' (pp 24–25). The medieval conception of Pilate as *os malleatoris*, the mouth or mask of the devil-as-hammerer, may be reflected in the Miller's use of his head as a hammer (lines 350–51) and in the emphasis given to his vocal organs (lines 559–60). His wearing of blue and white garments (line 564) is ironic, since those colors 'are traditionally associated with the faithful and the pure' (p 22).

1223 Rowland, Beryl. 'Aspects of Chaucer's Use of Animals.' *Archiv*, 201 (1964-1965), 110–14.
In Chaucer's mature works, animal images 'often have a significance beyond their immediate context and are applicable to a total portrait or situation' (p 111). Line 552 compares the Miller to a sow or a fox. The craftiness attributed to foxes is consistent with the thievery suggested by line 562 and with later references to a miller's dishonesty. The sow implies lasciviousness; accordingly, the Miller likes stories of *synne and harlotries* (line 561).

'The Miller, as his portrait emerges, is found to possess further physical or psychological qualities of the animals to which he was compared in brief proverbial phrase' (p 114).

1224 Scott, Kathleen L. 'Sow-and-Bagpipe Imagery in the Miller's Portrait.' *RES*, New Series 18 (1967), 287–90.
The Miller is compared to a sow (see lines 552, 556). Carved images and manuscript illustrations of a sow or a pig playing the bagpipe have survived. The combined image of sow and bagpipe, showing 'the ugly-sounding pipes in the arms of an ugly-sounding animal' (p 289), suggested distaste. 'As a man, the Miller is as physically coarse as the bristles of a sow, and he carries a musical instrument appropriate to his position in medieval society; as a type of glutton and lecher, he holds an emblem of the human stomach and of the male genitals; and as an aesthetic image, he squawls with both literal and symbolic reverberations. His pipes sound like the squealing of a sow, and in his drunkenness his voice sounds like both sow and bagpipes' (p 289).

1225 Steadman, John M. ' "An Honest Miller"? (Canterbury Tales, 555).' *N&Q*, New Series 9 (1962), 6.
A nineteenth-century tale connects the idea of a tuft of hairs with the character of a miller. It is probable that a 'folk-tradition concerning the honest miller's tuft of hairs in an unlikely spot already existed in the fourteenth century,' that Chaucer referred to a version of this tradition, and that the statement about the Miller's tuft of hairs was intended to suggest that 'he was honest, as millers go.'

1226 Thompson, James Westfall. 'The Origin of the Word "*Goliardi*." ' *SP*, 20 (1923), 83–98.
In line 560, the Miller is said to be a *goliardeys*. The word *goliardenses* or *goliardi* originally meant, according to Thompson, 'busy-bodies in or devotees of gluttony' (p 96).

1227 Utley, Francis Lee. 'The Last of the Miller's Head?' *MLN*, 56 (1941), 534–36.
The Miller is said to be able to break down doors with his head (lines 550–51). Other examples of this trait are mentioned, from late Roman to contemporary times. 'Thus while pachycephaly is without question a distinguishing feature, it is scarcely a vanishing one' (p 536). It appears as a motif in folklore and mythology, but rather than explain it in folkloristic terms 'we may perhaps content ourselves with more mundane hardheadedness' (p 536), given the documents that show that it is a recurrent real characteristic. Cf **1230**.

.228 Whitbread, L. 'Six Chaucer Notes.' 1978. See **659**.

The comment about the Miller's thumb (lines 562–63) may refer to 'the traditional view that a miller obtained his illicit gain and gold from the habit of pushing away for his own use some of the ground flour as it emerged from the millstones' (p 42).

1229 Whiting, B.J. 'The Miller's Head.' *MLN*, 52 (1937), 417–19.

The Miller breaks doors with his head (lines 550–51). This claim is feasible, for several nineteenth- and twentieth-century men are known to have performed similar feats. Thus 'we may be sure that between the fourteenth and nineteenth centuries stretched a long, thick-set line of heroes whose pachycephaly was exploited to stir the wonder and respect of their less gifted fellows' (p 419). See also **1229**.

1230 ——. 'Miller's Head Revisited.' *MLN*, 69 (1954), 309–10.

Although Whiting himself (**1229**), Wiley (**1231**), and Utley (**1227**) have already presented earlier and later examples of men who used their heads to break down doors, as the Miller does (see lines 550–51), Whiting here presents an example much closer to Chaucer's time, from one of Trevisa's additions as he translated Higden's *Polychronicon*. Trevisa mentions a Thomas Hayward of Berkeley, who breaks strong doors with his head. This passage probably dates from about 1385–1387. Further investigation might discover more information about a Thomas Hayward who was a miller and who was associated with Chaucer.

1231 Wiley, Autrey Nell. 'The Miller's Head Again.' *MLN*, 53 (1938), 505–7.

The Miller is said to butt or break doors with his head (lines 550–51). The practice was apparently not new: 'Butting heads aroused interest a thousand years before Chaucer's Miller showed his strength' (p 506). A fourth-century instance is cited. Cf **1230**.

✎ Part 24: The Manciple

See the Introduction, p xxxvii above, for a brief summary of criticism on the Manciple, and see the Index for further references.

232 Birney, Earle. 'Chaucer's "Gentil" Manciple and His "Gentil" Tale.' *NM*, 61 (1960), 257–67.

The character depicted in the Manciple's portrait in *GP* is appropriate also for the Manciple's own prologue and tale later in the *CT*. The *GP* portrait establishes the Manciple's 'shrewdness' and shows him to be a 'resourceful, impudent trickster' (p 259). *GP* also indicates that he is 'talkative' (p 261), since in the passages revealing his dishonesty it must be '*his* voice and *his* sardonic phrasing we hear echoed by Pilgrim Chaucer's' (p 261). The Manciple wants to triumph over others through his dishonesty, but also to receive approval from others. Chaucer's irony towards him begins with the first adjective, *gentil* (line 567), for although the narrator responds to the Manciple 'with his usual uncritical enthusiasm' (p 260), the Manciple would not have been 'gentil' by social standing and could not deserve that description 'by any nobility of word or deed' (p 260). He is 'gentil' only as the Summoner or the Pardoner is, 'in that topsy-turvy world of gullible Pilgrim Chaucer' (p 261). The characterization of the Manciple as the 'successful rascal' in *GP* (p 261) is mirrored in the style of his tale and its 'oily' diction (p 265), as well as in his interchange with the Cook.

233 Bland, D.S. 'Chaucer and the Inns of Court: A Re-Examination.' *ES*, 33 (1952), 144–55.

The development of the Inns of Court is reviewed. The Manciple is associated with '*a* Temple' in some manuscripts, with '*the* Temple' in other manuscripts (see line 567); it remains uncertain exactly which group of lawyers he serves. Historically, it is not clear whether a single Temple or two separate Temple societies existed in Chaucer's time, because the

fourteenth-century Temple records are lost. However, 'if there *were* two societies, then the obscurity [in *GP*] many be due to a wish on Chaucer's part
to prevent too close an identification of his Manciple, since there would be
only two men in such a position at the time. In fact, if the Temple records
for this period had survived, it is likely that the Manciple would be among
the most easily identifiable of the pilgrims' (p 153).

1234 Burnley, J.D. *Chaucer's Language and the Philosopher's Tradition.* Cambridge, England: D.S. Brewer, 1979.
Occasional comments on *GP* are included in this study of philosophical
concepts in relation to Chaucer's language. Discussing Chaucer's apparent praise of the Manciple, Burnley suggests that 'the *General Prologue*
description of the Manciple ... and the business of his masters ... both are
illustrative of such aspects of prudence as *yconomique, husbondrie* or *mar-
chaundisyng*' (p 56). Though prudence is a virtue, we are made aware that
higher and lower levels of this virtue exist, as Aquinas observed, and the
Manciple's prudence belongs to the lower kind. Thus 'it is inevitable that
when the lower kind of prudence is given praise due to the higher kind,
connotations of that higher value may be ironically present in our minds'
(p 57).

1235 Hughes, Geoffrey. 'Gold and Iron: Semantic Change and Social Change in
Chaucer's Prologue.' 1978. See **292**.
GP depicts a world undergoing social and economic change, a world in
which earlier ideas of common profit were being replaced by an increasingly individualistic materialism. In this context, 'the New Man of the
meritocracy is the Maunciple (though one can see New Men appearing at
all stages, just as the middle classes always seem to be rising). For he is the
most successful profiteer or "winner" of all, and he is —uniquely— without
personality, character or even body. He has no frame, no array, no mask.
He is pure native wit, honed by the hardness of the market place. *He* does
not need the security, let alone the uniform, of a "solempne and a greet
fraternitee" [line 364, on the Guildsmen]. He is the perfect, smooth administrator who can achieve anything, and feel nothing, the Machiavellian
prototype. One word gives us a clue to his sinister origins. In the second line [line 568] we are told that "achatours might take example" from
him. In statute 36 of Edward III (1360) it is enacted "Que le heignous
noun de *pourveyor* soit chaungé & nomé achatour" [Let the heinous name
of *purveyor* be changed and called achatour]. The purveyours had become
so unpopular that their name was changed by the cynical substitution of
terms to which we now give the name of "Orwellian." Not surprisingly, his
tale is about the changing of *wyf* into *lemman* and *white* into *black*' (pp
10–11).

1236 Mann, Jill. *Chaucer and Medieval Estates Satire.* 1973. See **363**.

The characterization of the Manciple 'may be linked with the dishonesty that Langland assigns to manorial officials, lawyers, and those who, like the Manciple, look after provision,' yet it is left uncertain whether the Manciple is dishonest or not: 'there is no certain evidence that the Manciple cooks the books, although the statement that he outdoes his masters suggests it' (p 174). If dishonesty is present, it is conveyed through the Manciple's own idiom, *sette hir aller cappe* (line 586); 'the phrase reveals the euphemistic way in which the perpetrator of an action represents it to himself. Such specialist, elusive idioms represent a refusal to apply absolute values to the practices of one's profession' (p 174).

1237 Rickert, Edith. 'Was Chaucer a Student at the Inner Temple?' In *The Manly Anniversary Studies in Language and Literature.* Chicago: University of Chicago Press, 1923. Pp 20–31. Rpt Freeport, NY: Books for Libraries Press, 1968.

The presence of the Manciple in *GP* supports other evidence that Chaucer had studied law.

1238 Severs, J. Burke. 'Is the *Manciple's Tale* a Success?' *JEGP*, 51 (1952), 1–16.

'Chaucer in the General Prologue stresses the fact that the Manciple is a "lewed" man by contrasting him with his "lerned" employers' (p 12). *ManT* is found to be suitable to the Manciple of *GP*.

❧ Part 25: The Reeve

See the Introduction, p xxxvii above, for a brief summary of criticism on the Reeve, and see the Index for further references.

1239 Barney, Stephen A. 'Chaucer's Lists.' 1982. See **149**.
The Reeve's portrait, which 'lists the subjects under the Reeve's professional competence' (see lines 597–99), exemplifies Chaucer's tendency to record 'the active and doing' functions of his characters, (p 209), as well as their states of being.

1240 Bennett, H.S. 'The Reeve and the Manor in the Fourteenth Century.' *EHR*, 41 (1926), 358–65.
Although this study mentions Chaucer's Reeve only in passing, it provides a general overview of a reeve's position. He was 'an essential unit in the manorial machine' (p 359), although he was usually of servile, not free, status. Appointment was annual, though some reeves (such as Chaucer's) held the position year after year; in certain cases a democratic election by the peasants of the manor determined who would serve. Although reeves were presumably illiterate, they were responsible for the compilation of their manors' annual accounts. They may have used 'tallies and notches on barn posts and the like' as an aid to their memories (p 363). Once a year a scribe would come to the manor to write down the detailed *compotus*, or annual financial reckoning, on the basis of the reeve's information. The account would then be audited, with the reeve held responsible for any arrears.

1241 Bennett, J.A.W. *Chaucer at Oxford and at Cambridge*. 1974. See **978**.
The Reeve comes from Baldeswell (see line 620), a location that is close to both Trumpington Mill and the Cambridge market. 'I suggest that Chaucer names Bawdswell as nailing him down to a particular part of Norfok that

puts him within easy reach of these two places' (p 88). The various duties of reeves are briefly discussed. 'When we consider that all these duties were discharged by necessity rather than by choice, and that reeves were so closely watched by auditors on the one side, and on the other by their neighbors ... it is not surprising that Chaucer depicts his reeve as thin, worn, tetchy, and uncompanionable' (p 89).

1242 Blake, N.F., ed. *The Canterbury Tales by Geoffrey Chaucer. Edited from the Hengwrt Manuscript.* 1980. See **95**.
The Reeve's beard is said to be shaven as closely as possible (line 588; line 590 in Blake's ed.). 'The absence of a beard at a time when beards were common suggests something sinister' (p 55).

1243 Coffman, George R. 'Old Age from Horace to Chaucer. Some Literary Affinities and Adventures of an Idea.' *Spec*, 9 (1934), 249–77.
This wide-ranging survey of literary images of old age contrasts the Reeve's portrait in *GP* to his personality in the prologue to his tale. The Reeve in *GP* is 'in the prime of his life — mature middle age. In the entire description there is not a single clear indication of old age' (p 273). In the Reeve's prologue, however, the details imply 'senile old age' (p 274). Chaucer may have forgotten the *GP* portrait, or have lacked time to revise it, or have been 'untroubled by the inconsistency' (p 227). In reply, see Forehand, **1247**.

1244 Curry, Walter Clyde. 'Chaucer's Reeve and Miller.' 1920. See **1208**.
The portraits of the Reeve and Miller (and their subsequent behavior) are ' "scientifically" correct according to the specifications of physiognomical lore' at the time (p 189). The Reeve's closely-cut hair, usually signifying humility, 'was doubtless a part of his general programme of hoodwinking his young lord' (p 190). The statement that he was choleric indicates that he was cunning and crafty. The lecherousness evident in his later prologue to his tale is anticipated in *GP* by his very small and slender legs, which signify, according to the physiognomists, lecherousness and also inner cowardice. Thus it is no surprise that he rides as far from the Miller as he can. Cf **209**.

1245 Dempster, Germaine. *Dramatic Irony in Chaucer.* Stanford: Stanford University Press, 1932; London: Humphrey Milford, 1932. Stanford University Publications in Language and Literature, 4. Doubly paginated as 3–102 and 247–346.
An example of dramatic irony is provided by 'the thanks with which the master of the Reeve accepts loans of the money pilfered from him' (p 80/324; see lines 610–13).

1246 Donaldson, E.T., ed. *Chaucer's Poetry: An Anthology for the Modern Reader*. 1958, 1975. See **63**.

'Symbolic of the close dealing and spare economy of the Reeve are his close-cropped head and beard and his skinny legs' (1975, p 1057). He may be riding at the end of the pilgrimage group (see line 622) to avoid the Miller, but the rear is also 'the best position from which to watch what is going on among any band of travelers, and it may be merely because of a habitual watchfulness that the Reeve brings up the rear' (p 1057).

1247 Forehand, Brooks. 'Old Age and Chaucer's Reeve.' *PMLA*, 69 (1954), 984–89.

A number of traits in the Reeve's portrait suggest that he is meant to be perceived as an old man. His sword is rusty because he is now too old to use it; he wears it only as a symbol of the youth that he wishes he again possessed. Coffman's viewpoint (see **1243**) that the portrait presents a middle-aged man in the prime of life misses the implications of the sword and other details. The Reeve is said to have been a carpenter, but that was long ago. His long surcote suggests the association of elderly people with fear of the cold; thus he wears a long, fur-lined outer garment to guard himself against the chill of April. He rides last in the group not only because he dislikes the Miller, who rides in front, but also because of his age. Just as certain details of the Wife's portrait in *GP* (eg, her deafness) are fully explained only later, so these hints in the Reeve's portrait are made explicit only in the prologue to his tale.

1248 Garbáty, Thomas Jay. 'Satire and Regionalism: the Reeve and his Tale.' *ChauR*, 8 (1973–1974), 1–8.

The humorous intention of the detail that the Reeve comes from Baldeswelle (lines 619–20) is discussed. Immigration into London from Norfolk, and particularly from the Eynsford area of Norfolk (including Baldeswelle), was especially heavy in the fourteenth century—and these immigrants were resented as constituting competition in the London labor market. 'Thus Oswald, the rustic Reeve with his rusty sword, comes from a narrow, confined area, fifteen miles across in Norfolk, which for years had been feeding immigrants into the city of London in extraordinary numbers .... There is no need to stress the history of frictions, petty ridicule, and sources of humor which a flood of immigrants from specific countries or even sections of one country have developed in the native population .... To the public eye the new arrivals undoubtedly represented a provincial type, awkward and gauche of appearance' (p 3). The possibility that Oswald too plans to become a London resident 'cannot be totally discounted' (p 3), but even if he does not intend to join the other Norfolk immigrants living in the city he 'would have been identified with this new group, and borne the onus of the second-class resident' (p 4). Later, when he imitates the students' Northern dialect in his tale, the effect would have been very comic: 'this man (who was already somewhat "beyond the pale" because of his origin and group identity, riding for several reasons at the rear of the pilgrimage) took it on himself to mimic a provincial dialect in his own barbarous jargon. What hilarious nonsense and what a brilliant connotative linguistic joke!' (p 7).

1249 Manly, John Matthews. *Some New Light on Chaucer*. 1936. See 362.
In the chapter 'The Host, the Reeve, and the Miller' (pp 70–101), Manly suggests that the Reeve may be modeled upon someone from Baldeswell, a person whom Chaucer would have met (or heard about) through his participation in the legal settlement of the Pembroke lands, which included Baldeswell. Chaucer may have been one of the two deputies appointed to investigate the management of the Pembroke estates. The 'malicious sketch' of the Reeve 'must have been highly entertaining to the great folk at court, all of whom were certainly familiar with the facts concerning the Pembroke lands' (p 94). The Miller may be someone from the same district or manor as the Reeve. In reply, see 1254; cf 1255, 1269.

1250 Mann, Jill. *Chaucer and Medieval Estates Satire*. 1973. See 363.
'Chaucer's Reeve is feared and hated like the rest of his class,' but the portrait gives the impression that his victims are not innocent—they 'are paralysed with fear because the Reeve knows about *their* malpractices; again winner and loser are united on the question of values. The question of right and wrong does not enter into their relationship; it is determined by the question of who can outwit the other. This significant deviation from the [usual] depiction of the innocent victim alerts us to the fact that Chaucer clothes the Reeve's behaviour in the same kind of ambiguities as he has used throughout the *Prologue*' (p 165).

1251 Moffett, H.Y. 'Oswald the Reeve.' *PQ*, 4 (1925), 208–23.
Chaucer's description of the Reeve shows an 'intimate knowledge of the manor' and its way of life; 'every allusion to the details of rural life is eloquent of the reality' (p 208). Documents that give precise information about agricultural life, especially the *Husbandry* of Walter of Henley, enable us to reconstruct what the responsibilities of the Reeve must have been. In Chaucer's time, the distinction between a reeve and a bailiff was disappearing, although earlier reeves had been villeins and the office had indicated servile status. 'Chaucer's Reeve is certainly an important official, holding the position of steward over one or more manors, with authority over bailiffs, and responsible directly to the lord as his accounts were checked by the auditors' (p 213). Many details about medieval agricultural management are provided.

1252 Olson, Paul A. 'The *Reeve's Tale*: Chaucer's *Measure for Measure*.' *SP*, 59 (1962), 1–17.

The *GP* portrait of the Reeve begins 'almost in the vein of caricature,' with Oswald depicted as 'one of those pinched and rigorous souls whose physical condition indicated a tendency towards hasty vengeance' (p 2). His position, however, would have needed a 'person of just and moderate temperament' instead, since the medieval reeve was 'the primary agent of the lord in the administering of economic and social justice to the peasants' (p 2). Through embezzlement and blackmail, the Reeve lives as if he were beyond justice. 'Oswald's art is the art of escaping justice himself while imposing his version of it on his underlings' (p 3). *GP* hints at the basis of his success in showing him with a priest-like shaven head and a friar-like tucked coat (line 621). Later, in his prologue and tale, the Reeve will more openly display a priestly attitude, for he has 'identified his purposes with the purposes of God and persuaded himself that his causes, right or wrong, are right' (p 14).

1253 Owen, Charles A. 'One Robyn or Two.' 1952. See **1219**.

Replying to Pratt (**1220**), Owen argues against identifying the Reeve of *GP* with the carpenter of *MilT*. It was in the Reeve's youth that he was a carpenter (see line 614), not recently, while the carpenter in *MilT* is an old man who has not left that trade behind. The two are also very different in characterization, for the Reeve is 'shrewd and careful,' while the carpenter in *MilT* is 'extremely gullible' (p 337).

1254 Powley, Edward B. 'Chaucer's Reeve.' *TLS*, July 14 1932, p 516.

The Reeve is said to have come from near Baldeswell (line 620). In 1360 Lionel of Ulster, in whose wife's household the young Chaucer served, became lord of lands near Baldeswell; in 1361 Lionel visited the area; 'with or without Lionel,' Chaucer may 'have found himself in Baldeswell.' This connection offers a better explanation for the Reeve's localization, Powley argues, than does the 'Pembroke interest in Baldeswell' proposed by Manly (**1249**, p 87). The Reeve is not being portrayed as 'an unprincipled knave,' as Manly judged, but instead as 'the competent but worldly servant of a manor.' In reply, see **1255**.

1255 Redstone, Lilian J. 'Chaucer's Reeve.' *TLS*, October 27 1932, pp 789–90.

The Reeve's portrait refers to a town called Baldeswelle (line 620). Replying to Powley (**1254**), Redstone argues that the connection between the family of Lionel of Ulster and Baldeswell was slight. Manly's earlier proposal for a connection through the Pembroke family (**1249**) is stronger — especially since the manor of Foxley Hall, near Baldeswell Village, was in fact administered by a reeve. In addition to the evidence suggested previously, there is a second Chaucerian contact with Baldeswell. In about 1385 Beatrice Roos, who held a manor there, was married to Sir Richard Burley, with whose brother Chaucer served on the Commission of the Peace for Kent.

1256 Schmidt, A.V.C., ed. *Geoffrey Chaucer: The General Prologue to the Canterbury Tales and the Canon's Yeoman's Prologue and Tale*. 1974. See **89**.

The name of the Reeve's horse, Scot (line 616), 'may be a pun: *scot* meant "tax" and the allusion may be to the customs or dues paid to the reeve of a manor. The Reeve would be "riding high" on his money' (p 147).

1257 Skeat, Walter W., ed. *The Complete Works of Geoffrey Chaucer, Edited from Numerous Manuscripts*. 1894–1897. See **3**.

Skeat notes that Sir Thopas had a dapple-grey horse, 'which has the same sense as *pomely gray*' (line 616), the color of the Reeve's horse (vol 5, p 51).

1258 Tupper, Frederick. 'The Quarrels of the Canterbury Pilgrims.' 1915. See **483**.

Lines 613–14 may be an addition made by Chaucer in order to facilitate the Miller's later attack on the Reeve. Chaucer had no tale against a reeve available for the Miller to tell, but he did have one against a carpenter; therefore he adjusted *GP* to make the Reeve a carpenter. The last line of the Reeve's portrait (line 622) may foreshadow the quarrel with the Miller, since the Reeve may be riding at the back of the group 'because his enemy, the Miller, rides in front' (p 268).

✒ Part 26: The Summoner

See the Introduction, p xxxvii above, for a brief summary of criticism on the Summoner, and see the Index for further references.

1259 Aiken, Pauline. 'The Summoner's Malady.' *SP*, 33 (1936), 40–44.

Although Curry (**1268**) identifies the Summoner's skin disease as *alopicia*, a kind of leprosy, according to Aiken the disease is '*scabies* of the dry variety' (p 40). If it were suspected to be leprosy, the Summoner would have been prevented from riding with the other pilgrims. Chaucer could have found his description of *scabies* in the *Speculum doctrinale* of Vincent of Beauvais, for the details correspond 'with remarkable fidelity' (p 40), including verbal parallels. All of the remedies Chaucer lists are recommended by Vincent for treating *scabies*. The medications do not work because, as Vincent points out, a cure requires a correct diet and abstinence from sexual intercourse. The Summoner, in contrast, is lecherous and 'persists in eating and drinking the very things which [would] most aggravate his condition' (p 44). Vincent's description combines five different authorities on this disease, but it is likely that Chaucer used Vincent's version directly, particularly since the 'knobbes' on the Summoner's cheeks find a parallel in Vincent but not in the other writers' details about *scabies*. In reply, see **1274**.

1260 Biggins, D. 'Chaucer's General Prologue, A 163.' *N&Q*, New Series 6 (1959), 435–36.

Responding to Baum's suggestion (**512**) that the Summoner's *burdoun* (line 673) involves an obscene pun, Biggins somewhat revises the interpretation, stressing the two meanings of the word as 1) 'ground melody' and 2) 'staff' (p 435). Shakespeare and other authors frequently link music with sexuality in word-play. Baum's proposed associations with words for young woman, jest, and mule are set aside as being only 'of marginal relevance' (p 435) to the pun on *burdoun*. [Despite the title, this item does not concern line 163.] See **1283**.

1261 ——. 'More Chaucerian Ambiguities: A 652, 644, D 1346.' *N&Q*, New Series 9 (1962), 165–67.
This article develops the suggestions of Biggin's related note (**1262**). Chaucer's remark 'Ful prively a fynch eek koude he pulle' (line 652), although it does not use exactly a pun, involves two meanings and can therefore be added to other lists of Chaucer's plays on language. The reference to pulling a finch contains 'a typically Chaucerian ambiguity of which both meanings are appropriate' (p 167). Lines 647–48 also contain intentionally ambiguous terms: *harlot* and *felawe*. Both the Summoner's own lecherousness and his activities as a 'confidence man' (p 167) exploiting the lechery of others are implied.

1262 ——. ' "Pulling Finches and Woodcocks": A Comment.' *ES*, 44 (1963), 278.
Commenting on the previous explanations of line 652 offered by Ericson (**1270**) and Kittredge (**1280**), Biggins emphasizes the ambiguity of the line. From one perspective, the phrase about pulling finches simply notes the Summoner's lechery. From another perspective, it refers to his blackmailing others 'on trumped-up or unofficial charges of fornication.' The irony of the Summoner's portrait is heightened 'when we realize that this fornicating rogue plunders his fellow fornicators.' Cf **1261**.

1263 ——. 'Chaucer's Summoner: "Wel Loved He Garleek, Oynons, and Eek Lekes", *C.T.* I. 634.' *N&Q*, New Series 11 (1964), 48.
Passages from Reginald Pecock's *Reule of Crysten Religioun* (dated 1443) are cited to show that the Summoner's 'dietary preferences, because of the lust they occasion, imperil not only his physical health but also his spiritual well-being': the eating of garlic, leeks, onions, pepper, and 'such othere scherpe thingis' was thought to be a cause of lechery.

1264 Bloomfield, Morton W. 'Chaucer's Summoner and the Girls of the Diocese.' *PQ*, 28 (1949), 503–7.
In the *FrT* the description of the summoner's connections with women clarifies what is meant by lines 663–65 of *GP*, which refer to the Summoner's relationships with the 'yonge girles of the diocise.' Although the term *girles* can sometimes refer to children of both sexes, Chaucer's use of it here implies young women, with the possible additional connotation (cf French *fille*) of prostitutes. The *GP* passage should be interpreted to mean that the Summoner had 'control (or influence) over the young women (or prostitutes) of the diocese, knew all their secrets and was their adviser

in everything' (p 507). The statement is ironic, for ideally the Summoner should control the girls according to Christian principles, since his office is part of the system of the supervision of morals, but in reality he controls them in such a way that they provide him 'profit and delight' (p 507): he uses their information about their companions for blackmail and takes his own pleasure 'as an extra dividend' (p 504).

1265 Bonjour, Adrien. 'Aspects of Chaucer's Irony in "The Friar's Tale." ' *EIC*, 11 (1961), 121–27.
The summoner within *FrT* 'is, in a way, the alter ego of Chaucer's own Summoner' (p 125) and the 'hallmark' of the Summoner's characterization is lechery (p 126). He may be 'the victim of his craft,' since lechery or involvement with lecherous people 'was the shortest way, if not the only road, to a successful and lucrative career' for summoners and other officials (p 126).

1266 Braddy, Haldeen. 'Chaucer's Bilingual Idiom.' *SFQ*, 32 (1968), 1–6.
Chaucer's 'naturalistic choice of words' or 'plainspoken element' helps him to 'reproduce faithfully' the 'idiomatic speech boldly enlivened with bicultural native expressions' that was in use in his time (p 6). The Summoner's pulling of a finch (line 652) probably means that he 'knew how to pull a young girl aside for his purposes,' but as for the *burdoun* he bears to the Pardoner (line 673), 'one finds it impossible to construe these lines as implying a homosexual relationship between these two pilgrims,' for 'the text appears to mean only that the ardent Summoner endorses the theme of the song by joining the Pardoner in a loud refrain' (p 4).

1267 Cawley, A.C. 'Chaucer's Summoner, the Friar's Summoner, and the *Friar's Tale*.' 1957. See **738**.
Chaucer's Summoner practices extortion and other abuses, as real-life summoners of the time did, but his unwholesome diet, disease, and lechery (perhaps perverted) are not necessarily general characteristics of summoners. 'The bad feeling between the Friar and the Summoner,' which becomes evident in their tales told against each other, 'may well be due not only to professional rivalry but to the natural enmity existing between a man like the Summoner and the outrageously heterosexual Friar' (p 174). Links between the Summoner of *GP* and the summoner of *FrT* include the exploitation of lechery — the Summoner of *GP* 'sells fornicators immunity from the archdeacon's curse' (p 174) — and the use of threatened excommunication for purposes of extortion. Similarly, there are links between the Friar of *GP* and the Friar as teller of his tale (verbal echoes and other similarities are presented).

1268 Curry, Walter Clyde. 'The Malady of Chaucer's Summoner.' *MP*, 19 (1921-1922), 395–404.

Chaucer's Summoner is dangerously ill, suffering from 'a species of morphea known as gutta rosacea, which has already been allowed to develop into that kind of leprosy called alopicia,' according to the medieval understanding of his symptoms (p 395). His fire-red face indicates the presence of gutta rosacea, but not even the most serious form of that skin disease could account for the details about his eyebrows, his narrow eyes, and the white 'whelkes' and 'knobbes' on his cheeks (lines 632–3), which are signs of leprosy. The 'stif burdoun' that he bears to the Summoner (line 673) and his crying out after drinking red wine may indicate that 'his voice has possibly that rough and husky quality spoken of by the medical men as an infallible sign of a leper' (p 401). According to the medieval authorities, the disease of leprosy was promoted by lechery, by the eating of onions, garlic, and leeks, and by the drinking of strong blood-red wine. The Summoner either has not paid attention to the medical authorities, or is unfamiliar with them, since he continues in those practices. The remedies that Chaucer mentions may have been taken directly from the medical books. Thus 'Chaucer's knowledge of medicine was more thorough and accurate than was once supposed' (p 403). 'Chaucer the scientist' created a figure corresponding to the medical descriptions of the type of leprosy called alopicia; 'Chaucer the poet' gave it 'the breath of life' (p 404). Cf **209**; in reply, see **1259**, **1274**.

1269 Dieckmann, Emma Pope M. 'The Meaning of *Burdoun* in Chaucer.' *MP*, 26 (1928-1929), 279–82.

The *burdoun*, which Chaucer uses with reference to the Summoner in line 673 (and also in *RvT*), does not mean the bass accompaniment to a song, as has been thought. Instead, it relates to the French term *Faux-bourdon* and its English version *Fa-burden*, which signifies a specific type of part-singing, one 'closely associated with a humming or droning sound,' monotonous and repetitious (p 280). A twelfth-century account of singing in England indicates that this was a style found in the North — which supports Manly's proposal (see **1249**) that the Summoner and the Reeve are from the northern part of England. Thus the 'Summoner sings *burdon* naturally in his great droning voice' (p 282).

1270 Ericson, Eston Everett. 'Pulling Finches and Woodcocks.' *ES*, 42 (1961), 306.

A passage from Dekker's *Bel-man of London*, 1608, is presented in support of Kittredge's viewpoint (see **1280**) that fornication is implied in the metaphor 'Ful prively a fynch eek koude he pulle' (line 652). Cf **1262**.

1271 Ferrie, Antoine. *Religion et gens d'église chez G. Chaucer.* 1977. See **241**.
Most of the pilgrims enjoy fine health, and their motivation for seeking St
Thomas's shrine is not to obtain physical healing, though the saint was
indeed associated with cures (see line 18). The Summoner, however, is
an exception. Having reached the end of his medications and ointments
as ways of dealing with his skin condition, he may perhaps be hoping for
a healing miracle ('il s'est peut-être mis en route, à bout de ressources,
escomptant un miracle en sa faveur,' p 451).

1272 Fleming, John V. 'Chaucer and the Visual Arts of His Time.' In *New
Perspectives in Chaucer Criticism.* Ed. Donald M. Rose. Norman, OK:
Pilgrim, 1981. Pp 121-36.
The Summoner's garland and buckler (lines 666-68) are 'preposterous'
when considered 'in terms of credible expectations of visual verisimilitude,'
but 'our experience of reading ... suppresses their preposterous character, so that we are quietly cajoled not merely to acceptance but to active
belief' (p 133). Chaucer is here exploiting Gothic painting's principle of
the grotesque, in which real and fantastic elements, or realistic elements
fantastically combined, are presented without comment. The Summoner's
buckler made out of cake — probably fancy bread, or cake in the modern
sense — may reflect an incident in Jean de Meun's *Roman de la Rose*, where
sinners use food as a bribe to ward off summoners and inquisitors. In this
light the Summoner's buckler indicates that 'he protected his criminal en-
terprises with appropriate bribes of his own' (p 135). Thus the Summoner,
'who wears a pub sign on his head and carries a pastry in his hand, is part
of the cakes-and-ale church that Chaucer detests' (p 135).

1273 Garbáty, Thomas Jay. 'Chaucer's Summoner: An Example of the Assimi-
lation Lag in Scholarship.' *MichA*, 47 (1962), 605-11.
Arguing that publication sometimes buries ideas, rather than transmitting
them, Garbáty uses the diagnosis of the Summoner's disease as an example. In the Middle Ages the Summoner's disease was called leprosy, but in
modern terms it is *Lues*, a secondary stage of syphilis. Curry (**209**) 'first
hinted at syphilis in a short and parenthetical sentence' (p 610) that has
since been largely ignored or mentioned only vaguely; standard sources still
say that the Summoner's disease is leprosy and fail to mention its venereal
associations, thus missing Chaucer's satire.

1274 ——. 'The Summoner's Occupational Disease.' *MH*, 7 (1963), 348-58.
The Summoner's disease has been thought to be leprosy (see Curry, **1268**)
or scabies (see Aiken, **1259**). However, a modern literary-medical diagnosis shows that he is suffering from secondary syphilis (*Lues II*), specifically manifested as 'a *Rosacea-like Secondary Syphiloderm* with *meningeal*

neurosyphilis' (p 352). Chaucer may have called the disease 'alopecia' or 'leprosy,' since the medieval terminology grouped several separate diseases under that name, but medieval medical texts identify the origin of this particular kind of 'leprosy' (p 353) with sexual activity. Therefore, regardless of the name, it is a venereal disease that is meant. Although earlier authorities had thought that syphilis was unknown in Europe prior to contact with the New World, more recent studies show that it had been present in Europe at least since the Roman era. Recognizing the venereal origin of the Summoner's disease aids in our understanding of Chaucer's satire against him. 'The face of the corrupt Summoner, watch-dog of morality, marks his own lechery' (p 358).

1275 Haselmayer, Louis A. 'The Apparitor and Chaucer's Summoner.' *Spec*, 12 (1937), 43–57.
Historical records on the office of the apparitor, or summoner, are reviewed. By Chaucer's time this office was associated with corruption: 'the apparitors had become a large and troublesome group of men who took advantage of the peculiar situation of their office to prey upon the people' (p 54), though such abuse was not universal, for some of these officers seem to have 'carried on their work without any exploitations' (p 55). In literary works, the apparitor had become 'a standard example of corruption and exploitation' (p 55). Chaucer's *GP* portrait of the Summoner is 'black and uncompromising, and completely lacking in any of the softening and humanizing touches which Chaucer uses in the companion portrait of the friar .... His descriptive method here stands in sharp contrast with the rest of the *General Prologue*' (p 56). Indeed, 'Chaucer's conception is more violent than necessary,' even given the antecedent historical and literary traditions (p 56), a situation which suggests that there may be a 'personal element' in the characterization: the Summoner may be based upon a historical individual whom Chaucer strongly disliked, 'an actual prototype, forgotten now except as an artistic creation' (p 57).

1276 Hinckley, Henry Barrett. 'Chauceriana.' 1916–1917. See **724**.
Several parallels to lines 637–38 suggest that speaking Latin when drunk was proverbial. (One of these parallels, printed incorrectly here, is corrected in Hinckley's brief note 'Corrigenda,' *MP*, 15 [1917–1918], 56.)

1277 Kaske, R.E. 'The Summoner's Garleek, Oynons, and eek Lekes.' *MLN*, 74 (1959), 481–84.
The Summoner's garlic, onions, and leeks (line 634) correspond to the leeks, onions, and garlic of Numbers 11:5. The Biblical reference and its medieval interpretations establish 'at least the strong probability that Chaucer is using this detail to deepen an already ugly picture of spiritual as well as

physical deformity' (p 483), since those foods were associated with general depravity, with the tendency to corrupt other people, with lust, and with other evil qualities.

1278 ———. 'Patristic Exegesis: the Defense.' In *Critical Approaches to Medieval Literature: Selected Papers from the English Institute, 1958–1959*. Ed. Dorothy Bethurum. New York: Columbia University Press, 1960; London: Oxford University Press, 1960. Pp 27–60.
Medieval commentators on Numbers 11:5, a passage in which leeks, onions, and garlic are mentioned, associate these foods with spiritual faults such as general depravity, the tendency to corrupt others, and blindness to non-material reality. The Summoner is said to eat these foods (line 49). They are related to his physical disease and also his spiritual deformity. [Kaske's viewpoints as represented in **1277** are incorporated here.]

1279 Kellogg, A.L. 'Chaucer's "Friar's Tale": Line 1314.' *N&Q*, New Series 6 (1959), 190–92.
In Wycliffe's description of false summoning, from his treatise *On the Seven Deadly Sins*, there occurs an analogue to the Summoner's letting a fellow have his concubine (see lines 649–51) and to other corrupt practices.

1280 Kittredge, G.L. 'Chauceriana.' 1909–1910. See **1149**.
The Summoner's pulling of finches (line 632) refers to fornication, not to fraud, as other examples of this phrase demonstrate. Cf **1262, 1270**.

1281 McVeigh, Terrence A. 'Chaucer's Portraits of the Pardoner and Summoner and Wyclif's *Tractatus de Simonia*.' *CF*, 29 (1975), 54–58.
The Summoner and Pardoner are simoniacs. When Chaucer suggests in *GP* that 'these practitioners of simony suffer from the physical defects of leprosy and homosexuality, he is borrowing from an ecclesiastical tradition which condemns the sin of simony by comparing it to leprosy and sodomy' (p 55). This tradition was well-known to Wycliffe, who used it in his *Tractatus de simonia*.

1282 Mann, Jill. *Chaucer and Medieval Estates Satire*. 1973. See **363**.
Chaucer's decision to include a Summoner may be due to influence from Langland. The Summoner's corruption corresponds to traditional attacks upon the behavior of officials of the consistory courts, but 'why is it a summoner, rather than an archdeacon or a commissary, whom Chaucer chooses to describe? Again, the stimulus seems to come from Langland, in whom scornful references to summoners are frequent' (p 140). In contrast to Chaucer's usual technique in the portraits, he here identifies a victim of a pilgrim's misbehavior—in this case, the *yonge girles of the diocise* (line 659). And yet Chaucer 'increases our sense of the Summoner's viewpoint,

even as he sharply distinguishes it from that of the narrator' (p 142). 'In the Summoner's portrait we do not oscillate between liking and condemnation, but between disgust and amusement; it is on this (comparatively) gentler note that Chaucer closes the portrait' (p 143).

1283 Miller, B.D.H. 'Chaucer's General Prologue, A 673: Further Evidence.' *N&Q*, New Series 7 (1960), 404–6.

Miller provides further passages in support of interpreting the *burdoun* of line 673 as meaning 'phallus,' as Biggins (**1260**) suggested. In the *Roman de la Rose*, the word only gradually develops this sense. In a ballade by Deschamps, however, the audience is expected to recognize this meaning at once, though the literal meaning, 'staff,' is also preserved. Chaucer might have taken the sexual sense from the *Roman*, although Deschamps' usage suggests that 'this sense of the word was already widely current in French' (p 406).

1284 Morris, Harry. 'Some Uses of Angel Iconography in English Literature.' *CL*, 10 (1958), 36–44.

Chaucer's Summoner has a 'fyr-reed cherubynnes face' (line 624). However, the standard medieval depiction of the cherubim was blue, not red (it was the seraphim who were shown as red). Chaucer might have been influenced by Italian images of red angels, which could have led him to assume that 'any of the angelic orders may be depicted in red' (p 38). It is more likely, though, that he 'came upon some work in which the iconography was corrupt' (p 38), so that the mistake was already present in his source. Two possibilities are suggested: the *De Proprietatibus Rerum* encyclopedia, which 'permits the assumption that the cherubim emit the same fiery glow as the seraphim' (p 39), and the Book of Enoch, which at one point mentions fiery cherubim.

1285 Pace, George B. 'Physiognomy and Chaucer's Summoner and Alisoun.' *Traditio*, 18 (1962), 417–20.

The Summoner, like Alisoun in the *MilT*, has black eyebrows (line 627). The *Physiognomy* of John of Metham (ca. 1449) states that black eyebrows show a predisposition to lechery. Although this text is later than Chaucer's time, the association between black hair and lecherousness goes back to Aristotle. 'Lechery stands out as the basic element in the Summoner's character' (p 419). The color of his eyebrows, which has been misinterpreted as related to his disease, reinforces his lecherous implications. By his office the Summoner ought to arrest fornicators, but his 'brows reveal that archenemy of lechery to be, ironically, lechery's epitome,' a man 'whose very eyebrows proclaim his hypocrisy' (p 420).

1286 Palmer, H.P. 'The Troubles of a Mediaeval Bishop.' *LQR*, 152 (1929), 172–84.

Selections from the *Register* of Grandisson, Bishop of Exeter during the reign of Edward III, illustrate the corruptions of the ecclesiastical courts.

1287 Patch, Howard R. 'Chauceriana.' *ESt*, 65 (1930-1931), 351–59.

A parallel to line 658, which mentions the Archdeacon's purse, occurs in Dante's *Inferno*, 19.69–72. However, it is not necessary to assume that Chaucer is alluding to this passage specifically. References to a purse are frequent in medieval Latin poems about simony.

1288 Peltola, Niilo. 'Chaucer's Summoner: *Fyr-reed Cherubynnes Face.*' *NM*, 69 (1968), 560–68.

Although Chaucer refers (line 624) to the Summoner's 'fyr-reed cherubynnes face,' in Christian art the cherubim were usually painted blue, not red. The Biblical cherubim represent the concept of monstrous sentinels with animal characteristics and (in Ezekiel) wheels. Chaucer's Summoner frightens children, as the sentinel-figure would, and reflects 'the circularity of the wheel' (p 563) in his garland and buckler. As for the color, although the visual arts show the cherubim as blue, there is confusion over the color in the *De sex alis Cherubim*, a work ascribed to Alanus de Insulis, whom we know to have influenced Chaucer; other writers too seem to have made the same mistake or change. It is possible that in English a pun on *cherubim* as *cherry = ruby* would have reinforced the concept of a red color. Chaucer's usage suggests sexual deviance: red faces are associated with fire, and he could have recalled the 'fire-red face of a Sodomite' from Genesis, or the fact that 'fire is also the eschatalogical punishment of a sexual invert' (p 568) in Dante's *Inferno*, 15.25–30.

1289 Robinson, F.N., ed. *The Works of Geoffrey Chaucer.* 1957. See **42**.

The term *assoillyng* (line 661) refers to absolution, and 'the passage implies an unmistakable doubt of its efficacy — a hint which perhaps comes as near to downright heresy as anything in Chaucer' (p 667). However, the remark 'need imply no more than a condemnation of the abuses of an avaricious clergy' (p 667).

1290 Ruggiers, Paul G. *The Art of the Canterbury Tales.* 1965. See **649**.

The Summoner's *burdoun* (line 673) perhaps recalls the trumpet in Dante's *Inferno*. His 'angelic visage,' like his life, is ironically the opposite of anything truly angelic (p 99).

1291 Schildgen, Brenda D. *The Conflict Between Art and Morality in Two Fourteenth-Century Poets: Juan Ruiz and Geoffrey Chaucer.* 1972. See **650**.

'The fact that no one wishes to share a drink with the Summoner is pathetically suggested by the narrator's remark [lines 649–50]. The Summoner must share his concubine in exchange for a drinking companion' (p 161–62).

1292 Spargo, John W. '*Questio Quid Iuris.*' *MLN*, 62 (1947), 119–22.
The meaning of the Latin words in line 646 has long been unclear. A writ that was 'current in English law from about 1300' (p 120) was designated by its opening words, *quid iuris clamat.* This writ summoned to court a person who was refusing to abide by the court's previous decision on a matter concerning legal title. The Summoner, who does not really understand the technicalities of the law, has simply picked up tags and bits of Latin in the courtroom. We therefore ought to leave 'the Summoner's tipsy mumblings in their duly impressive Latin' (p 121), rather than trying to translate them. As 'legalistic jargon' they have their own value (p 122).

1293 Weiner, Marc. 'A Case for Diagnosis, by Geoffrey Chaucer (1340?–1400).' *Archives*, 80 (1959), 87.
Part of the Summoner's portrait (lines 623–35) is offered, with a translation, as a set of symptoms from which one might diagnose his disease.

1294 Whitbread, L. 'Six Chaucer Notes.' 1978. See **659**.
The statement that the Summoner has a fire-red face (line 624) may involve word-play on a Latin legal tag, the *fieri facies* or *facias*, which was the name of a writ. This pun occurs in Nashe's *Unfortunate Traveler* (1594).

1295 Wood, Chauncey. 'The Sources of Chaucer's Summoner's "Garleek, Onyons, and Eke Lekes." ' *ChauR*, 5 (1970-1971), 240–44.
Chaucer knew Gower's *Vox clamantis*, in which a worldly prelate is said to prefer onions and leeks to manna — in other words, to prefer earthly vanity to divine concerns. Gower's description is indebted to Peter Riga's *Aurora*, a work with which Chaucer was also acquainted. He may have used these two sources in his description of the Summoner's diet (line 634). However, Chaucer also used the Bible directly. Aside from the specific details, the 'most notable difference between Chaucer and his models is the different degree of transparency' (p 243). The Biblical connection is very evident in Gower and in the *Aurora*, as is the spiritual interpretation intended. Chaucer, however, 'tacitly invites the reader to make both the connection and the interpretation' (p 243), reversing Gower's emphasis on the spiritual implications of the images and concentrating instead on the images themselves. Chaucer's version also differs from the others in transferring the negative trait about onions, etc, from the description of a priest to that of a summoner; his portrait of a priest (the Parson) is instead an idealized

one. Rather than producing a monotonous complaint, as Gower does in denigrating the three estates, Chaucer offers a varied and sophisticated social satire.

1296 Woolf, Henry Bosley. 'The Summoner and His Concubine.' *MLN*, 68 (1953), 118–21.

In line 650, it is possible that *his concubyn* means the Summoner's concubine — that he 'handed her over for a year to "a good felawe" in exchange for a quart of wine' (p 119). Similarly, in line 651 *hym* may be reflexive — the Summoner is 'maintaining his own innocence, not that of the "good felawe" ' (p 120). Line 652 may involve a pun on the idiom of pulling a finch, in the senses of committing both fraud and fornication: although the Summoner had temporarily given his concubine to another man, he continued to enjoy her, and thus cheated the man who had paid him in wine for her services. If so, 'it was certainly necessary that the Summoner exercise the utmost secrecy' in such an arrangement (p 120).

1297 Zietlow, Paul N. 'In Defense of the Summoner.' *ChauR*, 1 (1966-1967), 4–19.

A central difference between the Friar and the Summoner — who are not 'cut from the same cloth' (p 4), as has been thought — is that the Summoner's evil 'is written all over his outward appearance' (p 15), while the Friar's evil is concealed beneath an attractive surface. Thus the Summoner is openly a rascal; the Friar, however, is a thoroughgoing hypocrite, 'a rascal in disguise' (p 16).

✌ Part 27: The Pardoner

See the Introduction, pp xxxvii–xxxviii above, for a brief summary of criticism on the Pardoner, and see the Index for further references.

1298 Biggins, D. 'Chaucer's General Prologue, A 696–698.' *N&Q*, New Series 7 (1960), 93–95.

The Pardoner's claim to have a piece of St Peter's sail (lines 696–98) should be interpreted as referring not to Matthew 14:29, where Peter is said to walk on the sea, but instead to the incident reported in Matthew 4:18–22, Mark 1:16–20, and Luke 5:1–11. These passages pertain to Jesus's preaching from Peter's boat and to 'the marvellous catch of fish that followed' (p 94). There may be a 'submerged pun' (p 94) on *hente* (line 698), implying that Jesus caught Peter through the catch of fish. Chaucer's Pardoner, in referring to this incident, is making an 'inspired, truly audacious boast that he has part of the sail from the vessel owned by Peter *before* he became a disciple' (p 94). Developing Chaucer's implications, a play of John Heywood's includes a pardoner who claims that he has the bees that stung Eve in Paradise.

1299 Bloomfield, Morton W. 'The Pardons of Pamplona and the Pardoner of Rounceval: *Piers Plowman* B XVII 252 (C XX 218).' *PQ*, 35 (1956), 60–68.

The hospital of St Mary's Rounceval evidently distributed indulgences in the name of the Bishop of Pamplona. This hospital was notorious for abuses even before the major scandal of 1382. In the *Chronicon Johannis de Reading*, for example, a 1366 entry indicates that the brethren of the hospital 'were involved in a charge of forging a bull of excessive indulgence' (p 68). Chaucer's Pardoner 'who brought his pardons from Rome all hot, probably also had a few from Pamplona in his bag to continue to give offence to good Englishmen' — the draining away of English funds to the main house at Roncesvalles, in Navarre, would have been resented — 'and to anyone indeed who had the good of religion at heart' (p 67).

1300 Bolduan, Nils W. 'Chaucer and Matters Medical.' 1933. See **1112**.
On the Pardoner's portrait (especially lines 688–91), Bolduan comments,
'Is this not almost a classic description of the eunuch?' (p 1368).

1301 Christie, Sister Mary Joannes. *The Provenance of Chaucer's Self Portraits: The Pardoner and the Wife of Bath.* 1958. See **1137**.
In the chapter 'The Portrait of the Pardoner' (pp 181–231), Sister Christie
reviews scholarship on the Pardoner's characterization, finding that, because of discrepancies between the *GP* portrait and other information given
about the Pardoner, 'the details of the piece simply do not fit together' (p
194). This situation may be due to the incompleteness of *CT*. However,
it is also possible that Chaucer's audience would not have demanded 'rigid
consistency' in the characterization, for minds that were 'trained to work
on several levels of meaning would not have expected that every literal fact
could be made to operate on various levels simultaneously' (p 195). The
GP portrait includes many of the qualities recommended in Cicero's rhetorical plan for character-description, with details that reveal the Pardoner's
nature (inner and outer), his position in society, his manner of life, etc,
according to the Ciceronian pattern. In *GP* Chaucer used five of Cicero's
eleven qualities or categories of traits, leaving the others to be developed
in the Pardoner's later self-confession and tale. While the formal rhetorical
pattern is not followed in all respects, the *De Inventione* of Cicero 'supplied
the skeletal frame for the outline of this character' (p 227).

1302 Chute, Marchette. *Geoffrey Chaucer of England.* 1946. See **194**.
In including characters such as the Pardoner, 'Chaucer was running directly
counter to the whole spirit of his age. He had no moral purpose in describing
the Pardoner, and no religious purpose. He described the Pardoner merely
because the man was like that, which was a Renaissance point of view and
not a medieval one' (1977 rpt, p 257).

1303 Coletti, Theresa. 'The Pardoner's Vernicle.' *ChauN*, 1, 1 (1979), 10–12.
The Pardoner has a vernicle on his cap (line 685). The image is both 'a
vehicle for condemning the Pardoner,' since he does not conform to its
image of Christ, and also a carrier of 'an ambivalent hint of hope for him,'
since it 'calls to mind God's boundless love for man and the promise of
grace and forgiveness' (p 11). The vernicle 'suggests that *all* men are made
in God's image, that even the Pardoner is one of God's creatures' (p 12).
Cf Weissman, **1337**.

1304 Curry, Walter Clyde. 'The Secret of Chaucer's Pardoner.' *JEGP*, 18
(1919), 593–606.
Educated people in Chaucer's day would have assumed, according to the

principles of physiognomy, that they could judge people's characters from their physical features. The Pardoner 'carries upon his body and has stamped upon his mind and character the marks of what is well known to the medieval physiognomists as a *eunuchus ex nativitate*' (eunuch from birth, p 597). The indicative traits include 'wide-open glittering eyes, a long neck, a high-pitched voice, and a beardless chin' (p 598), along with the mental characteristics of deceitfulness, arrogance, sensuality and lustfulness, avariciousness, and general depravity. His long, stringy hair also implies 'impotence and lack of manhood' (p 596). Chaucer's Pardoner is thus a 'scientifically correct' (p 599) example of a eunuch according to the medical knowledge of his time. The portrait shows special similarities to the description of the eunuch given by Polemon, an authority cited by most of the medieval authorities on eunuchs. Chaucer may have had Polemon's description, or a version indebted to it, 'before him as he wrote' (p 600). The Pardoner is meant 'to be pitied rather than censured,' for given his condition 'he is compelled to follow the lead of his unholy impulses into debauchery, vice, and crime' (p 605). Since he is a social outcast, he preys upon society. Chaucer shows his own ability to appreciate, 'without judging too harshly, the point of view of even a *eunuchus ex nativitate*' (p 606). Cf **209, 1306, 1307, 1321, 1325, 1333**.

1305 Donaldson, E. Talbot. 'Adventures with the Adversative Conjunction in the General Prologue to the Canterbury Tales, or, What's before the But?' 1981. See **531**.
Discussing the seven uses of *but* in the Pardoner's portrait, Donaldson comments that the Pardoner 'evokes from the narrator a sequence of *buts* that seem to dramatize both an ill ease at first encountering that disturbing creature and a gradually achieved success at accepting him into the world of the pilgrimage' (p 357).

1306 Duino, Russell. 'The Tortured Pardoner.' *EJ*, 46 (1957), 320–25, 365.
Duino reviews the theories of Tupper (**482**), Kittredge (**317**), Patch (**407**), and Curry (**1304**) about the Pardoner's condition, with a preference for Curry's interpretation. 'Perhaps, in his gallery of the types of human nature, Chaucer wanted to include a man who had found Hell' (p 325). The Pardoner is comparable to Lucifer, for whom there is no turning back toward God, but also no peace.

1307 Ethel, Garland. 'Chaucer's Worste Shrewe: The Pardoner.' *MLQ*, 20 (1959), 211–27.
It is appropriate to use the Christian standards of the *ParsT* to pass judgment on the Pardoner (and the other pilgrims), since Chaucer's audience would have judged on that basis: 'when Chaucer in the *General Prologue*

specified "best sentence and moost solaas" as the grounds for judging excellence and awarding the prize, he could reasonably expect the award to be acceptable only if made in accord with the criteria his age accepted' (p 214). Christian standards were often violated, but nevertheless remained effective as standards. The Pardoner can be judged to be the worst of the pilgrims. He can be compared to the Monk and the Friar, since these three, being men of orders, have further to fall: 'in sin, as in tragedy, one must be of high station for magnitude of fall' (p 216). The Monk, while sinful, does not aim at the corruption of others. The Friar is worse than the monk, for he deliberately practices upon others, yet he lacks envy and has certain other admirable qualities. The Pardoner, however, exemplifies every one of the sins the Parson's tale identifies. His life is 'one great and grisly oath' against God (p 223). His evil may be traced to his condition as a eunuch from birth (see Curry **1304**). One alternative for a person so afflicted would be to accept the condition with good will. The Pardoner, however, has chosen the alternative of 'immortal hate,' trying to revenge himself 'upon God and upon men whose normality he mortally envied' (p 227).

1308 Fleming, John V. 'Chaucer's Ascetical Images.' *C&L*, 28 (1979), 19–26.
Chaucer seems to have been familiar with the ideas and documents of ascetic theology. The passage in the Pardoner's portrait (lines 680–87) that tells us that the Pardoner rode without wearing a hood, keeping his hood in his wallet which 'lay biforn hym in his lappe,' is a case in point. Chaucer indulges his taste for 'the cerebrally grotesque' (p 23) by depicting the Pardoner's purse, instead of sexual organs, in that position; the *Roman de la Rose* compares the Lover's members to a pilgrim's scrip. This image 'involves a privileged exegetical vocabulary which came to Chaucer through the literature of medieval asceticism' (p 24). Thirteenth- and fourteenth-century discussions of Christian perfection 'sometimes seem to be obsessed with what might be called the "purse question" ' (p 24). Should a Christian who wanted to live in perfection carry a purse? Bonaventure, for example, identifies perfect Christians 'simply as "those that bear no purse" ' (p 25). The literature of asceticism stressed 'the primacy of the visual imagination' (p 25). Chaucer discovered that its visual images, many of scriptural origin, 'could also inform the most powerful description of the imperfect creation which he saw about him' (p 25).

1309 Gafford, Charlotte K. 'Chaucer's Pardoner and Haze Motes of Georgia.' In *Essays in Honor of Richebourg Gaillard McWilliams*. Ed. Howard Creed. Birmingham-Southern College Bulletin, 63, 2 (1970). Birmingham, AL: Birmingham-Southern College, 1970. Pp 9–12.
The Pardoner 'has been lambasted for several centuries simply as a Romish

rascal and a homosexual liar' (p 9). However, 'could not Chaucer's Pardoner be considered as a heightened example of the human contradiction that, even though people often do not behave in both of two ways or do both of two things, they must have been originally designed and humanly prepared to have done either? Are only scoundrels, abandoned rascals, and eunuchs to see themselves reflected in the Pardoner?' (p 10).

1310 Halverson, John. 'Chaucer's Pardoner and the Progress of Criticism.' *ChauR*, 4 (1969-1970), 184–202.

Halverson reviews modern critical opinion about the Pardoner's sexual and spiritual condition and correlates it to such twentieth-century movements as phenomenology and Freudianism. In addition, a contrast in technique between the Pardoner's portrait and the Friar's is noted. In the Pardoner's description there is a lack of explicitness. His 'sexuality *is* his secret' (p 195), for we are given only Chaucer's guess and not a statement of fact about it. 'Chaucer maintains a comparative distance' from the Pardoner, 'confining himself to his physical appearance and to a description of his professional success' (p 196). In the Friar's description, however, 'the mendicant's venal and hypocritical ways are described as fact' and we are given 'an intimate portrait of the Friar's life, of which nothing is hidden from the poet' (p 196).

1311 Hamilton, Marie P. 'The Credentials of Chaucer's Pardoner.' *JEGP*, 40 (1941), 48–72.

The Pardoner is a canon regular of St Augustine, not a layman. He represents the hospital of St Mary Rouncival, a cell of the Augustinian priory of Roncesvalles in Navarre. His house was especially open to Chaucer's attack since it was the property of an alien priory and was already associated with abuses. The canons of the London Augustinian hospitals served as their own pardoners, so that it is likely that the Pardoner, representing such a house, is a canon. Since Chaucer had elsewhere satirized mendicant friars and Benedictines, 'it would be strange had he neglected the Austin canons, the most numerous and popular of the Regulars in England' (p 52). The Pardoner's references to his 'bretheren,' his preaching, and his reading of the 'lessoun' or 'storie' and singing of the offertory all indicate that he was in orders. Some manuscripts call him 'John,' a standard name for clerics. He wears the cap that is typical of a canon. His long hair and neglect of the tonsure show him to represent worldliness. Chaucer would have heard sermons condemning long-haired churchmen. The Pardoner's hair shows 'both humor and pathos,' however, for his scrawny locks are 'pitiful travesties' (p 61) of the abundant secular hairstyle he thinks that he is imitating. His papal licenses are genuine — a detail that constitutes an 'ultimate irony' (p 71), since papal bulls were not welcomed in England

and their importation was repeatedly forbidden; 'especially in Court circles with which Chaucer was allied, the papal bulls of the Pardoner would have been no recommendation' (p 71).

1312 Hendrickson, D.W. 'The Pardoner's Hair — Abundant or Sparse?' *MLN*, 66 (1951), 328-29.

Although some Chaucer editors are said to have referred to the Pardoner's hair as abundant, the text clearly indicates that his hair is sparse. In addition to the implications of *by ounces* (line 677), *colpons* (line 679), and the statement *thynne it lay* (line 679), the phrase *his lokkes that he hadde* (line 677) implies that he did not have very many.

1313 Kellogg, Alfred L., and Louis A. Haselmayer. 'Chaucer's Satire of the Pardoner.' *PMLA*, 66 (1951), 251-77. Rpt with slight revisions in Alfred L. Kellogg, *Chaucer, Langland, Arthur* (New Brunswick, NJ: Rutgers Univ. Press, 1972), pp 212-44.

Detailed historical information and documentation about the role of pardoners ('questors') shows that Chaucer's Pardoner, like the other pilgrims, is 'a generic figure' (1951, p 272). 'In attitude, practices, and credentials he is very much what a contemporary who had been in church during sermon time might have expected' (p 272). Among his added, individual traits, the reference to *Rouncivale* (line 670) is 'a particular name for a generic corruption,' since the foreign hospitals' failure to control the pardoners they employed 'had gained them an inescapable notoriety' (p 274). Thus the foreign name labels the Pardoner as belonging to 'the most ingenious and treacherous sort' (p 275). The fact that the Pardoner carries false relics also emphasizes his unusual corruption, for this abuse is referred to only infrequently in complaints against pardoners. In showing that 'this exemplar of spiritual abuse' rides with the Summoner, 'the man who should be putting him behind bars' (p 275), Chaucer is directing his satire against the corrupt system of justice. 'Chaucer's satire of the Pardoner is not upon the Pardoner but upon those who make the Pardoner possible' (p 276). The portrait expresses indignation against institutional decay in Chaucer's time.

1314 Kiehl, James M. 'Dryden's Zimri and Chaucer's Pardoner: A Comparative Study of Verse Portraiture.' *Thoth*, 6 (1965), 3-12.

Substantial differences are noted between Chaucer's art of portraiture and Dryden's. Chaucer remains closer to 'the Theophrastian model' (p 3), offers a more imagistically distinct description, and is more casual in tone and in management of the verse. There is also a difference of attitude: Dryden aims at 'devaluation, whereas Chaucer's portrait is engaged foremost in an almost fond portrayal' (p 11). He 'disvalues' the Pardoner somewhat (p 11), but not with 'detectable animosity' or completeness (p 12). Overall, Chaucer's portrait 'is a relatively generous and mellow one that omnisciently embraces the whole world, even the "worst" of it' (p 12).

1315 Lumiansky, R.M. 'A Conjecture Concerning Chaucer's Pardoner.' *TSE*, 1 (1949), 1–29.

Why is the Pardoner present on the pilgrimage? 'Either the pleasure of a vacation in the spring, sincere devotion, or the desire for social approval will pretty well account for the presence of the other pilgrims' (p 4), but these motivations do not account for the Pardoner's participation. Because his physical disability has barred him from normal satisfactions, the Pardoner 'finds his compensation in matching wits with normal folk and coming off best in the encounter' (p 3). 'Is it then too conjectural to suggest that the Pardoner, upon his return from Rome, encountered his friend the Summoner and learned of the plans for the pilgrimage, and that he then decided to join the company, determined to match wits with his travelling companions, and, if possible, to extract money from them?' Thus 'the Pardoner's joining with the Summoner in a lewd secular song and his aping of the newest fashions represent his effort to test the reactions of his newly-met companions' (p 5). It accords with Chaucer's overall characterization of the Pardoner throughout *CT* to see the Pardoner as initially joining the pilgrimage 'for the definite purpose of extracting money from the pilgrims in order to satisfy his desire "to get even with the world" by besting a more experienced group than his usual peasant audiences' (p 29).

1316 McAlpine, Monica E. 'The Pardoner's Homosexuality and How It Matters.' *PMLA*, 95 (1980), 8–22.

Previous commentary on the narrator's remark about the Pardoner, 'I trowe he were a geldyng or a mare' (line 691), has stressed the implications of *gelding* (usually explained as a eunuch) and have not adequately considered *mare* (to be most satisfactorily interpreted as homosexual). Homosexuality was long confused with eunuchry, hermaphroditism, and effeminacy; 'the lines between these various sexual phenomena were fluid in medieval theory' (p 13). The narrator himself is uncertain about the Pardoner's sexual status and finds the Pardoner's expertise in his profession as important as the sexual issue. 'The narrator sets an example of not reducing the Pardoner to his sexuality, an example that at other levels of response Chaucer means us to emulate' (p 14). Although the Pardoner sells forgiveness to others, he will not accept that 'easy out' (p 16) for himself; he 'requires true contrition, true purpose of amendment; he *does* believe that Christ's pardon is best' (p 16). Similarly, in his 'traffickings with relics, the plea for money is partly a camouflage for the plea for the redemptive kiss' (p 17). He seeks and asks for love. His song *Com hider, love, to me* (line 672) similarly suggests the Pardoner's inner desire for acceptance and charity. The vernicle that he wears on his cap (line 685) 'asserts the dignity of the Pardoner, whatever his sexual status, as part of Christ' and thus 'asserts the necessity of each reader's responding to the Pardoner in the context of Christian love' (p 19).

Chaucer's treatment of the Pardoner's condition is indirect and allusive — perhaps because Chaucer is being cautious or because he reflects the medieval view that this is 'the sin that should not be named' (p 18). In any case, since 'the facts about the Pardoner's sexuality are not given but must be established' (p 18), the audience is forced to interpret the Pardoner instead of accepting simple judgments. 'Chaucer may be seen as using his art, and especially its indirection and allusiveness, to challenge the sexual phobias of his readers' (p 18) and to make them see the Pardoner as genuinely one of the group of whom he has said, *pilgrimes were they alle* (line 26).

1317 Manly, John Matthews. *Some New Light on Chaucer.* 1926. See **362**.
In the chapter 'The Summoner, the Friar, and the Pardoner' (pp 102–30), Manly points out that the hospital of the Pardoner, at Rouncival, would have been familiar to Chaucer. There were repeated cases of the unauthorized selling of pardons or diversion of funds among Rouncival's alms-collectors. It is likely that 'so striking a person as the Pardoner' would have been known to Chaucer's audience (p 13).

1318 Mann, Jill. *Chaucer and Medieval Estates Satire.* 1973. See **363**.
The theme of homosexuality in medieval satire is reviewed. 'The Pardoner's homosexuality was originally linked with estates such as his in a *metaphorical* presentation of institutional corruption, but in the *Prologue* it has become both real, and the attribute of an individual' (p 147). Nearly all the *GP* relationships between individual pilgrims 'exist between pilgrims whose *estates* were originally linked, but in almost every case they have become merely *individual* relationships ... the most intense relationship between two pilgrims, and the one which most expresses their "individuality," is precisely that of the Summoner and Pardoner—that is (in Chaucer's world), a perverted relationship. The haphazard groupings in the *Prologue* suggest, not the free expression and association of individuals, but a specialised, blinkered approach, in which an individual's relation to the rest of society does not extend beyond his immediate family or friends .... If we are to read the Pardoner's homosexuality symbolically, I should prefer to define its meaning in accordance with this aspect of the *Prologue*, as a symbol of the perverted nature of merely individual relationships' (p 147). Satiric treatments of false relics in several sources are correlated to the Pardoner's corrupt practices, but nevertheless 'amusement, not disgust, is predominant

in the final picture of the Pardoner singing enthusiastically in hope of good pickings; in more ways than his skill in selling absolution, the Pardoner has resemblances with the "merye" Friar' (p 152).

1319 Manning, Stephen. 'Chaucer's Pardoner: Sex and Non-Sex.' *SAB*, 39 (1974), 17–26.
Manning emphasizes the importance of oral imagery in the Pardoner's characterization. When the Pardoner is introduced in *GP*, 'we see him riding along with the Summoner, and the two sing in duet "Com hider, love, to me" (lines 669–74). Thus Chaucer introduces a pattern of imagery which Freudian critics call *oral*, a pattern which basically involves taking in or spitting out of the mouth, and biting, along with the figurative connotations of those activities' (p 16). The Pardoner is 'unusually aggressive orally .... I suggest that the Pardoner substitutes oral aggression for phallic aggression' (p 21). When Chaucer compares the Pardoner to a goat (line 688), 'it is the voice which is compared to the goat' (p 21), continuing the oral imagery. Manning proposes that 'the Pardoner's being a gelding or mare is analogous to oral castration [which] is analogous to spiritual death' (p 25).

1320 Miller, Clarence H., and Roberta Bux Bosse. 'Chaucer's Pardoner and the Mass.' *ChauR*, 6 (1971–1972), 171–84.
In *GP* 'the Pardoner is the only ecclesiastical figure who is described against the liturgical background of the mass' (p 172; see lines 707–14). The last lines of the portrait 'present the Pardoner preaching in church during mass' (p 172). Given the sequence *lessoun* (epistle), *storie*, and *offertorie* (lines 709–10), the term *storie* 'might refer to the gospel' (p 173). In the allegorical interpretation of the mass by Amalarius, the epistle and the gospel signify 'the preaching of John the Baptist and Christ, preaching which is thrown here into sharp contrast with the preaching of the Pardoner' (p 175). Similarly, in this allegory the mass from the offertory onwards represents Christ's sacrifice, while 'for the Pardoner the coming of the offertory signifies only the necessity of filing his tongue to fleece his victims' (p 175). 'Thus the Pardoner deliberately perverts the meaning of the mass' (p 175). This theme is continued in his later prologue and tale.

1321 Miller, Robert P. 'Chaucer's Pardoner, the Scriptural Eunuch, and the Pardoner's Tale.' *Spec*, 30 (1955), 180–99. Rpt in *Chaucer Criticism*, ed. Richard J. Schoeck and Jerome Taylor, 1 (Notre Dame and London: Univ. of Notre Dame Press, 1960; 10th printing 1978), pp 221–44.
'It would be strange indeed if Chaucer had intended his characters to be recognizable as particular living individuals, or as scientific phenomena, and nothing more,' since a medieval author customarily built 'the surface or *cortex* of his work in such a way as to indicate some particular *nucleus*,

or inner meaning' (p 181). In the Pardoner's case, the detail of eunuchry in the *cortex* of the portrait is clarified by Scriptural references to eunuchs at Deuteronomy 23:1, Isaiah 56:3–5, and Matthew 19:12, and by medieval commentaries on these passages. The physical eunuch as described by Curry (see **1304**) is less important for the Pardoner's characterization than are two types of spiritual eunuch: one is a good man who accepts voluntary chastity, the other a sinful man who rejects grace and good works. The Pardoner as an ecclesiastic should be a *novus homo* or good eunuch, but he is instead a *eunuchus non Dei*, the sinful eunuch who lives the spiritually sterile life of the unredeemed *vetus homo*. The impenitent Pardoner is meant to contrast with the Parson, who resembles the good eunuch. Although the Pardoner should be working to increase virtue, his kind of increase is wholly material, as befits his spiritual eunuchry. Among the Canterbury pilgrims he represents a false ecclesiastic and a presumptuous hypocrite. In reply, see Thompson, **475**.

1322 Moore, Samuel. 'Chaucer's Pardoner of Rouncival.' *MP*, 25 (1927-1928), 59–66.
Medieval documents show that it was not unusual for hospitals to receive grants of protection for alms-seeking, or for indulgences to be granted for the benefit of hospitals. London records to this effect are cited. Thus it would be 'entirely appropriate' (p 64) for the Pardoner to be associated with a hospital. In 1382 the hospital of St Mary of Rouncival, which was one of the less important of London's thirteen hospitals, was involved in an incident in which persons who had collected alms on its behalf had evidently used the proceeds themselves. Therefore, Rouncival 'had at this time a certain notoriety' (p 65) because of false alms-collectors. Chaucer's audience would probably have interpreted the mention of Rouncival as an allusion to this incident; such an interpretation would presumably have been 'foreseen by Chaucer himself' (p 66).

1323 Mossé, F. 'Chaucer et la liturgie.' 1923. See **938**.
Mossé examines the liturgical references in the Pardoner's portrait, suggesting that *ecclesiaste* (line 708) means 'preacher,' rather than specifically 'ecclesiastic' in the sense of someone in orders. The references to *lessoun* and *storie* (line 709) imply that the Pardoner had a fine enough voice to read not only one of the lessons, but the whole office ('Chaucer voulait donc dire que son Pardonnaire avait une si belle voix qu'il était capable de lire non seulement une des leçons mais même tout l'office de matines,' p 286). *Offertorie* (line 710) has caused confusion, because preaching (line 711) does not take place after the offertory. Thus the *song* (line 711) cannot refer to the offertory in particular, but must mean the whole series of chants that does in fact precede preaching ('la partie de la messe qui précède la

prédication est tout entière occupée à des chants,' p 288). If *song* is given a collective sense, corresponding to modern 'singing,' we avoid attributing to Chaucer a major mistake about the liturgy.

1324 Movshovitz, Howard Paul. *The Trickster Myth and Chaucer's Pardoner.* University of Colorado Dissertation. 1977. Dir. Gerald Kinneavy. *DAI,* 38 (1977), 2768-A.

The Pardoner's portrait in *GP* 'gives contradictory and confusing evidence about his appearance and his sexuality.' Although most interpretations of the Pardoner have tried to reconcile such contradictions by discovering 'some essential fact' or inner motivation 'to put everything in proper perspective,' Movshovitz associates him instead with the traditional trickster-figure, 'whose purpose is to embody contradictions.' The trickster is 'a character of tremendous energy who is violent, deceptive, amoral, anti-social, and a figure who tries to mediate between polar opposites. An interpretation of the Pardoner as a trickster-like figure preserves the integrity of Chaucer's text by accepting rather than denying contradictory elements' [from *DAI*; diss not seen].

1325 Rowland, Beryl. 'Animal Imagery and the Pardoner's Abnormality.' *Neophil,* 48 (1964), 56–60.

The narrator remarks of the Pardoner, *I trowe he were a geldyng or a mare* (line 691), and Curry (**1304**) and others have taken him to be a eunuch from birth. However, the Pardoner is also compared to a hare and a goat, both of which animals were thought to be hermaphroditic or bisexual. Given these associations, along with other references to the Pardoner's wenching, lechery, etc, Chaucer was presenting him not as a eunuch but as a 'testicular pseudo-hermaphrodite of the feminine type,' in modern medical terms (p 58). He cannot function as a male, but 'at times he shows the typical desire of the deviate to conform to the sex in which he is reared, although physically he may be unable to do so' (p 58). The associations with the animals would have made the Pardoner's condition intelligible to Chaucer's audience. Thus the Pardoner 'stands revealed as an unhappy, frustrated creature, haunted by his own sexual inadequacy, conscious of his separation from normal life' (p 59). The Pardoner's relationship with the Summoner is explained by this interpretation — but not by the usual interpretation that he is a eunuch from birth, since individuals of that condition lack libido. See also **1327, 1328**.

1326 ——. 'Chaucer's Swallow and Dove Sittynge on a Berne.' *N&Q*, New Series 11 (1964), 48–49.

In *GP*, at lines 688 and 714, the Pardoner's voice is described in ways that correspond to the actual voice of a dove. Later, in the Pardoner's prologue to his tale, the way he moves his neck is compared to the motions of a dove. The *GP* portrait and the later depiction of the Pardoner thus use complementary traits to 'throw graphic light on human behaviour' (p 49).

1327 ——. 'Chaucer's Idea of the Pardoner.' *ChauR*, 14 (1979–1980), 140–54.
Rowland had earlier described the Pardoner as hermaphroditic (see 1325). Further evidence on medieval concepts of the hermaphrodite is presented here, showing that 'the values attached to the hermaphrodite were ambivalent. The hermaphrodite could be the image of perfection; it could also be an image of frustration or incontinence. Philosophically it meant an ideal unity; physically it was an evil and a misfortune' (p 148). Chaucer uses the 'traditional dichotomies inherent in the hermaphrodite as both monster and shaman' and draws upon the medieval viewpoint that 'the hermaphrodite's dual nature represented a duplicity, a doubleness of character' (p 149). The Pardoner's later behavior is credible, for in *GP* Chaucer has 'prepared for it by presenting a disastrous physical ambivalence as both counterpart and cause' (p 150). Cf 1328.

1328 ——. 'Thwarted Sexuality in Chaucer's Works' [Part II]. *Florilegium*, 3 (1982), 250–56.
Rowland had earlier suggested that the Pardoner is a hermaphrodite (1325). 'I now suggest, with additional evidence based on ancient and medieval authorities, that a contemporary audience might have found the diagnosis less exceptional than modern critics, and that Chaucer used the hermaphroditic condition as a complex central figure, reflecting it in imagery in both Prologue and Tale, in order to make a specific indictment' (p 254). In this context the Pardoner's relationship with the Summoner, and other details of the portrait, make sense. Cf 1327.

1329 Ruggiers, Paul G. *The Art of the Canterbury Tales*. 1965. See 649.
The Pardoner seems to be, on the physical level, 'a demonstration of the theory of evil as the absence or deprivation of a natural part' (p 123).

1330 Schaut, Quentin L., O.S.B. 'Chaucer's Pardoner and Indulgences.' *Greyfriar*, 1961, 25–39.
Schaut reviews the historical development of indulgences and their association with pilgrimages, pardoners, hospitals, and accusations of abuse. 'Upon first acquaintance a character such as Chaucer places before us may seem impossible outside the poet's imagination. But after examining the contemporary official documents we feel that nothing has been overdrawn' (p 36). Nevertheless, the Pardoner should not be taken as necessarily typical, for, like 'Chaucer's other men and women, the Pardoner is supreme in his kind'; in his portrayal 'have been fused all the worst characteristics of the class, each in its extreme manifestation,' as lines 692–93 imply (p 39).

1331 Scheps, Walter. 'Chaucer's Numismatic Pardoner and the Personification of Avarice.' *Acta,* 4 (1977), 107–23.

Line 691, which associates the Pardoner with a gelding or a mare, is impossible to interpret in precise physical terms, but by linking the Pardoner to two kinds of horses it links him to the sin of avarice. 'Gower portrays Avarice as a woman mounted on a horse whereas the other sins ride different animals' (p 117). 'The association of Avarice with the horse and the alternative iconographical representations of Avarice as both man and woman would, I think, serve to explain the "gelding or a mare" reference' (p 120).

1332 Schweitzer, Edward C., Jr. 'Chaucer's Pardoner and the Hare.' *ELN,* 4 (1966-1967), 247–50.

Because hares were thought to be hermaphroditic or to change their sex, the association of the Pardoner's eyes with the eyes of a hare (line 684) 'anticipates in its implication of sexual abnormality the line, "I trowe he were a geldyng or a mare" ' (p 249; see line 691). The *Eunuchus* of Terence, who was 'a major school author during the Middle Ages' (p 247), and the encyclopedic traditions refer to the ambiguous or abnormal sexuality of the hare. In addition, a further Christian symbolism may be implied, since, like other symbols, the hare could be interpreted both *in malo* and *in bono.* Hugh of St Cher 'explains that just as the hare is at once male and female, so the good prelate is both father and mother to those in his care,' but the Pardoner is 'the inversion of this norm' (p 249). The hare was associated with the Jews, who were seen as remaining in unbelief, and the hare was said to sleep with its eyes open. 'Eyes "glarynge" like a hare's may therefore be the unseeing eyes of a soul spiritually asleep, shining in the darkness of the privation of grace' (p 250).

1333 Sedgewick, C.G. 'The Progress of Chaucer's Pardoner, 1880-1940.' *MLQ,* 1 (1940), 431–58. Rpt in *Chaucer Criticism, 1,* ed. Richard J. Schoeck and Jerome Taylor (Notre Dame and London: Univ. of Notre Dame Press, 1960; 10th printing, 1978), pp 190–220; and in *Chaucer: Modern Essays in Criticism,* ed. Edward Wagenknecht (New York: Oxford University Press, 1959), pp 126–58.

Viewpoints toward the Pardoner and his tale are reviewed. Cautioning against Curry's assumption that physiognomical theory would have been widely known (see **1304**), Sedgewick remarks, 'I doubt very much that any of the pilgrims (except Chaucer and the Physician) were familiar, or needed to be, with the Physiognomies' (p 435). The Pardoner's *GP* portrait includes the themes of his later prologue and tale: 'irreverence, lust, shameless exhibitionism, physical impotency, avarice, superb skill as a charlatan' (p 445). Drinking, the only later theme that is missing in the Pardoner's *GP* description, is 'supplied by his association with the Summoner' (p 445). As for Chaucer's attitude toward the Pardoner, it is not appropriate to say that he either hates or pities him. As an artist Chaucer '*presented* him, fully-rounded and without reservation,' in a way that 'enables us to sharpen our senses against the scourge and blight of charlatanism' (p 458).

1334 Sleeth, Charles R. 'The Friendship of Chaucer's Summoner and Pardoner.' *MLN*, 56 (1941), 138.

Chaucer shows that the Summoner and the Pardoner ride together (lines 669–70). A document of 1355, from the register of the Bishop of Exeter, indicates that false pardoners sometimes connived with archdeacons' officials in defrauding the people. We are not explicitly told that this Summoner and Pardoner do so, but 'being familiar with Chaucer's objective method of satire, his habit of never drawing a damaging conclusion that he can trust his intelligent contemporary reader to draw for himself, we scarcely need further evidence of Chaucer's intention.'

1335 Standop, Ewald. 'Chaucers Pardoner: Das Charakterproblem und die Kritiker.' In *Geschichtlichkeit und Neuanfang im sprachlichen Kunstwerk, Studien zur Englishchen Philologie zu Ehren von Fritz W. Schulze*. Ed. Peter Erlebach, Wolfgang G. Müller, and Klaus Reuter. Tübingen: Gunter Narr, 1981. Pp 59–69.

Standop reviews several recent interpretations of the Pardoner, focusing on the apparent implausibilities and incongruities of the Pardoner's presentation in *GP*, in his self-revealing prologue, in his tale, and in its subsequent endlink. He rejects interpretations of the Pardoner's character that depend upon what he calls the heresy of psychological realism (the 'Häresie des psychologischen Realismus,' p 61). He also rejects patristic exegeses of such traits as the pardoner's eunuchry (which does not reappear after *GP*), his love-song, and his new-fashioned riding. Such interpretations go beyond what is evident in the text ('Man gibt vor, mehr über das Innenleben des Pardoner zu wissen, als der Text hergibt,' p 61), or impute to the text deeper meanings that the innocent reader can receive only with astonishment ('tieferen Gehalt [den] der naive Leser nur mit Staunen zur Kenntnis nehmen kann,' p 66).

1336 Storm, Melvin. 'The Pardoner's Invitation: Quaestor's Bag or Becket's Shrine?' *PMLA*, 97 (1982), 810–18.

The Pardoner 'stands between the Tabard Inn and Becket's shrine as the pivotal figure in the pilgrimage, the meretricious surrogate for what the other pilgrims seek at Becket's shrine' (p 810). His sexuality, 'whether perverse or merely lacking,' reflects his ecclesiastical functioning (p 812): 'Not only is he himself sterile, he is also the barren ground on which others waste their seed' (p 813). His companionship with the Summoner, 'whom

Chaucer portrays as an unsavory metaphor of the pilgrim,' suggests 'the relationship between pilgrim-lover and shrine-beloved' (p 813). Both the Pardoner and the Summoner imply fruitlessness, spiritual waste, and a distraction or diversion from the true goals of pilgrimage. The pilgrims become aware that 'the forces that would deter them from the pilgrims' way lurk not in the shadows of the Kentish woods through which they pass but in their midst' (p 816).

337 Weissman, Hope Phyllis. 'The Pardoner's Vernicle, the Wife's Coverchiefs, and Saint Paul.' *ChauN*, 1, 2 (1979), 10–12.

Extending the discussion of Coletti (**1303**), Weissman sees the vernicle on the Pardoner's cap (line 685) as 'the most conspicuous iconographic device used by Chaucer to establish a symbolic relationship between the Pardoner and the Wife of Bath' (p 10). Their antithetical headgear suggests the 'feminization of the Pardoner and the masculinization of the Wife' (p 11). The two pilgrims can be seen as inviting their contemporaries 'to experiment in transcending sex differences *in Domino*,' for in Christ there is neither male nor female (p 12).

338 Williams, Arnold. 'Some Documents on English Pardoners, 1300–1400.' In *Medieval Studies in Honor of Urban Tigner Holmes, Jr.* Ed. John Mahoney and John Esten Keller. Chapel Hill, NC: University of North Carolina Press, 1965. University of North Carolina Studies in the Romance Languages and Literatures, 56. Pp 197–207.

Williams supplies documents to supplement those presented by Jusserand (**312**) on the frauds that pardoners or *questors* were said to practice. Items given here concern conflicts between friars and *questors*; prohibitions against diocesan officials' giving aid to *questors*, against receiving false pardoners, and against confessing one's sins to false friars and *questors*; and a pardoner's license for Roncesvalles (see line 670). Nevertheless, the actual number of complaints recorded against pardoners is rather small. 'The picture of the friar which Chaucer gives us is certainly biased' and that of the Pardoner may also be unrepresentative (p 205).

339 Young, Karl. 'Chaucer and the Liturgy.' *MLN*, 30 (1915), 97–99.

It has been previously recognized that the Pardoner's terms *lessoun* (ie, *lectio*) and *offertorie* (ie, *offertorium*) pertain to the liturgy (lines 709–10). However, his term *storie* (line 709) — usually interpreted as a story, an *exemplum*, etc — is also a liturgical reference, to the term *historia*. In the liturgical sense *historia* has several meanings, most of them implying a series of narratives. Thus Chaucer's meaning might be loosely rendered, 'He well knew how to read either a single lesson or the whole string of lessons' (p 99). The passage provides further evidence of Chaucer's knowledge of liturgical terminology.

➣ Part 28: The Narrator's Comments and Apology for His Style

See the Introduction, p xxxviii above, for a brief summary of criticism on this section of the *General Prologue*, and see the Index for further references.

340 Baum, Paull F. 'Chaucer's "Faste by the Belle," *C.T.* A. 719.' *MLN*, 36 (1921), 307–9.
What did Chaucer imply by saying, at line 719, that the company was assembled at the Tabard, *faste by the Belle*? Although eight Southwark inns called the Bell can be identified, only two existed before 1600. Of these two, one was apparently a brothel. If this were the inn that Chaucer meant to identify, he is perhaps hinting that while some of the pilgrims were enjoying the hospitality of the Tabard, others might be patronizing the nearby house of a quite different reputation.

341 Crosby, Ruth. 'Chaucer and the Custom of Oral Delivery.' *Spec*, 13 (1938), 413–22.
'Chaucer, in accordance with the convention of his day, wrote primarily for a listening public' (p 432). Lines 715–24 show his concern for oral delivery: 'Chaucer's method of summing up what he has told and announcing what he is to tell ...indicates that he has in mind an audience who will be listening and who may need to be reminded of the course of the story' (p 418). Chaucer's use of stock phrases—'the conventional language of poetry intended for oral recitation' (p 420)—is also discussed, with some *GP* examples, such as *Bifel* and *on a day* (both in line 19).

342 Elliott, Ralph W.V. *Chaucer's English.* 1974. See **602**.
Lines 731–40 suggest the desire for verisimilitude: Chaucer's 'wording is sufficiently general to suggest that he was seeking a kind of verisimilitude

not merely in the speech of his vulgar characters' but in that of the other characters as well (p 369). Thus the *GP* labelling of a pilgrim's speech, as when the Merchant is said to speak *ful solempnely* (line 274) or the Wife to *carpe* (line 474), is reflected in the pilgrim's later presentation — though sometimes, as with the Prioress's French (lines 124–26), the label is not subsequently developed.

1343 Friend, Albert C. 'The Proverbs of Serlo of Wilton.' *MS*, 16 (1954), 179–218.
The collection of proverbs made by Serlo of Wilton in the twelfth century is 'the earliest written source ' (p 180) for several of Chaucer's proverbs, including the concept that words and deeds must resemble each other (see lines 741–42). Serlo's collection was used in the schools as late as the fifteenth century.

1344 Goodrich, W.J. 'Chauceriana.' 1904. See **721**.
The concept of words being cousin to the deed (lines 741–42) is traced to Plato's *Cratylus*, although Chaucer's application of the concept is 'quite foreign to Plato's argument' (p 122).

1345 Huppé, Bernard F. *A Reading of the Canterbury Tales.* 1964. See **295**.
Chaucer the pilgrim-reporter is 'the comic projection of most of what the poet hopes he is not' (p 28). Seeming to be 'yet another cheerful numbskull,' like some of Chaucer's earlier narrators (p 21), he sees only the surface of life. 'The narrator reports the masks; the author and we learn of the faces' beneath the masks (p 29). The narrator misinterprets Christ's speech (see lines 739–40), for Christ did *not* report external matters but spoke 'more often than not in parable, that is, in a manner just the opposite to that of realism' (p 27). Similarly, the narrator misinterprets Plato (see lines 741–42), for according to Plato true words 'will relate to the universal, the mathematical, the unchanging — they will be abstract' (p 28). Thus 'the narrator's "realism" is what Plato means by error' (p 28).

1346 Josipovici, G.D. 'Fiction and Game in *The Canterbury Tales.*' *CritQ*, 7 (1965), 185–97.
The conflict between 'the moral and the immoral, the edifying and the unedifying' (p 185), which is pervasive in the *CT*, is first openly enunciated in lines 725–42, the mock apology where the narrator's insistence on his 'purely reportorial status' (p 186) paradoxically establishes the poem's nature as 'an ideal world of fiction where right and wrong do not apply' (p 187). Since the narrator's relationship to the author is ironic, the narrator's claim to be 'a reporter dedicated to truth even at the expense of morality' (p 187) inversely frees the poem from reality. The Host, who near the end

of *GP* suggests the story-telling game and lays down its rules, is creating within the poem a version of the situation existing outside the poem, between it and its audience, for the whole work 'is not a veridical report but a game played by Chaucer with his readers' (p 189).

347 Leicester, H. Marshall, Jr. 'Reply to Robert Burlin' [letter in *Forum* section]. *PMLA*, 95 (1980), 881–82.

Replying to Burlin's criticism (see **589**) of his earlier article (Leicester **626**), Leicester here defends his use of critical terminology. On lines 725–50, he comments that 'the question in these lines is the extent to which the speaker feels (and fears) that he has falsified the pilgrims in his portraits of them; the corollary is the idea that the General Prologue itself may be far more the poet's portrait than an account of the characters. I take this corollary to be true, and I also take the issue to be one the poet-speaker raises consciously and conspicuously as part of his meaning' (p 882).

348 Renoir, Alain. 'Tradition and Moral Realism: Chaucer's Conception of the Poet.' *SN*, 35 (1963), 199–210.

The *GP* concept of the poet's task, 'quite simply to retell what he sees and to retell it *exactly as he sees it*' (p 201; lines 730–43), is not in contradiction with the concept of the poet at the end of *CT*. 'In both the *General Prologue* and the "retracciouns," we may suspect that Chaucer conceived of the poet as one working in the service of "moral vertu, grounded upon trouthe" ' (p 207).

349 Root, Robert K. 'Chaucer and the Decameron.' *ESt*, 44 (1912), 1–7.

In addition to the arguments presented by Morsbach (**381, 382**) to show that Chaucer used the *Decameron*, Root here proposes that Chaucer's apologies to the reader show similarities to Boccaccio's. The apology in *GP*, as others have pointed out, is similar enough to a passage in the *Roman de la Rose* that the *Roman* may be accepted as its source. In an extensive footnote Root traces the long background to the idea that words must be cousin to deeds (see lines 741–42). It is likely that Chaucer had read the *Decameron*, although he apparently did not have a copy of it at hand: we see here 'the sort of imitation that comes from memory rather than from the open page' (p 7).

350 Skeat, Walter W., ed. *The Complete Works of Geoffrey Chaucer, Edited from Numerous Manuscripts.* 1894–1897. See **3**.

Two passages from the *Roman de la Rose*, as well as one from Boethius's *Consolation*, express the idea that words must be cousin to the deed (vol 5, p 57; see lines 741–42).

1351 Taylor, P. B. 'Chaucer's *Cosyn to the Dede.' Spec*, 57 (1982), 315–27.
Chaucer was concerned with the relationships among thought, language,
and actions. The descriptions of speech habits in the *GP* portraits 'suggest
an accord between verbal habits and inward character' (p 319). The narrator's apology (lines 725–42), in which only the 'surface posture is a sop
to convention' (p 320), expresses all of Chaucer's 'own doubts and confu-
sions about the complex relations between intent, word, and deed' (p 319).
Chaucer's knowledge of Plato (see lines 741–42), derived through Boethius
and other sources, is reviewed. 'The apology as a whole moves from pleading the necessity of a vernacular and base speech to a suggestion — in
citing both Christ and Plato — that words both clothe morality and reflect
in their particular references a world of universals' — or that words *can* do
so. They usually fail to do so, 'and Chaucer suggests this failure simultaneously with his affirmation, for the same words that affirm a realism of
speech, deny it' (p 324). The word *cousin* means 'dupe' as well as 'relative'; thus this word 'belies the thing it identifies or the idea it expresses'
(p 324). Other terms in the apology-passage are also ambiguous. 'This
evidence suggests that Chaucer's view of language is that of a Christian
Platonist, and that he aspires towards a linguistic realism in which intent
informs deeds through the ministry of words. The evidence also suggests
that this aspiration is an ideal sullied by the practice of the real world' (p
325).

1352 Tupper, Frederick. 'The Envy Theme in the Prologues and Epilogues.'
JEGP, 16 (1917), 551–72.
This discussion of the conventional language pertaining to envy does not
examine *GP* directly. However, its survey of recurrent expressions of humility, self-excuses, complaints about envious detractors, statements about the
fear of misinterpretation, etc, provides useful background for the narrator's
self-excuse in lines 725–46.

ꙮ Part 29: The Host and the Establishment of the Storytelling Contest

See the Introduction, p xxxviii above, for a brief summary of criticism on this section of the *General Prologue*, and see the Index for further references.

1353 Bashe, E.J. 'The Prologue of *The Tale of Beryn*.' *PQ*, 12 (1933), 1–16.
The non-Chaucerian *Beryn*-prologue shows a clear understanding that each pilgrim is to tell *one* tale on each direction of the pilgrimage. This text 'supports a belief' that lines 793–94, which specify that each pilgrim will tell *two* tales each way, are 'a post-Chaucerian insertion' or 'an addition by Chaucer himself after the plan had already become circulated in its simpler form' (p 16).

1354 Bowden, Muriel. *A Commentary on the General Prologue to the Canterbury Tales.* 1948. See **104**.
The Host, drawn from the model of the historical Harry Bailly, is an opportunist and an 'extraordinarily vivid character' (p 292). He has 'the kind of presence that demands acceptance of his suggestions' (p 294). Bowden briefly indicates the regulations that applied to London innkeepers and the duties of being a lord's marshall (see line 752).

1355 Burrow, J.A. *Ricardian Poetry: Chaucer, Gower, Langland, and the Gawain Poet.* 1971. See **187**.
In Ricardian poetry (poetry of the era of Richard II) the circular structure, in which the narrative returns to its starting-point, is common. Had Chaucer completed the *CT*, 'he would have finished the work in accordance with the proposals made by the Host in his very explicit speech' at the end of *GP* (p 67). The Host's plan indicates that the journey will end at the

same place where it began, and that it will conclude in a mood of comedy and festivity.

1356 Delasanta, Rodney. 'The Theme of Judgment in *The Canterbury Tales*.' *MLQ*, 31 (1970), 298–307.

GP establishes the fact that the pilgrims are preparing themselves for a judgment by the Host (see the judgmental vocabulary of lines 778, 813–14, 816–18, and 833–34). This situation involves a parody of the Last Judgment. The Host, as 'a servant who is also master,' recalls 'the typological figure of another Servant-Master in the background' (p 299). The reference to a supper as a reward suggests Luke 22:27–30. Jesus there refers to his Father; Harry Bailly swears by his father's soul (line 781). The meaning of the judgment and the Host's interpretation of his role change as the work progresses. By the time of the Prologue to the *ParsT*, although the number twenty-nine recurs (see *GP*, line 24, and prologue to *ParsT*, line 4), the implications of Libra as judgment have replaced those of the Ram in line 8 of *GP*. Thus judgment is 'parodically foreshadowed in the function of the Host' (p 304).

1357 Derocquigny, J. 'Notes sur Chaucer.' 1910. See **595**.

The phrase *that is myn accord* (line 839) may mean, as it apparently does in a parallel passage of the French *Meliador*, that this is my judgment or my opinion.

1358 Everett, Dorothy. ' "If Euen-Song and Morwe-Song Accorde" (Canterbury Tales, Prologue, 830).' *RES*, 8 (1932), 446–47.

The Host's comment about evening-song and morning-song (line 830) is an ironic reference to a proverb, 'Even songe and morn songe beth not both on.' Given the proverb, it is perhaps not wholly surprising that certain aspects of the evening's agreement are treated ironically.

1359 Fisher, William Nobles. *Play and Perspective in the Canterbury Tales*. 1975. See **246**.

In the chapter 'The Canterbury Game' (pp 29–58), Fisher examines the establishment of the tale-telling contest. Chaucer emphasizes 'the voluntary accord that is necessary for the pilgrims to play their game together' (p 29). The Host begins by winning over the audience (*captatio benevolentiae*, in rhetorical terms). His offer to give the pilgrims his head (line 782) acts out the response he wants from the pilgrims in turn: since the head suggests not only life but also the will, he is indicating that he submits his will to the pilgrims and asks that they submit theirs to him. The Host thus 'demonstrates the sacrifice of self, of deviating will, that man must act out in order to attain ... ultimate alliance with God's will' (pp 31–32). This paradigm for reaching accord and aligning wills 'occurs again and again through the *Tales*, and everything in the poem is to be measured against this act of bringing wills into accord' (p 32). It is therefore appropriate that the penalty for discord should be harsh (lines 805–9, 833–34).

1360 Furnivall, F.J., and R.E.G. Kirk, eds. [names reversed on paper cover]. *Analogues of Chaucer's Canterbury Pilgrimage ... The Expenses of the Aragonese Ambassadors ... Including Their 4-Days' Journey from London to Canterbury and Back, 31 July — 3 Aug. 1415 ... .* London: Kegan Paul, Trench, Trübner, 1903. Chaucer Society, Second Series, 36.
Some idea of the expenses of a pilgrimage from London to Canterbury and return (cf line 806) can be gained from this information about the costs of the Aragonese ambassadors' journey in 1415.

1361 Gardner, John. *The Poetry of Chaucer.* 1977. See **252**.
Chaucer's characterization of Harry Bailly involves implications of a devil-figure, drawing upon medieval depictions of the devil as innkeeper. The name Bailly suggests 'imprisoning walls'; the promised supper suggests the hell-banquet that parodies the celestial banquet; *Host* taken as a pun equates him with 'a parodic Christ'; as in *SumT*, the devil might be present among men (p 240). However, 'Harry Bailly is by no means simply the Devil or even an essentially demonic man' (p 240), since he has positive functions too. Thus he is shown to have 'the doubleness — ambiguity — of all things earthly' (p 241).

1362 Gaylord, Alan T. 'Sentence and Solaas in Fragment VII of the *Canterbury Tales*: Harry Bailey as Horseback Editor.' *PMLA*, 82 (1967), 226–35.
Pursuing Harry Bailley's *GP* role as governor and judge and his criteria of *sentence* and *solaas* (line 798), in Fragment VI Chaucer offers a Literature Group, whose subject is '*the art of story telling*' (p 226). The reader will 'begin to see that Harry is lazy, but suspect that Chaucer wants him to work; he will see that Harry operates from simple rules of variety and diversion, but suspect that Chaucer acts from principles of art; he will see that it is Harry's main concern as host and editor that things should keep on happening, but suspect that it is Chaucer's purpose as architect and artist that the fragment should keep on developing. In short, he will begin to see that if Harry is the Apostle of the Obvious, Chaucer is the Master of Indirections' (p 235).

1363 Harlow, Benjamin C. 'Chaucer's Host: The Character of Harry Bailly.' *McNR*, 19 (1968), 36–47.
The Host's personality is reviewed. He provides continuity in the pilgrim-age, beginning with *GP*. He is genial, concerned with money, free to come

and go as he pleases, desirous of authority, impudent, forceful, 'a shrewd judge of men' (p 47), and a lover of good stories.

1364 Higgs, Elton D. '"What Man Artow?": Harry Bailly and the "Elvyssh" Chaucer.' *MHLS*, 2 (1979), 27–43.
In *GP* Chaucer establishes a contast between the personality of the narrator and the personality of the Host. 'Chaucer the Pilgrim-Narrator is the soul of tolerance and permissiveness, whereas the Host wishes to conform everyone to his own tastes and standards. This contrast is clear as early as the end of the General Prologue when the Narrator releases himself from any responsibility for either the propriety of the tales or the observance of strict social protocol in presenting the pilgrims. Immediately afterward comes the account of the Host's persuading the pilgrims to accept his plan for the tale-telling and his lordship on the journey' (p 28; lines 769–834). Where the narrator 'confesses his inability to do more or less than to present accurately what he has seen and heard,' Harry Bailly 'demands absolute obedience from the pilgrims' (p 30). The narrator is diffident; Harry is confident, even aggressive.

1365 Jack, Adolphus Alfred. *A Commentary on the Poetry of Chaucer and Spenser.* 1920. See **305**.
Jack suggests that Chaucer probably never intended to include a hundred and twenty tales in *CT*. Lines 793–94 represent 'an erring interpolation' (p 81) or a corruption of the proper reading. A word different from *othere* may originally have stood in line 794. For example, if *thuswise* is substituted and the passage repunctuated, it would mean that each pilgrim would tell two tales in all, not four.

1366 Keen, William Parker. *A Study of the Host in the Canterbury Tales.* Lehigh University Dissertation. 1967. Dir. J. Burke Severs. See also *DAI*, 28 (1968), 4133–34-A.
Keen summarizes previous analyses of the Host; the comparison between him and the Chorus of a drama goes back to 1747, for example. Keen's thesis is that 'the Host's primary role is to enliven the events on the fictional pilgrimage, usually in a comic way,' and that he is 'Chaucer's most important device' for setting the story-telling project in motion and keeping it running (p 23). In *GP* 'Chaucer presents a character whose manliness, wisdom, tact, solicitous attention to his guests, and imagination make him seem an ideal person to act as guide and master of ceremonies' (p 25). Like the Eagle in *HF*, Harry Bailly is comic in this role. The expectations created in *GP* are later sometimes fulfilled, but sometimes contradicted, 'with the result that the Host's actions continue to be fresh' as readers 'reshuffle their expectations' (p 25). The *GP* portrait is examined in detail. The

Host's literary criteria of *best sentence* and *moost solaas* (line 789) set him 'in the forefront of his age' as having a 'wide and liberal critical view' of the purposes of literature (p 53). His behavior in other parts of *CT* is also discussed: he meets challenges, some of which he does not handle successfully, but he recovers himself before relinquishing guidance of the pilgrimage to the Parson.

1367 ——. ' "To Doon Yow Ese": A Study of the Host in the *General Prologue* of the *Canterbury Tales*.' *Topic*, 17 (1969), 5–18.
The *GP* portrait of the Host prepares us for his behavior later. This portrait is set off from the rest by its placement at the end; the Host is the first member of the group to become the center of the others' attention. His portrait is also quite short. He is described more through the dramatic presentation of his words and actions than through descriptive details. In this way Chaucer can 'establish most vigorously the activeness' of this character (p 7). His *eyen stepe* (line 753) may suggest heroic qualities. *GP* indicates the Host's 'efficient service, his impressive appearance, his outstanding literary critical credentials' — he is a rather forward-looking critic, since the recognition of pleasure as a valid literary purpose was recent and unusual in medieval theory — 'his solicitousness, and the spontaneity of his imagination' (p 18). Nevertheless, small touches also prepare us for the difficulties that he will have in governing the pilgrimage group. For example, we are told that the Host would be a fit marshal *in an halle* (line 752), which praises him but also limits the praise to the relatively controlled environment of a hall. The realm in which the pilgrimage is to take place, however, is far wider than that.

1368 King, Francis, and Bruce Steele, eds. *Selections from Geoffrey Chaucer's The Canterbury Tales*. 1969. See **82**.
The imagery of the Host associates him with the Monk, the Wife, and the Miller. 'Like them, he displays a rather crude good fellowship' (p 361). 'With his mirth, his resounding blasphemies and his ignorance of spiritual values, he represents most vociferously in this work the outlook of secular man' (p 361).

1369 Lawler, Traugott. *The One and the Many in the Canterbury Tales*. 1980. See **330**.
Lawler suggests that we can infer, by the end of *GP*, that each pilgrim will tell only one tale, not four as the Host has proposed. At line 848, it is said that the Knight must tell *his tale*. The use of the singular form here 'is striking' and should lead us to expect that 'there will be only one tale apiece' (p 110).

1370 Leyerle, John. 'Thematic Interlace in *The Canterbury Tales*.' 1976. See
337.
We should not equate the Host's plan for the story-telling with Chaucer's
own intentions. 'As poet, Chaucer tends to treat members of the middle
class with a degree of ironic amusement, or even mockery. A self-important
publican who takes upon himself the uninvited role of guide for the pilgrimage, organizer of a tale-telling contest, and sole judge of the winner
seems likely to be presented with some irony, and his opinions, especially
his literary opinions, are to be taken uncritically only by the unwary' (p
107). On the interlace pattern that Leyerle sees as more fundamental to
CT than Harry's simple 'series of separate tales' (p 108), see the annotation
at **337**.

1371 Lumiansky, R.M. 'Chaucer's *Canterbury Tales, Prologue*, 784–787.' *Expl*,
5 (1946-1947), item 20.
The Host has shown the pilgrims that he is interested in money as well as
conviviality; 'Harry's gaiety is held in abeyance until after the bill is paid.'
The pilgrims' first response to his announcement that he has a proposal to
make is indifference. In lines 784–87 they do not register any enthusiasm. In
his next speech, however (lines 788–809), he makes a proposal that 'involves
neither annoyance nor expense for them.' The pilgrims 'now feel somewhat
contrite about their earlier suspicious dislike of the Host' and therefore 'now
bend over backwards in agreeing to Harry's suggestion and to his leadership
of the pilgrimage.' These viewpoints are incorporated in Lumiansky, **348**.
In reply, see Pearce, **1378**.

1372 Malone, Kemp. 'Harry Bailly and Godelief.' *ES*, 31 (1950), 209–15.
The Host is a literary creation, 'a figure of fiction, not a portrait of the
actual innkeeper of Southwark' (p 215). His wife's name does not agree with
the name recorded for the wife of the historical Harry Bailly, for instance.
The *GP* description gives him 'the superlative quality which we find in all
the pilgrims,' corresponding to 'the pattern of characterization regularly
followed' (p 210). The account of the agreement made between the Host
and the pilgrims shows a 'comic reversal of the customary relationships
between an innkeeper and his guests' (p 213), for here it is the guests who
obey the innkeeper's orders. The lordliness of the Host is comic, and his
scheme is 'nonsensical' (p 214) — few of the pilgrims could have heard a
tale being told on horseback, and the proposed fine for disobeying the Host
is huge. 'The absurdity of his program makes its adoption by the pilgrims
much funnier than the adoption of a sensible program could possibly be'
(p 215). He is 'one of the great comic characters of English literature' (p
215). These viewpoints are expanded in Malone, **359**.

1373 Manly, John Matthews. *Some New Light on Chaucer.* 1926. See **362**.
In the chapter 'The Host, the Reeve, and the Miller' (pp 70–101), Manly presents multiple historical sources that establish the existence of Harry Bailly, innkeeper of the Tabard in Southwark in Chaucer's time: the Host is thus modeled upon a historical individual.

1374 Martin, William Eugene. *Concepts of Sovereignty in The Canterbury Tales.* University of Pittsburgh Dissertation. 1971. Dir. Robert D. Marshall. See also *DAI*, 32 (1972), 5236-A.
In the chapter 'The "Game" Sovereign of the Pilgrims: Harry Bailly' (pp 27–50), Martin examines the formation of the pilgrims into a community, pointing out the similarities between this community and other medieval social organizations. Many of the pilgrims would have belonged to a guild or another association. 'The five guildsmen, their cook, Harry Bailly, the Wife of Bath, as a weaver, the Merchant and probably the Manciple and the Shipman would have been members of guilds. The Yeoman, the Miller, the Reeve, the Plowman and the Parson must have been part of the innumerable rural cooperatives at one time. The Man of Law and the Doctor of Physics [sic] were members of fraternal brotherhoods. The Clerk was a university student. The Prioress and the Monk helped to run their religious orders' (p 39). Except for its limited purpose and duration, the society the pilgrims constitute 'has all the features of a real society' — a sovereign ruler, laws and penalties, and an oath of loyalty (p 42). Additionally, this society is a game. 'The game society of the Canterbury pilgrims serves a similar function to the dream worlds of Chaucer's earlier poems,' allowing reality to be included but made malleable to human will (p 50). As sovereign, Harry Bailly presides over the process of making the pilgrims into an organization and trying to regulate human passions 'within an ordered framework' (p 50).

1375 Page, Barbara. 'Concerning the Host.' *ChauR*, 4 (1969-1970), 1–13.
Although the Host is indeed comic, his merriment is excessive in a way that corresponds to one of the stages of pride, according to Bernard of Clairvaux. Therefore, 'in terms of medieval psychology' the Host would be recognized as one 'type of the proud man' (p 5). He resembles the Wife of Bath in having a characteristic attitude of bravado that is temporarily 'undercut by a pathetic irony' (p 8) when he describes his own marriage. He is 'a time-bound and earth-bound man' (p 11) who represents the naturalistic world, the immediately present time, and in particular those qualities of 'the bourgeois man' (p 11) — as identified in estates-literature satire — that were open to criticism: social opportunism, faulty education, extravagance of expression, etc. Thus the Host is not merely a comic character, but 'a

remarkably complex artistic creation' (p 13) with multiple functions in the text.

1376 Payne, F. Anne. *Chaucer and Menippean Satire*. Madison, WI: University of Wisconsin Press, 1981.
The Host holds the traditional satiric position of the stock character *deus*, who 'gives the appearance of controlling the dialogue' and 'is characterized by the intent to give the figures in the central confrontation exactly what they think they want' (p 13).

1377 Pazdziora, Marian. 'The Sapiential Aspect of the Canterbury Tales.' *KN*, 27 (1980), 413–26.
Pazdziora collects examples of traditional ideas about time, death, transcience, fortune, marriage, etc, as expressed in the narrative portions of *CT*, and asks whether, in line 798, Chaucer is 'setting "sentence" over "solaas" ' (p 414).

1378 Pearce, T.M. 'Chaucer's *Canterbury Tales*, Prologue, 784–787.' *Expl*, 5 (1946-1947), item 38.
Pearce disputes Lumiansky's interpretation of lines 784–87 (see **1371**), arguing that the text does *not* show that the pilgrims were either bored or indifferent when the Host first proposed a plan. Nor is the Host shown as being pompous or overly concerned about money. The pilgrims agreed to his suggestions with alacrity, while 'they certainly would have rejected him if he had really been pompous — or a penny-pincher.'

1379 Pichaske, David R., and Laura Sweetland. 'Chaucer on the Medieval Monarchy: Harry Bailly in the *Canterbury Tales*.' *ChauR*, 11 (1976-1977), 179–200.
The *Canterbury Tales* should be read 'in part as a commentary on government' and the Host viewed 'as the focus of this commentary' (p 198). Initially, the Host is 'the obvious tyrant misgoverning a disordered society' (p 182). The Miller, leading the group with 'his harsh and discordant bagpipes, is something of an icon of disorder' (p 200). In the closing part of *GP*, the Host insists on '*his* governance, *his* judgment, *his* rule, and the facile imposition of that rule on the pilgrims' (p 183). The election that makes him governor is suspect, but the concept of an elected ruler is consonant with medieval political theory. The political implications are reinforced by such terms as *rebel, governor, rule, judgment*, and *judge*. Harry's behavior as monarch evolves in the course of the pilgrimage. In the prologue to *ParsT*, which provides a parallel to the election-scene of *GP*, Harry voluntarily relinquishes his role as governor. The presence of political concepts and advice in other Chaucerian works strengthens the argument for reading the Host's character in this way.

380 Pratt, Robert A., ed. *The Tales of Canterbury, Complete [by] Geoffrey Chaucer.* 1974. See **88**.

The Host's plan in *GP*, that each pilgrim will tell four tales, is more ambitious than the apparent later plans, that each will tell one or two. It is sometimes assumed that Chaucer later modified the *GP* plan, accepting the idea of a smaller collection of tales as he worked. However, the opposite is also possible — 'that as he completed tale after tale, Chaucer's ambition correspondingly grew, and that he revised the General Prologue to match' an expanded plan 'even before he had completed twenty-four tales' (p xxi).

381 Richardson, Cynthia C. 'The Function of the Host in *The Canterbury Tales.*' *TSLL*, 12 (1970), 325–44.

Harry Bailly 'represents the forces external to the artist that press him to be creative' (p 326): the needs of society and the awareness of time, death, and mortality. 'Time and audience are fused in Harry Bailly as the pressures external to the artist' (p 327). By putting the Host in charge of the pilgrimage, Chaucer is examining the relationships between art and society. The Host's game places the pilgrims in relation to each other; his inn represents both protection or guidance, and entertainment; and he himself is 'the middlest of the middle class' (p 327). His aesthetic principle of combining morality and pleasure, *sentence* and *solaas* (line 798), is typical for the Middle Ages. He sets the standards for the tales, although he does very little actual criticizing and should not be taken as a true literary critic. 'His remarks are simply the casual comments of a rather ordinary listener,' and therefore he 'exhibits the problems that most audiences present to any artist: instinctive and unreflective judgment and lack of sophistication' (p 333). He repeatedly refers to time or to brevity of speech; through him 'Chaucer was very likely trying to show the effects of time (the Host) on art (the tales)' (p 339). Despite Harry's limitations Chaucer does not reject him, since 'if Chaucer felt that morality guided art, and if the Christian duty of an artist was to illuminate life for everyone, then, logically, it was Chaucer's duty to serve Harry Bailly' (p 334).

382 Rickert, Edith. 'Godeleef My Wyf.' *TLS*, December 16, 1926, p 935.

Rickert reports historical documents which support the viewpoint that the Host's wife is named Godeleef, and which show Harry Bailly himself as being 'not merely a taxpayer but also one of the four controllers of the subsidy, two of the others being likewise innkeepers and the third a brewer.'

383 Scheps, Walter. ' "Up Roos Oure Hoost, and Was Oure Aller Cok": Harry Bailly's Tale-Telling Competition.' *ChauR*, 10 (1975-1976), 113–28.

Harry Bailly's concepts of literature are correlated to his character. He 'exemplifies traditional ideas of masculinity' (p 114) and shows an emphasis on bold speech and merriment. Eight of the eleven *GP* instances of the terms *mirth* or *merry* refer to him. His literary criteria are that stories should combine *sentence* and *solaas*, and that they should concern adventures that have befallen in the past. The bargain he makes with the pilgrims helps to 'assure him of a tidy profit,' and also makes it unnecessary, for the duration of their journey, for him to show 'the deferential, even obsequious, manner which we ordinarily associate with those whose livelihoods depend upon accommodating the public' (p 116). Harry Bailly becomes 'the arch-critic to Chaucer's arch-poet' (p 126). Within the context of the work, it is likely that the Host would award the prize to the Nun's Priest. However, the game that Chaucer is playing 'is as ironically, even comically, self-serving as Harry's,' since the true winner is 'the poet himself' (p 126).

1384 Schlauch, Margaret. *English Medieval Literature and Its Social Foundations.* Warsaw: Państwowe Wydawnictwo Naukowe, 1956.
GP is briefly described, primarily in terms of social-class structure. 'It was the confident, pushing Harry Baillys, active in many towns, who were thrusting aside old class inhibitions and preparing the way for the middle-class culture later to become predominant in England' (p 256).

1385 Williams, Celia Ann. 'The Host — England's First Tour Director.' *EJ*, 57 (1968), 1149–50, 1214.
'The gullibility of twentieth-century tourists might not be too different from that of these pilgrims under the dictatorship of Bailly' (p 1150).

1386 Winny, James, ed. *The General Prologue to the Canterbury Tales by Geoffrey Chaucer.* 1965. See **73**.
The Host and Chaucer 'share some significant points of likeness' (p 24). They are 'positive and negative aspects of the same blended personality' (p 25). As the organizer, 'the Host takes over Chaucer's literary function, while, as though to distract attention from his substitute's activities, Chaucer admits himself to the pilgrimage, as a minnow among the tritons' (p 25). The Host also shares certain features with the Monk: both 'are genial, expansive, pleasure-loving men of the world with authority of character, and both have "eyen stepe" and a robust physique' (p 126).

1387 Yamada, Toshikazu. 'About Harry Bailly in the Canterbury Tales.' *Nebulae*, 9 (1981), 177–87.
Not seen; listed in *A Bibliography of Publications on Medieval English Language and Literature in Japan* (Tokyo: Tokyo University Center for Medieval Studies, 1983), p 155, #1.

❧ Index

Unless preceded by 'p,' numbers refer to items rather than to pages. Boldface numbers identify the author or editor of the item, numbers in regular typeface indicate that the person or topic is discussed, and reviews are represented by 'r.' For example, the entry for Benson, Larry D., which reads 'p xxviii, 42, **103**, **149**, **419**,' means that Benson is mentioned on p xxviii in the Introduction and in item 42, and is the author or editor of items **103**, **149**, and **419**. The entry for Patch, Howard F., includes the listings **33**, 151r, and 1306, indicating that Patch is the author or editor of item **33**, wrote a review of item 151, and is mentioned in item 1306. Chaucer's works are indexed according to the abbreviations at the beginning of this book (eg, *The Romaunt of the Rose* is represented by *Rom*). Manuscripts are grouped together under 'manuscripts,' saints under 'saints,' references to the Bible under 'Bible.'

ABC 769
Adams, George Roy **139**, **140**
Adenet le Roi 643
adnominatio see rhetoric
Aeschylus 569
Aiken, Pauline **1108**, **1259**, 1274
Alan of Lille (Alanus de Insulis), 341, 648, 1288
alderman 1060, 1072, 1076
Alderson, William L. **97**
Alexander, Michael **141**
Allen, Judson Boyce **142**
Alyngton, Robert de 1003
Amalarius 1320

Ames, Percy W. **143**
Ameto, see Boccaccio
amplificatio, see rhetoric
analogues, *see* sources
Andersen, Jens Kr. **144**
Andersen, Wallis May **145**, **663**
Anderson, J.J. **284**
Anel 674
angels 1284, 1288
anger 140, 344, 482; *see also* Sins, Seven Deadly
animals 246, 438; ape, 1205; dog, 466, 754, 766, 768, 772, 779, 807, 808, 821, 838, 855, 869,